Model-Based Development

Model-Based Development

Applications

H.S. Lahman

✦Addison-Wesley

Upper Saddle River, NJ • Boston • Indianapolis • San Francisco
New York • Toronto • Montreal • London • Munich • Paris • Madrid
Capetown • Sydney • Tokyo • Singapore • Mexico City

The publisher offers excellent discounts on this book when ordered in quantity for bulk purchases or special sales, which may include electronic versions and/or custom covers and content particular to your business, training goals, marketing focus, and branding interests. For more information, please contact:

U.S. Corporate and Government Sales
(800) 382-3419
corpsales@pearsontechgroup.com

For sales outside the United States please contact:

International Sales
international@pearson.com

Visit us on the Web: informit.com/aw

Library of Congress Cataloging-in-Publication Data

Lahman, H.S.
  Model-based development : applications / H.S. Lahman.—1st ed.
      p.   cm.
  Includes index.
  ISBN 0-321-77407-8 (hardcover : alk. paper)
  1. Model-driven software architecture. 2. Application
software—Development. I. Title.
  QA76.76.D47L33 2011
  005.1—dc23   2011012733

ISBN-13: 978-0-321-77407-1
ISBN-10:   0-321-77407-8
Text printed in the United States on recycled paper at Courier in Westford, Massachusetts.
First printing, June 2011

Contents

Preface

Software development is an enormously complex intellectual activity. It is a relatively young discipline that is still rapidly evolving. It isn't done very well because everyone is still trying to figure out how to do it.

Nonetheless, there has been substantial improvement over the years in the way software is developed. A number of design methodologies have evolved to facilitate various aspects of software design. One was the Structured Design methodology, which provided a very intuitive approach that matched up well with the hardware computational models of Turing and von Neumann.

The Problem

While Structured Design was clearly superior to the ad hoc approaches that preceded it, it had an Achilles heel: the software tended to be difficult to modify when customer requirements changed over time, especially in large applications. At the same time, applications were rapidly growing in size and complexity. In addition, new languages, technologies, operating systems, data storage paradigms, UI paradigms, hardware, and whatnot were arriving on the computing scene with alarming speed. Yet business conditions were driving the need for faster time-to-market and reduced cost of software products.

The Hope

Consequently, a number of new design methodologies appeared that captured hard-won lessons about good and bad practices. They also presented revolutionary views of computing. One of those was the Object-Oriented (OO) paradigm, with the primary goal of ensuring that large applications are maintainable over time as requirements inevitably change during the software product's life cycle.

This book is about practicing a particular software design methodology, Model-Based Development (MBD), which is strongly based upon Shlaer-Mellor.[1] Employing

---

1. The methodology is named for Sally Shlaer and Steve Mellor. This methodology was originally expounded in the early '80s. Since then it has gone through several revisions, and there are several variations, of which MBD is one.

the OO paradigm in general and MBD in particular should lead to more robust and maintainable large applications.

This Book

Although the book employs UML as a notation, that is quite peripheral. There are plenty of good books that describe how to express a software design in UML, so UML syntax will not get much mention here. Similarly, this book follows a particular design methodology for MBD, but that is primarily to provide context for the real purpose of this book:

> The primary goal of this book is to describe why OO methodologies in general and MBD in particular advocate a particular way of doing things.

There is no single right way to design and develop all software. Too much depends upon the particular development environment, which includes everything from business goals through tools to group culture. In the end, a shop has to decide what set of tools will be most effective in its environment. To do that the decision makers need to understand why the MBD set of methodological tools works in many common situations. More to the point, the practitioners need to understand the fundamentals well enough to adapt them to particular situations.

Practicing OO design requires a unique mindset that is not intuitive in the world of hardware computational models. Rather than focusing on particular notations and methodologies, this book is really about how to *think* about software design. To that end, this book spends substantial time on the thought processes behind good software designs—even to the point of deliberately providing poor preliminary designs to demonstrate that the approach is self-correcting.

To achieve such understanding it is necessary to describe how traditional (pre-OO) approaches to software development failed in some ways and how the OO paradigm addressed those shortcomings. While Structured Development brought substantial order to the chaos of pre-1970 software development, it was not a panacea, and by the '80s it became clear that software still had serious maintainability problems that the OO paradigm addressed.

Similarly, one cannot describe why a methodology works well without discussing at least some of the underlying theory. Nonetheless, this is a book by a software developer for software developers, so a conscious effort has been made to describe theoretical issues in practical terms without mathematical rigor.

Because this book is primarily about building abstract OOA models, don't count on seeing a lot of OOPL code. As the methodology name suggests, the emphasis in this methodology lies in abstract modeling rather than writing traditional source language code. In effect, when a translation-quality OOA model is developed the *model is the code*. To put it another way, the notation of OOA modeling is UML augmented with an MDA-compliant Abstract Action Language (AAL). That notation is a 4GL[2] rather than a 3GL, but the model will be just as executable as any 3GL program. While the model is implementation independent, it is a complete, precise, and unambiguous specification of the solution for functional requirements.

As a final note, we would point out that the practical development experience of the author is measured in decades rather than years. This is definitely not a theoretical book, despite the emphasis on explaining why things are done. It is based upon what works in the real world.

Road Map

The subject matter of this book is limited to application development at the OOA level. This book is organized into three main sections. Part I provides historical perspective and an introduction to basic OO principles. The introduction includes a discussion of the problems with structured development that the OO paradigm sought to correct. Part II is about construction of a static structure for the problem solution. This section represents the largest differences between the OO paradigm and other approaches since it is where the OO paradigm's unique view of problem space abstraction is primarily manifested. Part III describes the dynamic aspects of the solution, particularly the rather militant use of finite state machines to describe behavior.

---

2. Computer languages are subdivided into generations that roughly correspond to historical innovation and increasing abstraction. The first-generation language (1GL) was machine code, bits set directly in hardware registers. The second generation (2GL) introduced symbolic names for things like instructions. Third-generation languages (3GLs) represented a major advance with notions like reusable procedures, block structure, and stack-based scope. 3GLs represented a huge advance in the size of programs that could practically be written, and they dominated software development for half a century. The fourth-generation languages (4GLs) broke with the previous generations by raising the level of abstraction to the point where the program could be specified in a manner that was essentially independent of specific computing environments.

Intended Audience

This book is primarily targeted at people with little OO experience. It is assumed that the reader has some cursory knowledge of UML.[3] The book also assumes that the reader has some software development experience, on the order of a couple of class projects in C. It assumes that the level of experience includes a general knowledge of computers and programming, essentially enough to be familiar with common acronyms like KISS.[4]

A secondary audience is the large number of converts to the OO paradigm from traditional procedural development environments. Many of these developers leapt directly into writing code in an object-oriented programming language (OOPL) since they already had substantial programming experience (i.e., believing that if one has seen one programming language, one has seen them all). Sadly, such converts have written huge volumes of bad OO code because no one told them why Object-Oriented Analysis and Design (OOA/D) is very different from Structured Analysis and Design (SA/D). If you are one of these, you will have to forget everything you ever learned about designing software and start with a clean slate.

The Role of Translation

A key characteristic of MBD is that it is one of a family of methodologies based on translation. That is, the methodology is compliant with the approach where a solution is modeled abstractly in a notation like UML and then a full code generator is employed to produce an implementation from that model automatically. Translation has some obvious advantages because it represents a logical extension of automation in the computing space that enhances productivity, enables economies of scale, and improves reliability. The downside is that it is not easy to do; the optimization problems faced for a model compiler are orders of magnitude more complex than those facing a 3GL compiler. Nonetheless, there are several commercial code generators available that provide 100% code generation for translation-based methodologies.

Although most of the translation approaches predate the Object Management Group (OMG) itself, they have been greatly facilitated by the Model-Driven Archi-

---

3. That isn't critical because the syntax is explained. In addition, books like Kendall Scott's *UML Explained* (Addison-Wesley, 2001) are cheap and quick reads that provide far more information about UML than you will ever need to record MBD designs.

4. Keep It Simple, Stupid.

tecture (MDA) initiative formalized by OMG. MDA has provided a much-needed standardization for plug-and-play tools and a conceptual framework for full code generation. Getting from an abstract, implementation-independent model to 3GL code or Assembly is a nontrivial task, especially in today's complex IDEs. That task greatly benefits from the formalism and concepts of MDA.

However, MBD is not tied to translation. The models produced in MBD are essentially the same as those that would be produced during OOA in traditional development and then manually elaborated to produce OOD models and 3GL code. The MBD models just happen to be more rigorously constructed than typical OOA models because code generators are quite literal-minded—they do what one says, not what one meant. There is nothing to prevent the developer from manually performing the conversion.

Acknowledgments

I am deeply indebted to the works of Steve Mellor and Sally Shlaer, whose methodology is the basis of MBD. They pioneered the translation approach to software development and provided the much-needed design rigor for OOA models. In addition, Steve Mellor is the best OO modeler I've ever encountered, and his examples have been marvelously instructive.

I am equally indebted to Rebecca Wirfs-Brock for her incredibly detailed and insightful reviews of the manuscripts.

Pathfinder Solutions provided a fertile testing ground for ideas. Greg Eakman, Carolyn Duby, and Peter Fontana were particularly supportive.

I would also like to acknowledge the remarkable patience and faith of Chris Guzikowski and Raina Chrobak at Addison-Wesley. I am also very appreciative of the editing efforts of Elizabeth Ryan, Diane Freed, and Chris Zahn.

Although this book was started after I retired, I am in debt to Teradyne/ATB for providing a world-class software development shop full of superstar developers who formed a crucible for many of the ideas in this book.

Finally, I am indebted to the myriad Internet correspondents over three decades that provided a sounding board for explaining the concepts in this book. Any clarity of expression that readers might find is largely the result of refining explanations in public forums.

About the Author

H.S. Lahman wrote his first software program on a plug board in 1957. That was such a character building experience that he spent the next decade as an exploration geophysicist employing cutting edge techniques in most of the major swamps, deserts, tundras, and jungles of the Free World. He then returned to school to learn about economics, operations research, and computing. For the next three decades he developed software in MIS, scientific, and R-T/E environments. He became an advocate of OO development in 1982. In the '90s he became an advocate of improved software quality and development processes.

Introduction

History is a nightmare from which I am trying to awake.
—James Joyce

Four decades ago a program of a million lines was regarded as huge, reserved for only the most massive mainframe systems in the bowels of the Department of Defense (DoD[1]). It was routinely estimated that to build such programs would require 1,000 engineers working for a decade. Today most of the applications on a PC are well over a million lines, and many are in the 10 million range. Moreover, they are expected to be built in a couple of years or less. So programs are growing ever larger while clients expect them to be developed with less effort.

In today's high-tech society rapid obsolescence is routine, and the economic model of the firm emphasizes growth more than ever before. These forces create the need for more, different, and better products in shorter time. Since all those new products depend upon ever-increasing amounts of software to run, the pressure on software developers to do their part to decrease time-to-market is relentless.

Developers are also assaulted on another front. Four decades ago the national average was 150 defects per KLOC[2] for *released* code. That was back in the good old days when no one had a clue how to go about writing "good" software. The GOTO and global data reigned, designs were done on blackboards and cocktail napkins, and the DEL key was the programmer's favorite. Developing software was the arcane specialty of a few mutated electrical engineers so, frankly, nobody really cared much if it was buggy.

Alas, such a utopia could not last. In the '70s and '80s two things happened. First, there was a quality revolution led by the Japanese that was quickly followed by the rest of Asia and, more slowly, by the industrialized West. This led consumers into a new era where they no longer had to plan on their car or TV being in the shop for one week out of six. Consumers really liked that. Second, soon after this the quality revolution software began to weasel its way into virtually everything. Suddenly software stood out as the only thing that was always breaking. Now that consumers were aware of a better way, they didn't like that at all.

---

1. This is a book about software, so we have to use acronyms. It is a union rule.

2. If you don't know what this means, you need to start with a more elementary text than this book. The important factoid about this statistic is that it refers to thousands of *raw* lines of COBOL code, a rather wordy language.

So while software developers were trying to cope with building ever-larger programs in ever-decreasing time, they suddenly found that they were also expected to get to 5-sigma defect rates.[3] To make matters worse, a popular slogan of the '80s became "Quality is Free." No matter that every software developer was certain that this was hogwash because software quality is a direct trade-off against development time. Sadly, the market forces were then and are now beyond the influence of software developers, so no one paid any attention to the wails of software developers. Thus the '80s brought new meaning to the term "software crisis," mostly at the expense of developer mental health.

The second major event was an extraordinary explosion in the technology of computing. Previously the technological advances were mostly characterized by new languages and operating systems. But the huge growth of PC software, the demand for interoperability among programs, and the emergence of the World Wide Web as a major force in computing resulted in a great deal of innovation.[4] Today developers face a mind-boggling set of alternatives for everything from planning tools through architectural strategies to testing processes. Worse, new technologies are being introduced before developers are fluent in the old ones.

Finally, developers are faced with a constant parade of requirements changes. The computing space is not the only domain that is facing increasing innovation and change. For core management information systems the Federal Accounting Standards Bureau (FASB), the IRS, and sundry other agencies in the United States decree changes with annoying regularity. Product competition causes marketeers to relentlessly press for new features as products are developed to keep pace with competitor announcements. Similarly, the standards, techniques, and technologies of the engineering disciplines are also changing rapidly as the academics strive to bring order to this chaos. The days of the "requirements freeze" and the project-level waterfall model are long gone.

To summarize, modern software developers are faced with an ancient problem: putting five pounds of stuff in a three-pound bag as quickly as possible without spilling any. We have better tools, methodologies, processes, and technologies today than

---

3. Assuming each line of code is an opportunity for one or more defects, 5-sigma represents a frequency of defects that is five standard deviations from a median of one defect per line. The defect rate corresponding to that level of quality is about 230 defects per million LOC—a thousandfold improvement over the norm of the '60s.

4. Interestingly, much of the core technology associated with the World Wide Web is really a rebirth of old technologies. I actually read an article recently in a fairly prestigious software development magazine where the author claimed the first markup language was invented in 1986. In fact, markup languages were commonly used two decades earlier. Sadly, that myopia meant that the industry learned nothing from the reasons why markup languages had been largely abandoned by the late '70s. But that is a topic for a different book.

we did a half century ago, but the problems have grown in proportion. The software crisis that Basic Assembly Language (BAL) was supposed to solve is still with us, which segues to this book's first Ingot of Wisdom:

> Software development is an impossible task. The only thing the developer can do is cope and keep smiling.

The State of the Art

A keynote speaker at a conference in 1995 asked everyone who used Microsoft Windows to raise their hand. Several hundred people did. He then asked all those whose system had crashed in the past week to keep their hands up. All but about a half dozen kept their hands up. The keynoter then asked everyone to keep their hands up who thought that Microsoft would go out of business as a result. All but a dozen hands went down. The keynoter used this to validate his assertion that good quality in software was not necessarily a requirement that was important to a software company's survival.

That conclusion is much less warranted today, as Microsoft discovered in its wars with Linux.[5] The keynoter was correct, though, that the key determining factor in a software company's viability in the marketplace is whether they deliver what their customers want. Broadly speaking, this can be viewed as an analogy of four buckets containing fluids representing reliability, features, ease of use, and availability (in the sense of time-to-market) where the cost of filling each of those buckets is different, as shown in Figure I-1. The end customer clearly wants all of those things but the vendor has a limited budget. So the vendor makes a decision that trades total cost against the mix of levels to which the buckets are filled. The marketplace then determines how well the vendor's decision provides *overall* satisfaction to the customer.

The decision about how much to fill each bucket is fundamentally a marketing decision. The marketeers earn their big bucks by anticipating what combination of levels will be optimal for a given total price in a given market. The task of minimizing the cost of filling each bucket lies with the software developers. Whenever the developer brings about a cost reduction, that reduction is directly reflected in a competitive advantage for that aspect of the product. The value of that advantage will depend upon the particular market niche. So, to measure the State of the Art of software

---

5. In fact, Microsoft learned its lesson well. Today's Microsoft products have pretty much caught up on the reliability front to the point where security is probably more of a competitive issue.

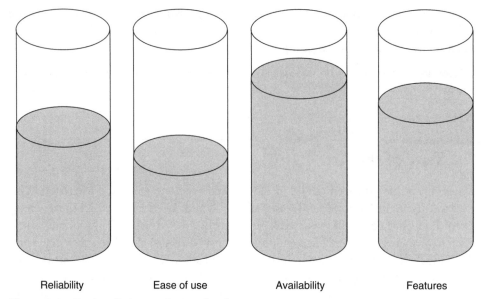

Reliability   Ease of use   Availability   Features

Figure I-1 *Trade-offs for conflicting development priorities*

development the question becomes: What tools are available to reduce the costs of filling the various buckets?

We have a variety of software tools to help us, such as version control systems. We also have lots of processes, ranging from XP (eXtreme Programming) to formal methods in clean room shops. And we have as many software design methodologies as there are methodologists.[6] We also have process frameworks like the RUP[7] and the CMM,[8] not to mention languages, integrated development environments (IDEs), metrics systems, estimating models, and all the rest of the potpourri.

> We have precious little data to sort out which combinations of the available methodologies, technologies, and practices are best.

The days are long gone when a couple of hackers could sit down in their spare bedrooms and come up with a killer application after a few months of consuming

---

6. An old but still amusing joke: What's the difference between a terrorist and a software methodologist? You can negotiate with a terrorist.

7. The Rational Unified Process (RUP) is not really a process. It is primarily a process framework that is highly tailorable to local development environments.

8. The Capability Maturity Model (CMM) is a true process framework in that it describes only what capabilities must be in place to produce good software, not how they should be implemented. Thus compliance with the CMM is a necessary but not sufficient condition for good software development.

lots of Jolt Cola and cold pizza. If you tell someone at a job interview that you wrote 100 KLOC last year, you can probably kiss that job off because hiring managers have figured out that the only way you can get that kind of productivity is by writing terminally unreliable and utterly unmaintainable crap. To effectively lower the cost of filling those buckets you need to go at software development in an organized and systematic way.

Because of this there is a lot of lip service paid to software engineering in today's industry rags. Alas, we are probably a long way from respectability as an engineering discipline. Software development is still an art, although it is more bilious green than black. The art lies in cobbling together a coherent development system that is appropriate for a given environment from a hodgepodge of disparate practices and tools. Instead of providing discipline for putting together such systems, our "software engineering" merely says, "Here's a framework and lots of alternatives to drape on it. Selecting the right alternatives and gluing them together correctly for the particular development environment is left as an exercise for the student."

What Works

Nonetheless, the reality is that the state of the art of software development has improved significantly over the past half century. The same number of people routinely develop much bigger programs with much better quality in shorter time, so we have to be doing something right. The tricky part is to figure out what things are more right than others.

Initially there was a collection of hard-won lessons based upon decades of rather rocky experience prior to 1970. For example, once upon a time FORTRAN's assigned-GOTO statement and COBOL's ALTER statement were regarded as powerful tools for elegantly handling complex programming problems. A decade later, programming managers were making their use grounds for summary dismissal because the programs using those features tended to be unmaintainable when requirements changed.[9]

All these hard-won lessons formed a notion of *developer experience*. The programmers who had been around long enough to make a lot of mistakes and who were bright enough to learn from those mistakes became software wizards. Unfortu-

---

9. The problem was that such statements changed the flow of control of the program "on the fly" in ways that were not directly visible in the code itself. Understanding other people's code is tough enough when sequence and branching is explicit. Such programs led to the acronym WORN—Write Once; Read Never.

nately, each developer essentially had to reinvent this wheel because there was no central body of knowledge about software development.

Starting in the late '60s a variety of methodologies for programming in 3GLs and for software design sprang up. The earliest ones simply enumerated the hard-won practices and mistakes of the past in a public fashion for everyone's benefit. Soon, though, various software wizards began to combine these practices into cohesive design methodologies. These methodologies were different in detail but shared a number of characteristics in common, so they were grouped under the umbrella of Structured Development (SD). Because they were rather abstract views—the big picture of software design—the authors found it convenient to employ specialized notations. Since many of the wizards were also academicians, the notations tended to be graphical so that theoretical constraints from set and graph theory could be readily applied.

SD was the single most important advance in software development of the middle twentieth century. It quite literally brought order out of chaos. Among other things, it was the engine of growth of data processing, which later evolved into the less prosaic information technology in the '80s, in the corporate world because acres of entry-level COBOL programmers could now churn out large numbers of reports that provided unprecedented visibility into day-to-day corporate operations. Better yet, those reports were usually pretty accurate.

Alas, SD was only the first step on a long road to more and better software development. As one might expect for something so utterly new, it wasn't a panacea, and by the late '70s some warts were beginning to show up. Understanding what those warts were is critical to understanding why and how object-oriented development evolved in the '80s.

Part I

The Roots of Object-Oriented Development

The Model-Based Development (MBD) approach to software development is fundamentally an object-oriented (OO) approach. So, to fully understand the methodology it is necessary to understand OO development in general. Because the OO approach is not as intuitive as traditional software development methodologies, we need to understand why the OO approach does things the way it does.

This part of the book looks at the historical context in which the OO approach was born so that we can understand the problems with traditional approaches that the OO approach sought to resolve.

Chapter 1

Historical Perspective

Problems are the price of progress.
—Charles F. Kettering

Compared to the physical sciences and the Industrial Revolution, software development is relatively new on the scene of human progress. It took more than a millennia for the physical sciences to play a ubiquitous role in modern life and it took the Industrial Revolution over a century to play a similar role. Yet computers and software have become an invasive and essential part of our lives in three decades. Alas, the road traveled has been a bit rocky.

This chapter provides historical context for *why* the OO paradigm was developed. To fully understand and appreciate the paradigm we need to understand what problems it sought to solve, so we start with a bit of history. We will then examine some weaknesses of the paradigm that dominated software development immediately before the OO paradigm appeared. Finally, we will provide a technical context for the rest of the book by examining some of the important technical advances made prior to the OO paradigm that were incorporated in it.

History

Essentially there was no systematic development at all through the 1950s. This was the Dark Ages of programming. It is difficult for today's developers to even imagine the conditions under which software was developed in those days. A mainframe had a few kilobytes of memory and paper tape was a high-tech input system. Western Union had an effective monopoly on teletype input devices that required several foot-pounds of energy for each key press—it was the machine that crippled programmers with carpal tunnel syndrome before the medical profession had a name for it. There

3

were no browsers, debuggers, or CRT terminals.[1] Basic Assembly Language (BAL) was the silver bullet to solve the software crisis!

In the late '50s and early '60s better tools began to appear in the form of higher-level computer languages that abstracted 1s and 0s into symbolic names, higher-level operations, block structures, and abstract structures such as records and arrays. It was clear that they made life easier and developers were far more productive, but there were no guidelines for how to use them properly. So this renaissance gave birth to the Hacker Era where individual productivity ruled.

The Hacker Era extended from the early '60s to the mid '70s. Very bright people churning out enormous volumes of code characterized this period—100 KLOC/yr. of FORTRAN was not unusual. They had to be bright because they spent a lot of time debugging, and they had to be very good at it to get the code out the door that fast. They often developed ingenious solutions to problems.[2] In the '60s the term *hacker* was complimentary. It described a person who could generate a lot of code to do wonderful things and who could keep it running.

By the late '70s, though, the honeymoon was over and *hacker* became a pejorative.[3] This was because the hackers were moving on to new projects while leaving their code behind for others to maintain. As time passed more special cases were exercised and it was discovered that the code didn't always work. And the world was changing, so those programs had to be enhanced. All too often it became easier to rewrite the program than to fix it. This was when it became clear that there was something wrong with all that code. The word *maintainable* became established in the industry literature, and unmaintainable code became *hacker code*.

The solution in the late '60s was a more systematic approach that coalesced various hard-won lessons into methodologies to construct software. At the same time,

1. My first program was written on a plug board in 1957. A plug board is essentially an extension of the hardware whereby one grounded TTL inputs, which normally float High (logic 1), with a wire to make a Low (logic 0). One wrote every single bit directly into the hardware. My program was a hello-world class exercise, but it took me two weeks to get it to work.

2. In the days of drum memories there was a fellow writing BAL who routinely optimized for the fact that there were two heads on the drum. He wrote his programs by physically separating the logically consecutive statements in his program by a distance that mapped to nearly half the circumference of the drum in address space. The exact placement was computed based on the number of cycles that the previously executed statement would take to execute and the drum rotation speed. This allowed the statements to be executed with something approaching half the latency for the drum rotation that a sequentially ordered program would have. The mind boggles that he could write programs that way, much less debug them.

3. With the advent of the Internet in the '80s, the term further evolved to refer to people who broke into computer systems for nefarious purposes.

programs were becoming larger and the idea that they had a structure to be *designed* appeared. Thus *software design* became a separate activity from software programming. The methodologies that began to appear during the twilight of the Hacker Era had a synergy whereby the various lessons learned played together so that the whole was greater than the sum of the parts. Those methodologies were all under the general umbrella of Structured Development (SD).[4]

The period starting around 1980 was one of mind-boggling advances in almost every corner of the software industry. The OO paradigm[5]—more specifically a disciplined approach to analysis and design—was just one of a blizzard of innovations.

Structured Development

This was unquestionably the single most important advance prior to the '80s. It provided the first truly systematic approach to software development. When combined with the 3GLs of the '60s it enabled huge improvements in productivity.

SD had an interesting side effect that was not really noticed at the time. Applications were more reliable. It wasn't noticed because software was being used much more widely, so it had much higher visibility to non-software people. It still had a lot of defects, and those users still regarded software as unreliable. In fact, though, reliability improved from 150 defects/KLOC in the early '60s to about 15 defects/KLOC by 1980.[6]

SD was actually an umbrella term that covered a wide variety of software construction approaches. Nonetheless, they usually shared certain characteristics:

- *Graphical representation.* Each of these fledgling methodologies had some form of graphical notation. The underlying principle was simply that a picture is worth a thousand words.

---

4. It was more well known as Structured Programming at the time, which was a bit of a misnomer because a common theme of SD was to provide software design using notations that were quite different than the programming languages of that era.

5. The first pure OO programming language, Smalltalk, appeared in 1972, but it was developed with the goal of providing better tools for simulation, and the mapping to general computation was not intuitive. It took about a decade for OOA/D to evolve to the point where general-purpose use was feasible.

6. The empirical data from those times was pretty varied and the quality wasn't very good, especially for the '60s. People might argue about the specific numbers, but it is unlikely anyone familiar with the period would argue that defects/KLOC had not improved by several integer factors in that period.

- *Functional isolation.* The basic idea was that programs were composed of large numbers of algorithms of varying complexities that played together to solve a given problem. The notion of interacting algorithms was actually a pretty seminal one that arrived just as programs started to become too large for one person to handle in a reasonable time. Functional isolation formalized this idea in things like reusable function libraries, subsystems, and application layers.

- *Application programming interfaces (API).* When isolating functionality, it still has to be accessed somehow. This led to the notion of an invariant interface to the functionality that enabled all clients to access it in the same way while enabling the implementation of that functionality to be modified without the clients knowing about the changes.

- *Programming by contract.* This was a logical extension of APIs. The API itself became a contract between a service and its clients. The problem with earlier forays into this idea is that the contract is really about the semantics of the service, but the API only defined the syntax for accessing that semantics. The notion only started to become a serious contract when languages began to incorporate things such as assertions about behavior as part of the program unit. Still, it was a reasonable start for a very good idea.

- *Top-down development.* The original idea here was to start with high-level, abstract user requirements and gradually refine them into more specific requirements that became more detailed and more specifically related to the computing environment. Top-down development also happened to map very nicely into functional decomposition, which we'll get to in a moment.

- *Emergence of analysis and design.* SD identified development activities other than just writing 3GL code. Analysis was a sort of hybrid between requirements elicitation, analysis, and specification in the customer's domain and high-level software design in the developer's domain. Design introduced a formal step where the developer provided a graphical description of the detailed software structure before hitting the keyboard to write 3GL code.

SD enabled the construction of programs that were far more maintainable than those done previously. In fact, in very expert and disciplined hands these methods enabled programs to be developed that were just as maintainable as modern OO programs. The problem was that to do that required a *lot* more discipline and expertise than most software developers had. So another silver bullet missed the scoring rings, but at least it was on the paper. Nonetheless, it is worth noting that every one of these characteristics can be found in modern OO development (though some, like top-down design, have a very limited role).

Functional Decomposition

This was the core design technique that was employed in every SD approach; the *Structured* in SD refers to this. Functional decomposition deals with the solution exclusively as an algorithm. This is a view that is much closer to scientific programming than, say, management information systems programming. (The name of the first 3GL was FORTRAN, an acronym for FORmula TRANslator.) It is also very close to the hardware computational models that we will discuss shortly.

The basic principle of functional decomposition is divide and conquer. Basically, subdivide large, complex functionality into smaller, more manageable component algorithms in a classic top-down manner. This leads to an inverted tree structure where higher-level functions at the top simply invoke a set of lower-level functions containing the subdivided functionality. The leaves at the base of the tree are atomic functions (on the scale of arithmetic operators) that are so fundamental they cannot be further subdivided. An example is illustrated in Figure 1-1.

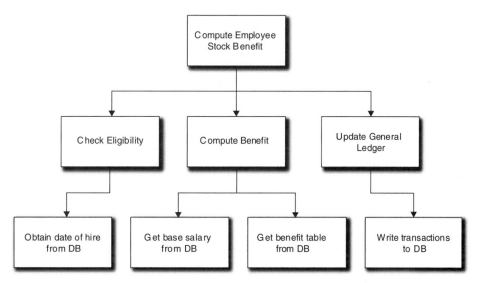

Figure 1-1 *Example of functional decomposition of a task to compute employee stock benefits into more manageable pieces*

Functional decomposition was both powerful and appealing. It was powerful because it was ideally suited to managing complexity in the Turing world of an algorithmic calculating machine, especially when the 3GLs provided procedures as basic language constructs. In a world full of complex algorithms, functional decomposition was very intuitive, so the scientific community jumped on functional decomposition like tickets for a tractor pull on Hard Liquor and Handgun Night.

It was appealing because it combined notions of functional isolation (e.g., the limbs of the tree and the details of the subdivided functions), programming by contract in that the subdivided functions provided services to higher-level clients, a road map for top-down development once the decomposition tree was defined, APIs in the form of procedure signatures, very basic depth-first navigation for flow of control, and reuse by invoking the same limb from different program contexts. Overall it was a very clever way of dealing with a number of disparate issues.

Alas, by the late '70s it was becoming clear that SD had ushered in a new set of problems that no one had anticipated. Those problems were related to two orthogonal realities:

- In the scientific arena algorithms didn't change; typically, they either stood the test of time or were replaced in their entirety by a new, superior algorithms. But in arenas like business programming, the rules were constantly changing and products were constantly evolving. So applications needed to be modified throughout their useful lives, sometimes even during the initial development.

- Hierarchical structures are difficult to modify.[7]

The problem was that functional decomposition was inherently a depth-first paradigm since functions can't complete until all subdivided child functions complete. This resulted in a rather rigid up-and-down hierarchical structure for flow of control that was difficult to modify when the requirements changed. Changing the flow of control often meant completely reorganizing groups of limbs.

Another problem was redundancy. The suite of atomic functions was typically quite limited, so different limbs tended to use many of the same atomic operations that other limbs needed. Quite often the same *sequence* of atomic leaf operations was repeated in the same order in different limbs. It was tedious to construct such redundant limbs, but it wasn't a serious flaw until maintenance was done. If the same change needed to be made in multiple limbs, one had to duplicate the same change multiple times. Such duplication increased the opportunities for inserting errors. By the late 1970s redundant code was widely recognized as one of the major causes of poor reliability resulting from maintenance.

---

7. A classical example is the zoological taxonomy that classifies all living things. Academics spent decades developing that taxonomy. Just as they were congratulating themselves on a job well done, someone brought home a duck-billed platypus from Australia. A hairy, egg-laying, web-footed marsupial with a bill simply did not fit into the taxonomy because several of its characteristics were determinants for very different limbs of the taxonomy. Modifying the tree would have been an arduous task; folklore says that zoologists at the time considered financing an expedition to Australia to exterminate the critters. Urban legends aside, to this day the placement of the critter in the tree is a matter of debate.

To cure that problem, higher-level services were defined that captured particular sequences of operations once, and they were reused by invoking them from different limbs of the tree. That cured the redundancy but created an even worse problem. In a pure functional decomposition tree there is exactly one client for every procedure, so the tree is highly directed. The difficulty with reuse across limbs was that the tree became a lattice where services had both multiple descending child functions and multiple parent clients that invoked them, as shown in Figure 1-2.

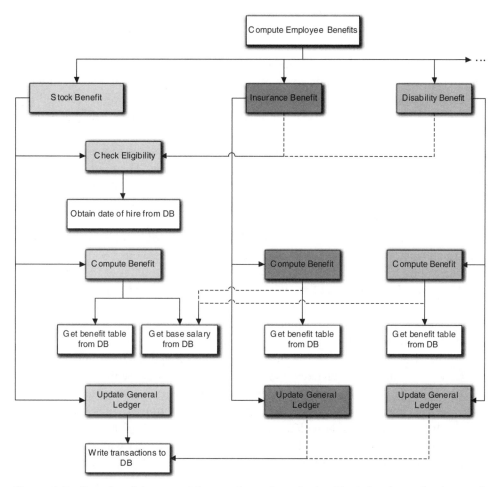

Figure 1-2 *Functional decomposition tree becoming a lattice. Shaded tasks are fundamental elements of different benefits. Dashed lines indicate crossovers from one decomposition limb to another to eliminate redundancy.*

Figure 1-1 has been expanded to include the computation of multiple employee benefits that all require basically the same tasks to be done.[8] Some tasks must be implemented in a unique way so the basic tree has the same structure for each benefit. But some tasks are exactly the same. To avoid redundancy, those nodes in the tree are reused by clients in different benefit limbs of the tree. This results in a lattice-like structure where tasks like *Get base salary from DB* have multiple clients that are in quite different parts of the application.

That lattice structure was a major flaw with respect to maintainability. When the requirements changed for some higher-level function (e.g., *Insurance Benefit* in Figure 1-2) in a particular limb, the change might need to be implemented in a descendant sub-function much lower in the tree. However, the sub-function might have multiple clients from other limbs due to reuse (e.g., *Get base salary from DB*). The requirements change might not apply to some of those clients that were in different limbs (e.g., *Stock Benefit*) because each limb where the sub-function was reused represented a different context. Then the low level change for one client might break other clients in other contexts.

The biggest difficulty for functional decomposition, though, was the implicit knowledge of context that came with depth-first processing. The fundamental paradigm was *Do This*. Higher-level functions were essentially just a collection of instructions to lower-level functions to do things. To issue an instruction to do something, the higher level function must (a) know who will do it, (b) know that they can do it, and (c) know that it is the next thing to do in the *overall solution*. All of these break functional isolation to some extent, but the last is most insidious because it requires that the calling function understand the much higher-level context of the whole problem solution. The higher-level function hard-wires that knowledge in its implementation, so when requirements changed for the overall context, that implementation had to be changed. This hierarchical functional dependence, combined with all the other problems just mentioned, resulted in the legendary *spaghetti code*.

Another way to look at this is through the idea of specification and DbC contracts. When a function is invoked, there is a *Do This* contract with the client invoking the function. That DbC contract represents an expectation of what service the function will provide. It does not matter whether the function provides the entire service itself (i.e., it is not subdivided) or delegates some or all of its functionality to lower-level functions. From the client's perspective, the contract with the function in hand is *for the entire service*. If the function in hand is a higher-level function in the

---

8. An example like this can be picked to death by bringing in other requirements that would ensure that, say, "Check eligibility" would have different requirements for different benefits. This is just an example of the structure issues, so it has been considerably simplified.

tree, the specification of what that function does is the specification of *all of the descending limbs*. The lower-level functions descending from the higher-level functions are extensions of it, and their individual specifications are subsets of the higher-level function's specification.

This means that all of the limbs descending from a given higher-level function in the lattice form a complex dependency relationship originating with the higher-level function. That is, to fulfill its responsibilities in the DbC contract with its client, a higher-level function depends on every descendant lower-level function doing the right thing with respect to its client's expectations. It is that dependency chain that is the real root cause of spaghetti code. A lower-level function's specification cannot be changed without affecting a potentially long chain of parent (client) specifications.

A similar dependency problem existed for sequences of operations. To modify the sequence in which the leaf functions were invoked, the implementations of the higher-level functions had to be touched. That is, the sequence was determined by moving up and down the limbs in a systematic, depth-first manner. That navigation of the tree was hard-coded in the higher-level functions' implementations. So to change the sequence, the implementations of multiple higher-level functions had to be changed. In effect, the overall solution flow of control was hard-wired into the tree structure itself, which sometimes required reorganizing the entire tree to accommodate small sequencing changes.

One way this is manifested is in doing unit tests of higher-level functions. Since the specification of the higher-level function includes the specification of every descending lower-level function, it is not possible to unit test a higher-level function *from the client's perspective* without working implementations of every descending lower-level function.[9]

> A strong case can be made that the primary goal of the OO paradigm is to completely eliminate the hierarchical dependencies resulting from functional decomposition.

It is not terribly surprising that no one anticipated these problems. They only showed up when SD's productivity gains were realized. As applications became larger, there were more requirements changes. Meanwhile, the functional decomposition trees were growing in size and complexity. Only when the benefits were realized did the problems show up.

---

9. A short-cut for unit testing was to stub the immediate child functions so that they returned or set variables in a manner appropriate for the test case inputs. Basically, though, this is just self-delusion. All you are doing is testing the test harness.

Lessons Hard Won

By the time the academicians began to ruminate about OT in the late '70s, a lot of crappy software had been written—enough so that the patterns that were common in that crappy software started to be painfully obvious. This led to a lot of papers and letters like Dijkstra's classic, "Go To Statement Considered Harmful" in 1968.[10] Those patterns represented the rather painfully learned lessons of software development (some of which were just touched on).

Global Data

One basic problem was that persistent state variables were recording the state of the system, and they were getting changed in unexpected ways or at unexpected times when they were globally accessible. This led to errors when code was written assuming a particular state prevailed and that code was later executed when that state did not prevail.

In practice such problems were difficult to diagnose because they tended to be intermittent. There was also a maintenance problem because it was difficult to find all the places where the data was written when, say, some new condition had to be added. So unrelated maintenance tended to introduce new bugs. This problem was so severe that by the late '70s every 3GL IDE had some sort of Find/Browse facility so that you could easily search for every place a variable was accessed. While convenient for the developer, such facilities didn't really help *manage* the state data properly. The problem was so pronounced that a functional programming paradigm was developed in parallel to the OO paradigm, largely to eliminate the need for persistent state data.

Elephantine Program Units

Once upon a time a fellow asked a colleague why he was getting a particular compiler error. The colleague hadn't seen the message before, but it sounded like some compiler's stack had overflowed, so the colleague took a glance at the code. The procedure where the error occurred was 1800 statements long, and there were several

---

10. E. Dijkstra, "Go To Statement Considered Harmful," letter to the editor in *Communications of the ACM*, Vol. 11, No. 3 (March, 1968), pp. 147–148. It seems astonishing now that back then this letter launched a debate about whether GOTOs really were bad, one that lasted nearly a decade. A rather famous guru defended GOTOs as a columnist in *Computer Language* magazine, writing one of the most convoluted 15-line programs I've ever seen outside a coding obscurity contest. It was incorrect, and he got so soundly flamed about it by a gazillion readers that he didn't put another code example in his articles for years.

procedures of similar size in the file. Printing the compiler listing used nearly half a box of paper! Since the compiler was doing file-level optimizations, it had too much to think about and committed seppuku.

As soon as the colleague saw the length of the routine he suggested that the basic solution was *Don't Do That*. At that point the code author indignantly lectured him for ten minutes on how screwed up the compiler was because it didn't allow him to code in the most readable fashion—like nested switch statements that extend for ten pages are readable! The sad thing about this anecdote was that it occurred around 1985 when people were supposed to know better.

Huge program modules led to loss of cohesion. The modules do too many things, and those things tend to have relationships that were all too intimate within the module. That tended to make them more difficult to maintain because changes to one function are not isolated from the other functions in the module. Another common problem was mixed levels of abstraction. Such modules tended to mix both high-level functionality and low-level functionality. This obscured the high-level processing with low-level details, a classic forest-and-trees problem.

Perhaps the worst problem of all, though, was that the larger the module, the more interactions it tended to have with other modules, so the opportunities for side effects were greatly increased. All modern approaches to more maintainable code advocate limiting the scope where side effects can occur. The simplest way to limit scope is to keep modules small.[11]

Software Structure

The word *architecture* started to appear in the software literature in the '70s because people were coming to understand that a software application has a skeleton just like a building or an aardvark. The painful lesson about structure is that when it has to be changed, it usually requires a great deal of work. That's because so much other stuff in the application hangs off that structure.

There are four common symptoms that indicate structural changes are being made to an application:

1. Lots of small changes are made.

2. The changes are spread across many of the program units.

3. Changes are difficult to do (e.g., hierarchies have to be redesigned).

4. The changes themselves tend to introduce more errors and rework than normal.

---

11. The acronym KISS—Keep It Simple, Stupid—was born in the '70s at least partially from this idea.

Such changes are commonly called Shotgun Refactoring, and in the Hacker Era there was a whole lot of it.

Lack of Cohesion

One correlation that became apparent early on was that changes were being made to many modules when the requirements changed. One reason was that fundamental structure was being modified. The other was lack of cohesion. Functionality was spread across multiple modules, so when the requirements for that functionality changed, all the modules had to be touched. Lack of cohesion makes it difficult to figure out how to modify a program because the relevant functionality is not localized. Because different modules implemented different parts of a given functionality, those implementations tended to depend on one another to do certain things in particular orders. Although it was usually easy to recognize poor cohesion after the fact, there were no systematic practices that would guarantee good cohesion when the application was originally developed.

Coupling

There have been entire books written about coupling and how to deal with it, so the subject is beyond the practical scope of this book. At the executive summary level, coupling describes the frequency, nature, and direction of intimacy between program elements. The notion of logical coupling grew out of trying to reconcile several different observations:

- Spaghetti code is difficult to maintain.
- Bleeding cohesion across modules resulted in implementation dependencies between them.
- If a client knows a service intimately, it often has to change when the service changes.
- If a service knows a client intimately, it often has to change when the client changes.
- The need to change two elements at once is directly proportional to the nature of access between them.
- The need to change two elements at once is directly proportional to the intimacy of access between them.
- Bidirectional intimacy is usually worse than unidirectional intimacy.

So the notion of coupling arose to describe dependencies between modules resulting from interactions or collaborations between program units. Alas, for a program to work properly, its elements must interact in some fashion. Consequently, developers were faced with a variation on the Three Laws of Thermodynamics: (1) You can't win; (2) You can't even break even; and (3) You can't quit playing.

When thinking about coupling it is important to distinguish between logical and physical coupling. Logical coupling describes how program elements are related to one another based on the roles they play within the problem solution. Physical coupling describes what they need to know about each other to interact *from a compiler's perspective*. Logical coupling in some fashion is unavoidable because solving the problem depends upon it. But it can be minimized with good design practice.

Physical coupling, though, is almost entirely due to the practical issues of implementing 3GL-type systems within the constraints of hardware computational models. For the compiler to write correct machine code in one module for processing—say, data passed to it from another module via a procedure call—the compiler must know how that data was implemented by the caller (e.g., integer versus floating point). Otherwise, the compiler cannot use the right ALU instructions to process it. So the compiler needs to know about the *implementation* of the calling module, which is a physical dependency on that implementation that is dictated by the particular hardware. The most obvious manifestation of this sort of coupling is compile-the-world, where many modules in a large application must be recompiled even though only one had a simple change.

Unfortunately, the literature has been concerned primarily about the frequency of access. Only in the late '80s did the deep thinkers start worrying about the direction of coupling. They noticed that when the graph of module dependencies was a directed graph without loops, the program tended to be much more maintainable. They also noticed that very large applications were becoming infeasible to maintain because compile times and configuration management were becoming major headaches. The challenge lies in minimizing or controlling the physical dependencies among program elements. The techniques for doing this are generally known as *dependency management*.

To date the literature has rarely addressed the nature of coupling. Since the nature of coupling plays a major role in justifying some MDB practices, it is worth identifying here a basic way of classifying the nature of coupling (i.e., the degree of intimacy), in order of increasing intimacy:

- *Message identifier alone.* This is a pure message with no data and no behavior. The opportunities for foot shooting are quite limited, but even this pristine form can cause problems if the message goes to the wrong place or is presented at the wrong time.

- *Data by value.* This form is still pretty benign because there is no way to distress the sender of the message and the receiver has full control over what is done with the data. It is somewhat worse than a pure message because the data may no longer be correct in the program context when the message is processed. This is usually only a problem in asynchronous or distributed environments when delays are possible between sending and processing the message. It can also be a problem in threaded applications where parallel processing is possible.

- *Data by reference.* Here we have the added problem of the receiver being able to modify data in the sender's implementation without the sender's knowledge. Data integrity now becomes a major issue. In fact, passing data by reference compounds the problems in the parallel processing environments because the receiver (or anyone to whom the sender also passed the data by reference) can change it while the sender is using it.

- *Behavior by value.* This curious situation arises in modern programs that pass applets in messages. This is similar to data-by-reference except that it is the receiver who can be affected in unexpected ways. The reason is that the applet is in no way constrained in the things that it does. When the receiver invokes the behavior it effectively has no control over and cannot predict a potentially unlimited number of side effects. If you don't think applets are a problem, ask anyone who deals with web site security.

- *Behavior by reference.* Though some languages from previous eras could do this by passing pointers to functions, it was very rare. Alas, in OOPLs it can be done trivially by passing object references. Like FORTRAN's assigned GOTO, it probably seemed like a good idea at the time, but it turned out badly. Today we realize this is absolutely the worst form of coupling, and it opens a huge Pandora's Box of problems. In addition to invoking behavior with potential for all sorts of side effects, the receiver can also change the object's knowledge without the sender knowing. Since the class' entire public interface is exposed, the receiver is free to invoke any aspect of the object, even those aspects that would cause a problem for the sender.

But worst of all, the encapsulation of the sender has been totally trashed. The reason is that the object whose reference is passed is part of the sender's implementation.[12] By passing it, a bay window has been opened into the implementation of the sender that invites bugs and presents a maintenance nightmare. (In OO terms, it defeats implementation hiding, which is a fundamental OO practice.)

---

12. This only applies to problem space classes that were crafted specifically for the problem in hand. General-purpose computing space classes like String, Array, and Complex_number are really just standardized data structures without significant behavior. In other words, they are simply extensions of fundamental data types.

This means the maintainer must track down every place the reference is used and verify that any change to the way it is used won't break anything. Even then, we can't be sure that someone won't change the receiver during another bout of maintenance to access the instance incorrectly. And even if everything just works, one still has to rebuild the receiver because of the physical coupling.

Because it is such a broad topic, space precludes dealing with coupling in this book. But it is important to note that the notion of coupling formalizes a flock of maintainability issues, and understanding coupling is fundamental to good program development whether you are doing OO development or not.

Technical Innovation

Prior to the OO paradigm all was not chaos, even in the Dark Ages of programming. The academicians were busily adapting mathematics to practical use in the computing environment. During their cogitations the academicians provided a mathematical lingua franca for the underpinnings of software development. This was a collection of theories and models that were particularly well suited to the computing environment. Today this mathematics is the basis of almost everything we do in software development.

This book takes an engineering approach to software development, so it is not going to trot out a lot of theorems. It is, however, worth a couple of subsections to briefly describe at the megathinker level the major relevant mathematical elements and how they influence software development. That's because those ideas still underlie the OO paradigm, albeit in a very well-disguised manner.

The Turing Machine

In the 1930s Alan Turing developed a detailed mathematical model of a theoretical calculating machine. The model was elegantly simple. It assumed all calculating processes were divided into fundamental, individual steps. Those steps could be expressed as a small set of atomic instructions to his machine. Once so divided any calculating process could be described in the following terms:

Sequence: A sequence of one or more instructions located consecutively in the program

Branch: A shift in the execution of the program from a sequence in one program location to another sequence at a different location in the program based upon the truth of some boolean condition

Iteration: A combination of sequence and branch that allowed a sequence to be repeated indefinitely until some boolean condition became true

The mathematics became heavily involved with precise definitions of things like *instruction* and *condition*, and then proving that a Turing machine with a finite instruction set could, indeed, successfully perform any arbitrarily complex calculation. To do so Turing had to examine various strategies for combining and nesting the basic operations.

The Turing machine is the most famous, but there have been a succession of models of computation developed over the years. These models belong to the general class of *hardware computational models*. It is important to realize that such models describe how a *computer* works, not how software is designed. In reality, almost the entire computing space is based upon various hardware computational models. Even exotic mathematical constructs like 3GL type systems have their roots in hardware computational models.

The OO paradigm represents the first major break away from the hardware computational models in creating an approach to software design that is, at least in part, independent of the hardware computational models.[13] That is not to say, though, that the OO paradigm ignores those models. Ultimately the problem solution has to be executed on Turing hardware, so the OO paradigm necessarily has to provide an unambiguous mapping into the hardware computational models.

Languages and Methodologies

As suggested, programs are written in a variety of languages. Initially programs were encoded as binary instructions directly into the hardware on plug boards that directly connected power rails to the hardware to form logic 1 and logic 0, one bit at a time. Instructions to the Arithmetic Logic Unit (ALU) consisted of binary words of a fixed size written directly into hardware *registers*. This was complicated by the fact that the hardware commonly subdivided those words into bit subsets called *fields*.

The first major advance in software development was the introduction of BAL.[14] As bigger problems were solved, software programs became larger, but people don't

---

13. Though the OO paradigm is unique in this respect, that uniqueness is not without its price. OO design is not as intuitive as construction approaches that are firmly attached to hardware computational models. While anyone who can spell "C" can learn OO design techniques, there is definitely a longer learning curve.

14. This was enabled by an advance in hardware technology that allowed one to provide binary instructions on media such as paper tape and punched cards that could be loaded into memory registers automatically. The hardware to do such things were the first peripheral devices that supported the ALU to make access to it more convenient.

think well in binary. BAL enabled hardware operations to be described symbolically with mnemonics like ADD, MOV, and JMP. BAL also enabled ALU registers to be represented symbolically as R1, R2, . . ., Rn. Finally, BAL enabled the developer to assign mnemonic names to memory addresses so that data could be named in a meaningful way. All these things were a boon to software development because they allowed the developer to think about the solution in more abstract terms than endless strings of 1s and 0s.

However, for BAL to work, all those mnemonics had to be translated into the binary view that the hardware understood. Thus was introduced the powerful notion of a program, called a *compiler*, to process other programs by converting them from one representation to another. (Primitive operating systems were already around to manage the housekeeping around running programs through the ALU, but they didn't significantly modify those programs.)

While all this made life much, much easier for the early software developers, there were still some problems. BAL was necessarily tied to the specific ALU instruction set, and by the 1950s hardware vendors were churning out a wide variety of computers with different instruction sets. What was needed was a more abstract description of the solution that was independent of a particular instruction set. This led to the introduction of FORTRAN (FORmula TRANslator) and COBOL (COmmon Business-Oriented Language) in the late 1950s. Just as BAL raised the level of abstraction of software programs above binary expression, this next generation of languages raised the level of abstraction above the ALU itself.

These 3GLs introduced a number of new abstract concepts for computing. These are the primary ones that characterized that generation of languages.

- *Procedures*. Procedures were blocks of instructions that could be invoked from anywhere in the program. When the block completed, control would return to the point in the program from which the procedure was invoked. This enabled a suite of instructions to be reused in different contexts, which was quite common in large applications.

- *Procedural message passing*. However, the data that was modified for each invocation context of a procedure needed to be different. Procedure parameters enabled a particular context to provide data that was unique to that context. Then such parametric data became a unique message sent to the procedure by an individual invocation context. This went a long way toward decoupling what the procedure did with the data from the source context of the data.

- *Types*. To provide that decoupling an abstract mechanism was needed for describing generally what the data is without the detailed semantics of source context. Types allowed the data to be defined for the procedure very generically (e.g., as an integer value). Thus a procedure to compute statistics on a bunch of samples could do so without knowing what the samples actually were; it only needed to know they were integers to compute things like means and T-Statistics. Thus, types at the 3GL level initially defined the implementation of data rather than the problem semantics of the data.

- *Stack-based scope.* Since procedures were called from other procedures, there was an inherent hierarchical structure for sequences of operations. Procedures needed to know how to get back to where they came from, and the notion of a *call stack* was born. The call stack provided a way to keep track of where you came from so that you could unravel nested procedure calls as they completed their tasks.

- *Procedural block structuring.* Procedures provided very useful building blocks for isolating functionality. Such modularity enabled a divide-and-conquer approach to managing complexity. The 3GLs extended this idea to provide modularity within procedures. This supported hard-won lessons like programs being more robust when groups of instructions had single entry and exit points.

Thus the 1960s was a time of profound revolution as software development moved from BAL to 3GLs. New concepts like procedural message passing and stack-based scope required a different view of construction than the only slightly abstracted Turing view of computing in BAL. Into the breach stepped the methodologists. As soon as 3GLs became widely accepted, the need for training developers in using them properly arose.[15] By the early 1970s it was clear that the larger programs enabled by 3GLs needed to be properly *designed*. That gave birth to a host of construction approaches under the general umbrella of Structured Development, as discussed previously.

Basically, those approaches recognized that solving large problems requires something more that just Assembly or 3GL coding skills. Somehow all those abstract constructs needed to play together properly to solve the customer's overall problem. Not the least of the problems was the recognition that programs needed to be maintainable. In addition, large programs needed a structural skeleton and, once in place, that

---

15. Initially this was largely driven by performance issues. The early 3GL compilers weren't very smart. So in the 1960s experienced programmers wrote "x = a + a + a" in FORTRAN instead of "x = 3 * a" because they knew the compiler was not smart enough to realize that one multiply instruction took an order of magnitude more ALU cycles than an addition and that ALU speed was measured in KHz rather than GHz. So the early methodologists were passing on these sorts of practical tidbits to posterity. But very quickly it became apparent that performance was not the only way to shoot oneself in the foot in a 3GL, and more sophisticated design advice was needed.

skeleton tended to be very difficult to modify because of the sheer number of disparate constructs hanging off it. So the methodologies quickly evolved to a more abstract level than 3GL coding, and the developer started looking at the Big Picture as a separate design activity from 3GL coding.

Programming languages are not the only representations of executables. There have been a large number of pictorial notations used to describe programs. It is no accident that every design notation from early HIPO charts[16] to today's Universal Modeling Language (UML) are often referred to as *graphical notations*. Such notations can express the abstract concepts needed for design very efficiently.

Most of the readers of this book will have some software development experience, so the previous discussion of languages and methodologies will probably be quite familiar. However, it was worth the review because there are several important things the rest of the book builds upon.

- A problem solution expressed in any language above binary machine language is a more abstract representation of the machine language that will actually execute on the Turing Machine. Another word for abstract representations of something more concrete is *model*. Thus a program in C is a model of the problem solution that will ultimately execute on the computer in the same sense as a UML OOA model is.

- Software development is continuously evolving towards more abstract ways of expressing problem solutions.

- Because of the ubiquitous presence of mathematics in the computing environment, the computing space is deterministic. For example, compilers, linkers, and loaders automated a lot of drudge work for early BAL and 3GL developers because mapping things like symbolic names to binary addresses is deterministic, even for complex multitasking environments.

Sets and Graphs

It is beyond the scope of this book to describe how ubiquitous various mathematics, especially set and graph theory, are in the computing space. However, a few implications of that are very important to the OO paradigm and MBD in particular.

---

16. HIPO charts were one of the earliest attempts at graphical descriptions of programs, so old that I forgot what the acronym actually means. When she reviewed this book, Rebecca Wirfs-Brock reminded me that it means Hierarchy, Input, Process, Output. Rebecca is a dear person and fine methodologist, but I am concerned that cluttering her mind with such arcane trivia might be displacing useful knowledge.

- The computing space is deterministic. That's because some kind of rigorous mathematics underlies everything in it, however well disguised that might be. This has enormous implications for automation.

- The computing space is disciplined. Everywhere we turn we are constrained by rules like those for language syntax, data structures, identity, GUI design, and so forth. In reality there is very little freedom in implementing problem solutions once we have defined the specific computing environment. Creativity in software development lies in designing solutions, not implementing them.

- The computing space is ultimately based on hardware computational models. However abstract our solution constructs are, the underlying mathematics ensures that they will all map unambiguously into hardware computation.

- The first methodological step in any software construction is expressing the ill-defined, imprecise, ambiguous notions of non-Turing customer spaces in notations that are complete, precise, and unambiguous with respect to the computing space. The mathematics underlying those notations that enable rigorous expression must necessarily be the same mathematics that underlies the computing space.

The methodologies of SD were not simply encyclopedias of a potpourri of hard-won lessons learned in the development trenches prior to 1970. Instead, they became cohesive philosophies of software construction that were based on solid mathematics. Every software construction methodology that has stood the test of time sits on that sort of mathematical platform, however informal its exposition might be and however simple its notation might seem. This was a two-way street; computing has been the driving force in developing entirely new branches of mathematics, from relational theory through type theory to exotic topological theories for non-Turing computation.

Normal Form (NF)

One of the most useful tools to evolve concurrently with SD was a particular branch of general set theory that underlies data storage and the static description of programs. That is, it formalizes and constrains the way data is defined, modified, and related to other data. E. F. Codd first defined it in the late '60s to describe relational databases.[17]

Codd's Relational Data Model (RDM) has since been incorporated into both the OO paradigm and extensions of SD. For example, the descriptor *attribute* associated

---

17. E. F. Codd, "A Relational Model of Data for Large Shared Data Banks," *Communications of the ACM*, Vol. 13, 1970, pp. 377–387.

with knowledge in OO classes is a term Codd introduced in 1970. A suitably arcane branch of mathematics with much broader scope has since been developed, called relational theory. The OO paradigm is based on that broader view.

We can avoid the mathematics of the set theory that forms the basis of NF here and provide the executive summary view because all one needs to know to develop good applications are the implications of the theory. Though NF is more broadly applied, it is most easily understood in terms of tables. The table itself represents an *n-ary relation* of table entities (the rows) that each share the same n *attributes* (the columns). That is, the table describes a set of entities that share characterization in terms of the attributes. Each attribute identifies a particular semantic domain of possible values. Each table entity (a row or *tuple*) has a unique identity and a set of specific values (the table cell values) for the attributes (see Figure 1-3).

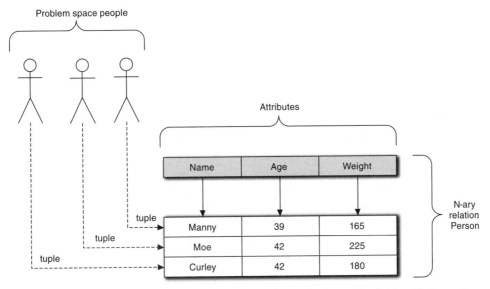

Figure 1-3 *Mapping of problem space entities to an n-ary relation. Each identifiable entity becomes a tuple in the relation. Each relation captures a set of unique values of characteristics that are common to each entity.*

In more practical terms, a column attribute represents a particular data semantic that is shared by every row in the table; it describes *what* the data in the cells of that column is. The cells then represent specific values for that semantic. Then each row represents a set of attribute values that is uniquely associated with the entity. The uniqueness is tied to identity; each row must have a unique identity that distinguishes it from other rows, and the attribute values must depend on that identity. In Figure 1-3 that identity is the name of a person.

In the more restrictive relational data model that applies to databases, some subset of one or more embedded attributes comprises a unique identifier for the table row, and no other row may have exactly the same values for all the identifier attributes. The identifier attributes are commonly known collectively as a *key*. Other attributes that are not part of the key may have duplicated values across the rows, either singly or in combination. But the specific values in a given row depend explicitly on the row key and only on the row key.

Relational theory is about the ways particular entities in different n-ary relations (tables) can be related to each other. For that theory to be practically useful, there need to be certain rules about how attributes and entities can be defined within an n-ary relation. That collection of rules is called *normal form*, and it is critical to almost all modern software development.

The kernel of NF has three rules for compliance:

1. *Attributes must be members of simple domains.* What this essentially means is that attributes cannot be subdivided further (i.e., their values are scalars). That is, if we have a table House with attributes {Builder, Model}, we cannot also subdivide Model into {Style, Price}. The problem is that the Style/Price combinations would be ambiguous in a single-valued attribute cell for Model in a row of House. So the House table must be composed of {Builder, Style, Price} instead.

2. *All non-key attributes, compliant with 1st NF, are fully dependent on the key.* Suppose a House table is defined with attributes {**Subdivision, Lot,** Builder, Model} where Subdivision and Lot are the key that uniquely identifies a particular House. Also suppose only one builder works on a subdivision. Now Builder is really only dependent upon Subdivision and is only indirectly dependent upon Lot through Subdivision. To be compliant we really need two n-ary relations or tables: House {**Subdivision, Lot,** Model} and Contractor {**Subdivision,** Builder}. (The RDM then provides a formalism that links the two tables through the Subdivision attribute that can be implemented to ensure that we can unambiguously determine both the Model and the Builder values for any House. That notion is the subject of a later chapter.)

3. *No non-key attributes, compliant with 2nd NF, are transitively dependent upon another key.* Basically, this means that none of the non-key attribute values depend upon any other key. That is, for House {**Subdivision, Lot,** Model}, if we have a Subdivision = 8, Lot = 4, and Model = flimsy, the Model will remain "flimsy" for Subdivision = 8 and Lot = 4 regardless of what other rows we add or delete from the table.

Generally, most developers depend on the following mnemonic mantra to deal with 3rd NF: *An attribute value depends on the key, the whole key, and nothing but the key.*

Other NF rules have been added over the years to deal with specialized problems, especially in the area of OO databases. We won't go into them here because they are not terribly relevant to the way we will build application models and produce code. However, the value of the three normal forms above is very general and is particularly of interest when defining abstractions and their relationships.

Data Flows

Data was a second-class citizen until the late 1960s.[18] Most of the early theoretical work in computer science was done in universities where the computer systems were solving the highly algorithmic problems of science and engineering. However, by the late 1960s there was an epiphany when people became aware that most of the software in the world was actually solving business problems, primarily in mundane accounting systems.

In particular, business problems were not characterized by algorithms but by USER/CRUD[19] processing of data.[20] For one thing, core business problems were not algorithmic rocket science—doing a long division for an allocation was pretty cutting edge.[21] On the other hand, those very simple calculations were done repeatedly on vast piles of data. What the business community needed was a way to handle data the same way the scientific community handled operations. This led to various flavors of data flow analysis. The basic idea was that processes were small, atomic activities that transformed data, and the processes were connected together by flows of data, as illustrated in Figure 1-4.

As it happens, when we make a data flow graph, it represents a breadth-first flow of control. The processes are self-contained and atomic rather than decomposed. So the problem solution is defined by the direct connections between those processes. The connections are direct and depend only on what needs to be done to the data *next*. If we want to solve a different problem, we change the connections and move

---

18. It was Nicolas Wirth who raised consciousness about the importance of data with his work on Pascal. In particular, one of his books was titled, *Programs = Algorithms + Data Structures*, whose egalitarian view was a quite seminal notion at the time.

19. USER = Update, Sort, Extract, Report and CRUD = Create, Retrieve, Update, Delete. All are simple operations on data.

20. This realization gave birth to data processing, which dominated the '60s and '70s. Later that morphed into today's information technology.

21. Obviously that is no longer true. Many large businesses have entire departments devoted to operations research, often larger than corresponding departments in universities. My earliest practical exposure to operations research was an algorithm to allocate an advertising budget to a variety of national, regional, and local media outlets (TV, magazines, etc.) for a Fortune 500 Company in the '70s. It was a pretty impressive linear programming application.

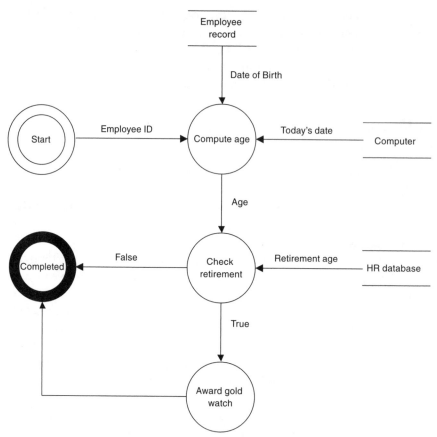

Figure 1-4   *Example of data flow diagram for computing whether a retirement gift should be given to an employee. Data is provided as flows (e.g., Employee ID and age) or is acquired from data stores (e.g., Date of birth and Today's date).*

the data through the same atomic processes differently. Data flows represented a precursor of the peer-to-peer collaboration that is central to the OO paradigm and will be discussed in detail later.

Alas, this view of the world did not mesh well with the depth-first, algorithm-centric view of functional decomposition. Trying to unify these views in a single software design paradigm led to some rather amusing false starts in the '70s. Eventually people gave up trying and lived with a fundamental dichotomy in approaches. For data-rich environments with volatile requirements, they focused on the OO paradigm as the dominant paradigm. Meanwhile, functional programming evolved to deal with the pure algorithmic processing where persistent state data was not needed and requirements were stable.

In many respects the purest forms of data flow analysis were the harbingers of the modern OO paradigm. As we shall see later, the idea of small, self-contained, cohesive processes has been largely canonized in the idea of object behavior responsibilities. Ideas like encapsulation and peer-to-peer collaboration have driven a breadth-first flow-of-control paradigm. But in two crucial respects they are quite different. The OO paradigm encapsulates both the behavior and the data in the same object container, and the data flows have been replaced with message flows. The important point to take away from this subtopic is that where SD was based on functional decomposition, the OO paradigm is more closely aligned with data flows.

State Machines

Meanwhile, there was another branch of software development that was in even deeper trouble than the business people. Those doing real-time and/or embedded (R-T/E) hardware control systems were experiencing a different sort of problem than maintainability. They just couldn't get their stuff to work.

Basically they had three problems. First, such control systems were often used in environments that were extremely resource limited. They didn't have the luxury of stuffing an IBM 360 into a washing machine or railroad signal. Second, the supporting tools that other developers used weren't available in their environment. This was especially true for debugging programs when they might not even have an I/O port for print statements, much less a source-level debugger.

The third problem was that they were dealing with a different view of time. Events didn't happen in synchronization with predefined program flow of control; they occurred randomly in synchronization with the external hardware, and that external hardware never heard of Turing unless it happened to be a computer. Their asynchronous processing completely trashed Turing's ordered world of preordained sequence, branch, and iteration. The tools have gotten better over the years, but the R-T/E people still have the toughest job in the software industry.

The tool that made life bearable for the R-T/E people was the Finite State Machine (FSM).[22] We have no idea who first wrote a program using an FSM, but whoever it was deserves to be in the Software Hall of Fame along with Ada Lovelace and crew. It basically enabled asynchronous processing in a serial Turing world. It also made marvelously compact programs possible because much of the flow of control logic was implicit in the FSM rules for processing events and static sequencing constraints represented by transitions, as shown in Figure 1-5.

---

22. If you have led a sheltered existence and don't know exactly what an FSM is or why it is a big deal, have patience. They are the primary topic of several later chapters. For those who have taken courses about finite state automata, it should be noted that the FSM used in software systems has added some capability over the classical theoretical machines.

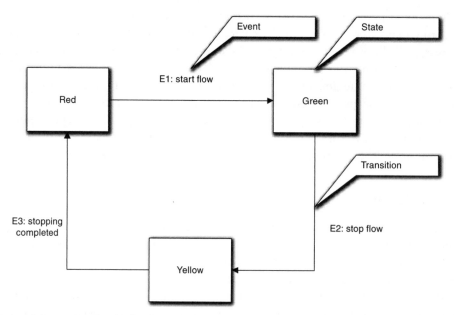

Figure 1-5   *Example of a finite state machine for a simple traffic light. The traffic light migrates through states in a manner that is constrained by allowed transitions. Transitions from one state to the next are triggered by external events.*

However, the really interesting thing about FSMs is that they happen to address a number of the same issues that are the focus of OOA/D. In particular, they provide an extraordinary capability for reducing the degree of coupling and truly encapsulate functionality. They also enforce basic good practices of OO design. If we were given the task of coming up with a single construct to capture *and enforce* core elements of the OO paradigm, the FSM would be that construct. But we will defer the discussion of how that is so until Part III.

Chapter 2

Object Technology

The real danger is not that machines will begin to think like men,
but that men will begin to think like machines.
—Sydney J. Harris

Structured Development (SD) revolutionized the way software was developed. It provided a systematic approach to software construction much more in line with the techniques more mature engineering disciplines regularly used. SD enabled much larger applications to be built much faster. By the late '70s it was becoming clear that despite being a boon to productivity, SD had some glaring weaknesses; those weaknesses were discussed in Chapter 1.

At the same time, OO methodologists were noting that an interesting side effect of the OO paradigm was that applications tended to be more maintainable. So around 1980 the emphasis on OOA/D switched gears in a subtle way. Until then the methodologies were primarily focused on expressing designs in terms compatible with the new OOPLs. They devised graphical notations of OOPL constructs, and their methodologies were geared to expressing basic design concepts in those notations.[1] But around 1980 the methodologists started to emphasize how OOA/D could be used to address the specific weaknesses of SD.

The remainder of this chapter is an overview of OO development at the executive summary level. We start with some basic elements of the construction philosophy underlying the OO paradigm. Then we move on to specific mechanisms and techniques that address the SD problems. The goal is to provide context by discussing how the OO paradigm addressed some of the problems of the hacker and SD eras. Most of the major features will be discussed in greater detail in later chapters.

---

1. In fact, the early Booch notation was sometimes referred to as "Graphical C++" because it incorporated several unique features of C++, like *protected*.

Basic Philosophy

The OO paradigm is rather sophisticated compared to previous software development approaches. It is not very intuitive in a hardware computational sense, so it requires a mindset that is rather unique. The paradigm is also comprised of a number of disparate concepts that need to play together. Here we will identify the fundamental notions that will be glued together in Parts II and III.

Maintainability

In the '70s there were a number of empirical studies of how software was developed. Two stunning conclusions came out of those studies.

1. Most software shops devoted over 70% of their development effort to maintenance.

2. The effort required to modify an existing feature often required 5 to 10 *times* more effort than developing the feature originally.

Clearly something was wrong with that picture. In the late '70s this became the software crisis, and the academic discipline of software engineering was introduced to address it.[2] At that time software engineering was primarily devoted to fixing SD to address the problems; if everyone just did SD *right*, then the problems would go away.[3]

After 1980 the primary goal of the OO paradigm became application maintainability. The OO gurus looked at the root causes of the problems (as described in Chapter 1) and decided that fixing SD was not viable. There were systemic problems like functional decomposition and marriage to hardware computational models that could not be fixed with a Band-Aid approach. Not surprisingly, the OO gurus saw the OO paradigm as the path out of the maintainability wilderness. So OOA/D methodologies sought to ensure that maintainable software could be constructed.

Maintainability is the primary goal of OOA/D.

Some wags have paraphrased Vince Lombardi[4] by saying maintainability is the only goal. Productivity for original development is very near the bottom of the list of

---

2. The term was introduced earlier, but it referred primarily to project management activities.

3. In the late '80s software engineering evolved into a more traditional process management view. But that's another story. . . .

4. I'm dating myself. Vince Lombardi was a legendary football coach in the '50s and '60s. When asked how winning ranked against other sports goals his answer was, "There are no other goals." Vince probably would not have been an ideal coach for Pop Warner teams.

goals. On the other hand, productivity for maintenance is very high on the list. Reliability is also high on the list because one of the main reasons traditional maintenance required so much effort was that the changes themselves were so complex they inserted defects. Everything in modern OOA/D is focused on providing more robust, maintainable, and reliable applications.

As a corollary, a fundamental assumption of the OO paradigm is that requirements are volatile over the life of a software product. If that is not the case, as in some areas of scientific programming, the OO paradigm may be a poor choice for development.

Problem Space Abstraction

Nobody likes change.

Developers don't like change because it means they need to maintain legacy code rather than moving on to wonderful new challenges. As it happens, the customers of software don't like change either. When change occurs in their domain, they will try to accommodate it in a way that will minimize disruption of their existing infrastructure (i.e., the processes, practices, policies, standards, techniques, and whatnot that are part of how they handle day-to-day operations).

When change filters down to the software as new requirements, it will be easier to incorporate if the software structure mimics the customer's domain structure.

This is a fundamental assumption underlying the OO paradigm. Essentially it assumes that all change originates in the customer's domain and must be dealt with there prior to defining new requirements for existing software. The customer will take the path of least resistance in accommodating that change in the customer domain. So the customer will have already done much of the work of accommodating the change as a whole before it filters down to the software. If the software structure accurately reflects the customer's domain structure, then the customer will have already done part of the developer's job.

These notions about change are why the single most distinctive feature of the OO paradigm is problem space abstraction. No other software construction methodology uses abstraction to anywhere near the extent that the OO paradigm uses it, and the OO paradigm is the *only* one that emphasizes abstracting noncomputing domains.

A major goal of the OO paradigm is to emulate the customer's domain structure in the software structure.

Very few customer domains are computing space domains; therefore those domains are not based on hardware computational models. They are enormously varied and rich in conceptual material. They are also very complex, much more so than typical computational environments. That complexity, variation, and richness would overwhelm any attempt at literally emulating it in the software.[5] So we need some way of simplifying the customer view and emphasizing the structural elements that are important to the specific problem in hand.

The design tool that does that is abstraction. Abstraction is ubiquitous in OOA/D. It is the primary tool for capturing the customer's domain structure. We will revisit problem space abstraction later in this chapter for an overview of mechanisms and come back to it throughout the rest of the book.

OOA, OOD, and OOP

In Chapter 1 it was noted that SD introduced two new steps, analysis and design, into the software development process. The goal was to provide stepping-stones between the customer space and the computing space that would lose less information in the translation of customer requirements to software implementation. The OO paradigm provides similar stepping-stones, but places a very different spin on what *analysis* means.

In SD, analysis was a hybrid of high-level software design and problem analysis. Many SD authors referred to it as problem analysis—determining what the real problem to be solved was. The OO paradigm assumes that one does problem analysis when one elicits and analyzes requirements. That is, problem analysis is a prerequisite to requirements specification because we can't specify requirements for a solution unless we know what the problem actually is. So object-oriented analysis (OOA) is quite different from SD analysis.

> OOA results in a full solution for the problem's functional requirements that is independent of particular computing environments.

In the OO paradigm, the OOA represents the customer's view of the solution because problem space abstraction expresses it in terms of the customer's domain structure. Because the OOA is expressed purely in customer terms, it can only address functional requirements. (Addressing nonfunctional requirements like size, performance, and security necessarily depends on *how* a specific solution is implemented.) As such, it is independent of the particular computing environment where the application will be implemented. Thus OOA is a true stepping-stone representing a problem space solution that is more readily mapped to the customer requirements. But because we use a notation that is based on the same underlying mathematics as the computing space, that customer view is readily elaborated into a computing solution.

---

5. A hardened 3GL programmer once said, "Give me a big enough computer and enough time and I will model the universe in real time." Good luck with that.

> OOD is an elaboration of an OOA solution that resolves nonfunctional requirements at a strategic level for a specific computing environment.

The definition of object-oriented design (OOD) is also different from that of SD, but less so. OOD is an elaboration of the OOA solution that deals explicitly with nonfunctional requirements at a strategic level. It specifies a high-level design view of the solution that accommodates fundamental characteristics of the local computing environment.

> OOP is an elaboration of an OOD solution that provides tactical resolution of all requirements at the 3GL level.

Object-oriented programming (OOP) resolves all requirements at a tactical level (e.g., specific languages, network protocols, class libraries, technologies, and whatnot). Note that the definitions of OOA, OOD, and OOP are more rigorously defined than their counterparts under SD. More important, there is a clear separation of concerns—functional versus nonfunctional requirements and customer space versus computing space—that is designed to manage complexity in large applications better.

Subject Matter

All OO artifacts—subsystems, objects, and responsibilities—represent some recognizable subject matter that exists in the problem domain. The term *subject matter* is difficult to define. The dictionary definition is that it is something to be considered or discussed, which is just a tad vague. But that simplistic definition does capture the notion of thinking about what the subject of an abstraction *is*. It also captures the very common team practice of developing abstractions by consensus. But this still comes up short in describing a rather rich concept.

> A subject matter defines and bounds the thing, tangible or intangible, that is being abstracted.

Alas, this definition, in its generality, is only slightly more focused on the OO paradigm than the dictionary definition. The problem is that the definition has to be readily mapped into the potentially infinite variety of customer problem spaces. But at least this definition introduces the notion that an abstraction must have clear boundaries, which is important to functional isolation, encapsulation, and separation of concerns. In the interest of providing more insight into the notion as it relates specifically to objects, it is useful to describe a subject matter in terms of the following qualifications.

- It has a cohesive set of intrinsic responsibilities relevant to the problem in hand.

- It is characterized by a unique suite of rules and policies.

- It is defined at a particular level of abstraction.

- It is readily identifiable by experts in the problem domain.

- Its boundaries are well-defined by experts in the problem domain.

- It is logically indivisible at the context's level of abstraction. (We will have more to say about logical indivisibility shortly.)

We do not model or code subject matter per se, largely because of the difficulty and ambiguity in defining it. Instead, we describe it in terms of obligations to know or do things. If everyone who touches a subsystem, object, or responsibility does not have a clear and consistent understanding of the subject matter (i.e., what it *is*), then inevitably there will be trouble. If you could only supply carefully crafted external documentation of one thing in an application, it should be subject matters.

Separation of Concerns

This is actually one of the more important concepts in the OO paradigm. The basic idea is that we should manage complexity through divide and conquer. Essentially, we manage complexity by decomposing the problem into smaller pieces that are more easily dealt with. This is not an original idea by any means; the functional decomposition that was central to SD did exactly this. What the OO paradigm brings to the table is a unique marriage of decomposition and a flexible view of logical indivisibility that is enabled by different levels of subject matter abstraction.

The OO paradigm essentially provides us with more tools for managing separation of concerns than SD did in the two-dimensional, hierarchical functional decomposition of sequences of operations. As a practical matter, there are four basic elements to separation of concerns in the OO paradigm.

1. *Cohesion*. Any concern is a cohesive concept that has well-defined scope and boundaries. Thus the notion of managing inventory is a cohesive concept in most businesses.

2. *Subject matter*. We can associate the concern with a specific, identifiable subject matter in some problem space. There is a body of rules, policies, data, and whatnot that one can associate with a subject matter called inventory management. Though conceptual, it is readily identifiable, and any domain expert will understand the subject matter semantics.

3. *Isolation*. We can encapsulate the concern using standard OO techniques. In the case of inventory management, the scale would dictate encapsulation at the application or subsystem level.

4. *Decoupling.* We separate the subject matter from other subject matters and minimize dependencies on the details of how it works across boundaries.

Note that the definitions of OOA, OOD, and OOP earlier are a good example of separation of concerns at the methodological level. The line in the sand between OOA and OOD separates the concerns of functional versus nonfunctional requirements. It also separates the concerns of the customer's domain from those of the computing domain. Separation of concerns is applicable all the way down to the responsibility level. As we shall see later in the book, responsibilities must be cohesive, logically indivisible, and intrinsic. That is just another way of saying that they represent a separation of very specific concerns away from other concerns.

Levels of Abstraction

Long before the OO paradigm, the idea of layering in products often conformed to the notion of levels of abstraction. The lower layers tended to be more detailed and less abstract with very specialized behaviors. Meanwhile the higher layers were more general and abstract with broadly defined behaviors. SD's functional decomposition provided a similar sort of ordering of levels of abstraction.

In software construction, there is a succession of abstract views as we move back from the 3GL program model, as indicated in Figure 2-1. As we move from top to bottom, we move from greater abstraction to lesser abstraction as more and more Turing detail is added. The nature of classes from OOA through OOPL code will also tend to move from abstract problem space abstractions like *Customer* to concrete computing space abstractions like *String*.

These stages represent quite different views. Thus the *OOA* represents a customer view of the solution and only addresses functional requirements while the *OOD* view is a computing space view that resolves nonfunctional requirements. Similarly, the Loader view of the problem is devoid of customer semantics while providing a view as close to the hardware computational models as one can get in software. Since the OO paradigm is based largely on abstraction, it figures that we should be able to use that to our advantage. As it happens, methodologically the OO paradigm employs levels of abstraction to assist in everything from defining overall application structure to dependency management.

Probably the most important application lies in defining overall program structure. While the original OO paradigm provided lots of tools and ideas, MBD has refined the notion of abstraction for this purpose more than any other OO methodology. We will talk about this in detail in Chapter 6. For now just keep in mind that a subsystem defines a level of abstraction, and all objects that implement that subsystem should be abstracted at that level of abstraction.

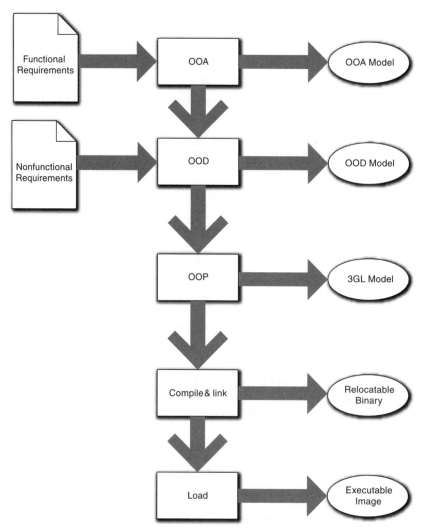

Figure 2-1   *Levels of abstraction in a typical OO development process. Abstraction decreases as we move down and more computing space detail is added. Each stage above "Load" provides a model of the actual computer instructions. Those models are a specification of the problem solution at the next lower level of abstraction. At the same time, every stage's output is a solution for the model specification of the previous stage.*

Problem Space Abstraction

At the core of all OO methodologies is the identification and abstraction of *entities* in some customer domain.[6] Those entities must be readily identifiable, but they can be either concrete, such as Car, House, or Person, or they can be conceptual, such as Contract, Law, or Obligation. In most customer spaces entities can be quite complex with multiple properties or characteristics. But those characteristics will be explicitly associated with the entity by the customer.

> The primary task of problem space abstraction is to identify entities in the problem space and their properties that are relevant to the problem in hand.

We call the abstraction of such an entity an *object*. So the basic notion of an object as a bundle of properties associated with an identifiable entity is a direct result of problem space abstraction designed to emulate the customer domain's structure.

If we look in an unabridged dictionary for a definition of *abstraction*, we find three distinct definitions. The first captures the idea of extracting particular characteristics. The second describes it as a conceptual generalization of the common essence of similar concrete things. The third captures the notion of a summary. The notion of *abstraction* in the OO paradigm has aspects of all three of these definitions. In the end, though, abstraction modifies reality and there are five ways that abstractions can modify reality.

1. *Eliminate characteristics*. Real entities usually have a large number of characteristics. Often many of these are simply not relevant to the problem in hand; for a dogcatcher facing a growling dog, knowing whether the dog is housebroken is merely a distraction.

2. *De-emphasize characteristics*. Another way to simplify abstractions is to just de-emphasize characteristics rather than eliminate them entirely. The criteria used to identify the different groups of critters in a phylum can be quite complex (e.g., warm-blooded, egg-layer, etc.). If we don't care about the details of the classification scheme, we could have a single attribute, *Critter Type*, where we provide values of "platypus" or "aardvark." In doing so, we have de-emphasized the entire classification scheme context to a single type descriptor.

3. *Generalize characteristics*. Sometimes the characteristics of individual instances have minor variations that are not important to the problem in hand. In this case we wish to generalize the characteristics in the application so that the differences

---

6. As we shall see, the notion of *customer* can vary with subject matter. In this book, an unqualified reference refers to the customer initially defining the requirements for the overall application.

disappear. If an application is printing a poster depicting the various snakes in the southeastern United States, it probably doesn't matter much that there are three broad classes of venom that help distinguish certain snakes for herpetologists. Poisonous versus nonpoisonous is probably good enough.[7]

4. *Emphasize.* An abstraction can select parts of the customer's problem space entity and place special emphasis on them. A metric for a process, such as defect rate, can usually take on values across a wide range. However, if we are doing statistical process control, we are only interested in whether or not a value lies within a predefined envelope or range. In that case we might decide to substitute a Boolean attribute for defect rate samples whose values represent *In Control* and *Out Of Control*. We are still viewing defect rate values, but a crucial aspect of that metric has been emphasized.

5. *Coalesce characteristics.* Abstraction is not limited to objects. It can be applied to the characteristics that comprise those abstractions. The idea here, though, is to extend the notion of generalization to capture multiple characteristics as a single abstract characteristic. A classic example of this is the mathematical notion of a complex number that contains both a real and an imaginary part. Most problem solutions that deal with complex numbers can be described without ever having to deal with the individual real and imaginary parts. In those cases it is fair to abstract the complex number into a single, scalar "value" in the OOA/D models.[8]

The last issue concerning abstraction is where they come from. The simple answer is that they come from the problem space. They represent entities in the problem space. So what is an entity? The following definition is useful.

> **Entity:** An entity is a real thing, possibly intangible, that is readily recognized as distinct by experts in a particular problem domain.

---

7. There is an adage among herpetologists that you can tell the museum guys from the field guys by counting their fingers. Clearly there are other circumstances where one wants a tad more detail about the nature of the venom of a particular flavor of snake.

8. This is why the Complex Number library class has become a de facto fundamental data type in many applications. If one overloads operators like "+" in an OOPL, the only time one has to think about the real and imaginary parts is when it is created. Typically that will be isolated to a low-level component in the application. For example, in electronic test equipment, a complex number is created when the Quadrature and Phase registers are read from the hardware but the 3+ MLOC of code on top of that manipulates it as a single, scalar value.

The entities from which we form abstractions may be concrete things, concepts, roles, or anything else in the problem space. The key aspect is that it is perceived to be a cohesive, identifiable *thing* by the gurus of the problem space.

> All entities and their object abstractions have unique identity.

This is a corollary to the notion that domain experts perceive the entity to be distinct. Each entity must be somehow uniquely identifiable, and each object abstracts exactly one such entity from the problem space. The notion of identity conveniently maps into the more rigorous set theory that underlies the OO paradigm and UML.

So what happens when we have an inventory bin full of 6-32×1 cap head screws? Does each screw have a name? Hardly. But an individual screw is still identifiable, if for no other reason than being the one picked from the bin. A DBMS will get around this problem by providing an artificial identity (e.g., an autonumber key) for each item. The OO paradigm has an even more subtle means of dealing with implied identity through relationships. Thus objects can be identified based on who they are associated with. For example, we might break up the notion of *automobile* into distinct objects like *body*. If the Automobile object is identified by a unique VIN number, then the *body* object may be uniquely identified as the only one associated with a particular, explicitly identified Automobile.

Encapsulation

One of the first problems attacked was hiding implementations so that other program units would not trample on them. In SD this was done through APIs, but they were usually only applied to large-scale program units. The OO paradigm formalizes the notion of implementation hiding through *encapsulation*; thus all implementations are encapsulated behind interfaces. The OO paradigm just made the notion of encapsulation so fundamental that it was applied to *all* abstractions.

> An abstraction incorporates two views: an internal one for describing **how** the abstraction works, and an external one for describing **what** the abstraction is about.

The combination of abstraction and encapsulation enabled a separation of semantics (*what* an entity was contractually responsible for knowing or doing) and implementation (*how* the entity knew or did it). The interface provides the external view while the stuff behind the interface provides the internal view. Thus the role of the interface subtly changed from a mechanism to provide module boundaries to a mechanism for hiding details.

Cohesion

In Chapter 1 we indicated that SD did not provide adequate guidelines for ensuring cohesion for application elements. That is, there was no systematic approach to cohesion. The OO paradigm provides a very systematic approach and uses cohesion explicitly as a design tool. Specifically, the OO paradigm depends on the problem space to provide cohesiveness. Thus objects are cohesive in that they provide a bundle of related properties that are unique to a specific entity in the problem space. A reviewer of an OOA model will always ask, "Will a domain expert easily recognize this object and be able to describe what it is just from the name?" Similarly, object properties are individually cohesive because they represent intrinsic, logically indivisible, and separably identifiable properties of a particular problem space entity *in the problem space*.

> Cohesion maps to distinct problem domain entities and their unique properties.

This linking of cohesion to what is recognizable as distinct (entities) and logically related (the properties that characterize them) in the problem space is one of the unique contributions of the OO paradigm.

Logical Indivisibility

Another rather unique feature of the OO paradigm is the emphasis on logical indivisibility. In traditional functional decomposition, only the leaf functions at the base of the tree had to be logically indivisible. In practice, such functions were usually one level above 3GL language operators like "+" and "-". That was because one decomposed until there wasn't anything left to decompose.

The OO notion of logical indivisibility is much more flexible because it depends on the level of abstraction of the problem and individual subsystem subject matter. Different OO methodologies recognize somewhat different levels of logical indivisibility.[9] MBD recognizes four fundamental levels of logical indivisibility:

1. *Subsystem.* A subsystem is a large-scale element of an application based upon encapsulating the functionality associated with a single, large-scale problem space subject matter. A subsystem is implemented with collaborating objects.

---

9. The main differences are whether one recognizes a "component" as being distinct from a "subsystem" and whether one can nest subsystems. These differences are not great because they are mainly about distinguishing really big units from not-quite-so-big units, and they mostly apply to systems engineering, which is partially addressed in Chapter 6.

2. *Object.* An object abstracts a single identifiable entity from a subsystem subject matter's problem space. An object has responsibilities to know and do things. Objects are abstracted in a manner that is consistent with the level of abstraction of the containing subsystem's subject matter.

3. *Object responsibility.* An object responsibility represents a single, fundamental unit of knowledge or behavior with respect to the problem in hand. The responsibility is defined at the level of abstraction of the containing object's subject matter.

4. *Process.* To describe the dynamics of behavior responsibilities one needs to express problem space rules and policies in terms of fundamental computational operations. These can range from arithmetic operators to complex algorithms defined outside the problem space in hand. A process is one or more cohesive operations on state data that are logically inseparable at the containing behavior responsibility's level of abstraction.

The OO notion of logical indivisibility means that the abstraction is self-contained, intrinsic, and cohesive such that there is no point in further subdivision *at the given level of abstraction.* That is, in any solution context the abstraction can always be contemplated as a whole. The OO paradigm then encapsulates that abstraction behind an interface so that its more complex implementation is hidden.

The power of flexible logical indivisibility probably isn't very obvious at the moment and you are wondering why such a big deal is made out of it. To see its utility you need to get some more methodological ducks in a row. However, an example might help to make the point. The author once worked with a very large device driver (~ 3 MLOC). In one high-level subsystem there was a single object knowledge attribute that was represented as a scalar data value at that level of abstraction. In that subsystem we were dealing with flow of control at a very high level and didn't care about the details. In a subsystem at a lower level of abstraction, though, that "value" expanded into more than a dozen classes, thousands of objects, and on the order of 10^9 individual data elements. It cannot be overemphasized how useful it is to be able to think about such complexity as a simple scalar knowledge attribute when dealing with high-level flow of control.

This flexible notion of logical indivisibility allows us to essentially "flatten" the functional decomposition tree so that we don't have tediously long decomposition chains. It also allows us to create different solutions by simply connecting the dots (behavior responsibilities) differently. We see examples of this in later chapters.

Communication Models

The world of Turing is inherently serial because one instruction is executed at a time and instructions are ordered. The reality is that things like distributed and/or concurrent processing are no longer limited to R-T/E. The simplistic days of batch processing in data processing systems are long gone. Today's software is interactive, distributed, interoperable, concurrent, and so on. Today's problems are inherently asynchronous. If one is building large, complex applications, one has to deal with it.[10]

In OOA/D behavior responsibilities are accessed asynchronously.

That is, it is assumed that a behavior responsibility can be triggered independent of the execution of any other behavior responsibility. In addition, there may be an arbitrary delay between the time the trigger was generated and the response is actually processed. In other words, one cannot count on a behavior responsibility executing serially in a predefined order immediately after some other behavior executes.

We will have a lot more to say about this in Part III on dynamic descriptions. For the moment all you need to know is why this is the case. The reason is that an asynchronous communication model is the most general description of behavior. If one can solve the problem under asynchronous assumptions, one can implement that solution as-is in any implementation environment: serial, synchronous, asynchronous, and/or concurrent. It may not be easy and one may have to provide a lot of infrastructure, but one can always implement it *without modifying the solution logic*. It is beyond the scope of this book to prove it, but that is not necessarily true for serial/synchronous solution designs if one tries to implement them in a truly asynchronous or concurrent environment. If one starts with a synchronous description and tries to implement in an inherently asynchronous environment, such as a distributed system, one may have to modify the solution logic in order to implement it correctly.

As R-T/E people can testify, getting an asynchronous communication model to work is not easy.[11] But once it is working, it will tend to be quite stable and fairly

---

10. Many OOA/D authors don't talk about asynchronous processing. Many consider it too complex and confusing for OO novices to grasp, so they just provide guidelines and rules that, if practiced properly, will hopefully get to the same place that thinking about asynchronous processing would. As an aside, I feel strongly that this view is both condescending and dangerous because it is difficult to practice those rules and guidelines properly if one doesn't know why they are really there.

11. This is another reason that many OOA/D authors avoid talking about asynchronous processing. There is less to teach and learn if one assumes a simple, synchronous world. That view even had merit through the '70s when virtually all applications were monolithic, stand-alone processes. Why confuse everyone with issues that only a small niche of computing (R-T/E) cared about? It is still relevant today for CRUD/USER applications, though the RAD IDEs tend to be very inefficient as they serialize networks and DB access. But that attitude just doesn't make sense in today's complex, interoperable application environments once one is beyond CRUD/USER processing.

easy to modify. More important, though, is that the OOA author does not need to worry about the details of concurrency and whatnot when forming the solution. The OOA model will Just Work no matter where it is implemented.

Knowledge is always accessed directly from its source when needed.

What this means is that when a behavior responsibility needs data to chew on, it goes directly to the data owner and gets a fresh value. In effect this means that we assume knowledge access is synchronous (i.e., the requesting behavior responsibility will pause until the knowledge is acquired). This assumption is necessary if one assumes asynchronous behavior communications in order to preserve developer sanity.

Message data is knowledge that represents a snapshot in time.

This corollary essentially means that in well-formed OO applications messages rarely have data packets because behavior responsibilities access the data they need directly.[12] This is in marked contrast with the traditional procedural context where procedures usually have arguments. If one employs an asynchronous behavior communication model, one cannot assume the data passed with the message will not become obsolete because of the arbitrary delays. So the only reason to pass knowledge in messages is because one *needs* the data to be bound to a specific point in the solution flow of control. An example of such snapshots might be data from multiple sensors that needs to be processed together from the same sampling time slice.

But if we *know* the implementation will be synchronous, why bother? Because what we know today may not be true tomorrow. If we create the OOA solution with a synchronous model and some future change in the deployment environment moves a subsystem or some objects onto another platform, we want that change to be relatively easy to implement. What we don't want is a shotgun refactoring of the flow of control. If one does the OOA solution right in the first place, that will *never* be a major problem later when the implementation environment changes.

As a bonus we will find that the added discipline in the OOA model will make it more robust and easier to modify when the functional requirements change. One reason is that the scope of access of data is limited to the method needing the data. Procedures provide a very convenient scope boundary in the computing space. That simplifies data integrity issues because one sees what data is accessed and when it is accessed within the method scope. But if data is passed one is necessarily concerned

---

12. We are talking here about OOA/D, not OOP. In very rare situations, tactical resolution for performance requirements can dictate that one limit the *number* of collaborations, so in OOP one may combine method invocation with knowledge access by passing data. But when one does that it must be an informed decision, and one may need to provide additional infrastructure to ensure the data is still timely by the time it is actually processed.

with where and when the data was acquired, which extends the scope of data integrity concerns back up the call stack to wherever the data was acquired.[13]

Breadth-First Processing (aka Peer-to-Peer Collaboration)

In Chapter 1 we discussed SD's depth-first, hierarchical functional decomposition and some problems associated with it. Again, objects save the day. Since objects have self-contained implementations due to abstraction, encapsulation, and logical indivisibility, they allow breadth-first communications. This is because if you tell an object to do something, it does it, and then it is finished because it is logically indivisible and self-contained.

From its clients' viewpoint it is atomic; an object is a single identifiable entity. Therefore, the important flow of control in the application is described in terms of object interactions (in OO terms, collaborations). This raises the level of abstraction of flow of control considerably. In fact, as we will see later in the book, when defining collaborations, one doesn't really care which object responsibilities are involved; the message is viewed as a collaboration between objects rather than between responsibilities (i.e., the receiving object selects the appropriate behavior for the message using its current internal state).

The value of the breadth-first paradigm shows up during application maintenance, particularly when debugging problems. Unless you have tried it, it is hard to imagine how powerful this approach is. In the author's experience when developing software like this, about two-thirds of the bugs fixed were diagnosed by inspection in a matter of minutes. In equivalent procedural code it was more like one-fifth.

> In the first pilot project the author ever did with the OO paradigm, the hardware guys were using the software as a diagnostic tool to figure out how the hardware should *really* work. So the hardware was changing underneath the software on essentially a continuous basis. We could usually have a hardware change correctly implemented in software before the hardware guys could finish breadboarding it.
>
> Just as we completed that pilot project, Marketing changed the performance requirements. To meet the new requirements we had to completely rework inter-task communications from shared files to shared memory and make fundamental changes to things

---

13. Functional programming relies on passing *all* state data as arguments. But functional programming limits the scope of data integrity issues in a different way through the concept of closure combined with the lack of persistent data. The passed data then represents the state of the entire problem solution at the moment the procedure was called, so the issue of timeliness effectively goes away.

like the way the hardware was initialized. We turned those changes in a week.[14] That totally astounded everyone familiar with the project because it would have taken a couple of months to do it if the application had been written procedurally like our other drivers up to that time. (The Marketeers had already fallen on their swords and told the customer privately that there would be a few months' delay based on past performance for similar changes!)

Another way of describing breadth-first flow of control is to say that collaboration between objects is on a peer-to-peer basis. At each point in the solution, the next action to be performed is triggered by a message that passes directly from the object raising the trigger condition to the object having the response. There is no indirection or middlemen involved in the collaboration. That is a direct result of abstraction combining with logical indivisibility to ensure that each behavior is self-contained.[15]

Elaboration versus Translation

Elaboration is characterized by a succession of stages—OOA → OOD → OOP—for developing the application where the developer adds value directly to each stage. The OOA is incrementally elaborated with strategic detail related to the computing environment until one has a completed OOD. At that point the OOA no longer exists. Then the OOD is incrementally elaborated with tactical detail to provide an OOP solution. This was the classic way OO applications were developed through the late '80s.

In contrast, the translationists draw a very sharp line in the sand between OOA and OOD. They preserve the OOA as an implementation-independent, abstract solution to the customer's problem. They then use a full code generator (known as a *transformation engine*) to translate the OOA into a code model (3GL or Assembly). The transformation engine essentially automates OOD and OOP.

The main advantage of the elaborationist approach is that everyone knows how to do it. One downside is a tendency to mire down in design paralysis because there is no clear criteria for when the OOA or OOD is completed. Another downside is that when porting to another computing environment, one can't separate the customer's problem solution from the implementation elaborations. Also, it is necessary to invest

---

14. The ability to turn maintenance that quickly on the pilot project was even more impressive for a number of reasons: We were new to OT, none of us had built an application before for the operating system (MS-DOS), the hardware we were controlling was analog and we had only done digital previously, and most of us had not previously used the implementation language (C++).

15. It has far more important implications for DbC because of the convenient direct mapping between triggering conditions and responses. Peer-to-peer collaboration enables DbC techniques for rigorously defining correct flow of control in the overall solution. But that is a topic for Part III.

in dependency management refactoring during OOP to make the 3GL program maintainable. And to preserve copies of the OOA/D models for posterity, one is faced with multiple edits for maintenance changes. But the biggest price is the redundant effort in providing implementation infrastructure that is reinvented for every application. In a typical 3GL program at least 60% of the code will be devoted directly or indirectly to particular technologies (e.g., XML) and optimization techniques (e.g., caching) that address nonfunctional requirements or tactical 3GL solutions. That code essentially gets reinvented for each application.

There are several advantages to translation:

- It separates the problem space solution logic from the implementation issues in the computing environment, allowing one to focus on these two problems separately. In practice this means that functional requirements (OOA) are resolved independently from nonfunctional requirements (OOD and OOP). This promotes specialization between application problem solving and implementation optimization.

- It allows the same OOA solution to be ported to different computing environments without change and with complete confidence that the problem solution logic still works.

- It allows a one-time effort to develop a transformation engine in a given computing environment. That transformation engine can then be reused to translate *every* application OOA to be run in that environment. In effect one has massive OOD/P design reuse across applications for a given computing environment.

- The exit criteria for completion of OOA is unambiguous because the OOA model is executable.[16] It is done when the tests for functional requirements pass.

- No dependency management refactoring is needed since only the OOA models are maintained as requirements change, and physical coupling is a pure 3GL problem.

- The OOA solution is roughly an order of magnitude more compact than a 3GL solution, which greatly improves communication and comprehensibility by focusing on the essential elements of the solution.

---

16. This might seem extraordinary, but it makes sense when one thinks about it. If the OOA model is rigorous enough for a transformation engine to generate correct optimized code, it must be rigorous enough to execute in an unoptimized, interpreted mode. All translation tools support such a mode and provide a test harness for applying the same test case data to either the model or the final executable.

Alas, there are some disadvantages to translation:

- The computing space may be deterministic, but it is also enormously complex. So providing adequate optimization in transformation engines is nontrivial; building a transformation engine in-house is not recommended. As a result, today's commercial transformation engines tend to be pricey. It took from the early '80s to the late '90s to develop optimization techniques to the point where translation code was competitive in performance with elaboration code. That is a substantial investment to recover.

- The OOA model must be very rigorous. Code generators do what one says, not what one meant, so the developer must use a good analysis and design methodology. Winging it is not an option, and the developer needs to learn about things like state machines because they provide the necessary rigor.

- Moving from traditional elaboration to translation is a major sea change in the way a shop develops software. Processes for everything from configuration management to test development will be affected because one essentially has a different set of development stages.

As indicated in the Introduction, MDB is a translationist methodology. The author believes that translation techniques are as inevitable as the conversion from Assembly to 3GLs in the '60s. Automation in the computing space has been inexorable since the '50s. When the author started out, his first program was on a plug board, FORTRAN and COBOL were academic curiosities, linkers and loaders were just appearing, and BAL was the silver bullet that was going to solve the software crisis. We've come a long way since then. Translation has already been institutionalized in niche markets, such as HPVEE and RAD IDEs for CRUD/USER processing. It is inevitable that general-purpose 4GLs will supersede the 3GLs.

However, the design principles of this book's methodology apply equally well to elaboration as they do to translation. Developing an application OOA model with MBD will lead to a highly maintainable application, and it will be a complete, precise, and unambiguous specification for the remaining elaboration stages. In other words, an MBD OOA model is what elaboration developers really should be providing anyway but rarely do.

The Message Paradigm

To be able to hide the implementations of knowledge and behavior, one needs a shield behind which those implementations can lurk. Thus every object or subsystem has an interface that hides its implementation. The notion of interfaces is hardly new.

That the OO paradigm employs them at the fine-grained level of objects is interesting, but not cosmological in importance. On the other hand, one of the most profound differences between the OO paradigm and other software construction approaches is the *way* interfaces are implemented.

> An interface defines a collection of messages to which an entity will respond.

This concept was what the OOA/D deep thinkers came up with to address a bunch of disparate problems. In so doing, they made the construction of OO software fundamentally unique and completely changed the way a developer thinks about constructing software.

Objects would communicate by sending each other messages, and the receiving objects would select some behavior in response to that message. This neatly decoupled the sender of the message from the receiver because the sender did not have to know anything about how the receiver would respond. This was potentially a very powerful and versatile approach. For one thing, in OOA/D a message can be quite abstract, representing with equal facility the setting of an interrupt bit in hardware, a timer time-out, or clicking a GUI control. For another, it allowed the receiver considerable latitude in responding. The receiver might respond to the same message with different behaviors depending upon its internal state. Or the receiver might ignore the message in some situations. Basically, this was a really good idea *provided the sender of the message had no expectations about what would happen in response to the message.*

> Messages are not methods. Messages are the class interface while methods are the class implementation.

This separation of message and method was the reason the why the OO view of interfaces led to a very different way of constructing software. Traditionally in SD's functional decomposition, higher-level functions invoked lower-level functions that were extensions of the higher-level function's obligations, so the higher-level function expected what would happen. Since specifications of the descendant functions were subsets of the higher-level function's specification, the higher-level function not only expected what the lower level function did, it *depended* on it. Thus the fundamental paradigm for navigating the functional decomposition tree was *Do This*, as we saw in Chapter 1.

But in the OO paradigm, the fundamental paradigm is peer-to-peer collaboration among logically indivisible entities and behaviors such that we can change the solution by simply reorganizing where messages go *without touching the method implementations*. Now messages become announcements of something the sender did: *I'm Done*. The announcement dovetails with DbC so that a message simply announces that some particular condition now prevails in the state of the solution.

As we shall see in Part III, this enables DbC to be used to rigorously define correct flow of control by matching the postcondition of the method where the message originates with the precondition for executing the next method in the overall solution's flow of control. Effectively, we have a poor man's formal methods to ensure correct flow of control.

In addition, we have excellent decoupling because all the message sender needs to know is what it did. Thus if all the message sender is doing is announcing something it did, it needs to know nothing about the responder. Similarly, since the receiver simply responds to a message, it doesn't need to know anything about the sender of the message. This drastically reduces coupling because the only shared knowledge is the message and its data packet.

The way methods in the OO paradigm are designed stems from methodological techniques for problem space abstraction. Those techniques ensure cohesive, logically indivisible, and self-contained responsibilities. But those techniques all assume the notion of *I'm Done* flow of control as an alternative to the *Do This* flow of control of SD. That is, the OO message paradigm ties everything together and without it those techniques would have limited utility. While problem space abstraction may be the most important distinguishing characteristic of the OO paradigm, the message paradigm is a very close second.

Before we leave the message paradigm it should be pointed out that MBD places more constraints on the message interface than other OO methodologies. At the object level in MBD almost all messages are simple knowledge requests or state machine events. One implication of this is that these interfaces are pure by-value data interfaces. This means that MBD explicitly prohibits the more egregious forms of coupling, such as passing object references to behavior methods.

Object Characteristics

This topic provides an overview of the basic building blocks of the OO paradigm. The word *object* is overloaded. The *Dictionary of Object Technology* has no less than seventeen formal definitions, and its discussion of the term covers fourteen pages.[17] To avoid that level of ambiguity, this book is going to stick to one set of definitions that is generic enough to avoid a lot of controversy:

> *Class.* Any uniquely identified *set* of objects having exactly the same responsibilities. The class itself enumerates the set of shared responsibilities that all its members have.

---

17. Firesmith, Donald and Eykholt, Edward, *Dictionary of Object Technology*, SIGS Books, New York, 1995, pp. 271–285.

Object. An abstraction of some real, identifiable entity in some problem space. The underlying entity may be concrete or conceptual. The object abstraction is characterized by a set of responsibilities. Objects with exactly the same *set* of responsibilities are members of the same class.

Instance. An object that is instantiated by software in memory (or indirectly in a persistent data store) during execution of a problem solution.

Responsibility. Abstracts a quality of a problem space entity as an obligation for knowledge (to know something) or an obligation for behavior (to do something). In the OO paradigm there is no direct way to express notions like *purpose*; such problem space qualities must be abstracted in terms of knowledge and/or behavior responsibilities. The underlying reason for this restriction is to provide an unambiguous mapping to the set, graph, and other mathematics that define the computing space. For example, a knowledge responsibility can be conveniently mapped into the notion of state variables, while behavior can be mapped into the notion of a procedure.

The relationships between these elements is illustrated in Figure 2-2. Customer space entities like Dick and Jane have unique qualities that we can abstract in objects in our conceptual design space. Those objects correspond directly to Dick and Jane. Since those objects have exactly the same sorts of abstract properties, we can group them in a class set. That class captures the notion of person from the customer domain. Eventually we will need to instantiate those objects in software at runtime as instances. Those instances will have concrete representation in memory locations where the properties become binary values.

Probably the most controversial definition just given is for *instance*. Many authors use *object* and *instance* as synonyms. In MBD we find it useful to distinguish between the conceptual design abstraction (object) that exists in the design whether the application is executing or not and the memory image (instance) of the abstraction at runtime. Usually objects are instantiated dynamically based upon the immediate context of the solution, and that instantiation has obvious importance to *when* things happen in the solution.

Attributes

Attributes define the knowledge for which each object of a class is responsible. The operative word here is *responsible*. Attributes describe the knowledge that any object of the class can be expected to *provide* or *manage*. A common misconception is that attributes represent physical data stores. Usually they do, but that is a coincidence of implementation because knowledge is commonly mapped to data in the computing

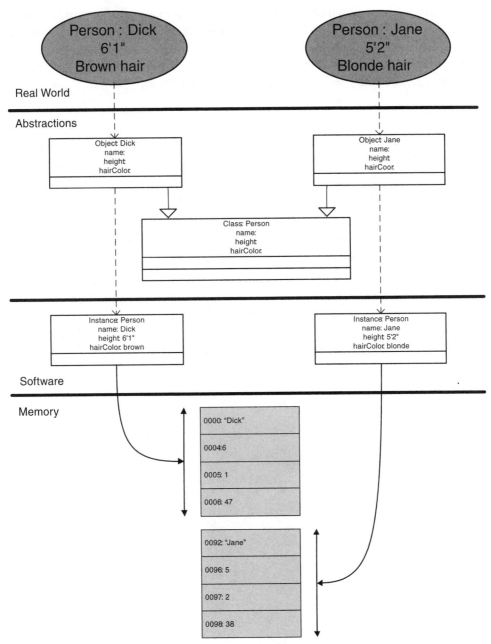

Figure 2-2 *The relationship between entities, objects, classes, and instances. Entities have qualities that are abstracted as object properties. Objects with the same property sets form classes. Objects are instantiated with specific values in computer memory.*

space. For our purposes here, attributes simply describe what the instance must know, not how they know it. That is separate from the *value* of what a specific object knows. Individual objects in a class set can have quite different values of a given attribute, or they may coincidentally have the same values for the attribute. The values of attributes depend solely on the identity of the owning object.

Methods

A method implements a specific behavior responsibility that all instances of a class must provide. Each method of a class is an encapsulation of particular business rules and policies for a particular behavior. Traditionally, the method name is used as a shorthand description to describe *what* the behavior is while the method body hides *how* that behavior is actually executed.

> The OOA/D only specifies what behavior responsibilities should do, not how they do it.

A behavior responsibility can be quite complex even though it is logically indivisible at the owning object's level of abstraction. To specify what a behavior method should do we need a special language that can specify such things in an abstract fashion consistent with the rest of the model. Therefore, we need an Abstract Action Language (AAL) that is designed to be a specification language rather than an implementation language.[18] While the syntax of most AALs is intentionally similar to that of 3GLs, they are really quite different things, as you shall see in Chapter 18.

---

18. In the context of OOA/D, all 3GLs, including OOPLs, are regarded as implementation languages that implement the OOA/D specification.

Chapter 3

Generalization, Inheritance, Genericity, and Polymorphism

> *So doth the greater glory dim the less:*
> *A substitute shines brightly as a king*
> *Until a king be by, and then his state*
> *Empties itself, as doth an inland brook*
> *Into the main of waters.*
>
> —Shakespeare, *The Merchant of Venice*

The basic operations of a Turing machine may be quite general in application and a boon to hardware developers, but it is extremely tedious to construct a program using only those basic operations. Most of the major advances related to languages and modeling have been directed at substituting abstract constructs that are more succinct for common combinations of Turing instructions.

That militant substitution began when BAL substituted instruction mnemonics for particular combinations of 1s and 0s. It gained steam as 3GLs added procedures, block structures, iteration formalisms, I/O constructs, and a host of other abstractions. Then graphical notations for high-level design concepts substituted simple bubbles and arrows that often represented collections of thousands of Turing instructions.

A primary contribution of the OO paradigm has been to formalize and standardize high-level abstraction, especially problem space abstractions, as spartan but rigorous substitutes for large collections of Turing instructions. Four important OO constructs are generalization, inheritance, genericity, and polymorphism.

Many people regard generalization, inheritance, and polymorphism as the hallmark characteristics of object orientation, which is why an entire chapter is devoted to them. Another view is that they are actually just mechanisms, albeit elegant, that implement the more fundamental OO ideas described in Chapter 2.

Generalization

Generalization is a very basic application of set theory. Recall that in Chapter 2 we defined a class as a set of entities that have the same properties. Set theory has the notion of subsets, as shown in Figure 3-1. The figure is called a Venn diagram, and the dots represent members of the set while the solid lines indicate the boundaries of set. Figure 3-1 represents the Venn diagram for a bank's accounts. The dots represent individual bank accounts that are owned by the bank's customers. In this case, all bank accounts must be either checking accounts or savings accounts, but not both. The boxes represent the boundaries of various sets of bank accounts: The outer box is the set of all of the bank's accounts, called a superset, while the inner boxes bound subsets of those accounts for Savings and Checking. We could add other subsets, say, for IRA accounts.

Each dot represents a uniquely identifiable member of every set whose boundary surrounds the dot. In this example, accounts are uniquely identifiable by a combination of the account's owner and the type of account. Note that it is possible for both a checking account and a savings account to be owned by a single customer, so we can't identify them uniquely just by owner.

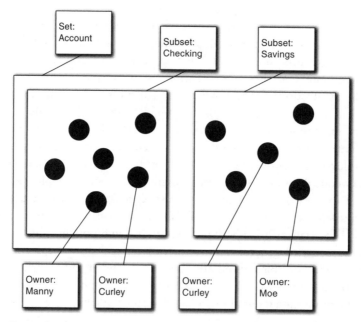

Figure 3-1. *Example of a Venn diagram for checking accounts in a bank. The overall set of all accounts can be subdivided into distinct groups of specialized accounts for checking and savings.*

If we look at a given dot in, say, subset Checking, that dot is also contained in the overall Account set. So we say that the entity is a member of set Checking and that it is a member of set Account. If we tidy up the terminology by using "A" as a shorthand for "member of Set A" and using "B" as a shorthand for "member of Set B," we can then say that a B is an A since there is only one dot and it is contained in both sets. You will see references in the OOA/D literature indicating that generalization is an "is-a" relation. This is exactly what they mean. In a Venn diagram, any given dot represents a single entity that is contained in multiple sets. So we can say that entity is a B and that entity is an A.

We also mentioned in Chapter 2 that classes are defined in terms of a set of responsibilities. In a Venn diagram we can label the individual sets easily, as in the diagram, but it gets messy to try to also enumerate the particular responsibilities that define a *particular* set. In the OO paradigm we care a great deal about those responsibilities since we need them to solve the problem in hand. So we need a different notation for the Venn diagram, such as in Figure 3-2. Each box refers to one of the same sets from Figure 3-1, but instead of showing entity dots we enumerate the properties that define the set.

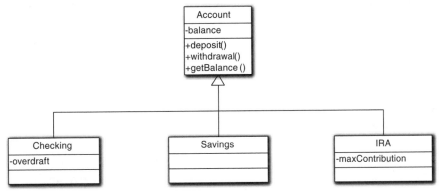

Figure 3-2 *OO generalization of subsets of Account having different properties that define each set. The properties of Account are shared by every member while the Checking subset defines a subset of Account members that also have the property "overdraft." Note that the Savings subset contains all the members of Account that do not have any other properties.*

The line connecting the classes indicates that a generalization is being shown, where set Account is the full class (known as a root superclass) while the sets Checking, Savings, and IRA are subset classes that contain only a subset of members of set Account. The dots are not necessary because the special connector tells us that we are really looking at a Venn diagram, and we can infer that every member of a subclass is also a member of its parent superclass.

Note that the properties we have indicated define set Account. How do we reconcile them with the properties we used to define the subsets? That's fairly straightforward. Every entity in the generalization (Venn diagram in tree form) is a member of set Account. Since since set Account is defined by the properties all of its members share, then all entities in set Account must have those properties. Similarly, the members of set Checking must have the properties that set Checking defines as shared *in addition to the properties defined for membership in set Account*. Since a member of set Checking is a member of set Account, it must have the all the properties defined for both sets.

The term *generalization* comes from the notion that set Account defines general or common properties for all of the entities in all descendant subsets. Conversely, another common term for the relation in OO contexts is *specialization*. Specialization captures the idea that a subset of the set Account have unique, specialized properties that not all members of the Account set have. You now know everything there is to know about OO generalization; it is a very simple organization of sets and subsets where the UML representation is just a Venn diagram in tree form.

All of the trickiness around generalization that you will see in the OOA/D literature deals with how we *interpret* generalization during problem space abstraction.[1] For example, you might have noticed that there was no mention of the word *object* in this explanation. That's because the generalization must exist for entities in the problem space before it can be abstracted into an OO solution. A common OOA mistake is to use generalization in the solution simply because it is elegant and makes life easier for the modeler. We will revisit this topic in great detail in Chapter 12.

Inheritance

If you thought generalization was simple, you are going to love inheritance. Inheritance is both one of the simplest OO concepts and one of the most overanalyzed. It is simple because it is just *a suite of rules for resolving object properties in a generalization*. In fact, in MBD it is a single, very simple rule that we already mentioned in passing:

> The properties of an object member of a leaf subclass are the union of the properties of its class and the properties of every superclass in a direct line of ascent.

---

1. A personal pet peeve of mine is that most OOA/D authors never mention sets and Venn diagrams. Instead, they leap directly to extracting generalizations from the problem space and generalize the structure rules from there. The result is that many novices have difficulty understanding it. But this is not rocket science, and you don't need a graduate course in set theory to understand what is actually going on. Once one understands the basic set/subset relation in terms of membership in class sets, the interpretation of generalization in the problem space becomes much easier.

That's it, folks.[2] Not exactly a mind bender, and it is intuitively obvious to anyone who recognizes that classes are just sets of objects. We resolve subset properties exactly the way we would do it in a Venn diagram, and the OO paradigm has just renamed that technique *inheritance*.

> Generalization, inheritance, and polymorphism are three entirely different things.

The confusion arises when authors start to talk about inheritance as if it were synonymous with generalization and polymorphism. As we shall see shortly, a special form of polymorphism is enabled by the *combination* of generalization and inheritance. If you keep these features separate in your mind, the paradigm will become a lot more intuitive.

Polymorphism

Polymorphism is a somewhat more complex topic than generalization and inheritance. Before getting into what it is, we need to dispel a common error in discussions of OO polymorphism. On online forums and even in the literature you will find people who refer to polymorphism as the substitution of *implementations*. While technically correct for some situations at the OOP level, this is not at all true for OOA/D.

A classic example of implementation substitution is a responsibility to sort an array. We can substitute a wide variety of sort algorithms (e.g., insertion, quicksort, etc.) for the implementation of the responsibility without affecting the results at all— the array will always come out in the designated order. That is, the *observable results* are unchanged when the implementations are substituted, which is because we employ encapsulation behind an interface expressly to hide the implementation, and we define the DbC contract in a manner that depends solely on the notion of ordering of a set.

> OO polymorphism in generalizations is about substituting behaviors.

For example, consider the concept of Prey with a responsibility to respond when attacked. If the Prey in hand happens to be a Pheasant, its behavior when attacked will be to take flight. If the Prey in hand happens to be a Rodent, the behavior when attacked might be to scurry down the nearest hole in the ground. If the Prey in hand

---

2. That's true for MBD, but things get slightly more complicated for methodologies that allow implementation inheritance combined with overrides. To support that, the rule needs to be modified so that one uses the first concrete implementation encountered while ascending the tree. We will talk about what implementation inheritance is and why MBD does not support it in Chapter 12.

happens to be a Gazelle, its behavior response might be to bound away. These are quite different behaviors by any reasonable definition of behavior, and they have quite different observable results. But through the magic of OO polymorphism we can sometimes substitute them freely.

The trick lies in our notion of how our Prey entity collaborates with other entities like predators. Consider a lion feeding on a kill when some sort of prey critter wanders too close. The lion might growl or do a mock charge to drive the critter off. The lion seems to be attacking, but its goal is simply to make the interloper go away. From the lion's perspective, it does not care *how* the critter goes away; it just cares that it goes away. So the lion is actually indifferent to responses of taking flight, scurrying down a hole, or bounding away when the lion sends the *attack* message. The lion's DbC contract with the prey critter can be expressed solely in terms of the prey critter leaving the immediate scene.

In effect we have raised the level of abstraction about what the DbC contract between the lion and the prey critter is so that the details of specific prey behaviors do not matter. But from the prey critter's perspective, each one actually responds in a very different way with different observable results.

Another key element is the separation of message and method. The lion sends an *I'm attacking* message to the prey. The lion sends that same message regardless of which particular flavor of prey critter happens to be there. So long as each flavor of prey critter responds to that message and leaves town in some fashion, the lion is satisfied.

The key ideas are

1. The collaboration is at a high enough level of abstraction that differences in the observable results of potential behaviors are not important *to the client*.

2. The DbC contract with the client is defined consistently with the collaboration's level of abstraction.

3. A mechanism exists to substitute different behaviors that satisfy (2) based on solution context.

This capability for substituting behavior in different solution contexts is a very powerful tool. However, as we shall see later in Chapter 12, we have to be quite careful how we use it lest we have Skyscrapers suddenly appear in our Pristine Landscapes. Managing that is tied to ensuring that the differences in observable results are acceptable in all collaboration contexts.[3]

---

3. As we shall see later in Chapter 12, managing observable results is what the Liskov Substitution Principle (LSP) is all about.

OO polymorphism does this by combining abstraction and encapsulation in a very elegant way. First, the semantics of the behavior are generalized through abstraction. This enables unique but similar behaviors to be viewed at a higher, more general level of abstraction where the details that differentiate the implementations are no longer important—a perspective where they all look the same.

Second, polymorphism takes advantage of the encapsulation interfaces that hide implementations to provide access to those implementations in a uniform way. Specifically, polymorphism depends upon the existence of a common interface for all of the substitutable behaviors. This enables the client to access each behavior in exactly the same way. This provides a degree of anonymity for the specific behavior from the client's view; the client doesn't have to know which particular behavior will be accessed. What they don't know about, they cannot depend upon, and we have effective decoupling.

The OO paradigm explicitly supports several ways to provide behavior substitution:

- *Ad hoc polymorphism.* Multiple behaviors are provided within a single responsibility, and one of those behaviors is selected at runtime when the method is invoked. This was the most common form of polymorphism in procedural applications, and it was manifested in "switch" statements within procedures where each "case" of the switch held a unique behavior. We can do the same thing within individual OO methods.

- *Inclusion polymorphism (aka inherent polymorphism).* Different behavior responses can be bound to a single message dynamically at runtime. This is the most common form of polymorphism seen at the OOPL level, and it is enabled by generalization. Essentially, the superclass provides an interface shared by the subclasses, but members of different subclasses provide their own unique behaviors. The Prey example demonstrates the inclusion polymorphism mechanism: The lion's messages are sent to the Prey superclass, and the individual subclass in hand provides a specific behavior such as takeFlight.

- *Overload polymorphism.* Substitution is achieved by overloading the same name with different behaviors. This most commonly appears in an OOP context when arithmetic or logical operators have their mechanisms substituted based upon the context of the objects to which they are applied. This is explicitly defined in the OOPLs, but it is usually implicitly defined at the OOA/D level. That is, in OOA/D it is *assumed* that fundamental operations on attribute ADTs are appropriate for the ADTs and will be implemented accordingly during OOP.

- *Parametric polymorphism (aka genericity).* This polymorphism occurs when behavior substitution is parameterized. That is, observable results are modified based on the values of state variables. This differs from ad hoc polymorphism in that there is usually just a single generic behavior that is executed, but the results of that execution can be drastically different based upon state variable values that the behavior eats. This is the most important form of polymorphism at the OOA/D level because it enables us to encode invariants while relegating details to configuration data. We will talk about this extensively in Chapter 5.

Ad hoc polymorphism is relatively straightforward and intuitive for anyone who has programmed in a procedural language. Overload polymorphism isn't of much interest to OOA/D because that view already abstracts the sorts of differences that overloading of names supports. We are going to concentrate here on the other two forms of polymorphism.

Inclusion (or Inherent) Polymorphism

Inclusion polymorphism is enabled by generalization. Conversely, it is inclusion polymorphism that adds power to OO generalization. Inclusion polymorphism employs superclasses to achieve both the necessary generality and the interface commonality. The generality is achieved through abstraction while the interface commonality is achieved through interface inheritance. By definition, the superclass represents the common characteristics of its subclasses. So, we collect similar but unique subclasses under a superclass, conceptually generalize their shared characteristics in the superclass, and then provide a common interface to those characteristics at the superclass level.

In Figure 3-2, the superclass class defines the basic responsibilities of *Deposit*, *Withdrawal*, and *GetBalance*. Each subclass implements the superclass' responsibilities. But in doing so, the subclasses can provide quite different behaviors with different observable results. The incoming message to the superclass is then dispatched to the specific behavior provided by the subclass in hand. Unless we were in the banking business we might expect those behaviors to be exactly the same.

However, at the detailed behavior level there are issues like legal restrictions (e.g., early withdrawal penalties for IRAs), policy restrictions (e.g., different posting delays for deposits), rules restrictions (e.g., overdraft protection for Checking but not Savings), reporting requirements (e.g., the bank's P&L and Balance Sheet), and lots of other stuff. This stuff inevitably results in different behaviors with different observable results because different business rules and policies apply for each subclass context.

Yet many clients have a much more basic view of Account characteristics like *Deposit*, *Withdrawal*, and *GetBalance* where those detailed differences are not relevant. It is the "Here's a pile of money, deposit it and don't bug me with the details of what that involves" sort of view. Inclusion polymorphism enables this by letting the client send a generic Deposit message to the Account superclass rather than the individual subclass.

Genericity

Genericity is one of those things that everybody uses without realizing it. Genericity is about substituting different behavior through parameterization. Essentially, we obtain quite different results depending upon the values (or presence) of input parameters to a single behavior responsibility. This idea has been around since Assembly macros, so we won't spend a lot of time on it. In fact, it has another name—parametric polymorphism[4]—that suggests it is just a special case of polymorphism.

Any method where different behaviors are possible depending upon the values of the method's arguments technically demonstrates genericity, so any method with an IF test of a parameter value could be deemed an example of genericity. However, most OO people would think of genericity in terms of *significant* behavior differences. It is left as an exercise for the student to come up with a good definition of *significant* in this context.

The unique thing that the OO paradigm brings to the table is expansion of the notion of what constitutes a *parameter*. The traditional view is that it is an input to a procedure. In an OO context the notion of parameter is expanded to include potentially any state variable that is accessible to a behavior method. Thus in the OO context, any knowledge attribute of any reachable object is potentially a parameter to a behavior responsibility.

This introduces a very powerful design pattern where we define generic behavior responsibilities in one object and relate that object to another object—a "specification object"—whose attributes parameterize the generic behavior. This enables us to instantiate the relationship between the objects dynamically at runtime. That is, we decide which specification object is the "right" one for the context dynamically. This is an enormously powerful technique, but it is so underutilized in today's OO development that we devote an entire chapter, Chapter 5, to it.

---

4. The 3GL type mavens have usurped this term to apply to a very special sort of type substitution. This book uses the traditional software definition that dates from long before formal type theory.

Chapter 4

MBD Road Map

> *He who knows the road can ride full trot.*
> Italian proverb

OO methodologies tend to be complex, and MBD is no exception. In addition, MBD represents a rather unique synergy of OO features that is difficult to appreciate until the whole thing is grokked, thus it is difficult to thread one's way through the forest without some context. This chapter provides a basic overview of some key elements of the MBD philosophy. That philosophy is basically an OO modeling philosophy; MBD simply provides a different emphasis than other approaches.

Problem Space versus Computing Space

This is unquestionably the central concept underlying model-based OO methodologies in general and MBD very much in particular. Very early in the development of the formal software design approaches a distinction was made between analysis, which dealt with the problem space, and design, which dealt with the computing space. This was originally formalized in Structured Development techniques in the late '60s. That eventually evolved into classical OOA and OOD modeling.

When computing moved out of university labs and into corporations in the '50s, it became readily apparent that the MIS types did not think about or describe problems the same way the computer scientists did.[1] They employed a different vocabulary and their problems tended to be more complex and diffuse. More important, their problems

---

1. Through the '60s *computer science* referred exclusively to designing computer *hardware*. There were no CS departments in universities; computer science was a specialty of the EE department. This still prevails in some schools, such as my alma mater (MIT), where a computer science degree is awarded from the EE department to this day.

were not defined with mathematical precision; they were inherently fuzzy and were expressed ambiguously in natural language.

The notion that requirements needed to be expressed more rigorously than natural language drove the development of a number of ingenious analysis techniques. The difference between the customer's problem space and the software developer's problem space was recognized, and analysis was regarded as a requirements specification technique rather than a software development technique. The job description of systems analyst was created, but that person usually lived with the customer and threw the analysis over a wall to programmers.

OOA and OOD are both aspects of solution design in the OO paradigm; both represent solutions to the customer problem.

When the OO paradigm was formalized in the '70s the founding gurus assumed problem analysis was part of requirements specification, so it was a prerequisite for OO development. They also felt there was a need to provide distinct stepping-stones for software design, so they made the separation of OOA and OOD central to the OO paradigm. They saw an OOA model as an intermediate stepping-stone *solution* to the problem on the way to developing the final software solution. The OOA model represented the abstract resolution to the customer's functional requirements that happened to be expressed exclusively in the customer's terms. In the 2000s this separation of the customer view of the solution from the computing view became further formalized in OMG's Model Driven Architecture (MDA) where the OOA model became a Platform Independent Model (PIM), and there is no confusion about the fact that the PIM is a model of a *solution* even though it provided an explicit bridge to the customer's domain.

Basically the Founding Gurus saw a continuum of solutions:

Requirements → OOA model → OOD model → OOP code → BAL → Executable

where everything to the right of a Requirements was a solution to the problem. Those solutions represented decreasing levels of abstraction and increasing inclusion of Turing detail moving to the right. Each step was viewed as a stepping-stone in incremental conversion of problem space semantics to computing space semantics.

At the same time, everything to the left of the Executable was regarded as specification of whatever was immediately to the right. In addition, each → implied a process that brought added value to the development. Thus a linker/loader brought explicit addressing, support services, and whatnot to the compiler's BAL code to produce an executable memory image; the compiler brought various levels of optimization for a particular instruction set, and so on.

Thus the OO paradigm formalized development by bringing several innovative notions to the table: incorporation of the customer's domain in the solution, stepping-stones in development, successive levels of abstraction, and the dichotomy of specification and solution. The dichotomy of specification and solution is particularly noteworthy because it was quite a new view of development. This dichotomy is summarized in Table 4-1.

Table 4-1 *Dichotomy of Process Steps as Both Solution and Specification*

Step	Solution Perspective	Specification Perspective
Requirements	None	Ambiguous natural language customer specification (e.g., use cases)
OOA model	Implementation-independent; pure customer perspective	Rigorous and unambiguous customer requirements; only functional requirements are addressed
OOD model	Strategic design with explicit identification of computing space techniques and mechanisms	High-level nonfunctional requirements are addressed
OOP code	Tactical implementation of design strategies	Low-level Turing-complete specification for compiler/interpreter
BAL	Locally optimized, relocatable executable	Detailed Turing machine specification for linker/loader
Executable	Actual Turing machine solution	None

While the OO paradigm formalized several discrete development steps, the OOA and OOD model steps represented an especially important demarcation. The OOA model was envisioned as a pure customer solution—one that could be used unchanged to guide the implementation of a purely manual system in the customer's environment, however inefficient that solution might be.[2] Only when shifting to the OOD model is anything included in the solution that is specific to a software solution.

This separation of computing space from customer space concerns is absolutely essential to translation-based methodologies like MBD. It enables a solution to be created in the OOA model that can be both tested and verified with the customer without worrying about the myriad details related to computers. More importantly, it provides a complete and unambiguous specification for the software that does not constrain the implementation choices for the transformation engine (or subsequent elaboration).

That separation also enables a great deal of skills specialization. If the OOA model is complete and unambiguous, then the transformation engine does not have to

2. To this day, that is a reviewer criteria for MBD OOA models. An unambiguous implementation path to a manual solution should be possible without altering the OOA model.

understand the semantics of the problem or its context in the customer's domain. It only needs to understand the semantics of the OOA model notation's artifacts (i.e., a meta model of the OOA notation). Thus, the transformation engine developer need not be expert in the customer domain and can specialize in computing space issues like caching strategies, network protocols, file systems, and the nuances of implementation language syntax.

Similarly, the application developer constructing the OOA model does not need to be expert in computing paradigms. The application developer simply needs to understand the basic rules for developing OOA models and the semantics of the notation syntax. Thus the application developer can focus on the customer's domain to ensure that the solution functionality provided is what the customer really wants and needs. To that extent, the developer of an OOA solution is roughly comparable to the systems analyst from structured development.

After appropriate implementation technologies have been selected (target language, infrastructures, libraries, OS, etc.), a transformation engine can be built for that environment[3] that will correctly construct an application *for any OOA model*. Better yet, if the transformation engine developers are clever people, they can provide computing space optimization as well—just like a 3GL compiler can optimize the instructions without knowing the semantics of the specific problem that the 3GL program is solving for the customer.

In the translation community this is known as *design reuse* because the transformation engine only needs to be developed once for the particular computing environment. That is a little misleading because the *design* being referenced is that of the transformation engine rather than the application. To the extent that the transformation engine is providing automation of design efforts that an elaboration application developer would have to provide in OOD/P, though, it is accurate. Design reuse is enormously powerful and provides virtually all of the productivity advantages of translation.[4]

---

3. This is commonly called a *platform*. This word traditionally has been referred to as simply the hardware and operating system. In a translation context a much broader definition is needed, so this book will usually refer to *environment* to convey that.

4. This separation of concerns is so important to MBD that all MBD model reviewers carry a kit containing garlic cloves, wooden stakes, and kindling so that they can properly dispose of any heretical application developer who includes implementation details in an OOA model. Implementation pollution of an OOA model is regarded as a mortal sin when practicing MBD.

Problem Space

It is fine to talk about separation of problem and computing spaces, but that doesn't explain what they are.

The problem space is the environment where a problem must be solved.

A key determinant of the problem space is that it is where the customer[5] lives. Whoever is defining the requirements has a particular domain in mind when doing so. Whatever functionality the software has is something that a human would have to do in that domain if there was no software.[6] That domain is the problem space. Note that a "customer" does not have to be a physical person. For example, the customer can be hardware if you are doing hardware control systems, or it could be another software application if your software is a component in a larger system. In those situations we typically personify the "customer" as if it were a person. In such cases, the problem space becomes the domain where the customer would live if it were a person.

Usually the problem space is clearly outside and unrelated to the computing space where software lives. This is the case in obvious situations like inventory control, point-of-sales (POS) order entry, portfolio management, air traffic control, and whatnot. It is slightly less clear for scientific applications like linear programming packages and weather forecasting systems that tend to be highly algorithmic, since Turing machines were designed to do algorithms.

Things start getting really tricky for R-T/E systems because the only hardware we can access with software has to look very much like a computer. But things really get murky when the software is for the computing space (e.g., a device driver or network router software). Interestingly, the most difficult software to model is that which is driven directly by computing space needs. It becomes difficult to identify an abstract "manual" solution in that domain because the entities we are trying to abstract from the customer domain are already implementation artifacts.

As a clarification, in this book any unqualified reference to *customer* refers to whoever defines requirements for the overall application and lives in the same

---

5. This book subscribes to a set of handy definitions stolen from Doug Rosenberg: A *customer* is whoever defines requirements; a *client* is whoever pays for the software; and a *user* is whoever actually uses the software. They may be, but are usually not, the same person.

6. Some software, like a heat-seeking missile controller, provides functionality that would be difficult for a human to do. A human might be able to do the computations on an abacus, but probably not before the missile missed and ran out of fuel—not to mention the implications of success for an on-board human doing the computations. But that just makes a manual solution infeasible in practice. The problem space and the computations still exist, at least conceptually.

domain as the client. That is, it is the business customer when there are several different customers defining requirements for different subject matters. That customer will typically know little or nothing about the computing space, and this is who the OO paradigm aims at when providing the OOA stepping-stone.

Computing Space

Fortunately the computing space is relatively easy to define.

> The computing space is the environment where a software solution is implemented.

The operative words are "software" and "implemented"; if those are both relevant, we are in the computing space where software developers (and transformation engine developers!) live. In some situations it may also be the customer space, in which case you may have more difficulty separating their concerns from design implementation concerns.

Essentially, the computing space is where all the tools, strategies, techniques, mechanisms, and processes related to software development and execution are encountered. Typically these include such things as:

- Implementation languages (C, Smalltalk, C++, Java Script)

- Technologies (TCP/IP, EJB,.NET, ESB, XMI)

- Hardware (instruction set, endian)

- Policies (interoperability standards, network protocols, two-phase commit)

- Paradigms (refactoring, coding standards, SOA, porting state via XML/XMI)

- Optimizations (look-ahead caching, stateless objects)

As the list indicates, just about everything that has anything to do with software lives in the computing space. Unless you are developing transformation engines, defining the computing space is only important to defining what OOA models are *not* about. One of the most difficult things for people new to OOA modeling to believe is that it is possible to develop a solution that doesn't somehow directly depend upon all this stuff.

There is another aspect of the computing space that is important to MBD and translation though. The computing space tends to be very mathematically based. Everything from basic data structures to dual processor optimization is invariably based upon unambiguous theorems from set theory, graph theory, relational theory, and so forth. This is crucial to translation because it enables the unambiguous specification represented by OOA model artifacts to be mapped deterministically into implementation mechanisms. It also enables optimization.

Transformation

As mentioned earlier, the basic development approach of converting an OOA model into an executable in a particular computing space is known as *translation*. The mechanical process of converting a particular OOA model into a 3GL or 2GL model is known as *transformation*. Technically it is possible to do a manual transformation, but that would be traditional elaboration. MBD is geared toward automated transformation by providing the necessary rigor to the OOA models that a code generator needs.

The process of transformation is beyond the scope of this book. However, it is very central to MBD, and many of the things in MBD are done to ensure the completeness, precision, and lack of ambiguity necessary for transformation.

This is not to say that the OOA modeling approach described in this book is not applicable to projects where traditional elaboration is used. The virtues of completeness, precision, and lack of ambiguity are applicable in any software development environment.

MBD **must** practice these virtues to support translation, but every model-based OO methodology **should** practice them.

Maintainability

In Chapter 2 the case was made that the primary goal of the OO paradigm is application maintainability in the face of volatile requirements. That discussion made the point that maintainability will be enhanced if the software structure emulates the problem space infrastructure. MBD is very much in tune with this philosophy precisely because the OOA model is the centerpiece of the approach. Throughout the later chapters you will observe a ubiquitous emphasis on problem space abstraction. That, in turn, drives MBD's emphasis on things like invariants and application partitioning.

Domain Analysis

The traditional view of domain analysis is that it is separate from software development. That is, it is concerned with describing the environment where the software is used rather than the software itself. This view is only partially correct. While true domain analysis often models things that are not of any interest to the software, it also models lots of things that are crucial to the software.

In the OO paradigm's formative years, OOA was often thought of as an analysis of the customer's domain that was broader than the software. Consequently, when formal Domain Modeling notations and techniques were developed, they were quite closely based upon the early OO paradigms.[7] One way to view an application's OOA model is that it is a subset of a full domain analysis. Assume that a Domain Model includes processes that are currently done manually and that need to be replaced with software. In that situation the OOA model should look essentially the same as the Domain Model because the OOA model describes the solution in the customer's terms.

In MBD we believe that developing an understanding of the customer's environment equivalent to Domain Modeling is essential to good software development. While the approach of MBD is somewhat different than traditional Domain Modeling and MBD goes considerably further in detail, the basic concepts are inextricably linked. So if you have ever done formal Domain Modeling you will recognize a lot of familiar stuff in MBD. Some of the ways Domain Modeling dovetails with MBD are

- *Understand the customer environment.* This is the primary goal because in MBD we want the software structure to parallel the customer's infrastructure. To build a good OOA model we must understand the broad context where the software is used. That context is most easily understood by examining an existing Domain Model.

- *Understand the customer solution.* In MBD we seek to understand how the customer would solve the problem without a computer. While this has benefits in facilitating model validation with the customer, the main goal is to represent customer infrastructure in the software structure.

- *Identify invariants.* A key goal in design is to identify invariants that apply to a class of problems similar to the one in hand. We then model the invariants, enabling the differences among the problem class members to be described in data. This makes the application more maintainable in the long term and reduces the application size, which enhances reliability. That's because requirements changes represent a new problem to be solved, one that happens to be closely related to the original problem.

- *Elicit, analyze, and specify requirements.* Technically, almost all development methodologies, including MBD, cop out and assume software development begins

---

7. In fact, UML can be and is used for both OOA models and Domain Models.

with an existing statement of requirements.[8] Unfortunately this utopian situation rarely exists in practice; when getting into the application details the requirements usually turn out to be incomplete, inconsistent, and ambiguous. The problem space focus of MBD enables developers to identify requirements problems, and to resolve them early and easily in Domain Modeling terms that the customer hopefully understands.

- *Use cases.* Since use cases are really a mechanism for specifying requirements, they are not directly a part of MBD. However, they provide a very convenient organization of Domain Model processes into specific application requirements, so the application developer should be prepared to use them. This is because use cases are ideal for partitioning requirements among subsystems and specifying method behaviors. In fact, MBD not only uses them, it strongly encourages creating them for individual subsystems after application partitioning to clarify how requirements have been allocated to subsystems.

Modeling Invariants

The basic idea behind modeling invariants is actually quite simple: Encode things that are unlikely to change and relegate the volatile details to external parametric data. Intuitively this makes a whole lot of sense, because if the code only contains things that don't change, it shouldn't need to be touched very often.[9] In addition, data is usually much easier to understand and modify than code, so if most changes can be done in data the developer will be more productive. While invariants are central to the MBD philosophy, we should point out that they really should be central to every software design approach, even non-OO approaches. Since the entire next chapter is devoted to invariants, we won't go into them further here.

---

8. The relatively recent advent of systems engineering as a discipline of software development addresses this by including the specification of requirements as one of the key activities. This just recognizes the practical reality that most customers can't or won't provide requirements at the level of detail software developers need. So one of the hats the systems engineer wears is that of the old systems analyst.

9. Well, duh. It might seem this is being an apostle of the obvious, but the sad reality is that most software applications make very little use of invariants. That's not really surprising because there is precious little reference to invariants in the software literature, aside from the relatively recent introduction of design patterns. As you shall see when we talk about them in detail, there is no rocket science here, and it is very difficult to explain why so few software gurus seem to have seen value in them.

Partitioning the Application

Invariants can be expressed in a lot of different ways. One way that is particularly interesting is the partitioning of applications. MBD places great store in careful partitioning of the application based upon subject matter, level of abstraction, and allocation of requirements through client/service relationships.

But partitioning the application is really a systems design activity, especially for very large applications. The partitions essentially provide a high-level structure for the entire application. Because it is important enough to the application side of MBD discussed in this book, we will provide a chapter to summarize the technique. The key idea to take away here is that application partitioning is the keystone of MDB development; everything else in the application design is built on that foundation.

A Static View

Since MBD is a modeling methodology, it should be no surprise that there are several different types of models employed. These can be broadly categorized as static and dynamic. The static models describe the organization and fixed structure of the application that is always present. This view is summarized in Table 4-2.

Table 4-2   *Static Models*

Structure	Model Artifact	UML Diagram
Large-scale organization; system partitioning	Subsystem, Component, Package, Interface, Dependency	Package, Component
Intermediate-scale organization; partition implementation	Class, Relationship	Class
Small-scale organization; knowledge and behavior organization	Knowledge and behavior responsibilities	Class

The Package and Component diagrams are syntactically the simplest diagrams in UML. At the same time they are semantically rich, and they may well be the most important for large applications. Essentially, these diagrams describe the overall organization and configuration management (e.g., release contents) of the application.

While the Class diagram identifies what behaviors are needed (methods) and where they are located, the Class diagram is primarily a description of the knowledge (attributes) processed in the application. Associations express intrinsic structural relationships among abstractions, not explicit communications. Taken together these diagrams provide a skeleton upon which the execution dynamics are based.

In OOA/D the static views are the primary place where problem space abstraction is done. The entities and their responsibilities are identified there. One also defines fundamental logical relationships among them that will be the basis for later dynamic collaboration. Those relationships already exist in the problem domain. To put it another way, the static model records problem space abstraction.

A Dynamic View

The dynamic models deal with the execution time view of what the application does. These models describe behavior and communications. They are summarized in Table 4-3. Generally only the first three diagrams—Sequence, Collaboration, and Statechart—are necessary for an OOA model. Use Case diagrams are sometimes explicitly identified to relate specific requirements expressed in use cases to model artifacts when developing larger applications.[10]

Activity and Object diagrams are not used in MBD because MBD employs an AAL to specify method dynamics. If you recall, an AAL is an abstract text language used to specify behavior within a method or state machine action. The AAL replaces the functions of the Activity and Object diagrams by specifying detailed behavior and instance access.

Table 4-3 *Mapping of Problem Space Structure to Models*

Structure	Model Artifact	UML Diagram
Synchronous messages among classes	Classes, Messages	Sequence
Asynchronous messages among classes	Class Roles (members), Messages, Associations, Roles	Collaboration
Class behavior	States, Events, Actions (methods)	Statechart
Functional requirements	Use cases, Dependencies	Use Case
Workflow; detailed behavior	States, Activities, Decisions	Activity
Snapshot of system state	Same as Class Diagram	Object

The Sequence and Collaboration diagrams are used to describe the communications among classes. Finite state machines (Statecharts) are used to describe all behavior in MBD that directly affects or reflects flow of control. MBD also supports subsystem and class methods (synchronous services) to describe behavior, but there are restrictions on what such methods can do. All method and state action processing is described using the AAL.

MBD primarily employs state machines to organize object behaviors. There are three reasons for this. The first is that an asynchronous behavior communication

---

10. In MBD uses cases are viewed as an input to design rather than an element of design.

model is the most general way to describe behavior. The second reason is that objects often have multiple behavior responsibilities, and there are often intrinsic constraints in the problem space on the sequencing of those behaviors. State machine transitions provide an excellent way of enforcing such constraints through static structure. The third reason is that the mathematical rules that govern finite state machines are an almost perfect match for enforcing fundamental OO notions like encapsulation, self-containment, logical indivisibility, and decoupling interfaces.

At this point you should have a pretty clear impression that the MBD view of behavior is probably not your father's view. The MBD view is very disciplined, and it requires the developer to be precise, rigorous, and very clear-headed about what is being described. The benefit of that discipline lies in relatively simple models that are very robust.

In this overview, though, we need to address a couple of popular misconceptions. One is that not everything can be described in state machines. That is quite true. But the exceptions are not directly addressed by the OO paradigm anyway because they are specialized algorithms. For the types of problems addressed in OO development, we can *always* find a means of expressing the solution essentials in finite state machines. There will be plenty of examples in Part III, but the key insight is to think of a state machine as being a way to express sequencing constraints on operations. Once we have that insight, state machines start to become obvious solutions for a lot of complex problems.

The second misconception is that rigorous approaches like MBD stifle creativity. The problem is that this notion confuses the discovery of the solution with the recording of the solution. The creative act lies in figuring out how to solve the problem in an elegant fashion. That is an intellectual activity quite different from writing down that solution.

Of all the things we do as software developers, the least creative is writing code.

That is true whether we are writing on a plug board, in BAL, in a 3GL, or in a 4GL like UML. Programming, in the sense of writing code, is essentially quite a boring mechanical activity at any of those levels. The creative part lies in figuring out what code should be written.

The reality is that the Turing machine is a highly deterministic and narrowly defined mathematical construct. Alan Turing deserves credit for being very creative in inventing it. But people writing programs in pure Turing constructs only deserve credit for perseverance, not creativity. The closer we get to the Turing machine the more deterministic the choices are and the less creative we need to be to make those choices.

Writing down an OOA model may be a lot more abstract and may enable a lot more wiggle room than writing BAL code, but any creativity advantage is relative at best. It is still a pretty mechanical process: "If I want to express *this* [brilliant idea], then I can only do it *that* way." All we do when moving to higher levels of abstract description above plug boards is reduce the amount of tedious recording, not the tedium of recording itself.

Sure, MBD has methodological rules that must be followed. But those rules exist to ensure that the solution *description* is complete, precise, and unambiguous. They also represent a minimum set of rules to achieve those goals. Every engineer, regardless of specialty, must work within the framework of design rules, and they are often a whole lot more detailed than those that constrain the typical software developer. The existence of reasonable constraints does not curtail creativity for a software engineer any more that it does for architects, civil engineers, mechanical engineers, or any of the rest.[11]

In MBD, accuracy of communication is paramount.

The OOA model is a medium of communication. MBD is, indeed, driven by the need to communicate properly with a very literal-minded transformation engine. To that end, the methodology is designed to ensure accuracy in the communication. That accuracy, though, is just as valuable when communicating with other developers.

Typically the models are developed as a team effort on white boards and are only committed to a tool when everyone is agreed. During highly creative sessions, the model is constantly modified. One of the advantages of rigor is that *everyone immediately understands exactly the same thing when a change is proposed*. The team may debate very creatively about whether the change is correct, appropriate, or even elegant, but they never misunderstand what the change implications are with respect to requirements because there is no ambiguity. This is an extremely valuable side effect of rigor.

---

11. If you look at the bookshelves of engineers in other disciplines, you will find at least one entire shelf devoted just to standards manuals. Those manuals provide rules on how to do things in excruciating detail. But you should probably not tell those engineers that their designs are not creative because they have too many standards.

Chapter 5

Modeling Invariants

When it is not necessary to change,
It is necessary not to change.
—Lord Falkland

The author believes that the notion of modeling invariants is more fundamental to MBD than translation itself. If you take away from this book a fervor for modeling invariants and never employ translation (or even the OO paradigm itself!) you will still have gained enough to significantly improve the quality of the software that you build. Your applications will be much smaller, they will be easier to understand and maintain, and they will be more reliable. That's not incremental percentages, that's integer factors.

Frankly, it is astonishing that the notion of modeling invariants has attracted so little attention in the literature of software engineering. For many years Steve Mellor was the only publicly visible proponent of the practice. In addition, Shlaer-Mellor and MBD are the only methodologies that explicitly integrate the practice. When presented on public forums the idea is often met with a sort of *I-knew-that* response that recognizes it as a good idea but assumes that everybody does it so there is no need to belabor the point. Alas, hardly anybody actually models invariants, and the best place to observe this lies in the way people partition their applications.

In Chapter 2 it was pointed out that modeling invariants was not an OO thing. One can model invariants using any software development methodology. It is simply a way of separating essential, stable structure from volatile details. However, the OO paradigm's emphasis on abstraction, encapsulation, functional isolation, programming by contract, polymorphism, and interface boundaries is a big help in getting a handle on it.

So Just What Is *Modeling Invariants?*

It is about capturing invariant aspects of the problem solution in the software while relegating detailed variability to external data. Unfortunately, this tastes good but doesn't have a lot of real meat in it. So it is time to flesh things out by providing a bit more beef.[1]

As it happens, the computing space is loaded with examples of invariants. For example, 3GL languages employ invariants that are abstracted for commonly recurring themes in Turing machine programs. Things like iteration constructs and I/O calls capture basic structural invariants while handling the detailed differences in parameters embedded in the constructs. Similarly, basic aggregate data structures (array, list, etc.) provided by most languages and in libraries are simply generalized sets whose implementation is parameterized.

The computing space is also loaded with design techniques that are really examples of invariants. Perhaps the most obvious examples lie in design patterns.[2] Every pattern represents a generalized structure that is common across many situations and provides a mechanism for describing the differences in situations as instantiation details. Even things as disparate as coding standards and network protocols represent variations on the theme of identifying and institutionalizing invariants. So we routinely use invariants. The problem is that they are someone else's generic invariants rather than our own problem-specific invariants.

The Invariant Side

First let's look at the notion of *invariant*. As the word implies, we are talking about something that doesn't change, something that is stable. So far, so good; nothing to boggle one's karma. But there is a qualifying spin on this notion in the MBD context.

---

1. Sorry about getting carried away with the metaphors. Sometimes when I think of Clara Pellor I get carried away with the lunacy of presidential campaigns. For those of you who are too young to remember, Clara did commercials. In one about fast food products she played a doughty old lady who asked in a strident voice about a competitor's product, "Where's the beef?" In a memorable moment in a campaign debate among Presidential candidates one candidate asked the other, "Where's the beef [in your position]?" In no small part, that irrelevant sound byte contributed to that opponent's loss. You really had to have been there.

2. If you don't know what design patterns are, I refer you to the GoF (Gang of Four) book: Gamma, Erich, Richard Helm, Ralph Johnson, and John Vlissides, *Design Patterns*, Reading, MA: Addison-Wesley, 1995. This book is required reading for anyone who wants to do serious OO development.

We are talking about a particular group of invariants—those things that are stable in the customer's problem space.

The problem space aspect is crucial because in the OO paradigm generally, and in MBD in particular, we strive to base software structure on the customer's infrastructures. That is because we believe that the customer will adapt to change in a manner that will cause minimal disruption to existing infrastructure.[3] If the software structure parallels that customer infrastructure, it should be minimally disrupted as well. And that implies maintenance with less pain.

The elegant thing about invariants is that they exist at all levels of abstraction. It is rather like a head of garlic. Around the outside there are a few big, rounded cloves. But as you peel away sheaths and cloves you find successively smaller cloves that become longer and thinner. Eventually one gets down to central cloves that are sized and shaped quite differently than the outer cloves.

The analogy is admittedly tenuous, but it underscores the point that invariants can be employed throughout the application, and that the scale and nature of those invariants will vary with the scale and context where they are applied. The big, large-scale invariants employed for application partitioning are usually pretty easy to spot. Alas, the little ones at the class and state machine level are often much tougher to recognize.

The developer must be aware that the notions of *customer* and *problem space* can be moving targets for large, complex applications, which presents problems for extracting invariants. For example, most applications have to store data persistently. It is quite common to create a subsystem to handle the actual data storage as a separate service to the rest of the application. The nature of that subsystem will depend in large measure on the nature of the persistence mechanisms (e.g., RDB versus OODB), which may be entirely transparent to the end user or customer of the software.

In such situations the *customer* becomes the database itself because it places constraints (requirements) upon the subsystem. The rest of the application is also a *customer* because of its needs (requirements) to store and access data in the database. While this changes the perspective on the subsystem's role as a service, it shouldn't change the fundamental abstractness of the subject matter description. That subject matter perspective provides the relevant invariants.

So for an RDB implementation of the service, the relevant invariant paradigm becomes the relational data model. While the rest of the application might think about a Clerk and the GUI subsystem may think about a Clerk Window with associated Controls, the persistence subsystem is likely to think about a Clerk Table with associated Clerk Rows instead of Clerk objects. Because the relational data model is

---

3. If you actually read the introductory chapters you might be tempted to view this repetition as a one-trick pony. I repeat things to make sure that important points sink in properly. Rest assured that if this is a one-trick pony, MBD has a lot of ponies—each with its own unique trick.

the core paradigm, application objects need to be recast in terms of things like referential identifiers, and identity itself becomes an explicit issue. The point is that to properly model invariants one must have a deep understanding of the problem space, regardless of what that space is. As a corollary, we must also isolate and encapsulate that problem space so that we can focus on only *its* invariants.

In a sense, the term *problem space* is a bit misleading in the invariant context because we seek invariants not in the problem itself but in the environment in which the problem exists. That is, the scope of the customer domain is necessarily broader than the problem itself when looking for invariants. It is, quite literally, the entire space in which the problem lies. One view of invariants is that they are characteristics common to a set of related problems, of which the problem in hand is one. A corollary is that to recognize invariants the developer needs to practice some degree of Domain Modeling or Analysis.

The rationale for this view is that when requirements change, they will likely require that we solve a new problem that is only slightly different from the original problem. So we try to describe in software the common aspects of solutions to a set of problems and relegate the differences in those solutions to data. In general, the more broad the class of problems resolved in software, the less likely that the software will have to change over time. To put it another way, when the requirements change it becomes more likely that they will simply identify a different member of the class of problems to solve. If so, the problem is already solved generically and we only need to modify the data to reflect the new member of the problem set.

Unfortunately, it is a lot easier to describe *what* one does when extracting invariants than it is to describe *how* to do it. There aren't a lot of cookbook guidelines because it is a relatively new technique, so the tools used in this book to describe how to do it are repetition and examples.

The Data Side

We now segue into the idea of using external data to describe detailed differences. This idea seems quite reasonable, but it begs the issue of exactly *how* we do that. The mechanism for converting data into different solutions is primarily based upon polymorphism, particularly parametric polymorphism. As you will recall, we use the term in the traditional software sense of obtaining different results from a generic behavior by providing different input data to the behavior.

Ad hoc polymorphism provides a clue. Those `switch` statements and cascaded `if…else` statements routinely modified behavior based upon state data. The OO paradigm simply offers an even more versatile technique through (a) extension of the notion of input parameters to all state data, particularly specification objects, and (b) dynamic instantiation of relationships to particular specification objects.

By binding instances together at runtime we get to select which state data (i.e., instance attributes) are to be used in particular circumstances. Thus, not only do we get to diddle with data values, we can also diddle with which sets of parameters to use. In particular, OO relationships tend to be instantiated based on a context that spans individual collaborations, so the relationship may be instantiated long before a particular collaboration method's invocation. More important, that context may be defined by someone other than the client in the collaboration. It would be getting ahead of the story to go into this in greater detail here, but have faith that this is really a very powerful technique that was pretty much unavailable before the OO paradigm.

Unfortunately, some magic is required to do invariants properly. It requires a different way of thinking about problems. Of all the activities of software development, identifying invariants depends most on the experience, judgment, and skill of the developer. The good news is that it is a very learnable skill. The only innate skill required is the ability to think abstractly, which is necessary to do OO development at all. It is also one of the essential things that separates *Homo sapiens* from all the rest so if you can't think abstractly, blame it on your parents.

There are no cookbook rules for doing it, so we will be spending a fair amount of time on examples, analysis patterns, and some (very loose) guidelines. But in the end you will have to rely on the time-honored paradigm of practice, practice, practice.

The Rewards

Because identifying invariants requires a lot of practice, it is important to understand why it is worth the effort. A major benefit of emphasizing invariants lies in maintainability of the application. External data is usually a lot easier to change reliably than application code because the side effects tend to be much more limited. As you may recall from the discussion of coupling in Chapter 2, data tends to be much more benign as far as dependencies go. We can misuse data, but it doesn't actually *do* anything by itself. In addition, data is often easier to change because it is so narrowly defined and simple. The context for changing it is usually very well focused, and we are modifying values rather than complex syntax. We can also provide tools that make the data updates more user friendly by automating tedious activities, such as finding the right data to change.

Nearly as important, though, is the impact on the development processes. When changes are done in data the software is unaffected. No code walking. No check-in and check-out of a flock of modules. No build cycle. No software configuration management. (There is configuration management of the data, but that is usually trivial compared to software configuration management.) And there is complete confidence that if anything breaks during testing, the problem lies in the data changes because the code wasn't touched.

What this often means is that the customers can manage the changes directly once you give them the proper tools. Usually this is nothing more than what they are already doing in some form anyway. They have to tell you what the change is, and that will very often involve specific data or identity. When you encode invariants you need to figure out how to express differences in data, and that data will necessarily be expressed in problem space terms. If it is in problem space terms, the user should be aware of it when the requirements change and use that same data to specify the requirements change. In effect, you have then moved requirements change management from executable program statements to a data entry problem in the customer's domain.[4]

But the most important benefit to maintainability is related to application partitioning. When system partitions are defined in terms of invariant and cohesive problem space structures it brings long-term stability to the system. When those partitions are encapsulated behind disciplined interfaces we have "firewall" protection against one partition doing rude things to another. And when those partitions are cohesive and are linked by client/service relationships, the scope of requirements changes tends to be contained. That is, you tend to have to touch a lot less stuff to effect the change.

A related benefit lies in large-scale reuse. MBD focuses on large-scale reuse rather than object-level reuse. Mechanically, MBD supports large-scale reuse through things like interface discipline. But the key to any reuse lies in defining semantics for the reuse subject matter that will stand the test of time. That is, reused elements could end up being reused in situations that were undreamed of by the original developers.

That requires a high degree of cohesion and well-defined subject matter boundaries. Since reuse is ultimately driven by the customer (i.e., the customer will trigger the requirements for those undreamed of reuse situations), the cohesion and boundaries must be stable in the customer's domain. To find that sort of stability in the customer's domain we must look for invariants in the customer space that define both the subject matter and its boundaries. If you do that, you will have a solid basis for long-term, large-scale reuse.

---

4. To defray visions of getting the customer to do all the work, there is no free lunch. The customer is not going to be keen on that unless you provide some very user-friendly tools. Configuration management of data may be easier but it won't go away, and synchronizing with customer activities may introduce a new suite of problems. There will also be a learning curve, and you better have a Plan B in case the customer screws up. In other words, the work hasn't gone away, you've just shifted into a more productive mode.

Another major benefit is reduced code size. Moving details out of the software and into external data simplifies the software. In effect we are moving a ton of if…else decision making into the external data. That leaves us with simpler code. It is not uncommon for code size to be reduced by integer factors when applying invariants.

A very important corollary of reducing code size is greater reliability. Generally, the number of defects is linearly related to code size over broad intervals. So if we reduce code size, we tend to reduce the total defects in the product as well. But what about defects in the data? Well, yes, one has to add those back in. However, there are several mitigating factors:

- Data is more regularly organized (e.g., tabular values), which makes it easier to change and less error prone.

- One only has to get values right, not complex syntax (e.g., in C using "=" instead of "==" in a conditional expression).

- Context is more focused because the semantics of the data values is narrowly defined, limiting the types of errors possible.

- Data has very limited intrinsic side effects.

- The data that supports invariants will be known in the problem space, so it will be easier to validate its correctness with the customer.

- The software uses all data of a given type exactly the same way (i.e., generically).

- Data can be formatted to reduce certain types of errors.

- Tools can remove tedious tasks and provide error checking.

- Configuration data are essentially system inputs, and errors in system inputs are almost always immediately manifested as incorrect results.

- Test cases can be automatically generated from the data to reduce the likelihood of escapes.

As a general assertion it is fair to say that errors in external data are less frequent than software errors (assuming we take some elementary formatting and documentation precautions), and when they do occur they are more readily found.

In the interest of truth in advertising, it should be pointed out that most of the code size benefits are realized at the class level when implementing individual subsystems. Nonetheless, applying invariants at the application partition level does have some indirect size reduction consequences. One way this happens is through cohesion. When a partition is highly cohesive, the abstractions needed to implement it tend to be rather simple, and the partition is more easily implemented. If the subsystems are each more easily implemented, it is likely that the application will be smaller. This is because complexity breeds interaction, so with reduced complexity there tends to be less interaction and exception handling.

Examples

As indicated previously, the best way to understand the use of invariants is by example and by practice. The more exposure we have to right thinking, the better off we will be. Unfortunately, we haven't shown enough of MBD to get into too many details, so the examples used here are rather superficial. The intent is simply to show the kind of thinking that is involved and how varied that thinking can be.

Bank ATM Software

This one has been used so many times in the literature that it has chestnut status. It is used here because a surprising number of authors have screwed it up royally by making a very elementary error in application partitioning. They made that error because they did not look carefully for problem space invariants. Figure 5-1 provides a hypothetical but plausible overall context for ATM software.

At this point we are only interested in three subsystems: *Account Management*, *ATM Controller*, and *Database*. Of those, we will focus primarily on the *ATM Controller* for this example. Basically these subsystem responsibilities can be broadly defined as follows.

> *Account Management.* This subsystem handles the basic business processing around individual customer accounts like checking, savings, overdraft, and so forth. It is responsible for creating and deleting accounts, debiting and crediting accounts, and mundane accounting tasks like providing audit trail data.
>
> *ATM Controller.* This subsystem is the software that actually controls the hardware in an ATM machine (e.g., keyboard, screen, card reader, cash dispenser, and deposit shredder). It talks to the rest of the bank's software over a network connection.
>
> *Database.* This subsystem handles persistence. Basically, it stores all the account data, audit trail logs, and other permanent data. Typically this is some big, honking enterprise database with fourteen levels of redundancy and whatnot, including some direct link to a vault at an undisclosed location under the Rocky Mountains.

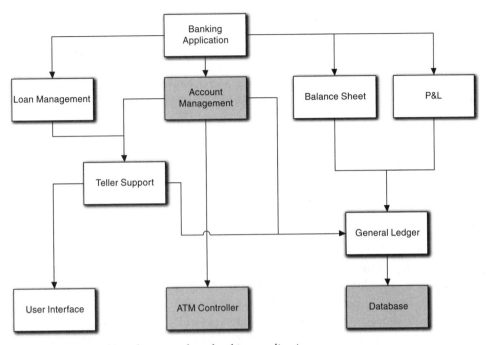

Figure 5-1 *Plausible subsystems for a banking application*

So far this seems like a quite plausible partitioning of the bank's software systems. Anyone familiar with banking systems would have little difficulty in identifying what these subsystems are about. Unless they were in the bank's IT division, they might not know what a relational data model is, but they would have a real good idea of what data needed to be saved and how important it was.

The problem here is not with what partitions are identified. It is with the way some authors designed them. Too many *ATM Controller* subsystems are designed with classes like *Checking Account*. In one, the *ATM Controller* subsystem was reading and writing data directly from the *Database* (i.e., it was generating SQL queries and sending them off through the network port). If software engineers were certified, doing things like this should be grounds for revoking their certification and assigning them to relatively harmless tasks like formatting printed reports or creating web pages.

A class like *Checking Account* belongs in *Account Management* because that's what that subsystem is about. But look at the description of *ATM Controller*. It is interested in hardware. It knows hardware. It probably even *likes* hardware. Hardware is enough for it to worry about, especially when every mid-level hoodlum in the country is trying to figure out a way of breaking into the ATM.

The *ATM Controller* subsystem talks to some entity on the other side of a network connection. The bank it is talking to may not even be the same bank that owns the ATM and installed the software! So why would the *ATM Controller* subsystem want to know anything at all about accounts, especially a particular bank's accounts? The only concept it needs to share with *Account Management* is the notion of *Message*, a message identifier and the format of a packet of data tied to that identifier.

> The fundamental subject matter of an *ATM Controller* is managing message traffic between the user, the hardware, and the network port.

It isn't the *ATM Controller*'s job to figure out if the user's account has enough balance to cover a withdrawal, apply overdraft policy, or any of the rest of that banking business. When the user requests a withdrawal, the *ATM Controller* should just forward that request to the *Account Management* subsystem and let it figure it out. When the *Account Management* subsystem decides it is OK to dispense cash, it sends a message back to the *ATM Controller*, which then talks to the cash dispenser hardware.

And the idea of the *ATM Controller* dealing directly with the *Database* is utterly preposterous. Consider how ecstatic the bank's DBA is going to be at the prospect of a customer remotely accessing enterprise DB objects directly from another bank's ATM through a 56Kb modem link. Also, do you really want exactly the same code for managing two-phase commit transactions in the *ATM Controller and* in the software for a real bank teller terminal? But it never should get to those sorts of implementation issues. If the *ATM Controller* has no need to understand the semantics of *Checking Account*, it certainly shouldn't know what part of that information should be persistent and what sorts of persistence mechanisms need to be used to ensure synchronization with the bank's General Ledger. The *ATM Controller* should not even know that the *Database* exists!

So where did these guys go wrong? The main problem is bleeding cohesion across subsystems. The cohesion problem is a direct result of not looking at the invariants of the *ATM Controller* subsystem. There are entities common to all ATMs, like the *Keyboard* and *Card Reader*. In addition, there are things common to most hardware control systems, like registers and interrupts. Moreover, the *ATM Controller* software is physically separated from the rest of the software by a distributed network boundary, which screams for simple, asynchronous data messages and separation of concerns across that boundary.

Taking these things together, they strongly suggest a focus on hardware control alone. By identifying general entities common to ATM control in particular and hardware control in general, the tentative abstractions identified are clearly quite different in nature than those in *Account Management*. A sense of quite different concerns for the two subsystems becomes apparent.

But the most important insight into invariants lies in realizing what the *ATM Controller* is really about. There is a set of concrete hardware entities—card reader, display, keypad, cash dispenser, deposit shredder, and network port—that the controller must deal with. How does it deal with these entities? It reads information from and writes information to their registers. In fact, it does virtually nothing except provide an order for transferring information among the various hardware entities' registers. What is the magic word we use in the OO paradigm for communicating between entities?

Message! The *ATM Controller* is about managing message flows. All it does is convert from one message format to another and ship messages around in a particular order. If it gets a message of type X from over *here*, it knows it should format a message of type Y and send it over *there*. To do that, it needs to know nothing about the semantics of the message content (i.e., what a *Checking Account* is). All it needs to know is what to do for each message type, and the mechanics of packing and unpacking each message type's data format.

The invariant behavior that we need to capture in the *ATM Controller* software is that of a message broker. If we raise the level of abstraction of the *ATM Controller* to this level we accomplish a great deal. First, let's look at the hardware side. Typically each hardware component of an ATM is manufactured by a different company and, competition being the backbone of a market-based economy, there can be multiple possible sources for each one. Does our *ATM Controller* software care?

Not a whole lot. We can easily describe the differences in components in configuration data. For example, the cash dispenser has to deal with a Dispense message that carries an amount. Typically the value is written to one or more registers and then there is another write to a separate register to tell the hardware to process the value. The number of registers and their addresses will probably vary from one manufacturer to another. Also, there are likely to be small differences in the way values are encoded to the registers (e.g., scaling, bit field sizes, etc.). But those differences can easily be described in data that specifies the number of registers, their addresses, their bit size, their endian, scaling rules, and any odd bit field formatting.

That data can be used to initialize an instance of a Cash Dispenser class. The Cash Dispenser will have a method, Dispense, for dispensing cash that will use the attribute values as parameters as it executes a generic routine to write the amount and trigger the cash dispensing. (We'll see a more specific example of how to do this shortly.) At this level a cash dispenser is not that complicated, so it will only require a modest amount of cleverness to design a Dispense method that will work for any cash dispenser on the planet—and probably any in our arm of the Milky Way galaxy—*provided the right external configuration data is provided.*

But what about the semantics of the messages? Can that really be abstracted so readily? Yes, Grasshopper, it certainly can within the limits of today's banking practices. There are not a lot of things the ATM's components can do, and those are pretty well standardized in terms of banking transactions. All the heavy lifting can be done on the other side of the network port by *Account Management* and *Database* based on *ATM Controller*'s announcements about its user's limited suite of activities.

In reality, an *ATM Controller* as proposed can be much more versatile. Suppose the bank decides to let the customer refinance a mortgage through the ATM. To do that, all we need is an additional suite of messages among display, keypad, and network port. The heavy lifting of loan approval, and so forth, will still get done on the other side of the network port. Clearly, message types, their data packet formats, and their destinations can be defined in external data fairly easily for something as simple as an ATM. With a little bit more creativity we can define message sequences (e.g., "If I receive message type A, I must send message type B") in terms of external configuration data because in an ATM those sequences aren't very complicated.

We can't go into detail here (though we will later) because we need more pieces of the puzzle first. However, defining the rules for dispatching messages for an *ATM Controller* in data is almost trivial. Basically this means that the bank can let the customer perform almost any financial activity with the bank without touching the *ATM Controller* software. All the new messages, display texts, and customer keypad responses can be defined through external configuration data. This is possible because the invariant paradigm of message broker does not depend upon understanding the semantics of message content any more than an e-mail program cares about the flaming in the message body.

If you are at all familiar with hardware control systems you will no doubt have realized that this paradigm potentially has much wider scope than just ATMs. We could develop the *ATM Controller* software in a fashion such that it could control a wide variety of hardware systems without changing anything except the configuration data. In fact, a much better name for the subsystem might be Hardware Message Broker. If you are beginning to suspect that this notion of modeling invariants brings new meaning to the word *reuse*, you would be right.

In addition to better cohesion, this train of thought leads to a better perspective on the nature of the subsystem boundaries. The network provides a very natural boundary, and the characteristics of network communications color the view of inter-subsystem communications. When combined with disparate concerns on either side, the boundary becomes more than simply a technical issue for efficient transmissions.

The boundary becomes an almost conceptual separation. On one side we have hardware and bank customers; on the other side we have banking and accountants. These are entirely different concerns and views, so the network interface becomes a medium of translating from one view to the other. When we consider the possibility of the ATM belonging to a different bank, it becomes even more desirable to minimize shared views; the least common denominator representation becomes attractive. In that context there is no need to pass objects across the boundary; we convert abstractions and minimize shared views through pure message interfaces that captures only the fundamental nature of the service invariants.

The point in the last couple of paragraphs is that this view of invariants is less about general rules and policies than about defining what subject matters *are*. The real insight here is understanding what the subject matter should know and do. We do that by seeking out its fundamental nature. Thus, the invariant in this example is what the intrinsic nature of an *ATM Controller* is. Once we grasp that, the generalization to classes of problems beyond ATMs becomes clear.

Hardware Interface

In the previous example we identified an *ATM Controller* as being concerned with managing hardware. However, that was the megathinker view of hardware communications. In this example we will deal with hardware communications at a much lower level of abstraction.

At a high level of abstraction we can think of all hardware interfaces in terms of reading and writing hardware registers. That's because almost all hardware provides an interface to software that is based upon the models for digital computation. We write values to registers, tell the hardware to read them, and read back values from registers when the hardware is done doing its thing (which it will announce by putting a value in a register to be read by the software).

For those of you who are not R-T/E people, the hardware guys provide the specification of the register semantics in what are known as *bit sheets*. The bit sheets identify registers by address, identify fields within the register {start bit, length} with a mnemonic, and provide a very brief and often unintelligible description of the field semantics. Registers usually have a fixed length in terms of bits. Things are complicated because values may not fit in a register, or fields may be split across registers, so reading or writing a single value often involves reads or writes of multiple registers. Finally, because multiple fields might be in a single register, one has to preserve the other fields' values when writing a value to a single field. (The R-T/E people refer to this as Read/Modify/Write[5] because we need to write the whole register. So we read the register, update just the embedded field, and then write the register.) The R-T/E people then build device drivers to run the hardware by talking to those registers.

A big problem that R-T/E software developers face is that the hardware guys are constantly changing the bit sheets as they do Engineering Change Orders (ECOs), or provide new and better circuit boards to do the same job, or simply to pull the chains of the software people. Because hardware real estate on circuit boards is precious, the hardware guys often move registers and redefine fields so they can fit everything on

---

5. To do this we need to provide bit-level masks and use arcane bitwise operators like XOR. That's why R-T/E people can do mental arithmetic in base 8 or 16. I actually knew a guy who could read aloud ASCII text in a hex memory dump as fast as I could read it aloud from a normal ASCII printout. R-T/E people definitely live in a different world.

the circuit board with feasible artwork.[6] So the bit sheets may be vastly different for two circuit boards that provide exactly the same functionality. Now the poor software guy trying to provide basic functionality for something like a cell phone finds that even though the phone works exactly the same way, the device driver needs to be rewritten because the bit sheets changed for a new card.

Historically, the R-T/E people actually pioneered modularity for exactly this reason. They provided a layer that would talk to the registers and provided a more generic interface to the rest of the software for the layer. Then all they had to do was replace that layer when the bit sheets changed. Today, though, we have a much better way to handle this problem so that we don't need to touch the layer at all.

But to reach that solution we need to think about the invariants of reading and writing hardware registers. We got halfway there earlier when we said that hardware control was about reading and writing registers. We read or write exactly one register at a time. We also read or write one problem data value at a time. Hence the basic problem is to put a single data value into one or more registers, and unless one is computing a gazillion decimal places for pi, the data value is going to fit into at most three registers.

In addition, we discussed how bit sheets provide a mapping between values and register fields. Here we are interested in the invariants of mapping values into defined fields in one or more registers. If you review the paragraph that described bit sheets, you will recognize that these things are always true:

- Registers are identified by addresses.

- Registers have fixed length in bits.

- Registers have one or more fields defined in terms of {start bit, bit length}.

- Fields have a designated identity represented by a mnemonic for the value that they store.

- Values may be split across fields in different registers. (The bit sheet will specify which field in which register has the lower order bits.)

---

6. "Artwork" refers to providing electrical connections between various points on the circuit board. Even a medium-sized board will have thousands of connections to make. Today most circuit boards have multiple layers so that the lands (thin conductive strips that make connections) can "cross over" other lands without shorting. In addition, land length is a problem because today's circuits run at such high clock rates that even a few inches can result in race conditions (synchronization problems for parallel signals). Long lands can also pick up noise at very high frequencies. Trying to find short, unobstructed paths is a very large np-Complete problem for circuit design, and often the hardware guy will have to move things around just to be able to provide feasible connections.

- If a register has multiple fields, one may need a Read/Modify/Write operation to set the value of a single field.

- If a value to be read or written is normally represented in more bits than the register field for it in the hardware, the value will need to be scaled.[7]

While reading and writing hardware registers is complicated, the list of possible processing activities is actually pretty short. Even better, those operations are so common that any R-T/E person can write them for a given value without much thought and possibly even when comatose. Better yet, the operations are easily separated and ordered sequentially. Thus, scaling a value to a field size is quite different than a Read/Modify/Write, and it will be done first. Best of all, the rules for those operations can be expressed exclusively in terms of bit sheet field specifications *that are simply data.*

That enables us to change the way we think about bit sheets. Instead of defining register fields, we can think of them as defining how individual semantic values are mapped into hardware registers. All we have to do is group together the bit sheet field specifications for the mnemonic corresponding to the value we want to read/ write, and we can "walk" those specifications in order to perform the relevant register reads and writes. And we can do that with very generic code that is parameterized with the bit sheet field definition values. A simplistic model for doing this is shown in Figure 5-2.

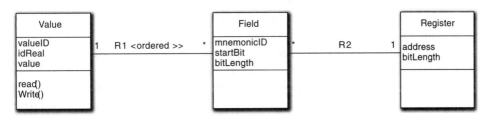

Figure 5-2 *Invariants of low-level hardware control*

The R1 relationship is ordered based on the bit sheet values so that one can split the Value over multiple fields in the proper sequence. R1 collects only the Fields that are relevant for the Value in hand. R2 then relates each Field to the Register containing it.

---

7. This wasn't mentioned in the bit sheet description, but hardware control registers are invariably integer values and almost always unsigned. One only sees floating- point register formats on computer CPUs and then usually on a dedicated FPU. So if the interface provides the values as a real number, it will also have to be converted to integer.

Value.read() and Value.write() are generic functions that know how to convert Value.value into one or more register reads or writes. They do that by navigating R1 and R2 to get the configuration information. For example, the Write() method will check if the bit length of the Field is less than that of the containing Register and, if so, will use a Read/Modify/Write. While the method code might be a tad convoluted, you can see that the method can determine everything it needs to know from navigating the relationships. So those generic methods capture the invariants of reading and writing registers and they are parameterized by the bit sheet data. (Recall the discussion of specification objects for parametric polymorphism; Register and Field are effectively specification objects.)

From an implementation standpoint the only trickiness here lies in getting the right bit sheet information. The values of the Register and Field objects are straight out of the bit sheet specifications. Since the registers and fields are fixed in the hardware, those objects can be instantiated at start-up from external configuration data (i.e., bit sheet data). The interesting part lies in instantiating the R1 and R2 relationships for a particular Value.

R2 is already fixed by the hardware as defined in the bit sheets, so we need to map a Value to its corresponding fields in the hardware registers. To do that we map valueID into the Field's mnemonicID, which can be provided through table lookups. Those lookup tables are instantiated from the configuration data as well.

The beauty of encoding invariants while relegating details to data in this case is manifested when the hardware guys change the bit sheets. All that changes are the data values in the configuration data; not a line of application code is changed. Better yet, we can reuse this layer across different device drivers; we just need to provide different configuration data.

The author helped develop a large device driver this way. The hardware had dozens of different cards, each with hundreds of registers. Over the life of that system dozens of new cards were introduced and there were hundreds of hardware ECOs. The device driver itself had over 250 KNCLOC of code. It was originally done procedurally without invariants. When we wrote it from scratch in an OO fashion we used invariants by putting the bit sheets in an Excel spreadsheet.[8] The software read the spreadsheet to initialize the specification objects and the lookup tables for relationship instantiation. The interesting data point was the change in maintenance effort. The old system required eight (8) full-time people to maintain it. The new version with exactly the same functionality required one (1) person half time for maintenance.

Caveat. Our version of the example model was somewhat more complicated than the one here because we addressed things like acquiring the configuration data and instan-

---

8. Note that this allowed the hardware guys to validate that we had captured the bit sheet data correctly in a very straightforward and reliable fashion.

tiation. There are also more elegant ways to capture the invariants than employed here, so consider this example a simplified version to make the point about invariants rather than an actual solution to communicating with the hardware.

Note that this represents a very different view of invariants than the ATM example. In the ATM example we used invariants to formalize our view of the *essence* of a subject matter; that is, the invariants described what the subject matter actually *was*. That, in turn guided how we abstracted the problem space. In this example, the invariants are basically a set of well-defined rules for converting the value view to the register view. Those rules would be readily recognized by any R-T/E developer as basic technique. Thus the tricky part was recasting some of those rules in terms of data and static relationship structure.

Depreciation

The notion of amortized depreciation is relevant to all commercial businesses. It is also a classic example of failing to recognize invariants because it is almost never implemented with them. The basic notion is simple. For accounting and tax purposes, assets are depreciated for a fixed number of years according to a specific formula based upon a base value of the asset at the time of its acquisition. Different formulas can be used for different types of assets. The business can often select the formula to use for a particular type of assets from a fixed set of choices. The rules governing how depreciation is applied are defined by organizations like the IRS and FASB. The most obvious solution is shown in Figure 5-3.

Figure 5-3 *Model for depreciation wholly contained in a single class*

We have an *Asset* class with a *computeDepreciation* behavior and attributes for *baseValue*, *assetType*, and *numberOfYears*. The *computeDepreciation* method implements the particular formula that the bean counters have deemed appropriate for this type of asset. So far, so good, except for a few niggling details.

- The formula in *computeDepreciation* is hard-coded in the method, so if the formula changes we must modify the implementation of *Asset*.

- Assets with different types may use different formulas, which means we need some sort of substitution of the formula with *assetType*.

- The notion of *asset type* may have other uses orthogonal to depreciation for describing what the asset actually *is*. This leads to a proliferation of combinatorial values for *assetType*.

- The powers that be regularly change the rules about what formulas and time duration can be used.

- The bean counters periodically exercise their option to change the formula and/ or duration for particular assets.

- The bean counters periodically add new assets with new types or change the types of existing assets.

Dealing with all that in a single method tends to get a bit clunky. One way around some of this is to use ad hoc polymorphism by putting a switch statement in *compute-Depreciation* that selects the correct formula to use based on the value of *assetType*. This can get messy when the bean counters add types because we need to add another case option to the switch statement for the new type. In addition, we may have several different types that can use the same formula. And we still need to perform rather delicate surgery on *Asset* when the rules change. For any reasonably large business, things get out of hand quickly. Figure 5-4 shows one of the more common solutions where generalization is used.

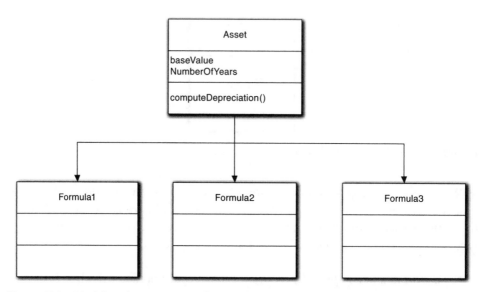

Figure 5-4 *Modeling depreciation with simple generalization*

This replaces ad hoc polymorphism with the more elegant inclusion polymorphism. Instead of a single monolithic switch statement, we now isolate a specific formula to a subclass. This is the approach used by the Because It's There School of OO Development; inclusion polymorphism is used because it is neat and uniquely OO rather than because the problem space requires it.

In many respects this solution is actually worse than the ad hoc polymorphism solution even though it looks more "OO-like." That will become clear as soon as we need to subclass assets based on some other criteria (e.g., capital versus nondurable equipment). To accommodate the formula-based generalization, we will need a combinatorial number of subclasses that provide every possible combination of the two orthogonal classifications. A common variation on this solution is to use the Strategy design pattern, as shown in Figure 5-5.

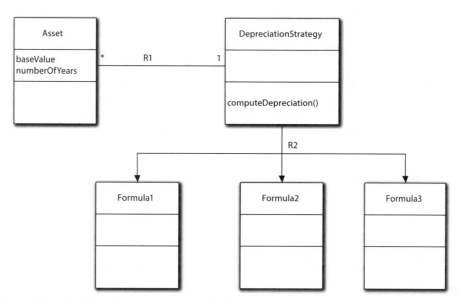

Figure 5-5   *Modeling depreciation using the Strategy pattern*

This eliminates any combinatorial subclassing because the depreciation algorithm has been removed from *Asset* entirely. However, it shares another problem with the previous example. If we want to add a new formula, we need to add a subclass. In addition, we need to modify the code that instantiates the R1 relationship. The only thing good about this solution is that it enables us to isolate and encapsulate the rules that determine which formula is the right one for the given *Asset*. In practice, that will usually involve the same sort of switch statement based on asset type as in the ad hoc polymorphic example, so we have just created some new objects that are close to being pure functions. Moral: Just because a neat feature exists in the OO paradigm does not mean one is required to use it.

To come up with a better solution that handles all the requirements in a quite elegant manner, we need to think about what the invariants of depreciation really are. In practice, the depreciation we compute is a single value that represents a fraction of the asset's base value. That single value represents the amount to be amortized in a particular accounting period after the asset was acquired. That is, what we really need to compute is

$$AmountInPeriod_t = baseValue * FractionInPeriod_t$$

We can compute the $FractionInPeriod$, for any formula for any year, t, after the asset acquisition without knowing anything about asset types as long as we know the total years of amortization. Thus for any year, t, all assets using the same formula for the same number of years of amortization will have exactly the same fraction of their base value for depreciation in that year.

The main insights here are (1) Computing the formula for a given amortization duration is always the same regardless of asset semantics and (2) Depreciation for a particular asset is nothing more than a fraction of its base value in any given accounting period. Both these insights represent useful invariants resulting from a decomposition of the problem until we were able to recognize essential elements. Why are these invariants useful? Consider Figure 5-6, which captures these insights.

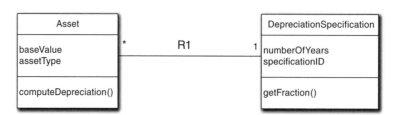

Figure 5-6   *Modeling depreciation invariants using a specification object*

The answer lies in the fact that they allow us to employ parametric polymorphism to solve the problem in a very generic fashion. The "formula" that *computeDepreciation* now uses is the one above, which is exactly the same for *any* asset. We get the value of $FractionInPeriod_t$ by navigating the R1 relationship and invoking *getFraction* with the desired value of t. All we have to do is supply it with the right value of *baseValue* for the asset. As in the inclusion polymorphism example, we get those by instantiating the R1 relationship correctly.

However, if we are clever about it, we can do that with a simple table lookup on *assetType* to yield the right *specificationID*. That mapping can be supplied in external configuration data rather then being encoded in executable statements. In addition, since *DepreciationSpecification* is just a dumb data holder, we can initialize all its instances from external configuration data as well. Then when an *Asset* object is created, we just do the lookup and instantiate the R1 relationship to the right instance in memory. The *computeDepreciation* behavior will then do the right thing for the asset.

Aside from a certain degree of elegance, the really neat thing is that we can add any number of new formulas and any arbitrary mapping between asset types and depreciation *without touching the application model or the resulting implementation code*. All we need to do is modify the external configuration data that defines *DepreciationSpecification* objects and the R1 relationship mapping between *assetType* and *specificationID*. That is, the actual computation of the formula is done once outside the application to supply the relevant values of $\mathrm{FractionInPeriod_t}$ for all combinations of formula and amortization duration in the definitions of *DepreciationSpecification*.

Now let's take it one step further. The bean counters always have to provide you with three pieces of information whenever anything changes for depreciation: the formula to use, the asset type it applies to, and the amortization duration. You can create a data entry tool outside the application that the bean counters can use to provide that data. The tool provides a nice GUI with a couple of text boxes for asset type, amortization years, and *specificationID* along with a pick list for existing formulas to use. The tool then executes the formula and creates the configuration data without the bean counter knowing anything about trivia, like file formats.

If we really want to get exotic we can provide a UI that enables the bean counters to even provide new formulas off the cuff. (Think: the same sort of formula wizard as in a spreadsheet.) Now, it is hard to conceive of anything that could possibly change related to depreciation that would require an application modification. Better yet, the application is a whole lot simpler with a "formula" that has a single multiplication and assignment. You are probably not going to insert too many defects with that, especially when you don't touch it in maintenance.

But haven't we just moved the problem out of the application and into the tool the bean counters will use? Yes, we have, Grasshopper. Think of it as creating a distributed application where the elements communicate through the configuration file. However, we rack up some major gains in doing so—even if the total code lines in the tool are more than we would have had in any of the other *computeDepreciation* examples.

- Multiple contexts or even applications may need to compute depreciation. The infrastructure for reading and using the configuration data will be exactly the same for all of them.

- Depreciation will be computed far more often for assets than the formulas will be modified. We are simplifying what we do most often.

- Modifying a production application is nontrivial, and in most shops it can be a major undertaking. No production application needs to be modified here for most (if not all) possible changes to depreciation requirements. We have reduced the requirements changes to a data entry problem.

- The configuration data has a fixed format regardless of the requirements changes. All that changes are the values. Thus we only need to get the data entry application right once.

- Similarly, one only needs to get the processing of the configuration data right once, regardless of how many times the requirements change.

- The concerns are very well separated and decoupled. Formatting the configuration data from a very basic UI is a very narrowly focused problem for the data entry tool that has no distractions about the context of how the data will be used.

- The path from customer (bean counter) to the implementation for the requirements is very straightforward without a lot of opportunity for any misinterpretations, and such.

- When requirements do change, things like parallel testing of new configuration data are greatly facilitated because we just run the production application as usual. In fact, we could have the configuration data printed out in a format that would be easy for the bean counters to validate because they provided it as input in the first place.

In the end this approach to depreciation is an enormous win. It is curious that no one seems to do it this way. The big insight is simply that the depreciation in any time period is a fraction of the base value. When you read the new "formula" you knew exactly where we were going and probably thought to yourself, "Of course! Why didn't I think of that?" The short answer is that most people don't think of it because they are not used to thinking in terms of extracting invariants from the problem space.

Before leaving this example, note that it represents a special spin on the notion of invariant, compared to the last example. In the hardware register case the invariants were simply there for the picking; one just had to think about the problem space a bit more abstractly. In this case we needed to recast the problem space from a traditional view of computing depreciation to a different view of what the essential computation actually was. We did that by decomposing the elements of the *process* of computing depreciation until we could see a new pattern emerge. To do that we had to step back and think about how we used the value we computed. Thus the real invariant lay not in the computation itself but in the context of using its results.

Remote POS Entry Example

The next example is for a remote point-of-sale order entry system. For simplicity, we are concerned here only with the customer being able to create and submit an order for merchandise remotely from the vendor. We are going to ignore all other order processing at the vendor once the order is received. In this case, let's assume there is a general merchandiser with a wide variety of items for sale in many different goods categories.

Let's further assume that some cross-functional team went out and beat the bushes with real customers to come up with the following set of requirements. (Though the list has the correct level of ambiguity, it is shorter than one in real life would be; this is just a representative example to make a point.)

- The goods need to be categorized in a hierarchy (e.g., clothing → men's → sportswear). The categories will follow the existing standard inventory classification system.

- The customer needs a convenient mechanism to navigate the goods categories.

- Major goods categories need to be immediately accessible from anywhere in the order entry process except order submission processing.

- A search facility must be provided to find all categories of goods or specific items.

- The customer can order one or more items. A list of currently desired items will be maintained. The customer needs to be able to easily review the list and add or remove items from it. The items in the list are not actually ordered until the customer submits the order.

- Customers need to be able to review every aspect of the order, including total cost adjusted for shipping fees, discounts, and taxes.

- Goods descriptions must be displayed in a consistent format. Required order attributes (size, color, style, etc.) must be separated from other descriptive material and emphasized.

As you read the list of requirements did you think: Web, Hyperlink, and Shopping Cart?

Bzzzzt! Thanks for playing. You have just flunked your first pop quiz on modeling invariants.

About a century ago Sears solved this problem by placing a mail order catalogue in a large fraction of the homes in the United States. That catalogue had solutions for every one of the listed requirements. For example, it had color-coded pages and an index for easily finding categories of items and individual items; it had an order form to record desired goods, and the customer could add or remove items from the form; and submission was clearly defined by mailing the order form back to Sears. The fundamentals of remote POS order entry have not changed in that time. The only things, aside from prices, that have changed are the implementation mechanisms.

Note that most general merchandisers still have mail order catalogues alongside their spiffy new web sites. This fact should be suggestive. It would be highly desirable to use the same software infrastructure for both mail order and web orders. For example, the order descriptions should be displayed the same way on the web and in the catalogue to allow reuse in the web display software and the print layout software. For consistency, all the item description information should be in one place. The same categorization, in fact, must be used because that is a standard referenced in the requirements. Also, the software that processes the orders would like to be indifferent about where the order originated.

The assertion here is that the OOA model should look exactly the same for the modern web implementation and the century-old Sears manual solution. One very good yardstick used by reviewers to ensure that OOA models are implementation-independent is that the model could be implemented as a manual system, like the Sears mail-order catalogue, in the customer's environment without changing the model. Essentially, this means that the OOA model must be sufficiently abstract to describe both a manual and a computerized solution.

We are not going to go through a detailed OOA model here to demonstrate invariants for this example. That is mostly a matter of class-level abstraction, and we will be dealing with that a lot more Part II. Instead, it will be left as a class exercise to think about how one would describe a solution abstractly enough that it would be accurate for such disparate solutions as web and mail order implementations.

Here is one hint of things to come, though. In the requirements, the notion of categories of goods was quite dominant. It would be very tempting to create a taxonomy of goods where every item type (class) was a leaf subtype in a monolithic generalization structure. After all, generalization is one of the distinctive characteristics of OT, right? And groups of items will share characteristics like *size* that can be captured in superclasses, right? For reasons we will get to later, that would be a serious error because it would invite major problems in doing maintenance as new categories and items were added and removed in the future.

For now just note that categories exist in the requirements for one and only one reason: to make navigation through the items easier for the customer. That context has nothing to do with the inherent characteristics of goods. Superficially there is a sharing of characteristics. For example, women's shoes and men's coats have a size, while refrigerators and air conditioners have an energy rating. But if you try to organize shared characteristics into a monolithic inheritance hierarchy for anything as complex and volatile as a general merchandiser's inventory, you will have nightmares about overweight duck-billed platypuses chasing you through mazes.

Once we recognize the role of categories as a navigational aid, we can focus on the invariants of navigation. Separation of a navigation representation from item representation can result in an elegant simplification where the entire navigational hierarchy is represented with only two classes, as shown in Figure 5-7. The object relationships that are represented by the reflexive parent/child relationship on Category contain all of the hierarchical information in a form that is ideally suited for navigating to the immediately higher or lower levels around a given category.

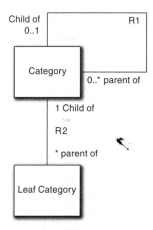

Figure 5-7 *Example of using a reflexive relationship to describe a tree hierarchy*

Figure 5-7 is a classic model of a hierarchical tree. The structure of the navigation is completely captured in the relationships. We can write the software for any hierarchical navigation (e.g., "walking" a web site like Amazon.com) from this model. The reason that Leaf Category is special is because we need to actually display inventory items when the user gets to that level. But we can accommodate even that in a generic fashion in Figure 5-8.

In this representation the Leaf Category class represents a *collection* of real items in the lowest leaf-level category. We can extend this by providing a Leaf Specification class that defines the attributes that are relevant for all the items in the leaf category. The Leaf Specification tells the Leaf Category how to interpret the data in the relevant Inventory Items. Essentially, this maps generic items' attribute values into characteristic semantics that will be relevant to the customer (e.g., the item's third attribute value, say 8 in an item instance, will always map into a women's dress size in the display).

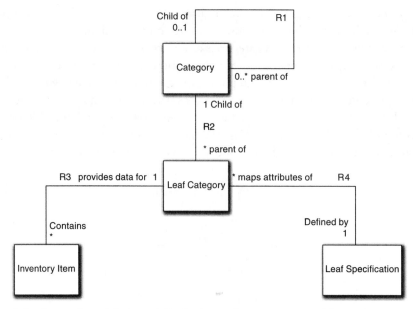

Figure 5-8 *Separation of the invariants for hierarchy navigation and hierarchy content*

The details of how to do this are a bit tricky so we will defer them until we get to class-level modeling. The important thing to note here, though, is that all the instances of Category, Leaf Category, and Leaf Specification and their relationships can be created at runtime from external data. This enables us to arbitrarily add or remove categories and item types without touching the software; it can all be done in the external data. Thus this marvelously simple model solves the entire navigation problem *and* enables virtually any type of new merchandise to be added to the inventory without changing the model.

Also note that we have specified the hierarchical POS category navigation but not the organization of Inventory Items. The requirements indicated they needed to be the same and that is fine. But the organization of Inventory Items doesn't really matter to the POS navigation problem, so we don't say how we know which Inventory Items go with a particular Leaf Category. All we need is a list of Inventory Items that goes with a Leaf Category, and that also can be defined in an external configuration file.[9]

9. Note the recurring theme in these examples of addressing requirements changes by modifying external configuration data rather than the application. This just reflects the fact that recognizing invariants goes hand-in-hand with parametric polymorphism. You will find that as you recognize more and more problem space invariants, you will be moving more and more of the maintenance out of the application. And that is a Very Good Thing.

We got to this model by stepping back and focusing upon the navigation problem invariants without worrying about the nature of specific goods. In doing that we recognized that navigation was about "walking" a hierarchical tree structure rather than generalization. That is, the relevant invariant is that navigation is about parent/child relationships between entities, not the inherent characteristics of the entities themselves. From there, modeling the tree structure alone was relatively easy.

Another key insight was that we don't care about how actual Inventory Items are organized. The requirements say that the categories will have to map the same way, but we do that outside the application where the configuration data is defined. That is, the rules for construction of the configuration data that defines R1 will be driven by the organization of Inventory Items. This is important to long-term robustness for two reasons. It means that requirements can change without affecting our POS software. Perhaps more important, it means we can focus on a much narrower problem in the POS without worrying about merging two different structures. That leads to an elegantly simple solution without any other concerns that drive *why* the Inventory Items are organized in a particular way. That simplicity would be impossible without having first decided that a POS was a different subject matter from Inventory Control that had different invariant concerns.

Chapter 6

Application Partitioning

So we grew together,
Like to a double cherry, seeming parted,
But yet a union in partition;
Two lovely berries moulded on one stem.
—Shakespeare, *A Midsummer Night's Dream*

If you destroy a bridge, be sure you can swim.
—Swahili proverb

In 1987 the author took his first formal training course in an OOA/D methodology. The first diagram described the large-scale, logical partitioning of the application, which today is known as a UML Component diagram. The instructor was asked how much time should be spent on the diagram. His answer was, "If you spend half a day, that is probably too long." That was the single worst piece of technical advice the author ever received. For a large application, that activity is the single most important activity in the entire development process.

Why Do We Care?

Every complex software application has a basic architecture that represents the structure or skeleton of the application. That structure provides a framework for the rest of the design elements. The framework acts very much like a back plane in electronic equipment that enables different modules to communicate in a disciplined way. That framework also supports plug-and-play for large-scale reuse.

Application partitioning organizes the application.

The essential work of application partitioning is to subdivide the application logically into subsystem modules. That organization necessarily affects how we think about individual subsystems when we design them. It also affects how we think about the way they will communicate with one another. Finally, and probably most important, it affects the way we allocate and isolate customer requirements *within* the application. If that organization changes, then it is quite likely that change will trigger a lot of rework in each subsystem. This is because those subsystems were built with particular assumptions about the way the application was organized. If those assumptions are no longer correct, then it is likely that fundamental changes will have to be made to the way each of those subsystems works.

Maintainability depends on a stable underlying structure.

Maintainable applications all share certain characteristics.

- The location of change is readily recognized.

- The scope of change is limited.

- The complexity of change is limited.

Application partitioning directly addresses the first two. The OO paradigm as a whole addresses the last characteristic by making detailed designs easier to modify. A change takes place in the subsystem defined to "own" the relevant requirements. (As we shall see shortly, client/service relationships explicitly allocate specific requirements to subsystems.) If subsystems are cohesive and subsystem boundaries are well-defined, then change will tend to be isolated within one or a few subsystems. However, change location is only recognized easily, and the scope of change is only limited if the organization of the subsystems—particularly their definitions—are stable over the life of the application. If the basic definition of the application structure is a moving target, then it is simply not possible to deliver on maintainability goals.

The OO paradigm and MBD in particular provide a systematic approach to application partitioning that will ensure long-term stability of the application structure. Better yet, it is a fundamentally intuitive methodology. So, the bad advice cited in the chapter opening was half right; once you get the hang of it, properly partitioning even the largest applications is usually measured in tens of hours and for a smallish application, half a day may be appropriate. The problem with the advice was that it didn't get across the idea that we *absolutely need to take whatever time is necessary to get it right*.

It is not possible to overemphasize how important partitioning is. The author worked on a large application with nearly two dozen subsystems where not a single subsystem's definition changed during more than a decade of heavy maintenance.

Subsystems were added for new functionality and their implementations were modified, but the original definitions of subject matters and levels of abstraction remained unchanged. That sort of semantic stability is enormously valuable over the life of an MLOC+ application.

It was a hardware control system for a large electronics tester (~10K control registers) capable of testing every digital component on something like a B-52 bomber. During that decade the underlying hardware was redesigned several times; not a single card in the system when the author retired had existed when the software was originally developed. Large chunks of functionality, such as diagnostics algorithms, were added on a plug-and-play basis. Over time it was run from a Wintel GUI, a Unix remote client, a customer's C program, an ATLAS test IDE, and as a component of a larger test system. There was a ton of maintenance done, and the final system was integer factors larger than the original. Yet after the first year of original development it was maintained by no more than *four* developers and usually only *one* developer, half-time. Many developers maintaining large R-T/E systems would kill to be able to work on something that stable.

Basic Concepts of Application Partitioning

Application partitioning is fundamentally a systems engineering task for large applications. Many OOA/D books do not even mention it because systems engineering is often viewed as a different trade union from OO development. However, the OO paradigm focuses on problem space abstraction, a very useful tool when trying to partition a large application for maintainability. That, combined with the importance of good partitioning, is why this is one of the largest chapters in the book.

As the last chapter indicated, invariants in the problem space should be ubiquitous in the design at all scales. The application structure will only have long-term stability if it is based on problem space invariants. Invariants ensure that the cohesion of the partitions is unlikely to change over the long term. When subsystem interfaces are defined in terms of invariants, that provides long-term decoupling of the subsystem implementations. That, in turn, prevents architectural drift as those subsystem implementations are modified during maintenance.[1]

---

1. You will note the emphasis on dealing with changes in the above commentary. Good partitioning is really a developer issue because the main justification is to ensure long-term maintainability. That is why the supplementary documentation that supports the component diagram and describes invariants in the problem space is more important than the diagram itself. When developers spend time on partitioning, they are doing themselves (and their progeny who will replace them on the project) a favor.

There are a number of specific ways that good partitioning improves maintainability. It is essential to understand that context in terms of why good partitioning is important and how it helps maintainability.

Cohesion. Cohesion is important because it helps to isolate change to the implementations encapsulated within one or a few interfaces. In addition, good cohesion facilitates good interfaces and mitigates against redundancy of function.

Interfaces. Strong interfaces enhance testability because they enable partitions to be tested on a stand-alone basis. They also enhance communications among different teams on large projects because they can be generalized and documented before the implementation is actually designed. On large projects they become the primary vehicle of communication for teams working on different subsystems. Once the requirements are allocated and the interfaces are negotiated, the developers of the individual subsystems can go their separate ways.[2]

Implementation hiding. Strong interfaces decouple clients from the niggling details of specific implementations. Since the details are the things most likely to change, strong interfaces tend to limit the scope of change through encapsulation.

Problem space abstraction. Good partitioning maps large-scale application structure into familiar customer infrastructure. Since customers accommodate change in a manner that causes the least disruption to their existing major structures, the major software structures will be minimally affected.

Invariants. Mapping partition boundaries against conceptual boundaries in the customer's environment that are unlikely to change will tend to provide long-term stability for the application framework.

Client/Service relationships. If partitioning reflects true client/service relationships, this effectively manages dependencies so that they form an acyclic directed

---

2. I was once hoisted on my own petard for this very reason by a Group VP. He announced a group development effort with another division on the other side of the continent. Several years previously we did a common project with that division, and it was a disaster because of logistics and different development cultures. So after the presentation I greeted him with, "Hi, Joe. Long time, no see. You know you haven't got a prayer in hell of carrying this off, right?" A year later we delivered the megabuck product with three days of effort required for integrating our stuff, and we didn't even have anyone on site for it! The reason was that Joe insisted that the project be run exactly as I had been preaching for years. The subsystems were defined and each division developed individual subsystems that were glued together by interfaces at system integration time. Interestingly, Joe was a Hardware Guy rather than a Software Guy. But he was also very sharp and could see the value of good application partitioning and how it could be mapped to mega project management. He was also a nice guy, so he didn't chortle too much.

graph. Any software engineering theoretician will be happy to give you twenty minutes on why acyclic directed graphs are *good things*.

If these points sound familiar, they should. The first five are pretty much the OO paradigm's central view of what class abstractions are about. As it happens, MBD treats application partitions almost exactly as if they were really big objects. The last point is just a well-established technique for managing software complexity.[3]

We need to take time out for a definition of our basic unit of large-scale encapsulation. Essentially the UML semantics are paraphrased in MBD as follows:

A **subsystem** is a large-scale logical unit of the software that abstracts a cohesive problem space subject matter at a particular level of abstraction and encapsulates that subject matter behind an interface.

This definition captures most of the critical ideas behind application partitioning. Application partitioning is about defining subsystems, and the MBD methodology addresses four activities in doing that: identifying subject matters, identifying levels of abstraction, defining interfaces, and allocating requirements. The rest of this chapter summarizes each of these activities.

Subject Matter

A subsystem is a part of the application that implements a unique subject matter. As indicated previously, the basic MBD view of a subsystem is that it is an object on steroids. More specifically, it has the following characteristics.

- It is an abstraction of an *invariant* problem space entity, usually conceptual.

- It encapsulates a subject matter that addresses a unique suite of functional requirements.

- It is logically cohesive.

- It has an intrinsic suite of knowledge and behaviors for which it is responsible.

- Its implementation is hidden.

- It is encapsulated behind a *pure message (event)* interface.

---

3. In fact, this view underlies a great deal of the dependency management employed during OOP to make OOPL code more maintainable. The notion of client/service also has familiar manifestations in things like client/server architecture and Service-Oriented Architecture (SOA).

- Its behavior is functionally isolated (i.e., it is not directly dependent on other subsystems' behaviors).

- It is uniquely identified.

The MBD view of a subsystem is even more constrained than an object because the interface used to encapsulate it provides more decoupling than a class interface.

The implementation of a subsystem is almost always done with objects. (Alternatively, we can nest subsystems to provide decomposition in very large systems.) The implementation of a subsystem is a set of objects that interact directly with one another. This is an important concept for MBD because it brings new meaning to the notion of *implementation hiding*.

The objects that implement a subsystem should be hidden from other subsystems.

This makes a lot of sense if we think about it for a moment and allow for the switch in implementation scale. Yet it is a notion that is very rarely expounded in OO books. As a result, we see lots of OO applications where problem space object references are passed routinely all over the application. Those references expose the implementation of some part of the application to the rest of the application *because they were abstracted to implement the source subsystem*. Not only do they introduce dependencies in the rest of the application on that specific implementation, they also give the rest of the application a license to kill (i.e., blow the sender implementation away).

A good example of why references should not be passed is the ubiquitous window handle in GUI applications. Often these applications will pass window handles all over the application. Since the OS Window Manager can be accessed from anywhere in the application, virtually anybody can update the GUI directly. Then the developers lament that porting their applications to a different platform with a different Window Manager is a big problem! In MBD, one and only one subsystem would have a subject matter that was responsible for GUI display, and any time another subsystem needed something displayed, it would talk to that subsystem rather than to the OS Window Manager directly.

The critical methodological ideas that affect design of subsystems are the following:

- Subject matters are unique. A particular suite of problem space rules and policies should only be found in a single subsystem.

- Subject matters are cohesive. The responsibilities are logically related in the problem space. A corollary is that the requirements to be addressed in the subsystem design are narrowly defined.

- Subsystems are self-contained. The design of a particular subsystem can be done in complete isolation from any other subsystem. A subsystem can be fully tested functionally in complete isolation (in effect, a unit test on steroids).

- The overall semantics of the subject matter (i.e., what it *is*) are invariant. The details may change, but its role in the overall problem solution context does not change.

When identifying subject matters, the most important consideration is the problem space. Whatever you identify as a subsystem should be readily identifiable in the problem space.[4] The application partitions should always be validated with the relevant customers. For all but the largest systems we are talking on the order of a dozen subsystems, so validation shouldn't be a major problem. There are a couple of key questions for that validation.

Does a domain expert recognize it immediately? The name of the partition should immediately evoke some perception of what the partition is about. If that perception doesn't line up reasonably well with your view, you have a problem.

Does a domain expert agree with the subject matter description? This is not absolutely essential at the nit level because it is in the nature of abstraction to make compromises with reality. But when summarizing the essence of a subsystem in a few sentences, the domain expert needs to keep nodding in the affirmative when reading them.

The last question is worth further qualification. Subsystem descriptions are done in natural language and, therefore, they are imprecise and ambiguous. Also, people provide their own filters based upon their psychological set, past experience, and preconceptions.

The value of subsystem descriptions is much more important for gaining consensus than for documenting the application.

The customer provides the requirements and you are going to have to allocate them to subsystems. You will find that a lot easier to do if you and the customer share *exactly the same* semantic view of the subsystems. This is because the customer thinks about and organizes requirements within the context of the problem space. If

---

4. An application can have several different problem spaces, each with their own domain experts. Some, like networking and database access, may be unknown to the application's end users. Thus, in a hybrid hardware/software system the hardware engineers become customers of the application because they define requirements for interacting with the hardware.

your application organization lines up with the customer's problem space organization, you are providing a customer-friendly environment for those requirements. If nothing else, scrubbing the subsystem descriptions with the customer will provide added insight into the requirements themselves.

It is beyond the scope of this book to get into detailed scrubbing techniques for natural language. The literature of both requirements elicitation and process improvement provides a wealth of material on this. I will only say that it is very important that you encourage detailed feedback on the descriptions. If you have never participated in formal consensus-gathering techniques (e.g., KJ diagrams[5]) you will be amazed at how much insight can be gathered and how many surprises there can be when people begin to discuss how they actually interpret written words.

As an example, consider a garage door opener. There will be a basic application subsystem, say Opener, that will contain the high-level logic for opening and closing the garage door. To do that it will have to send and/or receive events from a clicker, a drive motor, and an electric eye. Each of these hardware components is quite different with clearly different responsibilities, so we could separate them out into separate subsystems as in Figure 6-1(a).

On the other hand, we can make a case that the garage door opener software is about controlling hardware. That is, we could consider a single hardware subsystem dedicated to detailed register reads/writes for controlling the door motion. In that case we could combine talking to the individual hardware components into a single Hardware Interface subsystem, as in Figure 6-1(b).

So which would have greater clarity and cohesion? The answer, Grasshopper, is clearly: both. Which one is best will depend upon other information in the application problem domain. For example, suppose each hardware component comes with a software device driver from the hardware vendor and you don't plan to do a lot of hardware swapping. Those device drivers will be separate, realized components. The interface to them will be trivial; the total code lines to talk to those drivers might be a dozen function calls. In that case, you will probably want to go with Hardware Interface because the distinction between hardware components is largely transparent to the analysis.

Now suppose you have to provide a device driver doing direct register reads and writes for each hardware component, and you will have several different models with different vendor hardware components. Then you may want separate subsystems

---

5. An acronym for Kawakita, Jiro. The diagrams are a technique for building a high-level, summary consensus from a collection of low-level, individual statements that are related in varying degrees. A crucial initial step is to ensure that everyone understands each statement in exactly the same way. Invariably, at least half of the original statements will have to be modified in some manner to reach consensus.

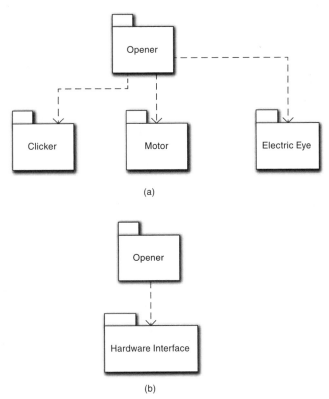

(a)

(b)

Figure 6-1   *Alternative component diagrams for a garage door opener*

even though they may be pretty small. The resulting design of the individual drivers will be significant, and it will have to be conveniently managed. The need for plug-and-play is an important requirement that justifies explicit isolation of the design for individual hardware components. Thus, clarity and cohesion are relative to the application context.

But what about reuse? If we define subsystems based on particular application contexts, won't that interfere with reuse? Yes, it might. But software development is full of trade-offs. Since you brought it up, though, the version in Figure 6-1(a) is likely to be better for reuse. Why? Because individual drivers can be readily substituted. We can probably come up with a very generic interface for each driver that will enable the implementations to be swapped transparently behind it. The Hardware Interface in Figurer 6-1(b) must necessarily coordinate specific drivers (i.e., make exactly the right driver calls). If we start to substitute drivers we could end up with a combinatorial number of Hardware Interface subsystem implementations.

Client/Service Relationships

Since subsystems embody functional subject matters, each subsystem must address some set of customer requirements. Good cohesion demands that the particular set of requirements that a subsystem resolves must be unique. (When large-scale customer requirements span subsystems, they are broken up into finer-grained requirements that can be individually allocated to particular subject matters, typically by a systems engineer.) In MBD, we do this by organizing subsystems in a directed, acyclic graph of client/service relationships or dependencies. Those relationships represent a flow of requirements from a client to a service.

At the top of the component diagram we usually have a single subsystem that provides overall high-level control over the problem solution. At the bottom will be very detailed and highly specialized services, so the graph forms an inverted tree. The level of abstraction is very high at the top and very low at the bottom. Reuse tends to increase as we move down the graph because detailed supporting services tend to be more generic (i.e., they apply to entire classes of similar problems). This is demonstrated schematically in Figure 6-2. The diagram groups subsystems into four broad categories: Application, which are very problem specific; Services, which are application specific but may provide reuse for very similar problems; Implementation, which tend to be highly reusable implementations of common facilities like database access; and Architecture, which represent placeholders for infrastructure like particular technologies. The Architecture group simply identifies computing space infrastructure the other subsystems will use, such as a particular operating system, so we usually don't clutter the diagram with dependencies to the Architectural subsystems.

It is important not to confuse this with communication. Communications can flow in either direction. For example, most applications will have a low-level service subsystem, the sole purpose of which is to communicate with the software user in a particular UI paradigm (e.g., GUI or web browser). The requirements on that subsystem—the semantics of *what* it needs to communicate—will be driven by the other subsystems in the problem solution that will need to communicate with the user. However, since the user is actually running the solution, most of the communications—the individual messages—will originate interactively with the user. Thus, requirements flow down from the problem solution while communication flows up from the user.

This architecture fundamentally influences the way we think about design, particularly for subsystem interfaces. Allocating requirements to subject matters using client/service relations requires a DbC contract between client and service. That contract will be manifested in the interface provided by the service, and the interface will reflect the invariants about how the service is used. The subsystem design then needs to directly support that interface. The client/service perspective combines with

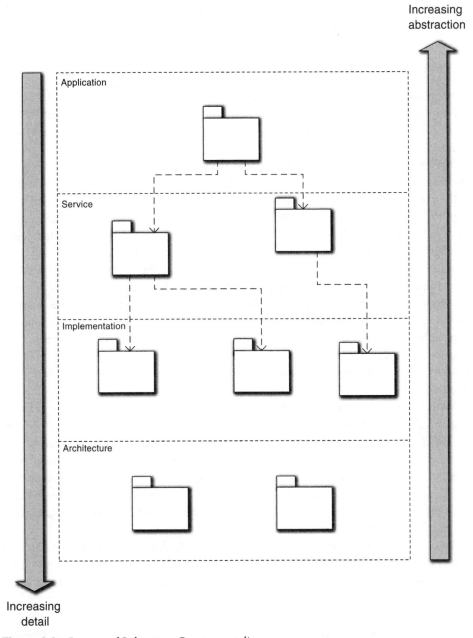

Figure 6-2   *Layout of Subsystem Component diagram*

DbC and invariants to overlay a very SOA-like[6] mindset on application structure and the design of low-level service subsystems.

Levels of Abstraction

Every subsystem is defined at a particular level of abstraction. When large subject matters are broken up to make them more manageable for a large project, that is invariably done by defining at least two different levels of abstraction: high-level control and low-level grunt work.

The level of abstraction of a subsystem is profoundly important to the design of the abstractions that implement the subsystem. All the objects of a subsystem will be at the same level of abstraction. This is the principal way that the OO paradigm deals with the flexible notion of logical indivisibility discussed in Chapter 2. This enables us to hide details and deal with the big picture in high-level subsystems while relegating details to lower-level service subsystems that are relatively myopic.

As an example, consider an application that solves different types of problems by applying the appropriate algorithms, as indicated in Figure 6-3. To do this it has to get instructions from the user, acquire data, select the best solution, execute the solution, and report the results; this quite clearly describes the steps in a high-level solution without mentioning anything specific about the details of individual steps. The solution has been abstracted so that we can delegate the grunt work for each of the steps to service subsystems. This is the central idea behind using abstraction to partition the application.

Similarly, the previous description dismissed things like data acquisition, reporting, and the UI as clauses in passing, despite that there might be thousands of LOC behind those subject matters. That's because they involve very detailed, pedestrian, and highly reusable processing. While selecting algorithms and implementing complex mathematics efficiently requires a certain creative flair, this sort of processing is highly standardized minutia that even entry-level developers can do in their sleep. Thus we have three broad levels of abstraction: overall coordination, complex analysis and algorithmic processing, and supporting grunt work.

Thus in Figure 6-3 the highest-level subsystem, Problem Solver, invokes the GUI subsystem to get user information, then invokes Data Acquisition to collect any data, then invokes Analyzer to select the best algorithm, and then invokes the proper algo-

---

6. For those of you who have led a sheltered development existence, SOA = Service Oriented Architecture. SOA is a popular modern paradigm for defining software architecture. The parallels to MBD application partitioning are striking to the point of suspecting plagiarism in the origins of SOA. However, SOA infrastructures tend to address a number of issues that are unique to IT (e.g., the ubiquitous dominance of the client/server DBMS model).

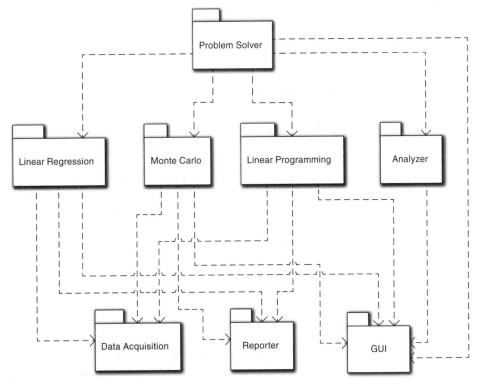

Figure 6-3 *Component diagram for a mathematics application*

rithm. We can describe that without knowing anything about the details. Problem Solver's mission in life then is to manage that *sequence*, not the actual activities.

Within Problem Solver we might abstract a Linear Program object that is a surrogate for a linear programming algorithm. At the level of abstraction of Problem Solver, that Linear Program object just represents a proxy for the actual algorithm. It might have interface methods like *Initialize*, *Solve*, and *Report*. Those methods would simply navigate the relationship to the actual algorithm.

Now we could include a flock of objects like Matrix in Problem Solver that would collaborate with the Linear Programming algorithm to actually solve the problem. After all, this application is about solving problems, and Problem Solver is the main subsystem to do that, right? Intuitively one can figure out that this would probably be a bad idea even without MBD or the OO paradigm. It would make Problem Solver hopelessly complex and obscure the high-level processing of selection, acquisition, execution, and reporting. The surrogate object in Problem Solver abstracts that away while still describing what is going on. Similarly, just looking at the names in Figure 6-3 gives us a warm and fuzzy feeling about separation of concerns and having a good handle on the big picture.

Interfaces

Every subsystem has an interface. These are also known as *bridges* in the translation community. This is because subsystem dependencies are different from object relationships, and they will be handled differently by a transformation engine. One unique thing about bridges is that they are two-way; the notion of a bridge refers to two pairs of input/output interfaces that talk to each other. When a subsystem's implementation needs to send a message to the outside world, it sends it to the subsystem's output interface. That output interface then forwards the message to the receiver system's input interface.

The reason we use subsystem interfaces is to minimize coupling and support large-scale reuse. However, the bane of reuse is syntactic mismatches, which we will talk about shortly. Two-way interfaces provide a mechanism to deal with syntactic mismatches.

In MBD these bridges are highly disciplined to ensure a high degree of decoupling. (Some translationists liken them to firewalls between subsystem implementations.) They are pure message interfaces: {message ID, [by-value data packet]}. In fact, MBD subsystem interfaces are almost invariably event based.

These are the critical things important to the later chapters.

- The nature of the bridge is two-way, where the sender of a message talks to its own output interface rather than directly to the input interface of the receiving subsystem.

- Messages are very basic communications. This often requires communications to be more fine-grained than we might have if we could pass objects or access behavior remotely.

- Inevitably, messages between subsystems require some sort of encoding and decoding by sender and receiver, respectively. This is the price of decoupling so militant that the only things shared by the subsystems are the structure and identity of the messages themselves.

- The communication model is always the more general asynchronous model. This usually implies some sort of handshaking protocols that must be incorporated in the subsystem design.

While bridges are highly constrained and those constraints must be honored in subsystem implementations, they provide huge benefits in efficiency, robustness, maintainability, and large-scale reuse.

Identifying Subsystems

Identifying subsystems is primarily an exercise in problem space abstraction. In fact, it is really the purest and simplest form of problem space abstraction because we are focused exclusively on large-scale structure in the problem space. There are no hard and fast rules for partitioning applications, but answering the following questions about candidate subsystems can be very useful. Basically, we seek insight into why the candidate subsystem in hand is different from others.

When abstracting the same entities as other subsystems, does the subsystem in hand have a different view of them?

This is critical for problem space entities.[7] Different subject matters have different rules and policies (behavior responsibilities), so entities in different subsystems should reflect that. We will tailor the object abstractions to the subject matter in hand to keep them simple within a subsystem. Since different subsystems do different things, we would have different views or tailorings of those entities when we abstract them as objects in our solution.

Is there a client/service relationship?

For this we need some definitions:

> **Client:** A participant in a one-way, binary collaboration that requests the professional services of the other participant

> **Service:** A participant in a one-way, binary collaboration that provides professional services to the other participant

Thus the client/service relationship just says that there is some collaboration context where one subsystem provides a service for another subsystem. That other subsystem becomes the client, and it defines requirements for the service to be provided.

To reiterate a point made earlier, this is not about communication; it is about requirements flows. In particular, it is about the nature of the subject matters and their role in the overall solution. We design our OO subsystems so that when a *specific* message

---

7. Note the emphasis on "problem space." There are lots of computing space data holder entities like String, Array, and ComplexNumber that we find convenient, and we even pass them across subsystem boundaries. But, as we shall see, these are usually abstracted as abstract data types (ADTs) for knowledge responsibilities. Here we are interested in problem space entities that have unique behavior responsibilities.

is sent during a collaboration, there is no expectation by the object sending the message about what will happen as a result; the message simply announces something the sender did. That is, the object sending the message is part of the implementation for the subsystem and knows nothing about external context; it is just *communicating*. So it has no idea whether the subsystem containing it is a client or a service in the collaboration context. The client/service "expectation" exists in the mind of the systems engineer partitioning the application for solving the overall problem.

Is the service more detailed than the client?

This is about the level of abstraction rather than the amount of detail. In the Problem Solver example earlier in the chapter, the actual algorithms could involve thousands of LOC while something like Data Acquisition might be a fairly trivial reading of file records and dumping values into memory arrays. The fact that Data Acquisition could be "cookbook" processing—it is very narrowly defined, largely independent of the implications of the data semantics for the problem, and clearly a supporting service—is what determines it as a low-level, detailed service at a lower level of abstraction, not the amount or complexity of processing.

Is knowledge shared with other subsystems?

What we are after here are the public knowledge responsibilities of the subsystem itself. The subsystem has responsibilities that are defined by its interface. Generally, it is a good idea for there to be a single "owner" subsystem for knowledge among subsystems.[8] When objects implementing different subsystems do share data, we need to make sure that data is used in different ways in those subsystems.

Is behavior shared with other subsystems?

Here we are focused on the public responsibilities of the subsystem, as reflected in its interface. While shared knowledge is sometimes forgivable, shared behavior is grounds for burning the developer at the stake. Subject matters should resolve unique sets of functional requirements, and functional requirements define what the software solution must do. Therefore, what a subject matter does should always be unique.

---

8. When objects that implement different subsystems share knowledge responsibilities, there is a need for explicit synchronization between those subsystems to ensure data integrity. Typically that will be implemented by the "owner" subsystem notifying other subsystems when its data changes. It is trivial to implement in an attribute setter, but somebody needs to "register" the subsystems that care.

Is the subject matter cohesive?

A subject matter is associated with what an identifiable problem space entity *is*. The nature of something is a bundle of logically related properties from an OO perspective, so the subsystem's knowledge and behavior responsibilities should be logically cohesive and intrinsic to the entity. Thus,

> Customer domains define cohesion, not developers.

Is the boundary clearly defined?

This is of critical importance to long-term stability. In an ideal world we want our subsystems to be defined so that it is obvious where customer requirements need to be resolved. Equally important, we do not want that to be a moving target over time. Ultimately that is up to the domain experts, so it is critical to scrub our subject matter definitions with them.

Unfortunately, our world is rarely ideal, and sometimes it will be difficult to gain consensus among domain experts. While gaining consensus up front on the way the problem domain should work can be painful, it will pay huge benefits over the life of the product.[9]

Could it be reused as-is?

While we focus on the problem in hand, the practical realities of software development force us to evaluate potential reuse from the perspective of the software shop's overall productivity. Fortunately, the way we define subject matters will almost always foster reuse. When we define subject matters and their interfaces in terms of invariants, that comes pretty much for free.

Is it bounded by a network in a distributed environment?

Technically this is a pure OOP issue and should not affect the OOA/D. In addition, like reuse, we generally get convenient distributed boundaries pretty much for free when we identify subject matters carefully. So this question is really a kind of sanity check. If you think a distributed boundary is going to go through the middle of your subject matter, it is almost certain you screwed something up.

---

9. In my experience most customers are not idiots. They realize that when they can't agree on what rules and policies go in what conceptual bins, they have a problem that will affect their own processes beyond the software in hand. So however grumpy they may be in the short term, they will appreciate your raising the issue in the long term.

Is it a different problem space?

As you will recall, an application can deal with multiple distinct problem spaces. Many of the guidelines above can be expressed in terms of identifying distinct problem spaces because a problem space is, by definition, a unique subject matter. So this is just a high-level criterion for recognizing a subject matter. When thinking about subject matters at this level, there are a few useful questions to ask:

Is there a domain expert that specializes in this space? If the customer can identify a specific person who understands this aspect of the business, then it is a pretty good clue that it represents a unique subject matter.

Is there a unique suite of formal standards that constrain the subject matter? The more complex and extensive such standards are, the more likely it is that they represent a unique problem space. An obvious example is the rate structures for a utility, which often require hundreds of pages of description.

Is there a substantial body of rules and policies that are defined outside the business context? Again, the more complex they are, the more likely it is that they comprise a unique subject matter. An example is the body of tax law. Things like complex mathematical algorithms also fall into this category.

Can it be abstracted in a unique fashion? This is equivalent to asking if there exists locally a unique, invariant pattern that can be abstracted. We've seen this before in examples like the GUI, which can be abstracted in terms of generic GUI design elements like Window and Control.

Does the customer see it as something different? Ultimately this is the clincher criterion. The customer is always right and will have some reason for viewing it as distinct. All you have to determine is exactly why the customer feels that way.

Bridges

Bridges between subsystems are a crucial element of MBD. The methodology is absolutely fanatical about decoupling implementations of subsystems, so it employs a very restrictive model of communications between subsystems. If you think of complex interoperability interfaces like CORBA when you think of subsystem communications, you are dead wrong. MBD subsystem communications are lean and mean without exotic facilities like remote object access or even RPCs.

The Message Paradigm, Yet Again

MBD treats subsystems as if they were objects on steroids. So all the same notions about implementation hiding, encapsulation, decoupling, and elimination of hierarchical implementation dependencies apply to subsystems—with a vengeance. Consequently, MBD limits inter-subsystem communications to the same pure messages that we've been talking about since the Introduction, so it is essential to provide communications that *enforce* those notions rather than simply supporting them.

The reason that MBD is so anal retentive about subsystems is because it is intended for large applications and supports large-scale reuse. When we define subsystems based upon problem space invariants, large-scale reuse becomes routine. Even higher-level service subsystems tend to become reusable across Product Line Architectures (PLA).[10]

Bridge discipline was so important in the original Shlaer-Mellor methodology that Steve Mellor borrowed the notion of *wormholes* from contemporary physics to describe subsystem communications. This notion captured the idea that messages disappeared into, or were spit out of, a portal to some mysterious rift of conventional space-time that was beyond the ken of mere mortals, much less application developers. Who could say where they went or where they came from in an infinite universe? Or what happened to messages sent? Or why received messages were sent? The only way Steve could have made bridges more mysterious would have been to describe them in Latin.[11]

But that image of surreal magic has value in MBD because it fosters the proper mindset for dealing with issues like coupling. It enables the developer to think about sending messages in terms of directing them to a darkly mysterious and bottomless wormhole rather than some particular subsystem. Given the unfathomable nature of wormholes, the developer had little choice but to use *I'm Done* announcement messages when talking to whatever lies outside the subsystem's subject matter boundary.

Perhaps more important, that notion of talking to a wormhole rather than some subsystem enabled another unique idea for implementing subsystem communications: the two-way interface. Traditionally OO interfaces were provided for encapsulation;

---

10. The PLA is something marketeers love. It enables them to provide a coherent message around disparate products. If you have never seen a PLA diagram, it is basically a tree viewed horizontally that has a main product line with branches for variants on the main product. The marketeers with MBAs from better schools will also use the PLA to *create* products to address different markets.

11. The devil made me do it. Steve and I go back a long time. When he reviewed a chapter from the book proposal for Addison-Wesley, his comment was, "It is a book that needs to be written. But I would hate to read it." Steve is a master of left-handed compliments as well as modeling.

they hid the implementation from the client when the client talked *to* the object. But that client's implementation talked directly to the service's interface. So traditional object interfaces are one-way, input interfaces. In contrast, in the realm of cosmology, wormholes are two-way; the same portal provides both an entrance and an exit.

This enabled even greater decoupling for subsystems than we normally have for objects. Instead of talking to an input interface that was unique to a subsystem, we talk to an output interface *provided by the subsystem where the message originates*. This has enormous implications for large-scale reuse. That's because a subsystem's implementation always sees exactly the same (output) interface no matter how the subsystem is used. So in a reuse situation we never have to touch *anything* in the subsystem implementation, not even to address messages. Even better, two-way interfaces provide us with a means for dealing with a major problem in software reuse: syntactic mismatches.

A common problem for all software reuse is syntactic mismatch among the provided interfaces in a new context. This happens because any complex semantic content can be accessed by multiple syntaxes (read: interfaces).[12] As a result, it is possible that the new client expects a different service interface than the one provided by the ported service subsystem. So even though the client and the service are completely agreed about the service semantics, they still can't communicate. As we shall see in a moment, the two-way interface enables us to resolve such syntactic mismatches without touching either the client's or the service's implementations.

Alas, it is easy to get carried away with metaphors, and the notion of wormholes is no exception. It plays nicely for asynchronous event-based behavior communications because there is no direct response. But what about synchronous knowledge access? The notion of a wormhole answering us with knowledge values kind of stretches the bottomless pit concept. Steve Mellor got out of that corner by inventing the notion of a *synchronous wormhole* where we had immediate access to knowledge. Thus the synchronous wormhole was a kind of Delphic Oracle that provided answers when we climbed the right mountain.

---

12. If you are not sure what we are talking about here, try this analogy. Write exactly the same program in C and in FORTRAN. The semantics of the problem solution that executes on the computer is exactly the same. However, the 3GL syntax used to represent that solution is quite different. If you want to solve that particular problem but you only have a C compiler and the program is written in FORTRAN, you've got a problem even though the FORTRAN program is quite capable of solving the problem. As another example, we just need to look at OTS class libraries for things like String and Array. The semantics is essentially identical because of the underlying mathematics, but different library vendors provide different interfaces to the classes, so we usually cannot swap library vendors without doing surgery on the applications.

The implementation of a synchronous wormhole at OOP time in a distributed environment must do whatever is necessary to ensure that the wormhole appears to the message sender to work exactly **as if** it were a direct synchronous return.

The notion of a synchronous wormhole makes a good conceptual analogy, but it just defers the issue of how the Oracle gets answers[13] until we actually implement the communications during OOP. It is beyond the scope of this book to describe exactly how we would do that, but essentially it means employing whatever computing space technologies (CORBA, DCOM, ESB, etc.) we have lying around the environment. What the notion of bridges brings to the table is the ability to encapsulate all that stuff in one place—the subsystems' interfaces.

The wormhole metaphor is used to hide complexity in the bridge implementation.

The important point to take away from this discussion of wormholes is that a bridge is more than just an interface, or even pairs of dueling interfaces. Among other things, the bridge concept exists to manage syntactic mismatches in large-scale reuse situations. That can involve substantial processing that is independent of what either subsystem does. The wormhole metaphor hides that complexity nicely by enabling the application developer to think during OOA/D in terms of a magical portal that accepts messages and spits out messages from/to a subsystem.

The Bridge Model

Now we can talk about the Bridge model. In the Bridge model we assume that every subsystem conceptually has both an input interface and an output interface. The objects that implement the subsystem send any outgoing messages to the output interface. The input interface dispatches any incoming messages to the appropriate objects in the subsystem implementation. This completely isolates the subsystem implementation from any knowledge of the outside world. The basic Bridge model is shown in Figure 6-4.

Generally, the *Input Interface* and *Output Interface* are defined once with the subsystem. They represent a single syntax for accessing the subsystem subject matter (input) or the external environment (output). They will move with the subsystem when it is ported to other contexts. Mechanically, whenever the objects that populate a subsystem need to send a message to the outside world, they talk to the subsystem's *Output Interface*. That interface re-dispatches the message to the appropriate receiving subsystem's *Input Interface*. (If you are familiar with design patterns, each interface is essentially a Facade pattern.) This completely decouples the implementations

---

13. Random factoid: Some modern archaeologists now believe the Oracle's cave was a source of hallucinatory natural gases.

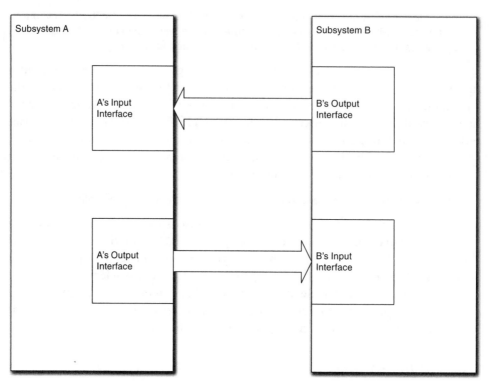

Figure 6-4 *The Bridge model for two-way bridge interfaces between subsystems*

of any two communicating subsystems because all knowledge of the other subsystem is limited to the *Output Interface* implementation, and even that knowledge is limited to just the other subsystem's *Input Interface*.

By postulating both an input and output interface for a subsystem, we have a very general way of getting around the problem of syntactic mismatch because the implementation of the *Output Interface* is regarded as part of the bridge implementation rather than the subsystem implementation. Thus the bridge itself can supply glue code to convert from one input interface syntax to another in the implementation of the *Output Interface*. Since client and service are agreed on the underlying semantics of the service, there must be a way to unambiguously convert between the syntaxes. That glue code depends only on the respective interface definitions; it is completely independent of either subsystem's implementation. So, we can insert a service subsystem into a new reuse environment without touching its implementation by simply providing new *Output Interface* implementations for the relevant communicating subsystems.

This enables a subsystem to be completely portable without any change. It also enables any subsystem to be swapped with only minor changes to the bridge code, and those changes in no way depend upon the subsystem implementations. This also means that we can employ exactly the same bridge model for in-house and third-party subsystems; at most we just need to provide a wrapper for the third-party subsystems.

While converting one interface syntax to another should always be possible, it isn't always easy. Just look at the contortions the interoperability protocols like CORBA or DCOM go through to pass object references across distributed boundaries. Fortunately, MBD makes this easier by limiting interface syntax to pure event-based, data-by-value messages. Though this was done to reduce coupling and make life easier for transformation engines, it also makes life much, much easier for providing bridge glue code.[14]

When client and service are developed together as part of the same project, it makes sense to negotiate interfaces that require minimal glue code. Such bridges are usually trivial 1:1 mappings, and even those can be optimized by the transformation engine. But there can be situations where the glue code requires an entire subsystem in its own right, though this usually only happens with third-party components.

Describing Subsystems

The partitioning of an application into subsystems is described in a Component diagram. For application partitioning there are only three relevant graphical elements: Subsystem, a classifier box with a predefined <<subsystem>> stereotype attached to the name; Dependency, a dashed line between client and service subsystem with an arrow pointing to the service; and Interface, which describes the subsystem responsibilities. Quite often we do not even include Interface elements because UML allows responsibilities to be enumerated in the Component classifier. They are primarily used to clarify when different clients define requirements for different service responsibilities.

The real documentation we need to provide about subsystems is typically attached to model elements as text tags. Because subsystems are so important, we need to describe them in some detail. This chapter subsection describes one fairly common

---

14. Not to mention being much more efficient. The canned interoperability interfaces offer developers tremendous convenience by supporting things like remote object access and RPCs. However, that convenience comes at a horrendous price in performance. It takes a *lot* of sophisticated code to support that kind of stuff across distributed boundaries.

approach to documenting subsystems. However, there are no standard rules for such documentation; use whatever works to ensure proper communication in your shop.

Subsystem Descriptions

Usually a paragraph or two is sufficient. The goal isn't to document the solution, only the containers for various parts of that solution. The objective here is simply communication—to just record as precisely as possible what the team thought each subsystem was relative to the customer problem in hand.

There are no hard and fast guidelines for what the description should address. But the following tidbits are often useful.

Is, not How. The basic idea here is that the primary goal is to describe what the subsystem *is* rather than *how* it does something. This perspective should dominate the description. Name subsystems with nouns, and then think of the description as a definition for that noun.

Responsibilities. It is often useful to clarify what sorts of responsibilities the subsystem has. At this point we should not yet know exactly what each subsystem will do, but we should have a pretty clear idea of what *kinds* of things it should know about and do. The notion of responsibility provides a more generic view than itemizing tasks or data.

Level of abstraction. This is an indication of the level of detail at which the subsystem will be implemented. Sometimes this is done by example, as in, "This subsystem deals with pin states only as an aggregate. It would not process individual pins." This is especially important when a large subject matter is split into an overall control subsystem and one or more subsystems that provide narrowly defined, detailed services. That division needs to be carefully defined.

Services. Sometimes it is convenient to describe a subject matter in terms of the services that it provides. This is somewhat different than describing responsibilities because the emphasis is on the client/service relationship. It is useful when subsets of responsibiltiies are closely related.

Invariants. It is often helpful to mention any relevant invariant that the subsystem represents. When the subsystem is implemented, this should help identify consistent class abstractions and processing metaphors. If the nature of the customer's business already has standardized definitions, those can be referenced.

Mission. Some people find it convenient to think of subsystems in terms of missions. The important thing is to keep the description of the mission abstract so that you describe what the mission is rather than how it is executed.

Though this is an individual style issue, it may be useful to anthropomorphize the descriptions. This has already been done several times in this book. For example, when talking about GUI subsystems, phrases like "it only understands pixels, Windows, and Controls" were used. This is useful because it suggests a customer-focused view where the subsystem could be a job description for some manual process. In fact, thinking of a subsystem description as a job description is not a bad metaphor.

Relationship Descriptions

In theory there are two pieces to the description of a Component diagram relationship. The first deals with the client/service relationship between application partitions. The second deals with bridges that support communication between partitions. The former is concerned with requirements flows while the latter is concerned with interfaces and message flows. These are quite different things and MBD deals with them separately.

In fact, bridge descriptions are usually not part of the Component diagram relationship descriptions. This is because bridges tend to evolve during the development since the details of interfaces are often negotiated between teams working on different subsystems. Typically the bridge descriptions will be in a separate external document from the UML model.

Because the subsystem description will identify the individual services and responsibilities, it is usually sufficient to describe the relationship with a one or two sentence summary of the client/service relationship. That's because we implicitly describe the sorts of requirements that the subsystem resolves in the description of the subsystem itself. Nonetheless, the relationship descriptions describe the nature of the dependency on the service so they are effectively a different "spin" on the requirements allocation. This is particularly useful when a service has multiple clients because the relationship descriptions can identify which particular services individual clients are expected to access.

It must be emphasized that we are talking about providing a general context for requirements rather than specific requirements. The intent here is to provide a guideline for when we must decide where original requirements and requirements changes should be implemented. In other words, good subsystem and relationship descriptions should make it fairly easy to allocate detailed requirements to specific subsystems later. Because this will also have to be done during long-term maintenance we want to keep the description stable, which means that we need avoid too much specific detail. Finally, the detailed subsystem requirements will be spelled out somewhere, like use cases, so we only need to identify who is driving those requirements and describe special situations.

Requirements Allocation

The actual allocation of requirements will typically be done by creating use cases for each subsystem. Because this is technically a systems engineering task, it is outside the scope of OOA/D so we won't go into it here. The key idea, though, is that somebody needs to break down customer requirements to the subsystem level. Hopefully the notion of client/service relationships will facilitate that.

An Example: Pet Care Center

As a practical example, let's consider some software to support a pet facility catering to upscale clients.[15] The Center will have the usual accounting software (e.g., General Ledger, Payroll, etc.), but that stuff has been done to death in the literature, so let's assume we are interested in software that tracks the processing of a pet through the Center. To avoid boredom we will skip the ten pages of detailed requirements from which we extract the high-level problem description. Instead, we will just provide a couple of paragraphs to describe the overall problem.

> The main purpose of the application will be to collect data about what happens for billing purposes. This includes charges for things such as medications, food, length of stay, facilities required, special handling, disposal, and whatnot. The primary outputs of the system are online transactions to an external invoicing system and ad hoc reports on pet status. Each transaction itemizes (with time stamp) an individual cost accrued for an account associated with the specific pet. Costs for things like facility use are accrued on a daily basis. The primary inputs for the system are a database, user input when a pet is registered, and online input by the staff (e.g., procedures completed). The database provides medication doses and costs, diets, allocations for facility use, costs of procedures, an similar generic information. The database is unique to this software application.

> The overall processing of a pet is in stages: admission, residency, preparation, treatment, and disposition. Some of these stages have multiple options. For exam-

---

15. In the book draft, the example was a Pet Euthanasia Center because I was seeking an example so far off the charts that no one could argue that OO techniques only apply to niches. However, *every* reviewer commented that it was in bad taste despite the fact that such centers already exist (in Southern California, of course). For the record, I am currently a cat owner and have owned a variety of turtles, hamsters, cats, and snakes, some of which had to be put down to eliminate suffering. So I have to wonder if those reviewers actually had pets.

ple, disposition can be the owner's responsibility[16] or, in the event of the pet's death, the processing may involve burial, cremation, memorial services, and/or organ donation. Each stage captures a suite of rules for determining things like medication and facilities required based on pet characteristics like size, species, and medical history—wherever possible barcode readers are used to facilitate progressing through the stages.

If you found the preceding paragraphs incomplete and imprecise, welcome to the wonderful world of commercial software development. Unfortunately, such flawed requirements are all too common. The goal from here on is just to provide an example of how we build a Component diagram and then document it. We begin with a summary of what might have been extracted from far more detailed requirements. The example exercise here is to laboriously "walk" through a mental process of identifying and documenting the subsystems and their relationships.[17] So where do we start?

The top is usually a good idea. We have multiple stages with apparently different responsibilities. Some or all may end up as subsystems, but somebody has to understand the overall sequence of processing to coordinate them. To do this, we stick a *Pet Tracker* subsystem at the top of the diagram to handle the pet's migration through those stages at a very generic level. Since we are in the early formative stages of defining the Component diagram, we don't attempt to be more precise about what it is yet; we will revisit it as we get more insight from the services.

An experienced MBD developer would recognize some very frequently occurring subsystems immediately: persistence in the form of the database, user inputs, and hardware control (e.g., barcode readers). We have already talked about how persistence and user communications are low-level services that should be encapsulated to hide their specific mechanisms, so we tentatively place *UI* and *DB Interface* subsystems near the bottom of the diagram. Similarly, messages to/from other systems and hardware are also a low-level communication service whose mechanisms need to be encapsulated,[18] so we put a *Physical I/O* subsystem with the others near the bottom of the diagram.

---

16. There may not be an owner. Walk-ins without owners are processed as charity cases.

17. I strongly believe that to understand OOA/D properly one needs to understand how to *think* about designs. Simply presenting a fait accompli solution doesn't explain how I got there. Throughout this book I try to focus on thought processes rather than the designs themselves. That includes making common mistakes because the design process is inherently iterative and self-correcting. But that only becomes apparent if one actually walks the path rather than taking a taxi.

18. In a more complex system we might separate hardware control from networking. Here, communications with other applications seem pretty trivial, so we lump it with hardware communications since ultimately networks are just more hardware.

The requirements talk about things like "facility," "cost," and "memorial services," but these seem more likely to be classes in a more generic subject matter or activities that take place outside the software. The only other entities the requirements talked about were the processing stages. We can make a reasonable case that each stage is a different subject matter with different responsibilities. But do we need to do so? In this case, maybe we don't because some of the subject matters will be almost trivial.[19]

For example, what is *Admission* really about? Most likely it is filling out one form with pet information and getting an account number to associate with it. The form itself will be handled in the *UI* subsystem, so all we have is a data holder class and some simple message exchanges with the database and whoever assigns account numbers. *Residency* is also fairly simple in that it really just determines the stall, cage, or whatever the pet resides in and what to feed it.

Whoa. Feed it? Why decide that in *Residency* rather than *Admission*? Let's look at this more closely. Actually, there seems to be two distinct responsibilities here: decide the diet and actually provide food to the pet over time. The first seems like something admission processing would do because it is related to the type of pet, which is first determined in *Admission*. In addition, the pet owner may wish to specify a special diet, or particular treatments may require a special diet. (The diet itself can reside in the database; all we need is to associate the diet identifier with it during registration or treatment.) Similarly, the diet may change during treatment. OK, make a note of that for the documentation. The actual diet will be in the *DB*, and the various stages will simply associate the diet identity with the particular pet.

The second responsibility seems like part of the residency because the notion of being resident is open-ended in time. Therefore, the residency just needs to be notified when it is time for feeding. It can get the diet from the *DB*.

But scheduling meals triggers another thought: There may be several things scheduled. When the pet transitions from stage to stage will have to be scheduled. If the pet dies and must be cremated, this likely will have to be scheduled based on resource availability. Medications during *Admission & Residency* may have to be scheduled. Having lots of stuff to schedule should suggest making scheduling a central notion of the solution. Should schedules be generated automatically, or will they be input by the user?

The requirements statement didn't say, so we need to talk to the customer again. However, we can be pretty sure there will be a *Scheduler* subsystem even if we don't know yet exactly what is being scheduled. That's because even if the user inputs the

---

19. We are cheating a bit because we haven't shown the detailed requirements from which the "high-level" overview was abstracted. In reality, we would have become familiar enough with them to make such judgments that are argued as intuitive or "likely" here.

schedule, somebody will have to store it in the database, generate events for its activities, and retrieve/display it. For instance, whoever prepares and/or delivers the food needs to know what to do and when. But since manual scheduling is a pain, the customer is odds-on to opt for automated scheduling either now or as a later enhancement. So tuck a *Scheduler* subsystem on the diagram in the lower half, but above the *UI*, *DB*, and *Physical I/O* subsystems, because it may use them as services.

Back to whether each stage is a subsystem. As long as scheduling is handled elsewhere, the *Admission & Residency* stages still don't seem terribly complicated; they just exchange some messages with other subsystems and provide user data entry. In particular, *Residency* really doesn't do anything except look up some data and compute a cost value when it receives a message that some event occurred (e.g., a meal was served or a day passed). It is hard to imagine these subject matters requiring more than a handful of classes in combination. In fact, we can almost envision a Pet class whose states were something like Admitted, Housed, Fed, and so forth. However, that would be getting ahead of the story by describing how the responsibilities were carried out. So slap yourself upside the head, Grasshopper, for even thinking that. Just put an *Admission & Residency* subsystem just below *Pet Tracker*.

OK, what about preparation? What's involved? We move the pet from its temporary abode to the *Treatment* facility, possibly tranquilizing it first if the treatment involves surgery or the pet has a nasty disposition. Again, that is not a complicated scenario; we might just slip something into the pet's last meal. It is difficult to imagine any need for a separate subsystem to encapsulate that subject matter. Since the preparation may be initiating the *Treatment* itself, we can safely combine the preparation stage with the treatment stage. To do this, we put a *Treatment* subsystem on the Component diagram next to *Admission & Residency*.

The pet gets treated in some kind of facility. In fact, there may be several facilities for radiology, operations, electroshock, and whatnot. Are these subsystems? Probably not in this application. Most of the actual activities in the Pet Care Center will be carried out by real people. The only thing relevant to this application is scheduling them and charging for them. At that level we just need to know the type of activity.

This is worth a bit more thought, though. Basically, the application records a bunch of pet and charge data, all of which it gets from real people through the UI. To schedule activities, it just notifies a real person that it is time to do something and that person eventually tells the software when it is done—again, all through the UI. In many respects this application is very much like the ATM controller; it is effectively just sending and receiving messages that happen to be related to scheduled activities. So far the only interesting functionality it seems to have is scheduling things.

If that is the case, do we really need subsystems like *Treatment* or *Admission & Residency*? We may not. But let's keep them as candidates for a bit because they may need to enforce business rules and policies. For example, we can readily imagine an admissions process that required things like credit checks, insurance processing, and whatnot. That level of business complexity might well warrant subsystem encapsulation. If they turn out to just be pass-throughs for decisions made in the core accounting systems, we can get rid of them later.

Another reason for keeping *Treatment* is that it may involve special hardware usage (e.g., X-ray, MRI, etc.). There may also be things like repeated treatments and diagnostic processes. Treatment may be quite different depending on the pet and problem. This sounds like more complicated business rules and policies that we might want to isolate and encapsulate.

So let's look at the *Disposition* stage. The pet may have to undergo an extensive period of rehabilitation with its own scheduled physical therapy sessions, special diets, and so forth. Even if there is no rehab, the pet may need to stay someplace until the owner comes to pick it up. Things get complicated if the Pet Care Center can't save the pet and it expires. It may then need to be buried or cremated, and there may be a need to provide a funeral service. This implies the pet may have to be stored someplace temporarily.

In fact, the entire disposition of the pet in the event it dies seems potentially complicated with a need for special scheduling and coordination. Storage is similar to preparation in that there really isn't much to it. Moreover, if the elected disposal mechanism is immediately available, no temporary storage would be required. If we reason that storage is also a form of disposition, it is easy to combine it with the *Disposition* subject matter.

But the other activities involved in actual disposal of the pet remains seem like a different subject matter. We might want to tentatively break those out from *Disposition* as a separate service, like *Remains Disposal*. The requirements indicated more complexity for *Remains Disposal* than any of the other subject matters. We can easily imagine fairly complicated scenarios combining everything from obtaining burial permits to reserving a cathedral.

Whoops. Burial permits? Reserving cathedrals? Wouldn't they be done before the actual disposal (e.g., while the pet was in storage)? No doubt. But the software doesn't actually do those things; it prompts the staff to do so. It is more likely the prompting would be done by *Scheduler*. That prompting will be scripted in a fixed sequence based on a strategy for disposal. Presumably the staff will select a particular strategy (e.g., cremation without services) based on the owner's wishes. Make a note of that.

Let's get back to *Remains Disposal*'s responsibilities. They are certainly more complicated than the other stages, but it is clear they are not so complex that it warrants breaking up *Remains Disposal* into specialized services like *Cremation*. Remember, this application is about tracking costs as a pet passes through the Center's processes.

Disposal will be notified of events that incur cost by the user or the hardware. All it really needs to do is compute the cost associated with the event. There may be several rules for this, but it isn't going to require fifty classes to encapsulate them. Make a note of that too.

While we are at it, let's think about levels of abstraction. Who coordinates activities like wakes, funerals, and cremations? If we let that be done in *Remains Disposal*, there isn't a whole lot left for *Disposition* to do except notify the pet owner and manage temporary storage of the remains. Alternatively, we could think of *Disposition* as providing high-level control and coordination of the pet's disposition in all scenarios. Since that high-level control would apply to disposition of a cured pet as well, that intuitively seems reasonable. In effect, *Disposition* makes decisions about what needs to be done and manages its sequencing at a high-level of abstraction. It then turns over control to *Remains Disposal* for the details.

As a sanity check, let's look at what *Remains Disposal*'s mission is if we move the high-level coordination out of it. We have already decided that the *Scheduler* subsystem is going to handle all things related to scheduling. Presumably, *Disposition* will tell *Scheduler* what events to schedule and the sequence. (There aren't very many combinations and each has fixed sequences, so *Disposition* probably only announces the combination and *Scheduler* manages the sequence.) But the activities are external and, given our conceptual view of the application processing messages, that doesn't leave a lot for *Remains Disposal* to do except compute simple cost values.

Hmm. Maybe this isn't as complicated as we thought, Grasshopper. What's really involved? The application tells a real person to get a burial permit, schedule a service, schedule a burial, and so on. For each task the person tells the application when that is done. The application then sends a message to a real person when it is time to move the pet remains around for each of those activities. The real person confirms that the pet has been processed and the application accumulates the charges. This doesn't sound like a bunch of complicated business rules and policies being applied to anything except the schedule, and much of that is likely to be "canned" for a handful of basic customer options.

Basically, this is just a handshaking protocol between the application and the staff or the Scheduler subsystem. Since *Disposition* is already dealing with coordination of the activities, it seems like it could handle that protocol as part of the coordination it is already doing. So it seems pretty safe to drop *Remains Disposal* as an important subject matter. Note that we can be pretty confident about this because we have already abstracted the fundamentals of what the application is doing in terms of sending and receiving messages (along with some scheduling responsibilities). The result of this preliminary partitioning are the subsystems in Figure 6-5.

That is probably it for identifying the subsystems in an initial Component diagram. At this point, it would be a good idea to go through a checklist of the criteria

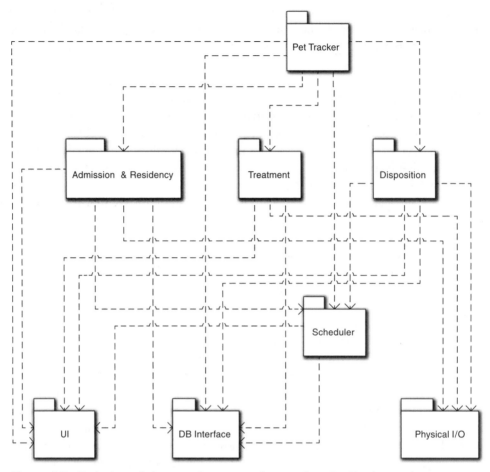

Figure 6-5   *Preliminary Subsystem Component diagram for a Pet Tracker application in a Pet Care Center*

from the previous chapters. We won't do that in detail here, but we will point out how these subsystems capture the key ideas of cohesive problem space subject matter, level of abstraction, and client/service relationships.

Cohesive. The subsystems are readily identifiable as having different responsibilities. While we have combined some subject matters, the resulting subject matter is still distinct from other subject matters and readily identifiable by domain experts. In addition, the subject matters are narrowly focused. We had little difficulty in recognizing inconsistencies and allocating responsibilities.

Based on problem space. This is pretty clear for all but *UI*, *DB Interface*, and Physical I/O. For these three they *are* problem spaces, just different ones from the customer's. One of the main reasons for encapsulating them was that they are unique paradigms distinct from the customer's problem space (e.g., Window/Control, relational data model, hardware read/write, and network protocols). The other service subsystems were taken directly from entities in the requirements. Three were explicitly defined as stages. *Scheduler* isn't explicit in the requirements, but it is doubtful that any domain expert is going to have a problem with it being an implicit need. *Pet Tracker* represents the purpose of the software in the problem space, but it is troublesome that it doesn't seem to have a lot to do.

Level of abstraction. We defined *Pet Tracker* as providing the overall control at an abstract level. The three subsystems in the middle of the diagram are all at roughly the same level of abstraction because they represent stages of the same process. They are less abstract than *Pet Tracker* because they address individual processes. *Scheduler* clearly provides services for the subsystems above it. Since it is a quite orthogonal subject matter, it may not technically be at a lower level of abstraction, but it is certainly at a lower level of semantic detail that would apply outside the context of pets and pet care centers. The three subsystems at the bottom of the diagram are at a lower level of abstraction because they represent detailed models of implementation paradigms in the computing space that support software applications.

Client/service relationships. We haven't talked about them yet, but implicitly we have identified them to some extent. We thought of *UI*, *DB Interface*, and *Physical I/O* as low-level services to the rest of the application. We described *Pet Tracker* as the coordinator of the stages in the process. The middle subsystems are those stages that *Pet Tracker* coordinates. Peripherally, we thought about the kinds of messages that these systems would exchange with external systems. To transmit those messages we need the low-level services of *UI*, *DB Interface*, and *Physical I/O*.

Before we can get a handle on the dependencies between these subsystems, we need to step back and get a grip on what the application is really about and what we expect to abstract in the subsystems. At this point it is often a good idea to take an initial pass at documenting the subsystems. This doesn't have to be very formal—a few bullet items may do—and doesn't require rigorous scrubbing. The purpose is to get everyone thinking along the same lines for what each subsystem is. The dependencies tend to fall out automatically as we define the subsystems.

We already noted that this application is about tracking a pet through a general process and associating costs with various activities in that process. It is worthwhile to think about how that tracking is done. A prerequisite for computing a line item cost is that some activity is completed, so the completion of an activity can be regarded as an event that triggers a cost computation. There are many mechanisms for announcing an event, such as the user completes an admission form and clicks a Submit button; an orderly swipes a barcode reader when a pet is fed; the system clock is polled to detect the end of a calendar day; and so on.

Various subsystems respond to those events. So far we have identified two sorts of responses. One will be nothing more than computing a cost and storing it in the *DB*. To compute the cost a subsystem needs relevant data, which is supplied either in the message data or is recovered from the database. Many of the triggering events will be generated by the staff through the *UI* as they announce completion of some activity like a treatment. Others will be generated by the *Scheduler*.

Hmmm. Storing a computed cost in the *DB*. How does it get to the Center's core accounting systems? We could post directly to the core accounting systems as costs are computed. But there are practical reasons why that might not be a good idea here. Typically you don't want to be posting tiny transactions individually to the enterprise DB when you could batch them. Also, immediate posting to an external system makes it more difficult to recover if somebody made a mistake (e.g., scanning the wrong barcode). Time doesn't seem critical here, except having a bill ready when a pet leaves, so maybe batching up costs in the local DB is a good idea. But when do they go to the external systems, and who sends them? Sounds like another job for the *Scheduler* to trigger updating other systems periodically. And this gives the *Pet Tracker* subsystem something to do. But we digress. . . .

The second type of response is what the staff actually does, such as feeding the pets at the scheduled time. Since those are human activities, the software is not concerned with them. However, the software does have to tell the staff what to do when it is time to do it, since most of the staff are probably making minimum wage and not necessarily self-starters. Essentially these sorts of responses mean the subsystem needs to provide an appropriate notification to the staff through the *UI*. To do that, the subsystem will probably need to obtain other information from the *DB,* such as the diet for a particular pet, for that notification. The events that trigger these sorts of responses will very likely be generated by the *Scheduler* subsystem.

In fact, there is a pattern that becomes evident for all the stage subsystems.

1. Receive an event from the *Scheduler* and decode it.

2. Obtain data from the *DB*, if necessary.

3. Send a message to the *UI* to notify the staff with any data from (2).

4. Receive an event from the *UI* when the staff completes the task and decode it.

5. Inform the *Scheduler* that the task is completed.

6. Compute a cost and post it to the *DB*.

Perhaps more important, these activities are very linear (i.e., they don't depend on other activities) and they only depend on the event identifier. So we have highly structured and very similar code for our activities. Moreover, at this point it has probably occurred to you that the subsystems representing the stages of the caregiving process don't do a whole lot. We can readily envision some infrastructure, such as lookup tables and whatnot, but essentially each event has a well-defined set of simple behaviors that are triggered by the event identifier.

The real intelligence in this processing lies in *Scheduler* as it decides when to generate particular events. In effect, we have defined all the important sequencing of activities in the application solution in terms of schedules. But even *Scheduler* isn't that complicated. It generates an event in one of two situations: to announce the next thing to do (e.g., move the pet to rehab) when it receives an event announcing completion of some activity (e.g., a treatment procedure is done); and to announce that the right elapsed time has passed in the schedule (e.g., it is feeding time).

Uh, oh. Where does *Scheduler* get stuff like the stage sequencing or feeding schedules? To answer that we need to look at what sorts of information it needs to do its job. Basically it needs the following sorts of "schedule" definitions.

Fixed periodic schedules. These are needed for things like feeding cycles and rehab time. Somebody has to tell *Scheduler* what the events are and the elapsed time between them. Does *Scheduler* need to know about *what* to feed the pets? No, that's a job for someone else, like the individual stages that respond with the right activity for Pet type. (In practice we will probably store diets in the *DB* for classes of pets and treatments.)

Stage transitions. Essentially the stage sequencing needs to be "hard-wired" into *Scheduler*. That's acceptable because it is an invariant to the way the Pet Care Center is run. (In practice that is likely to be trivial—just a lookup table that maps announcement events, based on event identifier, into the events to generate for the transition.) If we are clever about this when implementing the *Scheduler*, we can describe almost any "hard" sequence in the problem space this way as long as other subsystems tell *Scheduler* when they are done with individual activities. Note that we can map things like complex disposal sequences into stage transitions in the same way; the scale and scope are just smaller.

OK, so who provides this information? That's partially a design issue. For example, recall the discussion of invariants and parametric polymorphism in Chapter 5. The stage transitions are just a mapping among event identifiers from *Scheduler*'s perspective. Since event and stage identifiers are just data, the mapping can be defined in external configuration data. Then sequencing is not even "hard-wired" in

Scheduler; it is "hard-wired" in the configuration data, which can be changed without touching the application.

While stage transitions are likely to be invariant over the life of the application, other sequences might be somewhat more volatile. Therefore, we would probably like a user-friendly tool to modify the configuration data. That is a data entry problem much like entering pet information during registration, so it shouldn't be difficult to handle it the same way. But because that is much broader than individual pet admission, we would probably let *Pet Tracker* manage that sort of system-level data entry.[20]

What about periodic schedules? Superficially, those seem to be dependent on individual pets. But are they really? A pet's diet is likely to depend on the type of pet; if people don't get a lot of choice about meals in a hospital, why would pets be any different? It could also depend upon the type of treatment. Either way, though, the diet is likely to be predefined prior to the pet entering the Pet Care Center based on combinations of pet type and treatment. That's a job for the database; define the combinations once. Obviously, the same thing applies to the feeding schedule.

Again, all we need is a data entry facility for entering diet and schedule based on pet types and treatments. Managing that in a user-friendly way would also be a *Pet Tracker* responsibility. If this is an upscale Pet Care Center we might support special dietary rules for individual pets, in which case that data entry would be part of the admissions data. Obviously these same observations apply for any periodic schedule.

We can now take a stab at the dependencies on the low-level subsystems. This is summarized in Table 6-1.

As a practical matter, all the subsystems except *UI* will probably be clients of *Physical I/O* for barcode reading. The phrase "pet status" is a catch-all for any pertinent information about the pet, including charges made.

Note that our view of subsystem responsibilities has been significantly refined, especially since thinking about the sorts of events and responses we have, and the role of *Scheduler* in the overall solution. This has led to a rather simple event-based model of how things work, where the notion of a "schedule" drives almost all of the large-scale processing. This in turn has allowed us to anticipate parametric polymorphism in the solution so that the "schedules" are defined in terms of data and are stored externally.

---

20. We probably don't want janitors defining pet diets and how the facility works, so we probably need to provide some sort of user validation/privileges capability. That's something else *Pet Tracker* seems suited to manage. This is good because, in case you hadn't noticed, *Pet Tracker* hasn't had a lot to do. On the other hand, subsystems almost always turn out to be more complicated than we originally guessed, so we should expect this sort of thing to fill out *Pet Tracker*.

Table 6-1 *Dependencies for Pet Care Center*

Client	Service	Description
Pet Tracker	UI	Login and validation; display status; ad hoc queries; data entry for things like diets and feeding cycles
	DB Interface	Access pet status; configuration data entry; system DB data entry
Admission & Residency	UI	Admission form entry
	DB Interface	Store pet info: unique diets, schedules for feeding, pet status
	Physical I/O	Feeding barcode reader
	Scheduler	Announce completion of registration; obtain feeding/charge events
Treatment	UI	Inform staff; log procedure completion
	DB Interface	Pet status
Disposition	Physical I/O	Crematorium gas usage
	UI	Inform staff of activities
	DB Interface	Pet status
	Scheduler	Announce activity completion; obtain rehab or disposal event triggers
Scheduler	UI	Display/print schedules
	DB Interface	Access resource usage; schedules and resources

If you try to envision the code needed to implement the subsystems, you will probably conclude that it will be a lot simpler overall than you originally anticipated. Basically it will be an exercise in accessing lookup tables.[21] The use of invariants and parametric polymorphism is the immediate cause of that. However, they are enabled by the insights we had around *Scheduler*, the notion of *schedule*, and the use of events to announce that the state of the solution has changed. Perhaps most important of all, our abstract view of the way things work and how that maps into announcements of activities done by the staff interacting with the notion of *schedule* has greatly simplified our big picture view of what is happening.

The dependencies in Table 6-1 yielded the Component diagram in Figure 6-5. Coming up with such models is easy for experienced modelers but not necessarily so for novices. So it is worth spending a bit of time describing how the model elements can be traced back directly to First Principles of OOA/D in general and MBD in particular.

---

21. Something of an oversimplification. So far we have not discussed things like error recovery (e.g., the staff forgets to scan the barcode to announce completion of a stage). It is a good bet that most of the code will be involved in peripheral stuff like that.

Regardless of the level of abstraction, all communications are in terms of announcements. One subsystem announces some new condition in its processing. Another subsystem responds to that announcement by doing something.

First notice that we sneaked in the notion of *events* even though there wasn't a
state machine in sight yet. That's because events are pure announcement messages
that have no expectation of a particular response. As discussed previously on several
occasions, that communication model effectively eliminates implementation dependencies. But it goes a lot further than that in this design.

To analyze the dependencies, we needed to think about communications at an
abstract level. Using the asynchronous event model enabled us to think about
sequences of activities in terms of connecting conditions that prevail in the application solution as it executes. That was crucial to the *Scheduler* perspective of, "Tell me
what you did and I will let someone who cares know what to do next," enabling us
to isolate all of the invariant, systemic sequencing in *Scheduler* for stage transitions.
That is, *Scheduler* knows who cares about the condition, rather than the subsystem
that raised the condition, because that is a different set of business rules.

It was only a short step from there to realize that the same basic mechanism can be
used for more volatile sequences than stage transitions. In turn, that leads to the idea
that we can use the schedule metaphor for the mechanism (i.e., the stage transition
sequence can be represented as a schedule). This leap of faith is greatly facilitated, in
turn, by the fact that we already identified a *Scheduler* concept in the problem space
and have done some thinking about what the notion of *schedule* actually meant.

Of course, it didn't hurt that we had already thought about what the notion of
activity meant and had already expressed it in terms of a sequence of generic steps.
Bracketing those activities between a trigger event and an *I'm Done* announcement
event becomes natural once we are preconditioned to thinking in terms of event-
driven processing. That, in turn, provides a pretty easy mapping into the daisy-chaining implicit in the schedule metaphor. Ain't it great when a plan comes together?

Now let's look at the sorts of descriptions we might provide for the Pet Care Center. The intent here is to demonstrate the kinds of things we need to describe. The
specific descriptions will differ depending on the actual requirements, and the view is
biased by the author's personal preconceptions about what those might be.

Pet Tracker

This subsystem provides overall control and coordination of the progress of pets
through their processing at the Pet Care Center. The primary mission is three-fold.
Pet Tracker provides an entry point into the application when pets are admitted to
the Center. *Pet Tracker* provides an entry point into the application for ad hoc queries on pet status for staff and other interested application users. Finally, *Pet Tracker*

provides high-level facilities for data entry for configuration data and systemic database information that is independent of particular pets.

Pet Tracker collects cost transactions from the database on a periodic basis (or when a pet leaves the Center) and forwards them to the Center core accounting systems. *Pet Tracker* also provides ad hoc reports on past and current resident pets.[22]

Scheduler

This subsystem is the core of the application because all activity sequences are viewed in terms of a schedule metaphor. It has responsibility for generating schedules for individual pets based upon data in the database and information gleaned during pet admission. In creating schedules it provides resource leveling to avoid bottlenecks. It also has responsibility for updating affected schedules for resource utilization when a scheduling conflict arises (e.g., due to a pet going over its schedule when using limited resources).

The *Scheduler* also monitors the schedules of pets currently being processed and generates events to notify clients about scheduled activities. In doing so, it can incorporate lead times predefined in the database for certain activities to enable staff members time for preparations. The *Scheduler* manages timers to detect when activities are overdue.

The *Scheduler* provides events for specific sequences of activities, such as transitioning between processing stages. This is essentially a re-dispatch of activity completion events to the subsystem that needs to respond based upon the Center's rules and policies, which are defined in external configuration data.

The *Scheduler* provides an interface to support predefined queries on individual pet schedules and reporting on pet schedules.

Admission & Residency

This subsystem handles the responsibilities for admitting a pet to the Center and processing it as it awaits treatment and during rehab. Admission is contingent on whether suitable accommodations and other facilities for the pet are available. To admit a pet, the subsystem accepts data on the pet from the *UI*. It then invokes the services of *Scheduler* to create a schedule for the pet. That is sent to the *UI* and, if approved, the *Scheduler* is notified to store the schedule, and the pet data is also stored.

The responsibilities associated with pet residency are basically assigning an available location for the pet based upon pet characteristics (size, disposition, etc.) and

---

22. Note that our original concept of guiding a pet through the stages has disappeared. Once a pet has been admitted, that is an ongoing activity controlled by *Scheduler* now. *Pet Tracker* has just become an entry point for defining the infrastructure to support that ongoing process.

ensuring the pet is fed. The parameters for this assignment are pet data and configuration information in the database. Thereafter the subsystem responds to events from the *Scheduler* that announce necessary periodic processing, such as feeding and grooming. The subsystem then employs the *UI* subsystem to provide instructions for the staff. When the staff completes the tasks the subsystem is notified through the *UI* and barcode reader, and costs are computed. If a task is not performed within a predefined delay for the pet, an appropriate alarm message is sent to the *UI* to notify the staff.

This subsystem generates transactions to the database as costs are incurred for room and board. The charges are based on data for the pet and its type stored in the database.

Treatment

This subsystem handles the preparation and treatment of a pet. Based on data from the database, an event is sent to the *UI* containing any staff instructions for the preparation and treatment of the pet. The instructions are predefined based upon pet type/illness and are accessed from the database. The subsystem issues the instructions to the staff through the *UI* when a pet transitions into or out of the stage.

The staff informs the subsystem, who informs *Scheduler*, about any changes in the availability of specialized resources within the stage. Charges are accrued when treatment is completed.

All treatments are viewed as one or more individual medical procedures (x-ray, colonoscopy, mastectomy, etc.). When multiple procedures are required, the subsystem coordinates the sequence with the *Scheduler*.

Disposition

This subsystem is responsible for post-treatment care (rest, rehabilitation, etc.) until the pet is released from the Center. This subsystem is also responsible for processing a deceased pet. That processing may include storage, cremation, burial, and funeral services. The subsystem provides messages in the *UI* to Center staff members to initiate various activities in the disposition. These messages are triggered by events from the *Scheduler* subsystem.

The subsystem is responsible for knowing what pets are currently in the stage and their status.

Periodic charges for storage are accrued based on periodic events from the *Scheduler*. Charges for crematorium fuel are based on events from the *Physical I/O* subsystem that indicate the fuel consumption. Charges for disposal processing are accrued when the staff indicates that disposal is completed. All charges are computed from parametric data associated with pet type in the database.

Physical I/O

This subsystem provides an interface to the crematorium hardware. It identifies when the hardware is turned on and off. It also monitors fuel flow rate from sensors. The subsystem notifies *Disposition* when the system is turned on and off. When the cremation is completed it notifies *Disposition* of the average fuel flow rate.

The subsystem also manages data retrieval from various barcode readers in the Center that identify particular pets. The subsystem dispatches an event to the appropriate subsystem for the barcode reader identity.

Database

This subsystem provides an interface to an RDB database. The database contains data about pets, their schedules, various parameters based on pet type (medication, facilities required, and the like), and current charges. The data is highly specialized to the application. The database also contains configuration information (e.g., stage transitions) and systemic information (diets based on pet type/treatment, disposal options, etc.).

This database is separate from the Pet Care Center's core accounting systems. The only synchronization is periodic posting of costs to the core accounting systems.

UI

This subsystem provides communications between the other subsystems and the end user (usually a staff member). It must handle a variety of communication paradigms for form-driven data entry, ad hoc queries, predefined reports, and special notifications. The *UI* will be GUI-based on terminals at various locations in the Pet Care Center.

> **Caveat**. The example should not be taken literally because we were very sloppy about requirements due to space limitations, and everyone will have some preconceived notions about what they may have been. So it is quite possible other designs would work well for different preconceived notions. The important points of this example are (a) to demonstrate the level of documentation one needs, and (b) the thought processes, particularly abstracting essential elements of the processing and developing design metaphors used to arrive at *this* design.

Processes

Generally, it is a good idea to have your customer(s) present during the initial cut at identifying subsystems. The customers don't have to know any fancy notation, and you are talking about their problem space so there is no learning curve for them.

Make sure the whole team is there and emphasize that they should listen carefully to whatever the customers say. One of the many possible processes is

1. *Blitz*. This is a basic technique whereby everyone blurts out candidate names for subsystems. Each is accompanied by a sentence or two describing it. No suggestions are rejected at this time, even if the person suggesting it wants to recant. No candidate is criticized. The only goal is to provide a stream-of-consciousness list of *possible* subsystems. Each candidate's name and description are written on a yellow sticky note and placed on a white board for later consideration. People will usually run out of bright ideas within about five minutes.

2. *Preliminary scrub*. Each candidate is considered one at a time and scrubbed in a cursory fashion for a 1- to 2-sentence description that everyone can agree with. The idea is to eliminate those that are obviously not going to be subsystems. The most common reason for rejection is that it is too detailed (i.e., it is more likely to be an object within a subsystem). Another common reason is that another candidate conveys the intent better. Whatever the reasons, rejection requires two conditions: everyone agrees, and the decision is obvious. Don't spend a lot of time on this; it is just a preliminary screening.

3. *Organize*. This is a group effort where everyone mills around the white board and arranges the yellow sticky notes with the candidate names. High-level candidates are placed toward the top and service candidates that support higher-level candidates are placed toward the bottom. Candidates that people feel may be the same or very similar are placed adjacent to each other. Don't worry about specific dependencies. There may be some disagreement. Let people articulate why they feel their way is best and seek consensus. When in doubt, the customer's view should always carry the day. Though this is the first real opportunity to clarify the overall semantics, don't let it go more than half an hour or so.

4. *Eliminate duplication*. You now have a vague hierarchy of level of abstraction, some notion of service relationships, and have talked about at least some of the subsystems in more detail. Turn the discussion to eliminating candidates that can be included in other candidates. Focus on semantics that seems to have a high degree of overlap. If successful, combine the yellow sticky notes with the final subsystem on top. Don't overdo it; just merge the obvious candidates where there is consensus. When in doubt, don't merge. When there is disagreement let people talk it out, but don't let this go beyond fifteen minutes or so.

5. *Semantic analysis*. This is the crucial step where the customer's view is the most important. Ask the customers what they think each candidate subsystem is about. The developers should push back for clarification. In the end, everyone should be clear about the issues and questions earlier in this chapter—those

issues and questions should act as a mental checklist against the description. If other candidates were coalesced into the subsystem, check that their semantics has been properly incorporated. The discussion may remove candidates, merge candidates, or even add new subsystems. The customer is the driver here, and the developers would be well advised to take notes because the subsystem descriptions need to line up with the customer's view.

6. *Client/service relationships.* Here we identify the responsibilities of the subsystems and what sorts of services they provide. Use a dry marker to identify the relationships. Here the developers are likely to drive because they probably are more used to the notion of delegation. The goal is to allocate requirements in a broad-brush manner and get the level of abstraction right. The process is iterative with the previous step in the sense that allocating responsibilities also refines the semantic definition.

7. *Model.* The developers go away and build a Component diagram to designate the subsystems. Have someone with a good memory write up the subsystem and relationship descriptions as tags in the model. (It is usually a good idea to designate this person before the blitz so that they can take notes on discussions to refresh their memory later.) Subsystem descriptions are usually a couple of paragraphs; dependency descriptions are usually a couple of sentences.

8. *Review.* Review the model and descriptions with the team and customer. This is the final scrubbing and usually requires a dedicated but highly focused meeting. At this point, you want consensus at a rather pedantic level because you are dealing with natural language descriptions, so be prepared for some debates.

9. *Allocate detailed requirements and define bridges.* These are really separate activities from defining the Component diagram. For large applications, allocating the requirements can be a systems engineering task. Requirements are allocated as soon as the Component diagram is available, but defining bridges can be deferred because that will often be a matter of negotiation between the teams implementing participating subsystems in an original development.

There are lots of variations on this process. Choose whatever seems to work best in your development culture. Just remember that the key goals are consensus and communication.

Legacy Replacement: A Practical Example

There is an interesting process that is worth mentioning here because it provides a concrete example of the power of disciplined application partitioning. Software shops are almost always saddled with vast quantities of legacy code. Quite often it is poorly documented, difficult to maintain, and employs obsolete technologies so there is a strong desire to replace it.

There are basically three strategies for replacing legacy code:

Rewrite the entire application. Essentially, we create a brand new application and replace the old application with it once it is done. This is fine for small applications but is rarely feasible for larger applications because the entire development staff can't disappear for a few years to create the new application.

Purchase a replacement. This is just a trade-off between development effort and money. In practice, though, this can also be a major headache because the new system must be properly specified and managed for outsourcing. For OTS purchase we need substantial evaluation, and we may be seriously screwed if it doesn't work for all local contexts.

Piecemeal replacement. Here we replace modules individually in the old system over time in a prioritized manner. Traditionally, this has been a disaster. One problem is that it is very difficult to estimate the effort in excising old code to replace it with new code, so there is high schedule risk. The main problem, though, is that the standard techniques for identifying modules to replace are either on existing modules' boundaries or based on minimum cut set.[23] Either way, we are building the new application based upon the structure of the old application. But the most likely reason for needing to replace the old application is that it was unmaintainable because of lousy structure. So we just repeat the sins of the past and end up with a new system that is just as bad as the old.

The approach described next assumes piecemeal replacement, but it employs a rather novel way of identifying modules to replace. Instead of identifying modules in the old system somehow, we identify the subsystems we would want to have in the new application. We then apply the notion of two-way interfaces to drive the way we actually deal with the legacy application. Thus the Bridge model just described enables a technique to systematically isolate the new module in the legacy application that breaks up the development into phases that are much more manageable.

There are seven phases, or steps, in this approach:

1. Partition the ideal new application. This is essentially the first phase of an original development using the techniques of this chapter. This focuses on the application structure we want at the end of the replacement.

---

23. Minimum cut set is a graph theory approach where we use the call graph to identify clumps of nodes with related functionality that require a minimum number of graph edges (usually procedure calls) to be cut to isolate the module. The problem with this is that it does not reflect logical cohesion or frequency of access.

2. Select a subsystem and develop it using the same requirements as the legacy application. Again, this is standard initial development, including providing use cases for the subsystem. Fully test the subsystem, which you can do because of the nature of the interfaces.

3. Define an interface for the subsystem from (2) using the Bridge model. This would be the ideal interface we would use in the new application.

4. Identify the legacy code that resolves the same requirements as the new subsystem from (2). This is a routine, albeit tedious, job for reverse engineering tools and code inspections.

5. Insert the interface from (3) into the legacy code to isolate the code in (4) from the rest of the legacy application. This is the step with the highest risk, and it will be the trickiest because the legacy code will probably not be structured in a convenient manner. Consequently, we will probably have to perform some surgery on the legacy code just to access the interface. Use the implementation of the output interface to talk to the legacy code outside the code being replaced. The input interface implementation will be the one originally used to test the new subsystem in step (2). Note that the working legacy code that actually resolves the requirements remains in place.

6. Run the regression test suite on the legacy application with the interface in place. Since the code actually resolving the requirements (i.e., the code inside the interface) is the original legacy code, we are only testing whether it has been properly isolated. Because step (5) is difficult, there will be problems, but they will be well focused on the interface.

7. Once the interface works properly, excise the relevant legacy code from (4) and plug in the new subsystem. The implementation of the input interface is modified to talk to the new subsystem. Since that subsystem has already been fully tested in (2) and uses the interface already in place from step (5), this should Just Work. But you probably want to run the regression suite anyway.

8. If there are unimplemented subsystems remaining, go back to step (2).

There are several unique things about this approach. When we are done, we have exactly the new application that we want because each subsystem was created exactly as it would have been in an original development. This ensures that we do not repeat the mistakes of the past. Except for steps (4) and (5), this is normal development that the shop should be able to undertake without any special risk.

Steps (4) and (5) make the project much more manageable because they separate the concerns of isolating the replaced code from developing it. Though step (4) is nontrivial, tools from reverse engineering are especially suited to that task. The hardest part will be ensuring we have correct requirements, but we need those for step (2) anyway. We just have to find where those requirements are resolved in the legacy code.

Most of the project unpredictability and risk will be connected with the surgery on the legacy code needed to insert the new interface to isolate the code to be replaced. But inserting the new interface between the code to be replaced and the rest of the legacy application is a very narrowly defined task, and it is greatly facilitated by using a two-way interface so that glue code for syntactic mismatches can be isolated easily. The only big problem will be converting the surrounding legacy code to invoke the new interface. While tedious and error prone, it is deterministic because the resolution of requirements on each side is the same, so the underlying semantics of the functionality accessed must be the same.

Steps (4) and (5) are also "front loaded" in the sense that they get easier as the overall project progresses. That's because as more subsystems are replaced there will be more interactions with the interfaces of previously replaced subsystems. This means less surgery on the legacy code given that the previously replaced subsystems already provide exactly the interface we need. So, as we approach the end of the project the development effort and risk should approach that of the shop's normal original development.

The real key, though, is that steps (4) and (5) are *manageable* because their scope is very narrowly defined, making them easier to estimate, plan, and execute. It also makes risk much easier to evaluate when rummaging through the legacy code. But all that is only possible if a disciplined approach to application partitioning, "firewall" interfaces, and the Bridge model are used.

This approach is also versatile from a project management viewpoint. If the shop decides to replace more than one subsystem at a time, that can be done by largely independent teams since the only opportunities for toe-stepping are in steps (4) and (5). (The elapsed time for steps (6) through (8) is probably measured in hours.) The bulk of the work for each team should be in steps (2) and (3), so synchronization problems can be minimized.

What about requirements that change during the piecemeal replacement? The only situation that matters is when a change applies to both the legacy code and the subsystem currently under development, and customers can't wait until the new subsystem is in place. Then both the old and new code will have to be modified. But, assuming there is a reasonable change management process already in place, that just becomes a communication problem for the requirements.

Part II

The Static Model

In Part II we begin to discuss how the basic principles of OO development are applied in the MDB methodology. We start with the fundamental structure of the application, the application's skeleton on which everything else is laid.

This structure is intended to be relatively stable throughout the life of the application, so we refer to it as the static model. The distinguishing characteristic of the OO paradigm is problem space abstraction, and the static model is where the bulk of that is done. We identify the cornerstone elements of OO applications—objects—in the static model along with their properties and the relationships among them. By abstracting these from the customer problem space we ensure a stable structure for the software.

Chapter 7

Road Map to Part II

If the heart be stout, a mouse can lift an elephant.
—Tibetan proverb

In Part II we move from the overall systems engineering view described in Chapter 6 to the somewhat more detailed perspective of a particular subject matter or subsystem. That perspective is composed of two complementary views of a subject matter: a static model and a dynamic model. This section is about the static view; Part III will deal with the dynamic view of subject matter.

If you are into anatomical analogies, subsystems form the skeleton of an application. Because of the militant encapsulation of subject matters described in the previous chapter, it could be argued that the subsystem skeleton is really an exoskeleton that surrounds and isolates the critical portions of the anatomy. We can also make the analogy that the static model of a subsystem represents an internal skeleton because it provides a structure or framework for the subject matter over which the dynamic model is intimately laid.

But a more poetic view is that the static model is really the heart of a subject matter[1] because the static model is where OO problem space abstraction is most prominent. To build it properly we need insight into the essence of what problem space entities *are*. Thus the class abstractions composing the static model represent both the heart of the OO approach and the heart of the problem space subject matter. This overview identifies the basic elements of the static model that will be used in subsequent chapters. The other chapters in this section deal with each element in more detail.

---

1. In my experience all analogies applied to software development eventually fall apart. Picking such analogies to pieces wastes an enormous amount of bandwidth on software Internet forums. So if you don't like the analogy, just kiss it off to poetic license and ignore it rather than e-mailing me with a critique.

Unfortunately, this presents a problem because we are pressed for space and can't really do the topic full justice. Fortunately, there is already a good book on doing class modeling: Leon Starr's *Executable UML: How to Build Class Models*.[2] Another important book is Steve Mellor and Marc Balcer's *Executable UML*.[3] While the book is aimed at defining an MDA profile for translation, the examples are excellent. In addition, there are literally dozens of books that deal with the syntax of UML notation and how to manipulate it. So, rather than reinventing the wheel, we are going to minimize discussion of syntax and its interpretation while emphasizing how we apply OO principles to design.

What Is the *Static Model*?

Static is one of those overloaded terms in software development. In the context of OOA/D, though, it is very close to the traditional dictionary definition: "1. acting by mere weight without motion (~pressure), 2. relating to bodies at rest or in equilibrium, 3. not moving; not active."[4] Unlike the definitions often applied in computer languages, there is no implication of scope in the OOA definition.

A **static model** in OOA/D identifies fixed structure in the solution that is based upon problem space invariants.

In practice, negative definitions (i.e., not active) are often of limited use in understanding what's happening, so OOA/D subscribes to a somewhat more proactive quality for the notion of *static model* in the OOA context: The model defines a fixed structure implicit in the overall solution *context*. Thus OOA/D places a somewhat

2. Leon Starr. *Executable UML: How to Build Class Models*. Upper Saddle River, NJ: Prentice Hall, 2002. This is the most comprehensive book on class modeling available. IMO, it should be on every OO developer's bookshelf.

3. Steve Mellor and Marc Balcer. *Executable UML*. Upper Saddle River, NJ: Addison-Wesley, 2002. Steve is the best OO modeler I have ever known. When we first started out, we had a problem with a point about the Shlaer-Mellor methodology; we could not see a way around a particular form of implementation pollution. Several very bright people puzzled over it for weeks to no avail. So I cornered Steve at a conference to present the problem, which by that time I felt was irrefutable proof that some implementation pollution was unavoidable. Steve sketched out a solution—literally on the back of an envelope—with no implementation pollution. It took him all of thirty seconds to solve a problem that I and several other people in our group couldn't solve after weeks of effort. People like that are not good for one's ego.

4. *Merriam Webster's Desk Dictionary*. Springfield, MA: Merriam-Webster, Inc., 1995.

different spin on the idea of "static" that has connotations of (identifiable) structure and invariants rather than lack of motion.

Of the static models or views in OOA/D, two are required and one is optional. The last chapter described application partitioning, which is an inherently static view because we do not want the partitioning or allocation of responsibilities to change over time. We use the Component diagram to represent that static view because in UML it describes the deployment of logical deliverables. The Package diagram represents the static structure of the application from a configuration management viewpoint. The Package diagram is an optional documentation element in MBD because it deals with issues that are beyond the scope of this book.

The Class diagram is the primary representation of the static model for a particular subject matter where individual objects live. It will be the subject of this part of the book. In MBD, each designed subsystem will have its own Class diagram that describes the structure of that subject matter. In keeping with the notion of *static,* the Class diagram's primary function in life is to simply identify elements of the problem solution. The elements that it defines are

Classes. These identify the intrinsic properties shared by a set of objects. Objects do not appear explicitly in the Class model because they are instantiated dynamically, so their instances come and go based on solution context. We include classes because they define the structure of *any* object member of the set.

Responsibilities. From set theory, a Class defines a suite of properties that all members of the class possess. Member objects always have the property, so it is a static or structural element of the objects. In the OO context, a property is abstracted as a responsibility for either knowing something or doing something. Note that only the responsibility (*what*) is defined, not its implementation (*how*). The Class diagram simply identifies intrinsic responsibilities.

Relationships. These are logical ties between members of different classes. Such ties form the basis for collaboration among objects. A Class diagram relationship only defines the constraints on which objects can participate in particular collaborations. It does not identify specific participants in the relationship. In other words, relationships define the structure of participation in collaborations. In relational model terms, relationships are defined between n-ary relations.

Generalization. Generalization was discussed in Chapter 3. In the Class diagram we describe the structure of the generalization n-ary relation as a Venn diagram in tree form.

The reason the Class diagram is a static model is that it doesn't actually *do* anything. All it really does is identify things that will eventually do something (behavior responsibilities) and things that will support their doing something (knowledge responsibilities and relationships). The Class diagram then organizes those things so that the developer can easily overlay a dynamic problem solution. One can look at the Class diagram as a sort of parts list for the problem solution.

> The **Class diagram** identifies elements of the problem space that will be assembled into a solution for the problem in hand.

This pearl of wisdom summarizes several things that are worth discussing individually. The subject matter of any subsystem almost always represents a unique problem space. This is true even when we abstract the same underlying entities in different subsystems. Typically a subject matter defines a unique perspective with its own view of abstraction. It also represents some unique functionality that can be traced to particular functional requirements. Finally, a subsystem often captures a unique paradigm. Thus the Window/Control paradigm for a GUI and the Table/Tuple view of RDB persistence represent different problem spaces because each subject matter deals with different views, rules, policies, and paradigms when presenting and storing the same data.

The parts list defined in the Class diagram is a list of things necessary to solve a very specific problem. The context of the problem in hand is that of the subsystem's subject matter and its functional requirements. In other words, the problem in hand is limited to that defined by the subsystem's requirements—and *only* that subsystem's requirements.

> Classes, responsibilities, and relationships exist in the problem space independent of specific solutions. We simply tailor them to the problem in hand through abstraction.

We cannot emphasize enough how fundamental this is to OO development. By identifying building blocks abstracted from the problem space first, and then constructing a behavioral solution to a particular problem by cobbling together those blocks, the OO paradigm is fundamentally different than other software development approaches.

Knowledge versus Behavior

In the OO paradigm, knowledge and behavior are quite different beasts. In Chapter 2 we noted that one difference was the use of different communication models during collaboration. However, there are a number of other very fundamental differences. The obvious one is that behavior is dynamic while knowledge is static. But what do we really mean by that?

Clearly the *value* of knowledge changes with dynamic context. When we refer to knowledge as static, we mean that its semantics and structure do not change during the execution of the problem solution. Consider an object like a simple traffic light that has a knowledge responsibility to know its current color. The semantics is such that the traffic light always has a color. More to the point, every member of the traffic light set has a color with the same semantics. In addition, the number of allowed colors is limited to a particular value domain (e.g., green, yellow, red) and that constrains the semantics. But the colors of a traffic light can also have structure that transcends the basic semantics of *color* and its allowed value domain. That is, there is a predefined order in which the values can change: green → yellow → red → green → .... For any traffic light, the value of the current color changes with regularity, but the semantics of the current color and its structure are fixed.

The view of behavior is, in quasi-mathematical terms, a dual[5] of the view of knowledge. The notion of *value* is expressed in terms of the results rather than the behavior itself. Although every object member of a class has exactly the same behavior implementation, that behavior can yield different results based on dynamic context. Thus the value of the object's knowledge at any moment depends on the object's identity; it will be pure serendipity for two different objects to have the same value for the knowledge. But for behavior the results depend on the dynamic context, not the object identity.[6] So the same behavior could yield different results for the same object, or the same results for different objects, depending on the dynamic context.

This may seem like an arcane distinction, but it is quite important. One way that it is manifested is through polymorphism. Only behaviors can be polymorphic. The notion is essentially meaningless for knowledge because we substitute results directly by changing the value of the knowledge. More to the point, knowledge semantics are immutable with respect to DbC contracts. Green is green in a Traffic Light context and level of abstraction does not come into play. But entire behaviors can be substituted by changing the level of abstraction in a DbC contract, as we saw in Chapter 3.[7]

---

5. This notion is about the ability to interchange two entirely different representations of a solution based on a 1:1 correspondence of elements in each solution. The most famous example is the primal/dual approach to solving linear programming problems. We flip back and forth between representations because certain types of operations are more convenient in one representation than in the other. Later in the book we will demonstrate that often we have a choice in abstracting the problem domain in terms of knowledge or in terms of behavior.

6. A special case exists when the dynamic context happens to be the values of only the owning object's knowledge. But even then the dependence is indirect because the results depend on the knowledge, and the knowledge depends on the object identity.

7. This comes full circle to footnote 5. We can view polymorphic substitution as a convenience of representing the solution in terms of behavior. Similarly, simple value assignment is a convenience of representing the solution in terms of knowledge.

Practical Note

We have very strongly emphasized the notion that we develop the static structure of a subject matter in a Class diagram prior to worrying about the dynamics of the solution, particularly sequences of operations. This is very important to get the right frame of mind for OO construction. However, that frame of mind can be driven into the ground in practice.

The reality is that a subject matter must satisfy functional requirements, and functional requirements are pretty much all about behavior. Thus it is not possible in practice to identify the static solution elements needed to solve the problem without some idea about what behaviors will be required. Nor can we determine the necessary relationships without having some notion about how those behaviors will collaborate. Finally, the most useful form of requirements specification is use cases, where sequence is painfully obvious.

The trick lies in making behaviors and their sequencing peripheral to the development of the static model. We do this through abstraction, by thinking about them at such a high level of abstraction that they are barely recognizable. This is largely why OO development has its own special suite of buzz words and phrases used to describe OOA/D. Hence, classes have responsibilities rather than behaviors; objects collaborate rather than provide services; and an object sends a message rather than requesting an operation. This pedantic legerdemain enables us to raise the level of abstraction of the OOA/D away from the 3GL view of the computational model. That is,

> The OO nomenclature is just a mnemonic device to help the developer maintain the proper mindset.

Perhaps more important, the static and dynamic views of a subject matter are tightly linked together, and the subject matter development is not complete until both have been described. Therefore, in practice, the static and dynamic models are developed in an iterative fashion so that the static model may be modified to deal with issues uncovered during dynamic modeling.

Note that this is in contrast to application partitioning. The application partitions must be defined in the stone of problem space invariants. We may change the interfaces and the implementations of subsystems as requirements change, but the nature of the subject matter should not change as long as the customer remains in the same business. One way to rationalize the contrast is that application partitioning is defined in a single model for the entire application. That model is at a higher level of abstraction than the models for individual subject matters, so there should be no reason for it to change unless there are very drastic changes in the business requirements.

On the other hand, the static and dynamic views of a subject matter are on the same level of abstraction and they complement one another. Although complexity management urges us to develop those views separately, the views are still of exactly the same thing and need to be coordinated, hence there is iteration and feedback between the models when designing subsystems. The tricky part is to ensure the separation of concerns for static and dynamic models that provides a unique context for that iteration and feedback. Therefore tools, such as abstraction, and mental gymnastics, such as dealing in responsibilities, help us to maintain that separation of concerns.

Chapter 8

Classes

In this chapter and the next we explore the core of OO development—the recognition of objects. Everything else done in constructing OO software is predicated on objects abstracted from the problem space. So if we do not have the right objects the application will almost surely be fragile, will likely be difficult to maintain, and will often be incorrect. Yet this in not the largest chapter in the book, because problem space abstraction does most of the work for us.

Carefully defining subsystem subject matters narrows scope and provides focus. We get cohesion and logical indivisibility largely for free when we tie objects to identifiable problem space entities. The subsystem's level of abstraction anchors our sense of detail in objects. Getting the objects right may be critical, but we have a very disciplined approach for doing that. So this chapter is mainly concerned with special issues pertaining to abstracting entities and some "cookbook" techniques for identifying the ones we need in the first place.

Abstract Representation

So far abstraction has been emphasized without really defining what abstraction is all about. Since problem space abstraction is critical to the static model, we need to explore what it's about in more detail. Like many concepts, it is easy to define in the general terms of Chapter 2 but more difficult to map into specific situations. If there is any art in OO development, it lies in trying to abstract real problem spaces. In other words, *what* we need to do is pretty obvious, but figuring out *how* to do it with real problem spaces is not always so obvious. As a start, let's look at the traditional dictionary definition of abstraction[1] that recognizes certain basic ideas.

- *Object.* Something gets abstracted.

- *Classification.* Abstraction is classically associated with taxonomies.

- *Separation of ideas.* Concrete qualities are expressed in conceptual terms.

- *Separation of qualities.* Characteristics of a thing are viewed separately from the thing itself.

The OO definition of abstraction is surprisingly similar, indicating that the OO founding fathers had a fair to middling sense of the language when they chose words like *abstraction* and *class*. At this point, you might find it useful to review the essential elements of OO abstraction described in Chapter 2 as compared to the dictionary view.

Probably the most unique thing about OO development is the rather militant use of abstraction for tailoring the problem space view to the problem in hand. As the dictionary hints, traditional abstraction is primarily associated with rather static classification schemas in sciences like zoology and biology. In such contexts the rules and policies of classification provide a rigid framework of constraints on the abstractions.

In contrast, OO abstraction is highly proactive; it is an important tool for software construction rather than a constraint on it. We use abstraction as a technique for mapping the vast complexities of typical customer problem spaces into a more manageable form. In doing so we ensure that the abstractions culled from an often ambiguous or ill-defined customer problem space are consistent with the necessary rigor of the computational models.

> OO abstraction provides a mapping between the customer and computing problem spaces. In so doing it brings a semblance of order to chaos.

The importance of abstraction to OO development cannot be overemphasized. By the time we get down to writing individual statements in an OOPL, the die has already been cast for whether the application will be robust, reliable, and maintainable. Conversely, if we have properly defined the classes, responsibilities, and relationships, it will be hard to screw things up at the 3GL level.

Model of Something Real

Note that in the dictionary definition the emphasis is on abstracting a single property. However, in OO we abstract multiple properties from the underlying entity, and we

---

1. *Webster's New Twentieth Century Dictionary of the English Language Unabridged.* New York: William Collins Publishers, 1972.

need to have them play together properly in a dynamic solution (as opposed to a static classification schema).

So the OO object is an abstract surrogate for the entire underlying problem space entity that is suitable for manipulation in a dynamic solution. It provides a convenient placeholder for dealing with other OO notions like logical or physical indivisibility. But that leaves the issue of recognizing problem space entities open, which is the first goal in developing a Class diagram.

> A **problem space entity** is anything that has real and individual existence, tangible or in the mind, for a domain expert.

For *domain expert* we use the conventional meaning of anyone who is an expert on the problem space. This definition of entity is quite mellow in that it provides a whole lot of wiggle room for recognizing problem space entities. Basically anything can be a problem space entity as long as it is individually identifiable and readily recognizable by name by a domain expert. Nonetheless, it binds us irrevocably to the problem domain.

The easy things to spot are the tangible entities like people, automobiles, buildings, computers, and electric toothbrushes. These are also usually pretty easy from an identity perspective because they will usually have things like names and serial numbers to identify them. Some items, like bath towels, may not have explicit identifiers but are still recognizable individually by other means (e.g., the towel on *this* rack is *mine*; the towel on *that* rack is *yours*).

With intangible things one can be truly creative. Almost any concept is a candidate, such as: idea, contract, debt, and bondage. While we may have explicit identity for intangible things (e.g., loan number) that is the exception rather than the rule. Typically we must look for more indirect means of identifying individuals.[2]

An especially fertile source of intangible entities is roles. Roles are not just associated with people; they can be associated with almost any entity to imbue it with behavior. (In fact, Rebecca Wirfs-Brock, who was prominent in defining class properties in terms of responsibilities, tends to view most behavior in terms of roles.[3]) This is because, when dealing with solution dynamics, it is often convenient to anthropomorphize human behavior onto entities that we would otherwise think of as inert. Roles are ideally suited to such anthropomorphization.

---

2. Actually, the computing space provides a very efficient mechanism for distinguishing individuals: memory addresses. Each instance has a unique memory address. One essentially keeps track of individuals through careful initialization of references when instances are created. This is quite generic so one does not need any intrinsic property of the entity to use for identification. Thus two distinct software entities can be identical in the values of every property yet they are still individually identifiable.

3. Rebecca Wirfs-Brock and Alan McKean. *Object Design: Roles, Responsibilities, and Collaborations.* Upper Saddle River, NJ: Addison-Wesley, 2003.

In general, the problem is not identifying candidate objects from the problem space. As we shall see, techniques like object blitzes can produce integer factors more candidates than one actually needs. The tricky part lies in pruning the candidates to the minimal set that we actually need to solve the problem in hand.

Local to a Subsystem or Component

In Chapter 6 on application partitioning it was suggested that MBD treats the abstractions for each subject matter as completely independent abstractions, even when the same underlying problem space entities are abstracted in each subsystem. There are several related reasons why there are unique abstractions for each subject matter in MBD:

1. Each subject matter addresses unique problem requirements that are not addressed in other subject matters. Since requirements are primarily functional in nature, that implies the subject matter behaviors to resolve those requirements are also unique.

2. We wish to focus on the subject matter, so we want to abstract only those class responsibilities needed to resolve the subject matter's requirements. Therefore, we omit objects and responsibilities that are not relevant to resolving the subject matter's requirements.

3. Because we wish to abstract the unique invariants of the subject matter, we need to tailor our view of the subject matter to those invariants.

Look at it this way: Objects are abstract software design entities that map to problem space entities, and the mapping is one problem space entity to many objects with the constraint that each object must exist in a different subsystem. The constraint enables us to maintain uniqueness of identity within a subsystem and unambiguously map identity across subsystems.

As abstractions objects are not the same things as the entities that they abstract, so it is fair to have a one (entity)-to-many (objects) relationship among them. Thus, in the software design realm the objects in different subsystems are quite different *things* even when they share identity with a single problem space entity and each other. We simply use subsystem encapsulation to make referential integrity a manageable problem.

Logical Indivisibility

Recall the discussion of logical indivisibility in Chapter 2 where it was pointed out that the OO paradigm provides only three levels of logical indivisibility: subsystem, object, and responsibility. Despite there being only three levels of "decomposition," the notion of logical indivisibility is remarkably flexible in the OO paradigm because of the role that abstraction plays.

In Chapter 6 you may have wondered why the level of abstraction of a subsystem had equivalent stature with subject matter and client/service relationships. Logical indivisibility is why. When we start having objects collaborate it will be very important that they all have a consistent view of logical indivisibility. That is necessary so the messages generated on one side of the collaboration will be consistent with the responses to them on the other side.

> The subsystem level of abstraction drives what **logical indivisibility** means for particular objects and responsibilities.

For example, consider a Test object collaborating with an Instrument object. A detailed view of the Instrument might provide behavior responsibilities for the following: *set-up*, to initialize the instrument; *initiate*, to actually perform a measurement; and *fetch*, to provide the test results.[4] However, if the Test object is created at a higher level of abstraction, it might want to send a single *doIt* message because it views a test as logically indivisible at its level of abstraction. The semantics of the collaboration are the same for both objects, but the syntax of the collaboration makes collaboration impossible because of the different views of logical indivisibility.

Choosing a particular level of abstraction for a subsystem ensures consistency because it defines whether *doIt* is logically indivisible as a responsibility or whether *setup*, *initiate*, and *fetch* are logically indivisible as responsibilities. As we saw in Chapter 6, the Bridge model can handle the syntactic mismatch when the Test object is in a higher level subsystem and the Instrument object is in a subsystem at a lower level of abstraction. But if they aren't in different subsystems, then the subsystem determines which level of abstraction must be used within it.

Delegation

Entities in most customer spaces are complex. It is fairly common to find that an object abstraction needed to resolve even the limited needs of a subsystem subject matter results in a rather complex class. It is still cohesive by definition because it is bound to a single identifiable problem space entity. However, it may not be very manageable in the solution context. The simple answer to this is to break up the object into multiple objects that split the responsibilities.

---

4. This represents a typical test instrument driver interface for the VXI standard. Such a low-level interface is necessary for complex rack-and-stack test systems. If several instruments will be used concurrently, they must all be initialized prior to initiating any of their tests.

As a simple example, consider the notion of *car*. A car is potentially a very complex entity in the customer domain. One way to break it up might be through generalization via the notion of different models with different specialized responsibilities. But it is also made up of individual components, such as frame, body, drive train, wheels, and whatnot. If our software was managing an automated automotive assembly line, those components might actually have independent existence as parts in the inventory before they are added into the car. So we would naturally look to breaking up the notion of *car* into individual components and assigning certain responsibilities, like wheel size and body style, to them. It is also possible to employ conceptual notions like roles to break up objects. Thus we might separate the *strategy* for welding the body to a frame into a separate generalization when different styles of cars require different assembly line techniques.

This general process of breaking up entities into components and then assigning a subset of the original component's responsibilities to the new object is known as *delegation* because we delegate responsibilities to others. It is very useful, especially at the OOA level.[5]

Delegation is rooted in the problem space.

This is the crucial idea underlying proper delegation during problem space abstraction. The developer cannot simply make up convenient abstractions for the delegation; the delegation entities must already exist in the problem space. If you review the car example, it will be quite clear that the delegating and delegated objects all have obvious counterpart entities in the problem space. Aside from simplification of the abstractions, the relationships needed for delegation enable elegant solutions for complex dynamic problems . . . but that is getting ahead of the story.

Once delegated, a responsibility no longer belongs to the original object.

This is the second most important idea about delegation, and it is crucial to good maintainability. The whole point of delegation is to move a responsibility to a different object. Sadly, one of the more common mistakes in novice OOA/D is to keep the responsibility in the original class and have its implementation navigate to the delegated object and invoke its responsibility. That is, the original object still acts as a middleman in the collaboration between a client needing a service and the actual service provider, which clearly breaks the principle of peer-to-peer collaboration.

The problem with this will be manifested when requirements change such that the collaboration communication must change (e.g., the interface to the service changes,

---

5. In fact, almost all analysis and design patterns in the literature involve some kind of delegation. In Chapter 5, the specification objects we identified in each example illustrated delegation, where the responsibilities delegated from the original object were knowledge responsibilities.

such as needing an additional data element in a snapshot message data packet). The client and service are changed to meet the new communication requirement, which is unavoidable. But when there is a middleman present, the middleman must also be modified to accommodate the new communication requirement, even though its semantics in the overall solution are not affected by the change.

Class Notation

We are not going to spend a lot of time on the UML notation for Class diagrams. The subset of UML needed for a translation-quality OOA model is pretty minimal and straightforward. As indicated in Chapter 7, there are also lots of good books available for dealing with UML in general and the Class diagram in particular.

In a Class diagram we only represent the classes to which objects belong, not the objects themselves, so all we are defining in the Class diagram are sets and the object *properties* that make those sets unique. (We also describe relationships among classes in a Class diagram, but not in this chapter.)

Figure 8-1 does not show all the possible notation elements; we will burn those bridges when we get to them. In addition, some drawing tools offer optional features, such as class numbers and abbreviations, that are effectively tags to make full code generation easier (e.g., for lookup tables for classes and for type name mangling at the 3GL level). What we have shown here are the essential elements of a class that must be abstracted from the problem space: class identity, knowledge responsibilities, and behavior responsibilities. Note that there are three subdivisions of the class box. The top one is devoted to identity, the middle one to knowledge responsibilities, and the bottom one to behavior responsibilities.

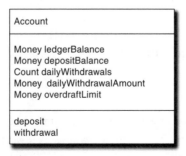

Figure 8-1   *Example of a UML Class definition. The top box identifies the class. The middle box identifies knowledge responsibilities. The bottom box identifies behavior responsibilities.*

Also note that the knowledge responsibilities have an abstract data type (ADT) associated with them, such as *Money*. The "A" in ADT indicates we don't care about how the knowledge is stored or physically represented. More important, at the level of abstraction of this class, each knowledge responsibility is represented as a scalar value of the ADT (i.e., the knowledge it abstracts is logically indivisible). For example, it is possible that for an international bank the notion of *money* is really a multi-valued descriptor that includes things like currency name and exchange rate in addition to the number of units.

This notion of ADT is very important to raising the level of abstraction of knowledge to a level that is independent of the eventual computing environment. It enables us to think of *value* as a scalar such that any pair of values with the same ADT may be manipulated regardless of the actual complexity of their physical representation. That is, we can be completely confident that any valid manipulation for the ADT in our model will just work for any pair of attribute values when implemented at the 3GL or lower level. Conversely, it enables us to keep track of the apples-and-oranges aspects of our knowledge. Thus when we describe the dynamics of the model, we will know that a *money* value and a *count* value cannot interact because they are different things.

In UML we have the following definitions.[6]

A class **attribute** is a knowledge responsibility of the member objects that is expressed as a scalar ADT.

A class **operation** is a behavior responsibility of the member objects.

A class **method** encapsulates an implementation of a class operation that produces a result consistent with the implied behavior responsibility contract.

The notion of *operation* carries a lot of baggage related to algorithmic steps, which defeats the point of decoupling properties from implementations through the notion of responsibilities. In addition, the OO literature quite often employs *method* to refer to a behavior responsibility, dating from long before UML. Up to now this book employed the more conventional definition, that a method is a behavior responsibility. Henceforth, though, we will use the UML definitions to be clear about the distinction between responsibility and implementation.[7]

---

6. More precisely, the MDA profile for using UML with MBD.

7. When we get to the dynamic description we will see that we do not define most operations directly; instead, we identify the state machine events that trigger state actions (operations). This is a convenience so that we do not clutter our Class diagrams with separate Interface model elements. The associated UML Statechart resolves the mapping of events to states and actions.

Identifying Classes and Their Responsibilities

In OOA/D we do not attempt to identify classes directly. There are actually several conceptual steps in getting the boxes onto a Class diagram:

1. Identify problem space entities that are candidates for resolving the subject matter.

2. Prune candidates that are redundant or not relevant to the problem the subject matter solves.

3. Identify the intrinsic properties of the problem space entities that are relevant to the subject matter problem.

4. Abstract the entity properties into object responsibilities.

5. Identify classes to organize sets of objects.

Do we literally follow this five-step script to do these things? No. In practice, steps 2 through 5 tend to be mashed together because they are highly interrelated. For example, the typical reasons for pruning candidate entities is that they don't have any intrinsic properties relevant to the problem (step 3) or there are other entities whose properties are more suitable to the problem in hand (steps 3 and 4).

The point here is that the list represents a suite of *conceptual* stepping-stones for migrating from the customer problem space to a Class diagram. As long as we generally follow this progression, things will tend to work out just fine. As it happens, the two most popular approaches to developing an initial cut at the classes in a Class diagram map closely to this sequence of steps.

Object Blitz

This is the most common form of developing an initial cut at a Class diagram, especially in a team development environment. It is actually based on consensus building techniques dating from the '60s that were developed to support systematic process improvement (e.g., Total Quality Management [TQM] employs several variations). Usually it is executed with a team gathered around a white board. There are minor variations, but here are the basic steps.

1. *Gather candidate entities without prejudice.* Team members throw out candidate entity names in a stream-of-consciousness manner. These are simply recorded (e.g., as a list on one side of the white board) without debate or justification. This usually takes only about five to ten minutes before team members run out of stream.

2. *Initial pruning*. Each candidate is considered in turn. Whoever originally suggested it provides a brief (one to three sentences) explanation of what they had in mind. The team has a short discussion (usually limited by a moderator to one to two minutes) to determine whether the candidate is viable *as described*. If there is full consensus that it is not viable (relevant to the problem in hand), it is rejected. Lacking full consensus for rejection, it remains a candidate by recording it as the title on both sides of a 3 × 5 card.

3. *Definition*. A definition is developed for each remaining candidate. It is usually better to delegate candidates to individual team members who write a preliminary definition for it to be scrubbed in the next step. The definition should describe what the entity *is*. The definition should be one to three sentences that describe what the entity is without details about what it knows or does. It is best for someone other than the original nominator to write the definition because this will immediately introduce a new perspective on what the entity is.

4. *Scrubbing*. Each candidate's definition is considered in turn. The team evaluates the definition and modifies it until a consensus is reached. The goal here is to gain a common understanding of what the entity is and how it is relevant to the problem in hand. Candidates may be rejected here if the scrubbing indicates that they are not relevant to the problem in hand. This should take one to five minutes per object.

At this point the 3 × 5 cards[8] define the initial cut at classes for the Class diagram. The Object Blitz is more focused on classes than objects as compared to the previous script. That's because recognition of entities and their generalization to classes of entities is essentially combined in a subliminal manner. (Remember: The class just defines properties of the member objects, so as soon as we have a single entity to abstract, we have a class to define.) Nonetheless, the progression from problem space entities to classes follows the conceptual script fairly closely.

All we have so far is a preliminary cut at classes. The details will undoubtedly change when we move on to identifying relationships and collaborations, which is why we can afford to place time limits on the various blitz steps to avoid analysis paralysis. If we don't get through all the details now, they will be resolved later. How-

---

8. Those of you with passing experience with OO development will probably recognize the cards as CRC (Class Responsibility Collaborator) cards. (Providing the responsibilities will be covered in the next chapter.) Providing CRCs was one of the earliest OOA/D techniques from the late '70s. They were adopted from the Table/Attribute cards commonly used to define RDB schemas in the mid-'70s. They went out of vogue when modern OOA/D notations were developed in the early '80s. They were revived for the OOP-based agile processes in the late '80s.

ever, we do have a framework for collaboration that is firmly anchored in the problem domain structure.

> Gaining a consensus understanding of the problem space is at least as important as identifying classes and responsibilities.

The reason that the Object Blitz relies heavily on consensus-building techniques is to help provide that crucial understanding. In particular, it ensures that everyone on the team understands the problem space the same way. If you have never used consensus-building techniques, you will have a rude awakening in step 4 when you discover how varied individual perspectives on a seemingly familiar entity can be.

Because the Class diagram is the skeleton upon which the solution is draped, it is essential that the team developing a subject matter have a consistent view of the semantics of that skeleton. Things like object and responsibility definitions tend to be quite concise because documenting the software is a secondary concern. In effect, they are simply mnemonic devices for a deeper understanding of the problem space. This deeper understanding stems from participating in the discussions that produced the mnemonic descriptions. To gain that understanding we have to do the exercise rather than reading the results of someone else's exercise.

Process note 1. In fact, the candidate classes developed in an Object Blitz provide a very good basis for project estimation. Because of the relatively fine granularity, the average effort time to develop classes is usually rather predicable (as is the 20% or so of new classes that will likely be identified subsequently). Typically, we can consistently estimate subsystem effort to within 5% to 15% once we have the Object Blitz results in hand. In one shop this was so successful that an Object Blitz for each designed subsystem was performed as a project planning activity rather than a design activity.

Process note 2. Because the Object Blitz is primarily focused on building team consensus about the software solution, most steps involve team discussion. Those discussions can easily get side-tracked, so to do Object Blitzes effectively some conditions must be met. The first is that there is a strong leader who can enforce limits on debates and cut off tangents. One of the most important things that the leader must enforce is that the team act like grown-ups. The goal here is a consensus on a *truth* that everyone can live with, not keeping score on who is right and who is wrong. The team leader must nip personal issues in the bud if they arise.

Another important condition is that some mechanism exist for resolving impasses where consensus cannot be reached. Ultimately that lies with the customer because the Class diagram is about abstracting the customer's problem space. So the deciding vote on class definitions and responsibilities is always the domain expert.

Ideally we would like a domain expert to participate in the Object Blitz and act as on-site arbiter.[9] Lacking an in situ domain expert, there must be a mechanism for capturing open issues to get feedback from a domain expert.

Use Case Variant

If we have subsystem use cases for the requirements, then there are variants on the first and fifth steps of the Object Blitz that can make life easier. For the first step, the team essentially considers a small group of related use cases one at a time and uses the same stream-of-consciousness technique to identify objects that would be relevant to resolving the collection of use cases. The team can literally call out objects as they scan the use cases. For the fifth step, the team just uses the use cases as a guide to identifying responsibilities. When the Blitz step is done it should be possible to "walk" the use case steps and point to at least one object responsibility that resolves that use case step.

Note that proceeding incrementally should not introduce problems when different groups of use cases are analyzed subsequently. That's because we are not defining a solution at this point; we are simply abstracting the problem domain structure. The underlying entities we abstract will still be there for subsequent use cases. If they are not relevant to the subsequent use cases, they can be ignored for those use cases. If they are relevant, then we just have more reason to abstract them.

Examples

In this subsection we develop some examples of identifying the classes for a given subject matter assuming an Object Blitz technique was employed. Because the next chapter is devoted to responsibilities, we limit the examples here to the first four steps in the Object Blitz. Even then we combine steps 3 and 4 because it is difficult to emulate group dynamics in a book. The examples will be carried forward for the remainder of the Object Blitz to the next chapter. Unfortunately, the specification of the subject matter requirements will be somewhat sketchy because there simply isn't

---

9. There is an added benefit to domain expert participation. Reviewing the results is not the same as participating in their development. Often the debates leading to a particular diagram can be very useful to a domain expert in determining whether the software developers are thinking about the problem space correctly. That is, the developer's own discussions are much more indicative of their understanding of the problem space than the bubbles & arrows in the final model.

space to do a good job on a requirements specification, so we depend on your general familiarity with the subject matter to fill in the gaps.

The goal in going through these examples is to provide some clues into the way we think about problem space entities, objects, and classes, so these examples are an educational tool, not problem solutions. If you are faced with designing exactly the same subject matter as one of the examples, you still need to do your own Object Blitz. The devil is in the details, and you will very likely have at least some different requirements. Therefore, you need to deal with your problem space specifically rather than cribbing an example from a book like this.

The Legendary Bank ATM Controller

This example is a favorite in the OO literature because the use cases are familiar to everyone who has an ATM card.

Subject Matter Definition

In Chapter 5 we indicated that the subject matter is that of *message broker*. This subject matter is really about reformatting and passing messages between the bank's accounting or persistence software (behind the network port) and the various hardware drivers. Thus the subject matter's decision making is based strictly on parametric information contained within the messages themselves. The decisions and sequences of operations map directly to use cases defined in the requirements and to handshaking protocols for security purposes (e.g., cash may not be dispensed until the bank software acknowledges posting).

Subject Matter Requirements

The bank ATM machine manipulates the following hardware elements: ATM card reader, input keypad, simple character UI, cash dispenser, an envelope processor, a receipt printer, and a network port. All banking decisions (e.g., whether a withdrawal request should be honored) and data persistence are handled by other subsystems on the other side of a network port.

The use cases can be summarized as follows. The customer is identified and then selects a transaction via the keyboard. When a customer transaction completes, the customer selects another transaction or logs off, and the ATM card is returned.

Each hardware element has its own realized device driver that handles basic operations appropriate for that driver. Though the UI is primitive, there will be another subsystem that deals with the mundane details of display. So this subject matter will communicate with that driver at the level of putString(...). Any response by the user will be through the keyboard. Synchronization between the keyboard and characters echoed to the display is handled by this subject matter.

Step 1: Get Candidate Entities

Normally this would be done with a stream-of-consciousness approach, but let's introduce a smidgen of discipline by first considering the easy entities, those that are tangible things in the problem space. There are several in this subject matter, so they would tend to be first out in an Object Blitz anyway. That list might look like the following:

ATM	Network Port	Character Display
Card Reader	Bank	Printer
Keyboard	Customer	Money
Cash Dispenser	Deposit Envelope	ATM Card
Envelope Processor		

So far this is pretty straightforward; any domain expert (e.g., an ATM hardware vendor) will be able to instantly provide you with a definition of each of these things. Things get a bit more creative when we look at intangible candidates:

Transaction	Protocol	Error
Message	Scenario	Display Template
Response	Scenario Manager	Display Factory
Use Case	Validation	Account

Some of these are a bit more obtuse (e.g., Scenario), so someone is going to have to put more words around them to understand how they fit into the solution. Also, you probably wondered why Use Case was in the list since it is a requirement description, not a solution entity. Remember, this preliminary list of candidates is without prejudice; no suggestion is rejected. The goal is to open the door to intuition, experience, and creativity to identify every entity that might conceivably be useful to the solution. That is best done free-form without any constraints or filtering, however well intentioned.

Step 2: Initial Pruning

This sort of analysis for each of the candidates in Table 8-1 would be typical.

Table 8-1 *Analysis of Candidate Objects*

Candidate	Resolution	Definition/Discussion
ATM	Replace	The image this conjures up is that of a controller that hulks in the center of a web-like network with tendrils throughout the solution; in other words, a "god" object with diverse coordination responsibilities. In the interest of making this more cohesive, we would probably narrow the definition to something like an initial dispatcher that maps an incoming message to an outgoing message. It would probably have a state machine with transitions that enforced the rules of sequencing activities. This narrower definition suggests a better name: Dispatcher.
Card Reader	Keep	Surrogate for the card reader device driver.
Keyboard	Keep	Surrogate for the keyboard device driver.
Cash Dispenser	Keep	Surrogate for the cash dispenser device driver.
Envelope Processor	Keep	Surrogate for the envelope processor device driver.
Character Display	Keep	Surrogate for the character GUI.
Printer	Keep	Surrogate for the receipt/balance printer.
Network Port	Keep	Surrogate for the network port device driver.
Bank	Eliminate	This subject matter is about processing messages that have enough embedded information for all decision making. The bank itself is on the other side of the network port (possibly on the other side of some third-party network host). In addition, this subject matter could easily be reused in other remote access contexts (e.g., stock market transactions). Essentially, Bank is just an actor on the other side of the network port.
Customer	Keep	This is very likely to be eliminated because it is really an external actor for the use cases. However, without looking at specific responsibilities we can't be sure yet; we might need a place holder for a customer ID.
Deposit Envelope	Eliminate	This is something that the device driver handles. All the relevant activities (e.g., time stamping) are presumably handled by the driver in a transparent fashion. That is, our subject matter only has to know the driver exists, not the envelopes it processes.
ATM Card	Keep	This is likely to be a dumb data object with attributes for account numbers, bank routing numbers, and whatnot that will be needed to construct messages sent to the bank over the network.
Money	Eliminate	Same argument as Deposit Envelope.

Continues

Table 8-1 *Analysis of Candidate Objects (Continued)*

Candidate	Resolution	Definition/Discussion
Transaction	Keep	We can't be sure yet, but there may be a need for some entity to understand specific business rules and policies about particular transactions (e.g., Deposit). For example, each transaction needs an identity so the Character Display can put up the right text.
Message	Keep	This is very likely a core abstraction, given our central subject matter definition. It may make Transaction redundant.
Response	Keep	This is rather unlikely because the collaborations will probably be handled by simply issuing messages that have the relevant data in their data packets. That is, it is unlikely that there will be a need to preserve message data beyond the initial processing of the message. However, we can't be sure until we look at particular responsibilities. (Note that we are looking ahead a bit based upon past experience with OO development, which is a prerogative that most developers exercise. But we need hard evidence that it will not be needed.)
Use Case	Eliminate	This is a requirements specification, not a solution entity. It will be fully represented in responsibilities and collaborations.
Protocol	Keep	The intent here is to capture the "handshaking" of network and device driver protocols. For the simple sorts of transactions necessary for an ATM it is unlikely to be necessary, but we can't know that yet.
Scenario	Keep	The idea here is that we may need an entity that has responsibilities for enforcing the rules of sequencing for a particular user request. This is similar to the postulated responsibilities of Transaction and Protocol. It is unlikely we will need all of them, and this will probably be the first to go because Transaction and Protocol are more cohesive notions.
Scenario Manager	Eliminate	The notion of Scenario is already dangerously close to procedural thinking (i.e., a high order behavior that coordinates other behaviors). This object would be completely over the top in that respect. It is difficult to imagine any relevant sequencing that cannot be handled in a peer-to-peer fashion among Message, Transaction, Protocol, and the various drivers.
Validation	Eliminate	Same argument as Response, but stronger. When validation is requested from the bank, the response message will directly determine the ATM's activities.
Error	Eliminate	Most error processing is an architectural issue that is handled in the OOD/P. In this subject matter the error processing is either on the bank side (unwinding a posting if the hardware fails) or a very simplistic GUI message. That can be handled by simply issuing the appropriate message (e.g., Dispenser-is-out-of-cash sent to the display).

Table 8-1 *Analysis of Candidate Objects (Continued)*

Candidate	Resolution	Definition/Discussion
Display Template	Eliminate	The idea here is to have a template that defines display properties (e.g., highlighting). The postulated GUI is so simplistic that this is probably not relevant (i.e., the display is fixed green-on-black).
Display Factory	Eliminate	Such an entity may exist, but it will be in the display driver.
Account	Eliminate	This is a notion that only the bank's software on the other side of the network port could appreciate. These sorts of semantics will be represented simply as an attribute value of ATM Card.
Dispatcher	Add	Replacement for ATM above. Thus far the dispatching seems simple enough that the subsystem interface could handle it, so this is likely to be a temporary placeholder for the interface.

Steps 3 and 4: Define and Scrub Entities

In the initial pruning we provided cursory definitions. In these steps we provide definitions that the application will have to live with. While these aren't written in stone because we are only scratching the surface of the solution, we still need to get everyone on the same page because that will make it a lot easier to identify responsibilities.

To do this properly, we have to anticipate responsibilities to some extent. The recommended way of doing this is to keep the use cases handy and envision which use case steps a particular entity would be involved with. This should be done at a very high level of abstraction though. We are not identifying responsibilities; we are just trying to understand the role the entity plays in the subject matter so that we can tailor the entity definition to that role. Table 8-2 provides the preliminary definitions a team might come up with for the remaining candidates.

Table 8-2 *Candidates after Pruning*

Entity	Definition
Dispatcher	Routes incoming messages from the network port or hardware units to the object that has the appropriate responsibilities to respond. May provide elementary formatting and data (e.g., an account number) to accommodate the needs of the receiver.
Card Reader	The Card Reader is a surrogate for an external hardware device driver. The device driver issues a message containing the relevant customer information when a card is inserted. The Card Reader will return the ATM card when transactions are complete, or eat it if it is invalid.
Keyboard	The Keyboard is a surrogate for an external hardware device driver. The driver issues a message for each customer keystroke.

Continues

Table 8-2 *Candidates after Pruning (Continued)*

Entity	Definition
Cash Dispenser	The Cash Dispenser is a surrogate for an external hardware device driver. The driver simply dispenses cash and provides status information.
Envelope Processor	The Envelope Processor is a surrogate for an external hardware device driver. The driver simply collects deposit envelopes, provides a time stamp, and stores them in the lock-box.
Character Display	The Character Display is responsible for displaying text on the screen through an external device driver. It also provides mapping of the display as a modifiable text string so that Keyboard characters can be properly echoed. It is essentially a character buffer that accumulates Keyboard entries and synchronizes them with the display. It provides rudimentary dispatching via a message to some other object when the customer's entry is complete.
Printer	The Printer is a surrogate for an external hardware driver. The driver simply prints information for the ATM user. The information and elementary formatting instructions are contained in the incoming message's data packet.
Display Specification	ADDED. This is the specification for the current display. It defines fixed text and the position, format, valid ranges, and other information needed to extract values from the display buffer for a particular transaction context. (Needed because characters provided one-at-a-time are buffered in the Character Display as echoed fields until the value is complete.)
Network Port	This is a surrogate for an external hardware driver. The driver formats all message traffic to/from the bank.
Customer	ELIMINATED. ATM transactions are independent and quite simple, so there is no need to persist state that is not already included in entities like an ATM Card. Nor is there any unique behavior responsibility for this entity that is relevant to the message passing focus of the subject matter.
ATM Card	The ATM Card is essentially a state holder for things like bank routing information needed to address messages to the Network Port across several individual transactions. It has no intrinsic behaviors that are relevant to the subject matter.
Transaction	This entity understands unique aspects of a particular transaction, such as display text and specifications for customer-provided values (e.g., it would instantiate the relationship between Character Display and Display Specification). It has a state machine whose transitions capture rules for correct processing sequence.
Message	ELIMINATED. The OOA is inherently event-based and events provide the basic {identity, data packet} form. That should be sufficient for this subject matter. That is, a message has no necessary intrinsic behavior responsibilities for this problem, and there do not appear to be any situations where the data packet information needs to be persisted after consumption of the message that would not be existing knowledge responsibilities in the entities we have.

Table 8-2 *Candidates after Pruning (Continued)*

Entity	Definition
Response	ELIMINATED. Same argument as for Message.
Protocol	ELIMINATED. We assume the Network Port device driver captures the protocol for that context, so all we need to provide are outgoing messages that can be mapped into that protocol. (Typically this comes free with asynchronous, event-based interfaces.) The only other candidate protocols can be handled by Transaction (particular use case sequencing) or Character Display and Display Specification (coordinating customer input).
Scenario	ELIMINATED. Given the current view of Keyboard, Character Display, and Transaction, there are no responsibilities left for this entity.

You will note that we have changed some definitions, added an entity, and eliminated some candidates. This is fairly typical of this stage as the team refines their view of the entities.

So What Is Missing?

If you have ever actually dealt with hardware controllers in general or ATMs in particular, you have probably already figured out that there is some stuff missing here. This is because there are other requirements that weren't mentioned, many of which are implied. The goal here was to demonstrate how we think about the subsystem, not to create a viable ATM Controller design.

However, it is worth spending some time on what is missing to make a different point. Some of the things missing are the following:

- *Start-up initialization.* When the software starts up, the hardware must be put into a known state and hardware self-tests will have to be run. In addition, most of the objects in the subsystem will be instantiated once at start-up.

- *Hardware self-test.* The hardware components will likely have self-tests that should be run to ensure they are in working order at start-up.

- *Routine system maintenance.* Somebody collects deposit envelopes, puts money in the cash dispenser, and does other as-needed maintenance. Whoever does that will probably want to run the hardware self-tests from the terminal and see the results on the display.

- *Error processing.* There are lots of ways the hardware can go awry in this system, ranging from the cash dispenser being empty to the card reader jamming.

- *Auditing.* Banks are very big on audit trails. They want to be able to trace problems to individual transactions. Most of that will be on the Bank's side of the network port. However, the Bank needs to be told about *everything* that goes on in the ATM Controller.[10]

Given our quite restrictive subject matter description, most of these things can probably be handled with a couple of new objects and some complexity in the dynamic description. What should concern you here is the level of abstraction.

It is quite possible that the provided hardware drivers will do a lot of this stuff so the ATM Controller can do its thing at a high level of abstraction that doesn't include things like detecting time-outs. If you were writing the drivers, they would be in another subsystem where you could allocate such details during application partitioning to ensure a consistent level of abstraction in this subsystem. But if the drivers come with the hardware and they don't do that sort of thing, then you may have a problem.

In that case you may want to consider providing a Hardware service subsystem where the individual driver surrogates live. Then the ATM Controller subsystem would just encode messages without knowing which hardware the messages were routed to. Now the ATM Controller can send a "time for self-test" message and get back either an "All's well" message or a "Broken" message with a diagnostic code in its data packet. Similarly, it could send a "dispense N dollars" and get back either an "I did it" message or an "I couldn't do it" message with a diagnostic code.

This enables our ATM Controller to provide very high-level control over what is going on that is more in keeping with our original vision of what the ATM Controller is about. Do you *need* a Hardware subsystem? That will depend on an analysis of the detailed requirements that weren't specified and the sophistication of the device drivers.

> Subsystem subject matters are almost always more complex than anticipated when doing application partitioning.

Another point of this digression on what was missing is that when you start to design a subsystem you may discover that it is too big, or that it has multiple levels of abstraction when you try to actually implement it. You will almost always recognize this when you do the sort of analysis described as you develop the Class diagram. If so, you break out some service subsystems.

Generally, it is easier to coalesce trivial service subsystems into their clients than it is to break up large subsystems after substantial effort has been devoted to their design. So when you are doing the Class diagram, if you even suspect things are getting out of hand you should reexamine your application partitioning. Since all you

---

10. Some auditors are so paranoid that they want every internal message (e.g., between the Keyboard and Dispatcher) logged to the bank immediately as it happens. They may provide a special binary Keyboard driver that logs every keystroke directly to the bank so they can detect back door code in the ATM Controller and unauthorized access.

are doing is breaking out service subsystems that this subsystem talks to, you will not affect other teams working on other subsystems, and it won't be difficult to get back to this model if it turns out that your concerns were unwarranted.

Pet Care Center: Disposition

Examples like the bank ATM are favorites of OO authors because the subject matter is largely familiar to any reader, so providing a lot of background information on the problem space is not necessary. The reason the Pet Care Center example is used here is to demonstrate that the OO approach is generally applicable, even for off-the-wall applications. We can make that point in this context with a single subsystem.

Subject Matter

The context here is a Pet Care Center in the mellowest part of Southern California. The Center will be a running example in the book because it has a lot of interesting activities. The most extraordinary activities, though, are associated with what to do with a pet that dies. Southern California has the highest density of pet psychiatrists in the world, so you can imagine the lengths pet owners might go to in honoring their departed pets. While the services of this subsystem might seem tongue-in-cheek, be assured that some pet centers really do provide such services.

The subject matter of the Disposition subsystem is to manage everything related to the pet that occurs *after* its course of treatment. That ranges from holding the pet until it is picked up by the owner to providing memorial services for deceased pets.

Subject Matter Requirements

The requirements for this subject matter are pretty basic. The subsystem tracks pets after their treatment. It tracks any rehabilitation, such as physical therapy sessions, and notifies the owner when the pet can be picked up. In the event the pet does not survive treatment, it tracks any processing around its remains, like storage, cremation, burial, shipment elsewhere, taxidermy, and memorial services. The services are predefined and associated with the pet in the database.

A schedule for migration though the process stages is predefined. The Staff[11] provides updates of status through the UI. The Staff needs to be alerted when critical schedule items are pending or when there is a schedule failure through the UI. The Staff can reschedule events (e.g., physical therapy sessions) when there is a schedule conflict. The Disposition subsystem will provide feedback on whether such changes are feasible, but the actual feasibility analysis will be in the Scheduler subsystem.

---

11. Staff here refers to human beings who staff the Pet Care Center. Communication with them is through a UI or printer.

Charges for residence or storage are accrued on a daily basis based upon the facilities required. Other charges are on a per-service basis and are accrued when the service is completed. Charges for cremation are a fixed rate plus a charge for the natural gas used (based upon monitoring of the hardware).

The subsystem interacts with the Scheduler subsystem by processing alerts concerning the schedule, providing the Scheduler with status information, and providing revised schedule information. That is, the Scheduler has all the schedule management responsibilities, including detecting conflicts. This subject matter simply maps Scheduler's events into notices for Staff.

Step 1: Get Candidate Entities

An initial Object Blitz might result in the following list of candidate entities that are important to the subject matter (this time without segregating tangible from intangible):

Pet	Storage Slot	Alert
Physical Therapy Session	Storage Temperature	Charge
Physical Therapy Technique	Disposal Technique	Staff
Residence Facility	Crematorium	Schedule Modification
Diet	Service	Status
Feeding Schedule	Schedule	UI
Pick-up Notification	Schedule Event	
Storage Facility	Critical Schedule Event	

Step 2: Initial Pruning

Essentially we follow the same pattern as we did for the ATM example. Table 8-3 reflects the probable results of this step.

Table 8-3   *Candidates from Object Blitz*

Candidate	Resolution	Definition/Discussion
Pet	Keep	Processing pets is the reason the subject matter exists.
Physical Therapy Session	Keep	Probably unnecessary because everything about physical therapy will be handled by Staff. But we can't be sure until we think about scheduling a bit more.
Physical Therapy Technique	Eliminate	This should be an attribute of Physical Therapy Session or simply code in a scheduling event that is relayed to Staff.

Table 8-3   *Candidates from Object Blitz (Continued)*

Candidate	Resolution	Definition/Discussion
Residence Facility	Keep	Charges will be based on this, and we will probably need to keep track of what facilities are used.
Diet	Eliminate	The diet will be kept in the database, and it just gets retrieved and passed through to the Staff in the UI.
Feeding Schedule	Eliminate	The Scheduler will generate the events, and they will just be passed through to the Staff via the UI. We also have a Schedule candidate that can be generalized to include this (e.g., via a type attribute).
Pick-up Notification	Keep	Probably unnecessary, but there may be some scheduling and penalty charge issues if the pet is not picked up in a timely fashion for which we need a placeholder.
Storage Facility	Eliminate	Storage Slot can capture everything we need.
Storage Slot	Keep	This is the unit on which charges are based for storing a pet's remains. We may also need to keep track of what facilities are in use.
Storage Temperature	Eliminate	This is likely to be an attribute of Storage Slot.
Crematorium	Keep	Probably unnecessary because we can think of disposal purely in terms of a process or technique for purposes of tracking charges and schedule. But the jury is still out because of the need to monitor the gas consumption; that might require an object to consume the gas.
Service	Keep	Providing services is mostly what the subject matter does, and charge accrual is largely built around this notion. The original intent here was to capture the notion of things like funeral services. However, there seem to be other services (physical therapy, taxidermy, etc.) that may warrant the same treatment.
Schedule	Keep	As you may recall, we have a separate subject matter to deal with scheduling issues, so it is unlikely this is necessary. However, it is conceivable that this subject matter needs a local view of a pet's schedule (e.g., for display with other relevant pets' schedules). It may also be useful as a surrogate for the Scheduler subsystem.
Schedule Event	Keep	This is also unlikely because the Scheduler subject matter will issue scheduling events that this subsystem may deal with as simple messages. But we don't know enough yet to be sure.
Critical Schedule Event	Keep	Same as Schedule Event, but somewhat more likely because this is likely to need an explicit behavior responsibility to respond to such an event.

Continues

Table 8-3 *Candidates from Object Blitz (Continued)*

Candidate	Resolution	Definition/Discussion
Alert	Eliminate	This is just going to be a message sent to the UI subsystem.
Charge	Keep	Similar to alert, this is likely to be just a message sent to the persistence subsystem. However, we can't be sure yet.
Staff	Eliminate	This is just an actor for the use cases. The relevant staff member is the user on the other side of the UI. So in this subject matter that semantics is captured in messages sent to/from the UI subsystem.
Schedule Modification	Keep	The Scheduler subsystem is responsible for processing schedules, so this is likely to be manifested as a message to the Scheduler. However, the need to provide interactive validation of the modification may require some degree of persistence to coordinate the collaborations between Scheduler and UI (e.g., if the modification is invalid, the message relayed to the UI might need information from the original modification).
Status	Eliminate	This is likely to be an attribute of Pet.
UI	Keep	The UI responsibilities are handled in their own subsystem. However, it may be useful to have a surrogate for that subsystem.

Steps 3 and 4: Definition and Scrubbing

Continuing the Object Blitz exercise, we might arrive at the results of the preliminary entity definition, shown in Table 8-4.

Table 8-4 *Preliminary Object Definition*

Candidate	Definition
Pet	A pet is the subject of the Disposal subsystem. This is likely to be a simple data holder object for characteristics that are important to charges, diet, etc.
Rehabilitation Session	RENAMED from Physical Therapy Session. A specific rehabilitation activity that has finite duration, requires resources, and requires scheduling.
Residence Facility	A specific facility for keeping the pet during its post-treatment stay at the Center.
Pick-up Notification	ELIMINATED. All the semantics can be captured in a Pet attribute (notificationSent) and in communications with Staff via the UI. The only things affected are penalty charges, the need for which can be handled by the attribute and a date. Resource conflicts for an over-stay can be detected in other ways, and Scheduler can be notified accordingly.
Storage Slot	A specific facility for storing a pet's remains characterized by size and temperature.

Table 8-4 *Preliminary Object Definition (Continued)*

Candidate	Definition
Crematorium	A furnace for cremating terminated pets. It is fired by natural gas, and the primary responsibility is to monitor the gas consumed during the cremation.
Service	ELIMINATED. This is a service provided by the Pet Care Center. There are five distinct classes of services provided in this subsystem: physical therapy and related post-treatment care; remains storage; remains disposal; memorial; and taxidermy. Post-treatment care is Staff activities that are triggered by Scheduler. Storage services can be handled via attributes. Disposal and Memorial services are sufficiently unique in nature and context to warrant being separate entities. Taxidermy will typically be outsourced so it can be combined with disposal.
Schedule	This is the schedule of rehabilitation or disposal activities related to a particular Pet.
Schedule Event	This is an event generated by the Scheduler subsystem that identifies a service to be performed at a particular time in a Pet's Schedule. This information is relayed to the Staff and it is monitored against the actual Pet status.
Critical Schedule Event	This is a Schedule Event that requires an immediate response by the Staff.
Charge	ELIMINATED. There appears to be no use for charges in this subsystem once they are accrued, so this should be just a message to the persistence subsystem when an activity is completed.
Schedule Modification	This is a change to a Pet's Schedule that is proposed manually by the Staff. It is a temporary object that exists to coordinate Staff input, Scheduler validation, and UI display.
UI	This is a surrogate for the UI subsystem. All messages directed to/from Staff are sent to or are generated from this entity.
Disposal Service	ADDED. A disposal service is one of burial, cremation, external shipment, or taxidermy.
Memorial Service	ADDED. A memorial service is one of wake or funeral.

A Few Final Points

At the beginning of the example we said the choice of the Disposition subsystem of the Pet Care Center was deliberate to demonstrate that the OO approach is generally applicable no matter how bizarre the subject matter. In this subject matter we are talking about physical therapy, cremations, taxidermy, and memorial services for pets. Yet the subject matter is readily described and abstracted. The deadpan description of the problem space analysis should make it clear that this is actually pretty mundane stuff.

In particular, note that with the exception of Pet and Memorial Service, all of the entities identified could have shown up with those same names in an application for the waste management industry. The text definitions of what they were would be somewhat different, but such definitions aren't directly implemented in software. In software we implement objects, relationships, attributes, computational procedures, and messages. Those things are always the same regardless of the problem spaces that they resolve. As long as there is a mapping between the things implemented in software and the problem space, the software will just work no matter how strange the problem space is. That is, the mapping is an exercise in design creativity for the software developer, but the OO artifacts of problem space abstraction are quite pedestrian within the paradigm.

Using Sequence and Collaboration Diagrams

If you are vaguely discontented about these examples, you should be. We've identified a lot of messages and dumb data holders but nothing so far gives us a warm and fuzzy feeling that *these* objects will resolve the subject matter properly. In particular, you will recall that when abstracting entities and their qualities we need to solve the problem in hand. How can we do it without some vision of what the solution is? The short answer is that we can't. There will be more said about this in the next chapter when we talk about identifying responsibilities. But we have the same problem here with simply deciding what problem space entities to abstract as objects.

One common way around that is to develop a very high-level Sequence diagram[12] as we construct the Class model. The candidate objects are put on the swim lane boundaries of the Sequence diagram, and then we note collaborations on the diagram as horizontal connections. The key is to not think about specific messages. Instead, we just use the Sequence diagram to jot notes on the collaborations. As we do this we talk through what each object's role is for that collaboration. The best way to do this is by tracing use cases through the Sequence diagram as shown in Figure 8-2 for the Pet Care Center: Disposition example.

This exercise provides two important things. One is obviously that we can validate a *plausible* sequence of collaborations that will solve the problem (use case scenario).

---

12. We are not going to describe Sequence and Collaboration diagrams because they are actually redundant in MBD. The translation tools can all automatically generate them once we have defined the other diagrams. So they really aren't part of the MBD MDA profile, and there isn't the space to describe them in detail. But any book on UML will give you all you need to know for this sort of rough analysis if you have never seen one before. For this discussion all you need to know is that vertical lines represent classes or objects, and directed horizontal lines represent messages between them. The diagram looks a lot like a competition swimming pool from above, so the space between vertical lines are often called "swim lanes."

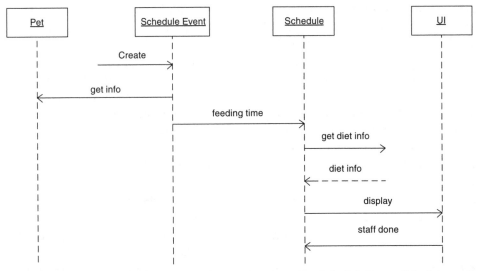

Figure 8-2 *Sequence diagram for collaborations among Pet, Schedule Event, Schedule, and UI entities*

The more subtle benefit is that we ensure that we have abstracted *all* of the entities we need to solve the problem in hand. That is, there are no swim lanes missing where one has no plausible collaboration to get to the next use case step. The crucial thing is to avoid getting carried away identifying messages. The use of the Sequence diagram that is suggested here is much more general, and it is intended to merely assist in the primary task of identifying classes and their responsibilities. To that end, let's see how we might "walk" a simple use case like the one that follows.

Use Case: Respond to feeding event from Scheduler.

1. Get diet data for indicated Pet.

2. Send message to Staff that it is time to feed pet; include diet information.

3. When Staff acknowledges feeding completed, generate charge and notify Scheduler.

What objects are likely to be involved? Let's go with *Pet, Schedule, Schedule Event,* and *UI* to see if they can do the job. When the external event is received from the *Schedule* subsystem we create a *Schedule Event* object and put the relevant data in its attributes. *Schedule Event* then announces it is there to the *Schedule* object.[13]

---

13. This is not how the dynamics would actually be done, but we don't want to get into those issues until the next section. For now, all we need is a *plausible* flow of control because we just need to prove that we have the right objects to solve the problem.

Let's assume *Schedule* knows what's involved in a feeding scenario (i.e., the actual object is a Feeding Schedule[14]) so *Schedule* will respond by sending a query to the database to get the diet information.

Oops. We have a surrogate for the *UI* but we don't have one for the database. A physicist's sense of symmetry says we are missing an object for the database surrogate. In this case it probably isn't a problem because the message is quite simple; the message identifier and *Pet* identity will convey everything the database needs to know. So these messages may be sent directly to the Persistence subsystem. (In the *UI* case the messages have more data, and we may need a state machine for handshaking with the Staff.) However, this sort of inconsistency should cause you to at least reconsider things.

Let's assume the database sends back an event with the diet information in the data packet. It will get dispatched by the subsystem interface to the *Schedule* object. The *Schedule* object then sends a message to the *UI* so the Staff can be notified. That message will have an identifier to indicate a feeding, and the data packet will have the *Pet* identity and the diet information. The *UI* object will forward that to the display and wait for a response from the Staff (in the form of another external event). When that response is received, it will generate a message so that the charge can be logged.

Oops, redux. Who is going to log the charge? We probably don't need another object because we already designated *Schedule* as being the major domo of the feeding process. Thus the acknowledgment that the feeding has been done can be sent directly to *Schedule*, which will compute the meal charge and send it off to the database.

Also note that the "get info" collaboration between *Schedule Event* and *Pet* doesn't have a response. That's because all *Schedule Event* is obtaining from *Pet* is knowledge it needs to talk to *Schedule*. In fact, *Schedule* might well do that directly. At this point we don't care because all we need is a plausible path through the use case. As it happens, one usually does not put pure knowledge collaborations on Sequence diagrams because they tend to clutter things. But "get info" is useful here because it covers a use case base (i.e., we need to know what type of *Pet* or what type of diet the *Pet* needs to ask the database the right question, and *Pet* would logically have that kind of knowledge).

It is now worth considering what *Schedule*'s role is in all of this. It doesn't actually do very much except send messages, but the sequencing of those messages is very important. In effect, the use case defines rules for the sequencing that need to be followed. What *Schedule* does is enforce those rules. It is getting ahead of the story, but *Schedule*'s main contribution here is to own a state machine whose transitions enforce the sequencing rules of the use case. That, in turn, ensures that the collabora-

---

14. Also getting ahead of the story here because this requires OO generalization, which we haven't talked about yet except generally. For now, just assume the *Schedule* object understands the steps involved in a feeding (e.g., cooking, preparation, etc.).

tions are done in the right order because *Schedule* needs to receive a specific triggering message to send the next message to someone else.

Something even more interesting about *Schedule* is that the notion of *schedule* has been highly tailored. This is not a schedule in the sense of a sequence of feedings at specific times; this sort of schedule is the Scheduler subsystem's problem. Here the notion of *schedule* is about the sequence of steps in a single feeding that must be performed to respond to *Schedule Event*. That is a pretty unique view of *schedule* compared to the way the term was used in the requirements, so we are abstracting a different problem space concept.

We probably would not have gotten to that concept from just the blitz scrubbing. It took the analysis of "walking" the Sequence diagram to get there. If somebody brought in a few six-packs and the team sat around awhile thinking about responsibilities, they might get there. They would certainly get there after stumbling around with the dynamics for awhile, but "walking" a use case through a Sequence or Collaboration diagram such as the one in Figure 8-2 would essentially *demand* that sort of view very early in the development.

Chapter 9

Class Responsibilities

Woe to him who fails in his obligations.
—Irish proverb

Identifying the intrinsic responsibilities of a problem space entity and abstracting them into an object is the heart and soul of OO development in the sense that these activities are the most common things you will do in solving the customer problem. Furthermore, the way that we abstract responsibilities is probably the single most distinguishing feature of OO development compared to procedural or functional development. This is where the OO rubber meets the developmental road, so we're going to spend some time here.

Attributes: What the Objects of a Class Should Know

Attributes define obligations for knowing something. In the static model we are interested in *what* an entity should know, not *how* it knows it. Thus it is important for the developer to maintain focus on the obligations rather than the values of what is actually known when constructing a Class diagram.

Definitions and Notation

The obligation to know a *color* is quite different than knowing the object is *blue*. This is because the obligation is an abstraction just like a class in that it captures the idea of a set, in this case a set of valid color values, more commonly referred to as a data domain.[1] If you recall the definitions of abstraction in Chapter 8, the notion of

---

1. Again, *data* carries emotional baggage. In the context of object attributes, the notions of *data* and even *value* are quite abstract. Both represent abstract views of knowledge, and the degree of abstraction is dictated by the containing subsystem.

color separates a property from the specific entity as an idea of the mind that stands on its own.

> An **attribute** is an abstraction of fact associated with an individual entity. The abstraction is associated with a class, while the value is associated with a member object.

So we look at *this* problem space entity and note that it is a *cube* while *that* problem space entity is a *dodecahedron.* From several such examples (and a little help from geometry) we can abstract the notion of *regular geometric shape* and attach it to a class definition that defines a set of objects that have various values of this characteristic. We then define an obligation for each entity having such a characteristic to know its regular geometric shape. This notion has a simple domain of values that includes *cube* and *dodecahedron,* among others.

In Figure 9-1 we have a class Rendering with two knowledge obligations. Note that notationally we name our attributes and prefix the name with an ADT identifier. The first attribute expresses an obligation to know what regular geometric shape it is. The second expresses an obligation to know what color its surface is.

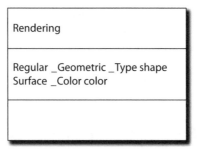

Figure 9-1   *Notation example for associating ATDs with knowledge attributes*

Note that there is no UML "+" or "-" qualification for public versus private. That's because we are defining intrinsic properties of the entity. The notions of public versus private access, so popular in the OOPLs, exist to address developer problems for 3GL maintainability when accessing knowledge. Since how a property is accessed at the 3GL level is not relevant to the customer's problem, we don't worry about it in the OOA model.[2] From another perspective, recall that we are talking about a static

---

2. For those of you that think we can ignore this because in translation we don't need to maintain the code, note that whether an attribute should be public or private is completely deterministic when mapped to OOP. We use UML Interaction Diagrams and abstract action language to describe the dynamics of the solution and, therefore, define access to knowledge. If the solution dynamics require that someone outside the object access its knowledge, then that responsibility is a public responsibility by definition and the attribute *must* be public. If the attribute is not accessed externally then it *may* be designated as private during OOP.

model here that is focused on abstracting entities. That view is intentionally quite myopic with regard to context, such as who has need of the obligation.

Not the Same as Data Storing

The cube and dodecahedron in the prior example are, themselves, abstractions of a set of properties (edge lengths and angles) that are highly constrained. This underscores the previous emphasis on logical indivisibility being a relatively major idea in OO development. In the context of *regular geometric shape*, they are scalar values that are not further divisible and, in this case, we capture them symbolically in the abstract values of *cube* and *dodecahedron*. This makes attributes different than data stores for a couple of reasons.

An attribute describes the nature of the knowledge, not its storage.

In 3GLs and databases values must be expressible in terms of a very limited number of storage types. This greatly restricts the notion of what a *value* can be. There is no such restriction for a class attribute. A class attribute can actually be implemented as an arbitrarily complex data structure *as long as at the level of abstraction of the subject matter we can think of it as a scalar*. Here we abstract the collection of properties that characterize *regular geometric type* into simple conceptual values of *cube* and *dodecahedron*.

This notion of abstraction-to-scalar is worth a couple more examples. Consider a telephone number. In most countries a telephone number is not a simple data domain. For example, in the United States a telephone number can be subdivided into {area code, exchange, number}. If it were to be stored in a relational database (RDB), it would have to be stored as separate attributes to be consistent with First Normal Form. However, we very rarely see an RDB where that is done because it would be highly inefficient.[3] So most database administrators deliberately denormalize their RDB by storing it as a scalar number or string. In those rare instances when a client actually needs to extract an individual semantic element of the number, that becomes a client exercise.[4] In effect, the administrator has abstracted the semantics up to a level where the telephone number as a whole is a simple domain.

---

3. The reason such denormalization is an idiom is that the most reasonable key for the individual elements would be the concatenation of those elements so there would be no nonkey elements in the table tuples. That leads to inefficiency in size (referential attributes *are* the tuple) and needless overhead in forming joins between tables.

4. This is so common for text values that SQL has actually institutionalized it by providing syntax to enable us to extract substrings from RDB string fields when forming a query dataset.

State

An OO application has two views of the notion of *state*. One is a dynamic view that represents the state of the processing. Essentially, this view identifies where we are within the sequence of operations comprising the solution at a given moment during the execution. We will deal with this sort of state in the next part of the book. The other view of state is static and is expressed in terms of values that persist across multiple operations.

The static view of state is manifested in state variables. Thus from an OO perspective, attributes are state variables. State variables are modified when something happens to change the state of the application. Typically that will be the execution of some behavior within the subject matter, but it can be something external that is simply announced as a message to the subsystem interface. There are assumptions and constraints that pertain to such state variables.

- State variables can be accessed instantaneously at any time as long as the owning object exists.

- Access to state variables is synchronous.

- State variables are only visible within the containing subsystem.

- Access to state variables is only available when navigating valid relationship paths. (We will talk about this in detail in Chapter 10. For now all you need to know is that this is the primary way the OO paradigm constrains state variable access to avoid the traditional problems of global data.)

The first assumption needs some justification. Consider that a method takes finite time to execute, and it has to access two different attributes: x from object A and y from object B. If there is concurrent or asynchronous processing $B.y$ might be modified after $A.x$ is accessed but before $B.y$ is accessed. That implies something changed between the accesses and, therefore, the values accessed may not be consistent with one another at the calling method's scope.

The short answer is that we don't worry about it in the OOA model because it is the transformation engine's job (or elaboration OOD/P's job) to ensure that the assumption is valid. The transformation engine is responsible for ensuring data and referential integrity *as if* access was instantaneous. That is, the application must be constructed by the transformation engine with whatever blocking of $A.x$ and $B.y$ from updates is necessary to ensure data integrity within the scope of the method accessing them. So that becomes the transformation engine application developer's problem, which is a different trade union.[5]

Abstract Data Type

In the previous example a shape attribute within the Rendering class was defined to be an ADT, *Regular Geometric Type*. This is yet another term that tends to be overloaded in the computing space. Here is the definition employed in OOA/D.

> An **abstract data type** is a developer-defined localization of knowledge that encapsulates the implementation of that knowledge so that it can be manipulated as a scalar.

This is a somewhat different spin than we usually see in the context of the type systems employed by 3GLs to implement OOA/D models. Those definitions generally substitute *interface* for *localization*, emphasize the access of the knowledge, and are more data oriented.

In the UML, the interface to a class' properties is separate from the class definition, so the notion of "interface" has less importance to the definition of a class' responsibilities. In addition, the idea of "localization" hints at cohesiveness, indivisibility, and abstraction for a particular problem space entity. Finally, the OOA/D view of *type* is more generic. That is, it is closer to the idea of set, category, or class than a formal interface with associated implications for client/service contracts.[6] The crucial thing to remember is that the operative word in the phrase is *abstract*.

A final point regarding ADTs is that they describe data and the operations on that data. We tend to get the impression from the OO literature that the only operations on knowledge are getters and setters (i.e., accessors commonly used in OOPLs to extract or set the value of the knowledge). In fact, there is nothing to prevent an ADT

---

5. This might seem like an insurmountable problem, but it really isn't. That's because MBD constructs the OOA solution specification so that it is relatively easy to do. For example, if the application is single-threaded without asynchronous events, then the engine doesn't have to do anything at all. Because of peer-to-peer messaging, integrity comes down to putting the messages in the right order, which the developer already did. By making responsibilities self-contained and accessing attributes on an as-needed basis, it becomes relatively easy to provide blocking mechanisms based upon method scope when the environment is more complex. Finally, we are very careful to separate knowledge and behavior access. Asynchronous and multithreaded processing is more complicated but still deterministic and manageable given the limited scope of access.

6. For what it is worth, I don't care for the term ADT precisely because it carries too much baggage from 3GL type systems. I would prefer *abstract data category* or *abstract data class* to be consistent with the rest of OOA/D. However, the term is very much entrenched in the literature. Just be aware that in OOA/D the term doesn't mean quite the same thing as it does in the OOPLs.

from having a whole host of operations. Thus an attribute whose ADT was *Matrix* might have operations like *transpose* and *invert* that modify multiple individual values within the matrix. Those operations are essentially "smart" setters for the *value* of the ADT. The key idea, with respect to abstraction and logical indivisibility, is that such operations can be invoked on the ADT as if it were a scalar value.

When operations beyond getters and setters are provided, though, we must be careful to ensure those operations do not trash the scalar view. That is, the operations cannot, by their nature, expose any further divisibility in the knowledge to clients. In the *Matrix* case an operation like *transpose* is fine because the multivalued nature of a matrix is not exposed to the client invoking *transpose*. However, an operation like *set element* does expose a finer granularity because an element value must be supplied rather than an ADT value.

Now let's carry this schizophrenia a step further. Suppose at the subsystem level we are interested in individual matrix elements, so we do need a *set element* accessor as well as *transpose*. This is a no-no for an ADT, so what to do? One solution is elevate the ADT to a first-class object. That is, we provide a Matrix class that has those knowledge accessors. How would we describe the Matrix class' knowledge? We would have a separate Element class that is related to the Matrix through a one-to-many relationship. The Element class would have a *set element* accessor. The *transpose* accessor of Matrix now becomes a behavior because it must navigate the relationship and invoke *set element* for each Element object. That is, it needs intelligence about Matrix' context as it collaborates with and modifies some other object's knowledge rather than just Matrix' own knowledge. As we shall see later in the chapter, that is the province of behavior.

ADTs and Contracts

Note that because the *shape* attribute in the Rendering example is limited to values that are regular geometric shapes, we have defined a constraint on what a Rendering object actually is. We have precluded Rendering objects from being fractal or amorphous. Similarly, the naming convention for the second attribute implies the constraint that the Rendering is always a solid. These constraints can be expressed in terms of DbC contracts. However, the enforceability of those contracts is quite different.

The first constraint is explicit and will limit collaborations regardless of how the developer constructs them. That formality enables the compiler or interpreter to check whether the developer screwed up by providing an invalid attribute value. But the constraint on being solid is implicit and can only be enforced by the developer in constructing the solution because it does not map directly to a 3GL type. That is, if the developer screws up it will only be manifested in an incorrect solution.

Strong Typing

If one defines attribute *X* as type *building* and attribute *Y* as type *helicopter*, then in an abstract action language an expression like *X + Y* is illegal. That's because the ADTs are clearly apples and oranges; it makes no sense to add a building and a helicopter no matter how we bend the notion of *addition*. The fact that the objects have different ADTs indicates that they are different sorts of things.

That same distinction would apply if we defined attribute *X* as type *money* and attribute *Y* as type *count*. Money and counts are semantically quite different things even though both their values may be represented by exactly the same storage type at the machine level. So even though arithmetic addition is legal at the machine level, the ADTs are arithmetically incompatible at the OOA level because of their different ADTs. Though the notion of *addition* is not limited to arithmetic operations in OO development,[7] it is limited to compatible ADTs.

This is an enormously powerful tool for ensuring that applications are robust. It is, in fact, one of the more important ways that state is managed in OO development. Assignments that change state variables are restricted to compatible ADTs. Perhaps more important, the context of access is restricted to expressions with compatible types. It is this sort of type enforcement that prevents circuit board schematics from appearing in the midst of one's Reubenesque painting.

Whoa! What about an expression like *X* * *Y*, where the *X* attribute is defined as the estimated weekly payroll (*money*) and the *Y* attribute is defined as the number (*count*) of weeks in an accounting period? Surely that computation would be a valid one, right? Very astute, Grasshopper. It would be a valid computation, and that sort of thing happens quite often. The short answer is that the developer has to explicitly authorize use of specific mixed ADT expressions, which we will get to when discussing abstract action languages.

Operations and Methods: What an Object Must Do

Abstracting attributes is relatively easy compared to abstracting behavior because we already have valid parallels in the classification taxonomies that already exist in the "real world." Static taxonomies such as the zoological phyla are relatively common, and those sorts of taxonomies are based upon the same general principle of charac-

---

7. It is quite plausible that one might want to add X and Y when both were *building* ADTs. Imagine urban planning software where complex building complexes are constructed by adding together multiple individual buildings.

terization through attribute values. The difficulty in abstracting methods is that they are inherently dynamic, and there are precious few examples of behavioral taxonomies in life outside software.

In the preceding chapters we talked at length about things like peer-to-peer collaboration, logical indivisibility, and intrinsic properties of entities. Those things make the construction of OO software fundamentally different than procedural or functional development. That difference is most profound when abstracting behavior responsibilities for objects. The real goal of the *I'm Done* mentality in replacing the procedural *Do This* mentality is to facilitate defining methods, not collaborations.

Get the methods right and the collaborations take care of themselves.

If we correctly abstract the object behaviors, then organizing the sequence of messages among those behaviors to provide the overall problem solution sequence is a relatively mechanical task.[8] A necessary condition of getting the methods right is to avoid thinking about context, which is what *I'm Done* is all about. The OO developer needs to ignore the implied sequencing in things like use cases when identifying object behavior responsibilities. To identify and specify behavior responsibilities all we need to know from the use cases are what the needed behaviors (steps) are. We connect the dots for the solution flow of control much later in the process.

As an analogy, we should be able to extract the steps in the use cases individually onto individual sticky notes, randomly scramble them, and then assign them one-at-a-time to objects. When doing so we would need to know nothing about the original ordering of steps. Of course, like all analogies, we can dissect it to irrelevance. For example, use cases are usually written at a coarser granularity than individual subject matters, much less classes, so a use case step may map into multiple object responsibilities. But the key idea that we map use case steps to responsibilities independent of the sequence of steps is still valid.

The final point to make here is that all those OO notions—such as self-contained methods, intrinsic responsibilities, *I'm Done*, logical indivisibility, implementation hiding, separation of message and method, and whatever else was hawked since Chapter 2—all play together in defining behavior responsibilities. They all methodologically conspire to ensure that we get the behavior responsibilities right. In other words, we get the behavior responsibilities right because the plan came together.

---

8. One wag asserted that in the OO paradigm, flow of control could be handled by a reasonably intelligent orangutan if one had a large enough bag of bananas.

Definitions and Notation

It's time to provide some formal definitions, starting by repeating some from the previous chapter.

> An **operation** is an object's obligation to do something.
>
> A **method** encapsulates the implementation of an operation as a procedure.

In other words, *operation* is the UML's term for the notions of responsibility or obligation. There are two views of behavior in MBD.

> Behavior responsibilities require that the object execute a suite of rules and policies that are unique to the problem in hand. These responsibilities are always associated with object state machines in MBD.
>
> **Synchronous services** are behaviors that access only attributes or capture algorithmic processing defined outside the subject matter problem space.

True behavior responsibilities are described with finite state machines in MBD, a topic discussed in Chapter 15. Because designing state machines is an extensive topic that justifies in-depth discussion in Chapter 17, we will not say a lot about them here.

The reason that MBD distinguishes between these two categories of behavior is because in OO development the categories are treated differently. The term *synchronous service* is rooted in the fact that accessing knowledge is assumed to be a synchronous activity, while accessing solution rules and policies is assumed to be asynchronous. Basically, the notion of synchronous service reflects the idea that pure knowledge access can be far more complex than simple getters and setters of values when we are dealing with ADTs. The *transform* and *invert* operations for the earlier Matrix example are synchronous services.

The notion of synchronous services is also useful for encapsulating algorithmic code that does not affect the solution flow of control. That is, the execution of the synchronous service modifies the application state but does not make decisions about the sequencing of operations unique to the problem solution. Such encapsulation makes life easier for transformation engines (and elaboration OOD/P developers) because it limits the nature of and scope for enforcing data and referential integrity. More important, though, the separation of concerns between knowledge operations and solution sequencing tends to provide a much more robust solution in the face of future maintenance.

Note that if an algorithm is defined outside the problem context, it must be expressed in a way that is not dependent on problem specifics, in particular the local problem solution's flow of control. The only way to do that is by having the algorithm be self-contained and by not enabling it to modify anything but data. Therefore, we can think of encapsulating such an algorithm, regardless of its complexity, as a single synchronous service to modify some pile of application knowledge. That is, it is just a "smart" setter.[9]

The third box in the Class is where we define operations. For the Matrix class in Figure 9-2(a) we have a standard suite of mathematical operations on a matrix. These operations are defined outside the context of any particular subject matter that might have use for a Matrix. The matrix itself is represented as a scalar knowledge value, *data*, of type 2DArray. The operations all execute against the entire matrix, so there is no exposure of individual elements. The *implementations* of those operations will necessarily have to be able to "walk" the actual array elements using well-defined mathematical algorithms. (Mathematical algorithms are defined outside the scope of any particular application problem space.)

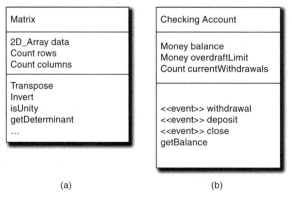

(a)   (b)

Figure 9-2   *Notation for behavior responsibilities*

The Matrix class is a classic example of a class that is a dumb data holder where all of the behaviors are synchronous services. Though the operations are algorithmically complicated, there is nothing that the Matrix does that can directly affect the problem solution other than through the state value of *data* (i.e., any control flow decision will be based upon some test, such as isUnity, of the *data*). Nor do any of the operations represent sequences or decisions that are unique to the problem solution context where a Matrix is accessed.

---

9. There is an exception that will be discussed under dynamics. When we allocate business rules and policies to state machine actions, a subset of those rules and policies may be relevant to two different states in the state machine. A synchronous service can be used to eliminate redundancy, regardless of the processing. In that case the synchronous service is equivalent to a private method in the OOPLs; it exists to simplify the object implementation and is not visible outside the object.

For the Checking Account class we have operations for withdrawing money, depositing money, closing the account, and checking the current balance. In this case, we can easily envision situations where the first three operations involve specific rules and policies, such as computing overdraft limits, that are unique to the subject matter (a particular bank's accounting system).

In addition, as a practical matter we know that things like deposits and withdrawals require collaborations with other objects (e.g., posting to a General Ledger, audit trails, etc.). Those collaborations imply decisions and predefined sequences that can be captured in terms of a succession of unique states of the execution itself. So it is quite likely that most of the operations of Checking Account represent true behavior responsibilities that we will associate with state machine states whose transitions reflect the valid decisions and predefined sequences. Therefore, invoking the first three operations will be done asynchronously using a state machine event, hence the stereotype <<event>> appended to each one. On the other hand, checking the balance is a pure synchronous knowledge access.

That's all there is to the required notation. The tricky part lies in the semantics we associate with those responsibilities. Also note that there is no identification of methods. We are only concerned with the operations in the Class diagram, not the implementations of those responsibilities. So the definition of methods is left to Part III, the Dynamic model, where state machines and abstract action language are described.[10]

Because MBD assumes an asynchronous environment for all problem-specific behavior responsibilities, the absence of the event qualifier indicates that the operation is a synchronous knowledge access or synchronous service.

Identifying Behaviors

The actual behavior responsibilities will usually be described when a state machine is constructed for the object and that topic is deferred to the next book section. Nonetheless, we need to identify them for the Class diagram. In so doing, we don't have to worry about state machines. The behavior responsibility still exists whether we associate it with a state machine state or not. The criteria identified in the following sections will work to ensure the responsibility is suitable for use in state machines. And those same criteria also apply to synchronous services.

---

10. Some translation OOA profiles do not even identify operations in the Class diagram; the third box is always empty. In our opinion, that is aesthetically inconsistent with what the Class diagram is about. While the results of a behavior may change dynamically during the execution based upon context, the obligation to provide a behavior is a static property of the object that is invariant over its life, so we believe it should be identified.

Cohesion

We have already talked about how an object represents one level of logical indivisibility in a subject matter and tying the object abstraction to a problem space entity. Those things provide a context for cohesion when defining responsibilities. The cohesion of knowledge responsibilities is pretty straightforward because they usually describe the entity itself quite directly. Behavior cohesion can be a bit trickier because we often use anthropomorphization to imbue inanimate entities or concepts with behaviors that a human would do if there were no software, so we often have a choice about what object might "own" something like a use case step.

An object's behaviors should complement each other in supporting the object's semantics.

When looking for a place for a behavior responsibility to live, we need to think holistically about the overall role of the object in the solution. All of the object's behavior responsibilities should play together well in supporting the object's goal. When we find bundles of object behaviors that are logically related within the bundles but not across the bundles, that is often a symptom of poor cohesion at the object definition level. Therefore, we should revisit the object definition and see if some form of delegation is needed.

As it happens, it is much easier to detect lack of cohesion when behaviors are individually atomic. With atomic behaviors it is usually fairly easy to recognize when they are just parts of a larger responsibility. Conversely, it is usually easier to spot the odd man out, so we need some guidelines for ensuring that individual behaviors are cohesive:

- *Self-containment.* This is the most important criteria because it is a necessary condition for abstracting intrinsic properties of problem space entities. The operation specification should be complete and fully testable without the need for invoking any behaviors from other objects.

- *Logical cohesion.* This means that the operation obligation is narrowly defined. Just as good individual requirements should be a statement of a single thought, so should the definition of behavior responsibilities. If you find that your description of the responsibility during scrubbing has *and* or *or* phrases, it is likely the responsibility is not cohesive and should be broken into multiple responsibilities.

- *Testable.* We should be able to provide a suite of unit tests for the responsibility that will unambiguously validate its correctness.[11]

---

11. A major advantage of the MBD approach to separation of concerns is that testing is usually quite easy to do and to automate at the class operation unit test, class unit test, and subsystem functional test levels. Providing test harnesses that are driven by external data is close to trivial, and they are usually pretty reusable across applications. (In fact, most translation IDEs provide built-in test harnesses.)

- *Fine grained.* This means that the object's individual behavior responsibilities should not be generalized to minimize collaborations or message traffic. The more we can define solution flow of control in message flows, the more robust and maintainable the application will be. So, it is preferable to have a lot of simple collaborations that are easily recognized rather than a few complex ones that provide a rigid structure.

If you have any experience with formal requirements specification, you should notice an eerie sense of déjà vu in these criteria. If we apply the same sort of rigorous approach to defining individual object behaviors as we apply to defining individual requirements, then we have made substantial progress down the path of OO Enlightenment. The elder statesmen of OOA/D were well aware of the principles of good requirements specification, and they actively sought to provide a traceable mapping to the OOA/D.[12]

Design by Contract (DbC) and Abstraction of Behavior

DbC originated with Structured Development but has been highly modified by the OO paradigm. We will talk about it in detail in the next section because it provides a rigorous technique for designing flow of control within the application. As a quick summary, when an object has an obligation, there is a clear implication that in satisfying that obligation the object is providing a service to some client. This, in turn, implies that the obligation itself can be formally specified in a contract between the client and the service. Thus the client provides a specification for a service and the service has an obligation to correctly implement that specification. This was the traditional Structured view and reflected the *Do This* philosophy of functional decomposition.

However, these notions of client and service need clarification in the OO context, and this is the best context to provide it. The notion of *client* is much more generic in an OO context and does not refer to a specific collaborator that provides a specification of the behavior. That's because the specific sender of a message shouldn't even know the actual receiver exists. In the OO approach, we abstract the object's responsibilities before worrying about who actually invokes those obligations. Nonetheless, the notion of a contract is very useful in thinking about object behaviors. The contract specifies what the given responsibilities are in a formal way for *any* client.

---

12. I once read a paper (alas, that I no longer have a reference to cite) in which the author made an interesting point about the contrast between OO development and Structured Development. The author asserted that OO development is requirements oriented while Structured Development is solution oriented. While I think that is a bit facile, I also think there is more than a little truth to it, especially when doing OOA modeling.

It might help to think of the client as one of many states that the solution passes through during its execution. Those states represent conditions that form a directed graph to determine what individual solution operation should be executed next. That determination implies that the solution itself must have specified what happens next. Thus the solution itself (or the solution designer) can be viewed as the client in the specification sense.

In OO development, DbC contracts are defined by the service, not the sender of the message.

This is easily seen in the way DbC contracts are supported in the OOPLs. Typically the OOPL provides syntax for specifying preconditions, postconditions, and invariants. Postconditions define the expected results of the behavior, and invariants define constraints on the execution. Both define a contract for what the operation must do, and they do so in a context-free manner (i.e., they can be defined with no knowledge of a particular client context). The interesting syntax is for preconditions, which define *what the client must provide*. Therefore, the only collaboration context relevant to an OOPL DbC contract places a constraint on the message sender rather than the other way around.

Synchronous Services

As indicated earlier, synchronous services are actually accessors of knowledge with complexity beyond getters or setters for simple attribute values. They are also used to eliminate duplication when different behavior responsibility implementations share low-level operations. In either capacity it is important to restrict what they do to make things easier for automatic code generation and to provide the robustness stemming from separation of concerns. To this end, it is useful to think of synchronous services in terms of a few very fundamental kinds of processing.

- *Knowledge accessors*. Essentially these are pure getters and setters for attributes. It is important that such services are restricted to only low-level operations that extract or modify the object's knowledge. (Most AALs separate accessors further into read or write accessors.)

- *Tests*. These are a special form of knowledge accessors that perform some sort of test on the object's knowledge. They always return a boolean value that is used for a flow-of-control decision. It is important that such services are restricted to testing. A test is a read-only operation in that it can extract the knowledge values to be tested but may not modify them, even by invoking a setter. Nor should a test compute a special value of knowledge; any knowledge to be tested should already exist in the form of an attribute or as an input argument to the test.

- *Transforms.* These are the most common sort of synchronous service. The basic idea is that the service transforms input data in the form of message data or object attributes into new values. However, transforms do not write those new values to attributes directly; that is left for separate knowledge accessors. Like a test synchronous service, a transform is a read-only operation. As a result, *transforms always return values.*

  The line between a transform returning a value and a knowledge accessor that is a complicated getter may seem thin, but there is an important distinction. The knowledge accessor is returning an existing ADT value that is defined by the attribute itself. Its complexity lies in dealing with the implementation of that attribute. In contrast, the value a transform returns is something else than the attributes it accesses. That "something else" is different knowledge than that accessed to compute it.

  Yet robustness demands that writing attributes be highly controlled, which is why we have write accessors. We preclude the transform from invoking the write accessor directly because we don't want to hide the rules and policies for doing the attribute write.[13] That is, we want those rules and policies to be exposed at the highest level of flow of control in the application rather than nesting them.

- *Instantiators.* These are synchronous services that instantiate or remove objects and relationships. Instantiation is a quite special operation that has important implications for referential integrity in the final implementation. To maintain our grip on sanity when developing an OOA model we need to make the assumption that objects and relationships can be instantiated safely in a synchronous fashion. Unfortunately, software implementations today are rarely this simplistic, therefore we have to provide manageable scope for such operations so that the transformation engine can enforce referential integrity efficiently. Because such management can present opportunities for things like deadlock, we need to get out of that scope as quickly as possible. That essentially means we don't want our instantiator synchronous service to do any more than it must.

- *Event generators.* An event generator simply generates an event. These are about as close as MBD gets to a fundamental operation in synchronous services.

---

13. As a practical matter, life is much easier for the transformation engine when managing data integrity if writes are limited to special accessors that don't do anything else. It is also important to providing concurrency because writes are usually critical "touch points" between threads. So we want knowledge updates to be highly isolated and readily recognized rather than nested within the scope of other operations.

While it is sometimes necessary to provide some trickiness for accessors and instantiators, that is never the case for event generators.

Most developers, especially those with R-T/E or DB experience, can buy into the need to keep instantiators simple so that data and referential integrity can be managed properly. It is a bit tougher to see why we are being so anal retentive about separating the concerns of access, testing, and transforming data. The justification is really the same for all five categories: robustness. When we do OO development, one of our primary goals is long-term maintainability. While it is futile to try to predict exactly what will change in the future, we can predict that systematically managing complexity by separating concerns in a divide-and-conquer fashion will make it easier to deal with whatever changes come down the pike. That's what encapsulation is about. If you religiously enforce these distinctions when identifying synchronous services, you will find that your applications will tend to be much easier to modify later because change will tend to be more easily isolated.

Anthropomorphizing

This is a very useful technique for abstracting behaviors for objects. It is especially useful when attributing behavior to tangible, inanimate problem space entities. The conundrum for OO development is that such entities typically don't actually do anything. The basic idea is to attribute human behaviors to the entity as if it were a person.[14]

There is a sound rationale for anthropomorphization. Software provides automation; the software exists to replace activities that people would normally do in a manual system. To replace the people, those activities need to be allocated to things rather than people. The traditional structured approach was to create a function that was a surrogate for a real person, usually called something like XxxManager. However, because the activities people perform are usually quite complex, that approach led to very large functions that needed to be broken up hierarchically by functional decomposition.

Since the OO paradigm strives to eliminate hierarchical dependencies, the OO solution was to eliminate the people surrogates completely and force the activities to be spread out over a bunch of objects that abstracted the structure of the problem domain. This very conveniently led to simple, cohesive collections of activities that could be encapsulated.

Anthropomorphizing is useful because it enables us to systematically distribute behaviors so that they can be more easily managed. It comes down to envisioning a herd of rather dense clerks with limited attention spans tasked with doing the opera-

---

14. This is not unprecedented in customer domains. For example, we say that a loom knows the pattern for a fabric. Software developers just do this sort of thing routinely.

tions needed to control various problem space entities. Because they are not very bright, we find it much easier to allocate very limited responsibilities to each of them. We then allocate each of those clerks' tasks to an entity they control.

Clearly, we don't think about all of that tedious allocation and indirection in the metaphor; we simply associate behavior responsibilities directly with the entity we are abstracting. Nonetheless, it can be a useful metaphor if we are having difficulty allocating behavior responsibilities and collaborations. Just imagine the dumbest conceivable clerk that could possibly control the entity, and then figure out what behaviors that clerk could handle. Then marry the entity and the clerk.

Choices in responsibility ownership are invariably rooted in anthropomorphization.

If you have any OO experience at all you have undoubtedly encountered situations where we could make a case for allocating a responsibility to either of two object abstractions. Such choices are always at least indirectly rooted in anthropomorphization. Furthermore, such choices almost always involve behavior responsibilities.

Allocating knowledge attributes is usually very easy to do once we have the right objects identified. That's because knowledge is a static property ideally suited to characterizing inanimate qualities. Behaviors, though, are things people do, and they need to be allocated to our objects. That gives the developer a whole lot more wiggle room for making design decisions about who will own those responsibilities.

The point here is that having plausible choices about where to allocate behavior responsibilities in the design does not reflect some inherent ambiguity in OO development. It is a pure mapping problem between human behaviors being replaced and the problem space structure. Like everything else in problem space abstraction, that mapping needs to be tailored to the problem in hand, thus choices in that mapping actually represent design versatility.

Process

Identifying responsibilities is very much like identifying classes, only the scale of abstraction has been reduced. Therefore, we can do the same sort of team consensus as the Object Blitz, except we deal with one class at a time. However, this can be a bit of overkill. The team already reached a consensus about what the entity is, which provides a fairly solid base for extracting properties. On the other hand, we need a team consensus on what the responsibilities are before the dynamics can be described.

So we advocate a compromise where we do a modified Object Blitz for responsibilities but in a somewhat more informal manner.

1. Perform the same stream-of-consciousness exercise as for the Class Blitz to obtain preliminary candidates for knowledge and behavior needed to solve the problem. (This assumes the team is already thoroughly familiar with the requirements.)

2. Scrub the responsibilities one at a time as a team in a manner similar to the Object Blitz. As a sanity check, identify what each behavior responsibility needs to know, and make sure that knowledge is in the list.

3. Create a very rough Sequence or Collaboration diagram as a team effort.[15] This is a throwaway just to assist in providing a broad-brush context for collaboration. No attempt should be made to identify specific messages. Just use the arrows between objects as a placeholder for expected collaboration based on a general knowledge of the object's subject matter.

4. Walk the Collaboration diagram. This works best with subsystem use cases but can be done with just external stimulus events. The team traces a path through the Collaboration diagram. As it traces the path, the team decides which responsibilities from the list go with which objects. Record the responsibilities and collaborations on the back of the 3 × 5 card for the object from the Object Blitz.[16]

5. Create formal descriptions of attributes and responsibilities. This is an offline activity where each team member independently develops simple text descriptions of the set of responsibilities allocated to them and revises the class description for consistency—all based on the team discussions of previous steps and the 3 × 5 cards.

6. Review the model documentation. The mechanics of review are an exercise for individual shops; there is a heap of literature on the subject, so we won't advocate any specific technique here. The basic idea is that the definitions are refined by whatever standard review process your shop has.

---

15. Collaboration diagrams are not required in MBD because they are redundant; the translation tool can create one once the other diagrams are completed. So we won't talk about syntax details. Basically they are just boxes for each class that are connected by arrows to reflect direct collaborations.

16. Different authors advocate more or less detail. At a minimum we want a list of objects that the object in hand collaborates with; better is some mnemonic about the nature of the collaboration (e.g., "gets sample data from" or "triggers measurement in").

7. Update the model descriptions. At this point we should be close to a final draft model of the classes in the subject matter. Throw away the Collaboration diagram.

During this process additional responsibilities to those in step 1 will be discovered. Attempt to resolve any disagreements about the nature of the responsibilities using OO criteria like self-containment, logical indivisibility, cohesion, and so forth. When in doubt, break up behavior responsibilities. As with the Class Blitz, we need some predefined mechanism to resolve irreconcilable differences. Ideally the customer is the ultimate arbiter because the responsibilities abstract the problem space.

Examples

Because we have not gotten to designing state machines yet, we are going to cheat a bit in these examples and pretend we don't use state machines. This is actually not a bad strategy for an initial cut at a Class diagram. In effect, the identified operations become placeholders for the rules and policies that we associate with states when designing the individual object state machines.

We are also going to cheat with the examples and not explicitly emulate the blitz process discussed earlier. This is mainly to save space in a situation where the detailed steps are fairly clear and the end product provides pretty good inherent traceability. We'll supply parenthetical comments to describe intermediate blitz reasoning in situations where things get tricky.

ATM

It is usually better to start with knowledge attributes for two reasons. They are usually easier to identify in the problem space, especially for tangible entities. More important, though, defining the knowledge provides a basis for defining behavior responsibilities. That's because almost all behaviors modify the state of the application as it is recorded in attribute state variables. Therefore, if we know what state variables are being modified it becomes easier to determine who has the responsibility for modifying them.

Table 9-1 represents a cut at identifying the knowledge responsibilities of the classes identified in the last chapter for the ATM controller software.

Now let's look at what behavior responsibilities these objects might have. The exercise here is to identify what sorts of rules and policies the state machines will eventually have to support. As suggested in the Process section, it is often useful to create a very rough Sequence or Collaboration diagram to assist in identifying the responsibilities.

Table 9-1   *Initial Cut at Defining Knowledge Responsibilities for ATM Controller*

Class	Attribute	Definition
Dispatcher	Transaction Table	A table that identifies what Transaction, if any, is relevant to the incoming message. The incoming message identifier is used to extract the transaction type. (The table will be used for instantiating a relationship to the appropriate Transaction instance for incoming messages from the network port. This is an example of abstracting a data aggregate into a scalar ADT. The structure of the table is a matter of private Dispatcher implementation; no one else needs to know anything about its contents.)
	Routing Table	A table that identifies who the subject matter recipient is for a re-dispatched message. The incoming message identifier is used to extract the recipient identity. (Note that in the ATM there is only one instance of each major component [cash dispenser, network port, etc.]. That means all the relationship navigation will be over 1:1 relationships, which means life is much simpler and a simple lookup table will do. Note that both Dispatcher tables are going to need some convenient representation of message identifiers, like consecutive integers. We don't care about that now; think of the tables abstractly.)
Card Reader	Active Card	A boolean flag to indicate the Card Reader is currently holding the customer's card. (It is unlikely this attribute will be necessary, but we don't know enough about the dynamics to be sure. The point here is that if we need to know this, then Card Reader is the entity that logically would be responsible for knowing it. Remember, we abstract what is necessary to solve the problem, so until we know whether we will actually need this, we need to track it.)
	Cards Eaten	This is a count of the number of invalid cards the Card Reader has eaten. (Again, this is unlikely to be needed unless there is some criteria for judging whether the Card Reader is malfunctioning based on eating too many cards. We need clarification of the requirements from the customer.)
	Read Errors	This is a count of the number of read errors that occurred since the last reset. (If needed, this is likely to be a data structure because there are several possible types of errors [e.g., card put in with the wrong orientation vs. a CRC failure on the data read]. Those errors are only of interest to the hardware and whatever software the bank has to analyze such data for all its ATMs; they are irrelevant to the ATM controller subject matter.)
	Reset Time Stamp	This is a time stamp to indicate the time the Cards Eaten and Read Errors were last reset to zero. (This is assuming requirements that weren't in the original specification. Such attributes often appear when an idea is triggered in the scrubbing [e.g., is there a need to compute error rates?] that gets clarified with the customer, resulting in additional requirements. If the developer's knowledge of the problem space suggests requirements are missing that needs to be checked with the customer.)

Table 9-1 *Initial Cut at Defining Knowledge Responsibilities for ATM Controller (Continued)*

Class	Attribute	Definition
Keyboard	Input Mode	The keyboard needs to know whether it should accept input from the keyboard or ignore it (e.g., baby Lucinda is being a brat). The valid data domain is: ACCEPT and IGNORE.
Cash Dispenser	Twenties Tens Fives	These are attributes that track the number of bills of each denomination the Cash Dispenser has available. (At first blush it seems like the dispenser should have a public responsibility to know how much cash it has so that we can check whether a withdrawal request can be met. However, it isn't that simple because the ability to meet a withdrawal depends upon the number of individual denominations. [If the customer wants $15, it is an invalid request if there are no fives, even if the dispenser still has hundreds in other denominations.] We don't want the other objects to understand the rules of policies of splitting up denominations. So we let the Cash Dispenser figure out if it can honor a withdrawal request. We will supply a fancy getter as a test synchronous service to answer that question as a boolean. Note that our Cash Dispenser is not quite as dumb as we originally thought; it will be a valid abstraction in our subject matter rather than just an interface to the hardware.)
Envelope Processor	none	This is a purely mechanical process, and there is nothing our subject matter needs to know about it.
Character Display	Buffer	This is the image of the character screen. It is defined by Display Specification, including embedded user values. When the customer hits Enter, Character Display will respond by extracting the customer's value and placing it in the data packet of a message it generates. (This assumes a particular, simplistic format for the ATM display where the customer makes choices by entering a value from the keyboard [e.g., choice "B"] rather than, say, moving a line highlight. Because the Character Display interacts with Keyboard, it will have a state machine.)
	Current Position	This is the index of the current position in the Buffer. (Note that we have no attributes to describe the screen position of stuff in the display. We are assuming that the text value will have embedded control characters that the simple-minded display driver can parse. That is, the Text attribute of Display Specification will have all that formatting information hard-wired.)
Display Specification	Text	The text for the display, including carriage controls, etc. Any value supplied by the customer will be initialized by spaces.
	Interactive Flag	This is a boolean to indicate whether the customer supplies an embedded value through the keyboard.
	Value Type	This is the type of a customer-supplied value, if any, to which the text will be converted. The data domain is NONE, ALPHA, NUMERIC.

Continues

Table 9-1 *Initial Cut at Defining Knowledge Responsibilities for ATM Controller (Continued)*

Class	Attribute	Definition
	Value Length	This is the length of the value in characters as it will appear in the text string buffer.
	Value Start	This is the index of the starting character of an embedded value in the text string buffer. (Note that Value Type, Value Length, and Value Start all have valid data domains [NONE, 0, 0] even when Interactive Flag is FALSE. We could have eliminated Interactive Flag by using Length = 0 as a flag value. However, that would mean Value Length is no longer a simple domain; it describes the length of a string *and* whether the display is interactive. When reducing attributes to simple domains we must be careful to ensure that other attributes have meaningful values throughout the life of the object, which is why NONE is part of the data domain of Value Type and 0 is part of the data domain of Value Length.)
Network Port	none	The plan is to have a very simple send/receive interface for the Network Port that is independent of the protocols, addressing, and whatnot. (That will mean, though, that every message will be constructed with some common information [bank routing number, customer account number, etc.] that the Network Port driver can use to resolve its issues for every message.)
ATM Card	Account Number	The identifier for the customer's account.
	Account Type	A code for the type of account. (Probably not necessary in this subject matter, but the bank will think it is important and, consequently, will expect it to be provided separately in data packets.)
	Bank Routing Number	The bank routing number for addressing a specific bank. (There will be other codes, such as a bank branch number. Essentially everything that is in the magnetic strip specification will be included in the ATM Card. We will just keep it simple here in the examples.)
	???	(Note there is no information about the account itself, such as maximum withdrawal amount. Those values will depend upon bank rules and policies, and they belong on the bank's side of the network port. The ATM just relays a withdrawal request, and the bank decides whether to honor it or not. So that sort of semantic information is irrelevant to the ATM controller subject matter.)

Table 9-1 *Initial Cut at Defining Knowledge Responsibilities for ATM Controller (Continued)*

Class	Attribute	Definition
Transaction	Type	A code to identify the transaction type. To keep the examples simple we will assume the only Transactions are DEPOSIT, WITHDRAWAL, and TRANSFER. Tentatively, we will use the Type attribute as a basis for parametric decisions. (As soon as we think about these types of transactions it becomes apparent that they represent quite different things. For example, a DEPOSIT transaction collaborates with only the Envelope Processor, the WITHDRAWAL collaborates with only the Cash Dispenser, while the TRANSFER collaborates with neither. However, they also have some commonality in that all three need a customer-supplied value. We will have more to say about this in a later chapter, but for now we point out that this screams for subclassing. It will also become apparent that the behaviors are somewhat different. So Transaction will become a superclass, but we haven't gotten there yet.)
	Amount	In this example, all three transaction types involve an amount of money. (You will note that a transfer requires at least one additional account number. To deal with this we need to cover subclassing first.)

Figure 9-3 is a Collaboration diagram that captures the envisioned collaborations from when a new ATM card is entered into the Card Reader to when the main menu is presented. Essentially, the boxes represent objects and the connections are messages between them. All we are providing is a rough guess at how the use cases get done so we can allocate behavior responsibilities.

Figure 9-4 is a Sequence diagram that captures the collaborations for a withdrawal transaction.

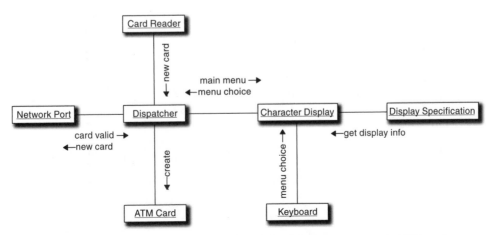

Figure 9-3 *Collaborations involved in reading and validating a customer's ATM card*

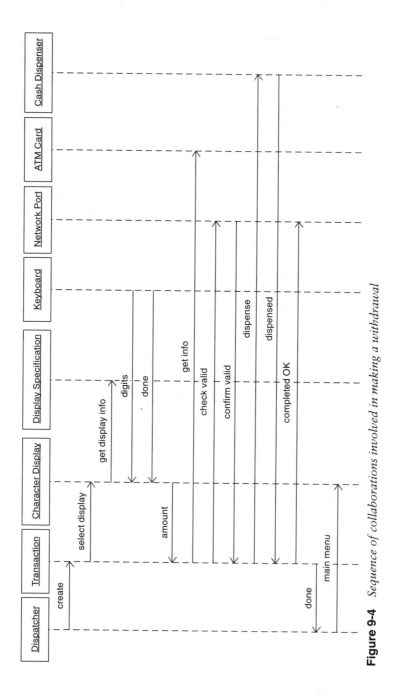

Figure 9-4 *Sequence of collaborations involved in making a withdrawal*

214

Astute observer that you are, you will no doubt wonder where the Deposit, Withdrawal, and Transfer objects came from in Table 9-2. They are subclasses of Transaction that represent specializations. We're not going to get to subclassing for awhile, so for now just understand that these new classes represent special cases of Transaction. They would have come into existence as soon as we started to do a rough Sequence or Collaboration diagram because not all Transactions have the same collaborations.

Table 9-2 presents the results of identifying the behavior responsibilities.

Table 9-2 *Final Cut at ATM Controller Responsibilities*

Class	Behavior	Rules and Policies
Dispatcher	Transaction	This is the primary behavior for the Dispatcher. It parses an incoming customer message, determines who should process it, determines the type of transaction, and instantiates the necessary relationships to the proper Transaction object. (That's a lot of stuff for a logically indivisible operation. However, this is where the flexible OO view of logical indivisibility comes into play. At the level of abstraction of the subject matter, all that processing is a response to the single notion of a *transaction*. That is, we always do *all* of that stuff *every time* when the message is received; none of it is done in response to some other message. Caveat: If use cases are modeled incrementally, we might not be sure of that and we might define separate responsibilities for a single use case. They would be coalesced later when it was apparent they would all be in the same state machine action, for reasons we'll get to when discussing dynamics.)
	Transaction Processed	Close out the transaction and reset for a new transaction.
	Card Processed	Request validation of the customer account.
	Account Validated	Reset to process a new transaction.
	Account Invalid	Notify Card Reader that the card should be eaten. Notify Display to provide an explanation.
	Card Eaten	Reset the system for a new customer.

Continues

Table 9-2   *Final Cut at ATM Controller Responsibilities (Continued)*

Class	Behavior	Rules and Policies
	Customer Done	Notify Card Reader that the customer's card should be returned. Reset the system for a new customer. (This behavior does not seem logically indivisible since the Card Eaten responsibility does the same thing. Good catch, Grasshopper; apparently you *have* been paying attention. Card Eaten is a bad name; it should really be something like Reset For New Customer. In fact, the Card Reader will acknowledge either eating the card or returning the card. Either acknowledgment will actually invoke the Reset For New Customer behavior. So that part of the behavior doesn't belong here. Recognizing that, though, is much easier if we are used to handshaking protocols for state machines, which we won't get to until the next section.)
	Hardware Error	Send Error to Display, notify bank, and shut down.
Card Reader	Read Card	This is the primary behavior; the customer data is extracted from the hardware magnetic strip reader and used to initialize the ATM Card object. (Since the Card Reader is acting like a "factory" object to initialize the ATM Card object, it has valid problem solution responsibilities. However, most of its behaviors are simply interfaces to the actual hardware driver in another subsystem.)
	Eat Card	The Card Reader processes an invalid customer ATM card.
	Return Card	The Card Reader returns the customer's card.
Keyboard	Key Pressed	If Input mode is ACCEPT, determine if the key pressed is Enter. If so, issue the appropriate message to Character Display and reset the Input Mode to IGNORE. Otherwise, inform the Character Display what character was pressed. If the input mode is IGNORE, ignore the message. (This is an external message because it originates with the hardware.)
Cash Dispenser DELETE(?)	Query Valid	Check if enough cash in the right denominations is available for the given amount. (This is actually a synchronous service and reflects some specific problem solution processing.)
	Dispense Cash	Dispense the indicated amount of cash. (This is just a mechanical hardware operation done by the driver. So this behavior is really just a surrogate for a bridge to the hardware driver. If the driver can service the Query Valid request we would not need the attributes in the subject matter either, and we could delete this object in lieu of a bridge. [We may want to keep the surrogate just to highlight the various bridges that are in play.])

Table 9-2　*Final Cut at ATM Controller Responsibilities (Continued)*

Class	Behavior	Rules and Policies
Envelope Processor DELETE(?)	Accept Envelope	Accept and time stamp the envelope. (This is a pure hardware activity so this behavior is just a surrogate for a bridge to the hardware driver. Since there is no interesting knowledge either, we would probably eliminate this class entirely unless we want to highlight the various bridges.)
Character Display	Initialize Screen	This is the primary activity. The Display Specification is used to provide formatting and whatnot. It just passes the text from the Display Specification through to the display driver. If the display type is interactive, set the Keyboard Input Mode to ACCEPT and set the Current Position to the start of the embedded value.
	Key Pressed	This indicates a key (other than ENTER) was pressed. Echo the character to the screen, save it in the buffer, and update the Current Position. (Things like backspacing, ignoring invalid characters, and guarding buffer overflow are also handled.)
	Enter Pressed	Extract the interactive value from the buffer, if necessary; notify Transaction; and clear the screen.
	Error	Clear the screen and display the Error text.
Display Specification	none	This is just a dumb data holder that is accessed by Character Display.
Network Port	Send Message	Construct a message in the appropriate format and send it to the bank. (The vision here is that the message provided is a {message ID, data packet} that reflects the originating context. Network Port will extract information about bank, account, etc., common to all messages from ATM Card. Network Port may also have a state machine to manage any network handshaking protocols. If there are such protocols, it would have additional behaviors to reflect that level of granularity in the external messages. The associated actions would just issue messages like protocol acknowledgments.)
ATM Card	none	This is just a dumb data holder that saves data needed by Network Port across multiple messages.
Transaction	Initialize	This is a common behavior for all transactions. The application is initialized to start processing for a transaction (e.g., issuing instructions to Character Display to provide a screen for the customer).
Deposit NEW	Process	Notify the Envelope processor to shred the envelope.
	Envelope Processed	Send Transaction Processed to Dispatcher. (The message will contain the amount the customer claims was deposited. Dispatcher will re-dispatch that message to the Bank via Network Port.)

Continues

Table 9-2 *Final Cut at ATM Controller Responsibilities (Continued)*

Class	Behavior	Rules and Policies
Withdrawal NEW	Process	Check if Cash Dispenser can honor the withdrawal. If not, send Error to Display and reset. If so, request Cash Dispenser to dispense.
	Cash Dispensed	Notify bank of successful dispensing and notify Dispatcher that the transaction has been processed.
Transfer NEW	Process	Notify bank of transfer.
	Transfer Denied	Send Error to Display and reset.
	Transfer Accepted	Send Transaction Processed to Dispatcher.

As you perused the behavior responsibilities for the first object, Dispatcher, your first thought was probably that some responsibilities were missing. For example, there were no responsibilities for telling the Cash Dispenser to dispense cash or telling the Envelope Processor to process a deposit. Those behaviors were delegated to other objects. Recall that Dispatcher should be cohesive, self-contained, and context-independent. The time to dispense cash or shred deposit envelopes is more logically determined in the Transaction object. That's because there are multiple activities in a transaction, some of which are unique to the transaction. So the most logical place to coordinate that is in Transaction.

You probably noticed the activities are all pretty trivial. Many of them could probably be implemented with one to two lines of code. All the complicated stuff has been allocated to the hardware drivers, leaving the most heavy-duty behaviors to be Dispatcher's Transaction behavior and Character Display's Initialize Screen behavior. You are probably wondering why we need so many classes, which might seem like a lot of "overhead" to you. Why not combine some of them so we at least have a dozen or so executable statements per class?

One answer is that there is a lot more code than in the solution rules and policies. Those rules and policies are what we need to solve the customer's problem; implementing that solution in software for a computer's computational model is a whole other ball game. The descriptions only vaguely mention things like instantiating relationships and formatting messages. In practice there will be enough 3GL boilerplate code to fill up these classes quite nicely in an elaboration process.

The more important answer, though, is that there are a lot of rules and policies that are implicit in the static structure of this model. For example, state machines will enforce sequencing rules that are only implied in Table 9-2. Thus for a Withdrawal transaction: We initialize *first*; *then* get customer input; *then* locally validate (the Cash Dispenser has enough money); *then* globally validate (gets the bank's authorization), *then* dispense cash, *then* notify the bank, and *then* clean up. Those activities are mostly generating messages to others but the sequence is critical.

Fixes Needed

You should have recognized several problems in the above responsibilities if you have ever used a bank ATM and you perused the example carefully. This is why modeling is a team effort and we have reviewers. If you didn't peruse it carefully, go back and do so now because there are a couple of points to make about robustness that won't sink in until you *understand the nature of the problems*. One useful technique is to "walk" use cases for deposit, withdrawal, and transfer through the Collaboration diagram. (The use cases can be mental; the reason this example was chosen is that it should be possible to picture oneself at an ATM doing those transactions.) These are the sorts of things you need to check.

- Is there a behavior to handle each use case step?

- Is there a behavior associated with each external message? Every external input message (from an Actor in use case terms) needs to have a designated responsibility to which the subsystem interface can dispatch the request.

- Is all the knowledge needed to perform the step available somewhere?

- Is behavior for the step self-contained and testable? A step is self-contained if all it does is modify attributes and send messages.

- Is the sequence of use case steps plausibly defined in the Collaboration diagram? We are doing static structure here so we aren't terribly concerned that we have defined collaborations exactly right yet. However, we should be concerned with any glaring inconsistencies, such as accessing ATM card information prior to creating an ATM card instance or having multiple ATM card instances around as a transaction is executed.

- What could go wrong? The issue here is not software correctness in the sense of design-by-contract. Rather, it is about problem space applications of Murphy's Law. We don't worry about the details of how Character Display deals with corrections the customer makes for typos from the keyboard. But we do worry about what happens if the withdrawal amount requested is more than is available in the account, what to do if the network connection times out, and what happens if the Cash Dispenser jams.

After you have done your homework and revisited the attributes and operations, come back here and compare to the critiques provided by the book reviewers.

- **Is there a behavior to handle each use case step?** There is as long as we have only three use cases and nothing ever goes wrong. This is not surprising because that's the way most software is built. We think about the obvious scenarios and how to implement them; we do the less obvious scenarios "later." The rest of these questions are aimed at breaking that habit and forcing us to think about the less obvious scenarios from the outset.

- **Is there a behavior associated with each external message?** No, because the customer is not the only Actor here. Relative to this subsystem, all of the hardware drivers we identified are also Actors because they collaborate with this subject matter. To see the problem, consider how the customer selects Deposit, Withdrawal, and Transfer. On some ATMs there is a dedicated key on the keypad for basic transactions. On other ATMs the customer selects from a screen menu. Our Collaboration diagram has made an implicit assumption that there are dedicated keys for this selection. That's fine if it is right, but the original requirements didn't define that, and there were no bridge descriptions for the hardware drivers.

A clear error here lies in handling printing. We blithely ignored transactions like balance checks. However, whenever a deposit is made, the ATM always provides a hard copy receipt for it.[17] Even if we decide we just need the bridge interface rather than a surrogate object for the printer driver, we still need a behavior that has the responsibility for encoding the balance and generating the message. And where does it get the balance it encodes?

If you are familiar with financial systems, especially in the banking industry, you will be aware that there is considerable paranoia about security.[18] There is also a

---

17. As it happens, I completely forgot about the entire printer in my original pass at Chapter 8! However, it is hard to miss when "walking" a Deposit use case through a Collaboration diagram.

18. With substantial justification, I might add. I happen to know the following anecdote is true because I had first-hand knowledge of it. Back in the late '60s some customers of a bank noticed a balance creep—their accounts were accumulating more money than they deposited. On the second of two successive statements the starting balance was larger than the ending balance on their previous statement. This magically added money to their account. The developer doing this was tricking out the auditing facilities by "depositing" nonexistent money to balance out cash withdrawals. Doing it via this technique didn't raise any flags in the existing auditing software. He was depending on the customers either not noticing or, if they did notice, not complaining. He got caught because he got greedy and started hitting up the "deposits" for significant money (i.e., $100+ at a clip). Eventually a customer, who wanted to spend this "found" money but was worried the bank might have made a mistake and would want the money back, asked if it was OK to spend it. The bank said yes because they didn't want to publicly admit that they had been ripped off. But the magical deposits stopped, and the developer gave back most of the money and became a "security consultant" as part of a deal to avoid doing time.

trend toward Just In Time servicing and whatnot. All of these things conspire so various people on the other side of the network port want a lot of information about the ATM itself. Hence there will generally be more data kept and reported. They may also want the ability for the bank to poll for things like cash on hand, status, errors, and so forth that have not been accounted for in the requirements. It is likely then that we are missing some sort of Status and/or History class that keeps track of additional information to support such queries.

- *Is all the knowledge needed to perform the step available somewhere?* Not quite, even for our three simple use cases. Note that for a balance transfer between accounts the customer needs to identify two accounts as well as an amount. The customer also has to define which is source and which is receiver, meaning that the display will have to support multiple values on one screen or present separate From/To screens to the customer. In the former case, Display Specification as we described it is inadequate, and for the latter case, we would need two Display Specification instances for that transaction. Either way we have some surgery to perform.

- *Is the behavior of each step self-contained and testable?* Yes. Though the behavior responsibilities are defined at a fairly high level of abstraction, it should be clear that they all either access knowledge synchronously (including synchronous services that are just glorified getters) or just send messages without depending upon the behaviors that respond to those messages. Therefore, we should be able to fully test any behavior without implementing anything else except knowledge attributes and their accessors.

- *Is the sequence of the use case steps plausibly defined in the Collaboration diagram?* Yes, except for printing and some error processing we'll talk about shortly. That's because we only have three quite trivial use cases in hand and there are lots of requirements, such as security and maintenance, that simply haven't been addressed.

- *What could go wrong?* The short answer is everything. The error processing defined so far is woefully inadequate. The problem does not lie in things like correcting user typos; that can be handled in the details of Character Display processing for a typical ATM (e.g., backspacing to erase a character). The problems lie in things like hardware failures, power outages, and network time-outs.

In many applications these sorts of errors are unexpected so they are handled by a default exception facility provided by the transformation engine. However, in an ATM they must be handled explicitly in the problem solution. That's because there is a synchronization problem between what the ATM hardware does and what is recorded in the bank's database. In addition, the bank customer is interactively involved. For example, if the bank approves a withdrawal, it can't simply post that withdrawal. Instead, it must lock the funds on the account (in case the account is accessed simultaneously) and wait for confirmation from the ATM that the cash was actually dispensed. Only then can it post the withdrawal to the general ledger in the database.

Unfortunately, lots of bad things can happen between the time the bank locks the funds and the ATM's acknowledgment. Some are easily handled, such as cash dispenser jams where the ATM just needs to tell the bank "never mind." But the acknowledgment can be delayed for a variety of reasons: A noisy line causes lots of packets to be re-sent, slowing things down; the network itself may crash; the ATM may have a power outage; the network as a whole may just simply be very slow today due to a denial-of-service attack on somebody; or the network may be locally slow because it is lunchtime and everyone is hitting their ATM.[19] Each of these contingencies may or may not require unique handling policies and protocols on both sides of the network port.

This is a kind of straw man because we didn't specify any requirements for handling such synchronization. However, in the real world, lots of requirements are implicit in the subject matter and business domain, so that really isn't much of an excuse. Anyone who has dealt with distributed processing and has any notion of a bank's paranoia over posting would realize there are some serious deficiencies in the specification of the responsibilities above, regardless of what the SRS said.

Your list of deficiencies may include things that haven't been mentioned. Don't lose sleep over it. We are not trying to design an ATM Controller here; we are only trying to indicate how we should try to think about that design. Space precludes a full design and a full answer to the previous questions.

Pet Care Center: Disposition

Table 9-3 and, later in the chapter, Table 9-4 represent the same drill as for the ATM example. The difference is that since you probably haven't actually used a pet care center (unless you live in Southern California), you have no use cases to compare, so

---

19. Being slow isn't a problem directly. But the software can't wait forever because of the potential for database deadlocks, so there has to be some sort of time-out check. If the software decides to reset and do something else after a certain time, there could be big trouble if the response finally arrives after that point.

we won't emphasize the things-to-fix gimmick. Table 9-3 lists the attributes. (The operations are listed in Table 9-4.)

Table 9-3 *Pet Care Center Knowledge Attributes*

Class	Attribute	Definition
Pet	ID	This is an internal identifier for the pet that is assigned when the pet is originally admitted (e.g., a patient number). (This is commonly provided when there is a need to access instances of the entity uniquely from a restricted set. All pets will likely have a name but it may not be unique.)
	Critter Type	A code that generally classifies the type of pet. The codes will map into an animal taxonomy but there will likely be special qualities (e.g., Vicious Cat).
	Height, Length, Weight	These provide data of obvious relevance to accommodations, rehab, and disposal.
	Status	The current status for the Pet. The data domain is IN REHABILITATION, AWAITING PICKUP, AWAITING MEMORIAL, AWAITING TAXIDERMY, and AWAITING DISPOSAL.
	Duration	The length of time in residency. (Probably not needed because we charge triggered by a daily event from Scheduler. Start/Stop time stamps might be more relevant. [That will depend on details about scheduling that we haven't talked about yet.] It is beginning to look doubtful that we need Residence Facility at all but we won't know for sure until we look at candidate behaviors.)
Rehabilitation Session	Type	A code that defines the nature of the rehabilitation. This will be used to identify the level of cost. (Cost likely also depends on Critter Type.)
	Duration	The length of time the session requires. (How about the time it actually takes? We only need that to deal with problems that will affect the schedule. We assume that the Staff announces the problem through the UI directly to Scheduler, or Scheduler can figure it out from the elapsed time when receiving some sort of *done* message.)
Residence Facility	Type	A code that defines the type of residence facility required. This will be used to identify the level of cost. (This is probably redundant with the Pet's Critter Type attribute; that is, the type of facility can probably be tied directly to the critter type. We won't know until we get into specific codes and behaviors.)

Continues

Table 9-3 *Pet Care Center Knowledge Attributes (Continued)*

Class	Attribute	Definition
Storage Slot	Slot Number	The storage slots have numbers to identify them. This will probably be more useful to the Staff for feeding and what-not than the pet's ID. Explicitly assigning a Pet to a slot will make scheduling easier. (Remember, these slots only apply to deceased pets.)
	Size	The data domain is TINY (goldfish, gerbils), SMALL (cats, possums, small dogs), MEDIUM (large dogs, sheep), and LARGE (horses) to describe the four sizes of storage available.
	Temperature	The data domain is FROZEN and COLD.
Crematorium	Current Gas Consumed	The gas consumption (cubic feet) for the current cremation. The value is reset to 0 between cremations.
	Cumulative Gas Consumed	The total gas consumption (cubic feet) in the current accounting period. (This really addresses accounting issues not in evidence yet.)
	At Temperature Flag	A flag to indicate whether the oven has reached the proper temperature. (This attribute will actually be discovered when we think about how the furnace actually works below.)
	Duration	The required duration for the Pet (based on size, etc.) once the optimal temperature is reached.
	Previous Meter Reading	This is the reading of the hardware's gas flow meter from the last time it was read. (This attribute will actually be discovered when thinking about how the furnace actually works below.)
Schedule	Cremation Flag	A boolean to indicate whether the Pet requires cremation.
	Taxidermy Flag	A boolean to indicate whether the Pet requires stuffing.
	Memorial Flag	A boolean to indicate whether the Pet requires a memorial service.
	Burial Flag	A boolean to indicate whether the Pet requires burial.
	Rehab Needed Count	A count of the rehabilitation sessions the Pet requires.
	Rehab Count	The count of rehabilitation sessions the Pet has completed.
	Rehab Frequency	A code that defines the periodicity of rehabilitation sessions (e.g., once a day). (The rehabilitation introduces some interesting strategic issues for the solution that are discussed in the accompanying text. That strategy determines how we abstract the object properties.)
	Pickup Flag	A boolean to indicate that the Pet requires pick-up by the owner.

Table 9-3   *Pet Care Center Knowledge Attributes (Continued)*

Class	Attribute	Definition
Schedule Event	Event Type	A code to identify the event from the Scheduler that announces it is time to do something. The data domain is: FEED, REHABILITATE, RESIDENCY CHARGE, STORAGE CHARGE, CREMATE, MEMORIAL, STUFF, and DISPOSE.
	Data Packet	A packet of data that is relevant to the particular event. (It is anticipated that only the UI will be interested in the data packet as it displays the event for the Staff or prints it out in a report. So we can treat it as a scalar within Disposition. Though this looks like a simple event message, we anticipate that it will have to be temporarily persistent in the subsystem [e.g., on request from the UI].)
	Critical Flag	A boolean to indicate whether the event requires immediate Staff attention.
Critical Schedule Event [DELETED]		(Common sense reigns and we realized that there was nothing in this event that could not be handled by simply adding the Critical Flag attribute to Schedule Event.)
Schedule Modification [DELETED]	Event Type	A code to identify the type of change the event announces.
	Data Packet	A packet of data that is relevant to the change. The data is generated from a form in the UI that the Staff fills in (e.g., with fields like Delayed, Delayed Until, etc.). (The UI will package the form data, and the Scheduler will interpret it so it becomes a scalar in the Disposition subsystem. At this point it becomes clear that Disposition is just a middleman, so the UI could send the message directly to Scheduler. That is, the change has no effect on this subject matter until Scheduler processes the change. At that point Scheduler will tell Disposition anything it needs to know about the new schedule by generating events at the right times.)
UI	none	This class is just a surrogate for the interface to the UI subsystem; it serves no purpose except as an address for messages.

Continues

Table 9-3   *Pet Care Center Knowledge Attributes (Continued)*

Class	Attribute	Definition
Disposal Service	Service Type	A code for the service type. The data domain is BURIAL, CREMATION, SHIPMENT, and TAXIDERMY.
	Location	The place where the carcass goes. (This option is encoded when the Pet is admitted and is only decoded for display, so we treat it as a scalar in this subsystem. Note that the service information is associated with a Pet at admission so it must be saved in the database along with the association. This isn't very relevant to Disposition but it is usually a good idea to make a note of such things when they come up for future reference when defining the database access. There may also be a need to provide the information for ad hoc UI queries from the Staff.)
	Service Cost	The basic cost of the disposal itself.
	Delivery Cost	The cost of delivering the remains of cremation or taxidermy, if any.
Memorial Service	Service Type	A code for service type. The data domain is WAKE and FUNERAL.
	Location	The place where the service will take place. (You will note that Disposal Service and Memorial Service look exactly the same. That does not mean they are the same, which will become clearer when we get to the behavior responsibilities.)
	Cost	The cost of the service.

You may be curious about the attributes for Schedule. Recall that in the last chapter we made subtle changes to the semantics of Schedule so that it described the activities that take place while the pet is under the purview of the Disposition subsystem. The basic vision is that this Schedule object understands the sequence of activities and it understands what to do (i.e., what messages to generate) when a Scheduler event occurs.

The implication is that if this Schedule object understands the detailed sequence of activities, the Scheduler does not need to understand them as well; otherwise, we are bleeding cohesion. In other words, we have made a design decision about who "owns" the activity sequence for a particular kind of disposition. This, in turn, implies that only large-scale disposition activities are scheduled through the Scheduler subsystem. For that, the Scheduler just needs to know the elapsed time before triggering an event and the type of event to trigger.

We made that decision based on the fact that the activities are unique to the Disposition subsystem, they are fixed for a particular kind of disposition, and they are executed end to end. The important point here, though, is that decision was, itself, triggered by the need to define the attributes of Schedule. We have a lot of leeway in abstracting the problem space, so to define those attributes we needed a strategic vision of the overall problem solution. So even though we hadn't thought very much about how the Disposition and Scheduler subsystems collaborate up to now, we needed to do so to abstract the Schedule object.

This is an example of a detailed subsystem design decision that could affect the communication bridges between the two subsystems. The *schedule disposition activities* semantics is quite different from *trigger an event after N hours* semantics; therefore, this is not something that can be handled in the bridge as a syntactic mismatch. So aren't we trashing our application partitioning efforts?

Not really, Grasshopper. The real problem here is that we had not allocated ownership and management of the disposition activity sequence when we defined the subject matters. Put another way, we left the borders of our Scheduler subject matter blurry. Nobody is perfect, including systems engineers.

So if we had been perfect and we had drilled down just a tad more about the level of abstraction of Scheduler, we wouldn't have a problem. All detailed schedules would be "owned" by the relevant client subsystems, and Scheduler would manage the sequencing among the various detailed schedules as if they were logically indivisible.

There are two points here. The first is that we should have been more careful in our application partitioning. Recall that we said it was the most important thing we do in developing large applications. If we had gotten the level of abstraction of Scheduler right, we wouldn't need to rework the bridge definitions and, possibly, Scheduler itself. As it happens we deliberately "overlooked" this when defining Scheduler just so we could emphasize what happens when we don't get things quite right.

> If subsystems are developed in parallel, always work from the top of the Component diagram downward.

The second point is that such a mistake is probably not fatal. Our encapsulation and separation of concerns is still pretty good, so the Scheduler bridge definition may need some work and Scheduler's implementation may need some work. But because Scheduler is still doing the same basic things, those changes should not be much worse than other requirements changes. More important, we are catching the problem fairly early in the design of the Disposition subsystem. If we design the Disposition subsystem before or at the same time as Scheduler, we will identity the problem before work on Scheduler goes very far. Since requirements flow from the top of the Component diagram to the bottom, it figures that we should do parallel subsystem development the same way; that is, we should develop the sibling subsystems of Disposal before the common service Scheduler.

Note the emphasis in this example on attributes that are aggregates abstracted as scalar values (i.e., Data Packet and Location). This is quite common when developing subject matters that have a relatively high level of abstraction. The main advantage of this is that it enables us to narrow the focus of our design, making the design compact and easier to understand because it is relatively uncluttered with detail.

Perhaps more important, it helps us abstract the interfaces to the subsystems, which enables us to define bridges in terms of requirements ("We will need the location data to respond to this message") instead of data ("We need the company name, street address, city, state, country, and postal code") or implementation ("The company name is a 50-character string, the street address is . . . "). In addition, the mapping of the data packet is isolated to whoever sends and receives the message, and the {message ID, <data packet>} paradigm is highly standardized, which enables us to apply some interesting reuse techniques.

Note also the emphasis on abstract, enumerated values for the data domains. This is also fairly common when we are trying to abstract complex entity semantics into knowledge responsibilities. Such data domains are ideally suited to preserving implementation independence while succinctly capturing complex semantics. In other words, they are well-suited to both raising the level of abstraction and extracting only views that are necessary to the problem in hand.

Now let's look at the operations in Table 9-4.

Table 9-4 *Behavior Responsibilities for Pet Care Center*

Class	Operation	Definition
Pet	Compute Charge	Most of the charges accrued are focused on a particular Pet, and somebody needs to compute them. Since the computations aren't complicated and the objects owning the required data are all reached by navigating through Pet anyway, it seems reasonable for Pet to compute the charges when triggered by events from Scheduler. (An exception is likely to be cremation because those charges depend more on the hardware.) The operation would use the charge type from the event to parameterize the computation.
	Initialize	There is probably going to be some set-up processing (e.g., residence assignment, Schedule creation, etc.) when a Pet comes under the purview of Disposition.
	Inactivate	Eventually the Pet somehow leaves the Center. At that time there will probably be some cleanup processing (e.g., archiving data, final billing statement generation, etc.) to be done.
Rehabilitation Session	none	This is probably going to be just a dumb data holder.

Table 9-4   *Behavior Responsibilities for Pet Care Center (Continued)*

Class	Operation	Definition
Residence Facility [DELETED]	none	(As pointed out in analyzing the attributes, the attributes could be owned by Pet. Since the Center's staff does everything, the only behavior we might have would be a trivial behavior to compute the cost of a day's stay. But we can have Pet compute its costs as well.)
Storage Slot	none	Just a dumb data holder for resource allocation and charge basis.
Crematorium	Start	This operation resets the Current Gas Consumption and At Temperature Flag. It presets the hardware to a suitable temperature. It reads the hardware gas flow meter and records the value in Previous Meter Reading.
	At Temperature	If the At Temperature Flag is not set, it invokes a system timer for the value of Duration. It sets the At Temperature Flag. It instructs the hardware to turn off the gas. It reads the hardware gas flow meter and computes an increment to Current Gas Consumption. (It is assumed here that the hardware will issue an event when the temperature reaches the preset value. This might also be implemented with a polling loop, but at this level we don't care.)
	Below Temperature	This operation instructs the hardware to start cooking again. It reads the hardware gas flow meter and sets Previous Meter Reading with that value. (It is assumed that the hardware will issue an event when the temperature falls significantly below the optimum temperature.)
	Stop	This operation instructs the hardware to turn off. The hardware gas flow meter is read and the value compared to Previous Meter Reading. If different, an increment to Current Gas Consumption is computed. Then Cumulative Gas Consumption is updated and the Staff and Scheduler are notified that Cremation is complete. (The assumption here is that this behavior is triggered by the system timer reaching the specified Duration.)
	Compute Duration	This is a synchronous service that computes the length of time the oven must be on, given the oven's optimum temperature and Pet characteristics. (The Crematorium computes this rather than the Pet because the algorithm is defined for the furnace, not the pet.)

Continues

Table 9-4 *Behavior Responsibilities for Pet Care Center (Continued)*

Class	Operation	Definition
Schedule	Dispatch Event	This operation processes an event from Scheduler. It re-dispatches the announcement to Pet (e.g., costs), the UI (staff notification), etc.
	Activity Completed	This operation determines the next activity to be done in the Disposition and sends a message to Scheduler to schedule it. (The vision here is that Schedule understands the order to "walk" the boolean flags. The flag determines what activity needs to be done next and Scheduler is notified. Scheduler then triggers that activity when it is due.)
Scheduler [NEW]	none	This is just a surrogate for the interface to the Scheduler subsystem. (It was discovered when noting that there are a number of messages to Scheduler as well as from it.)
Schedule Event	none	This is just a temporary data holder.
UI	Request Display	This is just a surrogate for the interface to the UI subsystem. (The UI also "sources" interactive responses from the Center's staff that are dispatched to the appropriate objects [e.g., announcing completion of a rehab session].)
Disposal Service	Contracted	This operation records the Service Cost of the service. A notification is sent to Scheduler if the date must be modified.
	Completed	This operation accrues the Service Cost. The Scheduler is notified and the relevant Schedule Event is deleted.
	Delivered	This operation accrues the Delivery Cost associated with TAXIDERMY or CREMATION. All of the relevant Pet objects are deleted.
Memorial Service	Contracted	This operation records the Service Cost of the service. A notification is sent to Scheduler if the date must be modified.
	Completed	This operation accrues the Service Cost. The Scheduler is notified and all of the objects relevant to Pet are deleted.

You probably didn't expect Crematorium to have the most complex behavior responsibilities in this subject matter. That should not be a surprise because we didn't say anything about how a crematorium actually worked in the requirements. In fact, the previous description might well be an oversimplification. For example, are we really going to do hamsters in the same size furnace we would use for a horse?

Also, at the level of behavior of turning gas on and off, we are assuming temperature sensors that are not in evidence in this model. We blithely dismissed all that as "hardware." But if we are thinking about timers in the analysis, wouldn't a temperature sensor be at an equivalent level of abstraction? All this should make us nervous about whether we are handling cremation properly. We can make a case at this point to make Crematorium a subsystem in its own right, one that explicitly described how sensors, gas meters, flow valves, ignition, and timers all played together. That would be far too much detail for Disposition's level of abstraction, so Crematorium would appear as nothing more than a surrogate interface class that accepted a Start message and issued a Done message with charges.

This would be an example of legitimate feedback to application partitioning. We find the subsystem to be more complex than we anticipated, and we need to provide a lower level of abstraction for parts of the subsystem. This results in delegation to a new service subsystem. As indicated in Chapter 6, this isn't a major structural change because we are simply delegating a service that only talks to Disposition and its responsibilities are dictated by Disposition's needs.

Before leaving these examples we need to address one area that has thus far appeared as magic. Specifically, where do all these object instances come from? "The stork brought them" is clearly not a satisfactory answer. The answer lies in design patterns, where the GoF[20] book is a reference that every OO developer should have. Typically we will have a *factory* object that exists to instantiate other objects and relationships. (The Pet's Initialize behavior might well act as a Factory for such initialization if it is pretty simple.) This is very handy because it standardizes the way applications are instantiated and enables us to isolate the rules and policies of instantiation (*who*) from those of the solution algorithm (*what* and *when*). In so doing it places those responsibilities in one place rather than dribbling them throughout the application.

When the idea of a Factory design pattern is combined with abstraction of invariants, we have a very powerful mechanism. It essentially enables the instances and relationships needing to be instantiated to be defined in external data that the factory object reads to do the instantiation. When dealing with invariants, it is very common for quite different problems to be solved simply by initializing different instance state data and linking instances with relationships differently. This can get quite exotic when we have tools like XML strings that can be parsed to define objects and their knowledge.

We didn't include any factory objects in either example because in both of these examples many of the objects can be defined at start-up. If they can be initialized at start-up, then initialization is usually relegated to a synchronous service at the subsystem level that is conceptually invoked via an "initialize" message to the subsystem interface at start-up. Therefore, the synchronous service effectively becomes a factory operation in the subsystem interface. In turn, that makes it a bridge, so it is outside the subject matter (albeit intimately related to it). In addition, we didn't include factory objects for the dynamically instantiated objects just to keep things simple.

---

20. The acronym refers to Gang of Four, the four authors in Gamma, Helm, Johnson, and Vlissides. *Design Patterns*, Reading, MA: Addison-Wesley, 1994.

Chapter 10

Associations

A poor relation—is the most irrelevant thing in nature.
—Charles Lamb, *Poor Relations*

It is probably safe to say that associations are the second most underutilized feature of OO development.[1] The problem is that although OO practitioners are well aware of them, they tend not to pay much attention to them. As it happens associations are extremely important to defining the structure of dynamic collaborations. They allow us to express business rules and policies in static structure rather than behavior responsibilities. Most important of all, they are the primary mechanism through which the OO paradigm limits access to knowledge. These advantages won't become entirely clear until we see how associations dovetail with the dynamic description in the next section. So for the moment you will have to be satisfied with just laying the foundation in this and the next two chapters.

Though the notation for associations is rather simple, the topic is not. Properly identifying associations in the problem space borders on being an art form because of the richness of the semantics associated with drawing a single line in a diagram. This is reflected in the fact that in UML the association artifact is the only artifact with a notation element (a role) that describes only what the developer was thinking and has no effect on the software solution. We could easily write an entire book on identifying problem space associations. Alas, we don't have the space but we strongly recommend that you include Leon Starr's book[2] on your reference shelf because it has the most comprehensive discussion on associations to date.

---

1. The most underutilized—and, ironically, also one of the most powerful tools in the OO arsenal—is parametric polymorphism, as indicated in Chapter 5.
2. Leon Starr, *Executable UML: How to Build Class Models*. Upper Saddle River, NJ: Prentice-Hall, 2002.

Definitions and Basics

The high-level definition of an association is the traditional dictionary definition: It is a connection. For purposes of OO development we just throw in a few qualifiers.

> A **relationship** defines the structure of a conceptual connection among object members of different classes.

> An **association** is the UML name for a relationship that does not involve subclassing (generalization).

Once again the UML has chosen to provide its own nomenclature rather than employing the generally accepted OO term, *relationship*. The existence of an association simply says that the individual members of two classes may be logically connected in some fashion. Structure is emphasized because an association says nothing about which particular members are connected. An association just describes constraints that limit which members of the classes may be connected. To that extent it is a set-based concept at the class level rather than the object level. This is important because it allows us to incorporate problem space rules that apply to groups of entities directly in the association definitions rather than in the dynamic description of object behaviors.

Each object will have its own unique set of connections instantiated to specific members of the other class. Even when the object can connect to several objects in the other class, the number of objects it alone can connect to is almost always a very small subset of the total members of the other class. This is illustrated in Figure 10-1.

Here the Physics member of class Course will only be actually connected to the Manny, Moe, and Curly members of class Student. Thus if we have a Physics object in hand, we cannot access any other member of the Student class except those three. From the perspective of Physics, Brad and Trevor may as well not exist, because only the indicated connections will actually be instantiated at runtime. Why just those? Because in the problem space there are rules specifying which connections can be made. In this case those problem space rules are defined by the notion of *course registration*.

In effect, once it is instantiated the relationship enforces those registration rules from the problem space. Even though all of the Courses are connected to Students and all of the Students are connected to Courses, when we look at a particular Student or a particular Course the connections are quite limited. This brings us to the Big Three concepts related to associations.

Instantiation. At some point in the solution we must decide exactly which objects are actually connected. This will be driven by problem space rules and policies, and it is the most important way to capture business rules and policies in static structure. It is also the way that we limit access to objects and, consequently, knowledge.

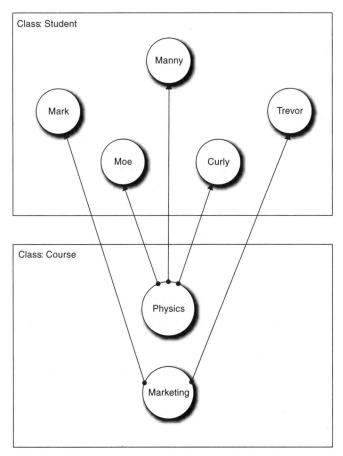

Figure 10-1 *Object-level instantiation of relationships between objects of different classes*

Navigation. When objects collaborate in a peer-to-peer fashion, they need access to each other. Since that access is restricted by associations, we route the message that triggers that collaboration by traversing a path of one or more associations. In short, we say an object *navigates* an association path to communicate with its collaboration partner.

Implementation. To be instantiated and navigated there must be some software mechanism that implements the association. At the OOP level there are many tactical choices for association implementation. But in the OOA model we don't deal with implementation issues, so we won't be talking about them in this book.

The rules and policies that govern instantiation are usually quite different than those governing collaboration. Association instantiation is about *who* participates in collaborations, while the collaboration is about *what* happens and *when* it happens. So we have another example of the emphasis of separation of concerns in the OO paradigm because we will usually instantiate associations at a different time and place in the application than we will define navigation.

Associations are abstracted from the problem space.

The definition of association navigation introduces the notion of a path of associations. Aside from an awful clutter of the Class diagram, we do not want to create a direct peer-to-peer association for every possible collaboration because that is not the way the problem space usually works. In most problem spaces the logical connections between entities of different kinds reflect fundamental concepts. Thus many People may populate a Nation, but not all of them are citizens with a right to vote. Similarly, many of those People may own Homes, yet there is no intrinsic connection between Nation and Home. Nonetheless, there is a path of connections between Nation and the Homes owned by citizens when the government decides it is time for an economic census.

Associations are always binary; they connect only two classes.

In our zeal for the emulating problem space structure in software structure, we want to ensure that our associations correspond to fundamental connections in the problem domain. Generally, the concepts underlying those connections are complex and the problem domain itself will endeavor to simplify things. One way it does that is by focusing on only two kinds of entities at a time. If you think about notions like contract, debt, and sale, they are almost always between two kinds of entities. There are a few exceptions, like parenthood, but even those can be reduced to binary associations.[3]

This constraint further dictates that peer-to-peer collaboration may involve navigating multiple associations in a path. This is an MBD constraint since the UML supports ternary and other multiclass associations.[4] The reason that MBD does not

---

3. As we shall see shortly, an association can have multiple participants (i.e., a Child has two Parents). If worse comes to worst, we can always provide multiple binary associations.

4. Why, I have no idea. In the decades I've been modeling I have never even been tempted to use a ternary association. There are probably a few rare problem space concepts where such an association might be plausible, but those can be expressed with multiple binary associations. *The Unified Modeling Language Reference Manual*, (J. Rumbaugh, I. Jacobson, and G. Booch. Addison-Wesley, 1999) cites an example involving {Team, Year, Player} for the purpose of tracking annual statistics for players on various teams. The example is, at best, contrived, because when a Player plays for multiple Teams in a Year, we would normally only be interested in the Player's annual statistics in the Year; at worst, the example violates 3rd Normal Form. (I know because I have written sports handicapping software.)

support more than binary associations is twofold: They are exceedingly rare in most problem domains, so we do not want to clutter a notation to treat special cases uniquely when they can be handled otherwise. More important, the intrinsic "forks" are inherently ambiguous in the context of peer-to-peer collaboration where we want to navigate a single path to a single object. At a minimum, we would need additional notational support to make the right navigation choices, and the UML does not provide that syntax.

A **collaboration** is a timely interaction between two objects. The participants in collaborations are primarily determined by associations.

Since associations exist in large part to provide structure for collaborations, it is about time to define this notion. Notice the emphasis on being *timely*. The timing of when to do things in the solution is critical, but who should interact is often invariant, at least across significant portions of the solution. So even though associations directly support collaborations, they are very different things, and the reasons for navigating associations in a solution are usually quite different than the reasons the association exists in the problem space.

An **association path** is a contiguous sequence of one or more binary associations.

Association paths are orthogonal to class semantics.

In Figure 10-2, if there is no direct association {A → B}, then for object A to collaborate with object B we will have to traverse a path of individual associations to get there. That path may involve navigating "through" the chain of individual connection {A → C}, {C → D}, {D → E}, and {E → B}.

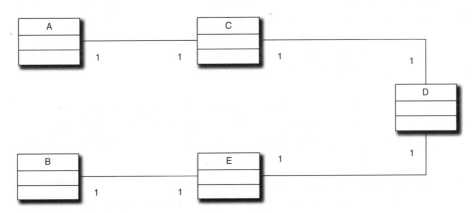

Figure 10-2 *Relationship path for navigating collaborations*

As we shall see in the section on dynamics, we can specify the association path without even knowing what the intermediate objects are.[5] In fact, transformation engines typically implement associations very much like aspects from Aspect-Oriented Programming (AOP); they are semantic structures that orthogonally cut across class semantics. The notion that we can implement, instantiate, and navigate associations completely independent from class semantics is very important to the OOA/D mindset because it allows us to decouple collaboration from specific object implementations.

> Association paths constrain access to objects because associations are instantiated at the object level.

> Associations are an enormously powerful tool for restricting access to state information.

As indicated in Figure 10-2, we instantiate associations on an object-to-object basis so that objects not involved in the association are not even visible, much less accessible. It is surprising that the OO literature rarely mentions associations in terms of constraining access to objects. In fact, though, this is the primary way that the OO paradigm avoids the traditional problems of global data even though object attributes are state variables that persist for the life of the object and are *theoretically* accessible by any other object in the Class model. Those problems are largely avoided because *in practice* associations restrict access on a need-to-know basis. The beauty of the technique is that it uses the problem space's own structure to enforce the restrictions.

But there is another, equally powerful implication of the role associations play in the OO paradigm. Associations allow us to separate the concerns of *who*, *when*, *what*, and *why* as they relate to collaborations. Generally, each of these concerns will have a separate suite of rules and policies that govern them in the problem space. The OO paradigm allows us to isolate each of those concerns so that they can be managed separately. That, in turn, enables much of the robustness of OO applications in the face of volatile requirements. To see that, let's look at how each of these collaboration issues is resolved in the OO paradigm.

- *Who.* Because OO collaboration is peer-to-peer, we need to make sure that the right two objects are collaborating. The primary mechanism the OO paradigm employs to restrict participation in collaborations is the instantiation of associations as just described.

- *When.* The developer provides the sequencing of activities at the UML Interaction Diagram level by connecting the dots of atomic, self-contained behavior responsibilities. Though usually done informally, it can be done rigorously by

---

5. This is in stark contrast to OOPL type systems where we must always know the full type of every object on the path. The ability to fully decouple associations from classes in OOA/D is one of the main reasons that physical coupling is not an issue in OOA/D.

employing the DbC techniques described in the next section. It is enabled by thinking about *when* in terms of announcing conditions that currently prevail in the solution with messages (*I'm Done*).

- **What.** This is a matter of problem space abstraction. We define the behaviors that encapsulate problem space rules and policies. It is crucial that we separate message and operation so that we can define operations as intrinsic behaviors that are context independent.

- **Why.** Basically these are the requirements that determine how the problem solution must work overall. It is the developer's vision of how everything plays together. It is this vision that extracts invariants from the problem space and identifies the static structure of the application.

Thus we have four distinct contexts for these issues and distinct mechanisms for dealing with them in the design.

Notation

Now that we know why associations are important, it is time to look at how we characterize them in detail. Graphically, an association is just a line in UML between two classes, but it is qualified by the following elements.

- **Discriminator.** The discriminator just identifies the association uniquely. Uniqueness is only required within subsystem scope, not across subsystems.

- **Multiplicity.** This defines the number of members of a class that may participate in a connection with a single member of the other class. Because of the symmetry, we have to define multiplicity on both ends of the association.[6]

- **Cardinality.** UML allows us to designate explicit numbers for multiplicity as well as ranges and other features. MBD does not specify cardinality because it is really only needed to address nonfunctional requirements. Since the OOA model does not deal with such requirements, it is unnecessary.

---

6. In the UML meta model, an Association is composed of multiple elements, including two Association Ends. So, technically, it is the Association End with which we associate multiplicity, conditionality, and role. However, the Association End is only identifiable in the Class diagram by the relative positioning of the qualifiers in the diagram. Thus this distinction is an arcane nuance that is important only if we are writing a transformation engine and have to read the model elements from a drawing tool that is UML-compliant. So in the rest of this book we will treat an Association as if it were a monolithic artifact with a set of symmetric properties.

- **Conditionality.** This defines whether participation is conditional (i.e., there may not be any participant in some situations). Like multiplicity, conditionality is specified for both ends of the Association. That is done by prefixing the multiplicity with "0.." if the Association is conditional. (The combined conditionality and multiplicity is read as "zero or one" or "zero or more.") No prefix is needed if the association is unconditional (i.e., there will always be at least one participant).[7]

- **Role.** This is the property mentioned previously where we explicitly indicate what the developer was thinking about when creating the Association. The role describes how a member of the class logically participates in the association. Like multiplicity and conditionality, there is a role for each end of the Association.

- **Constraint.** A constraint places additional limits on the participation in the collaboration besides multiplicity and conditionality. Constraints can take many forms, and we will talk about some these in greater detail later.

In Figure 10-3 an association exists (a line) between Employee and Company such that a particular Company has many (*) Employees but an Employee works for exactly one Company. The association roles are read as, "Company hires Employee" and "Employee works for a Company." The association discriminator is "R1," and the implied collection of Employees is constrained to be ordered in some fashion. The convention is that an end property is placed on the end of the line closest to the object of the role, which is usually a verb phrase.

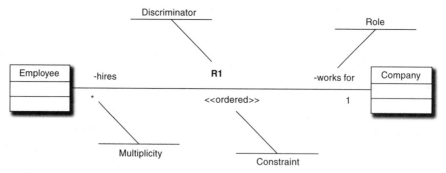

Figure 10-3 *Notation for UML associations*

---

7. For what it is worth, I really, really dislike the way UML handles this. Conditionality and multiplicity are quite different things, and combining them is misleading. Worse, it gets us painted into corners where nothing (the absence of a conditionality prefix) actually means something specific!

There is a special case, though, when the multiplicity is many on both sides of the association, as shown in Figure 10-4.

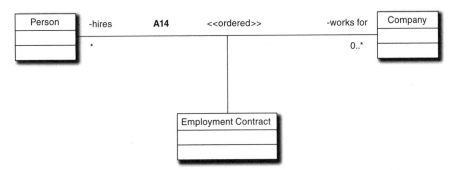

Figure 10-4 *Use of Association objects to qualify associations*

Now the multiplicity allows a Person to work for many Companies at the same time. For reasons we will get to next, many-to-many multiplicity is ambiguous in a pure binary association because it cannot be resolved solely in terms of class attributes (e.g., a single referential attribute as in an RDB). In relational data model terms, it would have to be resolved externally, say through an index. We'll have more to say about this sort of association later, but for the moment think of the third class, Employment Contract, as a placeholder for some mechanism to remove the ambiguity of reference.

The third class is known as an Association class. It may or may not have problem space semantics (e.g., the notion of an employment contract). An Association class qualifies the association in some fashion. If that qualification is about problem space semantics in addition to simple mechanical resolution of referential integrity, then we can use an Association class to qualify associations whose multiplicities are 1:* or even 1:1, as indicated in Figure 10-5.

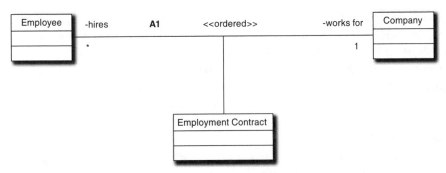

Figure 10-5 *Applying an Association object to relationships other than *:**

In Figure 10-5 the multiplicity is exactly the same as in Figure 10-3, but we still have an Association object to qualify the association. That's because additional problem space semantics is unique to that association, and we capture that semantics in the Association object.

That's all there is to the notation for Associations. You may feel that such a simple view of multiplicity and conditionality can't possibly be sufficient to justify all those assertions made previously about the power of capturing business rules and policies in association definitions. The rest of this chapter will be devoted to exposing why this very simplistic notation is actually an extremely powerful tool in constructing applications.

The Nature of Logical Connections

You probably noticed the repeated use of the phrase "logical connection" thus far. The reason why associations have roles even though the roles themselves don't affect the way the software will be implemented is because the developer needs to keep track of the reasons why associations exist. Thus, roles define the logic behind the connection. It is quite common for there to be multiple possible association paths between two collaborating objects. Usually only one of those paths connects exactly the right participants for the collaboration context, because the rules and policies governing the individual associations along the paths will be different. We use the roles then as mnemonic devices to keep track of the different rules and policies. Thus when addressing messages during collaborations, we need to navigate the right association path, and the right path will be determined by matching the logical connections of individual associations to the collaboration context.

> When associations are navigated, the sender of a message can have absolute confidence that the message will get to the right object without knowing anything about the rules of participation.

This is very important to long-term robustness in an application. Once an association is properly instantiated, it can be navigated in complete confidence for any purpose. When a Parent spanks a Child, the parent is always sure it is the Parent's Child and not the next door neighbor's Child. That's because the rules of instantiation required that Parent and Child be related in a familial manner to be connected. The Parent sending the Spank message does not have to understand those instantiation rules; all it needs to know is that it can send the Spank message to whatever Child participates in that association.

There is no rule that only one association can exist between two classes, as Figure 10-6 illustrates. In fact, the ability to define multiple associations is a powerful tech-

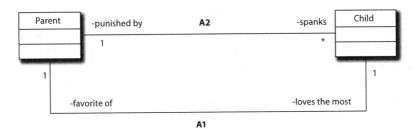

Figure 10-6 *Example of multiple associations between the same classes*

nique for managing collaboration complexity because it allows us to discriminate among different collaboration contexts.

By removing the concerns of participation from the implementation of Parent, we simplify Parent and make it more cohesive. It will also usually be more efficient because most problem space associations are navigated many times compared to the number of times they are instantiated. Elimination of tests to determine the *right* Child for those navigations should improve performance. Thus, as shown in Figure 10-6, the Parent can send a kiss to the favorite child by simply selecting the right association rather than searching through the entire set of children. In this case, having multiple associations will provide a significant performance benefit in practice.

Such performance improvements and consequent reductions in code size (by isolating instantiation to one place) is not serendipity. It is a direct result of correctly modeling the problem space. In the problem domain a Parent "knows" its Child—recognition is imprinted from birth in a highly efficient and transparent manner. So for any subsequent collaboration with the Child, the Parent does not have to think about that recognition; it already exists in mechanisms separate from any thought process around the collaboration.[8]

Multiple associations between the same classes should reflect different participation rules and policies.

This bon mot is directly related to the OOA/D set-oriented view of classes. In effect, the association defines a subset of set members on each side of the association. When two associations are instantiated at the object level for a given object, each association should define different criteria for identifying participating objects. That is, for a given object on one side, each association should normally produce a different subset of the objects on the other side.

---

8. Do not construe this argument as an advocacy for the notion that OO development is a cognitive model that somehow parallels human thought. The only point here is that recognition involves an entirely different mechanism than interaction, and the mechanisms can be instantiated at different times and in different ways. To interact we need to recognize, but don't need to understand, the mechanism of recognition.

Notice the weasel word *normally* in the last sentence. Depending on the specific nature of the criteria rules and policies, it is possible that both criteria might yield the same objects for some given object. In fact, when associations are both * associations, it is fairly common for the subsets of members yielded by each association to have some overlap. The point here is that both associations should not yield identical sets of objects for *all possible* instantiations.

Navigating to Knowledge versus Navigating to Behavior

As we have already mentioned, the OO approach separates knowledge access from behavior access. When we access knowledge, the access is synchronous, and we can't avoid knowing what particular knowledge is being accessed. This is because the only reason the knowledge is being accessed is that it is needed by the behavior in hand.

Fortunately, knowledge is static, so the coupling introduced in knowing what knowledge is accessed is relatively benign. That's because the knowledge always exists as long as the owning object exists. Association navigation ensures that we always get to an existing object, so that only leaves the validity of the data itself. But we access knowledge synchronously, so we know we are getting the latest, most up-to-date value.

In contrast, the *I'm Done* approach applies to behavior. Messages announce something happening in the solution, and the developer routes them to behaviors that care. Therefore, the sender and receiver need not know the other exists, and neither needs to understand the overall solution context in its implementation. So when we navigate relationships to behavior all we are concerned with is correctly *addressing* the message.

Once again, this reflects the basic OO practice of separating concerns. Through the use of associations, and the separation of message and operation, we separate the concerns of addressing and timeliness. The sender only needs to understand that it is time to send a message. The addressing is separated out into the association instantiation. The association of a specific behavior with the message is handled by the receiver. And all of this is managed by the developer at a higher level of abstraction than individual object behavior implementations when the collaboration messages are routed.

Association Roles

Ordinarily we would be tempted to capture the reason the association exists in the discriminator name, just as we capture class and responsibility semantics in their names. But doing this poses a problem because associations can be navigated in both directions, and there may be different rules and policies in different directions. So we identify a role for each end of the association to reflect our purpose in navigating in a particular direction.

Defining association roles properly is very important to good modeling. When addressing messages we need to select the correct association path when multiple paths are available. We use the roles as mnemonics for the underlying rules and policies of selecting participants. That, in turn, allows us to identify which particular subsets of candidate collaborators are appropriate for the collaboration context in hand.

Roles should almost always be asymmetric.

The main benefit to proper identification of association roles lies in the exercise of identifying them. This is because we are forced to think clearly about what the roles actually are within the context of the particular problem solution. One of the most useful tricks for thinking about roles properly is to ensure that each role captures a different thought. Each role represents a single object's view of the connection. Since objects abstract different entities and have unique properties, it figures that participating objects on each side of the association will have different perspectives on the nature of the association.

Whenever a reviewer encounters a symmetric association as in Figure 10-7(a), where each role simply rephrases the same notion of role, it should raise a warning flag. Symmetric associations can very rarely be justified. In Figure 10-7(b) the example provides some useful information about how each class views the collaboration.

Roles should add information not implicit in the participants.

The second problem with the first example is that it is virtually devoid of information content. The fact that one of the participating classes is named Employee already captures whatever insight the roles convey, so the roles are redundant. The level of abstraction is too high. Roles should be focused on the nature of the specific connection *within the subsystem's subject matter context.*

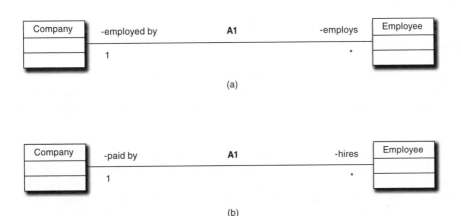

Figure 10-7 *Bad and good examples of role definitions*

In the second example it is clear that there is some sort of collaboration around hiring. That is, somewhere in the problem solution there will be a sequence of activities specifically related to hiring employees. Similarly, in the second example it is clear that the problem solution is going to have to deal with rules and policies related to payroll. That indicates a particular problem context, such as human resources. The roles might well have been {builds tools for, provides plans to} in another, quite different problem context for the same Company/Employee connection.

Roles should explain something about the connection.

The important thing here is that we are describing the *connection*, not necessarily a specific collaboration across that connection. There may be several client objects that need to collaborate with Employee for a variety of reasons. But if they want to limit the Employees they collaborate with to those employed by a specific Company, they all need to navigate through the A1 association.

Now clearly we can get carried away with detail and start devising roles like, "builds rear fender dies for all pickup trucks except those with extended or armored bodies." There is a trade-off to be made here between precision and brevity. We want the most precise description of the connection we can provide in a single phrase. Defining good role phrases is not an easy thing and it requires good vocabulary skills. If you tend to get frustrated trying to find things in a textbook using its index, then you probably want to be sure someone else reviews any role names you assign.

Facetiousness aside, role names should always be reviewed; the more eyes the better. Because formal reviews work best when they just identify problems (as opposed to solving them), we suggest that your process have some mechanism for group discussion of role names that are identified as a problem in a review. This doesn't have to be a big deal with a full team meeting, but a few people trading ideas will usually come up with something acceptable pretty quickly.

Association Paths

We already discussed the basics of association paths. Now we need to discuss some specific design issues around association paths. In Figure 10-8, one likely use case would involve a recruiter requesting student transcripts from the university.[9] Another

---

9. Those of you with just enough knowledge of UML modeling to be dangerous will no doubt think that some of the 1:* associations should be *:* associations (e.g., a Course has many Students and a Student takes many Courses). We'll address that later in the chapter. For the moment, just assume the application lives to do nothing more than place Course grades on Transcripts. In this case, the fact that a Student can take many Courses is not relevant to getting a particular Course's grades onto each of its Students' Transcripts. Remember that we only abstract what we need to solve the problem in hand.

use case scenario would involve a student's transcript being updated for the grade received from the teacher in a completed course.

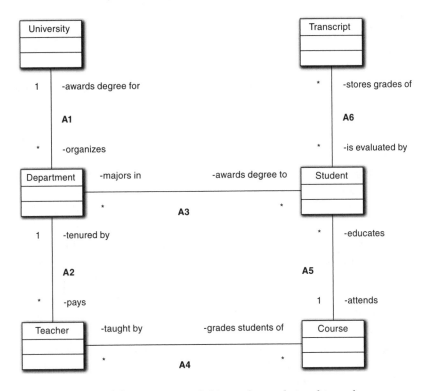

Figure 10-8 *Example of the separation of objects along relationship paths*

Do not add direct associations if an association path already exists that will navigate to exactly the same set of instances.

Corollary: Define the minimum number of associations necessary to solving the problem in hand.

In both these scenarios, a Transcript object needs to be accessed in a collaboration stemming from two different objects (University and Teacher) that are not directly connected to Transcript. We could insert a direct association for each case, but there are two reasons why that is not a good idea. First, it introduces clutter in the diagram. That clutter isn't too bad for two scenarios in a small model, but it will quickly become a rat's nest in a subsystem with 20 to 30 classes with dozens of use cases. As a practical matter we want to keep clutter down so that the model is more comprehensible.

But the most important reason is robustness. If we make a direct connection between University and Transcript, how do we select the right transcripts that the recruiter requested? To do that, University will have to somehow know which transcripts go with which students. (Even worse, the recruiter may want the transcripts for a particular department.) As it happens, the selection rules are already implicit in the association path University → Department → Student → Transcript. We can find *any* particular transcript, *any* group of transcripts for particular students, or *any* group of transcripts for a particular department by simply making the correct searches of the collections implicit in the 1:* associations.[10]

The second scenario leads us to another aspect of robustness. Consider how a student's transcript is updated when a teacher provides a course grade. Unless the school is a one-room university, it is actually rather unlikely the teacher updates the transcript directly. There is usually some bureaucratic process, like a departmental review, before a grade is etched permanently into the student's transcript. And by the time that process is completed, the update task has probably been delegated to some departmental administrative assistant who notifies some scion of officialdom, like a university Registrar, who then delegates it to the Registrar's AA to do the dirty deed.

For the moment let's assume that in the application modeled, the problem solution only cares about the recording of the grade, not the process of recording. For example, the actor in the use case for updating the Transcript may be the Registrar's AA. In that case it really doesn't matter, and we can abstract the bureaucracy into a direct association between Student and Transcript. But it is likely that the AA is working with a list of Students for a particular Teacher's Courses, and a user-friendly interface may want to provide that perspective in the UI form in terms of pick lists to define the search criteria in terms of Department, Teacher, Course, and Student. Quelle surprise! An association path already exists, Teacher → Course → Student → Transcript, that captures the fundamental problem space specification.

Now let's assume that at least some of that bureaucracy is important to the problem at hand. For it to be important to the problem at hand, some set of rules and policies explicitly defined by that bureaucracy must have relevance. At one extreme we need to model the entire process, which means we are missing a bunch of objects, like Registrar, and a bunch of collaborations, like the Teacher submitting a grade to the Department for review. In that case our model is pretty bad, and it might be time for some remedial training because we have missed some major requirements during problem space abstraction.

A more likely scenario is that we didn't miss by much. For example, the process of reviewing the grades may be an important collaboration between Department and

---

10. We will have more to say about this later in the chapter because it underscores a major difference between the OO and Procedural/Relational paradigms. For now just note that even though we still have searches, they will be much more efficient than for a direct connection. In effect we replace a single large search with multiple small searches. Even for O(ln N) searches, reducing N can significantly improve performance.

Teacher, but Registrar and all the AA-to-AA missives may be irrelevant. If that's the case, then the fix is relatively easy. We just have to add a responsibility to review the grade to Department and add another association between Department and Teacher, as shown in Figure 10-9.

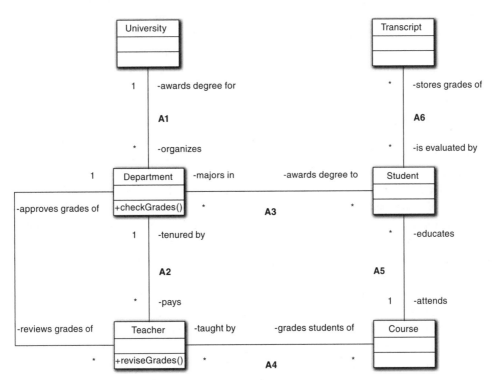

Figure 10-9 *Modeling departmental policy on reviewing student grades*

Now Department has the responsibility, checkGrades, to check the bell-curve distribution to approve the grades. If they are satisfactory, it will navigate to the relevant Transcripts and update them. Otherwise, it will issue a rude message to Teacher to revise and resubmit the grades. So Teacher has a responsibility, reviseGrades, to revise the grades and resubmit them to Department.

The basic thing to note is that the original structure of the diagram remains intact because we only added responsibilities to deal with new requirements. If we already had a direct association between Teacher and Transcript, we would have had to undo that. Trivial as this might seem, it is important to not have to undo things we have already done just to accommodate *new* requirements. (When existing requirements *change*, we usually do have to undo things, but that is a different context.) Though this example is pretty simplistic, the basic point is to capture only the essential structure of the problem space, which greatly increases the chances that new requirements will be additive.

The second thing to note is that once the new collaboration was introduced, the navigation to actually access Transcript—when it was appropriate to do so—was accommodated by the existing association structure, Department → Student → Transcript, because that structure had not changed. But how does Department know which Students must be accessed? That segues to the next point about association paths.

The obvious answer to that question is that Teacher includes the students with the grades as part of the data packet when submitting them for validation. But that just begs the question. How did Teacher get them? By navigating the Teacher → Course → Student association. Yet Teacher would have had to do that anyway when it navigated directly in the original direct association scenario (for the same reason that University had to navigate University → Department → Student anyway to select the right Transcripts for the recruiter).

But let's assume that Teacher does not submit a list of students and grades. Instead, Teacher simply announces to Department that grades are ready. In this scheme Teacher does post an interim grade to Transcript. Now Department navigates Department → Teacher → Course → Student → Transcript to get the grades for review. This scenario might be appropriate in a situation where grades were posted and students could request a review (in which case the new review collaboration is between Student and Department rather than between Teacher and Department).

The important point to note in these scenarios is that they are quite different but they require, at most, a single addition to the association structure, despite the fact that the responsibilities may be quite different and the flow of control, represented by message flows, is quite different. That degree of stability or robustness is only achievable if we include the minimum set of associations necessary to solve the problem in hand *and* we are careful to capture the fundamental logical connections of the problem space. This is why we define connections as simple binary connections before worrying about specific collaborations. It ensures a fundamental view of the problem space essentials.

Conditionality

Conditionality is conceptually quite simple but is often the source of great angst when trying to gain consensus on the proper problem space model.

An association is conditional if a valid situation exists in the problem space where an entity of one set is not related to **any** entity of the other set.

The first problem here is the notion of "valid." We use a broad definition that includes the implication of some span of time where life goes on normally *as far as the problem in hand is concerned.* Consider the example of getting new license plates for a car.[11] There will be some period of time between removing the old plates and installing the new ones when the car will not have plates, which is fine as long as the car is in a private driveway and is not driven until the transfer is complete. However, some people change their plates in the Registry parking lot, and that is technically illegal because the car is in a public lot.

As a practical matter, it is doubtful that even a registry cop would get bent out of shape about such a technical illegality. Nor can we imagine any need for software dealing with auto licensing that would care about that situation in its normal course of operation. We can, however, imagine situations where the lack of plates is important—such as driving without yet installing the new plates. Though rare, such situations have arisen and people have gotten tickets for it. So from the cop's viewpoint it is possible to have an interesting situation where a car is not fully registered even when the owner paid the Registry and got the plates.[12]

When you have the task of writing the control software for Robocop, you will probably have to make that association between Car and License Plate conditional on the Plate side. But until then, we still have a hard time imagining a software problem that would care about that situation. Most software would adopt the Registry view that the Car has been issued valid plates regardless of whether they were physically on the Car.

But wait! What about someone who lets their old plates expire before renewing the license? Now there is a real gap where even the Registry view has a Car VBN without a corresponding valid License Plate. Hmm. OK, that's another case where we need a conditional association that might come up in a much larger number of problem contexts. So when will this association ever be unconditional?

One possibility is the software that manages a fleet of Cars for a rental company. In that case there is likely to be a corporate policy saying we do not rent a car without valid plates, so any car without plates will be removed from the inventory the fleet management software accesses. Now from the fleet management viewpoint, a Car always has a License Plate and the association is unconditional. As a practical matter that will probably be handled by a query constraint on the database. In other

---

11. For readers not familiar with U.S. practices, most states license vehicles for one to ten years. At the end of that time we must renew the license and physically get a new set of plates to put on the car.

12. OK, nit picker, a lot of states define a special misdemeanor for driving without plates that is different than driving an unregistered vehicle. Give me a break; it's just an example.

words, when the fleet management software queries the database for available Cars, it will explicitly invoke the policy by querying for Cars that are properly licensed.[13]

This very simple and very real example has introduced a flock of issues that are tricky to resolve. But the resolution comes down to answering two questions.

1. Is there a reasonable situation *in the problem space* where the entities are unrelated?

2. Do we care about that situation for the problem in hand?

When answering those questions it is important not to get hung up on implementation decisions. Technically, any time you replace one participant in, say, a 1:1 association, there is some time duration where the entity is not related to any other entity. That's because instructions take a finite time to execute, which is a very real problem for asynchronous and/or concurrent processing. However, this is a referential integrity issue largely left to the transformation engine or OOD/P. So just model the problem space when defining associations. Between the methodology and the notation, there is sufficient context to resolve integrity issues unambiguously in the implementation.

Look for ways to eliminate conditional associations.

One reason for this bon mot is the trickiness. If you can find a suite of abstractions that clearly eliminate the conditionality, you also remove the angst over whether it really is conditional. But the main reason is that conditional associations require code to be executed for every navigation context. That is, we have to at least check whether the association is actually instantiated prior to every collaboration. In addition, conditionality usually implies some other behavior for that situation, such as recovery.

Figure 10-10 presents models for a hierarchy. The first example is an elegantly compact representation of *any* hierarchy to be navigated by some Client. The problem is that of the four association ends, three are conditional. This will complicate the code necessary to "walk" the hierarchy, because for every step in the navigation decisions will have to be made about whether the Node in hand is a root node, intermediate node, or leaf node in the hierarchy. In addition, the relevance of those decisions will depend on knowing whether we are navigating up or down the tree. That logic will be further complicated if we need to do depth-first or breadth-first navigations that require back-tracking.

---

13. Better yet, the inventory management software will understand all of the policies related to whether a Car is available for rental and will capture that in a database attribute of Car, such as an hasPlates or isAvailable boolean. This removes the need for the fleet management software to understand all those rules and policies by distilling them down to an available versus not available view. Just thought we'd mention this as a little plug for proper abstraction and separation of concerns in subject matters.

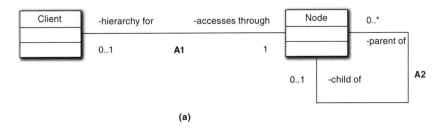

(a)

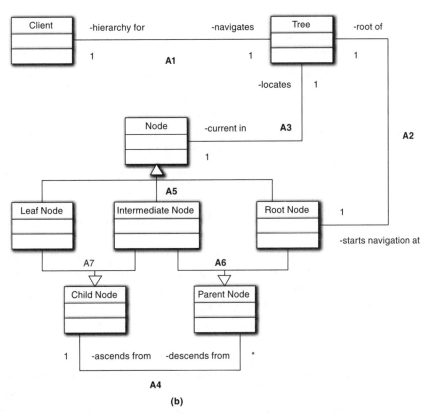

(b)

Figure 10-10 *A model of a hierarchical tree suitable for navigation in many contexts*

But things will be even more complicated if the nodes are not all created equal. For example, in the page hierarchy for a POS web site the content of the pages will probably be substantially different for leaf Nodes, where individual items are described, than for the root Node, which is likely to be a home page or something similar. That will create problems because code for various alternatives will be embedded in Node or, worse, in the Client who is doing the navigating. It won't be long before we have a god object, or a lot of bleeding of cohesion between Client and Node as Client must understand more about the details of navigation.

One answer to this problem is the second example in Figure 10-10. Here we have slipped in some material from Chapter 12 by introducing some superclasses. Fortunately, the relevant notation semantics isn't that big a deal here. All you have to know is that the superclasses in this case provide some very simple-minded commonality across the subclasses, and the subclasses represent disjoint subsets of the parent class' membership. In this particular case, all they provide is a definition of association instantiation. This can be summarized in Table 10-1.

Table 10-1 *Characteristics of Nodes in a Hierarchical Tree*

Superclass	Subclass Commonality
Parent Node	All members of descendant subclasses will instantiate an unconditional 1:* association with Child Node. (As a practical matter, this could be implemented with a vanilla pointer collection class.)
Child Node	All members of descendant subclasses will instantiate an unconditional 1:1 association with a Parent Node. (As a practical matter, this could be implemented with a simple pointer.)
Node	All members of descendant subclasses will have the nonreferential attributes that the Node class in the first example would have. (As a practical matter, every object in the hierarchy will implement the responsibilities of Node.)

Note that there are no conditional associations in this model. This model can correctly describe any hierarchy except the degenerate case of a single node hierarchy. While it is more complicated because of the additional classes, it does a much better job of making explicit the rules for any sort of hierarchical network. That will pay dividends when we actually describe the dynamics of whatever problem is solved by navigating the hierarchy.

The first benefit lies in encapsulation. Consider a POS web site where we would be representing the navigation hierarchy for hyperlinks. In such sites the actual content of root, intermediate, and leaf pages is usually different in significant ways. For example, the arrangement and content of panes will usually be different. Now we can easily encapsulate that logic so that it is completely transparent to the Client who is doing the navigating. There are no decisions to determine what to do when a Node object is accessed; the navigator does exactly the right thing because that is the only option. That is, the navigation rules are implicit in who the Node is (i.e., which subclass it is), and those rules are enforced when instantiating Nodes and their associations.

The second benefit lies in access. By inserting the Tree class we have defined a place for specific traversal algorithms, like depth-first search or breadth-first search, and even exotic tasks like determining the minimum sum of products for a boolean expression. That removes any responsibility for understanding the navigation from Client and isolates it in Tree. It has the added benefit that Tree can keep track of the current node in the traversal via instantiation of the Tree/Node association (A3) rather than Client.

Just as important, we can access the nodes through Node, Parent Node, and Child Node interfaces as the situation warrants. For example, we can navigate up and down the tree in terms of Parent Node and Child Node but then switch the view to the Node view to access the (nonreferential) responsibilities of the node. Again, separation of concerns between hierarchical navigation and node semantics will provide better modularity and simplify the dynamic description.[14] For example, we might isolate tree navigation in a separate subsystem from that where the semantics of the individual pages is manipulated. (We probably wouldn't do that because Tree already isolates that navigation adequately, but it underscores the idea of separation of concerns that the second model facilitates.)

Bear in mind, though, that sometimes the first example will be an adequate model. Where the second model shines is when the root, intermediate, and leaf nodes have differences in attributes or behavior. It is also useful when we must keep track of where we are within the hierarchy (i.e., the notion of current node), when we want to keep the traversal algorithm hidden from the Client, or when the traversal algorithm requires more complex processing like backtracking. If none of these things are necessary to the problem solution and are unlikely to be in the future, then the first example is likely to be sufficient.

Multiplicity

Compared to conditionality, multiplicity is usually pretty easy to figure out. However, it is not always without team angst when establishing consensus. Basically, multiplicity is pretty simple because we only care whether the connection is *always* to just

---

14. This simplification is something you will probably have to demonstrate to yourself eventually by directly encoding both models in an OOPL. When we speak of simplification we are not talking about code lines—because of the class declaration boilerplate, there will probably be a lot more keystrokes in the second model's implementation. The thing to measure is executable complexity. So when you are done doing it both ways, count the executable statements and the number of conditional statements. If the semantics of the hierarchy is at all complicated, you will be surprised at the difference. (You can also invoke code metrics like Halstead's or McCabe's, and they will demonstrate an even more dramatic reduction in complexity of operations.)

a single instance or not. If it is always only a single instance, the multiplicity is 1. If there exists any problem space situation relevant to the problem in hand where the connection may be to multiple instances, the multiplicity becomes "one or more," which we designate with an asterisk in UML. The only tricky part here is deciding what is relevant to the problem in hand.

When abstracting from the problem space only what we need to solve the problem in hand, often that involves simplification of the problem space, and one possible simplification is to reduce a one-or-more participation to a single participation. In the previous examples we had associations that represented the notion of a 1:1 "current" association. That is the most common example of specializing an inherently 1:* association into a 1:1 association by narrowing the temporal scope of participation. In other words, while many objects may be logically connected in the problem space, we may only be interested in *one at a time* to solve our problem.

There are basically two cases we need to consider. The first is the situation where the inherent 1:* association in the problem space is replaced by a 1:1. The second situation arises when we preserve the 1:* association in the model but then decide we also need a separate 1:1 association between the same entities.

Replacing a Problem Space "One-or-More" with a Model "One"

Clearly, the first thing to determine is whether a 1:* association exists in the problem space between the entities. If it does, then the question we need to answer is Do we care in our problem context? For example, is the "*" on A1 correct in Figure 10-11?

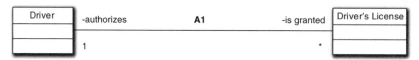

Figure 10-11   *One possible model of mapping drivers to driving licenses*

It is possible for a Driver to be licensed to drive by many jurisdictions and for different purposes, therefore a 1:* association exists in the problem space. If our application needs to know about all of the licenses during its execution, then we can't replace it with a 1:1 because we would have no way of navigating to any license other than the one in the association. This would be true for software that, say, revokes a driver's right to drive in a particular jurisdiction. To notify other jurisdictions with reciprocity agreements it would have to know about multiple licenses.

In contrast, consider the software that records the granting of a license in a particular jurisdiction. In that situation the software doesn't care how many other jurisdictions have licensed the driver. All it cares about is that the driver passed the qualifications and paid the fee in *this* jurisdiction. As far as that particular problem is concerned, a Driver has only one License.

> Unary multiplicity may be used on the source side of any association where the problem space collaboration is inherently one-way.

This conversion is fairly common for *:* associations in the problem space that are converted to 1:* associations to solve the problem in hand. The association of Student to Course in the Figure 10-8 University example demonstrates this. Clearly, a Student may attend many Courses and a Course may have many registered Students, yet the association in the example is 1 on the Course side. That's because all of the use case scenarios and hypothesized software missions provided assumed all we cared about was providing the Students for a particular Course. So the only navigation of that association was one-way via Department → Course → Student. That is, nobody cares how many Courses a Student is actually attending in the use cases. However, as soon as the software also needs to solve a problem like determining if a given Student took any classes from a particular Department, that is no longer true and the association must revert to the inherent *:* situation in the problem space.

While we can apply this sort of mental gymnastics whenever the problem in hand only requires one-way collaboration, it is wise to do so very cautiously. The danger is that we can be myopic about the requirements and overly constrain the solution relative to the problem space. The main reason why we employ the OO approach is to provide agility in the face of volatile requirements. One technique to do that is to ensure the software structure parallels the structure of the problem space.

When we "hard-wire" a one-way collaboration in the association multiplicity to simplify the model for a particular set of requirements, we need to be pretty confident that the sorts of changes that are likely in the future will not require two-way collaboration.[15] So, when in doubt, we should err on the side of the inherent problem space association. If we model the inherent problem space structure, it can be optimized by the transformation engine and we won't have to touch the model in the future.

Supplementing a Problem Space Association with a Second Association

In the Client/Node example of Figure 10-10(a), the traversal algorithm would likely be a simple dynamic iteration over processing individual Nodes. We would just use

---

15. Changing a 1:1 association to a 1:* association is annoying, but it is not a major structural change because the implementation will be well-contained around instantiation. So do not expend much angst worrying about specific changes; just try to envision the general class of changes that might happen.

the parent/child Node associations to obtain the next Node to process. Thus we are essentially just iterating over the set of Nodes in the collection, regardless of how we determine the order of processing them. That processing order is purely a matter for the dynamic description of the iteration, so the 0..1:* association is appropriate.

There is a notion of "current" Node in such an iteration, but it only applies within a single iteration cycle.[16] As soon as we need to keep track of where we have been we are in a different ball game because the notion of a "current" Node persists outside the iteration cycle. That is clearly true if we were executing some sort of breadth-first or depth-first search that requires backtracking. It would also apply, though, if the iteration is outside the scope of Client. For example. someone else might be asking Client for the "next" Node. Now other processing is going on between iteration cycles that has nothing to do with the iteration mechanics.

> Use multiple associations between classes whenever there exist collaborations with different participants.

The notion of *different participants* in this guideline is just another way of saying that we need a unique association path when the constraints on participating instances are different than for other sorts of collaborations or roles. That's pretty obvious for the case where we care about a particular current instance from among a set of available instances. The notion of *current* is a more restrictive constraint than the one on participation in the set of *available* instances. Let's revisit the Figure 10-8 University example to illustrate a much more subtle situation. In that example, the Department → Course → Student path restricted the accessed Students substantially compared to the University population as a whole.

But suppose we have a new requirement where we are only interested in, say, computing the average grades for all of a Department's Courses for both the Students that major in the Department and those that don't (i.e., we want just two averages). We still need the original associations to resolve the original requirements, but will they still work for the new requirements?

It's a trick question, Grasshopper, because it is intuitively obvious that they could if we had an attribute for Student that identified the Student's major. We just "walk" the same set of Students for all of the Department's Courses and incorporate each Student in the appropriate average based on the Student's major. So the real question here is Is that the way we should *want* to model things for both old and new require-

---

16. That scope and the notion of one-at-a-time processing is a direct mapping to the hardware computational models through the 3GL syntax. With very few exceptions we can describe any one-at-a-time iteration in terms of a single set operation. In fact, one AAL, SMALL, did not even support the notion of one-at-a-time iteration initially; all its operations were set operations. But Turing and von Neumann did not go that route.

ments? The answer to this question could easily lead to violence within the development team.

If we look at this issue purely from a problem space perspective, there is a quite natural association between Department and Student that captures the notion of some subset of all Students that major in the Department's discipline (i.e., the A3 association in Figure 10-8). Since the Students that major in the Department's discipline are clearly critical to the new requirements, that strongly suggests that we should use it somehow to resolve the new requirements.

The operative phrase is "use it somehow." There are two problems with this approach. One is that the association would be between Department and Student but we need grades for Students in the Department's Courses *that they took*. How do we get from the subset of Students majoring in the Department to their grades in particular Courses? There are ways to do it, but it will be messy with a lot of AAL code. The second problem is about how we separate the subset of Students that take the Department's Courses but major in different Departments. If you think about it, this is potentially an even bigger mess for the dynamic description.

> There are three ways to capture problem space rules: static structure, knowledge responsibilities, and behavior responsibilities. Always use the right one.

The point here is that the Department → Student association for majors clearly exists in the problem space, but it isn't all that useful for solving the problem in hand. Using an attribute for Major in Student and "walking" the existing association starts to look pretty good, especially when we realize that we have to visit every Student taking a Department's Courses anyway.[17]

But just to emphasize that such decisions are not always easy, note that there is a convenient way to use the Department → Student associations for majors to resolve the new requirements. We have two navigation paths: Department → Student → Course and Student → Course → Department, because the Course ↔ Student association can be two way. So we can easily compute the averages for Students majoring in the Department by navigating that path.[18] We will leave it as an exercise to figure out how to do something similar for the Students taking Department Courses that did not major in the Department. (As a hint, think: symmetry.)

---

17. Even if we need the Department → Student association for majors for other reasons, we do not have to use it to solve this problem. In fact, to instantiate the association collection with Students, we will probably already have a Major attribute in Student that we check when instantiating the association.

18. It would be less easy if we needed to compute the averages for individual Courses because the navigation Student → Course is in the wrong direction to summarize at the Course level.

These two solutions are a very close decision, which is why software developers get the Big Bucks. The final choice will probably be made based on what the team is most comfortable with and what other requirements need to be met. The advantages of the attribute-based solution are that it is simple and works with the existing structure. Its disadvantages are that it requires more dynamic support and is not very elegant in an OO sense. The advantage of the association-based solution is that it explicitly employs static structure in an elegant fashion. The main disadvantage is that if the way averages are computed is changed (e.g., to course-by-course), it might be more complicated to modify.

We have gone pretty far afield from pure multiplicity issues—this was somewhat intentional. You should take away from this subtopic the understanding that the concept of multiplicity is simple, but how it plays within the context of the overall problem solution can be quite complex. When we do OO development we are juggling a lot of Basic Principles that are individually quite simple. But the pattern they form is marvelously complex and a thing of beauty—once we get it right.

Selection versus Participation

We just indicated that we should use multiple associations whenever the participants are different in a connection for different collaboration contexts. If taken literally, that would almost always lead to multiple associations between objects, because we sometimes need to select a subset of instances from a 1:* or *:* association for a particular collaboration. For example, in our University example we might want to establish an honor roll by selecting all the Students registered to a Department who got straight As in that Department's Courses.

We can make a good case for such an association because the notion of *honor roll* is prominent in the University problem space. But do we want a special association of all Students who had straight As in core curriculum Courses, who played varsity croquet, and played lead kazoo in the school band? Probably not. So where do we draw a line in the sand between defining specialized associations and simply providing a dynamic search of a somewhat larger set?

If your answer is "It depends upon the size of the search," then you must have skipped Chapter 2. Go write on the blackboard, "Performance is a nonfunctional requirement. We do not do nonfunctional requirements in the OOA." Write it 1000 times and use squeaky chalk. Any search of an association collection for particular members in the OOA can be optimized by the transformation engine to a dedicated collection if performance is an issue. Therefore, we are interested in some sort of criteria that can be expressed in solution design terms.

The following criteria is useful to determine if selection warrants a dedicated association.

- *Locality of scope.* Here we mean that we do not care about the selection beyond the time it is made (e.g., within the scope of a single behavior responsibility). In the case of our Tree example, we created an association to capture the notion of *current Node* even though we had an existing association path to reach any Node. The reason was that we cared about that particular Node beyond the context of a single iteration cycle that processed the Node in hand. That is, we had to know about it because we might need to return to it later after some arbitrary amount of processing. If the scope where we care is very narrowly defined, then we may not need a dedicated association.

- *Commonality of superset.* This refers to whether there are multiple contexts that require a subset of a particular set. If those contexts lead to different subsets, then the differences in desired subsets can be handled by selection within the more general constraint defining the set from which they are all extracted. Thus we might want one subset of Students taking a Course who are honors students and another subset of Students taking that Course who major in the Course's Department. The subsets differ, but they are all derived from the same set of Students taking a particular Course. If the superset is already well constrained it may not be worthwhile to raise small differences in subsets to the level of associations.

- *Consistency of selection.* Here we mean that the same subset is always accessed from a given context. When a Student's grades are requested, it might be for Irving Frumpkin or Xerxes Trickleingens. That is, the particular member or subset of members varies from one navigation to the next for the same collaborative purpose. This sort of thing cannot be reasonably expressed as a structural participation because it is inherently dynamic.

In the end, though, choosing between additional associations is largely a matter of judgment. The key idea here is that the decision has nothing to do with performance. The choice should be made on the basis of which approach seems to have the best fit to the problem space for the problem in hand.

Constraints

Association constraints provide an additional limitation on the participants in a connection. This is actually just an alternative to expressing selections. The presence of an association constraint simply limits the connectable instances to a subset of those implicitly available based on the association roles, conditionality, and mutiplicity.

The UML supports the Object Constraint Language (OCL) to specify general constraints on associations. OCL enables us to provide a constraint at the attribute level. For example, we can restrict the association from Department to Student to include only students whose grade point average qualifies them for some special honor, like Dean's List recognition. Such a constraint depends upon the value of a GPA attribute, not the identity of the Student.

Such constraints are almost always inherently dynamic because attributes change over the life of the participants. Thus a Student may join or leave the Dean's List based on a single new Course grade. In MBD, all dynamic constraints on associations are dealt with in AAL. In other words, the relevant rules of dynamic constraints are encoded when the association is instantiated or as WHERE conditional clauses on association navigations. So in MBD, OCL is only needed to describe static constraints on associations in the Class diagram. Since static constraints beyond those in roles are quite rare, we are not going to talk about OCL at all, other than the very special situations that follow.

One fairly common constraint on * associations is that the collection is ordered. This is indicated by attaching the {ordered} qualifier to an association. All we care about is that the collection is somehow ordered. (This is similar to 1 versus * for multiplicity; different classes of implementations are required for ordered versus unordered collections.)

The second fairly common static constraint is related to association loops in the Class model. It is quite common for associations to form loops. Consider Figure 10-8 again. The set of associations A2, A3, A4, and A5 form a loop, so we could navigate from Student to Course via A3 → A2 → A4 or via A5. The interesting question is: Do we want to reach the same objects when navigating both paths from a given Department?

In Figure 10-8, the answer is no because there is no constraint requiring that. When we navigate A5, we get the set of Courses for which Students majoring in the Department have registered. When we navigate A3 → A2 → A4 we get the set of Courses that the Department's Teachers teach. But there is nothing to prevent a Student from registering for a Course in a Department that is not the Student's major. So typically we will reach a significantly larger subset of Courses navigating via A5 than we get navigating via A3 → A2 → A4. For the problem as stated, that is quite reasonable.

But what if we were only interested in Courses taught by the Department? That might be true if our problem were simply to correlate Student performance versus various Teachers *within the Department*. Now we don't care how many Courses the Students majoring in the Department take outside the Department, so we would exclude them from the A5 collection as if they didn't exist when we instantiated A5. In that case we would expect to reach exactly the same classes via both routes, right?

Not quite, Grasshopper. It is possible that a Teacher teaches a Department Course that is attended only by Students that are not Department majors.[19] We really do need to think these sorts of things through. However, the real problem here is worse than that. Associations are instantiated at the object level. Therefore, what we really need to consider is the situation when we have a particular Student, say Irving Frumpkin, and we want the Courses so we can compute his average. When we navigate A5, we get only the Courses Irving is taking. But when we navigate A3 → A2 → A4, we still get every Course taught by every Teacher in Irving's Department even though we started with only Irving.

The bottom line? In this problem space with these associations it just isn't reasonable to reach exactly the same Course objects via A5 versus A3 → A2 → A4 when we start from Irving. So when would we have such a constraint? The short answer is that we have such constraints when they are in the problem space.

In the situation of Figure 10-12, there is a problem space constraint that the pool of possible jury members for trials in a district must be registered voters of that district. There is another problem space constraint that says that Trials are presided over by a District Judge. Now if we are in a given District, say Eastern Middlesex County,

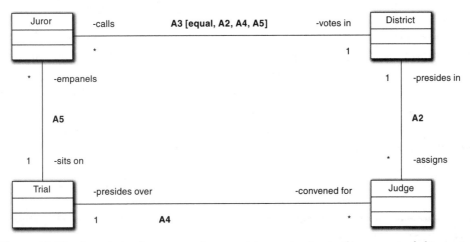

Figure 10-12 *Association loop constraints requiring navigation to the same set of objects via either path*

---

19. This is more common than we might think. As a physics major I was required to take a special flavor of physical chemistry that was taught by the chemistry department. However, to my knowledge no chemistry major ever took that course. That was because it was an elective for them, and they knew it was taught at 8 AM in an overheated lecture hall by a professor with the most monotone presentation I have ever encountered. So the only people taking the course were physics majors for whom it was required.

we can get to a set of Jurors navigating A3 or navigating A2 → A4 → A5. Either way, we always get to exactly the same set of Jurors—because the problem space *requires* that.

We designate that static constraint with "[equal, A2, A4, A5]" that qualifies the A3 discriminator. We read this to mean we get to the same set via A3 as we would get via A2 → A4 → A5. Now let's make a small change in the Class diagram and substitute Voter for Juror, as in Figure 10-13. Is the constraint still valid?

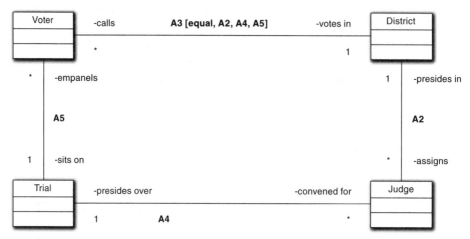

Figure 10-13   *Association loop constraints where the set of objects reached on one path must be a subset of the objects reached along another path*

Now we can have Voters who are not empaneled on juries due to age, infirmity, or whatever. So the set we get navigating A2 → A4 → A5 is a subset of the set we obtain by navigating A3, and the constraint is incorrect. This is another somewhat common situation.

Association Classes

We've already talked about these classes in Chapter 3 and when discussing definitions and notation here. The goal here is to talk about their importance when they are not simply a placeholder for a special implementation. If their only significance was to be such a placeholder, they would be superfluous because that is implicit in an association with *:* multiplicity.

The interesting situation exists when there is a real problem space entity that logically has the responsibility for understanding the rules and policies of connection.

For *:* associations those rules and policies are likely to be fairly complex, so it is likely that such an entity exists. That's because most problem spaces are pretty well organized around notions like divide-and-conquer, centralization of responsibilities, and separation of responsibilities. So *:* connections are usually converted to two 1:* connections in the problem space. (We will talk about such conversions in more detail shortly.)

> The value of including Association classes lies in encouraging the developer to think about the problem space rather than specifying the implementation.

We should always look for a problem space entity that logically captures the referential integrity rules and policies for the connection. The degree of attention devoted should be similar to that devoted to properly identifying association roles.

As an example, let's revisit the University example assuming our software has something more interesting to do than simply get Course grades onto Transcripts. Then it may become relevant that Students can take multiple Courses at the same time and Courses may be taught by more than one Teacher, as indicated in Figure 10-14.

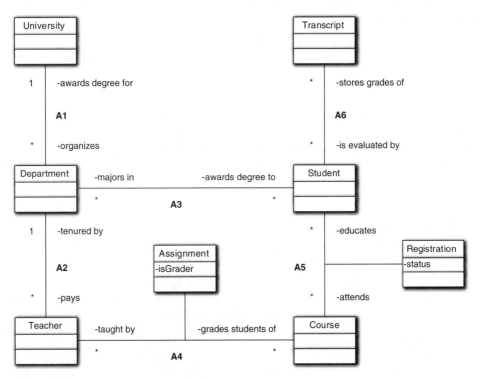

Figure 10-14 *Model expanded to deal with *:* associations*

The first thing to note is that we could easily find a problem space entity for the Student ↔ Course association because most universities require Students to register for each Course they plan to attend. So there is probably already an appropriate concept like *course registration* that captures the bureaucratic details. It is somewhat trickier to come up with a problem space entity for Teacher ↔ Course. But if we think about how teachers are matched up with courses in practice, we find that they are assigned there by a department. So there is likely to be a notion of *faculty assignment* in the problem space.

In fact, Department itself might be the associative object. There is no rule that an associative object can't have associations with other classes. Nor is there any rule that precludes Department from having a direct association with Teacher in addition to its role in assigning Teachers to Courses. Such associations are related to Department's other responsibilities in the problem solution.

The second thing to note is that both these entities are quite conceptual. This is very common with association classes because there is usually some problem space activity for assigning each individual connection. That activity needs to be abstracted into a class, probably through anthropomorphization, and conceptual entities are pretty useful for that.

> When looking for problem space entities for Association classes, look for activities related to forming the connection, and then seek a conceptual entity that would logically abstract that behavior.

The third thing to note is that the entities have interesting properties abstracted from the problem space. Thus, because most universities allow students to take courses as "listeners" rather than for credit[20] (i.e., they sit in on lectures but don't do the homework or exams), we have the notion of a Status for the connection. Similarly, we have can have different flavors of teachers for a course, such as lecturers and

---

20. One of my fonder undergraduate memories if of taking a graduate course in theoretical geology given by a visiting professor from Britain. Basically the course was about applying thermodynamics to geologic processes, such as mountain building (e.g., mountain building was caused by entropy changes deep in the Earth). It was way over my head, since what little I had ever learned about thermo had been long since forgotten. There were about twenty people attending the course. He used the English system, so the grade was solely based on a 3-hour final exam. I showed up for the exam and only two others were there; everyone else knew something we didn't and had taken it as a listener. After half an hour I had irrefutably established that I didn't even know what the questions were asking, much less the answers. About that time one of the others crumpled his answer booklet into a ball, tossed it in the waste basket, and walked out. Since the course was graded on a curve, I scribbled down a few thermo formulas and handed in my paper for a C. To quote Kenny Rogers, "Ya gotta know when to hold 'em and know when to fold 'em."

teaching assistants, so we can have interesting properties associated with those connections as well.

In other words, the Association class highlights the fact that there are real properties associated with connections themselves, rather than the classes being connected. When a student takes one course as a listener and another for credit, that difference can only be captured as an element of the particular connection. Moving the notion of "status" into the Student or Course would be ambiguous.

Alternatively, one could provide multiple associations between Course and Student; one for the set of Students taking the Course for credit and another for the set of Students taking the Course as listeners. That is a valid solution but it has the disadvantage of rigidity. If one subsequently adds the notion of pass/fail versus A–F grading as an option, one will have to create a new association and explicitly provide rules and policies for instantiation. However, if the notions of *status* and *grading policy* are captured as attributes, then the static model's associations are unchanged because all that is modified are knowledge responsibilities. This segues to the next point about Association classes.

The most important thing to note is that the Association classes can add substantially to our understanding of the problem space and the solution. In providing a better model they also help to isolate the connection rules and policies so that the application processing will be simpler. Though it is inappropriate to talk about dynamics here, note that with this model it is a whole lot easier to envision what the code might look like.

Look for Association classes for any association.

Like beer and breakfast, Association classes are not just for *:* associations. They can qualify any association where special knowledge or activities are associated with the connection instantiation that can be isolated in a problem space entity. If they exist, then including them will usually provide better insight into the solution. Of course, Association objects are relatively uncommon for 1:1 or 1:* associations. That's because the rules and policies of participation are usually simpler.

Reification

Because *:* associations are usually complex, it is desirable to try to manage this complexity through the principle of divide-and-conquer. One way to do that is to convert the single *:* association into two 1:* associations. This conversion is known as *reification*. The general structural transformation is shown in Figure 10-15(b).

In the reified model the * multiplicity could be on either end of the relationships, so in theory we have four possible combinations of 1:* associations in the reification. Choosing one depends upon how we want to think about the simplification. Figure 10-15(b)

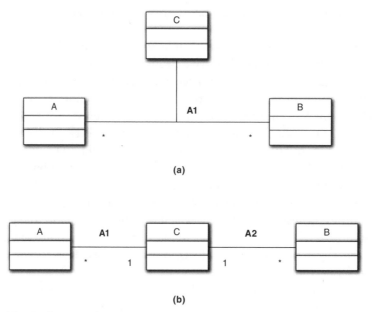

Figure 10-15   *Reification of a *:* association to two 1:* associations*

shows the most common approach where there is a C object instantiated for each A object and a separate C object instantiated for each B object. Each C represents a collection of Bs or As, respectively. During OOP we might implement C as a private embedded collection object within the A or B implementation.

Note that the association class, C, becomes an "ordinary" object in the reification. Since the OOA is about problem space abstraction, we would want C to be an identifiable problem space entity that is consistent with whatever view of multiplicity we chose. So we would not do an explicit reification in the OOA unless C could abstract an identifiable problem space entity. Essentially, we would leave any reification as an exercise for the transformation engine when there was no underlying problem space entity.

In fact, we rarely do reifications in the OOA model at all, even when the association class abstracts real a problem space entity. That's because the choice of multiplicities is usually an optimization issue (e.g., performance and heap resources). We only do explicit reifications in the OOA model when the problem space already makes the choice of 1:* associations—that is, when the problem space structure already uses one particular combination of association multiplicities. In that case, we make the reification explicit because we want to emulate exactly what the problem space does. So the main purpose in bringing up reification was to demonstrate that there is a convenient mapping the transformation engine can use.

Identifying Associations

Look for obvious associations first.

This seems to be belaboring the obvious, but it is surprising how quickly a team gets into arcane debates about obscure associations. It is usually a good idea to initially put any association that can't be agreed upon with a couple of minutes' debate into the Parking Lot[21] and look for another association to define. When the obvious ones where consensus is readily found are done, we go back to the others. Quite often the team finds that the obvious associations provide the necessary navigation paths once they are all in place.

If use cases are available, they provide a very good starting point for looking for "obvious" associations. Select a couple of use cases that represent the most basic functionality or the most common usage of the subject matter. The associations that will be navigated for those use case collaborations are very likely to be the ones most critical to the subject matter.[22] That is, those are the ones where it is most important to properly capture the problem space.

There are two reasons why we want to do the obvious or most critical associations first. One is that they are easy, which builds team confidence and gets the team into the zone. A far more important reason, though, is that such associations have a high probability of being correct interpretations of the problem space simply because everyone readily agrees about them. As such, they provide a good foundation as elements of more complex paths. That will help in determining what other associations are necessary and what their characteristics (roles, conditionality, multiplicity) are.

---

21. This is a term borrowed from standard techniques for managing meetings. The idea is that whenever an issue arises that was not on the agenda and shows signs of generating a lengthy tangential discussion, it is set aside into a "parking lot" (usually an area of a white board where the meeting chairperson jots such issues down). At the end of the meeting the parking lot items are evaluated into four bins: further discussion if time allows in the current meeting; topics for the next meeting's agenda; action items assigned to meeting members for outside work; and those to be ignored. The notion of a "parking lot" is a very effective tool for keeping meetings focused. In this case, it keeps the team focused on finding the obvious associations first and highlights those that may require further requirements or problem space analysis.

22. Recall that in the last chapter it was suggested that the team should employ a rough UML Collaboration Diagram to assist in organizing the team's thoughts. That same approach may be helpful here, but a lot of caution is required because it becomes very easy to create a peer-to-peer association for every collaboration. The goal here is to identify the *minimum* set of intrinsic problem space connections. So we *expect* collaborations to follow association paths rather than direct associations that peer-to-peer collaborations suggest.

While the order in which associations are discovered is pretty straightforward, identifying individual associations is not quite so easy. When we look at a railroad train schedule with arrival/departure times for a bunch of stations, it is fairly clear that there exists some sort of connection between pairs of stations—especially when we are already aware that railroad trains run on tracks. In most problem spaces there is no tangible connection between entities like railroad tracks, so we need to infer connections between stations by the sequence in time. Even when a tangible connection exists it may not have anything to do with the logical connection we need to make. Therefore, railroad tracks may be a useful cue to station connection for train-routing software, but they might be largely irrelevant to a solution that thinks of an end-to-end connection in terms of trip duration where total distance, maximum speed, and number of stops may dominate.

Once we get past the easy associations, the key to recognizing associations lies in understanding why we care about them. While an association represents a mundane structural description of how members of sets may be connected, the crucial issue is why we care that members of sets are connected. We care because they are used in collaborations between objects that are necessary to solve the problem in hand. Associations provide an overall structure to ensure that the *right objects collaborate*. Therefore, when trying to identify associations, we need to understand what associations will provide the best constraints on object access. So we usually look at finding the tough associations from the perspective of known collaborations.

Basically it all comes down to answering two questions:

1. Which classes need to collaborate?

2. Which objects within those classes need to collaborate?

The first question is about responsibilities and direct collaborations between them. We need the same kind of view of high-level collaboration that we employed in determining what entities to abstract and which of their properties to abstract. Let's "walk" through the reasoning for some of the associations in our University example to see how this works.

If our collaboration in the previous University example is to determine honors students for a department, we know that Department, Student, and Transcript will somehow be involved in the collaboration. It is a megathinker view of the collaboration because we don't need to know exactly how the collaboration works; all we need to know is what groups of entities are actually involved.

It is the second question that determines the associations, because it implies constraints on the collaboration. In the honors example we know a subset of Students is involved. Implicitly, our knowledge of the problem space requires that the subset be of Students who are degree candidates in a particular Department. We also know the collaboration requires that the Transcript grades for the Students meet the honors criterion, which will further limit the set's Students.

The natural association of Department with Students enables us to substantially limit the subset of Students *provided that association is limited to Students majoring in the Department*. As a sanity check we ask: Does that restriction make sense in the problem space? Yes, it does, because Students register as majoring in the Department. (The association between Student and Transcript is obviously 1:1 so that it is constrained as much as possible.)

So far this level of analysis involves a lot of selection (e.g., on grades) that is dynamic in nature. What we need to do is step back and look for the structural or static characteristics of the connections. The selection of honors students is a special case of the more fundamental connection between Department and Student. That connection already limits the association to Students who are degree candidates for the Department. A priori we have no way of knowing which degree candidates will qualify for honors; that will be determined dynamically by the grades in Transcript. But we do know that we can only consider Students who are degree candidates through the Department.

That constraint defines the roles for the association. Multiplicity and conditionality are now relatively easy to determine from the problem space. A Student is a degree candidate for one and only one (at *our* University) Department. The Department must have at least one degree candidate to justify its existence, and to be viable it needs many. Similarly, we know that each Student must have a Transcript, and a Transcript contains only the grades for a single Student.

Now we can double-check our associations by doing a mental "walk" through the honor roll collaboration's use case. Assuming we start in Department, can we determine the degree candidates? Yes, they are defined by the association. Can we determine each Student's grades? Yes, because we can reach the right Transcript through the unambiguous association connecting the student in hand to the right transcript.

Whoa! In my alma mater, honors were granted based upon overall cumulative rating *and* grades in the courses of the degree program. Grades in courses outside that department didn't matter except through the minimum cumulative rating. No big deal. There will probably be a cumulative grade point average (GPA) attribute in the Transcript that is updated whenever a new grade is added. This just introduces another constraint on which grades in the Transcript need to be looked at by the department honors committee. That means Course is also a participant in the collaboration, and it will be quickly determined that Department has a connection to the Courses that it alone administers.

Note that we didn't deal with the detailed dynamics of the collaborations to define the associations. All we care about is who is involved and how the participants are constrained. We don't care about particular messages, detailed behaviors, or sequences of operations. The last is a particular pitfall when employing use cases because they are organized by sequences of steps.

Look for collaboration connections in the use case steps, not the sequence of steps.

An obvious question is: Why not have a dedicated association between Department and Student just for honors Students? We would just do the same Transcript checking of all Students majoring the Department to instantiate that association with only honors Students. The answer to the question lies in recognizing that instantiating the association *is* the stated problem's solution.

Now the commonality of superset and consistency of access that we talked about earlier comes into play. If this were the only use case, then it would be correct to have a dedicated association. As we expand our view to other use cases, such as those already discussed, we will probably find that different use cases access the common superset of the Department's Students to obtain different subsets of Students for the use case context.

Make sure the connection is identifiable in the problem space.

This is essentially your sanity check on associations. The roles that are assigned to an association should make sense to a domain expert without explanation. This means that they have to be recognizable notions that are easily anthropomorphized. In order to identify the obvious associations it is useful to check the requirements and the problem space for descriptions of things that represent explicit connections. The sorts for things to look for are

- *Physical connections.* These are things like railroad rights of way, highways, and Ethernet cables that have significance to the problem. Typically they will be abstracted to something more generic like {precedes, follows} for a specific problem. However, a physical connection worth mentioning in the problem statement will almost always represent some kind of association that we need to capture.

- *Contracts.* Often there are implicit or explicit contracts between different sorts of entities in the problem space that are dictated by standards, laws, or other explicit obligations. Thus an association between Company and Employee has merit because of the concrete manifestation of an employment contract in the problem space.

- *Explicit relations.* These are most readily recognized by explicit relational vocabulary in the problem statement that effectively describes a role. Be alert for verbs like "has," "owns," and "uses." Also watch for verb-preposition phrases that imply associations like "defined by," "interprets for," and "sends to." In fact, any time the problem statement connects two different sorts of entities through some kind of verb, the odds are good there is an important association between them.

- *Explicit selections.* These are most readily recognized through explicit constraint vocabulary in the problem statement. These are often reflected in adjectives and adverbs that limit which members of a set of entities, like "largest," "flagged," and "past-due." Associated phrases that provide a comparison threshold or select on a property value, like "more than fifty," "all blue or green," and "only ripe," usually indicate a specific association exists. The trick here is that not all selections warrant a *unique* association. We want the minimum set of associations needed to solve the problem in hand. We may need to step back and seek out a more general connection for which the specific selection is a special case (e.g., the notion of commonality of superset).

- *Whole/part.* Clearly, entities that are part of another entity have a logical connection to it. Thus a Wheel may be identifiable on its own merits with unique responsibilities, but if we are assembling vehicles on an assembly line it is also a part of the Vehicle.

- *Specification/dependency.* Any terminology like "specifies," "initializes," "causes ...," "gets ... from," and "provides ... to" usually indicates some sort of logical dependency or specification connection.

Examples

For these examples it becomes simpler to display the diagram and then discuss the reasoning behind the way the associations were defined. The commentaries in the following tables are intended to capture the kind of thinking the development team would exercise. However, we will focus only on the simple associations because we haven't gotten to the chapter on subclassing yet.

The ATM Controller

Figure 10-16 is the most recent version of the ATM Controller Class model. You will note that the associations broadly reflect the sorts of collaborations we discussed when identifying classes and their responsibilities. The collaborations are reflected in the roles that we assign to the associations. This enables us to "walk" use case scenarios through the diagram to provide a sanity check that our structure is sufficient to solve the problem.

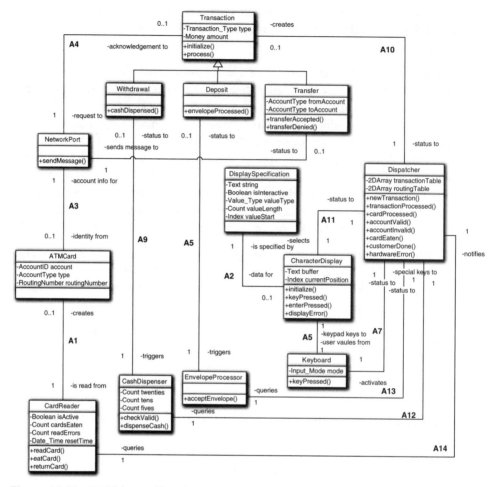

Figure 10-16 *Preliminary Class diagram for ATM Controller*

For example, a customer ATM card is inserted into the Card Reader. The Card Reader reads the data, creates a Card instance (A1), and notifies the Dispatcher (A14). The Dispatcher announces this to Character Display (A11) who puts up a welcoming screen and reports back to Dispatcher (A11), who activates the Keyboard (A7). The Keyboard then dispatches customer keystrokes to either Character Display (A6, if they are from the keypad) or Dispatcher (A7, if from dedicated keys). This dialog continues until Dispatcher knows what sort of transaction the customer wants.

Dispatcher then creates the appropriate Transaction subclass (A10) and transfers control to it with the relevant data obtained from Character Display. Transaction initiates a dialog with the bank via Network (A4), who gets addressing information from Card (A3). The Transaction also needs to obtain data (e.g., the amount) from Character Display (A10 + A11). At the appropriate point in the dialog, the Deposit or Withdrawal objects will collaborate with Envelope Processor (A5) or Cash Dispenser (A9), respectively. When the Transaction is complete, Dispatcher is notified (A10) and the Transaction instance is deleted. Dispatcher then collaborates with Character Display (A11) to ask the customer if there is another transaction. If so, the process is repeated. Otherwise, Dispatcher cleans up by initializing the Character Display (A11), deactivating the Keyboard (A7), and notifying Card Reader (A14) that the customer is done so that Card Reader can return the card and delete the Card instance (A1).

The reason we went through this scenario "walk" is to demonstrate something we talked about repeatedly in this and the previous chapters—the level at which we think about collaborations. (Until now we hadn't covered enough stuff to demonstrate it effectively.) We've said that we must be careful to keep our view of collaboration at a high level, and that is reflected in the earlier paragraphs. There is no identification of specific messages; in fact, some collaborations are explicitly described as collections of messages.

Nor does the description get into detailed behavior. For example, we only need to know that Character Display keeps track of characters from the Keyboard for specific input fields in a display buffer. That is sufficient for the collaboration between Transaction and Character Display. The fact that Transfer needs two values while Deposit and Withdrawal only need one is not of interest at this level, so we don't care how that is handled. Similarly, the entire networking and accounting protocol between Transaction and Network is blithely dismissed as a single protocol despite complexities like two-phase commits (see Table 10-2).

Table 10-2 *Association Descriptions for the ATM Controller*

Association	Commentary
A1	This is pretty self-explanatory. When a customer ATM card is read, the data needs to be stored someplace. We could have eliminated Card and let Network get the data directly from Card Reader, but Card Reader is a surrogate for a mechanical device that would have to read the card each time. This is cleaner and avoids the risk of subsequent misreads. Since a Card is created only when a customer is active, the association is conditional on the Card side.
A2	Also self-explanatory given the relative missions of Character Display and Display Specification. The one tricky thing is the conditionality on the Character Display side. The reason is that there are multiple Display Specifications but only one is attached to a Character Display at a time.

Continues

Table 10-2 *Association Descriptions for the ATM Controller (Continued)*

Association	Commentary
A3	Also fairly obvious, given our previous mission discussions. Since a Card is transient, the association is conditional on the Card side. We could eliminate the conditionality around Card by assuming it always exists and the Card Reader simply initializes the data for the current customer. Because of the way Keyboard and Character Display are activated in response to a card being inserted, this is a viable solution because there is no possibility that the wrong card information may be processed. However, that is fragile because referential integrity in the association depends indirectly on collaborations elsewhere in the model. The reality is that Card exists to hold information for the customer card currently in the Card Reader, and that information does not exist in the ATM's world when there is no customer card in the Card Reader. The transformation engine may provide such an optimization, but we don't in the OOA model.
A4	This association supports a potentially complex protocol between the ATM and the bank's accounting software where validation and posting require a whole lot of handshaking to complete a transaction. That collaboration is so complex that it is difficult to define good roles. The basic idea is that the customer has made a request and the bank needs to approve it. However, much of the hand-shaking is relatively trivial stuff like, "Yes, I got your message and I'm thinking about it." So we copped out a bit and described the Big Picture on the Network side and the Little Picture on the Transaction side. This is mostly a style issue, and many would prefer "+approves" to "+acknowledges to." The key is that everyone on the development team understands why the role was chosen and that the complexity is clarified in the association description.
A5	Self-explanatory. The conditionality exists because only one subclass logically exists from the ATM's view at a time.
A6	Given our assumption of a pretty dumb Keyboard, this is fairly obvious. The only trickiness lies in the fact that only keystrokes echoed to the display traverse this association.
A7	The basic idea here is that the Keyboard is ignored most of the time because we assumed dedicated keys did things like selecting transaction types, and it is activated only when data is needed from the customer.
A8	This is just the subclassing relation, and we haven't gotten to that subject matter yet.
A9	Same as A5.
A10	This association is more complicated than it looks. That's because lots of stuff can go wrong during all the protocol handshaking. Also, the hardware that Transaction accesses may fail. That all has to be announced to Dispatcher because Dispatcher has the high-level responsibility for dealing with failure modes.

Table 10-2 *Association Descriptions for the ATM Controller (Continued)*

Association	Commentary
A11	Another association with complicated communications. Dispatcher triggers the loading of the display and Transaction obtains data from the display via this association. However, the roles only describe the binary association between Character Display and Dispatcher; the association defines participation among members of only those two sets. That other collaborations take advantage of that participation is serendipitous.
A12	This association exists solely to allow Dispatcher to check the state of the hardware in case the machine needs to go offline.
A13	Same as A12.
A14	Same as A12.

Pet Care Center: Disposition

Table 10-3 describes the associations for the Disposition subsystem. (The full Class model is shown in Figure 10-17.)

Table 10-3 *Association Descriptions for the Pet Care Center*

Association	Commentary
A1	This one is pretty obvious; the Pet needs to be stored somewhere. It is conditional because not all Pets pass on at the Center.
A2	Also fairly obvious; the Pet means must be disposed. It is conditional because not all Pets pass on at the Center.
A3	A direct parallel to A2.
A4	Crematorium provides a special service for the Pet. This association is more complicated than the other disposal activities because of the hardware control. It is conditional because not all Pets pass on at the Center.
A5	Clearly every Pet needs a Schedule for processing through the various stages of the subject matter.
A6	The Schedule for the Pet is triggered by Schedule events from the Scheduler subsystem.
A7	A Schedule Event identifies and triggers a Disposal service activity.
A8	A Schedule Event identifies and triggers a Memorial service activity.
A9	Most Schedule Events are triggered through display messages to the staff.
A10	A Schedule Event identifies and triggers a Rehab Session activity.
A11	Rehab Sessions costs are charged to a Pet.

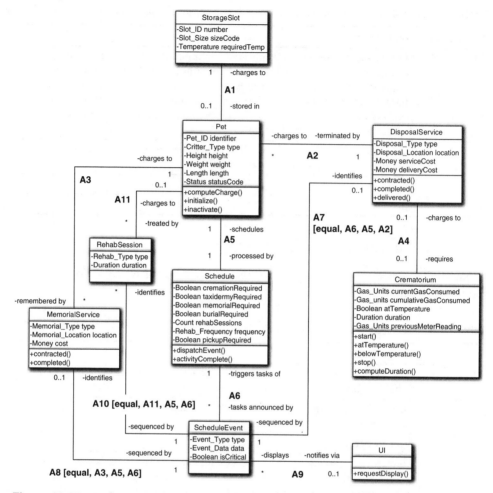

Figure 10-17 *Preliminary Class model for the Pet Care Center's Disposition subsystem*

The striking thing about the Class diagram is the "spider web" configuration of associations around Pet. That figures, because a Pet is the center piece of the subsystem and everything revolves around it. However, that is particularly true here because of the event-driven nature of scheduling activities. The real work in the subsystem is done when Scheduler dispatches its events to the right objects. Since an event is about a particular Pet, that addressing essentially is done by navigating paths that are spokes radiating from Pet.

Chapter 11

Referential and Knowledge Integrity

You can't get there from here. If you could, it would be too late.
—Old Borscht Comedy Circuit punch line

Referential integrity is essentially about making sure we access the right objects during collaborations. Knowledge integrity is about ensuring that any knowledge accessed is timely and consistent. While referential integrity applies to either behavior or knowledge collaborations, knowledge integrity is only concerned with knowledge access. In addition, referential integrity is about *who* participates in a collaboration, while knowledge integrity is about *what* is accessed and *when* it is accessed.

This all sounds quite straightforward, but in practice it has historically generated a great deal of angst. Methodologically, MBD defines assumptions and practices that greatly reduce the problems associated with integrity. The assumptions and practices most relevant to integrity have already been discussed in passing in prior chapters.

- Knowledge access is assumed to be synchronous, and operations access knowledge directly on an as-needed basis.

- Behavior access is asynchronous.

- All objects have unique identity.

- The static model (Class diagram) should be normalized.

- Collaborations are peer-to-peer using *I'm Done* messages.

- Behaviors are encapsulated as cohesive and logically indivisible operations.

- Finally, the transformation engine (or elaboration OOD/P) is primarily responsible for enforcing knowledge and referential integrity.

The last point is particularly important because it really drives how we construct an OOA model. The MBD construction practices ensure that the transformation *can* enforce knowledge and referential integrity in an unambiguous fashion. Thus, we are usually not consciously concerned about those issues when constructing the OOA model because the way we construct it largely defers those issues to the transformation engine.

In this chapter we will examine how these things play together to ensure that the OOA model can be implemented in a manner that enforces knowledge and referential integrity. We will also discuss a few common situations where the application developer must explicitly think about these issues.

Knowledge Integrity

This issue is concerned with two things.

1. *Timeliness.* Any knowledge accessed must be current with respect to the context where it is accessed.

2. *Consistency.* The value of any knowledge accessed must be consistent with other knowledge accessed in the context where it is accessed.

Note the emphasis on the context where it is accessed. Knowledge is always accessed by behavior responsibilities or from outside the subsystem. The behavior responsibility (or external actor) provides the context of access. That is why in OOA/D we want a method to access the knowledge it needs directly, rather than depending on other behaviors to provide the knowledge. This direct, as-needed access narrowly defines the scope where knowledge integrity must be enforced; the scope is bounded by a single operation. As we shall see, it also enables us to incorporate timeliness and consistency constraints in DbC preconditions for executing the operation needing the knowledge.

Timeliness

Timeliness relates to when knowledge values are updated within the problem solution context (i.e., at the right point in the solution flow of control). That is, the requirements will tell us when knowledge must be updated, and we just need to connect the flow-of-control dots so that happens before we need the knowledge. This can be resolved rigorously with DbC if we include the need for update in the precondition for executing the operation in hand. (We will discuss that DbC technique in Part III, The Dynamic Model.)

Since we don't think about things like concurrent processing in the OOA model, all we have to do is connect our behaviors correctly with messages so that we ensure knowledge is updated before it is needed. Usually that is fairly straightforward, and we have a rigorous DbC technique for those cases where it is not. It is straightforward because of the way we abstract behavior responsibilities and connect them with messages. (This will become more clear when we discuss dynamics and "handshaking" in Part III, The Dynamic Model.)

Consistency

The much nastier problem is consistency because there are several potential sources of inconsistency. One common consistency problem arises because of concurrent processing. In a concurrent processing environment there is a potential for someone else to be simultaneously writing the knowledge that we are reading. This is just a variation on the timeliness problem identified earlier in the sense that if someone else writes the value while we are using it, it is no longer current. Exactly the same mechanisms can be used for this sort of concurrency problem that we employ for timeliness problems, and we can make a simple assumption in the OOA:

> At the OOA level we assume that no knowledge accessed from the current context will be modified from outside that context as long as the current context is active.

This assumption makes life much easier because it defers the grunt work of enforcement to the transformation engine. Fortunately, as mentioned above, by limiting the scope of the current context, it is actually relatively easy to provide that enforcement.

A stickier problem for consistency arises when multiple bits of knowledge are needed by the same operation. Thus if we have a telephone number that is represented by multiple attributes for country code, area code, exchange, and number, we need all of those attribute values to be for the same telephone. If our timeliness constraint is honored when the operation is invoked, we can be sure they have been updated correctly. If we extend the above assumption to include all the knowledge the operation needs, the problem of race conditions as some of the values get changed while we are reading them also goes away. And as long as our Class diagram is normalized, we can be confident that we got the correct attributes when we navigated to the object owning them. Once again, the way we did problem space abstraction combines with a simplifying assumption so that this kind of consistency usually is not a problem.

Unfortunately, there are a couple of special situations where we need to pay attention: snapshots and dependent attributes.

Snapshots versus Immediate Access

We have emphasized thus far that it is important to access knowledge synchronously *when it is needed*. When we get around to talking specifically about messages, you will discover that it is relatively rare to have any attribute values in the data packet for a message that accesses a behavior responsibility. Usually the only time that happens is in messages going to or coming from another subsystem. The reason should be fairly clear at this point: We access knowledge directly, so there is no reason to pass it around. We only see knowledge passed around in synchronous services whose job is to deal with knowledge responsibilities explicitly.

But what if the solution wants an historical view rather than a current view? Then we could provide the historical view via message data packets. This sort of situation is known as a "snapshot" view where we collect knowledge responsibility values at a particular point in the solution for later processing. Behaviors operate on those knowledge values as a consistent set even though some or all of the underlying attribute values might have been modified by the time the behaviors actually execute.

This is most commonly manifested in sampling. Consider software that tracks readings from multiple temperature sensors on a mixing vat in a chemical plant. Typically the sensor hardware updates the temperature value every few microseconds. However, vat temperature can't possibly be regulated in that time frame, so we sample the temperature values and apply smoothing. A fairly sophisticated system might do the smoothing based on multiple complete sets of sensor readings. However, when the sensors are sampled may be a variable that describes the stability of the readings. That is, we sample more frequently when the values are changing relatively quickly, and we sample less frequently when the values are not changing rapidly. Thus the consistency rules are applied dynamically.

It should be clear that solving this problem is likely to require processing sets of temperature values that were recorded before the "current" set of sensor readings. To keep things straight, we will need to explicitly manage which samples are acquired and when they are processed. So the operations chewing on the samples can't go and get them on an as-needed basis; somebody will have to hand the samples to the operation, and that message data packet becomes a consistent "snapshot" of the state of sampling at a moment in time.

> When we must use snapshot message passing, consistency enforcement becomes the application developer's responsibility.

The transformation engine has limited psychic abilities, so it can't know when the scope of knowledge integrity has moved beyond the scope of the operation. Therefore, the application developer now owns the problem of knowledge integrity and must explicitly enforce it at the model level. Fortunately, once we realize that a snapshot is required, it is usually pretty easy to collect the snapshot values in a consistent manner.

Dependent Attributes

This is an exceptional situation that appears when a Class diagram is not normalized fully. The situation arises when the values of some knowledge attribute are directly dependent on the values of other knowledge attributes, which is technically a Normal Form violation. The classic case is the equation:

```
Mass = Volume x Density
```

Clearly there are situations when an object, such as Birthday Cake, might be logically responsible for knowing all three of these characteristics about itself. That's fine, but it creates a special knowledge consistency problem because Mass needs to be modified whenever Volume *or* Density is modified. That's something a code generator or OOP developer needs to know about so that consistency can be preserved. Therefore, we attach a notational adornment, a back-slash, to the dependent attribute in the class model, as shown in Figure 11-1.

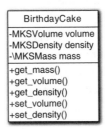

Figure 11-1 *Notation for dependent attribute (mass)*

The getters and setters are included, which you will recall we normally do not do by convention, to underscore another point. Note that there is no setter for Mass. That's because we have defined it to be a dependent variable so we can only modify it through its independent variables. This clearly makes sense, because if we attempted to change Mass we wouldn't know whether to modify Volume or Density or both. So, in addition to signaling the need to address knowledge integrity, the notation also enables the model compiler to detect erroneous attempts to write to the dependent variable directly.

What if the dependent variable is in another object? It seems pretty clear that if all the variables are in the same object, we could simply not provide a data store for Mass; since it can only be read, we could compute it each time get_mass is invoked. But how would that work if Mass is encapsulated in another class? Consider the situation in Figure 11-2.

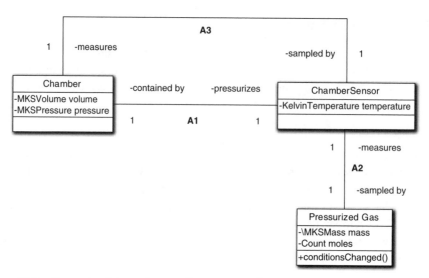

Figure 11-2   *Example of dependent attributes across classes*

In this case, the Mass of the Pressurized Gas is dependent on variables in two different classes. The computation here is deviously controlled by Boyle's Law,[1] which we need to figure out the density to get the mass. For whatever reason during problem space abstraction, it was deemed important to solving the problem that Pressurized Gas know its mass. That leads to a conundrum because Pressurized Gas needs to access other objects' attributes to know its own mass.

The "trick" here is that Pressurized Gas can use a data store for the mass attribute; we just need to ensure that it is updated whenever temperature or pressure is changed. We assume that Chamber monitors pressure and Chamber Sensor monitors temperature, both on some unspecified basis, so they need to notify Pressurized Gas when their attribute changes. This will Just Work provided we use synchronous services so that Pressurized Gas's mass is modified within the same action scope as the independent attribute is modified. That's because knowledge access is treated as instantaneous, and our unit of scope for knowledge integrity is the single behavior action that does the sampling.

The problem is that we can't just update mass directly via a setter; we have to be more circumspect about it by notifying Pressurized Gas that something has happened

---

1. For those who slept through freshman chemistry, standard density for a gas is defined at a particular pressure and temperature for one mole of the gas. That density has to be adjusted for the number of actual moles of gas in the Chamber using Boyle's Law: PV = nRT, where P = pressure, V = volume, T = temperature, n = number of moles, R is a constant. (Avagadro's Constant as I recall. If that's not right, my excuse is that my last chemistry course was fifty years ago.)

via conditions_changed. That synchronous service is invoked by whatever behavior in Chamber or Chamber Sensor detects the change to pressure or temperature, respectively. Why not just set it directly? The answer lies in separation of concerns and cohesion. To set it directly, whoever does the write would have to understand the formulas for computing it. It is hard to justify Chamber understanding that, much less Chamber Sensor. This leads to two generalizations:

> If the independent variables are not in the same object as the dependent variable, the owner of the dependent variable should be responsible for the rules of the dependency.

> If the independent variables are not in the same object as the dependent variable, the developer must explicitly provide synchronization.

The first point is just common sense; encapsulate the rules with the knowledge to which they apply. The second point simply recognizes that code generators do not have psychic powers. In the Pressurized Gas example, it is clear there is a lot of stuff going on in the surrounding context and the mass computation itself. That context will very likely provide its own suite of rules and policies for the circumstances when the mass value must be consistent. Therefore, deciding when to update the independent variables and when to notify Pressurized Gas that they have been modified will depend on much more than just the formulas. (We could make a case that the reason the developer is responsible for knowledge integrity here is that the model was deliberately denormalized, which segues to . . .)

Normalization of Attributes

We talked about normalization in Chapter 1, but it is worthwhile reviewing what we need to do to ensure that a Class diagram is in Third Normal Form. This is because normalization is important to knowledge integrity in a variety of ways. The most obvious way is institutionalizing the maxim of one-fact-one-place, which has been enshrined as a Good Practice since the origins of software development. It doesn't require an advanced degree to figure out that updating information is a lot easier if it is located in one place.

However, there are more subtle reasons for normalization. They involve keeping the information in the right place so that its value is unambiguous, and ensuring that the value is consistent with the level of abstraction. So we are going to "walk" through some of the practical implications of Third Normal Form in this subsection.

> 1NF. All knowledge attributes should be a simple domain.

This means that the semantics of the knowledge responsibility must be logically indivisible *at the level of abstraction of the containing subsystem*. If all you need is a string of digits to pass to a phone dialer device driver, then a telephone number is a simple domain. If you are allocating calls to telemarketers based upon country or area codes, then a telephone number is not a simple domain because it consists of several individual elements with unique semantics that are important to the problem in hand.

One of the most common violations occurs when attributes are used for "double duty" to hold normal values or some sort of flag value to represent a special case where normal values are not relevant. For example, we might define a Rectangle object with two attributes for the lengths of the sides, Major Side and Minor Side. However, for the special case of a square, the Minor Side is not relevant, so we might be tempted to provide a value of UNSPECIFIED to indicate the special case.

That's a 1NF violation because the semantics of Minor Side now has two orthogonal semantic elements: the length of the side and whether the Rectangle is square or not. To see that, note that it would be clearer if we used IS_SQUARE as a mnemonic instead of UNSPECIFIED. In other words, we must understand whether the particular Rectangle is a square to properly interpret the Minor Side length. Therefore, being a square is an important feature of Rectangle that represents a valid knowledge responsibility. That responsibility is quite different than knowing the length of a side, so it warrants its own knowledge attribute.

A variation on this theme is a Position class with attributes of Coordinate1 and Coordinate2 that is used for either polar coordinates (Coordinate1 is azimuth and Coordinate2 is distance) or Cartesian coordinates (Coordinate1 is the abscissa and Coordinate2 is the ordinate). This is extremely fragile because the context of access must somehow know which version of Position it has in hand, which opens the door for virtually unlimited foot-shooting. One fix, of course, is to add an attribute that identifies the coordinate type. But is that legal?

No, it's not. Adding the attribute does not change the fact that the domain of Coordinate1 is either an azimuth or abscissa coordinate but never both at the same time. The semantics of the value is still not a simple domain because an azimuth is not an abscissa. Whoever accesses that value must view it with different semantics to process it properly. As it happens, this is a very common situation whenever coordinate conversions are required, so we need a way to deal with the problem.

In OO development we deal with the problem through encapsulation. We implement the coordinates in one coordinate system or the other within the object. That implementation always uses a consistent semantic domain. We deal with conversion by providing alternative interfaces, such as get_azimuth, get_distance, get_x, and get_y and let the interface handle the conversion.

> If we want to optimize the implementation because the coordinates rarely change compared to the frequency of access, the transformation engine can provide private data stores for azimuth, distance, abscissa, and ordinate in the implementation that are synchronized when one of them changes. However, the public view of the *responsibility* will still be the generic Coordinate1.

An alternative way of dealing with the problem is through an ADT that combines Coordinate1 and Coordinate2 into a scalar by raising the level of abstraction. Then Position becomes the ADT and it is magically transformed from a first class object into an attribute. There is nothing to prevent us from then providing a descriptor with a type to indicate polar versus cartesian that can be used in manipulations. That's fair as long as we can manipulate Position without knowing its elements.

This is usually the preferred solution, and it is worth some effort to see if we can't abstract the clients of the coordinates so that they only need the abstract Location perspective. In effect, we are refining the level of abstraction of the subsystem in this particular context so that Location becomes logically indivisible within the subsystem.

2NF. All knowledge attributes depend on the full object identity.

Basically this means that if object identity is compound (e.g., identity is expressed explicitly in terms of multiple attribute values), then any non-identity attribute must depend on *all* of the identity attributes, not just some of them. Since many OO developers rarely employ explicit identifiers—much less compound ones—it would appear that this is pretty much irrelevant. Alas, that's not the case and 2NF is the most common source of Normal Form violations in OO development. In fact, it is because explicit identifiers are rarely employed that such violations are so common; they represent subtle problems that are less obvious without the cue of explicit compound identifiers.

Assume a typical subdivision with multiple house styles and a single prime contractor for each Subdivision. What's wrong with Figure 11-3? Given the context and the fact that House is the only object shown with attributes, you do not get points for quizmanship by responding, "the attributes of House." Which attributes are wrong and why?

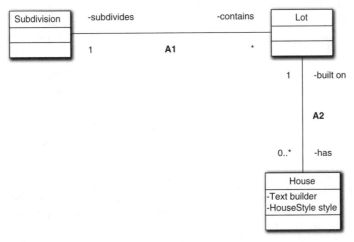

Figure 11-3 *An example of incorrect attribute ownership*

The problem lies with the builder attribute. It depends upon Subdivision, not House, so it belongs in the Subdivision class. While there is a unique builder for each House, the problem space defines the uniqueness of the builder at only the Subdivision level. That is, all Houses within the subdivision are built by the same builder, so associating it with the House is redundant. Contrast that with the notion of style, which is inseparable from House. Let's look at the same model using explicit, compound identifiers, as in Figure 11-4.

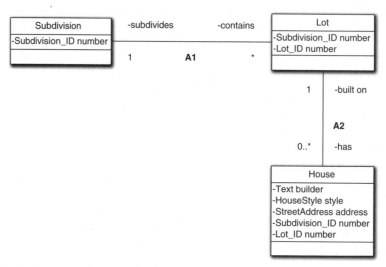

Figure 11-4 *An example of using compound identifiers*

In the diagram, the House address is an alternative identity to the compound identity of {Subdivision_ID, Lot_ID}. The compound identifiers used here are a special case known as *derived identifiers*. They represent a sort of logical decomposition where classes "cascade" identity from the general to the particular and the domain of individual identifiers is not unique to the class. Thus Lots in different Subdivisions might have the same number, but the lots' numbers within any given Subdivision will be unique. In this case, House.address represents a unique identifier for any House in any subdivision. In contrast, House.lot_number is only unique within the context of a particular Subdivision, so builder cannot depend on address because it only depends on lot number.

Note that the use of compound, derived, explicit identities makes it quite easy to resolve 2NF issues. We simply "walk" the candidate attribute up the chain of derived identifiers to the point where it is solely dependent on that identifier (or subset of compound identifiers). For this reason we strongly recommend that you provide explicit identifiers for classes in the Class diagram even though MBD doesn't require them, and you may not otherwise reference them in the model dynamics.

> 3NF. All knowledge attributes depend on the object identity, the whole object identity, and nothing but the object identity.

Going back to the Position example with an added Type attribute, this is not true because the values of Coordinate1 and Coordinate2 depend upon the new Type attribute rather than the identity of Position. That is, they depend upon another attribute that is not part of the object identity.

Fortunately, this situation is usually pretty obvious if we simply think about it for a moment when looking at the class attributes. It is also easy to fix by brute force. The simple approach is to simply break up the class via delegation.[2] In this case the notion of coordinates is pretty fundamental to Position, so it is unlikely we can identify a new class that captures a unique subset of Position semantics in the same sense that we can separate, say, Wheel from Car. So in this case we would probably employ subclassing by converting the Type attribute to a subclass: Position → {PolarPosition, CartesianPosition}. But that is fodder for the next chapter, so we won't dwell on it here.

Referential Integrity

As indicated in the chapter opening, referential integrity is about ensuring that we send messages to the right objects. This is largely accomplished by employing the practices established in the previous chapter for instantiating and navigating associations. Those practices can be summarized with two basic ideas.

- *Available participants.* Constraining the available participants in collaborations is what association instantiation is about. We encapsulate the static rules and policies that determine who qualifies to participate in a logical connection in an object that instantiates the association.

- *Selection.* When there are multiple potential participants we have the option of selecting one or some subset of those participants. Selection is based upon the properties of the individual participants and is inherently dynamic in nature.

We will deal with selection in Part III, The Dynamic Model. The remainder of this chapter just provides some details related to referential integrity to augment the discussion of association instantiation in the last chapter.

---

2. Don't forget to do that break-up in the problem space; the delegated objects must also be identifiable problem space entities.

Identity and Referential Attributes

First we need to talk about explicit identity and referential attributes a bit. While we don't *need* explicit identifier attributes in a Class diagram, they are often useful in resolving referential integrity issues. That's because the Class diagram is based on the relational model from set theory, and referential integrity is resolved with those rules. In other words, referential integrity in a Class diagram works *as if* explicit identity had been used.

However, object identity, when it does appear as explicit knowledge attributes, is somewhat more abstract than in a Data model for an RDB. The object identifier is often better thought of as an abstract handle for the object rather than as a value in a memory data store. Though explicit data values are common for concrete entities in the problem space, such as a customer's name, they are less common for conceptual entities like Meeting. Whether the identity has a concrete value or not, it is just *something* that uniquely identifies the underlying problem space entity.

> A **referential attribute** is a knowledge attribute that identifies some other object that participates in an association with the object in hand.

If you are familiar with RDBs, the notion of referential attribute is identical to that in RDB schemas, save for the abstraction of the identity itself. Unlike object identity, we never need explicit referential attributes in a Class model because we rely on the dynamics of relationship instantiation to provide the correct connectivity.[3] However, they are similar to association roles in that they can be quite useful for keeping track of what is going on in the model, especially if we are judicious about naming the referential attribute. A good referential identifier name can supplement the association role in clarifying exactly which object is relevant.

As an example, consider a high-rise building where individual elevators are clustered in "banks" of several elevators, as in Figure 11-5. Assuming a pedestrian numeric identification scheme, the first diagram captures the essential elements of the problem space. (All the attributes shown are object identifiers.) Unfortunately, it doesn't capture the notion of location. Typically, banks of elevators are clustered in different physical locations (e.g., north side versus south side). The second version does that for Bank because location is quality of a bank of elevators. Since it is unique, we can also use it as identity for a Bank. However, a particular elevator doesn't really care where it is. Therefore, it doesn't make sense for Elevator to view its bankID identifier in terms of location in the building floor plan. Nonetheless, Elevator.bankID still maps to Bank.location.

---

3. As we shall see in Part III, The Dynamic Model, AALs have explicit syntax for instantiating associations that does not use referential attributes, so they aren't used in code generation.

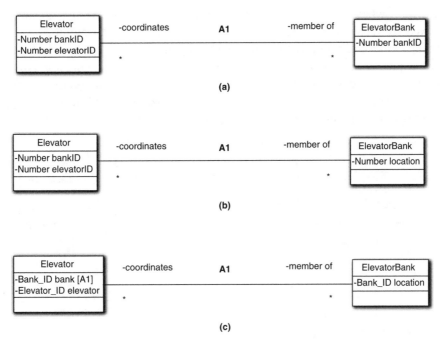

Figure 11-5 *Options for identity and referential attributes*

But doesn't that make it ambiguous (i.e., what the Elevator's bankID relates to)? In theory, the answer is no because it must map unambiguously to the identifier of a Bank, regardless of its attribute name. In practice, though, there is another problem with versions and parts (a) and (b) of Figure 11-5. The choice of Number as the attribute ADT is not a good one because it is too generic. Thus value of 1 could be either an Elevator identifier or a Bank identifier or a location identifier. More to the point, we cannot use both Elevator identifiers and Bank identifiers together in expressions because they are semantically apples and oranges, but we could use Bank identifiers and Bank locations in expressions since they both identify the same thing. In this simple example we are unlikely to screw that up, but it would be better to use more explicit ADTs, in Figure 11-5(c).

Note the inclusion of the association discriminator with the referential attribute. This indicates unequivocally that the attribute is a referential attribute for the A1 association. That is true even though it is also part of the compound identifier of Elevator. In addition, the correspondence between Elevator.bankID and Bank.location is made clear because of the ADT, BankID, that is unique within each class. All in all, the Figure 11-5(c) conveys much more information about what is going on in the model than the first two examples.

As a somewhat more exotic example, consider Figure 11-6. While the example is contrived to keep things simple, the basic idea is that the PartNumber ADT for firstItem and secondItem is the same, so how do you tell which association they map to? We explicitly indicate that by tacking on the association discriminator. Now it is quite clear what we meant regardless of how we named the attributes or their ADTs. So, we can name our attributes and ADTs to maximize the problem space mapping without worrying a whole lot about the referential mapping.

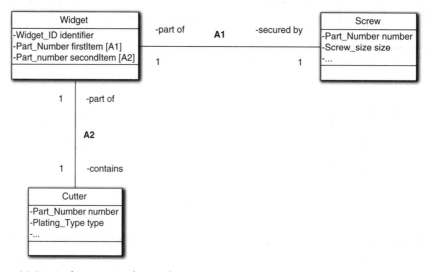

Figure 11-6   *Ambiguity in referential integrity*

Association Loops

An association loop is a graph cycle in the Class diagram. Such cycles are quite common in Class diagrams because we define associations as independent binary associations between classes. Since a class may have an arbitrary number of such associations with other classes, graph cycles are common.

Unfortunately, association loops present a problem for referential integrity. When an object from class A in a loop needs to collaborate with an object from class B on that loop, there are <at least> two possible paths to navigate from A to B. The problem is that the constraints on participation of the individual associations along those paths may be different, resulting in different sets of available B participants depending upon which path was navigated.

We've already seen the example in Figure 11-7(a) and examined some of the issues, but it is worth reviewing. If we take the association roles seriously, it is clear that the set of Courses we reach by A1 → A2 is not the same as the set we reach by

A3 → A4. Though A1 and A3 are explicitly tied to Department, and A2 is indirectly tied to Department, since a Course is taught by only one Teacher (in our example), A4 is not so constrained because a Student can take Courses offered by Departments other than that of the Student's major. Thus the set of available participants for A3 → A4 is substantially larger than the set of participants reached via A1 → A2.

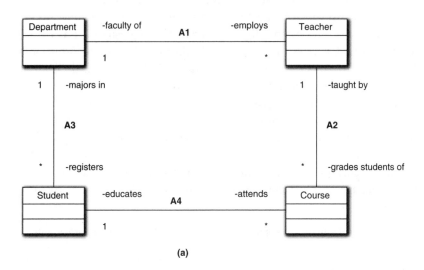

(a)

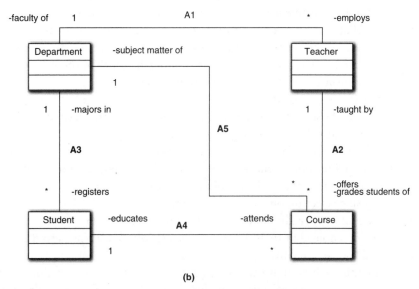

(b)

Figure 11-7 *Navigating the correct association in a collaboration*

The point here is that association loops provide the opportunity to go awry by navigating the wrong path in a loop for the collaboration in hand. For example, suppose this application exists to prepare a registry of students by department and a registry of courses by department. To do that, some object elsewhere in the application will iterate over Department instances and for each one will obtain a list of the Department's Students and a list of the Department's Courses.

Obtaining the list of the Department's Students is pretty obvious; we navigate A3 because that association essentially defines exactly the desired list as the set of available participants. A careless developer might then continue on to A4 to obtain the list of Department's Courses since the Department's Students will be attending the Department's Courses, right? Oops, now we get all the Student's elective Courses in other Departments. (We also miss Courses not currently attended by Students majoring in that Department.) Fortunately, that sort of mistake would require pretty epic incompetence for anyone with even a modest amount of problem space knowledge.

Instead, we navigate A1 → A2. Oops, now we get Courses outside the Department where the Teacher is a guest lecturer. This is less obvious, and this sort of arcane problem space detail is the kind of thing that can readily be overlooked when navigating associations.

Be wary of selections based solely upon the static set of available participants.

The problem here is that the associations reflect the problem space quite accurately but the problem itself requires a finer level of selection than just the available participants in the fundamental problem space structure; that is, the selection requires a dynamic adjustment for the particular collaboration. There is a tendency to equate the collaboration selection to the static participation, especially when they are almost the same.This sort of myopia results in navigating A1 → A2 to get the Department's Courses. The A1 → A2 path is so much better than the A3 → A4 path, making it easy to overlook that it isn't quite right either.

There are two ways to deal with these sorts of loop problems. We can define a direct association whose static participation is defined to be the desired set. The second example, in Figure 11-7(b), provides A5 to do exactly this. Though reasonable, there is usually a trade-off against diagram clutter if we create an association for every possible collaboration. Generally, we only add such associations when (a) they are critically important to the problem solution, or (b) there is no way to navigate the collaboration using selection on existing associations.

Note the use of "generally" above. As it happens, this is one of the exceptions where we have no choice but to add a direct association. But we need to describe the alternative to demonstrate why.

The second approach is to use selection based upon an attribute of Course. There is no apparent way to use selection on the associations in the example as stated because there aren't any handy attributes defined. However, it is relatively easy to add an attribute to Course that identifies the Department sponsoring the Course. Now we can navigate A1 → A2 and select conditionally on the basis of the Department associated with the Course being the same as the Department in hand. We could even navigate A3 → A4 and then select conditionally on the same attribute.

This will work quite well without A5, so why do we need a direct association in this case? The answer lies in what the Course attribute really is—it is a referential attribute. That's because (a) its value is the identity of a specific Department, and (b) its value is meaningless in the problem context unless that particular Department exists. The selection is being based, albeit indirectly, on identity.

> If selection is based upon the value of a referential attribute, there must be a corresponding direct association to the referenced class (unless the attribute is part of a derived identity).

That bon mot may seem a tad obtuse, but all it's really saying is that if we have a referential attribute to another object's identity, we need a direct association to the other object's class. That follows from the relational data model because embedded referential attributes exist to define such associations.

But why does this rule exist? The short answer is that it will make the application more robust. We could safely write abstract action language to instantiate Courses with the correct Department attribute value without A5. However, that construction will be fragile when we complicate things with guest lecturers and multiple Teachers for a Course. Those complications may alter where and how we get the Department value. For example, if initially we create a Course only when a Teacher is assigned, we might navigate through Teacher to Department to get the value. That becomes ambiguous if things change and multiple Teachers from different Departments are enabled.

Relational versus OO Paradigms: Worlds Apart

Previously we noted that the way RDB Data Models use relationships is quite different than the way associations are used in OOA/D. But until now we haven't had enough background to understand differences and their implications. It is important to understand the differences for a couple of reasons. Most software today uses an RDB for data persistence, so we need to know how to bridge the gap between the paradigms. Perhaps more relevant in the context is that a number of converts to OO development from RAD development have sought to migrate common RAD practices to the OO arena because they are familiar.[4] That migration rarely ends well, and it is important to understand why.

---

4. Alas, there is an entire cottage industry devoted to providing infrastructures to make query-based processing easier in OO development. That's fine for CRUD/USER processing, but OO development is overkill in that arena in the first place. Once we are beyond CRUD/USER processing, though, the query-based model leads to reduced maintainability and abysmal performance.

The relational paradigm[5] is very good at storing and finding data in a problem-independent way. It is a general mechanism and is ideally suited to ad hoc navigation of relationships. For example, in a 1:* relationship the relational paradigm places a referential attribute to the 1-side tuple in each *-side tuple. Navigation is very direct from a given *-side tuple to the related 1-side tuple. Conversely, we can always get to all the *-side tuples from a given 1-side tuple by searching the set of *-side tuples for the referential attribute whose value exactly matches the identifier of the 1-side tuple in hand.

That navigation in either direction is completely unambiguous regardless of the problem context, so you can always get to the data you need. More important, it always works for any two piles of tuples related through a 1:* relationship, so it is very general. It is also ideally suited to accessing large piles of related data (i.e., the notion of a dataset of multiple tuples created by a join across tables that selects sets of tuples from each table). That's because the uniform navigation of relationships makes it mechanically easy to cobble together complex queries that access lots of data in a single access. The key ideas here are

- Relationship navigation is primarily for collecting data aggregates.

- Relationship navigation starts at the table level.

- Relationship navigation is most efficient for accessing sets of tuples.

- Relationship navigation is very generic.

The price we pay for that generality is the *-side search we must conduct when we want to navigate from the 1-side tuple. In principle, that search is through all of the *-side tuples.[6]

In contrast, in an OO application we are solving a particular problem. To do that we migrate through a sequence of behaviors that are associated with particular objects, so we always have *a particular object in hand at any point in the solution.* More important, we need to reach the next behavior by sending a message directly to

---

5. Technically, both OO development and DBMSes make use of the same relational model. However, the common usage of the term *relational* is that used here: the query/join/table implementation paradigm associated with RDBs.

6. The DBA can provide optimization in the form of a special index for commonly used navigations. But then we are essentially using DBMS resources to address particular navigation problems, which defeats the goal of providing problem-independent storage and access of data. In addition, the resources needed can be nontrivial both in increased DBMS size and in overhead for adding/removing tuples since every index needs to be updated as well.

the single object that owns that next behavior. There are several key ideas in this description:

- Collaboration navigation is primarily for sequencing behaviors.

- Collaboration navigation starts at a single object.

- Collaboration navigation is peer-to-peer to a single object.

- Collaboration is about a single object-to-object message.

In a simplistic sense, we can summarize the differences between the paradigms as

The relational paradigm is about finding *data* while the OO paradigm is about finding *behaviors*.

The relational paradigm is about *managing* data while the OO paradigm is about *processing* data.

While we also navigate associations to obtain knowledge attributes, the primary goal in solution collaborations is to connect the flow of control dots of behavioral processing in the solution. Since we want tailor our solution to the problem in hand, we instantiate associations so that we can navigate from one solution step (operation) to the next with a minimum of difficulty. In other words, we want to use the nature of the specific problem and its domain to minimize searches. This is why associations are instantiated at the object level rather than the class level; it limits the size of the search set in *-side navigations to only those objects that are reachable.

In an application we **never** want to use relational paradigms like query-based processing unless the problem being solved is CRUD/USER.

Chapter 12

Generalization Redux

There can be only one.
—Duncan McLeod, *Highlander* TV and movie franchise

Thus far we have discussed the notion of *class* in terms of single set entities. The class defines the unique set of properties that all member entities of that class have. In Chapter 3 the notion of generalization was introduced via an overview. In this chapter we will get into some unique issues around generalization. Ironically, though generalization is very powerful, much of this chapter is devoted to the pitfalls of using generalization and will encourage you to be judicious in its use. To review from Chapter 3:

- A **generalization** is a relation that describes how specialized objects may be generalized.

- A **specialization** is a relation that describes specialized details of a subset of objects.

- Inheritance is simply a set of rules for resolving object properties in a generalization.

- Inclusion polymorphism enables substitution of behaviors within a generalization.

- Every member of a subclass *is a* member of its superclass.

- An object represents a single instantiation of the entire generalization.

- A generalization in UML is essentially a Venn diagram from set theory.

Basically the first two points are views of the same thing. OO generalization addresses a rather common situation in most problem spaces: The members of a class are clearly logically related, but some members have a few unique, specialized properties. OO generalization provides a convenient mechanism for describing that. In other words, generalization enables us to deal with minor variations in a set of closely related entities.

Subclassing

When thinking about generalization the obvious example is a taxonomy, as in a zoological taxonomy that classifies various critters. We start with a very generic critter, such as Animal. We then subdivide animals into phyla like Reptile, Amphibian, Fish, and Mammal based on some specific criteria such as living on land, in the sea, or both.[1] These subdivisions form branches where every member of the branch shares the same properties that were used to distinguish that branch from other branches. We can then further subdivide the branches in a similar fashion indefinitely.

Essentially this sort of subclassing represents categorization based on properties. The view in Figure 12-1(a) represents the common tree form that we might see in a paleontology class where the tree's branches represent evolutionary sequence as well as a division of properties. In OO development we are concerned with a more restricted view that is based purely on the subdivision of sets of properties. In set theory we employ a Venn diagram to describe such categorization, as in Figure 12-1(b). The dots in the figure represent individual critters. All the dots contained within a subclass boundary are members of that subset. Conversely, the subclass boundary encloses all members that share exactly the same properties. In the example, the Amphibian subset boundary represents the intersection of the Reptile and Fish subsets where members share the properties of being able to live both on land and in the sea.

Superclass: A set whose members are further divided into subsets and whose properties represent properties common to all of its descendant subclasses.

Subclass: A set containing a subset of members of some superclass based on a unique set of specialized properties or associations.

We organize the properties that are common to all members of two (sibling) subsets by placing them in a parent superclass. By creating multiple levels in the subclassing tree with individual subclassing relations chained together we can create quite complex hierarchical categorization around common and specialized property sets.

Notation and Rules

The subclassing association notation is quite simple. Each superclass and subclass is represented by a normal Class in the Class diagram. The subclassing relation is indicated by a special sort of association that looks like a garden rake. The teeth connect

---

1. True, that isn't exactly the way a zoologist looks at things; we'll address that issue a bit later. Here we are just interested in naïve plausibility at the megathinker level because the specific example is peripheral to conveying what the characteristics of a taxonomy are.

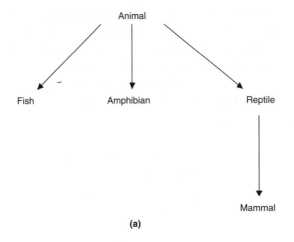

(a)

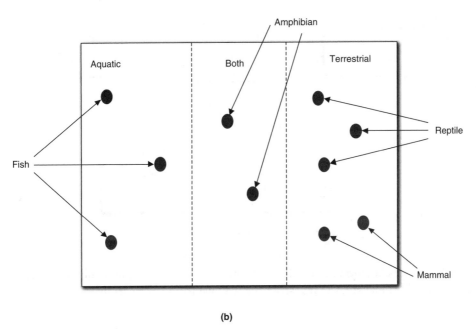

(b)

Figure 12-1 *Mapping of taxonomies into Venn diagram sets and subsets*

to the subclasses, and the handle connects to the superclass via a diamond symbol. Unlike an association, there are no roles, conditionality, or multiplicity. There is, however, a unique identifier to identify the association that is called a *discriminator*.

A subclass can, itself, be a superclass in another generalization. In other words, we can build complex hierarchical trees using subclassing associations. But at each level the superclass has its own unique subclassing association to its subclasses. Thus each subclassing association within such a multi-level tree must have its own discriminator.

Figure 12-2 represents an OO generalization view of our previous example taxonomy. There is some poetic license with the properties because we are just showing the notation, not a real taxonomy.[2]

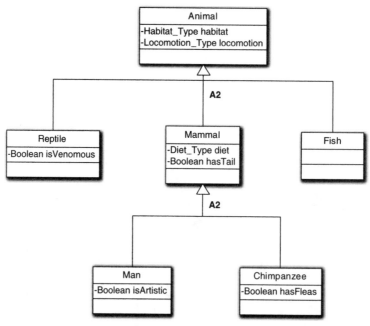

Figure 12-2   *Mapping a taxonomy into an OO generalization*

The OO subclassing relation differs from conventional sets and subsets because it has some additional rules that restrict the way we form the relation:

---

2. Biologists and paleontologists will be jumping up and down about the example because it doesn't make sense for a purist. For one thing, it is incomplete (e.g., no Avians). More important, the criterion for distinguishing the branches is ka-ka. For example, whales are mammals and sea snakes are reptiles, but they both live in the sea. Alas, we need an example that will be plausible to everyone over the age of eight and yet remain a *simple* example, so consider this a first step along an evolutionary path in model development.

1. *The set of members of a subclass is disjoint from the sets of members of its sibling subclasses.* That is, a given member of the parent superclass will be a member of exactly one descendant subclass.

2. *The union of members of all sibling subclasses is a complete set of members of the parent superclass.* That is, if a class has subclasses, then every member of that superclass must also be a member of one of the subclasses.

3. *Only leaf subclasses may be instantiated.* This is a crucial difference in the way the relational data model is applied to OO generalization compared to Entity Relationship Diagrams used in Data Modeling for RDB schemas. More on this below.

Technically UML does not require any of these constraints. But in MBD we would place the UML qualifiers {disjoint, complete} on each subclassing association. However, as a practical matter, since the MDA profile for MBD requires all single subclassing associations to be disjoint and complete, most tools supporting the profile assume it. The third constraint is really a construction constraint on the developer, so there is no UML notation for it; just make sure the subclasses defined are complete sets and this comes more or less for free.

A generalization is **disjoint** if a member of the superclass can belong to only one subclass.

A generalization is **joint** if a member of the superclass can belong to more than one subclass.

One reason the MDA profile for MBD emphatically requires these constraints is that they make life much easier for code generators without significantly affecting our ability to model the problem space. Far more important, though, is that all three constraints are really general OOA/D constraints if we want unambiguous model specifications. Unfortunately we can't back up that assertion until later in the chapter.

There is one important exception to the {disjoint, complete} rule that is needed to support multi-directed subclassing associations in the model, as in Figure 12-3. Whenever a class participates in multiple subclassing associations as a superclass, that is known as *multi-directional subclassing.* If the relations are disjoint they should have different discriminators. In Figure 12-3, the relations would be disjoint if a given Part could be a member of only one of the five subclasses.

If the associations are joint they should have the same discriminator, as in the figure. In Figure 12-3, a given Part can be both an InStockPart and a Nut. But the Part can be a member of only one subclass from each relation.

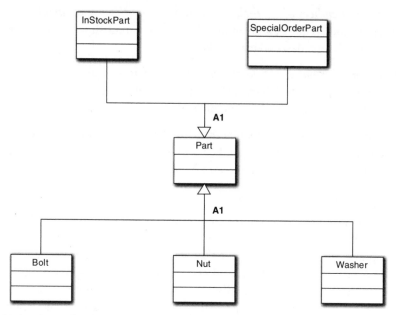

Figure 12-3 *Example of multi-directional subclassing*

Generalization and Specialization

As you no doubt recall, we identify classes based upon all the members having exactly the same set of properties. Figure 12-4 is a Venn diagram with the dots representing various critters where we are interested in specific properties of Humans. The subset boundaries surround members of the species that share the indicated characteristics. Since being a vertebrate is one of the defining characteristics of being a human (in zoological terms), that property set coincides with the entire set of humans; if it doesn't have an internal skeleton it isn't human, no matter who its mother was. On the other hand, humans can lose fingers or toes through accidents, cannibalism, and whatnot, so not all humans may actually have the proper count at a given moment in time, though the vast majority would.

No one would seriously contend that the subset of members who lost fingers or toes after birth were not Human in a zoological sense. Therefore, it would be hard to justify the notion that we needed to define separate classes for Human With Ten Fingers But Not Ten Toes and so on. We would not even seriously consider doing that for Humans who were *born* without the normal complement of fingers or toes due to birth defects. That's because zoological taxonomies are defined based upon subclasses having a large number of properties rather than individual properties, and some properties, like internal skeleton, are more important to categorization than others. Thus we can accommodate minor variations in the lesser properties.

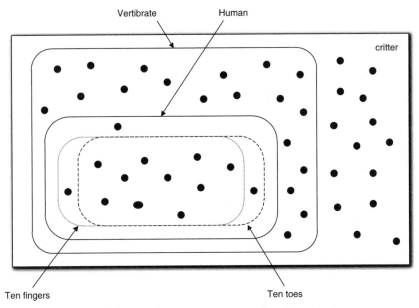

Figure 12-4 *Mapping of objects (dots) to containing subset boundaries*

The notion of generalization fits well with that fuzziness of definition. The collection of properties provides a general view of what a Human is without requiring that it be satisfied in every detail. However, if the membership of a subset is large and the details are sufficiently pronounced, then we can think of that subset of members as being specialized in a unique category. This is the case for Anthropoids whose members all share critical characteristics—internal skeleton, bearing live young, having hair, bipedal, and so on. However, it is quite clear that large subsets of Anthropoid members are quite different in the same ways. Nonetheless, all Anthropoids possess the same general characteristics.

Humans and Chimpanzees are significantly different in a very consistent manner, so a zoologist can tell them apart at a glance and a paleontologist can tell them apart by looking at a single bone. That's because the subsets of unique Human properties and unique Chimpanzee properties are large enough and consistent enough to warrant classification in their own right. Yet they share 98% of the genes in their genomes. Given that genetic similarity, it is difficult to deny that they are logically related in some fashion. Specialization comes into the picture by enabling us to think of Humans and Chimpanzees in general terms as Anthropoids for most of their properties and as unique specializations for a few of their properties.

Consider Figure 12-1(b) again. How do we relate Amphibians to Reptiles and Fish via generalization or specialization? In reality, Amphibians are very real denizens of our world, so they deserve their own class. They have the property that they live on land and they live in water. The other critters have the property of living on land *or* living in water, but not both. So Amphibian can't be a superclass for Reptile and Fish subclasses because all members of those subclasses do not share all its properties (e.g., a Fish does not live on land). That is, Amphibian can't be a generalization of properties common to both Fish and Reptiles.

What does work is to make both Fish and Reptile generalizations of Amphibian, as shown in Figure 12-5. There are a number of problems[3] with this, but the main point is that it is tough to justify Amphibian as a specialization when it is really just a merge of two classes' properties. The bottom line here is that even though generalization and specialization *usually* apply to OO subclassing associations, that is not always the case.

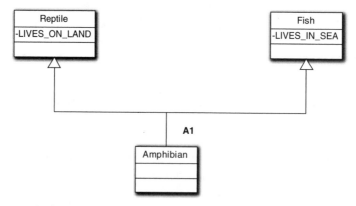

Figure 12-5 *Multiple generalization*

That is not to suggest that you should not think about subclassing in terms of generalization and specialization. On the contrary, they are quite useful concepts when applied generally. The zoological taxonomy was chosen deliberately as an example because, despite its familiarity to the casual observer, it presents a number of issues that affect OO abstraction when creating subclasses. The point here is simply that zoological taxonomies don't map exactly to OO subclassing, and it is important to understand why they don't. In particular, there is one crucial factor related to zoological taxonomies that was not even mentioned: They are based more on Darwinian

---

3. Give yourself a cookie if you noted that Reptile and Fish need additional subclasses to form complete member unions with Amphibian per the second rule of OO subclassing since there are reptiles and fish that aren't amphibians. Good luck on finding problem space classes that aren't thoroughly artificial, like NOT Amphibian. There are other problems that we will get to when we talk about multiple inheritance and composition.

evolution than property sets. Thus zoological taxonomies are not precisely defined when we look at them from the perspective of OO development, where objects' properties are limited to knowledge and behavior responsibilities. Things are further complicated by inheritance and polymorphism, as we shall see shortly.

Categorization

In the end, generalization is really just a form of categorization. We subdivide logical entities into component entities based upon some set of properties. The subdividing is driven by the general notion of generalization, and we have a set of mechanical rules in the form of normalization for organizing the properties in a systematic manner. We also marry a tree graphic with the existing notation for Classes in a Class diagram as a convenient way to organize everything.

> Keep subclassing simple.

This is the cardinal rule of good OO subclassing. It can be theoretically justified in terms of basic OO principles like cohesion. The more specialized properties that are involved in the subclassing decision, the more properties there are in the root superclass, because all members of all the leaf subclasses are also members of the superclass—along with their specialized responsibilities. So when looking at the union properties of all leaf subclasses, the very nature of specialization tends to break down cohesion of the superclass even if we adjust for the level of detail. For this reason, a reviewer should be very suspicious of subclassing trees with a large number of leaf subclasses. That sort of thing can almost always be simplified by employing some sort of delegation.

In addition, simplicity can be justified on a much more practical level. Software needs to be maintained, and adding specializations to an existing tree can be tricky because of the duck-billed platypus problem. Since requirements changes, unlike zoological taxonomies, exist in the future rather than the past, they are chaotically unpredictable. Thus there is a risk that the new class simply won't fit due to normal form problems or LSP problems (which we'll get to shortly), so the entire tree will have to be restructured. That can have some rather nasty implications for existing clients when using polymorphic substitution.

Another reason for simplicity is that the OO subclassing association is inherently static; it exists regardless of the specific dynamics of the problem solution. This means that we must change the relation to affect changes in what the application does, which effectively eliminates the possibility of using parametric polymorphism to apply changes through external data without touching the application itself. As indicated in Chapter 5, encoding invariants while leaving detailed differences to external data is a very powerful tool in OO design. Unfortunately, the subclassing relation is an impediment to doing that because of its static nature. Therefore, to maximize the benefits of parametric polymorphism, we should try to limit subclassing to situations where change is quite unlikely in the problem space.

All classes in a generalization must abstract entities from the same problem space.

As indicated earlier, all of the classes in a Class diagram (other than association classes) should abstract an identifiable set in some problem space. That applies to all the classes in a subclassing association, *including superclasses*.[4]

There is a further restriction on the classes in a generalization that they all abstract from the same problem space. (Though the subject matter of a subsystem usually implies a single problem space, there is no methodological tenet that requires that.) This constraint ensures cohesion by avoiding hybrid objects whose properties are unrelated, which we will talk about a bit more when we discuss composition later in the chapter.

Methodologically, it is good practice to carry this notion further by requiring that the abstracted entity should be of *obvious* relevance to the subject matter. When presented with a superclass of Things With Color, a domain expert should not fix you with a quizzical look and say, "So? I can grok that concept, but I thought we were looking for identifiable things specifically related to my Automatic Scenic Vista Painting Generator." In other words, the superclass entity should have a direct and clear semantic connection to the *particular* subclass entities in hand.

Superclasses should abstract problem space entities that have a specific is-a association *exclusively* to the members of their subclasses.

Recall how we got around the Normal Form violation for a color attribute for different classes. There isn't a Normal Form violation because the *color of* an Automobile is not the same thing as the *color of* a Mail Box or the *color of* a Star. That is, we can restrict the semantics of the *color of* responsibility to the class identity even though the values across classes may be the same (i.e., have the same data domain of taupe, puce, and fuchsia).

This is just an analogous view of the importance of a direct semantic connection between superclasses and subclasses. To justify generalization in moving the Color

---

4. Whoa! How can each superclass abstract an identifiable problem space entity if the object instantiates the whole tree? Good point, Grasshopper; you get a cookie for paying attention. Awhile back we mentioned that an OO generalization is also known as an *is-a* relation. An object is a member of every superclass in a direct line of ascent because the classes just define sets, not objects. Those superclasses just represent more general or abstract views of the same entity. Thus the notion of Vehicle represents a more abstract view of a given entity than a Passenger Car view *of the same entity*. The constraint here is that those more abstract *views* must be known in the problem space.

responsibility to the superclass, the semantics of the property must be generalized; we need a more general semantics for *color of*. Thus the *color of* the Automobile superclass entity needs to make sense in its own right just as the *color of* must also work for a Sedan subclass. For that to work, the superclass entity must be identifiable and its membership must be limited to the union of members of all of its subclasses. The notion of Things With Color is too vague because it includes virtually all concrete entities, not just those being related through subclassing in a particular problem context.

The generalization must exist in the problem space.

When we create subclasses we should not be subdividing software artifacts. Instead, we should be subdividing problem space entities. To apply subclassing the underlying problem space entities must have a recognizable structure to support that subdivision. For conceptual entities that is often quite easy because the problem space naturally subdivides concepts in terms of subsets. Thus we readily recognize that *employment contracts* and *prenuptial agreements* are both specialized versions of the general notion of *contract*. So an *employment contract* logically is a *contract* and subclassing is appropriate.

For many concrete entities, though, any decomposition is usually based on Whole/ Part. Thus an automobile may be decomposed into parts like drive train, body, wheels, and so on in your neighborhood chop shop. But once those parts are identified, they exist in their own right. So a *wheel* is not an *automobile* and subclassing is not appropriate. For concrete entities like Engine Block, subclasses are often based upon some problem space notion of *type*. (This is the dictionary sense, not the 3GL type system sense.) That notion may be manifested in something like a model number. Normally it will be characterized by a set of data attributes that will have fixed values for each model.

One of the interesting challenges in OO abstraction is deciding whether or not to create subclasses and, if so, exactly how to do it. In Figure 12-6, which view is correct? In the figure both versions seem equivalent. Every instance has a unique serialNumber identity. In both versions the instances for a specific model will have identical values for cylinderCount, weight, and cylinderVolume. Are they equivalent models?

If you were awake when we talked about normalization you will realize that the values in cylinderCount, weight, and cylinderVolume are dependent on engine model rather than the entity identity, serialNumber. That's a no-no because non-key attributes should be dependent *only* on the class key (identity attribute). So we can't use Figure 12-6(b) at all. However, Figure 12-6(a) looks a bit weird because the subclasses have no specializations. In addition, every member of a given model subclass will have exactly the same values for attributes like *weight*, which should make us

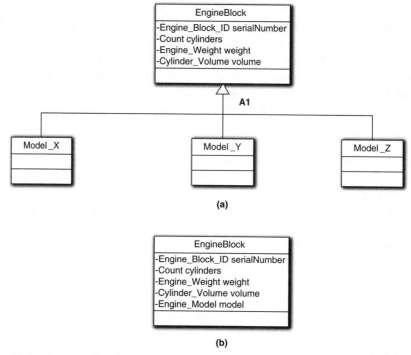

Figure 12-6   *An example of recasting generalization as knowledge*

suspicious that the value is not dependent solely on the object identity.[5] That should be a clue that Figure 12-6(a) may not be quite right.

To properly evaluate this let's look at the possible reasons why we might need sub-classing in practice to solve the problem in hand.

1. To collect common properties (generalization)

2. To separate specialized properties (specialization)

3. To support associations with other objects that may only collaborate with a particular subset of the members of the superclass

4. To enable inclusion polymorphism

The last reason is only of interest if the subclasses have different behaviors in response to the same message, but our objects appear to be dumb data holders. The

---

5. There are situations where this is valid, but they are uncommon enough that reviewers are going to want some darn good justification for that commonality of values.

third reason is actually fairly common, but so far there is nothing to indicate that this situation is relevant, so we can ignore it as well. That leaves us with the first two reasons, which don't seem relevant. All of this should prompt us to look for an alternative to generalization, especially when combined with our concern about identical values for the subclass members.

Consider Figure 12-7. We have abstracted the entire notion of "model" into its own class, each of whose instances have attribute values that are wholly dependent on the object identity, *model*. This directly and more clearly addresses the previous normalization issue. It also leaves the engine block to be the monolithic entity it naturally is in the problem space. In addition, we only need one object of Model for each model identity, and each object will have unique values that depend solely on the Model identity. With this model we have eliminated the generalization entirely. (What we have done is delegation, which we will be talking about in detail shortly.) So we are back to a variation on Figure 12-6(b) where we separate out an intrinsic concept.

Figure 12-7 *Parametric polymorphism as an alternative to generalization*

The points of this example are threefold.

1. We decomposed the entity (an engine block) in the problem space by recognizing a conceptual overlay (engine model) that was already intrinsically associated with the entity in the problem space.

2. Normal form can be a useful tool for recognizing problems.

3. The thought processes were driven by a desire to abstract the problem space naturally in the most intuitive manner for the problem in hand. Thus subclasses without specialized attributes did not seem natural.

It is fundamental to OOA/D design that whatever conceptual mapping we apply be known in the problem space.

Necessary condition: Any domain expert should be able to provide a fairly accurate description of each class in a subclassing association just from the name.

Sufficient condition: Members of each leaf subclass will have a clear and unique role to play in the solution.

This is the ultimate acid test for whether we have properly captured a subclassing association. In Figure 12-6(a), the notion of ModelX exists in the problem space, so the necessary condition for subclassing is satisfied. We rejected it because there was no obvious way that members of the ModelX subset contributed to the problem solution in some unique manner (given the requirements provided).

Fortunately, this example is about as tough as it gets for deciding whether subclassing is appropriate. As a practical matter, in the vast majority of modeling situations subclasses will be obvious because of different knowledge attributes being needed in different subclasses or the presence of unique behavior responsibilities for certain members. Thus any bridge architect will readily recognize that there is a difference between suspension bridges and cantilever bridges for the same reason you will be interested in distinguishing them as Bridge subclasses: They deal with different subject matters and have different provisions even though they are both bridges and share many characteristics. More important, it will be obvious that those differences exist to a domain expert, and there will likely be an agreed terminology for them.

Inclusion Polymorphism

Inclusion polymorphism was introduced in Chapter 3. As a quick review, let's start with a simple example. In Figure 12-8 the client, Problem, needs something sorted. It invokes a sort algorithm to do that. The differences between algorithms are typically performance issues that depend on things like the number of elements to sort.[6] That context is addressed by instantiating the association to the best algorithm, which will be a member of a particular subclass.[7]

From the client's viewpoint, though, they are all the same; they simply sort elements. So Problem sends exactly the same *sort(...)* message regardless of what specific algorithm implementation is invoked. To ensure this all we need is for each subclass of Sort Algorithm to provide an appropriate response to the *sort(...)* message. Thus the actual behavior implementation executed will be substituted based on which subclass member is at the end of the A1 association when Problem sends the *sort(...)* message. That association is instantiated dynamically based upon the context that determines which algorithm is the most appropriate. Substituting behavior

---

6. As a result, we would not expect to see this particular example in an OOA model; it is used here simply because it is so familiar. It is fairly common, though, for behaviors to be selected based on problem space rules and policies.

7. If you are familiar with design patterns, this will be immediately recognized as a Strategy Pattern that enables substitution of an algorithmic strategy based on dynamic (runtime) context. If you aren't familiar with design patterns, just note that this sort of problem is so common that it has been recognized as a reusable processing "pattern."

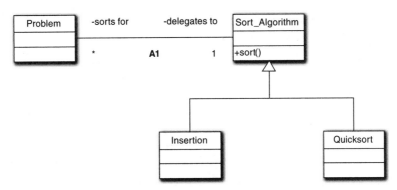

Figure 12-8 *Generalization to provide substitution of different implementations of the same behavior responsibility*

implementations transparently from the client's viewpoint based upon subclass instance is known as *inclusion polymorphism.*

Note that the association between Problem and Sort Algorithm is at the superclass level. An association with the superclass is how we define the scope of substitution. Such an association means that the client is indifferent to which subclass descendant actually implements the responsibility; it will accept the implementation of any leaf subclass that is a direct descendant. If there are multiple levels of subclassing, then the designated superclass will determine the overall "fan-out" of which subclass implementations are acceptable to the client navigating the association. (If some of the "fan-out" implementations are unacceptable, then the tree will have to be accessed at a different superclass.) The way we think of this is that the client navigates to a superclass that provides an interface. The instantiation of the association to a particular subclass member provides the actual implementation when the interface responsibility is invoked.

Figure 12-8 represents the purest form of inclusion polymorphism where only the implementation of the behavior is substituted. In that case, the execution results are not affected because the answer will be the same regardless of the algorithm employed. However, a less pure form, illustrated in Figure 12-9, is far more powerful where we actually substitute different behaviors that produce different results.[8] This enables the program results to change dynamically based upon runtime context without the client knowing or caring about it. In Figure 12-9 a completely different Benefit is computed depending on how the A1 association is instantiated.

---

8. Typically we substitute implementations without changing results to address nonfunctional requirements that are orthogonal to the functional requirements defining the behavior semantics. So at the OOA level, that sort of substitution is usually irrelevant, and we almost always want polymorphic substitution to change the results.

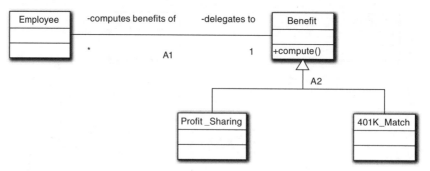

Figure 12-9   *Generalization used to provide different behavior responsibilities*

This is a very powerful OO technique because it separates the concerns of collaboration—like it is time to compute a benefit—from the concerns of defining context that depends upon a separate suite of rules and policies—like determining which benefit needs to be computed. When the *computeBenefit(...)* message is sent, the results are completely different depending on how A1 is instantiated. This becomes clearer when we expand the horizons a bit.

In Figure 12-10 we take some liberties with the UML notation because we do not define the subclass operation when it implements a superclass operation since it will have the same name. To demonstrate a point, though, we have indicated the subclass behavior implementations of the *attacked* behavior *as if* they were specialization behaviors unique to each subclass. Think of the subclass behaviors (UML operations) as describing how the subclass implements a response to the superclass' *attacked* message (UML interface element).

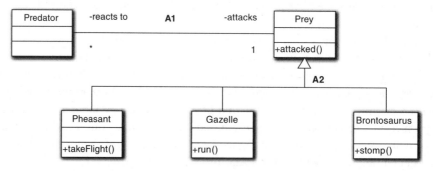

Figure 12-10   *Basic substitution of behaviors through generalization*

In this case, the superclass Prey defines a behavior responsibility for being attacked that will be shared by all members of all its subclasses. However, the subclasses don't respond in exactly the same manner. In fact, when we look at the subclass responses they are so different that it becomes difficult to conjure up a single method name that describes what they all do in the superclass.

Nonetheless, as long as the Prey's client doesn't care which response the critter makes once it is committed to the chase, the substitution is quite legal. It is also quite powerful because we are not limited to the conventional definition of "implementation." In this example, we are really substituting entirely different behaviors rather than different implementations of the same behavior.

That combination of disparate subclass behaviors and the client not caring about which is actually employed is both a blessing and a curse. While it leads to a very powerful means of dealing with context-dependent behavior substitution dynamically, it also opens the door to all sorts of problems that we will discuss shortly when we talk about LSP.

Why {disjoint, complete} Subsets?

We are now equipped to provide a better justification for these methodological constraints. Consider the Predator/Prey example from Figure 12-10. It is unlikely that a lone predator on the scale of a Velociraptor will want the behavior resulting from attacking an adult Brontosaurus. To exclude attacking a Brontosaurus, it wants to navigate an association directly to, say, a Gazelle. Then the Velociraptor is going to get a real big surprise if the member of the Gazelle subset that it attacks also happens to possess the properties of a Brontosaurus.

In other words, we insist on disjoint subsets to avoid exactly those sorts of set intersection surprises when navigating direct associations with a particular class. Whoever is navigating has a right to expect that *every* member of that class will have exactly the advertised set of properties without surprises. If we couldn't count on that, then the dynamic qualification we would have to provide every time we navigated an association would be an intolerable burden on the dynamic model, not to mention opening up copious opportunities for foot-shooting.

The need for complete subsets is a bit more subtle because it lies in a negative specification. Suppose we have a set of subclasses that are not complete. Then there will be members of the superclass that are not members of any of the subclasses. What if we want to access only members of the superclass that are not in any subclass? That subset membership is defined as not being members of any other subset. Such negative definitions can lead to nasty problems when the program is modified, especially when polymorphic access is used (see Figure 12-11).

In Figure 12-11(a), each subclass provides a different implementation of the fly() behavior. Let's assume that in the initial problem context the only other birds that were relevant were all flightless. To access only the subset of flightless birds, we need

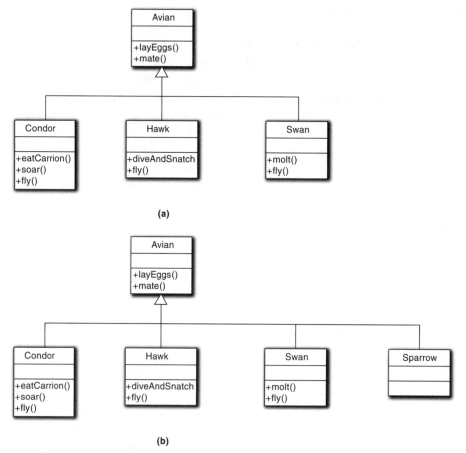

Figure 12-11 *An illustration of why the union of sibling subclasses needs to be complete sets of the parent superclass*

a direct association to Avian that selects member participants based upon not being in other subsets. That is already ugly because it involves testing the nature of the subclass, but it's possible. In addition, it looks strange because every subclass has a *fly()* property. This is because we can't put fly() in the superclass, even though it is common to each subclass, given that it doesn't apply to the other members of Avian. Thus the model looks like something odd is going on, but we don't know what because it is hidden in those "special" members of Avian.

Now suppose the requirements change and we have to add Sparrow, as in Figure 12-11(b). Now we have an ambiguity for whoever does the maintenance: Is Sparrow a new set of Avians that were not relevant to the original problem? Or were Sparrow members included in the Avians that were not subclassed originally? The original developer knows, but not necessarily a different maintainer, because the model is not clear about those Avians that are not members of explicit subsets. In other words, the original notion of flightless birds is not visible in any way.

This problem is especially nasty because it is quite likely the maintainer may not even think about it. The reason is that the problem lies in whoever was navigating that association to Avian to access those pure (not subclassed) Avians. In other words, the problem lies in the context of some existing collaboration that is probably totally unrelated to why the Sparrow subclass was added.

You may argue that in this case it doesn't matter because Sparrow isn't flightless, so the original collaboration is unaffected. True, but the maintainer can't know that without looking at the original collaboration context—*assuming the maintainer is even aware of it*. There are also other ways to break the client. What if Sparrow members are only now relevant (i.e., weren't previously instantiated) but they have no special properties *relative to the problem in hand*, so they are just lumped into the Avian superset? Now the condition for the Avian access is that the members selected aren't in any other subset and they aren't Sparrows; that is, the definition of what an Avian *is* has changed without telling the original client of Avian. That's why negative definitions are bad news.

A lot of words have been put around these two rules of subclassing, because it's amazing how few OO developers don't understand the sorts of ambiguities that violation of these rules introduces. Considering the potential for nasty problems during maintenance, violating these rules should be grounds for breaking the developer's thumbs. Even more surprising is how many OOPL designers do not seem to understand it either. All these problems could be completely eliminated if the language designers simply did not enable us to create a superclass instance without specifying a leaf subclass.

Multi-directional Subclassing, Multiple Inheritance, and Composition

The same generalization may be involved in multiple subclassing relations. That is, a superclass may have multiple subclassing associations with different subsets. This is known as multi-directional or compound subclassing. Some examples appear in Figure 12-12.

The interesting question in Figure 12-12(a) is: What properties does a leaf Product object have? A Product is either a StockItem or a SpecialOrderItem, but not both. Similarly, it is either a HardwareItem or a SoftwareItem, but not both. But can a Product be both a StockItem and a SoftwareItem? In this case, the answer is *yes*

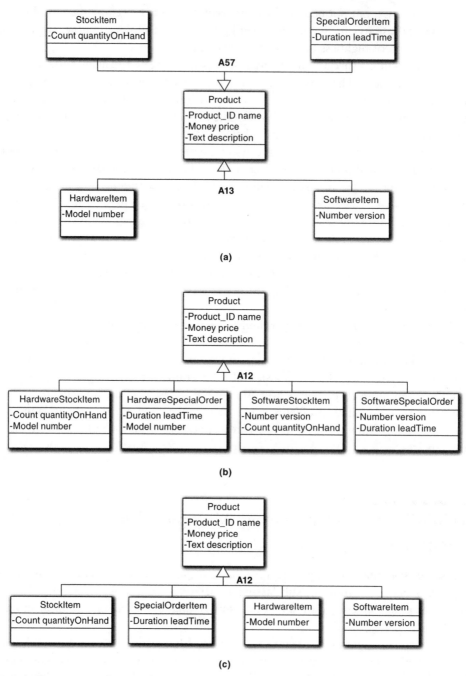

Figure 12-12 *Different generalizations for the same basic semantics*

because the associations have different discriminators, A57 and A13. Each relation represents an independent view of Product subsets, and every Product object will be categorized by both relations.

That means the individual relations are disjoint but the unions of subclass members of each relation both contain exactly the same members, which happens to be the complete set of superclass members. This is because both unions are independently complete sets of the same superclass, which effectively means that the number of subclasses of Product is combinatorial, as indicated in Figure 12-12(b) with a single subclassing relation. In other words, the compound subclassing of the in Figure 12-12(a) could have been expressed as Figure 12-12(b); they are equivalent. The value of the first view becomes apparent when we consider the combinatorial expansion if A57 and A13 each had, say, half a dozen subclasses. More important, the dual-relation view provides a separation of concerns that is much easier to understand.

What if the relation discriminators were the same in Figure 12-12(a)? It would mean that the relations were not independent views of the same Product members, which means that only the union of all subsets for both associations is complete. The subclasses remain disjoint sets, though, so a Product object would have to be a member of exactly one of the subclasses among the two associations without any combining of properties. In effect, that could be expressed as the third view in the Figure 12-12(c) with a single association. Again, the value of using multiple associations here lies in separating concerns so that the models are more understandable.

Use multi-directional subclassing to make the model more comprehensible.

Multi-directional subclassing enables us to view the root superclass generalization in different ways. However, it doesn't fundamentally change what the subclassing is and how the properties are resolved compared to an equivalent single subclassing association. In contrast, we can provide fundamental changes by combining multiple subclassing associations through composition. In composition, the associations "meet" at the subclass level rather than the superclass level. In other words, a subclass may descend from multiple superclasses.

Generalization resolves sets that entirely include subsets.

Composition resolves intersections between sets.

Going back to Figure 12-6, we could not employ generalization to extract the Amphibian properties because not all members of the Reptile and Fish sets had both properties. However, that intersection situation is represented exactly when Amphibian inherits from two different superclasses. The subset defined by the intersection is "composed" from the intersecting sets. Thus the concept of composition is just a mathematical dual of generalization.

Whenever a subclass descends from multiple superclasses we have what is known as *composition*. It is also known as multiple inheritance because the subclass inherits or resolves properties from more than one superclass. While subclasses in single or multi-directional subclassing are always objects of a single root source, subclasses in a composition are composed from multiple, often disparate sources.

Figure 12-13 is a classic example of representing a hierarchical tree, and every POS order entry site will have a similar representation somewhere to manage user navigation. We could represent such a tree with a single Node and a reflexive, conditional parent/child association, but this version eliminates the conditionality of the association. This is important because it converts dynamic rules embedded in the code into static associations, which reduces code size and opportunities for inserting defects. It also enables the LeafNode, RootNode, and IntermediateNode elements to have unique properties, which is likely necessary in most real-world POS sites.

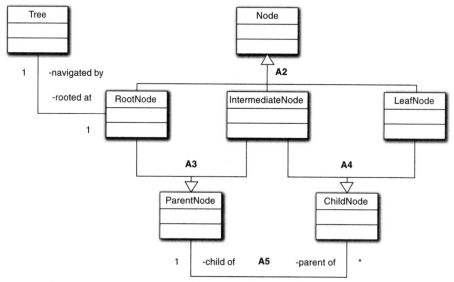

Figure 12-13   *Model of category navigation for a POS site*

Typically the traversal algorithm is placed in Tree and it "walks" the hierarchy. This representation enables that algorithm to be much simpler because it can determine exactly what to do next based upon the type of node it has in hand; there is no elaborate "memory" needed about the context of where it has been or where it is going. (Leon Starr provides some excellent examples of this sort of thing in his book, which we highly recommend.[9]) That is largely enabled by the use of composition in forming LeafNode, RootNode, and IntermediateNode.

---

9. Leon Starr, *Executable UML: How to Build Class Models*. Upper Saddle River, NJ: Prentice Hall, 2002.

The same rules of disjoint, complete sets apply to the individual associations. Inheritance is also the same; each subclass has the union of all relevant superclass properties. We just have to traverse multiple lines of ascendancy to collect that union. What makes composition unique is that the root superclasses can abstract quite disparate entities, which results in subclasses that are hybrids of potentially quite diverse properties.

That is not the case in the Node example because the notions of ChildNode and ParentNode are semantically closely related to the notion of a hierarchical tree. In fact, it would have been plausible to introduce another subclassing association between Node and ChildNode/ParentNode, making them a sort of multi-directional subclassing of Node. In that type of semantically cohesive situation, composition is reasonably benign.

However, composition is not a very OO notion because it can lead to serious cohesion problems. When the root superclasses are logically very different, the subclass tends to lose its cohesion. It can also lead to subclasses that cannot be directly mapped to problem space entities. This is most obvious when we consider the "-able" compositions common today in object-based interoperability infrastructures or RAD layered models. Such infrastructures tend to make extensive use of composition because it is a very convenient way to cobble together complex behaviors in a generic fashion that is independent of individual problem context. So when we need to, say, stream an object's attributes to a file, we make the object a composite by inheriting stream facilities from a Streamable superclass.

That works nicely for layered model and interoperability infrastructures because much of the grunt work can be handled transparently by hidden infrastructure implementations that understand the way the language compiler implements classes. In addition, such infrastructures are much more generic than typical applications, and their problem space is really the computing space. However, it presents a problem for mapping the object to the problem space in an individual application because such hybrids may not exist there. (In the streamable case, we are actually making a hybrid from two different problem spaces!) To see the problem, try walking into your nearest Honda showroom and asking to test drive a Streamable Accord. This is why one of the earlier guidelines in the chapter required generalization classes to be from the same problem space.

Composition is also heavily used in functional programming, and within that paradigm it is very useful because it "plays" very well with other features built around the lambda calculus view. Unfortunately, there is a tendency for developers to try to mix and match things that seem neat in different paradigms. Because multiple inheritance is a convenient way to implement composition in an OO environment, there has been a recent tendency to import composition as a mainline OO technique. Sadly, those efforts are often misguided because the OO and functional programming approaches are fundamentally incompatible. Construction paradigms exist as methodologies because their practices play together well in the overall context, providing a synergy that is greater than the sum of the parts. Cross-pollination of basic techniques between incompatible paradigms risks undermining that overall synergy. That happens when we apply composition in an OO context in a manner that results in subclasses that are not logically cohesive.

> Use composition **very** cautiously and insist on semantic cohesion among the root superclasses.

Most of the abuses of composition in an OO environment occur when dealing with hybrids from multiple problem spaces, as in the "streamable" example. That should actually be rather rare when practicing MBD because when separating concerns during application partitioning, we naturally tend to have subject matters that isolate particular problem spaces. For example, almost every MBD application will have separate subsystems for UI, persistence, and hardware access. Therefore, the notion of streaming to a file would be limited to the persistence access subsystem, removing the need for problem solution classes in other subsystems to have streaming facilities.

Nonetheless, we need to exercise great caution when employing composition. Always keep in mind that it is a technique that is characteristic of functional programming, not OO programming.[10] It should only be used within these constraints: (a) The root superclasses are logically related, and (b) the hybrid subclasses are valid problem space entities.

Before leaving the topic of composition, we need to note that composition is not tied solely to multiple subclassing. At the OOP level we can also implement composition by embedding classes within other classes. So using multiple subclassing and inheritance is just one (rather elegant) way to implement composition. In UML, the closest we can come to embedding one class in another is to define a composition association between them and the composition association isn't part of the MBD MDA profile. Thus, at the OOA level, all problem space classes are peers, regardless of what optimizations might be necessary in OOD/P to satisfy nonfunctional requirements. Thus the only classes that get embedded in other classes at the OOA level are knowledge attribute ADTs.

The last point to make before leaving this topic is about the special case in Figure 12-14.[11]

---

10. If you are a language maven you will no doubt point out that composition has been a stock feature of OOPLs dating back to Smalltalk. There is a big difference between being a supported language feature and being a basic construction paradigm. In this case the use of the feature needs to be seriously tempered with good methodological practice. This tempering basically says that cohesion takes precedence.

11. This example is paraphrased from *Executable UML* by Stephan Mellor and Marc Balcer. Boston: Addison-Wesley, 2002.

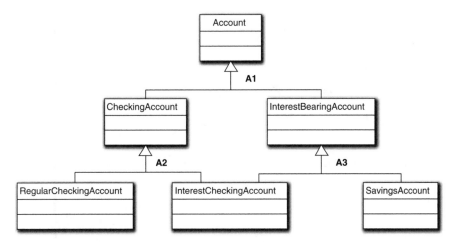

Figure 12-14 *An illegal generalization*

What's wrong with this picture? Hint: As Mellor and Balcer point out, the InterestCheckingAccount is illegal. The question is, Why? Because, by the rules of inheritance, it is both a CheckingAccount and an InterestBearingAccount. That is illegal because the A1 subclasses must be disjoint sets. This is easily seen by examining the corresponding Venn diagram in Figure 12-15.

The problem with Figure 12-15 is that there is nowhere to put the dots representing Interest Checking accounts. That's because InterestBearingAccount and CheckingAccount represent classes defined with different properties. All members of each class must have exactly the same properties as every other member of the class. Therefore, if we try to instantiate an Interest Checking account in the subset of Checking accounts we have a problem because the rest of the accounts in that group do not have the property of bearing interest. Conversely, we can't place those members among the Interest Bearing accounts because they have Checking Account properties that other members of the class don't have. The general rule of thumb is that the same subclass can't have multiple superclasses that derive from the same root superclass.

Liskov Substitution Principle

While superclasses are not instantiated, inclusion polymorphism depends upon being able to send messages to the instance in hand by knowing nothing more about it than it is a member of some superclass. This enables behaviors to be substituted transparently from the client's viewpoint. Alas, we must be a bit careful about that substitution.

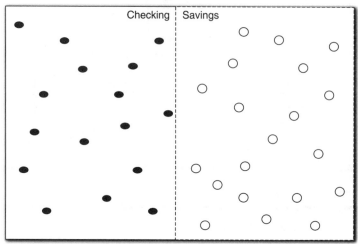

●   Regular checking accounts

○   Savings accounts

◐   Interest checking accounts

Figure 12-15   *A conundrum for mapping properties in terms of class sets. Where do interest-bearing accounts go?*

In 1988 Barbara Liskov[12] came up with a fundamental principle that constrains substitution in type systems, known as the Liskov Substitution Principle (LSP).

> If for each object o1 of type S there is an object o2 of type T such that for all programs P defined in terms of T, the behavior of P is unchanged if o1 is substituted for o2, then S is a subtype of T.

This is a definition that only a type maven could love, so try this paraphrase:

> Any client sending a message to an instance identified only as a superclass must be indifferent to which descending subclass the instance actually belongs.

If you are an astute observer you will no doubt notice that this paraphrase is not quite the same as Liskov's. Her principle is a constraint on the object types while ours is a constraint on the client's view of the substitution. Also, you should recall that OOA/D is about class systems rather than type systems. The main difference, though, is that if we interpret LSP literally, it is almost impossible to enforce in any practical OO application employing inclusion polymorphism, while the paraphrase is more feasible.

---

12. Barbara Liskov, *Data Abstraction and Hierarchy.* SIGPLAN Notices: 23, 5 (May, 1988).

That's because of the phrase "behavior of P is unchanged." Taken literally, this phrase essentially means that only implementations of the exact same behavior could be substituted, such as insertion versus Quicksort implementations in the sorting example earlier. But the real power of polymorphic substitution is achieved when we substitute different *behaviors* and get different results. In other words, when we use inclusion polymorphism we actually *want* different things to happen. We just want them not to be so different that the partner in the collaboration cares. Clearly, the program is going to behave differently (i.e., produce different results) if we substitute the behavior that actually responds when we send the same message. To see this, go back to the Prey example earlier in the chapter and speculate about the program results of the Predator attacking a Gazelle versus attacking a Brontosaurus. If LSP is so irrelevant to the way we use polymorphism, why make a big deal about it?

One reason is that LSP is a popular discussion on OOPL forums—there are endless discussions about whether a Square can be a subtype of Rectangle, often leading to amusing flame wars. That's because people keep trying to apply LSP quite literally to OOPL code. Given a literal view of program behavior, we can always find some special context where the program behavior, expressed as a DbC contract, can be broken. The reality is that LSP is virtually useless when literally applied to subtyping at the OOP level; it is simply too constraining to be of practical use.

Another reason for the online flame wars is that the participants are blinded by the merging of message and method in the OOPLs. The discussions tend to get bogged down in implementation details under the assumption that the client is requesting something specific to be done (*Do This*) at the superclass level. In many of those cases the problem would simply disappear if we could name the superclass method differently (i.e., treat it as a message that announces something the sender did).[13]

Recall that OOA/D is about class systems rather than type systems. Therefore, we need to recast the constraints in a manner that is useful for the design view of OO software construction. That recasting is represented by the paraphrase of the principle. Instead of worrying about the behavior results being the same, we worry about whether the client (more precisely: the collaboration context within the overall solution) cares about the possible differences in those results. In OOA/D we address this in several ways.

---

13. I am actually indebted to a fellow I know only by the online appellation of "Daniel T." for coming up with the Predator/Prey example that I have paraphrased. He originally made the point years ago on the comp.object newsgroup that many of the LSP violations people were debating simply disappeared if we weren't constrained by defining what was done at the superclass level through the method name. That is, if we define the response as "run()" at the superclass level for Gazelles, Rabbits, and Antelopes, then we are going to have a problem adding Pheasant or Brontosaurus as a new subclass. But if we describe the *message* as "attacked()" at the superclass level, it is unlikely there will be a problem adding those subclasses.

We treat messages as announcements of some change in the application state that was triggered by the sender of the message. Throughout this book we have been beating the drum that the message sender should have no knowledge about what the response to the message will be. So in that sense, LSP should *never* be a problem at the OOA/D level because the client *has no expectations*. In MBD we enforce this because we only define what events (messages) the superclass may accept on behalf of its subclasses, not their responses.

As pointed out previously, when we think of "client" we should take a more generic view of the collaboration in terms of DbC contracts between the receiver and *whoever* sends the message. If we access through a superclass we need to define a contract for that collaboration that applies for all members of the set, regardless of their subclass. One way to do this is by properly abstracting the invariants of the service to be provided. Symbolically we indicate that by providing an appropriately generic name for the behavior at the superclass level. This requires thinking carefully about the context of collaboration and the fundamental nature of the services provided.

In MBD we carry that further because we limit the context to a particular subject matter through application partitioning. This tends to narrow the view of what services are necessary. We also place a lot of emphasis on cohesion and, consequently, avoid complex subclassing trees. Also, we tend to look for other alternatives to subclassing in the problem space. Finally, our emphasis on association abstraction and navigation as a means for enforcing problem space rules tends to ensure that the contexts for superclass access are rather limited and well-defined. All these things tend to make LSP largely irrelevant at the OOA level.

Nonetheless, it is important to understand why LSP is important overall so that we can deal with those rare situations where it may come into play. In an initial development we can usually define a correct implementation where LSP is satisfied fairly routinely. LSP issues usually arise when we modify an existing subclassing tree by adding new classes somewhere in the tree.[14] Whenever that happens there is a risk that we will break an existing superclass access context. That is, the developer directed the message with certain assumptions about what will happen *in the overall solution context*. Changing the way behaviors are substituted can invalidate those assumptions.

That presents a very practical problem whenever we modify a subclassing tree that is accessed polymorphically. We must go to every client that accesses the tree via a superclass and verify that the client is still indifferent to the behaviors for all *new or*

---

14. We can also introduce LSP issues by moving the location of a concrete implementation from one superclass to another or by changing where a concrete implementation is overridden within the tree. Fortunately, MBD largely avoids these problems by not directly supporting implementation inheritance.

modified descendent subclasses. In the event that a client's indifference is broken, the client access context will have to be modified, which will probably entail a change to its implementation—serious stuff, because clients are supposed to be unaffected by service changes.

One way to think about this is to recall that the entire tree exists to resolve properties of a single object. Inheritance defines what behaviors the object actually implements by "walking" the tree. Thus the tree is, in a sense, part of the implementation of the object. To properly address a superclass message, the developer must understand that implementation. This breaks encapsulation and implementation hiding.

> Avoid polymorphic message addressing in the OOA; use it only when it clearly exists in the problem space.

Before sending in a death threat because this seems to indicate MBD is throwing out a characteristic OO feature, note that the context is limited to the OOA. We rarely see behavior taxonomies outside the computing spaces, much less polymorphic substitution of behaviors. Therefore, we should be suspicious about abstracting one from a customer problem space. As it happens, the primary use for inclusion polymorphism lies in the computing space, especially for OOP dependency management. One reason is that the computing space is about algorithmic computing, which means that we have exotic facilities expressly for manipulating behaviors. In addition, 3GLs are based upon type access and procedural processing, which is ideally suited to such substitution.

However, we do see a lot of data inheritance and we can have LSP problems with that. The model in Figure 12-16 actually appeared in an online LSP debate. Amazingly, the debate took up a huge amount of bandwidth over a couple of weeks without anyone realizing what the real problem was.[15] That was because the debate was focused on various proposed *behaviors* that operated on the data without paying much attention to the knowledge definitions themselves.

If you have been paying attention you will note that there is only one subclass, so the author was one of those who never heard of the complete subset rule. Right away this should indicate that something is wrong because it is kind of tough to come up with a proper name for a sibling subclass for Square that also *is-a* Rectangle.[16]

The real problem here, though, is that the common knowledge attributes in Rectangle aren't common. Square defines its own specification *for the same knowledge*

---

15. If you are wondering why I didn't spread enlightenment into the debate, I have given up. LSP debates on OO forums are as common as spring showers, and they are conducted primarily by type mavens who didn't bother to learn OOA/D.

16. Like maybe the superclass should be FourSidedPolygon and Rectangle should be a sibling of Square. Duh!

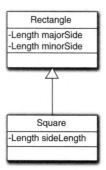

Figure 12-16 *Example of a knowledge LSP violation*

semantics. By the rules of inheritance, majorSideLength and minorSideLength are attributes that all of Rectangle's subclasses share. Therefore, Square should provide an implementation of them; instead, Square provides a different knowledge specification and implementation. More to the point, they are defined as *individual* properties of Rectangle that are part of the unique suite of properties defining the Rectangle class. This means Square cannot combine them into a single property like sideLength, even if the semantic made sense.

In fact, the semantic doesn't make sense because the representations of two distinct sides versus a single side are not the same since they are *defining* characteristics of the class of objects. The developer has chosen to abstract the essential nature of various polygons in terms of differences in the way sides are defined. At best they are only *equivalent* in particular contexts of use. It is that distinction of defining nature versus context equivalence that lies at the heart of the LSP problem. LSP insists that they should be equivalent in *all* contexts, but it is trivial to construct contexts where public access will be different for the two representations (e.g., someone invokes setMinorLength and setMajorLength with different values for a Square).

> You can redefine the *implementation* of a knowledge attribute in a subclass, but you cannot redefine the nature of the attribute.

If you take care not to violate this rule, you are unlikely to encounter LSP problems with your data inheritance and accessing of that data through a superclass.

Alternatives to Generalization

Though elegant, subclassing has a number of disadvantages. We've already mentioned that static structure tends to get in the way of encoding invariants while leaving detailed differences to external data. Another problem is that complex subclassing trees often reflect lack of cohesion in the root superclass abstraction. Complex trees can be difficult to modify because of the duck-billed platypus problem in the form of introducing LSP problems. For these reasons we have the following guidelines, in descending priority:

Prefer parametric polymorphism wherever it is reasonable.

Prefer delegation if reasonable.

Keep subclassing trees simple.

Keep subclassing trees to one level wherever possible.

As a practical matter, doing the last two usually involves at least partial use of the first two.

Delegation

There are at least two definitions of delegation currently in use. The more restricted one is that an object has a public responsibility it delegates to another object by simply relaying the message it receives to the other object.

In Figure 12-17 when ClassA gets a doIt() message, it simply invokes ClassB::doIt(). The key point here is that ClassA has a publicly designated responsibility that it abdicates to ClassB by relaying the client's message *as-is* to ClassB unbeknownst to the client.

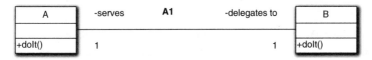

Figure 12-17   *Example of improper delegation implementation*

Once we delegate, the responsibility no longer belongs to the original object.

Unfortunately, this sort of thing is done all the time in OOP today, which is a sad commentary on developers' knowledge of OOA/D fundamentals. ***Don't do that!*** Behavior is a property just like knowledge and it is subject to normalization, just like data attributes. Two different classes should never have exactly the same behavior property because it violates Third Normal Form. (For those of you who are relationally challenged, it violates one-fact-one-place.)

It also violates the basic OO paradigm of peer-to-peer collaboration. If ClassB has the actual implementation of the doIt() behavior, then the client should be collaborating directly with ClassB rather than through a middleman (ClassA). When ClassA acts as a middleman, it is doing exactly the same thing that a higher-level function in a hierarchical functional decomposition tree does when it invokes a lower-level function to do something that is part of its own specification. Peer-to-peer collaboration in OO development is expressly intended to eliminate those sorts of hierarchical dependency chains.

To see why this is Not Good, think about what happens if requirements change and we need to change the interface to ClassB::doIt() by adding an argument to the data packet.[17] Clearly, the client needs to add the required data to the message, so it needs to change in addition to ClassB::doIt(). However, with this form of delegation we also need to change A since the new data must be passed through its interface. Thus we are forced to modify A when it no longer has anything at all to do with the collaboration between the client and B. This is especially bad in the OOP-level type systems because we must change the type signature of ClassA, which defines what ClassA *is*. So to accommodate a change in a personal collaboration between ClassB and the client, we need to change the *definition* of ClassA!

In contrast, if we remove the ClassA::doIt() responsibility from the figure, we have the second, more general form of OOA/D delegation. The basic idea is that objects in ClassA would originally have the doIt() responsibility, but to simplify ClassA we decide to delegate that responsibility to another object in another class, ClassB. We abstract ClassB to handle that particular responsibility. Now the client needs to navigate through ClassA to get to the responsibility. To do that, the client needs to know nothing about the ClassA semantics. Better yet, ClassA does not know about the message specifics, so it is unaffected by the requirements change.

The important thing to note is that when we do that splitting, each responsibility is "owned" by only one of the new set of classes. Since the classes were originally one, they will be related in some fundamental way by an association. Therefore, a client who needs to access the responsibility may have to navigate "through" the original object on the new association path to get to the right service-owning object. Though association navigation is more complicated, we preserve peer-to-peer collaboration and eliminate hierarchical dependency.

Delegations must exist in the problem space.

The same notion of problem space entity decomposition for subclassing decomposition applies to delegation decomposition. Proper delegation can't be an arbitrary splitting up of object abstractions. An object abstracts a single identifiable problem space entity and the class just defines a set of similar objects. If we split classes, we are also splitting the underlying entities that they abstract. To be a valid split, the

---

17. Yes, we should not pass a lot of data around in message data packets. This is just an example that needs to be familiar, so assume the new requirements demand that a snapshot of data be provided.

original underlying problem space entity must be logically composed of other identifiable entities. However we split the class, the new classes must represent those component entities from the problem space. In other words, the delegation must already exist in the problem space as we decompose the original problem space entity into its constituents at a finer level of abstraction.

Quite frequently the problem space decomposition will be conceptual, even for concrete entities. For example, a Person is not decomposable except from the viewpoint of an organ bank. However, the Person may play multiple roles in the problem context. Thus we can abstract a Role that has individual responsibilities that would otherwise accrue to a Person. Abstracting roles is far and away the most common form of delegation.

The two views in Figure 12-18 capture all the same responsibilities relevant to the problem in hand. But the delegation view is a clearer representation of what is being modeled.

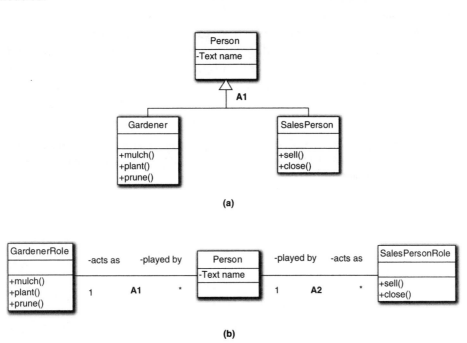

Figure 12-18   *Using role objects as an alternative to generalization*

Parametric Polymorphism

We already talked about parametric polymorphism extensively in Chapter 5 because it goes hand-in-hand with extracting invariants from the problem space. So we won't talk about it here, other than to mention that quite often it recasts behavior generalization to a data generalization rather than completely eliminating the generalization.

Basic Abstraction

Generalization, delegation, and parametric polymorphism just represent different approaches to abstracting the problem space. Whichever approach we choose, it will somehow include all the same responsibilities necessary to solve the problem in hand. But we have considerable latitude when identifying entities and responsibilities necessary to solve a given problem in hand. This is because customer problem spaces and their entities offer far more variety than computing space entities that are constrained by mathematical definition. Thus we get to apply a lot of *interpretation* to the problem space.

Subclassing, delegation, and parametric polymorphism are just examples of analysis patterns that are so common they warrant a degree of methodological formalization. There will be situations where you can avoid generalization by simply interpreting the problem space in a different manner so that independent entities are abstracted with properties defined differently to achieve the same solution goals. Because such situations will be unique on a problem-by-problem basis, there are no additional patterns to present as guidelines. All we can do is offer the following bon mot:

> When abstracting the problem space, don't accept the first plausible model that seems to address all the requirements. Look for and evaluate alternative abstractions and divisions of responsibilities.

Chapter 13

Identifying Knowledge

Knowledge is of but two kinds. We know a subject ourselves, or we know where we can find information upon it.

—Samuel Johnson, letter to James MacPherson

Most knowledge attributes are fairly easy to identify because they describe physical properties of inanimate objects in the problem space. Thus notions like *color*, *length*, and *part number* are easily recognized and abstracted as attributes. The next tier of attributes contains mildly conceptual but commonly used aggregates, such as *address*, a combination of street, city, and state; *name*, a combination of given and family names for a person; and *location*, a set of coordinates. Since they are commonly used in the problem space, they are also usually easy to identify, as in the examples.

The third tier of attributes represents a high degree of abstraction of the problem space. Because of the subtlety involved, these tend to be the most challenging for novice OO developers. One convenient way to classify these sorts of knowledge properties is the following:

- *Aggregates of data that we abstract as scalar ADTs in a particular subsystem whose level of abstraction is relatively high.* The trick here is to recognize that the level of abstraction of the subsystem in hand does not care about certain details. We tailor the knowledge abstraction to the abstraction of the subsystem.

- *A choice from among several possible abstract views of the knowledge.* This involves tailoring the subsystem's objects to the subject matter of the subsystem. In other words, we need to find the *right* abstraction for the problem in hand.

- *The direct result of anthropomorphization where we may have a choice about which problem space entity "owns" the knowledge.* These are situations when we must allocate to inanimate problem space entities the control responsibilities that a person would normally do. Similarly, there may be knowledge needed to support those control responsibilities that a person would normally know, so we have a choice about which inanimate object it is allocated to.

The goal in this chapter is to describe some practical techniques for uncovering knowledge attributes in the third tier. But first we need to review the proper mindset for uncovering knowledge attributes.

What Is the Nature of OO Knowledge?

Knowledge is not data—it is a responsibility for knowing something.

We abstract objects in terms of intrinsic responsibilities, which means we do not care *how* the object knows what it does; we are concerned only with *what* it should know. It cannot be overemphasized how important this distinction is to OOA/D. If we think purely in terms of responsibility, then we will have little difficulty with encapsulation.

The notion of *data* is highly overloaded in the computing space, and most of that overloading is related to how information is stored on a computer platform. Since we are dealing with OOA models in translation, we are only concerned with the customer's view of the information, not the computer's. Therefore, it is important to think of knowledge properties in a rather generic way, one that is independent of implementation details. In OOA/D, knowledge properties are always abstracted from the computing space through ADTs. So try to forget everything you have ever seen in 3GLs, including the OOPLs.

In Part III, when we talk about dynamics, we will see that in many situations knowledge and behavior are interchangeable, kind of like a physicist's view of mass and energy. Thus we often have a choice about whether an object needs to know something or do something to solve the problem in hand. Making that choice is about interpreting and abstracting the problem space, not the traditional computing space view of `algorithms + data = programs`.

OO knowledge is intrinsic.

Another important mindset issue lies in the fact that object responsibilities are intrinsic. A knowledge responsibility describes what an object knows *about itself*. In Figure 13-1(a), *events* is an intrinsic property of EventQueue even though it counts objects outside of itself. That's because EventQueue's fundamental mission in life is to manage Events, so it is a reasonable intrinsic responsibility for knowing how many Events it is managing at any given time.

Unfortunately, an all-too-common side effect of careless delegation is that an object knows things it shouldn't about the object to which it delegated responsibili-

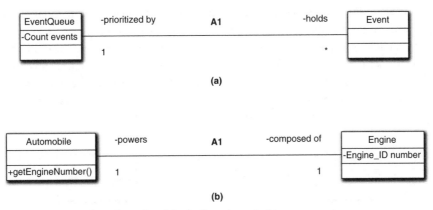

Figure 13-1 *Examples of good and bad allocation of object properties*

ties. That is reflected in Figure 13-1(b) where a client needing the serial number of an Automobile's engine would query Automobile for it rather than navigating to Engine to get it directly. As indicated in the last chapter, once the Engine has been extracted from Automobile to capture unique, delegated properties, those properties are no longer Automobile's. Therefore, Automobile has no business knowing anything about them; it becomes an anonymous waypoint along the navigation path of collaborations between clients and Engine.

Fortunately, this sort of problem is very easy to recognize in MBD when writing abstract action language. There are no 3GL-like getters when accessing knowledge,[1] so for a client to access the engine number from Automobile there would have to be an *engineNumber* attribute in Automobile, which would fail reviewer checks for normal form in the Class diagram (i.e., *engineNumber* would be an attribute of two objects from different classes with exactly the same semantics, value, and identity dependence).

Abstracting Aggregates

Because levels of abstraction differ among the application's subsystems, we need to push the notion of ADTs even further. We need to abstract the knowledge responsibilities to

---

1. In an AAL syntax we are always accessing the identified *responsibility*, not its implementation, so there is no need for the getter/setter subterfuge in the OOA/D. That is, the transformation engine *always* interprets the syntax as a getter/setter because the attribute is defined as an ADT.

be consistent with the subsystem's level of abstraction. As mentioned in Chapter 2, it is not uncommon for a scalar ADT attribute in one subsystem to map into an entire class, multiple classes, or even an entire subsystem when viewed at a lower level of abstraction. The tricky part is recognizing the high-level ADT abstraction in the subsystems at a higher level of abstraction. Unfortunately, our compulsions over the data view in the computing space encourage us to think in terms of aggregates of data rather than abstractions of information. These issues become apparent in Figure 13-2.

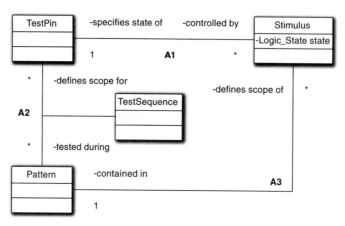

Figure 13-2   *Model of pattern-based digital testing. Stimuli are applied to tester pins sequenced in time by patterns (time slices).*

Figure 13-2 represents a view of the way digital hardware is tested when using a pattern-based tester. During each time slice, each tester pin is driven by a particular stimulus that is essentially a logic state (0 or 1) for the pin. (The set of stimuli and responses within a time slice is known as a *pattern.*) The stimuli in the time slices need to be sequenced in a particular order for a given test because the unit under test has internal state that is accumulated over many time slices. (The view in Figure 13-2 is actually greatly simplified; the real model involves nearly two dozen classes with a lot of unique data elements.) Now consider the architectural context of the full device driver for a digital test system, as shown in Figure 13-3.

(Again, this view of the application partitioning is vastly oversimplified; the actual device driver has roughly thirty subsystems.) In this, the DigitalTest subsystem has the model illustrated in Figure 13-2 because it needs to talk to the hardware via the PIO subsystem one pin and one time slice at a time. (Its mission is to load the stimuli into the tester's hardware memory.) But what is the view of a digital test in the Digital Unit Tester subsystem?

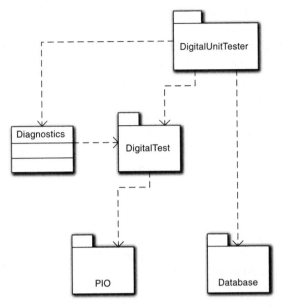

Figure 13-3 *Subsystem context for a tester of digital electronics*

In that subsystem we were interested in the overall control of the tester that coordinates things like selecting tests, executing them, and invoking diagnostics if the test fails. At that level of abstraction a digital test is monolithic (e.g., "run test 52C"). It might well be abstracted as a single Digital Test class that was a dumb data holder with the attributes *name* and *testData*. All the complexity of Figure 13-2 would be completely hidden by the *testData* ADT because at that level of abstraction there is no interest in the individual data elements within a digital test.[2]

Look for ways to deal with knowledge at its highest level of abstraction.

---

2. If you are curious about how this would be handled in the implementation, that is beyond the scope of this book; it is a job for translation. However, to give you an idea of what goes on, there are actually several alternatives. The most likely is that DigitalUnitTester asks Database for the test identified as "52C." It gets back the instance data for its DigitalTest class. In that case, the *testData* attribute would be a handle to a dataset extracted from the database. When it was time to execute the test, DigitalUnitTest would pass that handle in a message to the DigitalTest subsystem. The DigitalTest subsystem's interface would pass that handle to a factory class, which would decode the dataset and instantiate the relevant Stimulus and Pattern objects and their relationships. When that was completed, an event would be generated to whatever object kicks off the execution. In effect, the dataset is reduced to a message data packet by the transformation engine behind the scenes.

It is very important to be aware of the need to abstract knowledge when dealing with subsystems at a high level of abstraction. One way to do this is to put a mental boundary around data aggregates and determine (a) if there is some problem space abstraction that maps to that boundary, and (b) whether the current subsystem cares about any specific elements within that boundary. In fact, it is usually a good idea to look for ways in which the subsystem in hand can do its job without the specific elements in the aggregate, even when initially it seems intuitive that it does care about individual elements. For example, it might seem intuitive to manipulate the patterns as classes while hiding their individual stimuli in an ADT because at a high level, pattern-based digital testers manipulate patterns. In other words, patterns are a fundamental structural element of the tester, which is why we describe the class of testers as *pattern-based*. Nonetheless, within a particular subsystem in the application we can still extract an even more generic concept in the form of *testData* where even individual patterns are hidden.

If this advice seems vaguely familiar, it should. What is being advocated here is basically identifying knowledge invariants in the problem space by raising the level of abstraction. This is one reason why this chapter's leading quote is apropos. We need to separate the information we *must* have at hand from the information that is available elsewhere. As usual, the ultimate source of wisdom is the problem space itself. The point here is that we need to use abstraction and extract invariants from the problem space for knowledge attributes, just as we do for classes and behavior responsibilities.

When modeling a college that used pass/fail grading for freshman and letter grading for other years, we might be tempted to define an *isFreshman* attribute that determines how the value in *gradeValue* is interpreted, as in Figure 13-4. This is not a good way to define the Grade attributes for several reasons, but the one of concern here is that the value of *isFreshman* is not an intrinsic property of Grade.

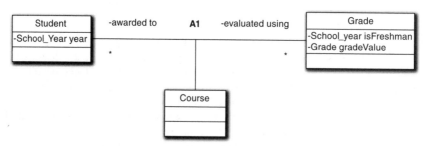

Figure 13-4   *A bad way to deal with pass/fail grading for freshmen*

In reality, the *isFreshman* value depends on the value of the Student's *year*. We can get into this sort of problem by thinking in terms of data, such as viewing *gradeValue* as consecutive integer codes, where 0 cleverly represents both fail in pass/fail and F in letter grading while 1 represents pass in pass/fail and D in letter grading. We are then faced with the problem of interpreting the value of 1 correctly,[3] so we introduce the kludge of *isFreshman* because that will be easier than going to Student to determine the year.

Pop quiz: Which of the following solutions is better when eliminating *isFreshman*?

(A)   Subclass Grade into FreshmanGrade and UpperClassmanGrade, where each subclass provides a different semantics for *gradeValue*.

(B)   Enumerate the data domain of *gradeValue* as {A, B, C, D, F, Pass, Fail}.

(C)   Use the existing codes, but let the client navigate to Student to determine how they should be interpreted.

(D)   Any of the above.

(E)   None of the above.

Technically the answer is (D) because the "best" solution depends upon exactly what the problem in hand is, and we could probably find a scenario where any of them could be viable.[4] The corollary is that there will be situations where one or more of them will be at least inconvenient. And if the application is complex, there may be multiple contexts for accessing *gradeValue* where there is a different "best" solution for each context. Making those sorts of decisions when tailoring to the problem in hand is why OO developers get the Big Bucks.

It is probably worthwhile to discuss what the relative disadvantages of these solutions are. In the subclassing case, A, the client will have to know what subclass it is accessing. We can't define *gradeValue* in the superclass because each subclass now has different semantics for it (as opposed to a different implementation of the same semantics). This means the client will have to navigate a direct association to the correct subclass, and we will have to make sure that is properly instantiated. Usually that will only be an optimal solution if different clients exclusively access either freshman grades or upperclassmen grades.

Using the existing codes, C is going to be wrong in almost any conceivable situation. To see this, think about the implicit assumption in the example that the year the

---

3. As mentioned previously, there are other reasons why this is poor modeling. One is that gradeValue is not a simple domain; it actually combines the {pass, fail} and {A, B, C, D, F} data domains for the {0,1} values so the attribute violates 1st Normal Form when we consider the semantics of the allowed values.

4. If you answered (B), you get half credit. If you answered "(F) Anything but (C)" you get full credit for spunk, for reasons we'll get to in a moment.

Student is in determines whether pass/fail is appropriate. What if the school decides to give pass/fail grades based on just standard Freshman courses and a freshman decides to take an advanced course; does the freshman get a letter grade? Now the interpretation of the grade depends upon the Student being a freshman *and* the course is a standard Freshman course. Surgery will be required on the client to obtain that extra information and process it properly. But that is likely to be completely unrelated to what the client is supposed to be doing with the grades *once they are properly interpreted.*

The basic problem is that the client must understand how the grade is assigned and that is probably none of the client's business. The only conceivable situation where this could be viable is if the only client is Student, who should already know what year it is in, and it was a one-shot application where we did not have to worry about the way grades were assigned being changed.[5]

That leaves us with reorganizing the data domain of *gradeValue*, B. This will almost always be a viable solution. For example, we can view the deficiencies of (C) as symptomatic of the overloading of code value semantics. With the indicated data domain, that overloading problem goes away, and the client is no longer concerned with how the grade is assigned; it just deals with the value as is. In Normal Form terms we are *defining* a simple data domain that includes all possible grade values. The downside of this is that the clients all have to deal with the entire data domain. That is, they must be prepared to deal appropriately with a Pass value as well as a B value.

But before leaving the pop quiz, note that (B) essentially combined *isFreshman* and *gradeValue* into a single ADT because the client no longer needs to access *isFreshman*. We will still need *isFreshman* in Student because somebody needs to assign the grade, and to do that they will have to access the right decision variables. But once the ADT value is assigned, any client can access that knowledge without knowing anything about Student.

That is an interesting bit of legerdemain since all we did was redefine code values so that the {0, 1} *data* was no longer ambiguous. In fact, the semantics of gradeValue was always {pass, fail, A, B, C, D, F} in the problem space! So in that sense the entire example and the pop quiz was a red herring. The real problem here is the mapping of abstract ADT values to numeric data values, which is the transformation engine's problem rather than the application developer's problem.

The main point in wandering this garden path was to underscore the point made earlier that knowledge responsibilities are defined in the problem space rather than the computing space. In the problem space there are seven flavors of the notion of a

---

5. If it was a one-shot, you probably wouldn't be doing OO development in the first place because volatile requirements wouldn't be an issue.

course grade. We can abstract those as enumerated symbols that are unique. Thus *fail* is not an *F* and *pass* is not a funny sort of *D*. Each is a uniquely identifiable *grade* in the problem space.

However, there is an even more important moral to highlight. The responsibility is for the Grade object to know the value of the grade. More important, it is *only* to know that value. The responsibility is not about how the grade value is determined or what we want to do with the value once it has been provided. Therefore, if we had not gotten side tracked by the circumstances of assigning a grade, how it is implemented, or what it is used for, we probably would have gotten directly to (B) without even thinking about it.

In part the side tracks were encouraged by referring to *data domain* in the example, which kept the {0, 1} view within sight.

> Attribute ADTs have an associated value domain. The most useful ADTs have purely symbolic values from the problem space.

It is often useful to think about attribute ADTs as values rather than data because of the numeric baggage that the notion of *data* carries in the computing space. If a HouseBoat has *price* attribute, the value of that attribute is very likely to be highly numeric. That's fine, because in the problem space it is a nice scalar number in most situations, but is also not exactly taxing on our creative talents.

In the OO paradigm we must abstract every problem space entity in terms of just two kinds of responsibilities: knowledge and behavior. That can get challenging when the qualities are inherently abstract. It also gets challenging when we need to generalize complex qualities as indivisible invariants. In both decision theory and economics there are very similar notions of *utility*, which represents a single abstract value of something that is not directly quantifiable or is an aggregate of other values. We need to get used to the similar idea that an ADT is a scalar value that can represent arbitrary complexity. Quite often we will need to think of that "value" symbolically.

Picking the Right Abstraction

> While knowledge is an intrinsic responsibility, we abstract it with the overall problem context in mind.

So far we have aggregated the *isFreshman* and *gradeValue* knowledge attributes into a single *gradeValue* ADT. Whether we were driven to that change by an aversion to value overloading, a perceived violation of 1st Normal Form, the dependence of *isFreshman* on *year*, a fear of added complexity in client behaviors, or simply having our aesthetic sensibilities offended really doesn't matter. The new abstraction will be a better one in most situations by many standards. We did that by changing the semantics of individual valid values of *gradeValue*. Instead of thinking of {pass, fail} as equivalent to or alternatives for {A, B, C, D, F}, we thought of {pass, fail} as additional unique and independent values of *grade*.

That change reflects a tailoring of the abstraction to the problem in hand. In other words, we changed the way we view the notion of "a grade" at a fundamental level for this problem solution by eliminating any ambiguity in interpreting the gradeValue in the problem context. In doing so, we created a single ADT whose scalar "value" is unambiguous for all clients in the problem context.

Knowledge abstractions rarely exist in a vacuum.

We also relegated any concerns the problem space might have about equivalence to whoever actually does the assignment of a grade. Encapsulating the rules and policies of *processing* a grade is a quite separate issue from defining our *gradeValue* semantics, but those decisions in the overall solution need to play together. When selecting that definition we needed some vision of how we planned to assign grades and how we planned to use them in the solution to the problem in hand.

As a practical matter for an example as simple as this one, we probably wouldn't think a great deal about that solution vision. That's because good OO practices like separation of concerns, decoupling, and whatnot would conspire to have us think in terms of assigning values and using values as different activities. Perhaps more important, limiting the responsibility to simply *knowing* the current value of the grade would lead us to viewing the values as distinct. So, to an experienced OO developer, (B) in the pop quiz would seem the most natural without worrying a great deal about how the values were assigned or used.

The change is a rather subtle one, but subtlety is what good abstraction is all about. Alas, there aren't a lot of cookbook techniques for doing that. It is primarily a matter of having the right mindset, which requires judgment and experience. The two key aspects of that mindset, though, are problem space abstraction (as opposed to data descriptions) and focusing on what is needed to solve the problem in hand.

One technique for doing that is to extract invariants from the problem space. When talking about invariants in Chapter 5, an example for doing depreciation was used. If you review that example you will see that the tailoring of the abstraction was primarily about the way we represent knowledge. In fact, the abstraction substituted a data structure for an algorithm. The key insight was recognizing that the formula could be broken up into two steps with an intermediate data structure. From the application solution's perspective, several executable formulas were replaced by a single, simpler formula and a data structure for knowing the period fractions.

In fact, one way to describe parametric polymorphism is that it is about extracting generic, invariant behaviors such that the detailed behaviors are handled through knowledge abstractions, thus we substitute knowledge responsibilities for detailed behavior responsibilities. That fundamentally changes the way we solve the problem in hand. So when we substitute a new semantic to combine *isFreshman* and *grade-Value*, we also change the way that clients will use the information to solve the problem.

That's one important reason why we abstract objects and their *responsibilities* before we worry about the dynamics of behaviors and connecting the behavior dots for the overall problem solution. When we define knowledge ADTs we are also defining the skeleton on which the overall solution will depend. Therefore, it is very important to come up with the best knowledge ADT for the problem in hand.

Abstracting What People Do

As we discussed in Chapter 2, when we abstract inanimate entities we tend to imbue them with control behaviors that people would normally provide in a manual solution. This is important because it actually enables us a lot of flexibility in allocating responsibilities. Thus the same inanimate entities abstracted in two different applications may not have responsibilities allocated in the same ways or even to the same objects. This doesn't violate the notion of abstracting intrinsic properties. It simply reflects that anthropomorphized behaviors only become intrinsic when they are assigned to the inanimate entity in the problem context. Technically that assignment is an interpretation of the problem itself.

Since some knowledge responsibilities track the needs of behaviors, their assignment to inanimate objects is also flexible, albeit a lot less so than behaviors. Anthropomorphized knowledge tends to be relatively rare, and we will have a lot more to say about anthropomorphizing in Part III, The Dynamic Model. Here we are concerned with knowledge that is usually discovered in an iterative fashion when allocating behavior responsibilities. For example, we tend to associate a knowledge attribute for *elementCount* whenever we deal with stack behavior. We may abstract a Stack object and it will go there. However, providing a stack might be necessary to implementing a behavior in an object abstracted for other reasons. The stack then becomes part of that object's implementation and *elementCount* will follow it.

As mentioned earlier in the chapter, the easiest knowledge properties to identify are those that really are intrinsic to inanimate objects (e.g., size, color, etc.). So it may be useful to make an initial pass at identifying such attributes as a "warm up" when forming a Class diagram; then we can attack the needs of the behaviors assigned to objects. It is important to note, though, that knowledge and behavior need to play together properly when dealing with anthropomorphization. The flexibility in assigning properties carries with it the need to make sure the assignments make the most sense *for the problem in hand*.

When in doubt make anthropomorphic assignments that seem most natural for the problem.

For example, suppose we have classes for Automobile and Bill Of Sale with a 1:1 relationship between them. Now we need to assign an attribute for *exciseTax*. Which object should own it? Most likely it goes with Bill Of Sale because generating a sale is when a excise tax becomes relevant. But what if this application is primarily about pricing the automobile and the Bill Of Sale is just a form that gets printed out once a deal is agreed? Then the information the dealer and customer are negotiating over is mainly associated with the Automobile. We might find it convenient to make the semantics be the actual money amount, rather than the tax percentage, and the computation—which a person would have to do if the software application didn't exist—of the amount might be assigned to Automobile. In that context it might make sense to put *exciseTax* in Automobile and let Bill Of Sale simply be a specification object for formatting the printing of data from Automobile and other relevant objects.[6]

The remainder of this chapter is devoted to a set of questions with answers you may find useful when trying to discover the knowledge attributes. The questions are an indirect reflection of the mindset issues we've been talking about.

What Does the Underlying Entity Know?

This is clearly the key question. The criteria for determining this is found in the context of the problem itself. We abstract only those properties we need to solve the problem in hand. So the question can be rephrased as: What does the underlying entity need to know to solve this problem? In practice we can further subdivide this by noting that there are things the entity itself needs to know to satisfy its own behavioral responsibilities, and there are things that the entity needs to know so that other entities can satisfy their behavior responsibilities.

Note that the only reason we need knowledge attributes at all is so that behaviors can do their thing properly. Knowledge attributes are state variables that preserve the application's state between the executions of behaviors, and that state can only change if a behavior does something to change the application state. Conversely, all MBD behaviors are essentially operations that do at least one of three things: modify the state of the solution (i.e., change states in a state machine), modify a state variable, or send a message. If the behavior does none of these things, then there would be no point in executing it because it would have no effect on the final solution results. Thus knowledge attributes are intimately related to the behavior responsibili-

---

6. Once we get there in the final draft of the model, we might consider renaming Bill Of Sale to avoid confusion with the real thing in the problem space (e.g., to Print Specification or Bill Of Sale Specification). Thus Bill Of Sale evolves from the original Object Blitz to a different abstraction in the final model as we refine our thinking about what is necessary to solve the problem. Design is an iterative process.

ties necessary to solve the problem in hand. So we have an alternative phrasing of the question:

What do the problem solution's behaviors need to know from this entity?

As a practical matter we usually provide an initial cut at the knowledge properties in the Class diagram before defining the specific behaviors (i.e., in MBD we define behaviors with Statecharts after the Class diagram is done). The point in the preceding paragraph is simply that we don't create the Class diagram in a vacuum. We always have some general notion of the behaviors necessary to solve the problem[7] even when creating the static models like a Class diagram. Therefore we need to consider the broad behavioral context when abstracting the knowledge responsibilities.

Many knowledge attributes are pretty obvious and can be extracted quickly from the problem space. After these are recorded, it is usually a good idea to make a pass over the Class diagram, one class at a time, to seek out those attributes that are less obvious *after the behavior responsibilities are identified*. For each class, determine what information would probably be needed to execute those responsibilities properly. Finally, decide what classes should logically provide any knowledge not captured so far.

What Subset of Entity Knowledge Should the Object Abstraction Know?

The goal here is to keep focused on the problem in hand. Typical entities in customer problem spaces are quite complex and can be viewed in many different ways. To manage that complexity we must be careful to select only a subset of the entity's properties that are of interest to the problem in hand. Because of the way we partition applications, we are really only interested in a part of the customer's overall problem—that which is related to the subsystem subject matter in hand. Each subsystem is an encapsulation of a view of a particular problem space, and we need to select for abstraction only the properties that are relevant to that view.

What Is the Subject Matter?

Subject matter is the key issue when deciding what knowledge properties to abstract. The subject matter will severely limit our view of the entity and what we need from

---

7. In fact, in MBD we recommend creating a very rough Collaboration diagram as part of the discovery of class abstractions. This is a throwaway and is not intended to be either rigorous or detailed. It is simply a mnemonic tool for recording the rough expectations for the overall solution.

it. This becomes most obvious when we "tailor" the subject matter by extracting invariants. Typically such invariants will greatly simplify our view by raising the level of abstraction and that will further limit what properties are of interest.

For example, dredging up our banking example, in a subsystem dealing with the business rules and policies of banking we need to know certain things about a Customer Account to deal with various transactions, such as the current balance and the overdraft limit. In that context, these are simple, independent state variables that will be expressed as knowledge attributes. In a GUI subsystem that presents them to a teller, they will be represented as Text Box instances with a large number of individual attributes, only one of which is the actual value. In an ATM controller, the balance will be necessary, but it will probably not be an attribute. Instead, it will simply be pass-through data in message data packets between the network port and the display device.[8] Things like the overdraft limit will not appear at all in ATM controllers because that only affects whether a withdrawal can be made, which is the Bank's decision. Thus the balance appears in all three subsystems but it is an attribute in only two, while the overdraft limit appears in two subsystems as an attribute but doesn't appear in the third at all. It is worthwhile going through the reasoning behind these different treatments.

> If it isn't in the requirements, you probably don't need it.

That is the situation for the overdraft limit in the ATM subsystem. The requirements for the subsystem will include what is displayed to the customer, what information the customer supplies, and what information the bank supplies. In today's ATMs, none of those inputs include the overdraft limit. As a sanity check we consider what the ATM does and, by implication, what it doesn't do. There is nothing in the subsystem requirements or the subject matter mission that deals with banking rules and policies for validating customer transactions, which is the only reason we would need the overdraft limit. In fact, those rules and policies are explicitly delegated to the banking subsystem on the other side of the network port. So the overdraft limit has no semantic value to the problem the ATM controller software is solving, and we can ignore it by not abstracting from the problem space.

> Be suspicious of any knowledge attribute that seems to only support rules and policies specifically allocated to another subject matter.

This guideline is hardly etched in steel tablets because we know that different functionality (reflected in different subject matters) can operate on the same data. However, in the case of something like overdraft limit, it is pretty clear that the prop-

---

8. In the simple-minded ATM we have been discussing, the balance is simply printed out for the user on a deposit slip or as a direct query by the user.

erty is carnally connected to the rules and policies of transaction validation. That's because the notion of *overdraft* really only exists in terms of banking policies.

Why is balance an attribute in a GUI subsystem supporting tellers but not in the ATM subsystem given that it exists in both as a display element? Good question, Grasshopper. There are two reasons that it is an attribute in the GUI subsystem. First, the notion of Customer Account is captured there, albeit decomposed into Window and Control abstractions. There is an explicit tie to entity identity via the Window instance identity and the relationships to Controls. In addition, the Controls provide similar identity mapping for balance versus overdraft limit. When the teller views the screen there will be no confusion about the fact that the teller is viewing a Customer Account with its Balance and Overdraft properties. While the GUI paradigm provides a very different view of the entity, the GUI subsystem still exists to display the banking subsystem's entities.

While that makes it likely that any entity property in the banking subsystem will be a property if present in the GUI subsystem, it doesn't mean that all entity properties from the banking subsystem need to be displayed. That will be determined by the requirements for the GUI subsystem (i.e., the GUI designer's specification), and if display is not required, the properties would not be abstracted in the GUI subsystem.

The second reason is that the value has to be persisted between GUI operations. The GUI has its own suite of responsibilities so that it can do lots of housekeeping while the values remain displayed. In addition, windows may be hidden from view or even closed temporarily while the GUI still keeps track of the data for later display. Thus the values must persist across GUI behaviors. This segues to why the balance value is present in the ATM subsystem but isn't a property of any classes implementing that subsystem.

Knowledge that persists across fundamental subject matter operations must be preserved in state variables.

The corollary is that if the knowledge does not persist across behavior executions within the subject matter, it may not need to be a class attribute, which is the case for balance in the ATM subsystem. The value is provided as external data that is decoded from one message data packet (from the network port) and encoded into another message data packet (to the display device) within a single behavior scope. It is purely transient within the ATM subsystem.[9]

---

9. Wait a minute! Doesn't the ATM UI have objects with persistent attributes just like the GUI? Not in today's ATMs where the UI is a character screen. The display is literally a text string with embedded positioning characters that is sent to the display device driver. It is sent once and the display remains the same until a new string is sent. When the user supplies values, they come from the Keyboard device driver; they coincidently also get displayed.

Note that an acid test for this sort of situation is that the value is not associated with any entity that the ATM needs to abstract. Since the ATM controller subject matter has no intrinsic responsibilities that would need to abstract a Customer Account, this test passes. An interesting question arises, though, if we find that we must save the value of balance across multiple behaviors within the ATM controller. Then we must save the value as an attribute, but where? The answer is to make it an attribute of an object that abstracts the notion of a message or transaction, rather than the Customer Account.[10] Given our description of the subject matter as a message processor, we can very likely map any persistence into a Message or Transaction object because the scope of persistence is very likely not to extend beyond a transaction's scope.

This brings up an interesting point about abstraction. Let's say we abstract a Balance Request subclass of Transaction with a *value* attribute that holds the balance in the context of a user's request for a current balance. A Balance Request is not a Customer Account, yet we know that its attribute and the Customer Account's balance attribute have exactly the same state variable value. Isn't something wrong with that picture? More specifically, isn't there a Normal Form violation somewhere?

The answer is no, because we have two entirely different subject matters on either side of the interface *that model different problem spaces.* Our ATM controller exists to re-dispatch messages between a network port, a user, and some hardware. In that subject matter domain, it is quite reasonable to abstract an entity like Balance Request that has a *balance* attribute. That entity is quite real, albeit conceptual, in the controller context. The semantics of the *balance* attribute is not that of an account balance; rather, it is simply a value that is, at most, constrained by some generic limits on size and whether it is integer or real. It could just as easily be the amount the user is requesting for a withdrawal.

To see this more clearly, suppose that instead we had abstracted Network Message rather than a subclass of Transaction. It would have a generic *value* attribute that could be a balance, a withdrawal amount, or a deposit amount. But that semantics would only come into play when we encode/decode the data packet using the message identifier to determine which hardware driver is relevant. In that context, the

---

10. If you recall the class model of an ATM controller I presented a couple of chapters ago, there was a Transaction entity. The subclasses of that entity did not include a Balance Request because nothing like the requested amount needs to be saved while processing an exchange of multiple messages with the banking subsystem. Suppose, though, that the collaboration between Dispatcher and Character Display became complicated enough for a balance display that it required executing multiple methods. Then we might need to temporarily save the value of balance we received from the banking subsystem until the Character Display was ready to receive it. Then we might need to abstract a class like Balance Request that has such an attribute.

message identifier is driving the processing, not the banking semantics of the value. The value is processed differently depending upon which device driver receives it, and all those device drivers care about is the numeric value itself.

Using the Balance Request abstraction may be more convenient for the problem in hand because we already abstracted Transaction. We will also name objects to provide a mapping to the underlying problem space. But we should not infer any particular semantics for the knowledge attribute that has Account semantics. In other words, the *balance* is just the value associated with a Balance Request in the ATM controller context. The fact that it is owned by something we call a Balance Request just provides us with a modicum of traceability when it is time to map that request into the banking software on the other side of the network port.

Those problem spaces coexist to the extent that the *value* attribute of Network Message will contain the same value as the balance attribute of Customer Account *in a particular request context*. Nonetheless, they are different problem spaces that can be abstracted independently. We, as omniscient developers, know how to map between those problem spaces. We can do so because we understand the context where the Network Message *value* attribute contains a Customer Account balance value and the context when it contains, say, the amount of a withdrawal request. We then provide software constructs to enforce the relevant mapping rules of those contexts across the subsystem boundary to ensure that the software works correctly in all cases. (Actually, the constructs come pretty much "for free" when we parse the message identifier.)

There are two points in this digression with the Network Message example. The first is to reemphasize that we must focus on the subject matter itself when abstracting knowledge attributes. The semantics of the value attribute of Network Message is not that of an account balance in that subject matter, even though we might specifically have a user request for current balance in mind when deciding we needed a Network Message object with a particular identifier. (The same is true for the Balance Request abstraction; the mapping lies in the Transaction identity.) The second point is that subject matters are often unique problem spaces that need to be abstracted independently even though there necessarily exist mappings between them.

The services a subsystem provides are dictated by external problem contexts, but the abstractions that implement the subsystem are dictated by only the subject matter, its problem space, and its level of abstraction.

So when evaluating what knowledge responsibilities are needed, be alert to shifts in the level of abstraction and the nature of the problem space being modeled. Try to avoid abstracting to the overall problem context.

What Is the Level of Abstraction?

The *value* attribute in the Network Message above is a good example of how the level of abstraction affects the way we abstract knowledge responsibilities. The Network Message entity is, itself, quite abstract because it represents a different problem space where we do not care about the semantics of the message content. As was indicated, this results in a very generic view of the *value* that only depends upon its properties as a data element. That is, in two different messages or transactions the semantics of the attribute could be quite different (e.g., account balance versus withdrawal amount), but the handling of the value will be pretty much the same (i.e., it will be forwarded to a hardware device driver as an integer or real number with specific maximum range and precision). Thus we need additional information, such as a message identifier or transaction type, to keep track of and map the semantics across subsystem boundaries.

> When in doubt, provide the most abstract view of knowledge that the problem in hand will allow.

In other words, we describe knowledge responsibilities with ADTs, so we should use them as fully as possible. Here the problem in hand is what is being solved by the subsystem, not the overall problem the application exists to solve. In solving the subject matter's problem, we seek every opportunity to extract solution invariants from the problem space. Invariants are always represented at a higher level of abstraction than particular solutions. However, it is not sufficient to simply recognize that all network messages look pretty much the same in a given context like an ATM controller (e.g., {message ID, <data packet>}). We also have to make sure that the way we abstract the entity's properties is consistent with that abstract view. If we follow the above guideline we will reinforce any invariants we have identified. More important, we will often uncover better entity abstractions, improve our solution collaborations, and even discover invariants from the bottom up when applying this guideline.

The other side of this abstraction coin is that we should let the level of abstraction of the subsystem itself drive the way we abstract knowledge responsibilities in the same way that it drives identifying entities. In the ATM controller subsystem we have defined the mission in terms of encoding and decoding messages and dispatching them. In addition, we pointedly omitted requirements related to banking rules and policies for things like validating accounts, approving withdrawals, and so forth. Thus the ATM controller's subject matter is very focused.

This subject matter has very detailed requirements concerning sequences of hardware operations, network protocols, and mapping messages to hardware components. In addition, in the overall banking system's structure it is a pretty low level service, equivalent to a UI. Nonetheless, it is actually quite abstract compared to the banking services subsystem as far as the semantics of banking is concerned.[11] The ATM controller subsystem has recast the banking semantics into message processing in a very mechanical but quite general way. So, when we define knowledge responsibilities we have to do so within the context of the way the subject matter abstracts things.

Even though our ATM controller is part of a banking system, we do not want to think in terms of business details like balances and withdrawal amounts. We will map to those concepts through the subsystem interface that defines the messages we process and through the way we encode/decode message data packets. But within the subsystem the entities and their knowledge are abstracted without that semantics. One of the most common ways to bleed cohesion across subsystems is to abstract a subsystem in terms of the overall business paradigm rather than just the nature of the subject matter in hand.

Does the Abstraction Need to Coalesce Entity Knowledge?

A lot of authors view the primary value of describing knowledge attributes with ADTs as strong typing; that is, it prevents Skyscraper objects from showing up in the midst of our Pristine Landscape. This is certainly valuable during OOP where the OOPLs employ type systems. However, at the OOA/D level it is really secondary to the ability to represent and manipulate complex data structures as scalar knowledge values. This ability is crucial to the flexible view of logical indivisibility that enables OO applications to avoid hierarchical implementation dependencies.

Look for opportunities to abstract data aggregates as scalar ADTs.

We've already talked about the way a simple attribute ADT in one subsystem can be expanded into complex structures involving multiple classes or even entire subsystems, so we won't repeat that here. However, we will emphasize that the developer needs to proactively look for opportunities to "hide" aggregates as ADTs.

At first blush, the obvious way to do this would seem to involve looking for aggregates (e.g., lists, arrays, etc.) where other objects in the subsystem do not need to

---

11. This is very common in service subsystems. They provide very detailed services for client subsystems, but those details are typically confined to a narrowly defined problem space. At the same time, those service subsystems employ problem space invariants to abstract away the semantics of the client. In other words, they abstract away any business semantics not related to their own subsystem. This ability tends to make service subsystems reusable across applications. Just thought we would point this out to reinforce the value of good application partitioning.

access individual members of the aggregate. Alas, if you just do this you will find there are few opportunities to abstract such aggregates into scalar ADTs, because the elements usually show up in an Object Blitz and we tend to express aggregates of them through 1:* and *:* relationships to other objects. So by the time we are looking for specific knowledge properties, we tend not to have obvious arrays and lists around.

More to the point, the elements show up as objects in the Object Blitz because we think we need them individually to solve the problem. By the nature of an Object Blitz, that is usually pretty well-founded, so it will be unusual to be able to eliminate both the element class and the * relationship. Nonetheless, blitzes aren't infallible so it is definitely worth a pass over the model to check for the possibility. The question to ask about any * relationship is: At this subsystem's level of abstraction, do we need to access objects of the *-side class individually?

So we need to look for aggregates in other ways. By far the most common is lumping together dissimilar but related attributes that we have already identified. A classic example is grouping {street, city, state, postal code} attributes into an Address ADT when it turns out the subject matter doesn't care about the individual elements. In a case like this it is usually pretty obvious, and before we have finished enumerating the individual attributes someone on the team will usually push back on why they are needed.

Therefore, we should keep an eye out for attributes that we initially think are needed individually but where we can raise the level of abstraction so that they aren't needed. In Figure 13-5 we have a very simplistic view of artifacts in a fantasy computer game. The Skeletal Model and Segments are one way of representing movement of the artifact at a scale that is computationally feasible. The game artifact, the Ogre, is subdivided into connected elements, Segments, that can be moved individually to provide articulation. To make things easy, we have included only the knowledge attributes of Segment for this discussion, and the obvious question is: How can we abstract some or all of those attributes into a single scalar ADT?

First, think about why we are modeling this. That is, what is the subject matter? Let's assume this is a high-level subsystem that exists to manage the game semantics. It enforces the rules of the game itself, such as Ogres always attack Heroes. It deals with the game actions at the level of the Ogre attacking a Hero and swinging a sword at the Hero's head. Those "high-level" movements are then relayed to some graphics rendering subsystem that does magical algorithmic things to create a smoothly flowing display. Given that context, how do we abstract the knowledge attributes of Segment?

One fairly obvious notion is *position*. We have five attributes that supply a very detailed view of where a particular limb element is at any time. Do we really care about that when thinking about swinging a sword at the Hero's head? Not really. We

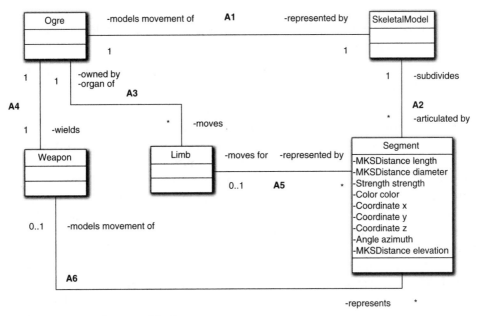

Figure 13-5 *Simplistic model of a computer game*

will care a lot about it in a very low-level service subsystem that contains all sorts of exotic graphics algorithms for display rendering, and we will care a lot about those details in a lower-level subsystem that deals with the physics of motion, collisions, and whatnot. But we probably don't care much about the specific location of the Ogre's forearm in the game logic subsystem.

What about the other attributes? It might be tempting to abstract these into something like *segmentData,* or we might make a case for *length* and *diameter* being abstracted as *geometry.* There wasn't enough information provided about the game semantics yet to make that call. For example, suppose the Hero always attacks the longest limb or targets an injury (low strength) first. Then we would need the length and/or strength attributes explicitly to target things like sword swings. But if we only needed strength, then *geometry* would probably be a good abstraction.

But to keep things simple, let's suppose we don't need any of the attributes. Now *segmentData* is looking pretty good. Could we also include *position* in that as well? Maybe. This depends on who the game artifact interacts with. It was already suggested that there are likely to be multiple supporting subsystems. Clearly *geometry, position,* and *color* are things the display rendering subsystem would need to know. But a subsystem that just computes movement trajectories for things like swinging a sword would not care about *color.* A combat subsystem that resolves damage would care about *strength* and *geometry* (for lopped off limbs) but not *position.* The point here is that even though we might be able to use *segmentData* to capture everything from the perspective of the subject matter in hand, it would not be desirable from the perspective of communicating with other subsystems.

> ADTs that are passed to other subsystems need to be abstracted consistently with the other subsystems' requirements.

With this in mind, *segmentData* is probably not the best choice because it contains irrelevant information for a particular service subsystem.

Having analyzed options for how to express Segment's attributes into ADTs, let's switch gears and say that was a waste of time because it was a trick question. Given the simplifying assumption that this subsystem does not care about *any* of the attributes individually, we really don't need Segment, much less its attributes. To see this, think about whether this subsystem would even need to manipulate *segmentData* or its variants. This subsystem is about Ogres swinging Swords at Heroes' heads. We have already relegated details for display rendering, movement physics, and whatnot to service subsystems. Why would we need an abstraction that enables swinging a sword to be approximated for graphical and combat resolution?

The answer is that we don't need *segmentData* for any reason other than to pass data to service subsystems. So why do we need to pass the data to service subsystems? Because the Skeletal Model has been defined in this subsystem. Why? Good question, that.[12] A skeletal model is a mathematical technique for solving different problems: display and movement resolution. It is basically a design strategy for dealing with an entirely different suite of requirements for things like graphics rendering and motion physics. *It has nothing to do with the Game semantics at the level of an Ogre swinging a Sword at a Hero's head.* So if we eliminate the Skeletal Model and Segment classes, the whole problem of abstracting attribute ADTs becomes a non-issue. In the relevant subsystems, there will be views of the Skeletal Model with all the attributes needed for that subsystem.

In case you are wondering, those models will very likely be instantiated via parametric polymorphism from external configuration data. This enables this subsystem to cause the corresponding Skeletal Model to be created in the service subsystem by simply supplying identity and some basic type information (Big Nasty Ogre versus Little Annoying Ogre) that the game system already logically knows. That information will be used to access the correct configuration data to initialize all the attributes properly. Ain't it great when a Plan comes together?

---

12. It was mentioned in Part I that a good way to elicit requirements is to ask "why" repeatedly; this is true for things like abstracting attributes as well. Pushing back by asking why we need an abstraction until it is fully justified is an excellent technique for getting to the right level of abstraction, as in this case.

Part III

The Dynamic Model

In Part II we learned how to define the stable structure or skeleton of the application. But that structure simply exists; it does not actually do anything to solve the customer problem. To actually solve the customer problem a software application must engage in computation.

But that computation must, itself, be done systematically, and it must be complementary to the static model. This part is concerned with developing such a systematic and consistent approach to specifying the dynamic computations needed. That systematic approach has a conceptual framework we call the dynamic model. The cornerstone element of the dynamic model, the object state machine, plays essentially the same role as the object did in the static model.

Part IV

The Dynamic Model

Chapter 14

Road Map to Part III

> *Every one is responsible for his own actions.*
> —Tamil proverb

While Part II was devoted to the static structure of the software solution, this part is devoted to the dynamics of the solution. Previously we examined what objects are, what they know, and how they are logically related. Now it is time to focus on what objects do.

Part III Road Map

In the translation methodologies in general and MBD in particular, the notion of dynamics has two parts: the structure of behavior, as captured in finite state machines (FSMs); and the actual algorithmic content, which we capture in an abstract action language. The use of finite state machines is mandatory in MBD for several reasons.

- Transitions define sequencing constraints from the problem space. Capturing such rules in static structure tends to simplify the executable code and enhance reliability.

- Certain types of sequencing errors can be detected and handled quite generically in a state machine infrastructure. Such errors can be detected in one place, the event queue manager, and handled in one place rather than having the detection code littered through many contexts.

- Interacting state machines are very unforgiving. Logical errors are very often immediately manifested. This makes it difficult to get them to interact properly initially, but once they are working they tend to be remarkably robust.

- State Transition Tables (STT) and State Transition Diagrams (STD) provide a high-level view of flow of control. This high-level view facilitates maintenance to a degree that is difficult to believe until we have actually used them. For example, in the author's experience roughly 70% of all logical errors can be isolated to a single state action by simply inspecting the relevant STDs for a few minutes.

- Interacting state machines are the best approach to dealing with the asynchronous communication model that is used in OOA/D for behaviors.

- The rules of finite state automata that govern state machines happen to rigorously enforce a number of OO fundamentals, such as encapsulation, implementation hiding, and peer-to-peer collaboration.

All of these things are important, but the last is the most significant by far. If we were to try to design a mechanism to *enforce* good OO practice, it would end up looking very much like object state machines.[1] Unfortunately, using state machines is not very intuitive to most newcomers to software development, which is why three full chapters are devoted to them.

State machines are not just for breakfast.

Sadly, the conventional wisdom contains a myth that state machines are only applicable to certain types of software development, specifically arcane areas of real-time embedded (R-T/E) programming. *This perception is utterly untrue.* Once we get used to using state machines it becomes clear that they can be applied to describe any behavior that is appropriate for OO design. The key insight is that state machines capture sequencing rules among behaviors in a very elegant manner. To the extent that sequencing of operations is absolutely critical to dynamics, state machines actually provide a very general tool for managing dynamics. In addition, most applications will be simpler, more robust, and more reliable for having employed them.

It's All about Behavior

Software is ultimately computational; it executes a solution to a problem that consists of a sequence of a very large number of tiny operations. Those operations may manipulate data, and the operations may be organized into clusters, but ultimately there will be no useful results without the solution doing a lot of mundane computa-

---

1. Or their more general brethren, Petri Nets. We use finite state machines rather than Petri Nets because their special constraints map better into the constraints of good OOA/D practice.

tion. All the object behavior responsibilities that we abstract as necessary to solving the problem in hand must execute.

The computational nature of software remains in place, but at the OOA level we have done a lot to organize it in particular ways. We have been very careful to define what data the behaviors chew upon. We have been careful about defining associations that restrict what data the behaviors chew upon. We have organized combinations of logically related knowledge and behavior responsibilities into objects that are abstracted from real entities in the customer's problem space. When we define behavior responsibilities, we define them in terms of intrinsic, logically indivisible responsibilities. All of that static structure defined in Part II was focused on one objective: providing a stable framework for specifying the behaviors that will be executed in the solution and the sequence in which they will be executed.

If you are unfamiliar with state machines, we will be discussing them in nauseating detail in the next few chapters. For the moment all you have to know is the summary in Figure 14-1. A state machine consists of states and transitions. A state is a condition where a particular suite of rules and policies apply, represented by the circles. We move from one state to another via a transition, which is a directed line between current and next states. The transition is triggered by an external event that carries a data packet with it. In the figure the alphabet is abstracted as individual data elements: a, b, c, and so on. Each state has an action that executes the relevant rules and policies when the state is entered, and that action processes the incoming alphabet according to the rules and policies of the state. That action is a behavior responsibility because it executes the rules and policies that prevail for the condition.

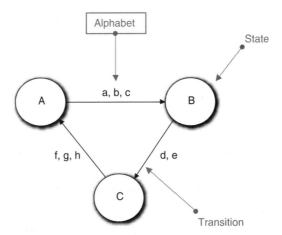

Figure 14-1 *Notation for a Finite State Automata (FSA)*

Particular events trigger transitions, so the state machine must be in the right current state to transition when a particular event is consumed. That is, there must be a transition exiting the current state to which the event is attached; otherwise, an error condition is raised. Thus the combination of events and transitions provides constraints on the sequencing of actions. A fundamental assumption of FSMs is that in a state, the action cannot know what state the machine was in previously or what the next state will be.

Now let's look at the properties of state machines and see how they line up with OO practice (see Table 14-1).

Table 14-1   *Comparison of State Machines and OO Practice*

FSM Property	Description	OO Characteristic
State Isolation	State cannot know prior state or next state	Cohesion, encapsulation, self-containment
Alphabet	State actions operate only on input alphabet	Collaboration (self-contained), collaboration (attribute access), message versus method
Event	Pure message triggers transition	Message versus method, messages as announcements
Transition	Limits next state	Collaboration

The fact that a state represents a condition where a unique suite of rules and policies apply, when combined with the constraint on knowing nothing about where it is going or where it is has been, provides a very rigorous encapsulation of a self-contained behavior. While the rules on processing an alphabet are more restrictive for finite state automata, they are generally relaxed for software state machines so that they match up exactly with the way the OO approach handles state variables. In other words, the action can obtain its alphabet either from the incoming event or by directly accessing state variables within the constraints of association navigation.[2] The notion of a state machine event very clearly corresponds directly with the notion of a message in OO collaboration.

The rules that govern valid transitions place rigorous constraints on the way collaborations can be executed. That is, it is the developer's job to make sure that a state machine is sent only events that will be valid for it *when the event is consumed*. Thus transitions provide constraints on behavior sequencing during collaborations that are

---

2. This is another reason why we want knowledge access to be synchronous. It essentially makes attribute access indistinguishable from parameter access from the method's perspective. However, direct attribute access makes data integrity issues much easier to manage than when data is passed via messages.

analogous to the constraints on attribute access provided by association navigation. Providing this analogous suite of (static) constraints on behavior sequencing is one of the main reasons MBD chooses to employ object state machines to describe all behavior. If we simply define methods without the state machine infrastructure, there is no explicit, structural mechanism for enforcing such sequencing rules.

Object state machines define collaboration.

Because of the way we abstract objects, they tend to be rather simple. Thus we expect that their behaviors, as expressed in state machine actions, should be rather simple. One of the main things we do when we use state machines is provide a rigorous framework for collaboration. The sequencing rules inherent in the transitions constrain interactions between objects. Those constraints drive how the objects must collaborate when we connect the dots for the overall problem solution. This will become much more obvious after we talk about DbC in a state machine context later in Part III. For the moment, just hold the thought that the actions may implement the behaviors but the state machine structure provides the skeleton for collaboration *between* behaviors.

As was mentioned, state machines are very unforgiving—precisely because of the sequencing rules implicit in the transitions. When we do not have the sequencing quite right, a transition error will be raised very quickly because the state machine is in the wrong state to consume the event. That's because those sequencing rules are explicitly incorporated in the static structure of the state machine itself. Without state machines to provide the necessary condition checking, the developer would have to encode it explicitly in the behaviors in every relevant context where the behavior is invoked, which would lead to very verbose, fragile, and redundant code.

The importance of strictly enforcing sequencing rules in the static structure of state machines cannot be overemphasized—it makes a huge difference for both code size and overall reliability. As a bonus, when the static structure constraints are violated it is very easy to detect, and we can provide that detection in the architectural infrastructure that the transformation engine provides. So, as application developers, we do not even have to even think about detecting the errors. The bad news is that you are likely to generate a *lot* of unexpected errors the first time you execute the overall model. The good news is that once you get them all fixed, you can be quite confident you have gotten the solution right.

Getting state machines to interact correctly usually requires implicit protocols for collaborations. Such protocols are known as *handshaking*. At its most basic level, the idea behind handshaking is that a message is not sent until the receiver announces that it is ready to accept the message. In effect we create a dialog between the objects that ensures that the solution steps will be executed in the correct sequence. The UML Interaction diagrams are classic examples of defining handshaking sequences, whether we employ object state machines or not.

Object Life Cycles

Complex behaviors that are related almost always entail some sort of sequential process; they must be performed in a set of steps that have a predefined order. Because the order is predefined, those steps are always executed in the same order no matter how many times the overall behavior is repeated. Such sequence and repetition is fundamental to hardware computational models. One way to think about the sequence of steps in an overall behavior is to think of the sequence as a life cycle of the overall behaviors, where the individual steps are stages in that life cycle.

In an OO environment this notion of life cycle is even more appropriate because we organize individual behaviors into cohesive suites in objects that represent problem space entities. Those entities very often have obvious life cycles in the problem space. For example, the construction of an automobile on a production line goes through a life cycle of growth from nothing to a fully assembled (mature) automobile. We can easily associate stages with that life cycle where various components are assembled: framing, drive train assembly, body assembly, and so forth. In the extreme, the notion of an instance of an object in a software application very clearly has a birth-to-death life cycle that never extends beyond a single execution of the software itself.

This notion of life cycle is just an analogy, but it is very pervasive in many problem space entities, computational sequences, software execution iterations, and the notion of objects being instantiated. Thus any construction paradigm based on the notion of life cycles is likely to be quite general in application.

That is especially true when we abstract objects as a collection of cohesive but stand-alone behavior responsibilities. Inevitably there will be some constraint in the overall solution that defines the order in which those individual responsibilities are executed. Thus, each responsibility has a designated *place* in the overall solution algorithm that defines a relative order. We use static transitions to define those sequencing dependencies as intrinsic constraints on the objects' behaviors *in the problem context*.

When objects collaborate to solve the problem, those collaborations form sequences that are often repeated, forming small cycles of collaboration within the overall solution context. The sequencing of those interactions between objects is what we capture in the state machine transition rules. Thus the "stages" of the state machine life cycle are really determined by the sequencing of its interactions with the outside world. There are four ways to capture those sequencing rules for interaction.

1. Enforcing the order in the implementations of behaviors that invoke other behaviors (i.e., "hard-wring" the sequence into method implementations)

2. Providing elaborate checking at the end of behaviors to determine what to do next

3. Daisy-chaining messages explicitly so that the order is enforced

4. Enforcing the sequencing rules in an explicit static infrastructure.

The first approach is classically procedural in nature because it is based on functional decomposition, so it usually results in hierarchical implementation dependencies. You definitely do not want to go there if you are doing OO development. The second approach is tedious, bloats the application, and is usually error prone. You don't want to go there unless you have a predilection toward masochism. The third approach is basically what the OO developer does if there is no explicit infrastructure to enforce the sequencing rules; the developer simply chains together operations in the right sequence. The problem here is that the developer has to get it right in *every collaboration situation,* and when it isn't right that may not be readily detectable.

The last approach is exactly what a state machine life cycle provides. The transitions define the allowed sequences between one stage of interaction and the next within a suite of external collaborations. This has two big advantages over the third approach. First, it only needs to be done once when defining the life cycle of the object. Second, state machines are very unforgiving. When the sequence is wrong you *always* get an error. This makes finding logical sequencing problems in message generation much easier. The developer still has to get the message generation right, but it will usually be painfully clear immediately when it isn't right.

Returning to the myth that state machines are just a niche tool, it should be clear that the opposite is actually the case. State machines provide an elegant mechanism of managing the sequences of operations that are inherent in *any* computational processing. More important, they actually enforce problem space rules on sequencing in a manner that makes it much easier to get the solution right.

Asynchronous Solution

In Chapter 2 it was noted that knowledge access is synchronous while behavior access is asynchronous in OOA/D. Now that we have the static structure under our belts we can expand upon the notion of asynchronous behavior communication. This is one of the fundamental things that distinguish OO design techniques, yet it is rarely explicitly mentioned in the OOA/D literature outside translation contexts. The author's speculation is that translation grew up in R-T/E where there is simply no choice about rigorously making that distinction, while outside R-T/E methodologists choose to capture the distinction indirectly in design guidelines, principles, and rules.

The reason that an asynchronous model is employed for behavior collaboration is that the OOA model (aka MDA PIM) needs to be independent of the computing environment. Providing a synchronous versus asynchronous implementation is a decision that depends explicitly on the computing environment and nonfunctional requirements. An asynchronous model is the most general description of behavior collaboration. As indicated in Chapter 2, a synchronous implementation is a special case of asynchronous implementation. But to make this clear, we need to digress with some definitions because there is a lot of misunderstanding in the industry about the differences between synchronous, asynchronous, and concurrent implementations.

> In synchronous processing, the order of execution of operations is deterministic in time for a given suite of inputs.

> In asynchronous processing, the order of execution of operations is nondeterministic in time for a given suite of inputs.

Basically, this means that in a synchronous implementation the order of execution is predefined; it will always be exactly the same for any set of input data. Basic procedural flow of control, where a calling procedure pauses until the called procedure completes, is a synchronous mechanism because it guarantees that all procedures will be executed in a fixed order. Thus all 3GLs, including the OOPLs, are inherently synchronous in nature; we have to bootstrap special software artifacts, such as event queue managers, to deviate from the synchronous model.[3]

Essentially, asynchronous processing means that there is an arbitrary delay between when a message is sent and when an operation is executed in response to that message. So if we send multiple messages, the order in which the responses are executed is arbitrary. (There are some exceptions needed to preserve the developer's sanity, which we will get to in the next chapter.) Note that this *requires* that the message be separated from the method, which is so fundamental to OOA/D that we have belabored it in almost every chapter of this book.

In asynchronous processing, the order of execution is not explicitly defined, and we can have different orders from one execution to the next even though the input data is identical. This view tends to be counterintuitive in a Turing world where the notion of a fixed sequence of operations is one of the cornerstones of the computational model. Unfortunately, the real world tends to be asynchronous when we deal with large problems. For example, network transmissions, particularly on the Internet, are notorious for having arbitrary delays due to traffic and routing problems. In Figure 14-2, assume Application A sends two messages, X and Y, to Application B and Application C, respectively.

We would intuitively expect the responses from Application B and Application C to be in the same order that the requests were issued by Application A, as indicated in

---

3. Fortunately for us translationists, that bootstrapping all lives in the transformation engine and supporting infrastructure.

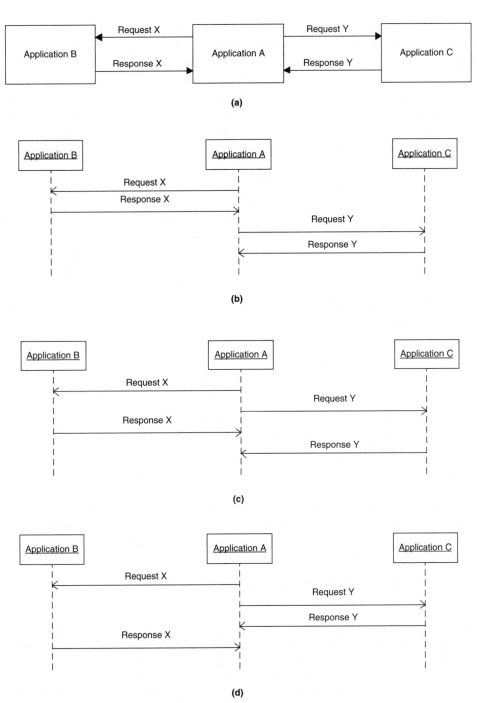

Figure 14-2 *Alternative sequences for message passing in a distributed environment*

Figure 14-2(b). (In fact, Figure 14-2(b) represents a pure synchronous view if Application A pauses to wait for the response to Request X before sending Request Y.) However, on a network there is no guarantee of that because A does not wait for a response. Request X might be delayed so that Request Y could be consumed first, or Response X could be delayed to produce Figures 14-2(c) or 14-2(d) from Application A's perspective. Any time we have processing that is load sensitive based upon something external to the problem solution, we have a potential for these sorts of physical delays. For example, the delay in recovering data from disk may depend upon the load placed on the DB server by other applications' requests.

The notion of perspective is important when dealing with asynchronous behaviors because there is another source of asynchronous behavior besides physical delays, as in a network. Whenever the stimuli to an application are in arbitrary order, we have inherently asynchronous behavior. The message loop in a GUI application is a classic example of this. The user makes essentially arbitrary selections from menus and so forth that determine what the user wants to do. That ordering is entirely at the whim of the user. Therefore, from the application's perspective, the order of requests for its functionality are in arbitrary order even though the data involved may be the same from one session to the next. So the user can ask for information on customer Ben and then customer Jerry in one session while asking for customer Jerry and then customer Ben in another session.

> An alternative definition of asynchronous processing is that the order in which external messages are presented for consumption is arbitrary.

This sort of arbitrariness in the order of external requests is just a variation on the notion of delays, albeit more general.[4] That is, we can *interpret* the variation in stimuli sequence in terms of delays. From the application's viewpoint it always has the capability of processing a request for customer Ben or processing a request for customer Jerry, and the user requests both. As far as the application knows, the user always makes the requests in the same order, but there is a different arbitrary delay in their delivery from one session to the next. Thus the notions of message delays versus message ordering are just different perspectives of the same inherent arbitrary nature of communication ordering.

> Asynchronous behavior is not the same as concurrent behavior.

---

4. So why lead with the less general notion of delays? We want to make sure that we construct our methods and collaborations in a way that decouples the message sender from the receiver. The best way to do that is by assuming an arbitrary delay between the generation of the message and the response to it. This assumption prevents us from even being tempted to make the sender dependent in any way on the response. Therefore, the best way to construct OO software at the OOA/D level is by always assuming delays.

One of the more common sources of confusion for novice developers is the difference between asynchronous behavior and concurrent behavior. As previously indicated, asynchronous behavior is about the ordering of messages or delays in responding to them. That is, asynchronous processing is about scheduling *when* a behavior is executed.

Concurrent processing involves the simultaneous execution of multiple behaviors.

Thus concurrency is about parallel execution of operations. If we have an application where only one method executes at a time, that application is not concurrent. Nonetheless, it can be asynchronous as long as the events that trigger each behavior's execution are not presented in a predefined order. Using the previous example, if the application can only access customer Ben's data or customer Jerry's data but not both at the same time, it is inherently nonconcurrent.[5] However, from the application's viewpoint there is no way to tell which the user will request first during any given session, so the processing of those requests is inherently asynchronous.

Now suppose the application *can* process a request for customer Ben's data and a request for customer Jerry's data at the same time. Now the application is concurrent whenever the second user request arrives before the processing of the first request completes. (Note that it is still inherently asynchronous as well, since either message could be first.)

Now suppose the user can request both customer Ben's data and customer Jerry's data in a single request. Internally, the processing of customer Ben's data is still a separate activity from processing customer Jerry's data. As a design decision, the developer will probably decide to always kick off processing for customer Ben's data first, immediately followed by kicking off processing for customer Jerry's data.[6] Now the order of kickoff events is predefined, so the application is synchronous. Yet it is still concurrent if the processing of the second event starts before the processing of the first event completes.

It is crucial to understand that asynchronous and concurrent processing are two very different things. Ironically, one reason this understanding is important is because in OOA we *always* think about asynchronous behavior communications while we *never* think about concurrent behavior processing! Understanding the difference explains why we can and do separate the two issues.

---

5. The word is used advisedly. There is a tendency in the literature to equate *synchronous* with *nonconcurrent*. However, that overloading of synchronous can be confusing because they really are different things. It is convenient because they tend to map 1:1; concurrent processing is almost always implemented with asynchronous communication while nonconcurrent processing is almost always implemented with synchronous communications. Just beware of the *almost*.

6. That decision mechanism may be as simple as "walking" a predefined list of customers.

We can ignore concurrent processing in the OOA because it is a pure computing space implementation. The fundamental logic of the application will be correct whether parallel processing is used or not. That's because we use parallel processing to address nonfunctional requirements like performance. Since our OOA solution to the customer's problem is supposed to be independent of decisions made around nonfunctional requirements, we defer the decision to provide parallel processing or not.

Similarly, the decision to use a synchronous implementation versus an asynchronous implementation is a computing space decision. Alas, this situation is a bit different because we still need to have *some* model of behavior communications to define collaborations in the OOA. Since synchronous execution is a special case of asynchronous, we choose the more general model for the OOA and defer the decision to implement synchronously.

Time Slicing

Before leaving the topic of asynchronous/concurrent behavior communications we need to address a related topic. In the computational models of Turing and von Neumann there is no direct way to implement concurrency. In fact, with the advent of multiple processor ALUs, the academics had to work overtime to come up with entirely new branches of mathematics to deal with parallel computation.[7]

The main idea behind things like threads is the notion of time slicing, which is necessary if we have only one processor. If we have two sequences of machine instructions, each encapsulated in a procedure, and a single processor, we can emulate parallel processing by alternating the execution of statements from each procedure. Even though only one instruction from one procedure is executing at a time, from the perspective of an external observer the procedures both *seem* to execute in parallel. That's because they both seem to start at about the same time and finish at about the same time. That's because we subdivide the overall execution time into small time slices, and in each time slice we allocate the processor to a single procedure.

While this model of parallel processing is rather simplistic because of issues like instruction pipelining, it still conveys the general idea behind the practical implementation of concurrency. We just use things like threads to apply the scope of concurrency across multiple program units (methods). The onus is on the developer to ensure that the processing in one thread does not step on the toes of another thread's processing. That is, the developer must be careful about defining threads that may access shared data.

---

7. Alas, so far all that new math has not yet been implemented in the engineering of 3GL optimizing compilers except in very rudimentary ways. Instead, the developer is given constructs like threads to bootstrap the most complicated part—deciding what sequences can execute concurrently without stepping on each other.

The reason for bringing this up is because it demonstrates the sorts of issues the translation engine must address. This indirectly justifies a number of practices that are incorporated in OOA/D in general and MBD in particular—practices like separation of message and method; the use of object state machines; encapsulation of methods as logically indivisible, self-contained, intrinsic behaviors; treating knowledge access as synchronous while behavior access is asynchronous; and peer-to-peer messaging. All these things play together to manage scope in a way that makes life easier and deterministic for the transformation engine to implement things like concurrency.[8]

Synchronous Services

In a strict sense, not all behavior occurs in state machine actions, despite the previous discussion. Nor is all behavior asynchronous. Some behavior resides in what we cleverly call *synchronous services*, methods that are invoked directly rather than being triggered by events. MBD constrains what sorts of behaviors can be placed in synchronous services. But to understand those constraints we need to digress a bit into what constitutes *behavior*.

Thus far we have not distinguished among different sorts of behavior. That was fine so far because we were not dealing with the dynamics of solutions directly. Now, though, we need to identify certain characteristics of behaviors.

A problem-specific behavior is one that is unique to the customer problem in hand.

An invariant behavior is one that can be applied to multiple customer problems.

The overall solution to the customer's problem is expressed in terms of problem-specific behaviors. When we talked about abstracting behavior responsibilities from the problem space that are necessary to solving the customer's problem, we were talking about problem-specific behaviors. These behaviors make the developer's solution for functional requirements unique. In practice, though, we often apply algorithms and whatnot that are not unique to the problem in hand. Such algorithms are generic or invariant relative to the customer problem space and can be applied to many different customer problems. Often we will "glue" together a number of such generic algorithms in our unique problem solution.

This picture is complicated by the abstraction of application partitioning into subject matters. In this view, any subsystem that can be reused in different applications is generic with regard to a particular application solution. Yet we abstract the content of service subsystems the same way we abstract the root problem subsystem. Application

---

8. Note that if the development is manual elaboration, following these practices is even more useful. They essentially enable a more cookbook approach to OOD/P that will pay dividends in productivity (less rework) and reliability (fewer defects).

partitioning effectively changes our perspective about what a problem-specific behavior is and what an invariant behavior is. Thus each subsystem has its own subject matter problem space. When we abstract behaviors from the subject matter problem space, we are abstracting problem-specific behaviors *for that problem space* even though the application customer may not even know they exist.

For example, suppose we have an application that allocates a marketing budget to various advertising mediums (TV spots, newspaper ads, magazine ads, billboards, etc.). The overall solution will be all about notions like demographics, market size, media appeal, and region. Since it is a complex problem we may decide to use a particular mathematical operations research technique to solve the problem, say, a linear programming algorithm. Linear programming is a commonly used optimization technique, and the algorithm is self-contained.[9] So the only thing about the algorithm that is unique to the budgeting problem is setting up the data the algorithm needs. That setup is problem specific because it depends on the semantics of the advertising context, such as demographics. But the linear programming algorithm itself is an invariant.

As a practical matter, the linear programming algorithm is fairly complicated, so it is likely we would encapsulate it in its own subsystem. For that subsystem the problem space is now a particular branch of operations research. The linear programming algorithm involves a bunch of standard manipulations of matrices in a particular sequence. We would likely abstract a number of specialized Matrix objects and would associate behaviors with them, such as *transpose* and *invert*. Those operations are defined in a much broader mathematical scope than linear programming, thus they are invariants relative to the subject matter's problem of linear programming optimization.

The key point here is that our perception of what is problem specific and invariant is much like special relativity; it depends upon where the observer is standing. In particular, it depends upon which subsystem we are developing at the moment.

Problem-specific behaviors are organized by state machines.

Invariant behaviors are usually encapsulated in synchronous services or subsystems.

While our view of what is problem specific and what is invariant depends upon subject matter context, once we have established the appropriate perspective we need to be fastidious about where we put each sort of behavior. We put problem-specific behaviors in state machines because we use state machines to solve the subject matter problem via collaborations while state machine transitions define constraints on the sequencing. That's because we need a disciplined way of connecting the dots for the

---

9. Being self-contained means that it operates on a great gob of data that is organized in a particular way. Other than supplying the data and extracting the results, there are no other interactions with the algorithm. So, conceivably, we could encapsulate the entire algorithm in a single procedure.

overall solution, which is the creative part of solving the problem. Since invariant behaviors are defined elsewhere, we aren't concerned with their internal flow of control because that is predefined. Therefore, we encapsulate them so they don't distract us from solving the problem in hand.

The most common use of synchronous services is for objects that exist to hold knowledge. A classic example is a String class that we might use in OOP to manage text characters. Such an object has no intrinsic properties that are unique to the problem in hand. For example, if our String class is an ADT for a person's *address* in the problem domain, the operations that the string class provides depend in no way on the problem semantics of *address*. Its intrinsic behaviors are solely manipulations of its knowledge (individual characters), even though they may be fairly complex, such as concatenation. Thus a String has no life cycle that is relevant to the problem in hand, so we would put all of its text manipulation behaviors in synchronous services.[10]

A similar logic applies to the Matrix abstraction in the prior example. The operations on a matrix's elements can be quite complex algorithmically. But in the linear programming context they are self-contained data manipulations that are not at all dependent on a specific problem context like linear programming. Similarly, the entire linear programming technique is independent of a specific problem context like allocating marketing budgets. It is just so complex that it warrants being its own subsystem rather than being encapsulated as a synchronous service.

Generally we can classify synchronous services as the following:

- *Accessor.* The behavior reads or modifies the object's knowledge. These are usually quite simple because they are limited to getting the value of the object's knowledge or updating it with a new value.

- *Tester.* This behavior tests the value of the object's information. For example, we might want to know if the current knowledge value is equal to a particular value.

- *Transformer.* This sort of synchronous service transforms the object's information in some way. The classic examples are behaviors like *transpose* and *invert* that might be associated with a Matrix object.

- *Instantiator.* These synchronous services are used to instantiate objects and their associations.

---

10. Actually, since String is a class that would normally only appear during OOP, we would not abstract those operations in an OOA model. (Remember, a knowledge ADT is abstracted as a scalar value.) We simply used this example because it should be familiar to the reader. However, if we encounter a subject matter where the individual characters were of interest, then we might have a String *class* in the OOA model with those responsibilities. That class would still be a data holder and the operations would be problem independent.

There are three important characteristics of synchronous services that follow from this description. The first characteristic is that they are, indeed, *synchronous*. Unlike generating events, the synchronous service is invoked directly and the caller cannot continue until it is completed. The reason is that the client is accessing the object's knowledge, which must be synchronous access in order to ensure data integrity. Since all synchronous services are ultimately invoked from state actions and we use an asynchronous model for behavior collaboration, this means that a synchronous service is *an extension of the invoking state machine action.*

The second characteristic is that they do not collaborate with problem-specific behaviors of other objects. Since we describe all significant problem-specific behavior with state machines in MBD and state machines provide the framework for behavior collaboration, this means that synchronous services should never generate events. This constraint is a direct result of the services being synchronous and being limited to operations on a narrowly defined set of data.[11]

The third characteristic of synchronous services is they do not apply rules and policies that are unique to the problem in hand. Drawing this line in the sand is usually easy for experienced OO developers, but it tends to seem quite arbitrary for novice OO developers. The problem is that if we want to get picky, any modification of data is behavior by definition. More to the point, modifying data is usually what behaviors live to do.

Sometimes we can use the uniqueness of the problem space as the criteria, as we did with the *transform* synchronous service of a Matrix object. We can stretch that to a conversion from *volts* units to *millivolts* units in an attribute setter because the conversion rule exists outside the specific problem's space and the need to convert is implicit in the ADTs of source and target values. But what about a getter that computes the value of *salaryCost* by multiplying *baseSalary* by *burdenRate*?

The formula represents a business rule, but one can argue that it is dictated by invariant, external accounting standards. In the end, deciding whether business rules and policies can be in a synchronous service usually comes down to whether the knowledge change is intrinsic to the knowledge and does not depend on the overall solution state. In practice, this means that if there are constraints on *when* the knowledge can be modified relative to modifying other object knowledge or invoking object behaviors, then that constraint needs to be captured in a state machine transition so those rules and policies would have to be in a state machine action.

---

11. A more practical reason is that since events connect the dots of flow of control, we want to be able to see that flow of control at a consistent level of abstraction. If all event generation is limited to state machine actions, we only need to look at those actions to follow what is going on. That is, nothing about flow of control is hidden in nested synchronous service calls. This makes the application a lot easier to debug when something goes awry with state machine interactions.

Avoid nested synchronous services.

Keep synchronous services simple.

You will greatly reduce the risk associated with making the wrong guesses about using synchronous services versus state actions if your synchronous services are self-contained. They will also be more robust during maintenance if you keep them simple. In particular, it is a good idea to limit the content of each synchronous service to the categories identified at the start of the topic.[12]

Action Languages

Many moons ago, before MDA and UML, the dynamics of state actions and synchronous services were described using a special sort of Data Flow Diagram known as an Action Data Flow Diagram (ADFD). ADFDs are rarely used today because centuries of experience have provided us with very elegant text-based languages for describing algorithms. So by the mid-'90s, almost all the commercial translation tools had converted to using a text language to describe dynamics rather than the traditional ADFD. Alas, this conversion was not painless. Some of the early AALs quite literally mimicked the ADFD by mapping one process to one statement. This led to a very verbose syntax where every atomic process—read accessor, arithmetic operation, write accessor, etc.—had to be in a separate statement. That effectively eliminated compound expressions such as one typically finds in 3GL code. Worse, each such statement had to be on its own line. The end result was carpal tunnel syndrome for the developers and AAL code listings that killed more trees than the hard-copy printouts of the ADFDs! Fortunately, most modern AALs have adopted more conventional and compact syntax.

A far more serious problem, though, was the level of abstraction of the text AALs. Some vendors figured that if we used a 3GL directly as the action description language, we could save a lot of transformation processing and make the learning curve for the developer much easier. So a number of translation tools in the late '80s and early '90s decided to use C++ as the action description language.[13] As it happens, those tools effectively became precursors of the round-trip tools that are common today.

---

12. Obviously, you are not going to put an entire linear programming algorithm in a single synchronous service. When the processing is complex enough to warrant development outside of the application model using other techniques, then all you need to do is invoke that processing from within the model.

13. The language was augmented with preprocessor directives that linked the C++ syntax to model elements. Thus the only true code generation needed was replacement of the preprocessor directives with C++ code derived from the graphical diagram element semantics.

Unfortunately this was a very slippery slope, because using a 3GL language to describe the dynamics completely trashes the level of abstraction of UML, which should be a 4GL. That's because a 3GL is a language for implementing the design while the OOA model specifies the design. Moreover, in an MDA context the PIM should be independent of the choice of such languages. In addition, particular 3GLs introduce computing space implementations like stack-based memory scope management. But worst of all, from a language like C++ we can encode any strategy, access any available technology, and address any nonfunctional requirements. In other words, the developer can do anything that could normally be done during OOP. Thus, using a 3GL to describe dynamics opens a huge door for implementation pollution of the model that effectively destroys its value as an abstract design specification.

The AAL described later in Part III has a level of abstraction that is consistent with the rest of the OOA model and independent of particular implementations. Using such an AAL to describe detailed dynamics is the only way to obtain the advantages of a true 4GL problem solution.

Mealy versus Moore versus Harel

In Figure 14-1, a model for state machines was described where the relevant rules and policies were contained in an action executed on entry to a state. There are actually a number of different models for implementing finite state automata in state machines. The model described is known as the Moore model. In the Moore model, the state action is executed as a new state is entered, and it is quaintly called an *entry action*.

Another common model is the Mealy model where the action is attached to a transition rather than entry to the state. In this model we can have different actions associated with different transitions when there are multiple transitions to a given state. The Mealy model arose because of a conundrum with Moore when the practicalities of action execution were considered. A state machine must always be in some state, which implies that the transition between states is instantaneous. However, if an action is executed on entry to a state, this creates a problem because actions, in practice, take a finite time to execute. The Mealy model gets around this problem with the notion that the action is executed when the triggering event is "consumed" by the state machine, which enables the transition to be instantaneous upon completion of the action.

Mathematically, the Mealy and Moore models are fully convertible; any Mealy model has an equivalent Moore model and vice versa. There are some situations where a Moore state machine will have additional states compared to the Mealy version, but the logical equivalence holds.

MBD employs the Moore model.

MBD is adamant about using the Moore model. That's because the Mealy model effectively associates the action with consuming the event. In other words, the notions of message (event) and method (action) are merged. From there it is a very short step to regarding the event as an imperative to do something (*Do This*). The MBD position is that we should avoid even the temptation to define collaborations in terms of imperatives, so MBD insists on rigorous separation of message and method to ensure events are regarded as announcements (*I'm Done*). By associating the action with entering the state rather than the event, MBD ensures a purist separation of the announcement message and the response action.

So how does MBD deal with the conundrum of an entry action taking finite time when the transition needs to be instantaneous? The short answer is that we don't worry about it because it is an arcane theoretical issue. The engineering answer is that there is a logically equivalent Moore model for every Mealy model. If they are logically equivalent, then we can solve the OOA problem for the customer with Moore models. If that doesn't satisfy you, then consider these two fundamental assumptions of MBD object state machines.

1. An object's state machine can consume only one event at a time.

2. The current state of an object's state machine is not visible outside the object's implementation.

If these two practical rules apply, then it really doesn't matter if the transition is instantaneous or not. The current state is only of interest for internally dispatching to the proper action. Prior to consuming an event, the state machine will be in a state. When finished consuming the event (i.e., when the action has completed execution), the state machine will be in the new state. Since the current state is externally inaccessible, any delay in transitioning cannot affect the solution results as long as only one event is consumed at a time.

Another popular state machine model found in OO contexts is the Harel model. The Harel model extends the Mealy model to include a notion of inheritance between distinct superclass state machines and subclass state machines. The Harel model also supports a notion of history about prior states that can be used to modify transitions. Using the Harel model can result in very elegant expressions of very complex interactions. This can be very useful for describing behavior at the subsystem level.

> If you are tempted to use Harel for an object state machine, you probably have a serious problem with object abstraction.

The problem is that MBD does not use subsystem state machines; it only uses state machines to describe individual object behaviors. We take pains to provide cohesive abstractions of problem space entities that are self-contained, logically indivisible, and context-independent at the subject matter's level of abstraction. We also tailor our object abstractions to the subject matter, which narrows the potential responsibilities. Those techniques tend to result in rather simple object abstractions. If the behavior of an individual object is so complex that it must be expressed using a Harel model, then it is very likely that the object has too many responsibilities, or it is not abstracted at the correct level of abstraction for the subsystem subject matter.[14] If you are ever so tempted you should immediately look for a delegation in the problem space, as described in Part II.

The Learning Curve

Novices to OO development usually find it relatively easy to define abstract classes and relationships from the problem space. There are even mechanical techniques, such as Object Blitzes described in Part II, for identifying objects. Unfortunately, it often takes awhile before they get the knack of defining the *right* abstractions and getting them to play together properly. That is, the art of defining static structure lies in *what* we abstract from the problem space rather than in abstraction itself.

Exactly the opposite is usually true for dynamics. Novices often have difficulty in recognizing *any* life cycle in objects, which is why the myth arose that using state machines is a niche technique (i.e., they can be used everywhere except *my* problem). However, once the initial hurdle is overcome and they start to recognize life cycles readily, it becomes a fairly mechanical process to ensure that the state machines are well formed.

By the time the developer gets to the point of describing what goes on *within* state actions and synchronous services, the OO paradigm looks pretty much like procedural coding. Only the level of abstraction is different. As long as the responsibilities were properly defined during problem space abstraction, it is pretty hard to screw that up. And if we do screw it up, encapsulation and implementation hiding ensure that it won't corrupt the rest of the solution.

So in Part III we are going to emphasize how we think about life cycles and provide some guidelines for making sure the life cycle is properly formed. An AAL will be described briefly, but only to the extent of describing how their level of abstraction is different from that of 3GLs.

---

14. Personally I have a problem with history as well. Even though Harel actions do not directly make use of it, the notion of making use of past state history seems like a violation of the FSA idea that a state cannot know where it has been. Arguing that we are just modifying transitions and not the actions themselves strikes me as an overly facile rationalization. In addition, history makes implementation enormously complicated. For example, the UML specification of Harel history (as of v2.0) is ambiguous, so the transformation engine vendor has to make implementation assumptions to support it.

Chapter 15

The Finite State Machine

Who changes his condition changes fortune.
—Italian proverb

Condition makes, condition breaks.
—Scottish proverb

In this chapter we get down to the meat of describing the dynamics of the problem solution. The most basic tool for doing that in MBD is the finite state machine (FSM). The FSM is probably the most elegant and important general mathematical tool applied to software development.[1] More important, it is extraordinarily applicable to OO development. That's because the rules for FSMs explicitly enforce basic OO principles. We would be hard pressed to design a tool that provides the same degree of rigorous enforcement of things like encapsulation, implementation hiding, separation of message and method, and peer-to-peer collaborations.

As an added bonus, the asynchronous assumptions underlying FSMs fit very nicely into the context of OOA modeling where we need to be independent of specific computing environments. As has already been pointed out several times, an asynchronous description is the most general description of behavior. Since FSMs can only interact asynchronously, using them forces us to develop an OOA model of solution behavior that is independent of the computing environment and has no hierarchical implementation dependencies—just as we should.

The rest of this chapter is devoted to the basics of identifying FSMs in the problem space.

---

1. Before you send in your cards, letters, and death threats to laud the importance of the computational models of Turing and von Neumann, note the use of the qualifier "general." The computational models, while mathematically defined, were created specifically to address the problem of computation. The finite state automata theory that underlies FSMs was developed independently and was not applied to software development until the late '40s.

Basic Finite State Automata

The underlying mathematics for FSMs is Finite State Automata (FSA). In an FSA there are three essential elements:

1. *State.* This is a unique condition where a specific suite of rules and policies apply. In an FSA those rules and policies determine how an input *alphabet* is to be processed in that state. An important rule for FSAs is that the rules and policies at a given state may not depend in any way on what the previous state was or the next state will be (i.e., they are self-contained and only depend on the alphabet and the condition). Diagrammatically, an FSA state is traditionally shown as a circle that is labeled with a unique state identifier.[2]

2. *Transition.* This is just a change in state indicated by an arrow from the current state to the new state. Triggering a particular transition is controlled externally to the FSA itself; the FSA just enforces the rules for valid transitions from a given current state.

3. *Alphabet.* The mathematical definition is a bit arcane, but for our purposes we can think of the alphabet as some set of input values provided when the transition is triggered. The rules and policies of the new state operate on the input values. If there are multiple transitions into a state, then they must all have the same alphabet. Diagrammatically the alphabet is usually an enumeration of variables attached to the transition.

Figure 15-1 illustrates a simple FSA. Note that state X cannot be reached from either of the other states—a classic case of you-can't-get-there-from-here. This is rather unusual for software situations, particularly object life cycles, but it is occasionally seen.

In FSAs there are some assumptions that cannot be realized in real software. The FSA is always in some state (i.e., the transition is instantaneous). Similarly, the rules and policies that process the alphabet take no time to execute. Finally, the rules and policies operate only on the input alphabet (i.e., there is no persistent data in the FSA). The main differences between FSMs, as applied in OO development, and FSAs lie in the handling of these assumptions.

The basic definitions of state and transition remain the same. The notion of alphabet, though, is considerably expanded to include state variables (the knowledge attributes of objects) that are persistent across states. This is necessary to address the

---

2. Most UML drawing tools use a rectangle with rounded corners. That's because it is user-friendly to put additional information in the state, such as a description of the condition's rules and policies, that fits better in a rectangle.

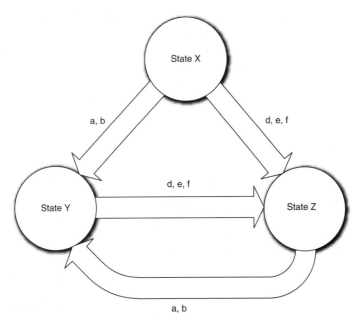

Figure 15-1 *Example of an FSA life cycle with constraints on the sequences in which states may be accessed*

fundamental dichotomy of object abstraction in terms of both knowledge and behavior. Since knowledge is accessed synchronously in OOA/D, accessing attributes is not significantly different than accessing input parameters as long as the processing is self-contained.[3]

Since the notion of accessing knowledge includes the possibility of modifying it, the scope of activity of the alphabet processing is greatly enlarged by this expansion of the idea of what an alphabet is. That's because the processing can modify knowledge attributes in addition to providing an alphabet for outgoing transitions. That immediately introduces issues around data integrity in real software. One of the reasons that OO development emphasizes things like encapsulation, abstracting *intrinsic* responsibilities, and peer-to-peer collaboration is to better manage data integrity by managing the scope of change. This is in part why the FSA paradigm is so useful—it limits the scope of the rules and policies that are executed in a state by ensuring they are self-contained.

> An **action** implements the rules and policies associated with the state condition. A state machine action is an object method.

---

3. This is one reason why attributes are accessed directly by methods on an as-needed basis. It ensures that the alphabet is unambiguously defined *at the time the state is entered*.

In an FSM we encapsulate business rules and policies in an *action*. The action's processing is that associated with the particular condition's rules and policies. That containment of processing is very important when it is time to implement things like concurrent processing because it rigorously defines the scope of change.[4] That containment is further enhanced by the introduction of a conceptual infrastructure to support object FSMs: the event queue. The introduction of an event queue decouples actions from one another.

> An **event** is a message that announces some change in conditions within the overall software solution.

Events are FSM artifacts that are associated with transitions. Technically an event announces some change in the condition and that announcement triggers a transition. We need events because we have multiple interacting FSMs in a typical OO subsystem, so that quasi-mystical "external trigger" of the FSA is quite concrete in an OO subsystem. It actually originates in another object FSM with its own state conditions to worry about. In addition, we need some mechanism for passing around the alphabets from one object FSM to another. So, we introduce the interpretation of *event* as a message between FSMs that triggers transitions, and the event message's data packet represents at least part of the alphabet.

What about the assumptions of instantaneous transitions and actions in the FSA? So glad you asked, Grasshopper. That is, indeed, a conundrum, because software actions require finite time to complete. Also, in an asynchronous model we could potentially have the state machine processing two actions at the same time if the events appeared quickly. The answer is the event queue. All events directed to the FSM are enqueued by the event queue manager for later processing. The event queue then "pops" the events one at a time to ensure that the FSM only consumes one at a time (i.e., the event queue manager waits until the object FSM has completed any current processing before popping the next event from the queue). This very neatly gets around the finite execution time problem for state actions because the event queue manager serializes[5] the processing to ensure the state machine doesn't step on itself.

---

4. Since we are talking about 4GL PIMs primarily in this book, we are not going to go into implementation details. Note, though, that standard concurrency techniques like thread management, semaphore blocking, and whatnot are a lot easier to implement correctly when the scope of change is known to be limited to a single procedure. (Usually state machine actions conveniently map 1:1 to 3GL procedures.)

5. This notion of serialization is quite common in the RAD IDEs that largely hide asynchronous processing. Invariably, behind the scenes that infrastructure is event-based, and there is an event queue manager somewhere that enables events to be serialized. To this day many RAD tools refer to the public hooks they provide to invoke developer code "on events."

However, the event queue manager is really an implementation issue. Typically it will be a reusable library class and the details of instantiating it will be determined by nonfunctional requirements. Therefore, we need to raise the level of abstraction and never explicitly create EventQueueManager objects in an OOA model. The concept is abstracted in the idea of events as special messages and in certain assumptions the developer can make. Then the event queue manager is just an implementation infrastructure to support the message passing concept. There are assumptions the developer can make when designing collaborations.

1. Only one event at a time is consumed by a given FSM. The event queue in the implementation takes care of this, so the developer can rely on this assumption.

2. Multiple events from the same sender FSM to the same receiver FSM will be consumed in the same relative order that they were generated. This is crucial to proper management of data integrity in an asynchronous behavior model with state variables; without this rule the developer's mind will tend to boggle. It can occasionally be a pain for the transformation engine to enforce, but we simply can't live without it.

3. Self-directed events will be consumed before external events directed to same FSM. Self-directed events are generated by an FSM to itself. They are often a symptom of poor design, which will be addressed later. However, there are some rare situations where they can be useful, and this rule is necessary for those situations. Thus the developer can rely on this prioritization within the event queue manager.

Note that the introduction of event messages is quite consistent with the OO separation of message and response (method). In an object FSM, the event is a separate model element that is associated with the transition. In fact, we can fully design object FSMs without considering events at all and then, in a later pass, we can determine where events are generated and associate them with the relevant transitions.

One interesting implication to underscore the distinction between event and transition is that we could associate the same event with multiple transitions in the FSM. This means that the response to the message (i.e., condition rules and policies to be executed) could be different depending on what the *current condition* of the object is. In effect we have the potential for behavior substitution without the subclassing infrastructure usually associated with inclusion polymorphism—it is done within a single object! This sort of substitution is not possible in a pure FSA model because only the alphabet is defined for the transition, not an identifiable event.

There is one final issue that was discussed briefly in the part road map: Exactly when is the action executed? In a pure FSA, it is executed on entry to the state. An

FSM that has the same rule is known as a Moore FSM (known in UML as a *behavioral state machine*). As indicated in the Part III road map, there is a theoretical conundrum related to finite action execution time. The people who worry about such things came up with the Mealy FSM (known in UML as a *protocol state machine*), whereby the action is associated with the transition and it is executed when the event that triggers the transition is consumed.

Alas, there are other deeply philosophical OO issues at stake because of the implications of the Mealy model *in an OO context*. Mealy is just not a good fit with basic OOA/D technique. In the Mealy model the key implication, which is supported by many OOA modeling tools, is that we could have different actions on different transitions targeting the same new state. If we have gone that far, then we could have different alphabet parameters for those actions. That is pretty far removed from the original FSA definition. In particular, it pretty much trashes the fundamental state definition that it is a condition where a *unique set of rules and policies always apply*. In effect the Mealy view says that there are multiple sets of rules and policies that *might* apply.

However, that is not the big problem with Mealy. The real concern is with how we select a particular set of rules and policies from among the alternatives to be executed when the state is entered. They are selected based upon the context (i.e., the particular transition/event).[6] Alas, one of the fundamental rules of FSAs is that the rules and policies can't depend on what the last state was. At this point it seems that the theoretical mapping to FSA theory is getting pretty thin indeed. But the back-breaking straw is that it opens a Pandora's box of temptation in an OO context by enabling the action to be mapped directly to the event.

In an OO context events are supposed to be messages that announce some change in the state of the application. The OO paradigm separates message and method precisely so that those announcements can be made with no expectation of what will happen. This enables the behavior implementation where the event is generated to be independent of what will happen as a result. But if we map the resulting action directly to the event, that decoupling goes away. There is now an explicit expectation of what will happen when a particular event is generated. That is a very procedural mindset that invites one to create implementation dependencies in the sender implementation. Removing that temptation is why...

In MBD we only use the Moore model for object FSMs.

---

6. In theory, we could have different actions for the same event on different transitions. (I have always suspected this was what the Mealy authors had in mind.) However, in practice, Mealy models are almost always constructed with 1:1 mapping between action and event, which is the tendency we seek to avoid by using Moore models.

For the previous discussion we need to clarify the difference between a condition in an object FSM and a condition of the overall solution. Since the object has a much narrower focus than the overall solution, object FSM states tend to be subsets of the overall solution's conditions. In general, the DbC postcondition of an FSM action maps closest to a condition of the overall solution. However, the overall solution includes things like data integrity constraints for every attribute in the entire application, most of which are irrelevant to a particular object's responsibilities.

Notation

Figure 15-2 represents the graphical view of a State Transition Diagram (STD) in UML, which is the traditional name for such diagrams. It is called a *statechart* in UML. The state is represented as a box with rounded corners that is divided into two sections. The state condition identifier is placed in the upper section of the box. A natural language description of the state goes in the lower section. In MBD this is usually a natural language pseudocode for what the action does. (Most tools enable the description view to toggle between the natural language description and the actual abstract action language [AAL] specification for the behavior, but we'll deal with that later.)

Figure 15-2 *Relationship of events to state machine transitions*

The arrows in Figure 15-2 represent the allowed transitions. The event that triggers the transition is associated positionally with the transition. It has a unique identifier and a mnemonic description of the event. Generally, we do not include the passed input values in the event message in MBD, although most tools allow that. There are a several reasons for this, including that the alphabet tends to clutter the diagram. Another reason is that we usually apply MBD with tool support and the full event description is just a click away. The main reason, though, is that we look at the Statechart diagram to view the solution flow of control. At that level of abstraction the specific arguments are peripheral details.

There is a special situation that applies when an object is created and must be placed in an initial state. This is a one-time event in the life cycle, and it is sometimes known as a "create" event. This is represented by a "floating" transition into a state that has no source state. The floating end is terminated with a small solid circle. We also use this notation to indicate a set of transitions from substates, as in Figure 15-3.

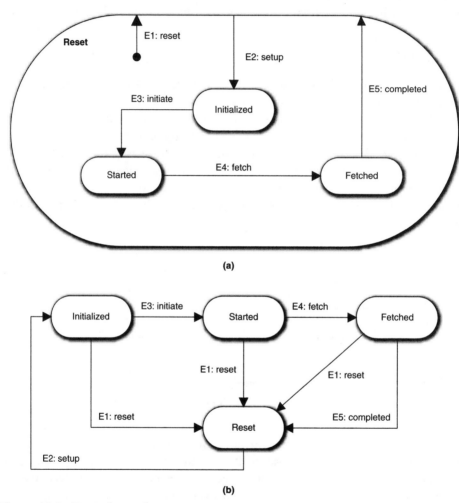

Figure 15-3 *Equivalence of superstate notation to peer states*

Figure 15-3 represents one variation of representing state machines that is worth discussing: superstates. The notion of superstates was originally expounded in the Harel model for FSMs. As indicated in the previous chapter, MBD does not employ the Harel model. However, we do provide a superstate artifact that is handy for reducing diagram clutter. As shown in Figure 15-3(a), a Reset state performs an action to reset some test hardware. The main structure indicating a basic life cycle progression[7] is: Reset → Initialized → Started → Fetched → Reset.

The problem is that the E1:reset event can be issued at any time to halt the current sequence, which results in a transition back to the Reset state from every other state. There are two reasons why it is advantageous not to draw those transitions explicitly. One is the clutter of the additional transition lines in the diagram that distracts us from the important processing and sequencing constraints. In a simple example like this that is no big deal, but in a more complicated FSM we would have ugly cross-overs and whatnot for the transitions. More important is that the E1: reset event will only get issued when some sort of exceptional situation arises in the external world (i.e., the normal return to Reset is just from Fetched via E5:completed). Thus the top diagram clearly shows the normally expected life cycle without any distraction for rare scenarios.

It must be emphasized that this is not the Harel view of superclasses. In Harel, the Reset state would probably be called something like Active and it would have some behavior that was executed when any of the E2, E3, E4, or E5 events was processed, such as ensuring that a port connection to the hardware was available. That is, the superset state would have some unique behavior shared by all of the contained sub-states. In the MBD approach that is not the case. Reset is just another state in the life cycle, with its own unique rules and policies that only get executed when a transition is explicitly made to it. The superstate is basically a pure notational artifact to reduce the number of transition lines necessary on the diagram. Thus part (a) in Figure 15-3 is semantically equivalent to part (b).

There are a couple of commonsense conventions necessary for properly interpreting an MBD FSM with superstates:

- Events from *all* contained substates to the superstate are indicated with a "floating" event with an origin inside the superstate. The E1:reset event is an example.

- Create events that set the initial state of the FSM to the superstate when the object is instantiated are represented as "floating" events to the superstate whose origin is external to the superstate.

- Events to the superstate from only one or a subset of substates should be shown explicitly because they are not common transitions for all substates. The E5:completed transition is an example where it is only valid if the FSM is in the Fetched state.

---

7. In the test hardware industry, the Setup [the hardware] → Initiate [the test] → Fetch [the results] has become a de facto standard, and virtually all test hardware provides an interface to support it.

- Events from the superstate to one or a subset of substates should be shown explicitly because they are not common for all substates. The E2:setup transition is an example to show the only way out of the Reset state.

Essentially these rules simply remove any ambiguity about whether a particular transition is common to all substates or not.

The state machine structure can also be described in tabular format in a State Transition Table (STT) as shown in Table 15-1. The rows are the current state while the columns represent the possible events that the object will accept at least some of the time. The cells have three possible entries: the new state, if the event results in a valid transition; "can't happen," if the event is not valid for the current state; and "ignore," which means the event will be consumed but no transition takes place and no action is executed.

Table 15-1   *FSM View of State Transition Table*

Current State/ Event	E1: reset	E2: setup	E3: initiate	E4: fetch	E5: completed
Initialized	Reset	CH	Started	CH	CH
Started	Reset	CH	CH	Fetched	CH
Fetched	Reset	CH	CH	CH	Reset
Reset	Ignore	Initialized	CH	CH	CH

The FSM view of the STT is somewhat different than a classical FSA STT because it is not possible to ignore an event in an FSA. We include Ignore in MBD because the notion of a message being relevant to an object *some of the time* turns out to be a fairly useful feature. A classic example of this is the OS window manager for a GUI that generates a gazillion WM_MOUSE_MOVE events as a spastic user moves the mouse when the cursor is in hourglass mode. This enables the object to traverse several states where it doesn't care about mouse movement until the task in hand is completed, so it ignores them. But when the task is completed it transitions to a state where the hourglass is turned off, and it is ready to accept the movement events and respond appropriately.

Note that this notation is almost childishly simple. Yet FSMs are enormously powerful tools for describing behavior in an OO context. Effectively using that power requires that we appreciate the elegance with which FSMs enforce OO principles. Most of the rest of this chapter and the next will be devoted to showing how to think about FSMs so that the power is unleashed.

The Role of Design by Contract (DbC)

Long before OO development, the notion of software contracts between client and service was introduced to facilitate modularization and API design. In the '80s, DbC was formalized for OOPLs in terms of inline correctness assertions for method preconditions, postconditions, and invariants. These were defined as:

- *Precondition.* Some set of testable conditions about the inputs and state variables that must prevail before the method can execute. Basically, a precondition tests whether the overall state of the application is ready for the method to execute.

- *Postcondition.* Some set of testable conditions about outputs and state variables that must prevail after the method completes. Basically, postconditions test whether the overall state of the application is correct after the method completes doing its thing.

- *Invariant.* Some set of testable conditions about state variables that must prevail for the entire time the method executes. Basically, an invariant tests whether the overall state of the application is consistent throughout the time the method is executing. As a practical matter, invariant assertions were only written for the state variables that the method touched (i.e., a "white box" view).

As it happens, preconditions and postconditions are enormously important to FSM interactions. In some cases a DbC analysis is the only practical way to get them to play together properly. However, we use a somewhat different spin on DbC in an FSM context. At the 3GL, level correctness assertions are primarily focused on ensuring data integrity, while in OOA models we also use them to validate timing.

We use DbC to design FSMs and collaborations.

One way the difference in views is manifested is that in MBD we view a precondition as the condition that must prevail for the method in hand to execute rather than as a constraint on inputs. Since part of that precondition for execution is that the required inputs are available and consistent, the views are equivalent in that respect. What MBD adds to the notion of a precondition is algorithmic sequence. Our notion of precondition includes the position of the method among the many individual steps of the overall problem solution.

In a Moore model, an FSM state is identical to a DbC postcondition. The FSM state represents a condition where the action's rules and policies prevail, which is the same as saying it is the postcondition for executing the action on entry to the state. Since an FSM state change is triggered by an event generated in a different FSM action and we think of events as announcements of some state change, the postcondition of the action generating the event must be the precondition for the responding action. This enables a very rigorous technique for determining where events should be generated and where they should go.

Conceptually, the technique is trivial. We just have to compare the precondition of the state in hand to the postconditions of other states and, when a match occurs, generate the event in the action of that matching postcondition. The tricky part lies in properly determining the precondition of the state in hand. That precondition has two elements:

1. The behavior responsibilities that must execute before the behavior in hand in the overall solution flow of control

2. The attribute values needed by the method and the criteria for their timeliness and consistency. (Essentially this is the traditional DbC view of the OOPLs.)

As a practical matter, for the first element it is usually easier to identify the last responsibility to execute in the flow of control that is a prerequisite for the execution of the method in hand. Unfortunately, that is not always so easy. The reason is that the elements are not as independent as they might seem.

Consider a method that accesses six different attributes. Each of those might be owned by a different object. More to the point, they may be set in six different methods. In effect, executing each of those setting methods becomes a prerequisite for executing the method in hand. In addition, there may be several methods that modify attributes those setting methods need. So which one is the last method that needs to execute before the method in hand? To figure that out, we need to work backwards and reconstruct the entire chain of data updating dependencies. That sort of backtracking would be a challenge for a grandmaster-level chess program.

Use a UML Sequence diagram to keep track of dependencies when resolving DbC flow of control.

However, it gets a whole lot easier if you have already resolved some of the preconditions of other methods. It also gets easier if we have a convenient format for keeping track of those dependencies and for thinking about flow of control in the large. The tool for doing that is a UML Sequence diagram. If you are modifying flow of control in an existing application, figuring out how to do it can literally take just a few seconds if you have a Sequence diagram from before the change.[8]

---

8. Most tools that support translation can automatically generate a Sequence diagram from the model. That diagram can be immensely helpful during maintenance to determine how the flow of control needs to be modified.

When you are initially defining the flow of control, it is recommended that you use a white board[9] Sequence diagram to keep track of what you are doing. For that the following process is useful.

1. Start with an external subsystem input event. The action that processes that event becomes your starting point.

2. Take a guess at what action should be executed next in the flow of control sequence from the action where you are. If there are no actions left without trigger events, you are done.

3. Determine the precondition for executing the action identified in step 2.

4. Compare that precondition to the postcondition of the action in hand. If satisfied, the action identified in step 2 becomes the action in hand and you go back to step 2. Otherwise, you go back to step 2 and make a different guess.

The value of this approach is that the backtracking to reconstruct chains of data dependencies is largely eliminated. That's because the approach takes advantage of the fact that you already have a pretty good idea of how the application flow of control should work at the object collaboration level; thus the guess at step 2 is a very educated guess. In addition, wherever you are in the process, you already have documented a bunch of known dependencies in the Sequence diagram, so you already know what the last action to execute is.

Alas, there is still a problem. You could have two sequences of processing that start at the same point but are essentially independent. Such sequences are represented schematically in Figure 15-4. Using this approach as is will tend to lead you down one of those sequences until you reach a "join" point, J, where the action to execute will depend on the last action of both threads (D and Z). If you traverse the {B, C, D} sequences first, then the precondition for J will not be satisfied by D alone, and we are faced with figuring out that Z is the last *other* action. To avoid that, try to do a breadth-first "walk" by checking whether there is more than one "next" action at each action. That is, check whether there is more than one valid guess in step 2 (e.g., B and X in the figure). If so, validate and keep track of each one before moving on to a new action.

---

9. Unless you are a Red Belt Superstar, do not even think about entering the Sequence diagram decisions directly into the model as you make them. Everyone always screws up somewhere along the line and has to revise early sequences. That's a lot easier to do on a white board than in the model. Making mistakes is part of modeling. Fortunately, the DbC technique will uncover them before they do any harm.

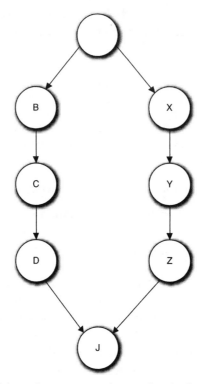

Figure 15-4 *Example of dependence on completion of multiple processing sequences*

Besides the rigor that can be used to validate collaborations, DbC is important because it raises the level of abstraction of collaboration. It enables us to design state machines and describe their actions without worrying about generating events. In theory, once object FSMs are defined, we could backfill the collaborations at the UML Interaction diagram level to encode the overall solution sequencing using DbC to determine the message events.

Looking for State Machines

This is unquestionably the toughest part of MBD for newcomers. Even if we don't buy the conventional wisdom myth described in the Part III road map, it is usually tough for developers to identify FSMs in the problem space if they have never worked with state machines before. It is even more difficult to abstract them correctly.

As indicated in the road map, there are two issues that must be resolved: whether the object has true problem space behaviors (i.e., that the responsibilities are not better thought of as knowledge accessors) and, if so, whether there are fixed sequencing constraints on their execution in the problem space. The rest of this chapter is devoted to guidelines on how to resolve those issues.

Knowledge versus Behavior

The first task in developing state machines is to identify what knowledge is and what behavior is. As the Part III road map indicates, synchronous services are a form of behavior but they are very restricted; they are essentially operations on knowledge properties already defined as attributes. So we have an early decision to make: Do we represent the problem space in terms of knowledge that we manipulate using synchronous services, or do we represent the problem space in terms of pure behaviors whose sequencing we manage with state machines?

Alas, this is not always a clear decision. This is best illustrated by considering what may be the simplest possible example: an On/Off indicator on a machine that must be green when the machine is On and must be red when it is Off. You no doubt recall that in the Part III road map we said that we use FSMs to capture sequencing rules in the problem space. In this case there seems to be a sequencing rule: When the light is green, the only possible change is red, while if it is red, the only possible change is to green. Does this mean we need to capture that sequencing in an FSM?

In this simple case the answer is probably not. If we had to have an FSM for every possible data value change, our models would be terminally cluttered for no useful purpose. The real issue here is the nature of the responsibility. Is the color of an On/Off indicator inherently knowledge (its current color) or behavior (some activity important to solving the problem)? Intuitively, an On/Off indicator seems like a pretty inactive object in the scheme of the overall solution, and changing the color doesn't seem to have an associated activity that is crucial to the overall problem solution flow of control. (Writing to the hardware to physically change the color would probably be a behavior, though, if different instructions were required for each color.)

However, if we implement this object as a dumb knowledge holder with nothing to actually do, we may still have a problem. If we provide a synchronous setter like setColor(color), then we move the rule for determining the color to some other object. In effect, ensuring the right sequencing becomes someone else's rule to enforce. Does that seem reasonable? Shouldn't that rule logically belong to an On/Off indicator? In fact, now that we think about this, why would anyone except On/Off indicator even know what colors are valid? Now we're getting into some interesting areas about our vision of how the objects will collaborate to solve the overall problem. This is the kind of trouble we get into when we start thinking about what we are doing.

Again, in this simple example the answer is fairly obvious. We really should encapsulate as much about the indicator colors as we can within On/Off indicator. Our application will be more robust if we remove those decisions from the collaborating client contexts. For the On/Off indicator to change, something else in the application was turned On or Off, and in *that* context On/Off is all that matters. So are we back to having a state machine, such as shown in Figure 15-5?

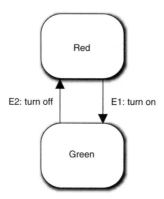

Figure 15-5   *A very basic state machine for a traffic light*

This is certainly plausible. We have cleverly converted the context's view of On/Off into the indicator's Red/Green view by the way we mapped the events to the transitions, and we have completely hidden both the actual colors and how they map to On/Off. Nice work, Grasshopper.

This sort of FSM might be reasonable in R-T/E where the software may have to write to the hardware to change the lamp color. This might involve some special formatting that is significantly different for red and green. Such formatting would represent different rules and policies. If so, that hardware control may be important enough to the problem (e.g., device driver software) to warrant thinking of it as a behavior with unique rules and policies.

Look for ways to recast behaviors as knowledge.

In general, though, we should look for ways to recast behaviors in terms of knowledge. That's because manipulating data is usually easier, less complicated, and less error prone than organizing behaviors. Let's suppose this On/Off indicator is an object in a higher-level subsystem where we aren't worried about the details of the hardware. The question now becomes: Do we need an FSM to capture the constraints that Off always follows On and On always follows Off?

The odds are that the answer is no. The operative word is *Indicator*. This entity just shows us something that it knows, a status, which is basically knowledge that can simply take on different values. So, by its nature, an Indicator just tells us something we need to know. If we provided an FSM to capture every possible rule for setting all our knowledge values, we would complicate our model and end up with something like the Keyboard with an event for every key value.

But what if this object is a surrogate for a hardware device driver that needs to have hardware registers written whenever the status changes? And what if those writes are quite different for each state? Then aren't those writes behaviors that implement unique rules and policies of hardware control? The answer is a definite maybe. Complex hardware writes might be a necessary condition for using an FSM, but they are not necessarily a sufficient justification.

We can think of any hardware register write as setting a knowledge attribute where the register itself holds the knowledge written.[10] In addition, hardware reads and writes are usually very low-level activities compared to the level of abstraction where we might think about some entity being On or Off, so those writes probably don't affect flow of control in the overall solution where the Indicator status is important. Therefore, they don't directly represent unique business rules and policies that are necessary to resolve the subsystem subject matter where the On/Off indicator is abstracted.

That reasoning strongly suggests a simple knowledge-based abstraction. But the critical thing we need to think about is the sequencing of On and Off status. Who sets the status? Whoever that is needs to understand the sequencing. That is, they need to understand when the Indicator should be On and when it should be Off. If correct sequencing is important to the problem solution (e.g., the requirements say it would be an error to try to set the Indicator On if it was already On), then we need to be concerned about cohesion and whether the client needs to understand that sequencing rule or the Indicator.

Again, in this simple example it is likely that whoever sets the Indicator already has some notion of On and Off in its own context or the status is implicit in some system user's actions (e.g., pressing the Power button). So it seems reasonable that Indicator is just a dumb data holder to keep track of what someone else is doing. In addition, there are tricks we can use to limit what the client needs to know, such as providing a *change* message that just toggles whatever status is currently there. That removes the need for the client to know exactly what the status is; it just needs to know that something changed, and Indicator needs to know about that.

---

10. In fact, in R-T/E applications it is very common for the attributes of hardware surrogates to map 1:1 to register fields. The hardware surrogate is then just a dumb data holder with attribute values we get or set. That mapping can become complicated, as the example on hardware control in Chapter 5 demonstrated. The important thing is that such complexity is usually at a lower level of abstraction than the subsystem where we manage what the hardware should be doing.

OK, now let's take the example a step further and do a Traffic Light. The Traffic Light has three colors, red, yellow, and green, that are cycled in a particular order for particular durations. (To keep things simple for the moment, let's assume we have a different Traffic Light object for each direction.) We only have one *color* attribute. Do we still want to abstract the Traffic Light purely in terms of knowledge?

To decide that, we need a vision for collaboration. It is hard to imagine a context that does not involve timers here because the light cycles have fixed duration. Then the change is triggered by the timer's time-out event, which is really convenient when we are using an asynchronous behavior collaboration model. So the questions are: Who triggers the Timer, and who catches the timer event?

Imagine this Traffic Light object is in an automated system where the traffic lights have fixed timing. In this case it makes sense for the overall system to initialize Traffic Light to a known state at start-up and then kick off an infinite loop of interactions between Traffic Light and Timer. That is, Traffic Light would understand the cycle. Traffic Light would start the Timer each time it changed to a new color using the appropriate duration for the new color. Traffic Light would switch to the proper next color when it got the Timer's *durationCompleted* event. Thus Traffic Light and Timer perform an endless collaborative dance around the G → Y → R → G cycle. Since durations are likely to be different for each color, an FSM makes a great deal of sense here because of the nature of the collaborations between Traffic Light and Timer.

In contrast, suppose the system was a very sophisticated traffic management application for an urban area that adjusted cycle times on the fly based on actual traffic conditions detected by various sensors. In this scenario it is quite likely that some other entity is charged with monitoring sensors, analyzing data, and adjusting individual traffic light cycles (in fact, probably a whole subsystem!). In that context, what role would a single Traffic Light object have? Probably not a very big one. All the traffic flow decisions would probably be made elsewhere, and Traffic Light would just be, at most, a hardware surrogate or, at the least, a dumb data holder for the current light status. In this situation we are back to a knowledge-based object like On/Off indicator.

But maybe not. Suppose our traffic manager analysis only wants to deal with changing the traffic flow. It might think in terms of *startFlow* and *StopFlow*. Now when Traffic Light receives the *stopFlow* message, it would have to switch to Yellow and start the Timer for a fixed time, then switch to Red. But processing the *startFlow* message just switches from Red to Green. Now we are back to a collaborative cycle to be managed between Traffic Light and Timer. In addition, Traffic Light is enforcing nontrivial rules about processing a change in colors. So we again need an FSM; it is just a different one from that needed for the fixed-durations scenario above.

Hopefully you have come away from this discussion with these important insights.

- We can trade knowledge for FSMs, and vice versa, when representing the problem space.

- Even seemingly very simple entities can raise complex design issues because all the abstractions must play together in the design.

- Deciding between knowledge versus FSMs is dictated by the problem itself since the decision is fundamentally one of abstracting the problem space.

- Deciding between knowledge and FSMs is often critically dependent on the big picture of how objects will collaborate.

- We should look first for knowledge-based solutions.

- When sequencing of behavior is critical to the solution, we usually need an FSM.

Managing Sequences

Most of this book so far has railed against thinking about solutions in terms of sequences of operations. This was in the context of developing the static framework of the application. Now we are dealing with dynamics, and we can't avoid dealing with sequences of operations because they are defined by the requirements. However, we can be disciplined about what sequences we think about and how we think about them in the dynamic description.

> State machines capture constraints defined explicitly by functional requirements or implicitly in the way the problem domain works.

When identifying states and transitions, we identify operations where the requirements or a domain model explicitly indicate that one operation *always* precedes another. Such requirements are explicit constraints on the sequencing of behaviors in the overall solution. If the behaviors happen to be responsibilities of the same object, then we want to think about using an FSM to describe those sequencing constraints.

It is in our interest to capture as many of those constraints as we can in transitions. Doing so enforces the constraint in static structure, which minimizes the amount of dynamic description we need to enforce the constraint (i.e., the selections and condition testing to make sure it is the right time to invoke the behavior). As it happens, FSMs are ideally suited to this, because once the transitions are defined we need only ensure that triggering events are generated in the right place, and we have DbC to ensure that. This is a much less verbose and less error-prone way to ensure the sequencing constraints are properly managed.[11]

Step 1. Identify responsibilities with sequencing that are explicitly constrained in requirements.

The first step in developing an object life cycle is to identify the behaviors relevant to requirements' sequencing constraints. Sometimes doing so will result in groups of small responsibilities where it is the sequencing of the *groups* that is constrained by requirements, not the individual responsibilities. Recall that an FSM state is a condition whereby a unique *set* of rules and policies apply. We will group those small responsibilities into a single state action to be such a set.

Whoa! Doesn't such merging into a single state action fly in the face of logical indivisibility of behavior responsibilities? The answer is that we also have flexibility in defining the level of abstraction of logical indivisibility. In effect, we are using the requirements constraint on a group of individual responsibilities to determine the correct level of abstraction *for collaboration*. In other words, we *start* our design at a low level of abstraction for logical indivisibility because it is easier to evaluate the sequencing constraints if the individual responsibilities are narrowly defined. But the problem constraints drive the actual level of abstraction where we end up because they define a degree of commonality among the detailed behaviors.

Note that this is inherently an iterative process. As we refine our view of logical indivisibility, that will be fed back in terms of more abstract behavior responsibilities identified in the Class model, and it will also refine our overall vision of the solution when we define other object FSMs. It is also the reason that we don't try to define detailed collaborations before we define the FSMs. We need the collaborations to be done at the right level of abstraction, and this step—where we let the requirements drive the level of abstraction—is important in ensuring that. If we design interacting FSMs with detailed messages based on our original view of logical indivisibility, we are likely to create FSMs that are too complicated.

A classic example of this is a common problem cited by those who believe FSMs are ill-suited for certain problems. The problem is to represent keyboard entry of words into GUI text boxes. The critics postulate an FSM based upon a unique event for each key on the keyboard. This requires a set of transitions through states that migrates through every possible incremental combination of valid characters. A partial example is shown in Figure 15-6(a) where each state is a unique concatenation of a particular sequence of characters. Clearly, such an FSM is just not practical for more than a few valid and very short words.

---

11. In my experience, conversion to MBD from traditional procedural techniques resulted in roughly a 50% reduction in released defect rate. Unfortunately, the data we collected could not determine the exact reasons for the reduction, but my gut feeling is that at least half of the improvement was directly attributable to describing behavior with FSMs.

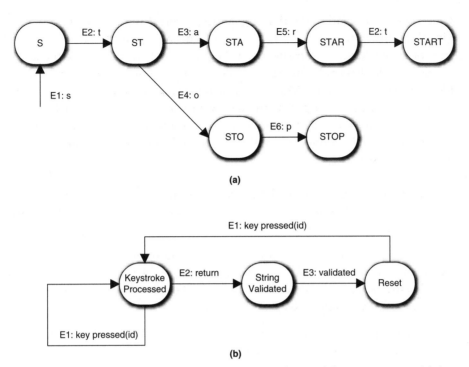

(a)

(b)

Figure 15-6 *Example of a really bad state machine and a much better way to model the semantics*

The FSM in Figure 15-6(b) is superior because the level of abstraction of the sequencing constraints has been raised. Now all keystrokes except one from the hardware or OS look exactly the same. Nonetheless, the FSM honors the very basic keystroke sequencing constraint that a valid word be formed. We just don't do the word validation in the object that processes raw hardware keystrokes. That is the real problem with the critics' example: It hypothesizes poor object semantics and separation of concerns.

It would simply never occur to an experienced OOA developer to even think about an FSM like Figure 15-6(a) because the object semantics would not have that word validation responsibility when the Class model was done. The semantics of a Keyboard abstraction is polling the hardware, converting hardware codes to ASCII, applying modifiers like Shift being pressed, and (possibly) concatenating keystroke codes in a buffer. That is at a much lower level of abstraction than thinking about whether valid words are formed. (In fact, the word *validation* might not even be in the same subsystem as the hardware control represented by the notion of a Keyboard! The idea of a Keyboard might only be relevant to a specialized service that the UI invokes.)

Aside from encapsulating the right semantics, Figure 15-6(b) is interesting in the way in which abstraction is used to capture the sequencing constraints. Note that all keystrokes except Return are treated as if they were equivalent. Raising the level of abstraction of the keystroke messages is critical to eliminating the combinatorial problems of the first example. When we raise the level of abstraction, the individual letter values are relegated to parametric data values in the event data packet. Essentially we have reformulated the sequencing constraint to be consistent with the notion of external validation. That is, the Keystroke Processed state consolidates the set of basic processing steps.

1. Check for temporary modifier keys. These are Shift, Control, Alt, and so on that modify the ASCII codes for all subsequent keystrokes until they are released. Record the state and exit.

2. Check for special keys. These are Caps Lock, and so on that modify the ASCII codes until they are pressed and released again (i.e., they are treated as individual keystrokes but they affect the way the keyboard interprets other keystrokes in terms of ASCII codes). Record the state and exit.

3. Encode the proper ASCII code for the hardware keystroke value given the current effects of modifier and special keys.

4. Concatenate the ASCII keystroke value into a temporary string buffer.

This is a good example of a number of logically indivisible operations that can be combined because they apply to every keystroke except Return, and these operations always have to be done before other operations, like validating the word in the string buffer. In fact, we could abstract all four of these operations into the more general notion of updating the state of the Keyboard.

Note the spin this model places on validation. We only validate the string in the buffer when the user has indicated the string is done (i.e., hitting the Return key). That makes the Return keystroke special, and it draws a line in the sand that divides the activities for processing all other keystrokes from the activities of validating the word and resetting for the next entry. Thus we can summarize the new overall processing constraint at the new level of abstraction as follows:

1. Collect the text box string one character at a time. This action includes the four behaviors above.

2. Validate the string.

3. Reset the text box after validation processing.

You will note that this is exactly the life cycle that the second example shows. Quelle surprise!

Note that this segues back to the point made previously: that we should look for ways to abstract behavior in terms of knowledge. Encoding modifiers and special keystrokes as state variables is a very elegant way to simplify the behavior of the keyboard and, in this case, it is one way to eliminate the critics' combinatorial problem. As such, the example is a good demonstration of how we marry knowledge and behavior to provide a simple solution for a superficially complex problem.

Now suppose the Keyboard did not queue up a buffer of keystrokes; instead, it simply forms the ASCII code and sends it to someone else. Now we have an entirely different situation where the last two steps are no longer relevant. What does this say? Obviously we have only one state, so there are no sequencing constraints to capture, which tells us that our Keyboard does not need an FSM. We could view processing the hardware keystrokes as simply knowledge setters for attributes like *ASCIICode*, and the ASCII code would be forwarded as a simple knowledge attribute value.[12] So in this case the entire object becomes a simple data holder or even an attribute in another object.

It is worth reviewing the essential insights that led to the second solution rather than the critics' because we need to design the *right* FSM while we are at it. First and foremost was separation of concerns. It was critical that our Keyboard object should not be distracted by the rules and policies for validating words; it should stick to the narrower focus of converting hardware register values to ASCII codes. That is logical indivisibility and cohesion in action at the object level. Another important insight was abstracting the invariants of text box string processing. Our FSM was focused on the stipulated problem in hand (i.e., termination via Return). If we had been modeling the Keyboard for a word processor, we might have had a suite of delimiter characters that would indicate the end of a word.[13]

However, though the transitions we ended up with were tailored to the problem in hand, the life cycle states were intrinsic *once we properly abstracted what the object responsibilities were*. To put it another way, the states represented an extraction of invariants from the problem space at a higher level of abstraction than in the critics'

---

12. A common solution for this sort of notification when something changes is the Observer pattern. If there is only one client who cares, though, it can be implemented much more simply.

13. Actually, if we needed to abstract a Keyboard for a word processor context, it would probably not accumulate characters. The rules for processing tokens are very complex (e.g., underscores, slashes, etc.) and we would want to encapsulate all of them. In addition, those parsing rules are clearly more the concern of word processing than the concern of converting hardware representations. So the Keyboard would very likely provide one character at a time to someone else.

solution. A key insight in this solution is the way the sequencing constraints are abstracted. That is, in turn, reflected in the states, the transitions, and the nature of the events. Throughout this book, abstraction has been promoted as the defining element of OO development, and this is just one more example of how ubiquitous it is in OOA/D. This all segues into . . .

Step 2. Isolate the behaviors in states and enforce the sequencing constraints in transitions.

This sounds a lot more cookbook than it actually is. Hopefully, the reasoning in the previous example illustrates the sorts of issues and techniques that are relevant. Probably the most important element of the proper mindset is the notion that OO FSMs are abstractions, and both the object responsibilities and the FSM need to be at the right level of abstraction. That may require some iteration and creativity to get right. Fortunately, though, practice makes perfect, and it doesn't take all that much learning curve to get good at it.

Self-Directed Events

The topic of managing sequences would not be complete without a discussion of one of the most controversial issues in FSM design. It is possible for an FSM action to generate an event to its own FSM that causes a transition. If you recall, we even have a special rule for prioritizing such self-directed events. Unfortunately, self-directed events tend to be badly overused, especially by novices. In fact, there is a school of FSM design that argues we should *never* use self-directed events.

The reason is rooted in the FSA notion that transitions are triggered externally to the state machine. The FSA state conditions reflect conditions in the *environment* of the FSA, and the FSA simply organizes them in a disciplined model, thus how we decide the state should change is not the FSA's concern. However, we have bent the FSA rules before to provide OO FSMs, so this theoretical issue is not completely compelling.

A much more practical problem has to do with the notion of a sequence of operations itself in a software context. In Figure 15-7, assume the actions for State1 and State2 each result in a set of machine instructions and imagine the sequence of instructions that the CPU "sees."

Figure 15-7   *Context for self-directed events*

The point here is that if the State1 action generates the E1 event, then there is no point to having the two states. There is no flow of control circumstance where the State2 action's instructions do not seamlessly follow the State1 action's instructions. In effect, all we have done is artificially subdivide an otherwise monolithic Turing sequence of operations. To put it more bluntly, all we are doing is using FSM state actions to organize our behaviors into classical *procedural* units. Anything that even hints at procedural organization is going the have the reviewers lighting the kindling under our feet.

Now suppose E1 is generated externally. The CPU may see the full sequence as above, but that will be serendipity because we don't know *when* that event will be issued. Within the logic of our overall solution, a ton of instructions might be executed between the executions of the State1 and State2 actions.

Use synchronous services to organize complex monolithic sequences, not FSM states.

The mechanism MBD uses for connecting the flow of control dots is interacting FSMs. Don't dilute that by using states and transitions for other purposes. The benefit of keeping the FSMs pristine will not become apparent until you are debugging or doing maintenance. At that point we need to be able to count on a transition representing a fundamental element of flow of control without having to rummage around in the action details. A lot of debugging and change analysis is done just by looking at boxes and arrows without the action details.

Having argued strongly that self-directed events are usually symptomatic of poorly formed FSMs, how is that reconciled with the opening of this topic where it was hinted that some self-directed events are justified? In MBD we do sometimes employ self-directed events, but we are very careful about when we do so. The reason is that in object FSMs we have conditions that depend on the timely update of state variables (knowledge attributes). There are situations where the handshaking necessary to ensure data integrity would require additional states and transitions (and sometimes additional objects!) that might distract from the overall purpose of the interacting FSMs.

Figure 15-8 represents an object with the role of broadcasting a message to multiple recipients, collecting acknowledgments that the recipients received it, and determining whether some recipients did not acknowledge the message within some elapsed time after the broadcast. The Broadcasted action saves the count of messages sent and initializes a Timer object that returns the E3:expired event. The Acknowledged action counts the acknowledgments and, if it matches the number sent, it shuts down the Timer. The key rule that must be enforced is that the object cannot start another broadcast until the current one has completed, either by receiving all the acknowledgments or experiencing a time-out. That is captured by the fact that E2:message is only valid for the Ready → Broadcasted transition. One problem is that the E4: All acknowledged event is self-directed.

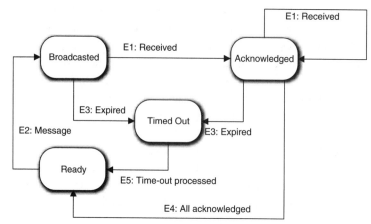

Figure 15-8   *A state machine that broadcasts messages must wait until all messages are acknowledged or a time-out occurs before broadcasting another message.*

The tricky part here is getting to the Ready state when the recipients have acknowledged. We could delegate the responsibility of counting acknowledgments to another object that exists purely to count the entries. The E1:received message would go to that object and it would do the counting. When the counts matched, it would send the E4:all_acknowledged event back to the object in hand.

That's valid, and the conservative school of FSM design would argue that it is more robust. It may be somewhat more robust, but it is probably overkill for several reasons in this situation. First, we have to create an artificial object that may have no counterpart in the problem space just to get around a self-directed event. Second, that object needs its own FSM to be designed. Third, it needs to be initialized by the Broadcasted action with the count to check. Fourth, the interactions may get complicated when there is a time-out (e.g., what do we do with the E1:Received events if the allowed time has already elapsed?). Fifth, that other object might only have one state. Finally, perhaps most important of all, providing such infrastructure just distracts from the core problem of broadcasting messages and collecting responses. So in a case like this, opting for the self-directed E4:all_acknowledged event to keep things simple will usually be the best choice.

> Try to justify self-directed events in terms of resolving both the FSM and state variable (knowledge attribute) views of "state."

Note that this is a clear case where persistent state variables across FSM state actions are relevant. The count needed is accumulated across transitions. Probably more important, that count seems to logically belong to the object doing the broadcasting. Thus the self-directed event is really just combining two views of object "state," which provides some additional rationalization.

Another problem in the example FSM lies in getting to the Ready state after a time-out has been processed. Here, no obvious state variable update is involved, which should make us rather suspicious because we have no rationalization about marrying different views of object state. In fact, someone reviewing the example state machine would probably be bringing out the matches and kindling. That's because there is an obvious and simple way to avoid the self-directed event from Timed Out to Ready.

To see that, think about the basic purpose of the Ready state. It enables us to enforce the constraint that the object is not already busy processing a message (i.e., the condition is that the processing of any previous message is done). This provides an anchor for the E2:message transition that captures the sequencing rule. However, after processing the time-out, is the object any less done processing the current message than if all of the recipients have acknowledged receipt? No. When the object is in the Time Out state, it is just as unoccupied as when it is in the Ready state. So instead of the Timed Out to Ready transition with the E5:time_out_processed being generated, we should just have a transition from Timed Out to Broadcasted triggered by the E2:message transition. The example is an interesting contrast of reasonable and bad practice.

Handshaking

Since we are employing an asynchronous model for behavior communications, we have to live with handshaking as a Way of Life. When two objects, both with embedded sequencing constraints, need to collaborate, we need a mechanism for keeping the collaborations synchronized. That is, we need to ensure that the receiver is in the right state to accept the event that the other object sends. Alas, this is complicated by the fact that an important assumption of asynchronous communications is that there can be an arbitrary delay between when an event is generated and when it is consumed. Thus, in theory, it is possible to generate event E2 after E1 but have E1 consumed before E2. In fact, this is rather common in distributed processing.

However, in the OOA/D we make a couple of assumptions, which we've already talked about, that greatly simplify these problems. The important assumption is that there is a single event queue for all events processed in the subsystem. The second assumption is that only one event is popped at a time, and its action completes before popping the next event from the queue. The third assumption is that the event queue is FIFO; events are popped in the order in which they were placed on the queue.[14]

14. An exception is self-directed events, which are usually given priority over external events for a given receiver FSM. However, one goal in providing a self-directed event is almost always to ensure that the state machine does get to the right state to process external events.

These assumptions conspire to ensure that events within the subsystem are consumed in the same order that they were placed on the event queue. Fortunately, these assumptions are fairly easy to enforce in the implementation even in distributed and/ or concurrent environments. But transformation is a different trade union so we won't go into that here.

The basic problem comes down to making sure the events go on the event queue in the right order. That's not always easy when there are long, parallel chains of processing. It gets more complicated when the knowledge needed by an action at the end of one of those chains is updated somewhere in the middle of another chain. An example is shown in Figure 15-9. The figure is just a flow chart that represents the *algorithmic* sequence in the solution if {A,B,C} and {X,Y,Z} were readily recognized individual sequences in the problem space.

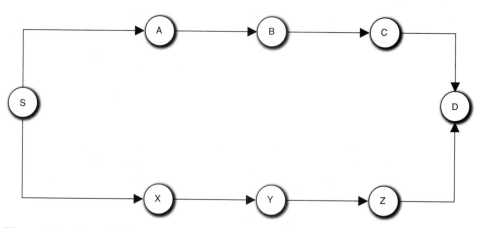

Figure 15-9   *Overall solution sequence context for executing multiple state actions*

The S action kicks off both sub-processes and the D action must wait until both C and Z execute, but it doesn't care which one completes first. This might arise if B needs data from A, C needs data from B, Y needs data from X, Z needs data from Y, and D needs data from both C and Z. Since D is indifferent to which sub-process finishes first, we could make an arbitrary design decision to serialize the sub-processes, as in Figure 15-10.

One of the problems with simple flow charting was that it was easy to miss more subtle dependencies. Suppose that Z also depends on data updated by B. If these sub-processes were in different parts of the application, that might not be so obvious, especially if the requirements call out the sub-processes individually that might result in some myopia about what processing was important. Assuming our due diligence with DbC uncovered this dependency, then connecting the dots in Figure 15-10 was wrong. So how do we correct it? One way is to reverse the order of the serialization so that S triggers A, C triggers X, and Z triggers D, shown in Figure 15-11.

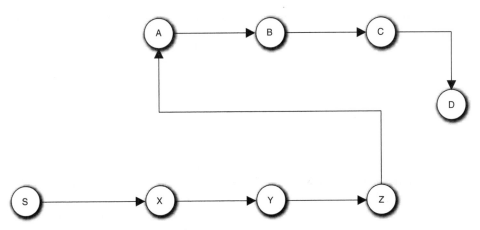

Figure 15-10 *Serialized version of Figure 15-9*

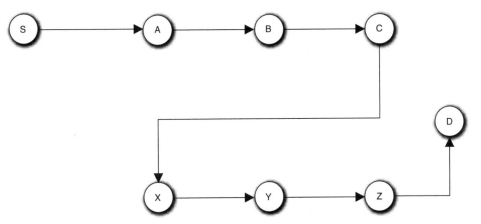

Figure 15-11 *Revised serialization to ensure data prepared by B is available to Z*

OK, so far so good. But now let's assume that {A, B, C} are behaviors of one object while {X, Y, Z} are behaviors of another object. Now we have four self-directed events that should raise a warning flag. At this point it may help to make things a bit less abstract. Let's assume these two objects are different flavors of test instruments, say, an Ammeter and a Voltmeter. Now the three behaviors of each object might represent different implementations of {setup, initiate, and fetch}. Finally, assume the requirements say that our application must be compatible with the VXI standard, which decrees that {setup, initiate, fetch} must be independently accessible so we can't coalesce them as we did when initially talking about self-directed events. Are we now forced to use self-directed events?

No. What we need to do is step back and look at what the real sequencing constraints are.

- $A \rightarrow B, B \rightarrow C$

- $X \rightarrow Y, Y \rightarrow Z$

- $C \rightarrow D, Z \rightarrow D$

- $B \rightarrow Z$

These are the only constraints that we must honor in the flow of control. As long as each individual dependency is handled correctly, we can order the processing of all the actions in a wide variety of ways, of which Figure 15-12 is just one example.

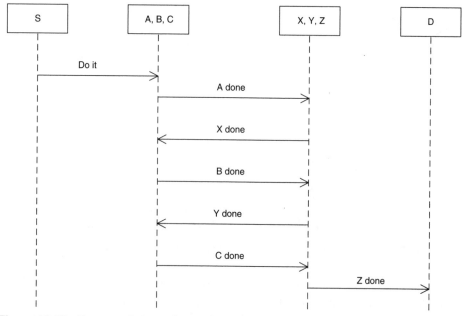

Figure 15-12 *Sequence diagram for synchronizing the sequence in Figure 15-11*

Now *Do it* from S triggers A, *A done* triggers X, *X done* triggers B, *B done* triggers Y, *Y done* triggers C, *C done* triggers Z, and *Z done* triggers D. You can easily verify in the Sequence diagram that all of the actual constraints have been honored. Given our more realistic test instrument interpretation, this is actually a better picture of what is really going on in synchronizing the instruments.

The real benefit of eliminating the self-directed events this way, though, is that maintenace will be easier to do. We would not want to coalesce the actions even if the VXI standard weren't an issue. For our simple example, we could manage the sequences in a monolithic fashion as in Figure 15-11, but the self-directed events would encourage us to combine the actions (which would be harmless for this example). If you have any familiarity with rack-and-stack hardware test systems, it should be clear that future requirements might require the actions to be separated.[15] So, when the requirements change you would have to un-combine them and rearrange the messaging. By avoiding the self-directed events we get to the right place in the original development, so all we have to do during maintenance is rearrange the events. (As a bonus, the Sequence diagram makes it clear that the sequencing of messages is not tied to the sub-processes.)

A useful tool for getting a handle on handshaking situations is the UML Activity diagram. We can create a rough, throwaway AD for the relevant use cases to show "touch points" in the uses cases among multiple objects. That can be useful in figuring out how to deal with the synchronization.

Some Examples

As we've already indicated, for novices there tends to be a bit of magic in recognizing life cycles in problem space entities that we can abstract into object FSMs. In addition, the steps indicated and the issues raised might sound fine, but they are a tad general for easy application in real software projects. Unfortunately, there is no cookbook approach to the learning curve. So the best we can do now is provide a few examples to demonstrate how we should think about looking for life cycles.

Garage Door Opener

This is a classic starter project for novices because it is quite simple, but it demonstrates a number of interesting features. Let's assume we have identified the following objects as relevant: Clicker, which triggers opening or closing the door (ignore registration and whatnot here); Door, for which we are controlling opening and closing; Electric Eye, which detects obstacles to closing; Position Sensor, which determines if

---

15. A clearer example would be if the instruments are a function generator and an oscilloscope. Then the oscilloscope requires the proper function to be set up and generated first. In effect, this means that both instruments need to be set up before either is initiated, and they must be initiated in tandem.

the door is fully open or fully closed; and Controller, which talks to the hardware elements. The question is: Does Door have a life cycle?

If we think about what a garage door controller actually does, it isn't a whole lot. If the Door is closed and the Clicker is clicked, the hardware is told to open the door. If the Door is open and the Clicker is clicked, the hardware is told to close it. If the Door is closing and an obstacle is detected, the hardware is told to open the Door. When the Position Sensor indicates the Door is fully opened or closed, the hardware is told to stop moving it. (This last is probably done directly in the hardware, but this is just an example.)

If you have a few years of non-OO development under your belt, the answer will be obvious. There is only one object that actually does anything and that is the Controller. So the Door has no life cycle. Of course, that answer is dead wrong or we wouldn't have chosen this example. Just because an object has an "–er" at the end does not mean it coordinates everyone else. In fact, such a name would immediately make an OO reviewer suspicious because it screams of being a high-level node in a functional decomposition tree that coordinates the machinations of minions at lower levels in the tree.

Look at the descriptions of what the objects are. Which one is moving (i.e., changing state)? It appears in every sentence describing an activity. More telling, it appears in those sentences that describe conditions (e.g., "If the Door is open..."). If there is one object here that is active, it is the Door. In fact, it is the only object that really needs to do anything; the others are really just surrogates for the hardware.[16]

So what kind of life cycle does Door have? Obviously there should be states for Open and Closed. Is that it? No. The problem is that it takes awhile to actually get from one state to the other and things can happen in that interval, like the Clicker was clicked again or the Electric Eye detected a beaver standing in the doorway. To properly capture the constraints implicit in the problem description as transitions, we need more states. In particular, we need Opening and Closing.

Note that in Figure 15-13 we have four states and six transitions but only three events. (The actual number of events will depend on the specific hardware.) That essentially means we are capturing a lot of rules in the static FSM structure—more than we probably thought there were when reading the problem statement. Note that this FSM is quite intuitive.

---

16. In fact, they will probably just be data holders. To start the motor to close the door we will send a message to Controller to start the motor in a particular direction. That will map into a hardware register write. In fact, we might want to consider changing the name from Controller to Motor, since that is the only hardware that is actually being manipulated in normal operations.

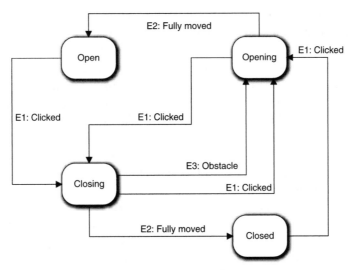

Figure 15-13 *State machine for controlling a garage door*

Automated Home Kitchen

Let's assume we need to write the controller for an automated home kitchen that will prepare a complete meal unattended. One of the many objects will be an Oven that is used to cook the meal. Given that this is one element of an automated process, does Oven have a life cycle?

We can make a case that it is a dumb data holder. It just records the start time, temperature, and duration of the cooking cycle for some other process that emulates the cook. However, that phrase, "process that emulates the cook," should set off alarms. Our software is replacing the cook with an automated system, thus the software will be doing things the human cook would have done. We could create a Cook object to play that role, but we would essentially be creating a god object that controlled all the behaviors.

In OO development, the way we avoid this is through anthropomorphization. We allocate the actions that a human cook would have done to inanimate entities in the problem space, such as an Oven. That allocation enables us to separate concerns when managing complexity. So our Oven is likely to have behavior responsibilities that are a small subset of what the human cook would normally do. What sorts of behaviors are those likely to be? The Oven needs to be initialized by setting temperature, and so forth. It also needs to be preheated. A human cook would have to perform a set of discrete actions on the Oven before actually putting the roadkill in for cooking, and those are constrained to a particular sequence. That, in turn, suggests states like Inactive, Temperature Set, Preheated, and Cooking.

Another way to look at this is to think about how the notion of Oven fits into the overall notion of Automated Home Kitchen. The objects that we abstract for the Automated Home Kitchen will have to collaborate with one another, which implies that there are some rules about sequencing activities. Thus Robotic Handler cannot put the roadkill in the Oven unless the Oven door is open. In addition, the Oven will have to interact with objects like a Timer. In the overall scheme of automatically preparing a meal, there will be a whole lot of recipe-like operations, many of which will be constrained to be in a specific sequence. This is particularly true for automation, where we need to be quite explicit about trivial things like opening doors. So our Oven may also have states like Door Open and Door Closed to support the necessary collaborations with other objects.

We want to capture as many of those sequencing rules as we can statically in FSM transitions. With this minimal description we can't say for sure what the states and transitions for Oven are, or even if it will have a life cycle in the final model. However, the discussion should make it clear that there *could* be one, that it might be fairly complicated, and that we need to at least evaluate it.

Air Traffic Control System

In an ATC there is a notion of the position of an aircraft. That notion combines radar data, altimeter data, and error envelopes. (Actually, several data from different types of radar and from the aircraft itself are combined in the notion.) There is also complex analysis to associate raw radar data with a particular aircraft.[17] Even more complicated analysis is necessary to determine error envelopes in three dimensions for collision avoidance processing. As a result, the Position data that is ultimately displayed on the controller's console is the end result of complex processing from multiple subsystems. The question is: Does the Position have a life cycle?

Probably not. The keyword that recurs in the description is *data*. The processing necessary to construct and refine a Position object may be quite complex, but that will most likely be done by a combination of other objects. However, this was a bit of a trick question. There is another view of Position that may be relevant. Aside from the data itself and the processing to provide it, there is another set of sequencing constraints around the notion Position. Those constraints are related to the processing necessary to *construct* a Position.

This processing is done in a specific sequence from the time raw radar data is acquired until the time the Position is displayed for the controller. We must correlate

---

17. When two aircraft are low on the horizon at a substantial distance it becomes difficult to determine which radar image belongs to which aircraft, even if they are actually several thousand feet apart.

raw positions from different radars, then associate the collection with an aircraft transponder, then include altimeter data, then adjust the altimeter data for weather conditions in the aircraft's location, and so on. And that is just to get the data. Additional analysis is required for things like error envelopes, flight path tracking, and, finally, symbolic display on the controller's console. One way to capture those sequencing constraints is via transitions in a state machine that reflect the state of the Position in the processing sequence. That state machine would probably reside in some other object (e.g., Position Constructor) because Position itself has quite a bit of knowledge already, but the notion of a construction life cycle for Position is still valid.

There are two points to this example. The first is that an FSM is there in the problem space to abstract as a life cycle, and we need to think about it. After due diligence we may decide that particular abstraction is unnecessary to the overall ATC problem solution, but we still need to make that a deliberate design decision. In other words, we are deciding whether we need the life cycle to solve the problem in hand, not whether one exists.

The second and more important point is that life cycles are abstractions just like everything else in OO development, meaning that we need to be prepared to view the problem space in different ways. We can't simply dismiss Position as a data holder; we need to look at the big picture from different angles. In reality, once you start looking for life cycles you realize that there is almost always some bizarre problem context where virtually any pedestrian inanimate object has a conceptual life cycle. The following example is a case in point.

Rock

This is your garden variety stone outcrop, as in a road cut. For most people there is simply not much to it—it's just that hard, dull grey, bluish or reddish stony thing. To the trained eye of a field geologist, though, the outcrop is a wealth of information about the history of the rock. To a mineralogist, the rock is actually quite complex, being composed of several different mineral crystals or even other rocks. Similarly, to a petrographer who studies the microscopic structure of the rock, it has exotic chemistry and there are many clues about its evolution. On closer examination, a paleontologist may find fossils in the rock that shed light on its age and evolution. Still, that just indicates complexity that requires special training to recognize, and it is all just data, right?

Au contraire. It depends upon your perspective on viewing rocks. To demonstrate that, though, we need to digress a moment to Geology 101. In geology there is a conceptual model quaintly known as the Rock Cycle. All rock we see today originally cooled from a liquid form called *magma* to form *igneous* rock, which basically means crystalline. (The lava that flows out of volcanoes is a classic example of igneous rock formation.) Once it solidifies at the surface it is exposed to erosion by wind, water, temperature changes, and other mechanisms. Erosion breaks down the rock into tiny fragments that are carried away and deposited somewhere else as sediment. Erosion can even modify the rock chemically. These fragments are eventually buried, so they are subjected to increased heat and pressure, which causes them to consolidate into *sedimentary* rock. Depending upon depth of burial, time of burial, temperature, and pressure, both igneous and sedimentary rocks can be further modified chemically and physically to form *metamorphic* rock. In extreme cases, conditions can be so harsh that metamorphic rock completely melts to form magma. That magma may subsequently cool, repeating the cycle by forming igneous rock. All rocks we see today on the Earth's surface have been through this Rock Cycle, shown in Figure 15-14, several times.

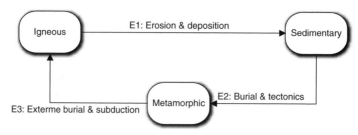

Figure 15-14   *The legendary Rock Cycle*

Now suppose you are tasked with constructing software that simulates the life of a portion of a continent for a mining company. The mining company is keenly interested in this sort of thing because different types of rocks have different minerals. In addition, we have found all the easy resources lying around on the surface, so they have to predict what is under the surface. Since drilling and mining to "prove" resources are very expensive, they want to do it in areas with the highest probability of success. By simulating a mountain building episode (aka *orogenic cycle*, yet another life cycle of interest), they may be able to predict where the most beneficial rocks have formed. Now the Rock Cycle becomes critically important to the simulation because they need to identify where the clumps of igneous, sedimentary, and metamorphic rocks are today as a result of continental drift millions, or even hundreds of millions, of years ago.

> Conceptual processes have sequential constraints in the same way that solution operations have sequential constraints.

There are multiple points to make here. One is that no matter how inert an entity might seem, there is usually some perspective where it has a life cycle, however arcane and special the perspective may be. In this case that perspective is historical and only of interest to a unique academic discipline. Next, it is not the rock itself that does something today; it is the way it evolved that provides the life cycle. That segues to the third point: The problem context itself can determine life cycles, in much the same way that anthropomorphizing human activities onto inanimate objects provides life cycles. That is, we map an evolutionary process onto the rock instead of human activities. The last point, to quote a famous pool player, is that, "I was jus' showin' off."[18]

---

18. My undergraduate training was in geology and I spent nearly a decade doing field geophysics, so I couldn't resist. BTW, they never send you to Paris to look at rocks, so I have an intimate knowledge of some of the best swamps, jungles, tundras, and deserts in the world—which accounts in no small part for why I do software today.

Chapter 16

States, Transitions, Events, and Actions

Choosing each stone, and poising every weight,
Trying the measures of the breadth and height,
Here pulling down, and there erecting new,
Founding a firm state by proportions true.
—Andrew Marvel: *The First Anniversary of the*
Government under Oliver Cromwell

In the previous chapter we dealt with identifying when state machines are necessary and how to recognize object life cycles. In this chapter we will get into the structural details of how state machines are constructed. The structure is the more mechanical aspect of developing state machines, so this chapter will just flesh out the basics that were described in Chapter 14. The goal in this chapter is simply to establish the proper mindset for developing state machines.

States

Recall that a state is simply a condition where a particular set of problem space rules and policies apply. The natural language notion of "state" as a *condition of being* is actually pretty useful here. The tricky part lies in the fact that there are at least two perspectives on the notion of *condition*. One perspective is that the object has a state of being, pretty obvious since we are designing object state machines. The second perspective is somewhat less obvious: that the subsystem as a whole has a state of being.[1]

---

1. Which is, in turn, a subset of the overall application's state of being. However, our encapsulation of subsystems ensures that when designing FSMs within a subsystem we only need to worry about the subsystem's context.

When discussing the static description of the solution the notion of *intrinsic* object properties that were independent of particular collaboration context were emphasized. While we selected the entities and responsibilities to abstract based on the general needs of the problem solution, we were very careful to isolate them and think of them in a generic fashion. Alas, as a practical matter we cannot design state machines without considering context. Thus we need to explicitly consider the context of the overall problem solution in terms of the subsystem's state of being. The important mindset issue, though, is that we should think of the application in terms of conditions rather than algorithmic sequences.

One way this is reflected is through DbC, which enables us to rigorously determine where and when to generate events by matching state preconditions and to other states' postconditions. But that only works when we have designed the object state machines so that their states are complementary to the big picture of the overall application's migration through *its* states. Similarly, the subsystem perspective came up in the last chapter when we discussed how handshaking depends on collaboration context. Those constraints exist only in the perspective of the overall subsystem state of being.

> We can consider the overall problem solution as a migration through state machine states. Then each object state machine state should map unambiguously to one state in the overall solution machine at a time.[2]

The importance of this metaphor lies in two important corollaries. The first is that each state in the conceptual subsystem state machine simultaneously *maps to a single state in every object state machine*. One can think of the conditions for each object state machine state as a subset of the conditions that prevail in some state of the overall solution, as illustrated conceptually in Figure 16-1. That's because every existing object with an object state machine is always in some state, and intuitively that state should map to the state of the overall application.

The second corollary is less intuitive. *Each state in an object state machine may map to more than one state in the subsystem state machine.* There are two reasons for this. The first reason is that we may reuse object behaviors (re-invoke their rules and policies) in different contexts in the overall problem solution. The second reason is related to the fact that we do not continuously execute object rules and policies; they are executed only when the state is entered.

> Any object state transition occurs in lockstep with some transition in the conceptual application state machine.

---

2. This is a conceptual metaphor to explain how the object and application perspectives map to one another. Do *not* waste time trying to design big, honking application state machines. We focus solely on object state machines explicitly to avoid that level of mind-numbing complexity.

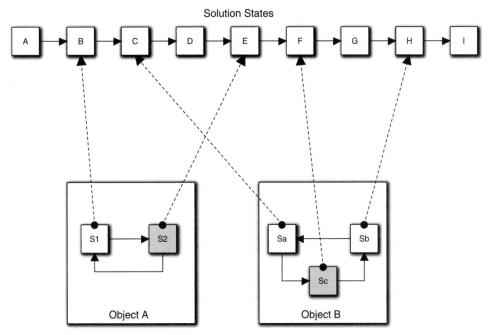

Figure 16-1 *Mapping of state machine states to overall solution states. Shaded states are current states of the object state machine. So, by implication, for Object A to be in state S2, the overall solution must have already proceeded to at least state E. Similarly, state S1 must have prevailed from solution states B through D.*

This is really the point of the condition metaphor. There can be no change in an object state machine unless there is a corresponding change in the state of the overall solution. On the other hand, individual object state machines provide enormous flexibility for the solution because their transitions don't have to map 1:1 with a sequence of transitions in the conceptual subsystem state machine. Thus the same object state machine state can "slide" through a succession of subsystem states because the object is not directly involved with that aspect of the solution; the object stays in the same state while the application migrates through its states. For example, in Figure 16-1, Object A's S1 state remains the same while the solution migrates through its states B through D. But at least one object FSM will transition whenever the solution transitions to a new state.

To summarize this discussion, the key points are

- Transitions represent changes in the overall solution's condition.

- Instead of thinking in terms of a sequence of operations, we think of flow of control in terms of transitions between states both at the object level and at the subsystem level.

- Since object actions are triggered by transitions, the proper time to apply a suite of business rules and policies is when something happens in the overall solution to change its state. (This is the basis for the DbC techniques already discussed.)

This notion of migrating through subsystem solution states and object states is critical to MBD because it quite neatly ties together both state variables and algorithmic sequencing in a single concept. So, it is important to consider how state variables enter the picture when mapping object state machines to the overall solution. That is, ensuring that the data is ready is just as important as the sequence of solution operations when determining collaborations and, consequently, identifying states and transitions. For example, in Figure 16-2(a) we have a fairly mundane sampling and filtering controller. Filter1 and Filter2 each process different data from the original samples in Figure 16-2(b). Figure 16-2(c) is a Collaboration diagram for a set of objects that abstract the processing. Figure 16-2(d) is a state machine for the Collector object.

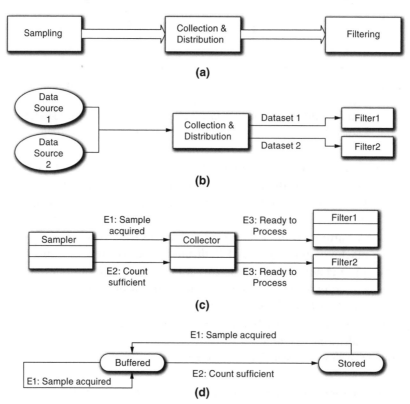

Figure 16-2   *Different views of a sensor sampling application: (a) overall block diagram; (b) filtering of separate datasets; (c) collaborations; (d) collector FSM*

Sampler collects and counts sample values from some hardware in the form of two sets of related but different data as a single overall sample in time. It forwards that sample's data, one value at a time, to Collector. At the same time, Sampler counts the samples it has acquired. When the count hits a threshold, Sampler generates E2 and resets (Figures 16-2[c] and 16-2[d]). Collector buffers up the data in the overall sample until enough have been collected. At that point it copies the buffered samples to public attributes in other objects as a "snapshot" of the data sampling. Since this is a synchronous knowledge update we are assured that the objects always have consistent data. Collector understands which objects should get which subsets of data from the sample set. Since the filters need to process complete sets of consistent data, Collector notifies them when a new complete set is ready.

This is a quite plausible solution, and many applications doing similar things would have this sort of flow of control. However, the logic within the Collector is likely to be complicated, particularly in the Stored state. If we think about breaking up the processing in the Stored state of Collector so that a state is dedicated to each kind of filtering, we would have a problem with the way Sampler triggers the actual data storing because that is tied to a single state condition (i.e., the overall sample count threshold has been met). But if we think about things a bit more we will note that Filter1 and Filter2 are really tied to the individual subsets of data that Sampler collects. It is basically serendipity that both sorts of filtering happen to need exactly the same snapshot in time, and it is a convenience of implementation to bundle the two sets of data values in a single sample data packet when both subsets are acquired at exactly the same time.

Figure 16-3 explicitly captures this independence. That is, Sampler is really generating two independent streams of data that are processed independently. Sampler generates separate E2a and E2b events for the streams as the data is obtained. This will actually be a more robust model because we can change that policy tomorrow without affecting any of the downstream processing. That more robust solution became evident because thinking about separating the data updates for the E3 events caused us to recognize the intrinsic independence of the sampling sets and filtering in the way we modeled the data collection.

Now for extra credit: What is wrong with the Figure 16-3's state machine?

The problem lies in what the Buffering state actually does. The description blithely implied that it is some sort of temporary storage for sample value sets until they can be distributed to other objects in a consistent fashion, implying that the storage is limited and that it gets reused once the values have been distributed. In other words, there has to be some sort of clear-and-reset behavior when the values are written, which was probably done in the Storing state of the original model. We now have two states for the old Storing state. How does each state know whether it is safe to

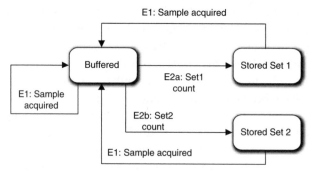

Figure 16-3 *State machine for an object managing buffering and storage of samples*

reset the buffer for the data? In other words, how does it know that *both* subsets of values have been distributed when it is distributing only one subset?

The answer is that it can't (more precisely, it shouldn't) because the processes are independent. What we will have to do is implement the buffer storage differently so that the two subsets of data are separated. Then only the relevant set of data for the E2a or E2b event is reset in the appropriate state. Since that is a matter of private knowledge implementation, there is nothing really wrong with the state machine per se. The point is that there is no free lunch. We have to look at the big picture when designing state machines and that may include the way the object's knowledge is implemented.

To get a handle on states, we need something a tad more substantial than the notion of *state of being*, especially when we define transitions. Alas, a state of being is kind of like art; we know it when we see it. Recall the example of a garage door opener in the previous chapter where the Door had states for {Open, Closing, Closed, Opening}. This seems intuitive enough for a simple example using 20/20 hindsight. But you may also recall that the Closing and Opening states were added in a second bout of navel contemplation (aka an iterative design pass), so they weren't quite that intuitive initially. Also note that {Open, Closed} and {Opening, Closing} convey different ideas; the first pair is inherently static while the second pair in inherently dynamic. The point here is that there are several ways to view the notion of *state of being*.

- *What the object is.* This is a static view like {On, Off} or {Open, Closed}. It is the purest view of *state of being*.

- *What the entity is doing.* This is a dynamic view like {Opening, Closing} or {Heating, Cooling} where the entity being modeled is conceptually performing some activity on a continuous basis and all we are providing is the trigger. This situation is common in control systems where the activity is what the underlying hardware entity being modeled actually does. In that situation the rules and policies encapsulated in the state's action provide initialization, setup, and/or initiation of the activity. This distinction between what the underlying entity does and what the object state's action does is important. We do not want to define a state condition in terms of what the associated object behavior is, but we can define it in terms of what is happening *as a result*.

- *What role the object is playing.* Because we anthropomorphize human behavior onto inanimate entities, it is common to think in terms of roles that the object migrates through during the problem solution.[3] The key here is to think about what the role itself is rather than the rules and policies that it executes. In the previous Collector example, the {Buffering, Storing} states could be viewed as roles the Collector plays within the overall solution.

We could summarize these views by saying that we define states in terms of *why* their rules and policies need to be isolated. While the previous suggestions are useful, they are not the only possible views. The real key is that we need to abstract the state condition as something different than the rules and policies associated with the state condition. In fact, just coming up with good state names is a very useful exercise and should not be done casually, because providing names that do not simply describe the behavior isn't easy if the behaviors haven't been encapsulated properly, so we have a check on prior development.[4]

Transitions

Transitions are rather straightforward; they represent a change in condition from one state to another. However, a more practical view is that they express a sequencing constraint from the problem space or problem solution. Usually the rationalization that determined the need for a state machine in the first place will go a long way

---

3. Rebecca Wirfs-Brock was a pioneer of role-based design. Her methodology is rather different than MBD, but her book *Object Design: Roles, Responsibilities, and Collaborations* (Addison-Wesley, 2003) is an excellent presentation of this perspective. Within the context of MBD I think the overall perspective on roles she presents is quite valuable, and I think the book should be on every OO developer's reference bookshelf.

4. This notion of checking on prior design work becomes a recurring theme when dealing with dynamics. The static structure that we developed is the skeleton on which the dynamic view is hung. So it is fairly common to uncover difficulties in the static structure when focused on the dynamic description.

toward determining what the sequencing constraints are in the problem space. Since the responsibilities have already been abstracted to be cohesive and logically indivisible, we are left with just connecting the dots for the problem context. In many cases, the constraints will be fairly obvious because, after all, we are modeling a life cycle.

> In defining transitions we sequence conditions, not behaviors.

This is really the key mindset issue for defining transitions. While we necessarily need to think about the overall solution context to some degree, we want to keep that thinking as pure and abstract as possible. In particular, we want to avoid thinking about a sequence of operations, as in the steps of an algorithm. That's because the traditional view of a sequence of operations is inherently synchronous, and with our asynchronous OOA/D behavior model we cannot guarantee that the operations will be executed contiguously. We can guarantee what condition must prevail for the object to execute the operation *whenever it is time to do so*. Once we know what the conditions are, we can order them relative to one another.

While transitions represent constraints on how the object collaborates with the rest of the world, we need to avoid thinking about the specific events that trigger the transition. Determining where and when events are generated is a logically distinct design task for connecting the dots in the overall problem solution. When we define transitions we are dealing with the supporting static structure for the overall solution flow of control. That static structure is expressed purely in terms of the underlying entity's intrinsic life cycle and we want to focus our thinking as much as possible on that life cycle.

> Like object responsibilities, life cycles in object state machines are highly tailored abstractions of the underlying entity's actual life cycle.

Note that defining states and transitions is very similar to defining objects and responsibilities in the Class diagram. We use abstraction to *select and tailor* what we need from the underlying entity based on the problem in hand. But *what* we abstract are still intrinsic properties of the underlying entity. Thus the states and transitions represent a unique view of the intrinsic entity life cycle tailored to the context of the specific overall solution. It may seem like a fairly minor distinction, but that mapping of context view to intrinsic reality is both ubiquitous and fundamental to OO abstraction. Nurturing that dichotomy in our mindset will pay dividends by removing the temptation to create behavioral dependencies.

A viewpoint that some newcomers to state machine sometimes find useful when looking for states and transitions is to think in terms of *situation* rather than *condition*. Because we use the Moore model in MBD, most objects are really doing nothing at all when they are in a state. (The rules and policies associated with the state were executed when the state was *entered*.) In other words, most objects spend most of their time sitting on their thumbs just waiting for something to happen. However, where they are waiting (i.e., their current FSM state) may be a determining factor in what they will be capable of doing when and if something happens.

As a contrived analogy, imagine a fireman who can be either on duty at the firehouse or off duty at home in bed. When the fire alarm sounds the fireman can respond effectively, or not, depending on where he is. When at the firehouse the fireman has access to the proper equipment to respond because of the location. In fact, it is having access to the equipment that is a *condition* of being ready to respond to the fire alarm rather than the physical location of home versus firehouse. It is easy to anthropomorphize a notion of the fireman (or object) being in a good situation (i.e., the right place at the right time) when the alarm (or event) occurs. Being in that situation enables the fireman to respond (transition to fighting the fire). Thus the notion of *situation*, where the dictionary definition has dual meanings of location and condition, can be useful.

Transitions implicitly define when we cannot get there from here.

Regardless of how we view a state machine state, the definition of transitions still comes down to determining what possible states may immediately follow the current state in the overall solution. As constraints, though, what we are really defining are the state migrations that are not possible. Omitting a transition between two particular states (or a reflexive transition to the same state) is essentially saying that there is no possible solution context where the object should migrate between those states. Obviously, we do not design state machines based on the transitions we can't have, but it is a useful sanity check on the transitions we do have to explicitly verify that all the possible omitted transitions really cannot happen in any solution context.

Events

Events are simply messages.[5] We call them events because they announce something noteworthy happening in the application. The crucial mindset issue is that the noteworthy happening occurs *elsewhere* in the application from the object having the state machine that responds to the event. (You may recall this is why we frown on events that are self-directed.) Because objects collaborate on a peer-to-peer basis, that noteworthy happening will be the execution of an action in another object state machine. As indicated earlier in the discussion of states, that noteworthy happening

---

5. FSA gurus have a more rigorous definition that only a mathematician could love, so this is just the OOA/D spin.

will also map to a change in the condition of the overall problem solution. Therefore, the event message announces both changes simultaneously.

This has some important methodological implications.

Events do not identify transitions.

In fact, transitions have no unique identity. That's because to execute a state machine we do not need transition constraints to have unique identity since the transition has no unique, intrinsic characteristics. Since the only thing that distinguishes one transition from another is the state of origin and the state of destination, the STT expresses everything we need to know about transitions. So if you've seen one, you've seen them all. However, the transition only tells us *where* we can go when something happens. We need to know *when* to go, which is what the event provides, so we need to *associate* the events with the transitions for their happening to be noteworthy.

An interesting implication of the separation of event and transition lies in ignoring events. Recall that in an object state machine we can ignore events in the STT. They are consumed, but the state machine does not execute any rules or policies or change state. That is a uniquely OO view of state machines. In effect, it means that a happening may be noteworthy in the external context where the event is generated, but it may not be noteworthy in the current context of the listening state machine.[6] This is a manifestation of the way the OO paradigm separates the concerns of the object that has changed the application state from the concerns of the object that might care about that change. Thus having the added flexibility of determining whether there will be a response at all becomes a local option.

Another manifestation of the flexibility of separating events from transitions is that we can associate the same event with multiple transitions that do not share the same origin and/or destination states. In effect, this provides us with a form of polymorphic behavior substitution for individual objects so that the rules and policies executed in response to the event can be quite different even though the event is generated by the same noteworthy external happening. In other words, the rules and policies that prevail depend on when the happening occurs relative to the receiver's life cycle.

This sort of thing is actually quite common. For example, in the Garage Door Opener example of Figure 15-13, the E1:clicked event was assigned to four different transitions: Open → Closing; Opening → Closing; Closing → Opening; and Closed → Opening. Thus the resulting rules and policies could be either for the Opening state or the Closing state, depending on the current state of the Door when the Clicker was clicked.

---

6. You were probably wondering, Grasshopper, why that stilted phrase, *noteworthy happening*, was used. Now you know.

While this might seem like just a cute feature, it is really very important. Imagine for a moment what the code would look like if we did not use a state machine and needed to account for all of the possibilities, such as the pet cat playing with the Clicker as if it were a mouse; basically, we would have a rat's nest of IF statements to deal with the various combinations. However, in the state machine solution there probably won't be any IF statements and the action code is likely to be trivial. This is because all the rules and policies were captured statically in the states, transitions, and event assignments. And a crucial enabler for this was the E1:clicked event that could be assigned to multiple contexts. (Of course the cat might cause the motor to overheat, but that's a hardware problem.)

The event context is not the transition context.

This is the most important implication of the separation of events from state machine transitions in an OO context. Events announce something happening externally. The semantics of the response context may be very different than the semantics of the happening context. In the Garage Door Opener example of Figure 15-13, the semantics of generating the E1:clicked event is about pressing a button on the Clicker control, while the semantics of the response is about opening or closing the door.

But the person doing the clicking knows the semantics, right? She wants the door to open or close; otherwise she wouldn't be clicking, right? Maybe so. But the person doing the clicking is not the Clicker. The button press is an external stimulus from the application's perspective and it has no open/close semantics. (To see that, imagine the cat playing with the clicker; the cat isn't trying to open or close anything except the clicker box.) From the software application's perspective the Clicker is just a surrogate object for some simple-minded hardware.

However, this segues to the notion of mapping. It is the developer who provides a mapping between what the person doing the clicking wants done and what the Clicker, Door, and their collaborations abstract. One major piece of that mapping lies in designing the state machine states and transitions. Another major piece lies in generating events and assigning them to transitions in the state machines. That assignment provides a mapping between the context of the event generation and the context of the response. Since the OO paradigm emphasizes encapsulation of abstractions that are highly tailored around intrinsic context, the need for such mapping is quite common. The separation of events from transitions is crucial to being able to provide that semantic mapping in a flexible manner.

The last implication of the separation is related to when we assign events. Previously we discussed how we could theoretically apply DbC to generating events by assigning them to transitions after we had designed all the object state machines in the subsystem. That is possible as long as we think of events as pure announcement messages. Conceptually, we want to think of events as a way of connecting the flow-of-control dots for collaborations in the overall problem solution. In other words, defining collaborations is a separate development stage that we can execute after designing the object state machines.

However, as noted in the introductory discussion of DbC in Chapter 2, that is rarely done in practice by experienced state machine developers because they are necessarily thinking about collaborations as they design the state machines and the mapping is often fairly obvious to the experienced eye. Nonetheless, if you are not accustomed to developing interacting state machines, it is strongly suggested that you initially follow the purist approach: Don't generate events or assign them to transitions until after you have made an initial pass at designing all the subsystem state machines. You will find that, as a novice, generating and assigning the events involves significant iteration over the state machine designs because things won't match up quite right. This is fine, and it will be an excellent learning exercise.

Before leaving the topic of state machine events we need to address the idea of polymorphic events addressed to a superclass in a subclassing hierarchy. If we employ the Harel model for state machines, the topic becomes mind-numbingly complex. Fortunately MBD does not use Harel, so we will just ignore that possibility. In MBD any superclass state machine is really just a notational convenience to avoid duplicating states and transitions in each subclass state machine. There are two manifestations of this.

In the simplest manifestation, all the subclasses share exactly the same life cycle, in which case the superclass state machine is also the complete state machine for each subclass and we are just drawing it in one place. So what is the point of having subclasses if they all have the same life cycle? Conceivably the subclasses could have different data accessed by synchronous services, but that would be quite rare in this situation. Another rather uncommon justification is that subclasses exist to support explicit relationships that only apply to subsets of members. A much more common reason is because the subclasses have different behaviors associated with the states. In this case the superclass events trigger the behavior substitution of inclusion polymorphism. All we have to do is provide the specialized action method for each subclass and map it to a superclass state.

The second manifestation is somewhat more complicated and occurs when the subclass state machines are different but share some of their states and transitions. In this case, the superclass state machine captures only the shared states and transitions as a matter of notational convenience to reduce duplication in the subclass state machines. However, conceptually there is no superclass state machine in this case. Each subclass has a single state machine that merges its specialized states and transitions with the common ones from the superclass. This becomes a pure mechanical issue for mapping transitions between the superclass states and the subclass states, which will be provided by the transformation engine. Again, the subclass state machine is free to provide a specialized action for the superclass states, so we have the same sort of polymorphic substitution as in the first manifestation.

In both manifestations the notion of a superclass event has an important limitation: It must be a valid event for every subclass in the entire line of descent from the superclass. The events will be polymorphic if the subclasses associate different actions for the superclass state.

Keep any polymorphism simple, and implement it at the leaf subclass level.

This is much simpler than the Harel view where superclass events can be "short-stopped" by superclass actions that execute before the subclass actions and dispatch can be made to subclass states based on history.[7] If you encounter a situation that you feel you cannot resolve with this simplistic view, then it is time to review the object abstractions because there is a problem with cohesion. In such situations, look for a delegation resolution with multiple objects.

Actions

You may have discerned a pattern to the mindset issues so far in that states, transitions, and events are regarded as distinct, quasi-independent features of state machines where each has a unique suite of design criteria or issues. That is astute, Grasshopper, because the same thing applies to state actions. States and problem context *limit* what the entity is responsible for doing. Transitions *constrain* the sequencing of what the entity does. Events determine *when* the entity does what it does. Actions are about *how* the entity does its thing.

Unlike everything we have talked about so far, actions are not the least bit static. As soon as we step into the specification of a state action we are in an entirely different and highly dynamic world compared to the static structural views described thus far. All of the static structure described in umpteen chapters exists to support the dynamics described within state actions. It is only with state actions that we get to anything remotely resembling traditional software programming. So if states, transitions, and events are different critters, then state actions are extraterrestrials.

Action rules and policies are intrinsic to the entity.

---

7. Just to be clear, Harel is actually orthogonal to OO subclassing. Harel provides a form of subclassing *for a single state machine*. In OO subclassing the subclasses have different state machines. However, we might be tempted to eliminate subclasses by employing Harel for a single class' FSM.

This is probably the most important aspect of defining state actions because it is the easiest way to go wrong, especially if we are used to traditional procedural or functional development. We have already hammered on the need for responsibilities to be intrinsic when they are abstracted. At the action level, we flesh out those responsibilities with the detailed business rules and policies that need to be executed. At that level we also need to make sure we describe that execution in terms of intrinsic rules and policies that do not depend in any way on anything going on outside the object (other than knowledge being available). In order words, we need to think of the relevant rules and policies in quite generic terms as we specify them.

Fortunately, the way MBD works already goes a long way toward ensuring that we will not be tempted to pollute our actions with external behavior dependencies. For example, the event-based asynchronous model prevents us from using data returned by invoking other objects' behaviors (e.g., the traditional procedural function return that immediately introduces an implementation dependency). Similarly, the restrictions MBD places on synchronous services preclude sneaking in behavioral dependencies via the back door. The way we abstract objects and responsibilities from the problem space severely limits the opportunities for foot-shooting.

Nonetheless, all that methodology cannot fully insulate us from temptation, so we need to be vigilant. Because we are dealing with business rules at a different level of abstraction and from a different perspective, it is fairly common to discover small problems with the objects, responsibilities, and state machines when we start to specify state actions. Therefore, be prepared for an iterative design process where you modify objects, responsibilities, and knowledge implementations.

Keep action data needs simple.

This is a corollary of the previous point about the need to think in terms of both data and operation sequencing. When responsibilities were identified in the static view, the emphasis was on cohesion of the *behavior*, not the data it accesses. When it is time to create state machines, though, we must consider data integrity issues because of the compound nature of action preconditions. The simpler the data needs of the action, the easier it will be to define preconditions and, consequently, rigorously ensure that execution is done at the right time.

Doing that is actually a lot easier than it sounds. Behavior responsibilities exist to modify the state of the application, which is represented in an OO context by state variables (attributes). If the behavior executes but no attribute was modified, then we cannot prove that the responsibility was satisfied.[8] So if we were careful about defin-

---

8. Note that I am careful to refer to the object's behavior *responsibility*. When we employ state machines it is fairly common for state *actions* to do nothing except generate an event. Object responsibilities are always implemented as actions, but some actions do not explicitly implement problem space rules and policies. Such actions are part of the implementation of constraints on the sequencing of behavior responsibilities.

ing behavior responsibilities as cohesive and logically indivisible, they will tend not to modify a lot of attributes. So, in practice, this guideline is more of a checklist item on how we have defined the responsibilities and state conditions. When we find that we are modifying several disparate attributes, we should be suspicious that the action encapsulates distinct sets of rules and policies that might be separated in time by different solution contexts.

Actions should be self-contained.

Actions only modify attributes, instantiate objects and relationships, and/or generate events.

Actions do very few things and we want those actions to be self-contained. Both instantiation and event generation are fundamental processes so they are implicitly self-contained. However, manipulating attributes could be done in a synchronous service and we invoke those services directly from actions. So there is a potential loophole here because the synchronous service could invoke other synchronous services, forming an indefinitely long chain. This is why we made such a big deal about synchronous services only modifying knowledge. If a synchronous service could instantiate or generate events, we break the containment of the invoking action.

Thus the acid test for actions being self-contained lies in unit testing. We should be able to define tests for every object responsibility based on six things.

1. Defining a known application state in terms of attribute values accessed by the object's actions

2. The current FSM state of the object

3. The ending FSM state of the object

4. The resulting state of the application in terms of attribute values modified by the responsibility

5. Events generated, including data packet content

6. New objects and relationships created

The first two items are the initialization required while the last four items represent observations of the results. As a practical matter, unit testing of an application developed with MBD tends to be very simple and the unit testing is easily automated. Most translation IDEs provide a built-in test harnesses for that.

Obviously, this depends upon having been disciplined about defining synchronous services so that they really are knowledge responsibilities and don't invoke endless chains of other object synchronous services. Evaluating the self-containment of the action being specified is the last line of defense against spaghetti code. When defining state actions that invoke synchronous services, you should double-check those synchronous services to ensure they really are just manipulating knowledge directly.[9]

The last thought on the mindset for dealing with state actions is related to exit actions. Exit actions are associated with exiting a state; that is, they are executed whenever there is a transition out of the state, regardless of what the next state is. From a purist viewpoint, exit actions are inconsistent with the Moore model used by MBD. That's because the state represents a condition where a *single set* of rules and policies apply. If we execute those rules and policies on entry to the state, then there should be nothing left to execute on exit.

As a practical matter, though, exit actions are similar to self-directed events. We do not want to use them casually, but there are situations where they can reduce the number of states and transitions in the state machine. Usually the underlying reason is the same as for using self-directed events: management of state variables, which are orthogonal to behavioral state machines. So, like self-directed events, as a reviewer you should demand solid justification for employing exit actions.

The Execution Model

If you would like a highly technical description of the execution model for MBD, you will have to go to a source like OMG's execution specification. When a bunch of academics start debating the nuances of runtime execution, it tends to bring new meaning to words like *arcane* and *obtuse*. Fortunately, such detailed descriptions are mostly only of interest to the developers of transformation engines. For the developers of application OOA models, life is much simpler: Essentially the developer can make several simplifying assumptions about execution that the transformation engine developers will have to support. Most of these assumptions have already been covered, but here is a quick review.

- *All knowledge access is synchronous.* Basically this means that the developer can assume the data is immediately available and consistent within the scope of a single state action. In other words, knowledge access is instantaneous, and the transformation engine will provide a mechanism to ensure the integrity of the data (e.g., nobody else will be writing it while it is being read).

---

9. There are situations where synchronous services can be nested, such as a subset of knowledge changes that are common to multiple actions. But reviewers will want a good justification if synchronous services are nested.

- *There is always an event queue for each subsystem.* Since all behavior responsibilities are captured in state machines in MBD, this ensures that message and method are separated, and that behavior implementations are decoupled. The transformation may eliminate the event queue in a synchronous implementation, but the application modeler cannot depend on it. Note that this event queue is conceptual; it will not explicitly appear in the model.

- *There is only one event queue per subsystem.* The OOA developer only needs to worry about functional requirements, so there is no need to be concerned about concurrency, distributed processing, and other complications due to addressing nonfunctional requirements or deployment. Those concerns all belong to a different union.

- *Only one state action is executed at a time in a subsystem.* That is, the event queue pops one event at a time and waits until the associated action completes before processing the next event. Essentially, this assumption makes the state action a basic, indivisible unit of computation.

- *Multiple events between the same sender and receiver will be consumed in the same relative order that they were generated.* Though the asynchronous communication model enables arbitrary delays between generating and consuming an event, there are limits to how arbitrary the delays can be. In this special case, the delays cannot change the relative order of events. This is essential to the notion of handshaking to synchronize state machines.

- *Events generated by a state machine to itself will be processed before events generated by other state machines.* This was discussed in Chapter 14. While not essential, it makes life much easier for ensuring data integrity.

- *Algorithmic processing within FSM actions and synchronous services employ the same execution model as the 3GLs.* Essentially this means that the detailed dynamic specification of behavior works the same way in an AAL as it does in the 3GLs.

These assumptions combine to provide an asynchronous model for behavior. There is a host of issues the transformation engine developer needs to address to make these assumptions valid, but that is not the application developer's problem. The only real problem the developer has is the asynchronous model. For most developers who have not dealt with asynchronous models, there is apparently a major hurdle: If there is an arbitrary delay between when a message is sent and when the response is triggered, how can we be sure that things will get done in the right order? As we discussed previously, the answer to this is simple: The event queue makes it

Just Work. The R-T/E people adopted the interacting state machine paradigm precisely because it brought order to an inherently asynchronous environment.

To put it another way, the "arbitrary delay" between when an event is generated and when it is consumed is really about how many events are already on the queue when it is pushed.[10] So if there are no events on the queue, it will get executed right away, and the only delays will be the wait until the sender action completes and the queue does its processing. If we put events on the queue as soon as the noteworthy happening occurs, they will get popped before events from other noteworthy happenings that occur subsequently. This is because events are only generated in state actions, and we only process one state action at a time with our single event queue. Thus the event queue maintains the order of noteworthy happenings so that they are responded to in the order they occurred. As discussed in the previous chapter, handshaking is the tool we use to ensure that events get on the event queue in the right order.

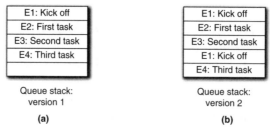

Figure 16-4   *Serializing events through the event queue*

Alas, life is rarely so simple. The previous logic applies to events generated by interacting state machines *within* the subsystem during the normal course of subsystem processing. There is another source of events that is truly asynchronous: external events from outside the subsystem. A priori we have no control over when those events are pushed onto the queue. Suppose the subsystem "daisy-chains" a suite of processing activities in response to an external event, E1, as in Figure16-4(a). Let's further suppose that due to the way knowledge is distributed among the objects,

---

10. In reality there may be other delays, such as network delays in distributed processing. Generally, these will be manifested by things like handshaking protocols that we may have to accommodate explicitly in the model as part of the requirements. Alternatively, it may be possible to deal with them in the transformation engine. For example, we may have an infrastructure available, such as CORBA support, which will already serialize the protocols so that they seem synchronous. In that case the event is external and the subsystem will only "see" it (push it on the queue) after the serialization.

whoever responds to E4 accesses data that was modified by whoever responded to E1. If so, then we are in trouble if another E1 event is pushed onto the queue before the response to E3 completes, as in Figure 16-4(b). That will cause the data modified by the first E1 event to be overwritten before the response to E4 gets to it.

The short answer to this problem is: Deal with it. As the subsystem developer you have to know when asynchronous external events will be a problem for your design and, in those cases, you will have to provide serialization explicitly in the model. Fortunately, it is relatively easy to do because subsystem interfaces are event based in MBD, so the external event just goes onto the subsystem's event queue. Most of the time it won't be a problem because you will design your subsystem interface around a protocol when subsystems interact, just like your objects within the subsystems.

For example, if most of your instructions come from the software user via a GUI, your subsystem is likely to have a natural exchange of user requests and subsystem results so that there is no need for the user to submit additional requests until the processing is completed and the results have been supplied. If you can't trust the user to wait, you can enforce that by having the GUI ignore random user interactions when waiting for results (e.g., give the user an hourglass cursor). The GUI will stop ignoring the user interactions when it gets the results from your subsystem.

However, whenever asynchronous external events can be a problem, the most common answer is usually serialization. In other words, we introduce an explicit queue into the application model to temporarily hold the external events until the application is ready to process them. This queue is unrelated to the event queue that manages object collaborations. It needs to be explicit because it is a necessary element of the solution design.

Another solution is to design the subsystem interfaces so that the subsystem can solicit a request from the client subsystem when it is ready to process. Usually, though, this just moves the explicit queue to the client. An exception is handling hardware interrupts. Since the interrupt is just a bit set in some hardware register, we can just poll the interrupt bit as a knowledge attribute at a convenient point in the software processing rather than modeling the interrupt as an externally generated event.

Naming Conventions

As in the rest of MBD, naming conventions for states and events have a dual role. They obviously provide documentation for posterity. Providing good names has a much greater value because they force the developer to think about what is being modeled. Coming up with good names for states and events is not an easy task, so it forces us to focus on the essence of the life cycle and the problem context. In this sense, providing good names is very much like extracting invariants from the problem space.

Naming states is relatively easy because there are essentially only three basic approaches. The preferred approach is to name states for the condition or state of being they represent. Thus in the garage door opener example of the last chapter, the states {Open, Closing, Closed, Opening} are pretty clearly tied to the notion of *door state*.

The notion of state condition is closely tied to the preconditions for executing the state's rules and policies. Since those preconditions are often compound (e.g., "Execute the permanent store after a complete set of samples has been collected, pre-processed, and temporarily stored."), it can get interesting when we are looking for a single pithy word or phrase. Nonetheless, this is the best way to name states, so we should take some time to find that pithy word or phrase.

The second approach to naming states is to name them consistently with the Moore model. That is, the state is named after what the rules and policies accomplished when they were executed upon entering the state. In effect we are naming the state for the postcondition of executing the rules and policies rather than the precondition. This will usually be indicated by a past tense verb (e.g., Samples Stored). Usually this is easier to do because we have already isolated our behavior into a cohesive, logically indivisible unit, so it is often fairly clear why we are doing it.

The third approach is a variant on the second where we name the state for the role that the action plays in the object life cycle. While valid, this is a last resort because it is often hard to distinguish between the role the rules and policies play in the solution and what they actually do. That is, the idea of role is more closely associated with what the rules and policies are than with the notion of state of being or condition. This becomes a slippery slope that can lead to naming states for their actions, which is a very procedural view of the world.

Naming events can be close to an art form. The problem is that we have one foot in the object, since the event triggers a transition in the object's life cycle, and we have the other foot in the context, since the event is generated by some noteworthy happening in some other object in the overall solution context. This tends to lead to some degree of schizophrenia since the context of generation may have quite different semantics than those of the receiving object's life cycle.

There are two possible approaches and each has ardent advocates. One approach is to name the event for the receiver context (i.e., the receiving object's view of what causes the transition). The logic behind this is that if we are doing event generation in a separate development step from designing the state machine structure, then we are doing some form of DbC to determine where the event should be generated. In that case the generation location is arbitrary compared to the precondition of the receiver's state.

The second approach is to name the event for the sender context (i.e., the generating object's view of what happened). The logic behind this approach is that the event is a message announcing that something happened. The only way we can "announce" something happening in a simple message is through the message identity. Therefore, we name events for what happened in the sender's context.

MBD is partial to the second approach in an OO context because it is more consistent with the OO view of separation of message and method where messages are announcements. It is also more consistent with the general OO notion that we design interfaces to suit the client rather than the service, and the event is basically an interface message. However, that can sometimes get awkward during maintenance if the location where the event is generated needs to change. If the new location has a different semantic context than the original, we would want to name the event differently, which would mean modifying the STT of Statechart diagram for the receiving state machine. If we name events for the receiver context, then this is not a problem and we just have to move the event generation, which we would have to do anyway.

As a practical matter, when there is a wide disparity in sender and receiver contexts we seek to raise the level of abstraction until the event name has an interpretive "fit" to both sender and receiver contexts. This reduces the likelihood that the event name would need to change during maintenance and makes documentation sense in both contexts.

Chapter 17

Developing State Models

*The proof of the pudding is in the eating,
but not if the eater is a poor judge of pudding.*

—Anonymous epigram

Alas, anyone can whip together a state machine. When the whippers are incompetent one will get bad state machines, as the Keyboard example in the Part III road map indicated. The main ingredient of state machine design competence is the right mindset, as discussed in the previous chapter. In this chapter we will discuss a more detailed approach to designing state machines that will help avoid foot-shooting when combined with the right mindset.

Most of the work in state machine design is actually done when one allocates behavior responsibilities to the class. If one religiously applied good OO problem space abstraction in identifying classes and responsibilities, much of the battle is already won. All you have to do is identify sequencing constraints among those responsibilities and you will have the core structure of the state machine.

Designing State Machines

The best way to think of an object state machine in an OO context is in terms of an intrinsic life cycle.[1] That life cycle consists of a set of states of being and constraints on migrating through those states. The states of being are determined by the intrinsic nature of the underlying problem space entity, while the constraints are determined by the overall solution context.

---

1. The notion of *cycle* here is looser than the notion of a closed graph cycle. While most objects' life cycles are closed because iteration is fundamental to computation, that is not necessarily the case. Thus one can think of born → live → die as an object life cycle.

Step 1: Identify the level of abstraction of the behaviors.

This is arguably the most important step in designing state machines. The idea here is to figure out what behavior the state machine manages and, more importantly, at what level of abstraction that management occurs. If you did a good job of documenting what your objects and responsibilities *are*, then most of this will be done already. Then your only remaining concern is expressing collaborations in terms of that level of abstraction.

This is all rather esoteric, and it probably won't mean much until we get to some examples later in the chapter. The main point here is to regard the state machine as a control structure for the object-in-hand's role in the overall solution. We want the overall state machine structure to be consistent with the subsystem's level of abstraction and the object's mission within the subsystem subject matter. From that perspective, the specific behavior responsibilities we have identified for the object are black boxes that will be encapsulated within state machine actions. Thus we are only interested in how the state machine connects up those black boxes, not what those black boxes actually do in the solution.

For example, consider changing a simple Traffic Light's color. There are several possible views of collaboration corresponding to different levels of abstraction of the collaborations, such as: setRed, where the determination of color is the client's responsibility; toggle, where the color details are handled in the Traffic Light implementation; and haltTrafficFlow, which has nothing directly to do with Traffic Light's color. The level of abstraction of those views will determine whether we need a state machine at all and, if so, what collaborations it may have (e.g., with a Timer for yellow to red). Thus for setRed, we can probably cast all of the Traffic Light's responsibilities in terms of knowledge, but for haltTrafficFlow we will be capturing problem space rules about the red $\rightarrow$ yellow $\rightarrow$ green cycle that might better be captured in behavior responsibilities.

One of the most common mistakes in state machine design is to let the state machine design be driven by detailed behaviors. In fact, we will quite often combine multiple individual behavior responsibilities in a single state action.[2] Alas, the author has seen state machines with literally dozens of states, most of which are connected by self-directed events. Each state action dutifully encapsulated a single logical behavior responsibility from requirements. The problem was that in the actual solution context the precondition for executing many of those behaviors was exactly the

---

2. So why did we bother defining "atomic" responsibilities in the first place? The reason is that it is much easier, conceptually, to merge them when needed than it would be to break up monolithic responsibilities later; later on we might already be biased into a false notion of what "atomic" is in the collaboration context. That is, the monolithic responsibilities might incorrectly drive our notion of the level of abstraction of collaboration.

same, so the states merely represented algorithmic steps in a single basic behavior. Those behaviors with the same precondition should have been coalesced into a single action where the sequence would simply be the order of steps within the action. Doing so would have eliminated the self-directed events and reduced the overall state machine size to a handful of states.

Requirements line items do not map 1:1 to state actions.

This is because in the context of collaboration with external objects, the granularity of the collaboration may be much coarser than the granularity of the individual, logically indivisible behavior responsibilities within requirements. To put it another way, collaboration is about *when* those line items must be resolved. Logically, the collaboration context that determines when they must be resolved may be the same for several of them. We capture the *when* in transitions while we capture the *what* of individual steps in actions. Therefore, your first task in designing a state machine is to examine the level of abstraction of the collaborations to determine when things should happen.

Step 2: Identify the "hard" states.

The first cut at an object state machine should be done purely on the basis of identifying intrinsic states of being that are relevant to the problem in hand. The so-called "hard" states are those that represent concrete or physical states like {Open, Closed} for a garage door. These will usually be fairly obvious.[3] This view of the life cycle forms the kernel view of the intrinsic entity nature. The so-called "soft" states like {Opening, Closing} probably won't show up until you try to resolve the sequencing constraints.

Step 3: Allocate behavior responsibilities to state actions.

Start out with one responsibility per state action. Now we switch gears and think of the state not as a state of being, but as a condition that enables that set of rules and policies. For each state, we select the appropriate behavior responsibility that should prevail when the object is in that condition. It is important to keep this view abstract. A behavior responsibility may implement multiple individual rules and policies from requirements, but we only care about the overall responsibility (i.e., the *set* of rules and policies determines *what* the responsibility does, not the individual rules and policies within that set that determine *how* it does its thing). A common novice mistake is to start writing actions before the state machine structure is completed.

---

3. That's true once one gets a bit used to designing state machines. Don't get bent out of shape if states of being don't seem to pop out of thin air when you first start out. That's normal and it takes some practice.

When all you have are "hard" states, the odds are you will have a couple of behavior responsibilities left over. For example, in the garage door example in Chapter 15, there are no special rules and policies for the Open and Closed states. All the action does is send a message to the Motor announcing that movement is completed (i.e., the condition has been achieved) so that it can turn itself off. This should be a big clue that there are some missing states because responding to the beaver in the doorway is something those states aren't handling.

Step 4: Combine behavior responsibilities in state actions, if necessary.

When one considers collaborations, it may be necessary to combine the responsibilities that we so carefully made logically indivisible into a single state action. This is where we have to start keeping one eye on the overall problem solution context. When we combine responsibilities in an action, we raise the level of abstraction for *logically indivisible* so that it is consistent with the collaboration context—which we didn't directly consider when defining the static structure. Thus responsibilities that were logically indivisible as individual entity properties may not be in the special circumstances of particular collaborations.

Of course, one needs to be careful when raising the level of abstraction. It is important to be quite sure that *all* the possible collaboration contexts *always* need *all* the combined responsibilities to prevail *at the same time*. This sounds more complicated than it really is. In practice it is a whole lot easier to coalesce fine-grained elements than it is to recognize the need to decompose coarse-grained elements. Perhaps more relevant, since our subsystem is quite narrowly defined from application partitioning, there probably are not going to be a whole lot of collaboration contexts to worry about. In addition, the level of abstraction that we defined for the subsystem helps a great deal in figuring out the level of abstraction of collaborations.

The rigorous acid test for whether rules and policies can be combined is DbC. If the preconditions for executing two responsibilities are exactly the same, then they can be combined. That's because those preconditions will both match the same postcondition of an external object's action, so the triggering condition always occurs at the same time in the solution. Typically one doesn't need to think about it so formally, though. The fact that some set of rules and policies is the logical response to the same announcement will usually be pretty clear.

In fact, if one employs a rough Collaboration diagram to keep track of collaborations as one develops state machines, it will usually be obvious by inspection that a single collaboration will trigger multiple responsibilities when the responsibilities have been defined more finely than the collaborations. Therefore, it is strongly recommended that you use a white board Collaboration diagram to "rough out" collaborations.[4]

---

4. I must emphasize that all one is doing is keeping track of collaborations, not messages. At this point we just need to know roughly who is talking to whom and when they are doing so. It would be premature to try to pin things down to individual messages.

Step 5: Add states as necessary.

There are two reasons for adding states. The obvious one is that there are behavior responsibilities that have not been accounted for in the existing states. The less obvious one is to facilitate collaborations. These are sometimes known as "handshaking states" because in networking and R-T/E domains one often encounters communication and hardware protocols that require an exchange of synchronizing messages in a predefined sequence. This exchange is commonly known as *handshaking*, as I described in Chapter 15.

If one has behavior responsibilities that don't seem to fit into the existing states, one needs to provide a home for them. Alas, one can't simply add a box to the Statechart, assign the responsibilities to the action, and make up a random name for the state. Adding states is probably the activity in state machine design where a proper mindset is most important. The state needs a rationale to be added. The rationale requires the state to represent an intrinsic state of being of the underlying object *and* to map into a condition for executing the associated behavior. If the rationale cannot satisfy both these goals, it is time to revisit the allocation of responsibilities to the object and/or the expected collaborations.

Keep in mind that when adding states one is providing static structure as the framework on which the dynamic solution rests. For robust and maintainable software, that structure needs to be stable. One way to provide stability is to map the state to an invariant in the problem space, such as an intrinsic state of being. In doing so, though, we need to be selective about what invariant to map. That selection is driven by how the object collaborates with other objects within the specific problem solution. In other words, the selection must be consistent with the object's collaborations.

One way that is manifested is through collecting behavior responsibilities into actions when there are multiple "left over" responsibilities. It may not be possible to put them all into a single state because of the constraints of collaboration. That is, the preconditions for executing some of the responsibilities may be different than for others. Those different preconditions essentially represent different collaboration contexts. In that situation the responsibilities need to be allocated to multiple new states. (In a sense this is a form of delegation within the state machine.)

Another way collaborations come into play is through handshaking. Typically, handshaking requires additional states. Quite often those states will not actually *do* anything. That is, there will be no associated behavior responsibility for the state action to execute. Such states are characterized by simply generating an event in the action to announce that the state condition had been achieved. For state machine novices this leads to an obvious question: If the state has no prevailing rules and policies, why do we need it?

The answer lies in the handshaking we talked about in Chapter 15, and we need to amplify on that discussion a bit for this context. Basically, handshaking introduces the notion of a handshaking protocol that essentially allows the receiver to tell the sender when it is safe to put an event on the event queue. Thus, the sender must wait until it is told it is safe to execute the problem action. There are lots of variations on the protocol, but the essential elements are a communication like the following:

Sender to Receiver: I just did X.

Sender to Receiver: I just did Y.

Receiver (internally): Now I get to do my thing because X and Y are both complete.

The premise here is that the Receiver needs to do something that depends upon both X and Y being completed. But the Receiver cannot depend on the Sender doing them in any particular order. More important, from the Sender's perspective they are unrelated activities. That is, X and Y will be done in different actions associated with different states. Recall that the rules of FSA preclude a state knowing whether another state has been executed. Therefore, it cannot be the Sender's responsibility to send an "X AND Y are done" message. The Receiver must somehow wait until both are done because that is the precondition for doing its thing. Typically that "waiting" will require an additional state.

In Figure 17-1 we solve that problem by allowing either E1 or E2 to transition to Waiting, whichever comes first. Then when the other event arrives it will trigger a transition to Did Something Else. In this case the Waiting state action does nothing at all.

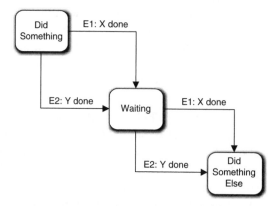

Figure 17-1   *FSM that must wait for two events before proceeding*

Extra credit question: What happens if two E1 or two E2 events arrive?

That would certainly be a problem, Grasshopper—if it could happen. It would not happen if the Sender's life cycle was constrained so that the actions doing X and Y always alternated, which is quite common because most life cycles form a true graph cycle. If you recall, we also have a rule saying that events from the same sender to the same receiver must be delivered in the same order they were generated. That rule exists to facilitate exactly this sort of situation. It ensures that if E1 and E2 are generated alternatively, they will be consumed alternatively.

But what if the Sender state machine cannot guarantee that E1 and E2 will alternate? The state machine in Figure 17-1 won't work properly and we have to fix something. The fix depends upon the specific requirements. The following cases apply.

1. The problem space demands that X and Y must both be done as matched pairs. In this case the Sender FSM's transitions must be modified to reflect the constraint. If this is not possible (e.g., X and Y are actions in different state machines), we have to find some other way to express overall flow of control to force them to be executed in pairs. In other words, we will have to provide special handshaking around the execution of the X and Y actions before the object in hand does anything.

2. X and Y must both be done at least once, but we don't care if they are done more than once. One way to handle this is by introducing two wait states, as indicated in Figure 17-2. One would handle repeated events with reflexive events, which are harmless since the wait states don't actually do anything.

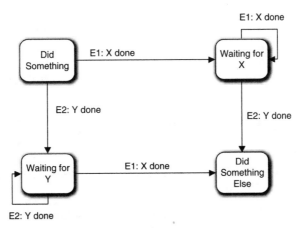

Figure 17-2 *A variant of Figure 17-1 where activities can be repeated*

In other words, the solution depends upon how the requirements specify the collaboration. Now let's look at how we might use handshaking to force X and Y to be done in pairs.

Sender to Receiver: I just did X.

Receiver to Sender: That's nice.

Sender to Receiver: I just did Y.

Receiver to Sender: That's nice.

Receiver (internally): Now I get to do my thing because X and Y are both complete.

Here the premise is that the Receiver needs to do something after X is done but before Y is done. So the Receiver tells the Sender when it is safe to do Y. In this case, no "wait" state is required because the Sender will be unable to transition to the state that executes Y until it gets a confirmation from the Receiver. In other words, the handshaking protocol is built into the Sender by splitting the X and Y responsibilities and providing a transition between them to capture the sequencing constraint.

The Sender FSM might look something like Figure 17-3. The Sender's basic life cycle is A → X → Y → B, and the Receiver has synchronized that life cycle with its own by providing the "That's nice" acknowledgments. For its part, the Sender provides the "I just did X" and "I just did Y" announcements, which synchronize the Receiver's life cycle to the Sender's. Thus handshaking makes Sender and Receiver dance partners who keep in step through their respective life cycles.

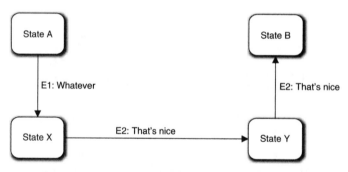

Figure 17-3 *Using handshaking announcements to "walk" through a life cycle*

Now let's look at a bit more context for the overall solution. Figure 17-4(a) represents a solution to a problem sequence where the overall solution requires activities to be executed in the order shown in the diagram. In particular, Object B should respond to Object A doing the Y behavior before it responds to Object C doing the C behavior. As an exercise, try to see if you can detect an ambiguity in the Sequence diagram concerning that constraint. (Hint: Suppose Object A and Object C execute concurrently and one has a much higher priority than the other.)

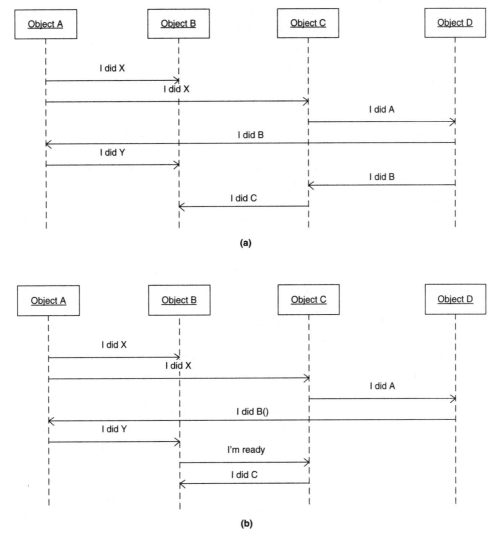

Figure 17-4 *Using handshaking to ensure one Object state machine is ready to accept events from another*

The problem lies in the order that Object B will consume the "I did Y" and "I did C" events. In a true asynchronous environment one cannot guarantee that the "I did Y" event will be consumed first. For example, if Object C executes at a much higher priority than ObjectA, then the action that generates "I did C" may complete and push that event onto the event queue long before the Object A action that generates "I did Y" completes and pushes that event. That's because Object D essentially provides a fork in the processing with two different paths leading to Object B doing things. If the things that Object B does must be done in a predefined order, then we must provide some sort of synchronization for those two paths to make sure the "I did Y" and "I did C" events get pushed on the queue in the correct order.

An unambiguous solution is presented in Figure 17-4(b). Instead of Object D creating a processing fork by issuing two different events, there is now only a single possible sequence for putting events on the event queue. To do that we had to introduce a trivial bit of handshaking between Object B and Object C, where Object B tells Object C when it is ready to accept the "I did C" event by issuing the "I'm Ready" event.

Note that Object C's C behavior is now triggered by the "I'm Ready" event rather than the "I did B" event. This gets back to the points made in the previous chapter about naming conventions and separation of message and method. The Object C state machine is unchanged; all we have done is associate a different event with the relevant transition. But because the context of the event generation has changed, it makes sense to use a different event message.

This also underscores my earlier point about constructing object state machines independent of context by making sure states have a problem space rationale. While we extract states and transitions with one eye on collaborations, the basic structure should be independent of context. The specific event that will trigger the transition is a context detail, while the state machine structure is an intrinsic problem space invariant of the underlying entity. That decoupling allows us to significantly change the overall solution flow of control without touching anything except where the triggering event is generated.

What about the fork produced when Object A generates two "I did X" events? That's not a problem, because the only possible sequencing constraint that could be relevant is that Object B responds to "I did Y" after it responds to "I did X." In this case Object A is generating both events, and it can't possibly generate the "I did Y" event until after it receives the "I did B" event, and it can't receive that event until it generates the "I did X" event to Object C. As long as Object A pushes the "I did X" event to Object B before it pushes the "I did X" event to Object C, the event queue will make things Just Work.[5]

This notion of daisy-chaining events through the event queue and synchronizing via handshaking is really crucial to good state machine design when state machines must interact, as object state machines do during collaborations. If you feel the least bit shaky about why the two forks in the original Collaboration diagram are a potential problem and how the second version fixes the problem with the second fork, you

---

5. There's a second reason. Recall from the last chapter that one of the rules the modeler can count on the implementation enforcing is that events between the same two sender/receiver objects will be consumed in the same order they were generated.

should spend some time "walking" the diagram as described in the preceding paragraph. You need to convince yourself that if events are pushed onto the event queue in a serial fashion everything will Just Work. (You also need to convince yourself that forks leading to different linear paths back to the same state machine can be a problem if the state machine itself has constraints on which responding action must be executed first.)

If you have never used state machines before, it will take awhile to fully appreciate what a marvelous invention the event queue is. The way in which the event queue and handshaking protocols combine to bring order to arbitrary delays and asynchronous processing has a quite magical aspect.[6] Perhaps more important, once one gets the collaborations to work, the state machine approach tends to be very robust and often yields very simple runtime code. Recall the garage door opener example in Chapter 15 where the actions had almost no executable code. All the business rules were elegantly handled by the FSM structure and the sending of messages at the right time.)

One final point on handshaking. You will note that Figure 17-4(b) does not require us to add states to the Object C or Object B state machines. That's because this example barely qualifies as handshaking; the "protocol" is simply that Object B tells Object C when it is ready to respond to Object C. This is actually the more common situation where one just reorganizes the daisy-chain of event generation. The handshaking issue was raised here because it is one possible reason for adding states to an object state machine.

Step 6: Add transitions.

This will usually be somewhat anticlimactic because just to recognize the states you will need to understand the overall collaborations, which implies knowledge of the sequencing constraints. Where you will encounter problems with this step is realizing that the behavior responsibilities may not map quite right when you try to map the requirements onto the state machine, which is exactly what happened with the garage door example when identifying the need to add {Closing, Opening} states. The door controller needed to do things while the door is moving, and those things didn't quite hang together when we tried to map them into static {Open, Closed} states. In effect we had more transition circumstances than we could map between just two states.

There isn't a lot of art here. Basically one is evaluating sequencing constraints and mapping them into a Statechart. The easy ones are those explicitly identified in

---

6. When I was first introduced to the notion of asynchronous communications my instinctive reaction was: This can't possibly work and, if one could get it to work, one's mind would be turned to mush in the process. I spent a lot of time in the ensuing couple of years looking for exceptions, but there was always a simple and elegant reorganization of collaborations that saved the day. So eventually I gave up looking and took it on faith.

requirements (including sequencing implicit in use cases). The green → yellow → red sequence of a traffic light is an example of a requirement that would likely be spelled out explicitly. The less obvious ones are those that are implicit in the nature of the problem space. That the pet cat could play with the garage door clicker until the motor burns out is less likely to be dealt with explicitly in the requirements.

Step 6A: Identify the life cycle invariants in the problem space.

A far more common problem is that the requirements are simply incomplete. It is assumed the developer has enough problem domain knowledge to fill in the gaps. Thus the specifications for an automated cooking oven where the food is loaded and unloaded by a robot are unlikely to mention that the oven door needs to be open before the robot loads the food. However, computers tend to be very literal minded and not very bright, so one must be very explicit about such details in the software specification. Therefore, the developer needs a systematic approach to adding transition constraints, and the best way of doing that is to look for invariants in the problem space. The question to answer before defining transitions is: In this problem context, is there some sequence of collaborations that is always done in the same order?

The operative phrase in that question is *problem context*. The issue is not some sequence of operations in a preconceived solution algorithm. Rather, it is about the problem space context in which the specific problem lives. Try to identify sequencing constraints that apply for any inputs to the solution that are reasonable. Thus, having the automatic oven's door open is necessary regardless of what food will be cooked, the temperature it will be cooked at, and the duration of the cooking. Better yet, look for an invariant that applies to variations on the problem in hand. Best of all, look for an invariant that applies to a whole class of quite different problems. Before loading anything *into* a container one needs access to the container. That applies to refrigerators, grain silos, and garbage cans as well as ovens.

The more general the invariant is, the more robust its implementation will be in the face of requirements changes.

This was already mentioned a few chapters ago, but it was worth mentioning again. State machine transitions are static definitions of the structure. Capturing business rules and policies in static structure is usually a good idea because it simplifies the dynamics. But one downside is that static structure tends to be more difficult to modify when things change. So one wants to capture things about the business in static structure that are very unlikely to change unless the business itself changes (in which case the software as a whole will be in deep ka-ka).

Therefore, it is a good idea to step back a pace or two and mentally work through the anticipated collaborations to see what sequences are fixed by the nature of the problem space. One way to do this is to walk through the relevant use cases and understand why their steps are ordered in a particular way. (The final example at the end of this chapter does exactly that.) Is the order just a convenient description for a Turing environment, or is there something fundamental in the problem space that is dictating the sequence? The more abstract and generic the invariant seems to be, the more confidence you have that you have uncovered an intrinsic life cycle constraint. Fortunately, you already thought about problem space invariants when abstracting objects and responsibilities, which should make recognizing the particular spin for collaboration sequences easier to spot.

As mentioned previously, having a rough Collaboration diagram of the collaborations will tend to help. The Collaboration diagram presents a rather high level of view of the flow of control. Such a high-level view makes it easier to evaluate collaboration sequences around a particular object. That is, the view presents the sequences that *might* be, thus helping you to focus on those that *must* be.

Step 7: Associate events with the transitions.

This is where the overall solution dots are connected. Typically one assigns the event and determines where it will be generated at the same time. Being able to do that ensures that the state machines interact together correctly. By the time you get here, things should be pretty clear, because everything you have done so far was done with one eye on collaborations. So it is usually fairly routine to determine where the events are generated. In those cases where it is not all that clear, one can fall back on the formal DbC technique that we discussed previously.

Naturally, things don't always go so smoothly. One common problem is that it seems like there are several different places where the event might be generated. This may be quite valid. For example, if you can generate errors from multiple contexts, you may have a single object that lives to process those errors (e.g., communicate with the user via a UI subsystem). A more common problem is that the precondition for transitioning to the receiving state is compound, and different conditions are satisfied in different places in the subsystem.

There are two ways to deal with this problem. One is to reconnect the messages so that the action where one condition is satisfied generates the event that triggers execution of the action where the other condition is satisfied. That is, one creates a single linear sequence for pushing events on the event queue such that the compound condition is incrementally satisfied in a cumulative fashion. Then one generates the event to the object in hand where the last condition of the compound condition is satisfied. This is the preferred method for most such situations. It is commonly referred to as *daisy chaining.*[7]

---

7. Don't ask why. Originally it had its roots in sexual innuendo. However, the phrase became part of the lexicon of R-T/E software development decades ago, probably because women R-T/E developers were about as rare as Tennessee snail darters back then.

The second approach is to employ handshaking so that the receiver "waits" for events from both contexts to arrive before providing a response. Figure 17-1 was an example of this. As an alternative, one delegates the synchronization to another object. This object's sole purpose is to "wait" for events announcing the various conditions, and then it generates the final event when all the conditions have been met. There are two reasons to avoid this approach. One is that it is more complicated. Another, more aesthetic reason is that one is "hard-wiring" the solution algorithm into an object implementation.

It is tempting to use a dedicated object when the individual condition contexts are unrelated, so there is no natural reason for one to be triggering the other. One may also choose this approach when daisy-chaining the sequence for the first approach seems too fragile (i.e., it is difficult to organize properly and is likely to have to change during maintenance). However, the real justification for this approach should be that an entity already exists in problem space with such synchronization as an intrinsic responsibility. Unfortunately, in most customer spaces that will be a human being whose responsibilities you need to anthropomorphize. Therefore, the dedicated object will probably be abstracted from the computing space or some esoteric conceptual space like design patterns.

Examples

Probably the most effective way to describe state machine design is to walk through the thought processes for some examples. We'll use the ATM Controller example. You might want to go back and review the static descriptions of that example before continuing here.

Recalling the discussion of the ATM Controller, it was suggested that there really wasn't a whole lot of processing and most of the objects were either hardware surrogates or dumb data holders. The most likely entities to have a life cycle relevant to the problem are the Dispatcher, Character Display, and Transaction. The Dispatcher clearly needs to understand the ordering of hardware operations and display; essentially, its role in the application is to act as traffic cop for messages from the user. Character Display needs to initialize the screen, process a stream of user keystrokes, update the screen, and let Dispatcher know when the user has finished entering a value. Superficially that sounds like a single procedure with a loop over reading keystrokes, but there is enough going on to take a closer look. More important, each of the activities is triggered externally, and there is a definite sequence in which they need to be done. Transaction does the real "banking" work, such as it is, by communicating with the Bank and triggering certain hardware activities.

ATM Controller: Character Display

First, let's look at Character Display. In the rough Collaboration diagram in Figure 17-5, we see that the collaborations are not too complicated. Since Character Display will talk directly to the OS window manager to actually present a display, there is another player not shown. Typically, though, the OS window manager presents a serialized (synchronous) interface, and it is realized so we won't bother showing it in the Collaboration diagram. So, the level of abstraction of the collaborations seems to be reasonable. There is a pretty clear order in these collaborations: The screen must be set up first, then the user types in a value, and finally the value is sent off to Dispatcher.

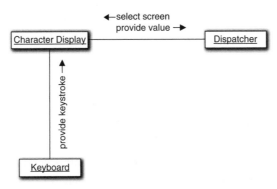

Figure 17-5 *Preliminary cut at collaborations for the Character Display object*

Are there any "hard states"? There are some obvious states related to sequencing operations, but there really aren't any obvious, intrinsic states of being that leap out here. However, there are three clumps of processing that must be done in sequence based on the Collaboration diagram: initializing the screen through the OS window manager; processing keystrokes from the Keyboard; and extracting a value. Note that those responsibilities are invariant with the type of screen; we will do the same things for deposits and withdrawals. (Transfers are trickier, but we'll get to them later.) Thus we can think of the conditions that prevail for executing each set of processing as a kind of "hard" state simply because it is so obvious and invariant.

Basically all Figure 17-6 represents is a mapping of the collaborations directly into states. (More precisely, I have mapped the collaboration responses into states by casting the conditions for executing the responses into states.) Note that the state names are all past tense descriptions of the response. This is a quite common naming convention for states where the state is named for the postcondition of executing the response. That is very consistent with the Moore model of state machines where, you no doubt will recall, the action is executed on entering the state. In this case, the state-of-being condition for the state happens to be pretty obvious. That is, most experienced developers would think of these as "hard" states. Therefore the diagram represents completion of the first three steps of the process suggested.

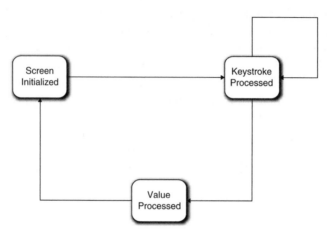

Figure 17-6   *Preliminary state machine for Character Display*

You have no doubt noticed that we have four transitions in the state machine but we had only three collaborations in the Collaboration diagram. Recall the discussion of modeling a keyboard from the section road map; this is the proper way to handle the keyboard input. As it happens, each transition involving Keystroke Processed represents a single collaboration with Keyboard. Note that we have effectively combined a gazillion states for individual keystroke sequences (the view described in the Part III road map example) into a single state. That legerdemain was accomplished by raising the level of abstraction of keystroke processing to an invariant that could be parameterized.

Now we have a state machine that seems to handle all the collaborations. In addition, it is quite easy to envision what the actions for each state do. The action for Screen Initialized reads the Display Specification, formats a buffer, keeps track of where the value will be in the buffer, and ships the buffer off to the OS window manager. The action for Keystroke Processed inserts the key value in the buffer and echoes the character to the right place in the display. The action for Value Processed extracts the full value from the buffer and ships it to Dispatcher. So everything seems to fit together properly.

Or does it? It is time to look for additional states and transitions beyond the obvious "hard" states and transitions. What about user errors? As long as the user catches typos, we can handle that in the Keystroke Processed action simply by doing the right thing in the buffer with the Backspace key value. In addition, for the simplistic ATM we have in mind we only have a numeric keyboard, so we don't have to worry about alphanumeric typos. The code might start getting complicated and we might need a few smart private synchronous services to access the buffer, but that really doesn't concern us here. That sort of processing is pure implementation and won't affect our problem solution flow of control.

Don't let action implementation complexity drive state machine design.

This segues to another important practical point about OO development in general. We use OO to solve an overall problem for the customer. We use OO techniques to isolate and encapsulate major program units so that their implementations can be decoupled for better maintainability. But once we have identified logically indivisible units in the overall solution flow of control, we pretty much wash our hands of those units' implementations. Essentially we are making a trade-off in managing complexity whereby we ignore implementation details in order to get the big picture right.

Is there anything else in the problem space that we are overlooking? What about aborts? Is there a $nevermind key the user can press at any time to abort processing? Can the user do something dumb, like stomp away without retrieving their account card when informed they have insufficient funds? In such cases there may be situations where the Character Display could be left in a state that is not suitable for the next activity. This is a place where a Ready state may be useful as the state where the Character Display is always ready to accept a *new* screen request. One would have a transition from both Screen Initialized and Keystroke Processed to get to the Ready state to accommodate resets, aborts, and so on.[8]

The point here is that it's best to step back and look at the whole problem space in addition to the specific use cases that seem relevant to the object in hand. When performing this sanity check, look for unusual scenarios. If you do, then the last question in the previous paragraph should make you realize that the state machine described so far won't work properly for all situations.

The problem is quite common in software development—we tend to be myopic about "normal" use cases. What happens when the ATM user tries to make a withdrawal without sufficient funds? This state machine works fine for specifying the withdrawal amount. Dispatcher will then select a new screen to announce that there are insufficient funds. So far, so good. What's wrong is that the announcement screen may not have an amount to fill in (we can't assume the user will always want to try a lesser amount). Typically the user will be given a menu of keys to hit to decide what to do next. Character Display must map that keystroke into a message to send to Dispatcher.

---

8. If that is done, it might be convenient to make Ready a superstate where those transitions are implied, as discussed in the last chapter.

In fact, we have screwed up big time here[9] because there are probably several other screens (e.g., the start-up menu) where the user does not fill in a value or just selects a choice that Character Display returns to the Dispatcher. Our state machine is quite myopic about dealing only with the common Deposit and Withdrawal requests; nor does it seem to deal with the account selection needed for a Transfer.

There is no need to panic, though, because abstraction and cohesion come to the rescue, and this is easy to fix. One possibility is to subclass Character Display based on the sorts of screens one might have (e.g., get an amount, select a menu item, information dialog, etc., where each member of the category has unique value processing or lack of it). Then each subclass has a unique state machine to process its particular flavor of screen.

That's a valid approach, and it would certainly be preferred for sets of complex screens. Effectively one creates subclasses to deal with the invariants of each screen category and employs Display Specification to provide details like text labels for individual category members. In this case, though, we need to look for a simpler solution since the UI is a cretin. In our simple ATM context, the user will do one of four mutually exclusive things:

1. Press a single key that has special semantics in the screen context, such as a menu selection,

2. Provide a value,

3. Simply close the screen (via Enter), or

4. Provide multiple values.

The Keystroke Processed state can do the right thing for the first case *if it knows the first situation prevails*. All we need is a type attribute in Display Specification that the Keystroke Processed action can access to decide what to do (i.e., map the key value to an event to send to Dispatcher or process the key value as a digit in the value in its buffer).

All that remains is to make sure our transition constraints will work properly for the single key case. They will if there is a transition from Keystroke Processed to Screen Initialized for the selection of the next screen. Such a transition would be triggered by the Dispatcher in response to the announcement that the special key was pressed. That's fine except for one detail: the relationship to Display Specification.

---

9. In practice we would be unlikely to make this mistake. That's because when we defined the knowledge responsibilities for Display Specification, we would have been forced to think carefully about *all* of the possible screens. With that inventory fresh in mind, we probably would have realized managing a user value is not the only thing Character Display does.

That relationship must be re-instantiated for the new screen to be displayed based on the user's selection. Screen Initialized could do that.

OK, by applying KISS, our object and its state machine are kept simple and cohesive for the menu case. We already deal with the second and third activities, which leaves us with the Transfer transaction where the user is probably going to have to provide at least two values.

One could provide subclasses based on the number of values to retrieve. Or simply break up the screens to collect one value at a time. One could also provide an outer iteration around Value Processed and store values in attributes.

However, there is a much simpler solution, given our simplistic view of the character UI. Whether the user supplies one, two, or N values, they are just locations in our display buffer. The Display Specification can define the number of fields and their individual locations. That is, the user isn't done (presses Enter) until all the fields have been provided. So Value Processed can use Display Specification to extract all the fields at once.

The only problem is keeping track of which field a given character provided by Keyboard is in within the Keystroke Processed action. Since the user will usually not fill each field with digits, there will have to be some way for the user to move to the next field, such as an arrow key. The Keystroke Processed action can take care of that since the arrow keystroke just indicates a predefined skip in the buffer. That skip defines where in the buffer the next character is stored and what position on the screen to echo the next character. Keystroke Processed is now somewhat more complicated, but none of that complexity affects flow of control; the same buffer is being modified, and the same buffer will be interpreted by Value Processed. Therefore, handling multiple fields can be done in the implementations of the existing actions.[10]

Now let's think about how the user can screw things up. Fortunately, the UI is so simple there aren't a lot of ways. The ATM may have a key called Main Menu or something that the user can click at any time to start over from the beginning, which is effectively an abort of current processing. The Keystroke Processed action can detect that key just like any other special key. It would probably be best to let Dispatcher figure out what to do with it, just like the other special keys.

We haven't given the user a lot of keys to play with, so about the only problems around values entered will be an invalid value or a missing value. Detecting an invalid value will be the bank's or some other object's problem, and that will happen

---

10. We are getting pretty close to the point where we might need a separate subsystem for the UI, though. So far things are simple enough that we can hide the processing in the implementation. But if the UI gets more complicated with things like nonnumeric fields and several ways for the user to navigate between fields, the mechanisms and mapping through Display Specification become complicated enough that we might want to design them explicitly as a separate problem from controlling the ATM hardware.

long after Character Display has done its thing by extracting the value. But a missing value is something Value Processed can detect. To be consistent it, would probably be best to simply announce the problem to Dispatcher and let it figure out what to do.

If the user hits arrow keys when only one value is required or hits the wrong arrow key to navigate to a field, it can probably be handled by simply ignoring them in Keystroke Processed.

The last problem is a time-out when the user failed to complete a transaction because a not-too-bright mugger lost patience. How the machine responds will depend on banking policy and, possibly, the hardware, so we won't get into it here. There are two other very interesting things to think about for this scenario, though. One is where the time-out event is coming from. You seem to have forgotten something in your model, Grasshopper. You don't have a Timer object. Shame on you.

Actually, you lucked out, Grasshopper, and there is no shame in it. In event-based processing, timers are so ubiquitous, especially in R-T/E, that they are regarded as an infrastructure object like event queues and we usually do not show them explicitly in the OOA model. So the time-out event will magically appear.

The next interesting question is: Who should respond to the time-out event? The problem is that the time-out probably has lots of implications besides the display. Certainly the processing of the current user transaction may need to be aborted. That gets tricky if we are in the middle of a withdrawal and the bank has already put a hold on the customer's account pending the actual cash dispensing. But if the user is not responding at all, perhaps the whole session needs to be aborted. Then one needs to do something with the user's ATM card and reset the entire machine so another customer can use it. Clearly, responding to the time-out is not a Character Display responsibility.

The potential for a universal reset of multiple ATM components is a distinct possibility, so we should think about this and how it would affect the Character Display. Assuming somebody else manages the overall reset, we can probably count on the fact that the reset will involve putting up a new screen, even if it is just the ATM logo for when no customer is actively using the machine.

So the overall strategy for managing errors is the same as handling special keys: Report it to Dispatcher and let Dispatcher figure out what to do next. That will very likely involve putting up a new screen, and theoretically that could happen when the Character Display is in any state.

In Figure 17-7, the Screen Initialized state becomes a superstate. In this example we are only eliminating one transition, so the superstate notion is overkill. I was just demonstrating the sort of thinking that would lead to its discovery. Display Specification will have a type attribute to indicate the general category of screen to parameterize the action processing. Character Display will potentially generate a variety of events back to Dispatcher for different screen contexts (categories), and we will have to keep that in mind when we deal with Dispatcher's state machine.

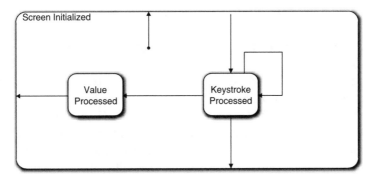

Figure 17-7 *Updated FSM for Character Display object*

Note that in this discussion did not follow the last three steps of the design process discretely. They became somewhat jumbled together in dealing with various special cases. That's not terribly unusual. The approach described is intended to be a guideline. One should definitely address each step somehow, and it is often useful to do so in a systematic (ordered) way. But the order is not crucial. In any intellectual exercise that requires creative thinking, one sometimes needs to just go with the flow.

Also note that this discussion touched on a number of issues that imply iteration over work already done, from requirements elicitation through the static model to possibly other state machines. This sort of tweaking is inevitable in any complex human intellectual undertaking, so get used to it. Hopefully the general OO and specific MBD practices will minimize the amount of rework required. That minimization is a major reason why we use methodologies for design.

ATM Controller: Dispatcher

For the next example, let's look at the ATM controller's Dispatcher object. When we defined classes like Deposit, Withdrawal, and Card, we discussed possible functionality that we might ascribe to them. For the moment, try to forget all that as we "walk" through this example, because the point is that the methodology itself is self-correcting. We want to approach this as if we decided that Dispatcher was a controller object at the heart of the ATM that coordinates all messages. That is, every message goes to Dispatcher and is re-dispatched to the right place. So, tentatively, Dispatcher is a god object controlling everything else.

This is a common mistake when one has just enough knowledge to be dangerous. It's possible to get the level of abstraction of the subsystem right (managing messages rather than banking semantics) but then get carried away with the notion of dispatching messages. Going hand-in-hand with the controller view, there is commonly an overreliance on use cases to drive structure. So rather than directly applying the process steps described earlier, we will take a more direct, use case-driven approach. That should demonstrate that applying basic design principles will get us to the right place anyway.

The first question we should ask ourselves is: What is the Dispatcher's mission in life? It is actually the heart of the ATM Controller *as we have defined it*. As it happens, we have defined the ATM Controller to be rather simple-minded; all it understands is the routing of various messages to and from different hardware elements. As the name implies, the Dispatcher takes in an input message, reformats it, and forwards it to the right hardware element. If that were all that there was to it, then we would not need a state machine; a single method with an embedded switch statement would do it.

However, there is a bit more to it. There are some implicit rules about the ordering of input messages, such as the user must supply an amount via Character Display before the Cash Dispenser can be told to dispense cash. Intuitively the Dispatcher might seem like a good place to capture those rules in terms of transition constraints. So our basic life cycle is essentially the invariants of the sequence of interactions with the user (via Character Display), the Bank (via the Network), and the ATM hardware elements (Cash Dispenser, et al.). If we happen to have a suite of use cases that specify the user interactions, the logical place to start is by mapping their implied sequencing constraints into a state model. So let's look at how that works for some informal use cases.

```
Use Case 1: User authentication.
User inserts ATM card in reader.
Validate card information with Bank.
If stolen, display message and eat card.
If invalid, display message and eject card.
If valid, display main menu.
```

Let's assume that the Dispatcher has an Idle state where it sits between users (i.e., when there is no card in the Card Reader). In this case it is pretty easy to map a state condition for each use case activity: Card Inserted; Card Read; Card Stolen; Card Invalid; and Card Valid. Each state will have a unique action to perform, in order: Request information from Card Reader; request validation from Bank (via Network); instruct Character Display to show a relevant display and then instruct Card Reader to eat card; instruct Character Display to show a relevant display message and then instruct Card Reader to eject card; instruct Character Display to display the main menu. Such an FSM is shown in Figure 17-8.

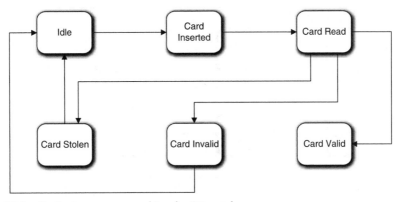

Figure 17-8 *Preliminary state machine for Dispatcher*

So far, so good. Note that since we are designing the intrinsic life cycle, we are not worried about what the specific events are that trigger the transitions or where they come from. Let's look at the next use case.

```
Use Case 2: Withdrawal
User selects Withdrawal from main menu
Display amount request screen
Validate amount with Bank
If invalid, display message
If valid,
    Dispense cash
    Query additional transaction
    If none, eject card, clear display, and print record
    Else, display main menu
```

We can do pretty much the same thing for this use case, which just adds states and transitions to the state machine we already have, as shown in Figure 17-9.

Note that the mapping of states to use case lines is not exactly 1:1 for this use case. That's because we aren't mapping activities; we are mapping states of being or conditions in a life cycle. In addition, we have one eye on the general sorts of collaborations we will have with other objects. Also note that the actions in most of our states are trivial; they just generate messages to hardware objects. That is exactly what Dispatcher is supposed to be doing. So the states are just way points where Dispatcher waits for an announcement that some triggered activity has completed.

There is a bit of trickiness here in that if the user has another transaction, we would have to go back to the Card Valid state. That's because that is where the message to display the main menu is requested so we can dispatch to a menu selection. In other words, we are reusing the state and its action. But there is a problem with the state name because for this use case we aren't validating the card. So, if we are going

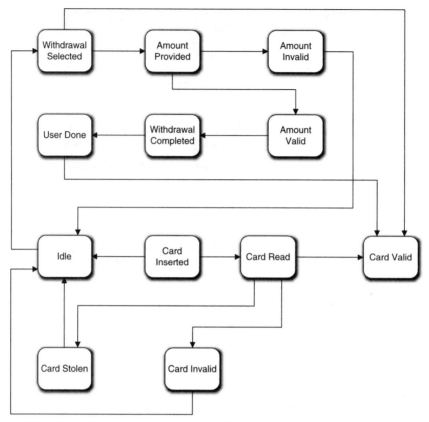

Figure 17-9 *Dispatcher state machine updated for withdrawal transaction*

to be properly anal retentive about the state model, we need a more general name that covers both contexts, such as Ready For Transaction.

Alas, proper state names are the least of our problems here. We should be worried about the size of the state model because we have twelve states and at least two more major uses cases—Deposit and Transfer—to go yet. Also, Card Valid is beginning to look more like Idle than Idle itself. Finally, we might also be concerned about a pattern emerging around the Ready For Transaction (nee Card Valid) state. The cycle for each use case starts and ends with the Ready For Transaction state if the user has multiple transactions. Each of our other transaction use cases will very likely have the same pattern around that state so, we will end up with a "flower petal" pattern where multiple mini-cycles look like petals on a flower around the central state (the stem). Such a pattern suggests blobs of unrelated processing, and that suggests a lack of cohesion in the object abstraction. Similarly, large state models suggest too many disparate behaviors.

So a reviewer is going to want a lot of solid justification for such a state machine. In this case we might justify it on the basis that most of the states don't actually *do* anything in terms of algorithmic processing; they are basically placeholders for the transition constraints on the sequencing. While that can be a valid justification, it is *very* thin, and we should still look for some way to simplify the state model. There are basically two ways to do that.

One approach is delegation, where we allocate some of Dispatcher's responsibilities to other objects. For example, the entire first use case might be handled by the Card object because it is a one-time validation when the user's card is inserted. That is, when the Card is created, it could "walk" the validation sequence and, if valid, could then turn over responsibility for managing the main menu and subsequent transactions to the Dispatcher or Transaction. Before doing that, though, we need to make sure such a delegation is reasonable in the problem space.

We can rationalize that by stepping up a level in abstraction and looking at what the use case itself is doing. It is validating a user whose surrogate here is Card. At that level, validation seems like a reasonable responsibility for Card, assuming a bit of anthropomorphization. What about Dispatcher? Are we usurping its mission of talking to the hardware (i.e., bleeding cohesion across objects)? Yes, but all we are really doing is limiting *which* hardware messages it coordinates from the overall problem perspective. That is, Dispatcher doesn't really know anything about the semantics of the messages; it just enforces some sequencing and mapping rules *for the messages that it does process*. The delegation decision is made on the basis of the semantics of the messages themselves.

So we can rationalize such a delegation in the problem space. But a good sanity check is whether doing so will disrupt our existing model. Card already has relationships with Network and Card Reader, so those collaborations are OK. However, to implement the use case Card would also have to collaborate directly with Character Display. It is hard to rationalize any relationship navigation path to get there with the present Class Model. Transaction might not even exist when the validation is done, and connecting to Dispatcher through the Card Reader hardware doesn't provide a warm and fuzzy feeling.[11] However, we can fix that by adding a direct relationship between Card and Character Display or Dispatcher. That isn't what many would regard as a major modeling change, so I don't think there is a problem with the delegation from

---

11. When dealing with relationship connectivity, one shouldn't be overly concerned with physics. When dealing with logical connectivity, such navigation is entirely possible, especially in this case where Card Reader is really a surrogate for hardware. Nonetheless, one should avoid major Acts of Faith when thinking about relationship navigation. Here the problem space perspective of logically connecting through the hardware just doesn't feel quite right.

that viewpoint. So in this case we could add the relationship[12] and create a state model for Card that handled the first use case. That state model would be exactly the same as the "flower petal" for the first use case.

Unfortunately, that still leaves us with the flower petal problem for the other transactions. Can we delegate the transaction use cases individually? How astute of you, Grasshopper. Yes, and we already have convenient subclasses of Transaction that could hold state models for the sequencing constraints of each transaction. If we can rationalize delegation to Card, we can certainly rationalize delegation to Transaction subclasses for each transaction use case. Nor will such a delegation disrupt the model very much.

As a practical matter, any experienced OO developer would have recognized these delegations as soon as the use cases were inspected. We walked through developing the Dispatcher state model this way deliberately because this kind of "flower petal" complexity crops up fairly often when requirements are not as conveniently organized as the presentation of the use cases. The real issue here is recognizing the problem when it does occur and doing something about it. As it happens, we probably would have recognized the problem much earlier when we identified the responsibilities of Card and the Transaction subclasses in the Class model. This is what was meant about getting to the right place even if one gets off on the wrong foot. When warning flags like large, complex state machines and suspicious life cycle patterns show up, we are forced to step back and look at the big picture again.

So what is the second way to solve the problem? To answer this question we need to think about whether we need Dispatcher at all now. Superficially there is nothing for it to do now if the main use cases are delegated to objects that collaborate directly with the hardware.[13] An interesting question, though, is whether we *want* those objects to talk directly to the hardware. Recall that our original justification for Dispatcher was to map messages to the specific hardware elements. In that respect we are usurping Dispatcher's decoupling prerogatives if we make other objects aware of specific hardware elements.

As a practical matter this does not have to be a big deal, because in each case (so far) the object collaborates with Character Display and whatever hardware element is on the end of a particular relationship. So we can let Card Reader, Cash Dispenser, et al. provide the formatting appropriate for the hardware element. Then the objects

---

12. To Dispatcher for reasons that will become clearer in a moment when we talk about the Main Menu.

13. Actually, error processing (displays, hardware resets, etc.) is something we would probably like to centralize, and Dispatcher might be convenient for that. That would be an entirely different functionality than our current view, so we will ignore it for the moment. But hold that thought because we will be back to it in a couple of paragraphs.

generating those messages don't really have to know about specific hardware; they can simply announce what they have done to whoever is there. Therefore, a full delegation solution where we essentially eliminate the need for Dispatcher is a viable solution in this specific situation.

But the question we need to ask now is: Are there still some sequencing constraints that are better enforced centrally than in the individual delegates we have defined? In other words, are there some higher-level invariants common across use cases that we can capture in Dispatcher?

The answer to these questions lies in abstracting the problem space. Finding a higher level of abstraction for the state model is the second way to resolve the complexity problem. Look at the given uses cases and imagine two more for deposits and transfers that will be very similar to the withdrawal use case. See if you can identify some higher-level sequencing that is common to them all. (Hint: Find a way to describe specific operations so that the same description could be substituted in each use case. That may require combining some detailed use case steps.)

In this case there are three things each use case does if one steps back far enough to view them. They each retrieve data from the user, they each display something, and they each trigger or authorize some hardware activity. The data is different, the displays are different, and the activities are different, but each use case controls the sequencing of doing those things. This allows us to abstract the collaborations to "give me my data"; "put up my display"; and "do my activity." An object initiating such collaborations controls their order, but it doesn't need to know anything about the details of where the data is, what the display is, what activity is done, or who performs the activity. Therefore, Dispatcher could act as middleman and provide a mapping for "my" to the details.

The FSM in Figure 17-10 captures the sequencing of these basic activities. If you compare it to the FSM in Figure 17-9—which would now be in Card or Transaction—you can probably readily imagine the handshaking that would go on to have these two FSMs march through the transaction in lockstep. (This FSM has fewer states, but the Transaction has other collaborations.)

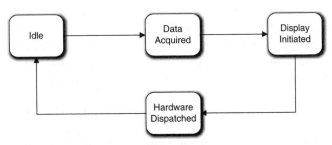

Figure 17-10 *Dispatcher state machine after delegating processing to other objects and capturing invariants*

This FSM is not really an alternative to delegation, though; it is complementary to the Transaction FSM. Just from the state names we can tell that this FSM is at a higher-level of abstraction. Given the way we arrived at it, it represents a quite different view that is really about how the hardware elements are coordinated. So we probably need this FSM in *addition to* the delegation. The value of that will become clear when we look a bit deeper into the problem.

That FSM is fine as far as it goes, but some activities are missing. For one thing, the ATM logo needs to be displayed when there is no active customer. Not a big deal; we can do that in the Idle state. Just because we have a Display Initiated state does not mean that every screen needs to be triggered from that state. So far the rules and policies that are relevant to Display Initiated are those related to displaying a *transaction* screen.[14]

What about things like the Main Menu screen most ATMs have? That screen needs to be shown first thing when the user successfully logs in and also when the user completes a transaction. The first question is: Who manages that? The short answer is: Nobody. Stop thinking like a C programmer, Grasshopper. When the ATM card is successfully read, that screen can be triggered from the Card Valid state of Figure 17-8. All we need to do is add a transition from Idle directly to Display Initiated. The Display Initiated state will do exactly the sorts of things it does to put up a transaction screen.

What is broken in that situation is the transition from Hardware Dispatched to Idle in our new Dispatcher FSM. When the hardware is done, that signals the end of the transaction and we want to put up the main menu. So the transition should go from Hardware Dispatched to Display Initiated.

But what about those special keys the customer presses when selecting a menu item? To answer this we have to think about what those keys might mean. For our simple-minded ATM Controller, let's assume that they mean either the user is completely done with the ATM and wants to go hit the bars, or the user selects another transaction. Both of these bring up some interesting issues for the ATM in general and this FSM in particular.

If the user wants to go away, the ATM needs to give back the ATM card and return to the Idle state. We could do that by simply providing a transition from Display Initiated to Idle and let the Idle state check the Card Reader for a card and, if so, eject it. That's not a good idea because the Card Reader might jam and we would need to process the error. However, we know that Hardware Dispatched could have a malfunction for any hardware operation, so it probably will be set up to deal with that already. (It isn't now because we haven't gotten there yet, but it should be.)

---

14. We could have named the state Transaction Display Initiated and I wouldn't get bent out of shape over it. However, one can easily get carried away trying to put too much information in a name. In this case there are other possible screens that might be triggered from Display Initiated, as in the next paragraph.

So for this situation we should take advantage of Hardware Dispatched to eject the card from Card Reader. This means we need a direct transition from Display Initiated to Hardware Dispatched. And when the "card ejected OK" message comes back from Card Reader, that event should transition from Hardware Dispatched to Idle. So we still need the transition to Idle; we just use it for a different event context.

For the situation where the user selects a new transaction, we have some stuff to do. We need to delete the current Transaction object (if there is one), instantiate the new Transaction object, and turn control of the processing over to it. We also have to instantiate the proper relationships to the Transaction object. Together, those are a whole new set of nontrivial rules and policies. If Dispatcher owns them, we need a new state, say, Transaction Instantiated.

Let's say we do that. We need a transition from Display Initiated to Transaction Instantiated that will be triggered by a "new transaction" message for the selection. Once Transaction takes control, the first thing it will do is try to put up the right screen to get the user's data. So we also need a transition from Transaction Instantiated back to Display Initiated. So far so good.

One can argue, though, that giving Dispatcher responsibility for managing the instantiation of Transactions and their relationships could detract from the cohesion of Dispatcher. In fact, one reason we have several flavors of established design patterns for object construction is because the rules and policies of instantiation typically are quite different than those that govern collaboration. That's a valid argument, and you wouldn't be docked for relegating that to a separate "factory" object. It would be the case if the associated processing was complex or unique decisions had to be made to instantiate properly; that clearly would be fodder for isolation and encapsulation.

In this situation, though, there probably isn't much to it. As a practical matter we only have one Transaction at a time, and the only knowledge it has that depends on identity it gets from the user through the display (i.e., an amount). So we would probably instantiate one of each flavor of the Transaction subclass at start-up. Then all we have to do to "create" a transaction is instantiate two relationships to the relevant instance for the Transaction subclass object. That's not rocket science, so I would probably opt for simplicity and do that in a Dispatcher state.

We have one problem left with this state machine. There is the potential for malfunctions in the hardware and some possible user errors so far. Hardware malfunctions are probably terminal and one needs the same special processing around all of them that leads to an ATM belly-up shutdown. At a minimum that processing is going to involve putting up a screen to tell the user there is a problem; telling the bank a repair is needed; ejecting the ATM card (if possible); and shutting down. We could put that processing in a single Dispatcher state, but it would be better if a dedicated Hardware Error object owned that processing.

There are several reasons why. Error processing of that level of complexity is not something that seems like the Dispatcher should own; it is quite different than the rest of Dispatcher's processing. It probably requires handshaking with the bank. There may be a required sequencing for the hardware shutdown and there are other sequencing rules (e.g., the ATM card should be ejected before shutting down the machine). So we don't want to clutter Dispatcher's state machine with all that. Those sequencing rules apply to a specific context, error processing and graceful shutdown, so they should be encapsulated. So make a note, Grasshopper, that the Class diagram needs to be updated for the new object. Finally, the FSM itself is getting pretty big.

It might still be convenient and consistent to have a Malfunctioned state in the Dispatcher FSM, though. That state would trigger processing by relaying the error to the external Hardware Error object. There would be a transition from Hardware Dispatched to that state. There would probably be a transition from that state to Display Initialized as well since the user needs to be told about the problem. Such a state makes it explicit how a hardware malfunction fits into the overall scheme of things without burdening Dispatcher with the details. In addition, the Dispatcher is still the central point for hardware communications.

What about user errors? From the discussion of Character Display, we know the big one, an invalid amount, will be handled by Transaction while the little ones (typos) will be handled internally by Character Display. So there really isn't anything to manage for Dispatcher.

Figure 17-11 represents the updated version of Figure 17-10. The most obvious difference is that there are a lot of transitions, and they are mostly around Display Initiated. The number of transitions really isn't a problem. It just looks messy because we haven't put specific events on the transitions. If there were events, they would be quite different because they reflect very different triggering contexts.

The central role of Display Initiated is somewhat more worrisome because the life cycle tends to take on a "spider" pattern around it. A reviewer is going to look very closely at such a state machine. But one can rationalize that this is one of those situations where such a pattern can be justified. This is because the display has a central role in both the way transactions are processed and the way special situations like errors are processed. I can also argue that the Dispatcher's mission is to decouple banking transaction processing from the hardware. To do that, Dispatcher manages messages, and many of those messages are necessarily directed to the display. More important, Dispatcher is enforcing constraints on different sequences of messages where each sequence happens to involve a display.

Before leaving Dispatcher, we need to discuss the current vision of what the Hardware Dispatched state action actually does. Basically, it interprets a code in the incoming event data packet and generates an event with a data packet that is a copy of everything in the incoming event data packet except the code Dispatcher inter-

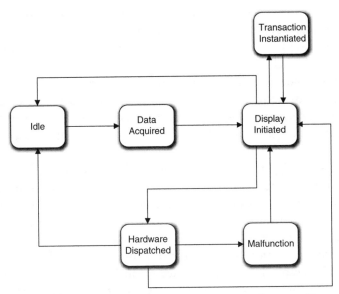

Figure 17-11 *Dispatcher state machine updated to handle hardware malfunctions and transaction instantiation*

prets. When interpreting the code, the Dispatcher also selects the right hardware surrogate to target, probably via a table lookup. The hardware surrogate will interpret the data packet and convert it into a physical hardware read or write.

As a practical matter, though, objects like Cash Dispenser are unlikely to have state machines. Ultimately one is reading or writing values in hardware registers to control the hardware. A hardware register is just a memory location, like an object attribute. For all practical purposes, all one is doing is reading and writing knowledge, which is inherently a synchronous activity. So the "methods" of hardware surrogates like Cash Dispenser are really just smart setters for the hardware's knowledge.

In fact, device drivers largely reflect this; they provide a synchronous interface where each command is implemented separately from other interface commands. So whether Dispatcher calls a Cash Dispenser method, invokes a device drive method directly, or does direct register writes, the "events" to the hardware are really going to be synchronous service setters. By providing hardware surrogates like Cash Dispenser we are introducing additional decoupling from the specific hardware registers, but we should think of the messages as synchronous services to be invoked by Dispatcher.

There are a couple of important points about this discussion of Dispatcher worth reviewing. We have subtly changed the mission of Dispatcher. Although we didn't mention it explicitly, Transaction and Card talk directly to the network port rather than through Dispatcher. That's because some of the transitions are necessarily triggered by the bank, and once one has delegated management of the individual transactions it makes sense for the network events to go directly to those FSMs since no interpretation is needed.

It also provides more coordination of the processing than simple message re-dispatch. For example, we have accommodated several bits of new functionality by defining more transitions and associating different contexts (events) with those transitions. Nonetheless, Dispatcher doesn't really *do* much except the original message reformatting we intended.

To that extent, Dispatcher is an excellent example of how FSMs can manage sequential processing without executable statements. All of that coordination is done through the handshaking that provides events for the transitions. As a result, there is no explicit central coordination of the processing for the various use case scenarios; it is all managed through FSM transition structure and FSM interactions.

Such an elegant solution is enabled in no small part by the way we managed abstraction. The Dispatcher FSM migrates through its states in lockstep with the Transaction FSM. But that synchronization was not the primary goal of the FSM designs. We came up with the Dispatcher FSM working independently with the use cases at a different level of abstraction where we extracted invariants from the *set* of use cases in a holistic fashion. It was those invariants that we captured in Figure 17-10 that enabled the FSMs to play together.

Another important point is that we were able to accommodate a lot of additional processing without changing those core states. We added a couple of states and several transitions, but we didn't change the original core action responsibilities of the states or their roles in the original transaction use cases. If you think about it, we accommodated a boatload of additional scenario content between Figures 17-9 and 17-10, but the FSM differences are rather minor and the original actions are essentially the same. So this example also demonstrates the truth of an assertion made earlier in the Part III road map: It is not easy to get interacting FSMs right, but once they are right they tend to be very robust in the face of volatile requirements.

ATM Controller: Deposit

Previously we tentatively identified a Deposit subclass of Transaction to capture the semantics of the user making a deposit. The analysis is pretty much the same as what we decided to do for the Withdrawal use case. In fact, this is one of the interesting issues about this life cycle, but we're getting ahead of the story.

We are well along that road with the invariants just discussed: display a screen, get user data, and request a hardware action. That's fine for pinning down the level of abstraction and identifying "hard" states. But it sounds a bit procedural because it is oriented around telling others what to do. That's probably OK here because the mission of this object *in the problem space* is to enforce problem space rules about the sequencing of activities. That is, the object itself doesn't really do much except to format and dispatch messages in the right order.

So let's look at the use case and see how this vision fits. For this object, the following use case could be relevant.[15]

```
Use Case 3: Deposit
User selects Deposit from main menu
Display amount request screen
If invalid, display message
If valid,
     Accept deposit envelope
     Query additional transaction
     If none, eject card, clear display, and print record
     Else, display main menu
```

You will note that this use case is almost exactly like the Withdrawal use case. This should not be a big surprise because of the invariants we identified. So we have the basic display, data access, and hardware access sequencing. We also have some cleanup to do at particular points in the processing of the transaction. Note that the processing is quite linear except for the cleanup activities. Intuitively, it seems obvious that the use case steps also define constraints in the sequencing that must be honored (e.g., we must validate the amount before dispensing cash). So tentatively we might expect something like Figure 17-12.

Note that the linearity is boggled by the transitions around Amount Error Displayed. Why not use a superstate for that? The main reason is that it can only be reached from one state. We use superstates to eliminate transitions from several states going to one state.

Now to the point of this exercise: What's wrong with this state machine?

The design process says we should check for activities that can be combined in a single state action. Should ejecting the card, clearing the display, and printing the record be in their own states? In this case they are done as a group only after the customer is finished with the ATM. In fact, it doesn't matter what order they are done in, so there is no *intrinsic* sequencing constraint to enforce among them. Therefore, we should get rid of the Card Ejected, Screen Cleared, and Record Printed states with

---

15. Use case purists would probably get uptight about this being a stand-alone use case. They would argue that it is really just a variant, along with Withdrawal, of a single use case because of the similarities. Well, that's just tough. The point of use cases is to cast the requirements into a form that is readily understood, and this is the best form for my exposition.

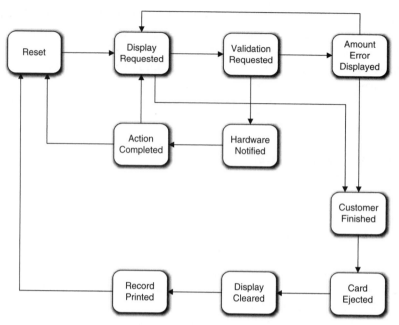

Figure 17-12 *Preliminary Deposit state machine*

their transitions and let the Customer Finished state action just push three different events onto the queue at the same time.[16] The modified FSM is shown in Figure 17-13.

Fair enough. But now we still have six states, yet when we talked about invariants across transactions we only came up with "display a screen," "get user data," and "request hardware action." So can we eliminate more states? Probably not, for a couple of reasons. First, the invariants don't describe everything the transaction needs to do. For example, we have to process errors. OK, maybe we could add another invariant activity, "process error," because all the transactions are likely to need to do that. But that won't work so well because of the second reason.

The second problem is that our Transaction object needs to collaborate with other objects. For example, to validate the amount it has to talk to the Bank at the other end of the network connection. So conceptually we may just have "request hardware action," but in practice we need to define what that means in terms of collaborations. In this case half of our states can be viewed as simply supporting collaboration

---

16. In this case there is a subtle trap when interpreting the use case. These three "states" were activities in the same line in the use case and were associated with a single decision, suggesting an "atomic" requirement. Don't combine activities into a single action just because the use case puts them together. You need to validate the order independence explicitly rather than relying on the cosmetics of the use case organization.

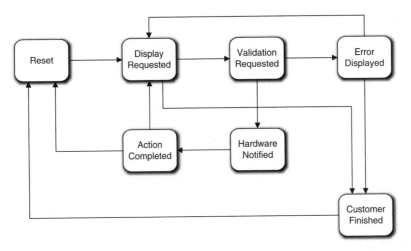

Figure 17-13 *Update Deposit state machine to eliminate states with same condition*

sequencing constraints. To put it another way, half our states reflect our Deposit just waiting for someone else to do the grunt work. Thus they exist to support the sort of handshaking that was discussed previously.

That handshaking sneaked into the FSM as a fait accompli because we mapped those states to the use case steps. The use case was probably subdivided into steps because the customer already understands the kinds of protocols that would be required to deal with the deposit as a manual teller activity. In practice, the state machine designer would keep one eye on the other state machines and would verify that the states resulting from that mapping really do accommodate the necessary exchanges of synchronization messages. The handy way to do that is to scribble notes to oneself on a white board Collaboration diagram.

However, the invariants might be reflected in another way. Compare Use Case 2 and Use Case 3. They are virtually identical. The only difference lies in some specific references such as "Deposit" versus "Withdrawal" and "Accept deposit envelope" versus "Dispense cash" in two activity lines and the validation activity in the Withdrawal. From a software design viewpoint we could combine those two uses cases as:

```
Use Case 4: Transaction
User selects choice from main menu
Display amount request screen
If Withdrawal, validate amount with Bank
      If invalid, display message and exit
Execute transaction in hardware
Query additional transaction
If none, eject card, clear display, and print record
Else, display main menu
```

Again, use case purists will get bent out of shape here, but we are trying to make a point about software design, not requirements specification. Now go back and look at the last state machine proposed and determine what changes need to be made to accommodate this use case. Answer: The only change to the state machine would be to accommodate the validation.

So we could actually use the state machine that was developed for Withdrawal provided there was a transition to go directly from Amount Provided to Hardware Execution Completed (aka Cash Dispensed). There is nothing in that state machine that depends upon whether the transaction is a Deposit or a Withdrawal except the processing around validation. There will be a several differences in the actions associated with the states because the right event messages need to be generated to the right collaboration objects. But those don't show up at this level of abstraction because we are using the FSM to capture invariants of the processing.

We have seen exactly this sort of situation before when we discussed subclassing and state machines. One has a set of state machines for the subclasses that are almost the same for all the subclasses except a few local states and the actual actions associated with the states. We can use the convenience of a superclass state machine to describe the states and transitions that are common among each of the subclass state machines and only need to define the Amount Valid and Amount Invalid states and transitions in the Withdrawal subclass.[17] Note that this sort of thing maps very nicely to use case variants whenever the variants can be expressed in subclasses, as is the case here.

The only remotely tricky processing would be around a Transfer. That requires two values to be processed and the message goes to the network port hardware rather than an ATM hardware element. Because of the way we have currently defined Dispatcher, the routing is not a problem and the values are just passed through from the Character Display. So all we have is a slightly different formatting of the event data packet in the state action. Alas, that is a theoretical toe stubber.

If you recall the rules for FSAs, the alphabet on each transition to a given state must be identical. So the Amount Provided state technically can't be the same for Deposit/Withdrawal and Transfer. As it happens, we have a clever way around this in the OO paradigm. We can make the event data packet itself an ADT, which hides the specific implementation and content behind abstraction. That allows us to have the consuming action "parse" the data packet based on embedded codes. However, one needs to be cautious about this: It hides a synchronization issue between sender and receiver because the encoding/decoding of the data packet needs to be consistent.

---

17. But be sure to keep in mind that in MBD we use the superclass state machine as a notational convenience to avoid duplication in the subclasses. That is, there is no Harel-like inheritance.

This sort of synchronization is significant to the basic problem solution here, so it should be more explicitly dealt with in the solution model. For this reason we want the Amount Provided state to be a subclass state. A different event will have to be used in the subclass state machines, which requires that the relationship navigation must be explicit to the subclass.

If you have committed the ATM Class Model to memory you will note that each Transaction subclass already has its own associations, which means that all clients will be navigating those specific associations so there will be no polymorphic events. It also enables us to employ different event data packets because conceptually each subclass state machine is unique.

We have gone through a rather laborious analysis of these examples, including some deliberate false starts, intentionally to try to demonstrate how an experienced state machine developer thinks about state machines. Developing state machines is not very intuitive to the newcomer, so the extra verbosity is the best way of conveying the proper mindset.

Chapter 18

Abstract Action Languages

I have often wished that there were a language in
which it would be impossible to tell a lie.
—G. C. Lichtenberg

We have spent most of this book discussing static structure. Even the chapters on FSMs were primarily about using state machine transitions to capture problem space sequencing rules in static structure. Eventually, though, we need to describe what the software *does*. An AAL describes what a behavior responsibility does within an individual state machine action.

The AALs are text based and superficially look a lot like 3GLs, because what they describe is primarily algorithmic and is expressed in terms of algorithmic computation. That is, the business rules that are left over after capturing as much as possible of the problem space in static structure are invariably fairly low-level computations. Depreciation is defined by *this* formula. The memory manager employs *that* least recently used algorithm. Half a century of experience has demonstrated that the 3GLs are a pretty good way to express computation.

Because the AALs borrow heavily from 3GLs, the learning curve for AALs tends to be very short for anyone who has even modest conventional programming experience. Consequently, this is going to be the shortest chapter in the book. In fact, the real goals of this chapter are twofold:

1. Describe how AALs differ from 3GLs

2. Demonstrate that the implementation details littering 3GL code are not relevant at the 4GL level

The first is the easiest because it really comes down to the level of abstraction. UML combined with an AAL that is compliant with OMG's execution semantics is a true 4GL. What makes it a 4GL is independence from specific computing environments.[1] That independence is only possible if we raise the level of abstraction to a very high level that would map just as easily to an abacus and smoke signals as it would to a modern desktop hooked into the web. As we shall see shortly, modern AALs are very simple and very abstract.

But for that abstraction to work it must be tied to some conventional notion of problem solving *in the problem domain*. This is why we spent so much time on problem space abstraction to define the static structure. As we shall see, the AAL syntax is very closely integrated with UML graphical syntax. Since the static description is militantly rooted in the customer problem space, we can tie the behavioral description directly to that skeleton rather than the hardware computational models. So while the AAL syntax may look a lot like 3GL syntax and things like arithmetic operators are used the same way, the AAL is inextricably bound to the rest of the UML graphical model.

In no small part, the simplicity and abstraction of AALs is due to OOA/D design principles that lead to logically indivisible responsibilities. Everything we have talked about so far leads to small, narrowly defined state actions that are completely self-contained. So when we set about describing what goes on within a state machine action, we don't have a whole lot of complexity to describe, which enables us to focus on the customer's view of the necessary processing.

This segues to the second goal of this chapter: demonstrating that the solution description need not be encumbered by computing space paraphernalia. Shedding computing space technologies, techniques, and practices is often the most difficult thing for novices to the OO paradigm to do. The reality is that OO designs are *simple*. But that can only be demonstrated by carrying through some of our examples where we can see how little executable AAL code is needed.

AALs and ADFDs

Today almost everyone uses text-based AALs, but this was not always the case. Originally, before UML, the modeling notations were fully graphical and chose to express behavior in a special diagram called an Action Data Flow Diagram (ADFD). It was closely based on the traditional Data Flow Diagram (DFD) used in many Structured

---

1. In MDA terms, the model is a Platform Independent Model (PIM). This is essentially OMG's name for an OOA model. The basic idea is that the model describes the solution in such a fundamental way that we should be able to provide a mapping from that specification to any specific implementation environment. That, in turn, depends on the existence of metamodels for both the PIM representation and the specific computing environment.

Programming methodologies. Text-based AALs replaced ADFDs primarily because they were easier to change during maintenance and because text is actually a more compact means of describing algorithmic processing. But a brief summary is worthwhile because typical AAL syntax is rooted in the ADFD notation.

An ADFD had essentially three primary elements:[2]

- *Process*. A fundamental, self-contained, logically indivisible unit of behavior. A process operated on input data to produce output data. In DFDs these were all what we would call transform processes. In ADFDs, though, they could be any of the fundamental processes discussed in the Part III road map.

- *Data flow*. A connection between processes that represented a flow of data from one process to another. In effect this was a message data packet.

- *Data store*. A set of related state variables. This was another divergence between Structured DFDs and OO ADFDs. In Structured Programming the data store was usually a database record while in the OO context it was an object.

The basic idea of the original DFDs was that an application could be described as flows of data among processes. ADFDs introduced the idea of special kinds of processes and objects as data stores.

Unfortunately, this led to some amusing verbosity in the early AALs that simply mapped ADFD syntax to text syntax. For example, if we quite literally mapped each process to a text statement in the syntax, and we had specialized processes to read, modify, and write attribute values, a simple increment of an attribute might require three separate statements like:

```
tmp = Customer.age; // read accessor
tmp = tmp + 1;      // transform
Customer.age = tmp; //write accessor
```

Fortunately, modern AALs take advantage of compact syntax to perform such an increment in a single statement. They also do a better job of defining what a fundamental process is. Nonetheless most AALs are easily mapped directly into an ADFD representation. With UML the ADFD became an Activity diagram with specialized processes.

There is no inherent restriction on the linguistic model for the language (declarative, imperative, predicate, etc.) but imperative AALs are the most common. In fact, most AALs are based upon existing procedural languages expressly to provide familiarity for converts from traditional development. However, AALs are very abstract,

---

2. There were some other bells and whistles, but these are the important ones for mapping to text-based AALs.

so they offer far fewer syntactic options than typical 3GLs. AALs tend to be set oriented for their operations because OOA/D models are very focused on relationship sets. One language was so set oriented that it originally had no construct for element-by-element iteration (e.g., a C "for" loop).

AAL Syntax

The AAL used in this book is a generic sort of syntax that does not represent any particular AAL.[3] Thus almost all AALs have individual statements for generating events, creating instances, instantiating relationships, and accessing knowledge. The biggest single difference between ADFDs and AALs is that the AALs usually provide individual arithmetic and logical operators so we can embed what trivial test and transform processes do directly in the AAL code. That is, 3GL-like expressions may be mapped into ADFD transforms (or vice versa, depending upon our perspective). The AALs also usually supply additional syntax for things like iteration.

The AALs are pretty simple because of their high level of abstraction; in some cases the entire AAL syntax definition fits on a single page. In addition, the syntactic elements are fairly intuitive once we are familiar with the rest of the elements of a UML Class Model. Table 18-1 describes the syntax. To keep things simple some of the options for more exotic situations (e.g., selecting a relationship for navigation based on role) are omitted.

Table 18-1   *Summary of AAL Syntax in Terms of ADFD Processes*

Syntax Element	ADFD Process	Description/Syntax
DO	None; handled by manual loop	Perform element-by-element iteration over objects in a set obtained by relationship navigation or obtained from a Class.
		DO set-reference-name [WHERE (expression)] {statement-block}
		DO CLASS class-name [WHERE (expression)] {statment-block}

---

3. Curently most AALs are proprietary because they were developed for specific tools. As of this writing a battle is raging within OMG as the various vendors attempt to get their AAL blessed by OMG as the "official" AAL. I have chosen the high road and don't want to get involved.

Table 18-1 *Summary of AAL Syntax in Terms of ADFD Processes (Continued)*

Syntax Element	ADFD Process	Description/Syntax
WHILE	None; handled by manual loop	Perform element-by-element iteration.
		WHILE (expression) {statement-block}
CALL	Realized transform	Invoke realized code in a procedure.
		CALL service-handle ([parameter-name = expression, ...])
LINK/ UNLINK	Instantiate relationships	Instantiate a relationship between two objects.
		LINK object-reference relationship-ID object-reference [ASSOCIATIVE object-reference]
		UNLINK object-reference relationship-ID object-reference
IF	Test	Provide conditional processing, possibly alternatives.
		IF (expression) {statement-block} [ELSE {statement-block}]
GENERATE	Generate event	Generates an event.
		GENERATE event-name [(object-reference.attribute-name, ...)] TO object-reference
CREATE/ DELETE	Create/delete instances	Create an object instance.
		CREATE class-name ([attribute-name = expression, ...])
		DELETE object-reference
Navigation	None	Specifies relationship navigation in the Class model as a chain of relationship references starting with the object in hand. Used to obtain object references to address events, access attributes, or invoke synchronous services.
		Object-reference=THIS -> relationship-ID [-> relationship-ID, ...]
Declaration	None	Declare a temporary variable for computation.
		abstract-data-type variable-name [= initial-value]
Statement-block	None	A block of statements that are executed in sequence.
		Statement; ... END;
Accessor	Accessor	Access a knowledge attribute.
		Object-reference.attribute-name
Invocation	Transform	To invoke a synchronous service or built-in method.
		Object-reference.service-name (expression, ...)

Continues

Table 18-1 *Summary of AAL Syntax in Terms of ADFD Processes (Continued)*

Syntax Element	ADFD Process	Description/Syntax
Operators	None	Arithmetic, logical, bitwise, and unary operators for expressions (syntax similar to C).
		Arithmetic: +, –, *, /, %, **
		Logical: <, <=, ==, >=, >, &&, ||
		Bitwise: AND, OR, XOR
		Unary: +, –, !
Expression	None; transform; test	Construct logical or arithmetic expressions.
		Syntax is the same as C.

Attribute assignments are done with the write accessor on the left of an "=" and the arithmetic/logical expression with read accessors that computes a value on the right. In my simple syntax statements are terminated by a semicolon. The conventions for Table 18-1 are: CAPITALS indicate keywords; [] denote optional elements; and ellipses indicate 0 or more repetitions.

An interesting question is: If AALs are so abstract, why do they have bitwise operators? The operators are introduced simply to enable us to write basic transforms inline in the AAL code. As it happens, this AAL is explicitly specified for use in R-T/E environments, and in that domain bitwise operations are equivalent to the + and – of debits and credits in an accounting domain.

Another, related question is: If AALs are so abstract and platform independent, why hasn't OMG blessed a single AAL as the standard for all applications? One reason is that AALs tend to be domain specific. Thus, an AAL designed explicitly for accounting domains might have a special operator for allocations. That is, one uses the AAL that best fits the way the customer thinks about problems. In contrast, we often choose 3GLs based on computing domain criteria, such as performance.

Examples

Garage Door Opener

Recall the garage door example where we had an FSM with four states: *Open, Opening, Closed,* and *Closing.* Let's assume we have a Motor object whose job it is to write to the hardware. Assume the hardware has one 2-bit register with two 1-bit fields for *direction* (0 = forward or open; 1 = reverse or close) and *initiate* (0 = stop;

1 = start).[4] Further assume we model *Motor* with a *register* attribute and provide *set-Direction()*, *start()*, and *Stop()* as the interface for accessing that knowledge. Finally, let's assume the *GarageDoor* is connected to *Motor* via a 1:1 association called A1.

Let's first consider the object state machine we discussed previously. What is the AAL for each of the states? For the *Open* state, all we need to do is tell the *Motor* to stop:

```
ref = THIS -> A1; // navigate to the Motor over the A1 association
ref.stop();       // invoke setter
```

The association navigation simply says that we should obtain a reference to the object on the other end of the A1 association. In this case, that is pretty simple since the association is 1:1. What happens if you screw up and the object at the end of the association doesn't have a stop() synchronous service? The same thing that would happen in any a strongly typed OOP—the model simulator or transformation engine would say something rude about your skill with AAL, because the Class diagram will tell it what is actually on the other end and what properties it has.

Similarly, for the *Closed* state we need to tell it to stop.

```
ref = THIS -> A1; // navigate to the Motor
ref.stop();       // invoke setter
```

For the *Opening* state we need to set the direction and start the Motor.

```
ref = THIS -> A1;        // navigate to the Motor
ref.stop();              // in case Clicker was clicked again
ref.setDirection(0);     // invoke setter
ref.start();             // invoke setter
```

Finally, for the *Closing* state we need to do the same thing with a different direction.

```
ref = THIS -> A1;        // navigate to Motor
ref.stop();              // in case Clicker was clicked again
ref.setDirection(1);     // invoke setter
ref.start();             // invoke setter
```

In an AAL we usually have the same freedom to provide symbolic literals for the direction that we would have in a typical 3GL.

So let's look at the code for the *Motor*'s synchronous services. What do we need to do to stop the motor? We need to set the *initiate* field in our register to 0. Let's assume the *initiate* field is the least significant bit and the *direction* field is the second

---

4. In practice, there are likely to be two write-only registers for start and stop. Simply writing to the registers will cause the motor to start or stop, respectively. But that's a level of detail only a hardware guy could love. As stated our example enables us to use some of those neat bitwise operations to complicate the AAL.

bit. Do we care about the direction? No, because we explicitly set it correctly in the GarageDoor state machine whenever we start it, so we don't need to worry about read-modify-write. So our stop() setter is pretty basic:

```
stop()
    register = 0;
```

which ensures the *initiate* bit is set to 0. Similarly, setDirection is always done before start(), so we can overwrite the Initiate field. But when we write a 1 we need to make sure it gets into the 2nd bit. One way to do that is like this:

```
setDirection (direction)
    Register = direction * 2;
```

Since twice 0 is still 0, this is fine for forward. For reverse, 2 * 1 = 2, which is 10 in binary and will set the second bit to 1. R-T/E people, especially the ex-EEs, love this sort of arcane elegance and can do it in their sleep. But lesser mortals might want to be more explicit about what is happening with something like:

```
SetDirection (direction)
    IF (direction = 0)
        degister = 0;
    ELSE
        degister = 10b;    // assign binary value
```

Things get more tricky for the *start()* setter because we need to preserve the value of the *direction* field. So we need to do a read-modify-write:

```
temp = Register;      // read both fields to a temporary variable
temp = temp OR 1;     // set initiate field to 1; bitwise OR.
Register = temp;      // write back both fields.
```

That's it, folks—all the AAL code for a garage door opener. Seventeen executable statements. Garage door controllers are pretty simple, but 17 executable statements?!? In addition, note that each individual action is almost childishly simple. The fact that the AAL is so simple and so highly compartmentalized really represents the culmination of everything we have talked about in this book so far. It is simple because we have captured domain rules and policies in static structure like the state machine transitions. It is highly compartmentalized because the way we did problem space abstraction forces us down the path of separation of concerns and logical indivisibility.

But more important, it is worth considering how we might need to modify this model if requirements change. The sorts of things that might change are introducing multiple clickers, more problem sensors, multiple doors, and some sort of clicker registration procedure. Let's look at each of these.

- *Adding clickers.* Our model doesn't change at all because we don't care which clicker is clicked so long as it is registered. The clickers are external actors that all send the same message. At most we might have multiple instances of a *Clicker* surrogate object.

- *More problem sensors.* Again, virtually no effect because the response to a problem is either to stop the door or open it. We might have to add another couple of transitions to account for different problem responses. In the worst case we would have to add another state to the object state machine to account for simply stopping the door where it is rather than opening it.

- *Multiple doors.* All this means is that we will have multiple instances of *Garage-Door*. Presumably something like clicker identity will determine which clicks go with which door. That dispatch can be handled by the bridge because the clicker is an external actor. Or, if we have *Clicker* surrogate objects, we just need a 1:1 association between *Clicker* and *GarageDoor* to handle the routing of the message. (A similar multiplicity of instance associations comes for free in our existing A1 association for Motor and garageDoor; all we have to do is instantiate it properly and the existing AAL will Just Work.)

- *Clicker registration.* OK, this gets a little trickier and we will probably have to introduce a new object like *Registrar* that manages the registration protocol. That object will instantiate the associations between *Clicker* and *GarageDoor* instances. But our model of *GarageDoor* and its collaborations with *Motor* will be unchanged.

In fact, in all situations except introducing more problem sensors that require different responses, our model of how *GarageDoor, Motor, Clicker,* and *Sensor* collaborate doesn't change at all. This translates into a system that is going to be very maintainable in the face of change. So AAL simplicity for the dynamic description and compartmentalization are really just manifestations of achieving the more important goal of the OO paradigm: to produce maintainable software.

Before leaving this example, here's an extra credit question: Given the AAL code above, what is wrong with the FSM for the *GarageDoor* object? (Hint: Recall that we defined an FSM state as a condition where a unique set of rules and policies apply.) You will note that the AAL code for the *Open* and *Closed* states is identical. That's a no-no because it violates the notion of a *unique* set of rules and policies. Dealing with issues like this is what makes software design an iterative process.

So what to do? It might be tempting to coalesce the *Open* and *Closed* states into a single state, such as *MovementCompleted*. The problem with this is that the E1:Clicked event becomes ambiguous; we don't know whether it should transition to the *Opening* state or the *Closing* state. UML supports conditional transitions, so we could make the transition to *Opening* or *Closing* be dependent on the value of a state variable (attribute) that we set appropriately during our actions. The *Opening* and *Closing* states could record the last known direction, and since our actions execute as the state is entered there would be no confusion about reversing direction.

But before we perform surgery on the FSM, it might be a good idea to consider how we came to have the same actions for the *Open* and *Closed* states. We got to this situation because of the way we chose to define the *Motor* object. In particular, we separated the responsibilities of setting the direction from those of starting and stopping the motor. This made starting the motor slightly trickier but trivialized stopping the motor by sending it exactly the same message whether we want to stop closing the door or we want to stop opening the door. In other words, we raised the level of abstraction of Motor from stop-closing or stop-opening to stop-whatever-you-are-doing.

Conceptually, the *Open* action's policy is that the door must stop closing or being closed and the *Closed* action's policy is that the door must stop opening or stop being open. Those policies are intrinsic to the nature of the condition and they are different. It is only the *Motor* that raises the level of abstraction of the collaboration so that opening and closing aren't relevant, and that is reflected in the message used to announce that the policy prevails. So it was a trick question and nothing needs to change.

However, the distinction between the nature of the rules and policies that prevail for a state condition and the way we communicate the state condition during collaborations is important. In this case the *Open* and *Closed* states really didn't have any explicit rules and policies; the rules and policies were captured in the semantics of the conditions themselves and the FSM transitions that limited how we got to the state. The ref.stop() message simply announced that the state condition prevailed.

ATM: Character Display

In Figure 17-6 we have three states for the *CharacterDisplay* object. The actions for these states will likely be the most complicated in the entire ATM Controller subsystem, so it is worth seeing how bad AAL coding can get. By way of review, here are the attributes that we defined in the Class diagram for this object.

- *buffer.* This is a typical character buffer for a character display. The number of characters is (line count × characters per line). It is assumed the OS will manage the *buffer* mapping in terms of lines.

- *currentPosition.* This is simply an index into *buffer*, assuming *buffer* is a linear array of characters.

In addition, the following attributes from *DisplaySpecification* will be relevant:

- *text.* This is an image of the screen character buffer with all fixed characters already on place.

- *interactiveFlag.* A boolean for whether the user must supply a value through the keyboard.

- *valueType.* This describes the type of data, if any, the user will have to provide (NONE, ALPHA, NUMERIC).

- *valueLength.* The maximum length of a user-supplied value in characters.

- *valueStart.* The character number where a user-supplied value begins in the *buffer.*

For the *Screen Initialized* state we need to make some assumptions about how the application talks to the OS. An ATM machine is going to have a pretty primitive OS where the display is just a video buffer and whatever is in the buffer will get displayed. There will also be control values that must be set to determine simplistic visual features such as foreground/background color, blinking, and so forth. The control values could be embedded in the video buffer on a byte-by-byte basis, or they could be a separate, parallel buffer. In any event, both the control values and characters will have to be written directly into video memory for the OS to process. This is starting to look tediously complex . . . we haven't even gotten into issues like 16-bit versus 32-bit color.

Fortunately, we don't have to worry about any of that because it is all platform specific and our solution needs to be platform independent. As long as we are getting the fixed text characters from *DisplaySpecification*, we can get the default background colors, entry field highlighting, and whatnot from *DisplaySpecification* because they aren't going to change. All we have to do in this object is load the data into video RAM and echo any data entry characters the user types into the video buffer.

So, we will assume that *DisplaySpecification:text* is an ADT that actually contains all the necessary display information, including fixed characters. In effect, it becomes a handle for a blob of bytes that we can load as-is starting at the video buffer address for the length of the video buffer. Better yet, we can assume the RTOS provides a video device driver that has a convenient interface to do this.[5] Therefore we would

---

5. If it doesn't, then somebody will have to write one. Since such code is low-level implementation code, it would probably be done as realized code outside the scope of this problem design. (We could do it in AAL, but that would be much like writing a square root routine in Access macros.) It would clearly be reusable for any other application that needed to talk to a character display using this particular RTOS. So we are just doing what the RTOS vendor should have done in the first place.

essentially be calling an OS system service to do the actual loading. Then the entry action for *Screen Initialized* will look like:

```
Reference specRef;     // declare handle to Display specification

specRef = THIS -> A2;
IF (specRef.interactiveFlag)
    currentPosition = specRef.valueStart;
ELSE
    currentPosition = 0;
CALL videoLoad (buffer = specRef.text);
```

We just navigate to *DisplaySpecification*, set the current position in the *buffer* to the start of the interactive field (if necessary), and call the video driver's interface for mass loading of the video buffer content. (The mapping of the arguments to however the device driver manages parameters would be defined in the transformation rules for accessing things like OS system services. AAL does this in a somewhat more verbose way because it enables the CALL to be mapped to more complex communication mechanisms than simple inline procedures, such as interoperability protocols in distributed applications.)

The *Value Processed* state is also quite simple. It just extracts the value the user provided from the buffer, checks it for proper numeric characters, and sends an appropriate message to the *Dispatcher*. Note that we only get to *Value Processed* if the user needs to supply a numeric value; special keys for menu choices will be processed by the *Keystroke Processed* state. Again, we assume our display device driver has a high-level interface for extracting a substring from the character display buffer. We also assume we have library utilities to check strings for being integers and to convert ASCII text to integers.

```
Integer value = 0;     // temporary variable for value
String valueText;      // for copy of user's input
Boolean isInteger;     // result of check for numeric
Reference specRef;
Reference dispatcherRef;

specRef = THIS -> A2;        // navigate to Display Specification
dispatcherRef = THIS-> A11;  // navigate to Dispatcher

// extract value's characters form display buffer
valueText = CALL getSting (start = specRef.valueStart,
    length = specRef.valueLength);

// check if value is an integer
isInteger = CALL validateInteger (text = valueText);
```

```
// inform dispatcher
IF (isInteger) {
    value = CALL convertTextToInteger (text = valueText);
    GENERATE valueObtained (value) TO dispatcherRef;
    }
ELSE
    GENERATE userInputError (INVALID_INTEGER) TO dispatcherRef;
```

There are a couple of interesting things to note here. This looks pretty much like a 3GL program because AAL is usually designed to use 3GL-like syntax to reduce the learning curve. As indicated previously, methods tend to be algorithmic, and the 3GLs represent decades of evolving efficient text languages for algorithmic processing, so this should not be a surprise.

Note, though, the lack of detailed processing. The action relies heavily on realized code to do the grunt work, in this case library functions for low-level activities like checking for numeric values. This is much more common in AAL than in typical 3GLs because the AAL mindset is to only deal with things that represent unique rules and policies for the problem in hand. Modern 3GL code is often written in a highly modular way with heavy reuse through libraries and whatnot, so a pure 3GL action would look very much like this because the library functions are pretty obvious. But when writing AAL code developers are religious about trying to identify and encapsulate realized code. As a result, they will often delegate blocks of code to realized status that are considerably larger than 3GL developers would put in the library function. There are only two criteria for doing so:

- The realized code must capture processing that is defined in a much broader context than the problem in hand, such as mathematical algorithms. That is, the realized code should be readily reusable when solving quite different problems. It should not implement any business rules or policies that are unique to the problem in hand.

- The realized code must be accessible as a synchronous service transform process. More specifically, the input data is limited to the argument data, and only that data is transformed into new results data. That is, the realized code is completely stand-alone and not dependent in any way on anything accept its CALL arguments.

There is no point in going into more AAL code examples here because they all tend to be simple and look pretty much the same. This is because everything we covered in this book so far has been indirectly aimed at ensuring that object state machine actions are simple, self-contained, highly focused, and logically indivisible, so they will rarely be larger than the examples already provided. When they are larger it is almost always because the actions are instantiating multiple objects and their relationships, since providing a single action scope is the easiest way to ensure referential integrity. But in those cases instantiation is the *only* thing being done, so the individual operations are severely limited.

We can argue that this chapter represents the culmination of everything in the OO paradigm in general and MBD in particular. Ultimately it all results in small, self-contained, highly focused, and logically indivisible behavior responsibilities. Such behaviors are easy to maintain when requirements change, and they are easily chained together to provide complex problem solutions. Traditional Structured Development provides a similar sort of divide-and-conquer approach and had the same goal of small, self-contained, highly focused, and logically indivisible operations. But it resulted in a rigid hierarchical decomposition structure that was difficult to maintain, and it did not ensure the software structure emulated the problem domain structure. The OO paradigm evolved around a systematic approach to problem space abstraction, a flexible view of logical indivisibility, a dedication to invariants, the notion of capturing business rules and policies in static structure, and the separation of the resolution of functional and nonfunctional, and the resolution of nonfunctional requirements. All those things combine to ensure that writing object behavior responsibilities is anticlimactic.

Glossary

3GL *See* Third generation language.

4GL *See* Fourth generation language.

Abstraction
The result of emphasizing certain features of a thing while de-emphasizing other features that are not relevant. An abstraction is defined relative to the perspective of the viewer.

Accessors
Expressions that read or write specific analysis data atoms.

Action
Made up of zero or more action language statements attached to an operation, state, or transition.

A fundamental unit of behavior specification that represents some transformation or processing in the modeled system, be it a computer system or a real-world system. Actions are contained in activities, which provide their context. *See* Activity.

Action Implementation
Analysis actions translated into the target language.

Action Sequence
An expression that resolves to a sequence of actions.

Activation
The initiation of an action execution.

Activity
A specification of parameterized behavior that is expressed as a flow of execution via a sequencing of subordinate units (whose primitive elements are individual actions). *See* Action.

Actual Parameter
Synonym: Argument.

Aggregate
A class that represents the whole in an aggregation or whole-part relationship. *See* Aggregation.

Aggregation
A special form of association that specifies a whole-part relationship between the aggregate or whole and a component part. *See* Composition.

ALU *See* Arithmetic Logic Unit.

Analysis
Development of a platform-independent UML model for the analyzed problem domains in the system. Analysis results in a model of the problem domain that is independent of implementation considerations. Analysis focuses on what to do; design focuses on how to do it. *Contrast:* Design.

Analysis Actions
Model specified action language associated with states, transitions, or operations.

Argument
A binding for a parameter that is resolved later. An independent variable.

Arithmetic Logic Unit
The hardware where core computation is done in a computer. The term has largely replaced Central Processing Unit (CPU) because of the complexity of modern computers such that multiple discrete hardware units now interact to handle core computation.

Association
A relationship that may occur between instances of classifiers.

Association Class
A model element that qualifies an association. It is a placeholder for complex resolution of references in *:* associations. It can also capture additional problem space information about associations.

Association End
The endpoint of an association, which connects the association to a classifier.

Association Link
Establishes a connection between the specified class instances.

Attribute
In UML terms, a structural feature of a classifier that characterizes instances of the classifier. An attribute relates an instance of a classifier to a value or values through a named relationship.

In OOA/D terms, an attribute is a knowledge responsibility of an object or subsystem.

Attribute-Value
A mechanism for associating a particular value with a mnemonic identifier.

A-V Pair
A descriptor containing and attribute identifier and corresponding attribute value.

Behavior
The observable effects of an operation or event, including its results. It specifies the computation that generates the effects of the behavioral feature.

Behavior Responsibility
A behavior responsibility represents an obligation on the part of an object or subsystem to do something. Behavior responsibilities typically capture problem space rules and policies that must be executed to solve the problem in hand.

Binary Association
An association between two classes. A special case of an n-ary association. It defines how objects of the classes may be logically connected.

Boolean
An enumeration whose values are true and false.

Boolean Expression
An expression that evaluates to a boolean value.

Bridge
A logical connection between subsystems that supports communication during collaborations.

Build
The process of compiling and linking the translated implementation code, realized code, and implementation libraries into the deliverable system.

Call
A synchronous invocation of a behavior responsibility.

Cardinality
The explicit number of elements in a set. *Contrast*: Multiplicity.

Child
In a generalization relationship, the specialization of another element, the parent. *Contrast*: Parent.

Class
A classifier that describes of a set of objects that share the same specifications of features, constraints, and semantics.

Class Diagram
A diagram that shows a collection of classes, their responsibilities, and their relationships.

Client
An object that requests a service in a DbC contract for a collaboration. *Contrast*: Service.

Collaboration
An interaction between objects or subsystems manifested by a message passed between them. In an OO context, the message announces a state change in the message sender. Usually some behavior responsibility of the receiver will be invoked when the message is consumed.

Compile Time
Refers to something that occurs during the compilation of a software module.

Component
An independent unit of processing with a well-defined interface that can be used with other components to build a system. A modular part of a system.

Composite
A class that is related to one or more classes by a composition relationship.

Composite State
Any state with nested states (sometimes called a superstate).

A state that consists of either concurrent (orthogonal) substates or sequential (disjoint) substates. *See* Substate.

A technique for creating hybrid objects through generalization. The object inherits responsibilities that are logically orthogonal to its primary responsibilities in the problem space.

Concurrency
The occurrence of two or more activities during the same time interval. Concurrency can be achieved by interleaving or simultaneously executing two or more threads. *See* Thread.

Conditionality
Specifies whether there must always be at least one participant in an association or not. *Contrast*: Multiplicity.

Context
A view of a set of related modeling elements for a particular purpose, such as specifying an operation.

Deliverable System
The set of executable elements that constitute the software product to be verified and delivered.

Dependency
A dependency relationship indicates that one class refers to another class. One class might, for example, use the definitions in another class. A dependency is always uni-directional.

In a subsystem, Component diagram dependencies represent the flow of requirements from a client to a service subsystem.

Deployment
One possible implementation of a PIM on a target platform and target system topology.

Design
The process of defining the high-level structure of a software solution. For example, OOA and OOD represent different aspects of design for a given problem solution.

eXtensible Markup Language (XML)
An open, extensible ASCII-based standard for describing data. It employs HTML-like markup tags and A-V descriptors.

Finite State Machine
A formalization of states (conditions of being), actions associated with those states, the valid transitions between them, the external triggers of the transitions, and the data that state actions use. FSMs provide a very disciplined mechanism for managing complex, asynchronous processes.

Fire
To execute a state transition. *See* Transition.

Fourth Generation Language
There are many possible definitions, but the one employed in this book is a language that is independent of particular computing space environments. That is, the language describes a problem solution in customer terms and abstracts away computing space details.

FSM *See* Finite State Machine.

Generate event
To create an instance of the specified event and queue it for dispatch to the specified instance.

Handle
A pointer that enables a program to access some resource, such as a library function.

A handle is a data type. It is a generic reference without a specific type. The user of a handle cannot invoke specific responsibilities of the entity being referenced.

IDE *See* Integrated development environment.

Implementation Libraries
Realized system components supporting a specific compiler, language, or operating system environment.

Integrated Development Environment
A suite of discrete programs that are integrated seamlessly in a common framework and presenting a single UI.

JVM (Java Virtual Machine)
The runtime system responsible for the execution of Java bytecodes produced by compiling Java source code.

KLOC; KNCLOC
Thousand Lines Of Code; Thousand Non-Comment Lines of Code.

Knowledge responsibility
An obligation for an object or subsystem to know something. Note that such an obligation does not require a concrete and persistent data implementation, such as a memory register. In OOA/D the object simply needs to provide a value when queried.

Link
Instantiate an association between instances of two objects from diffent classes.

LOC
Lines Of Code

Marking
A name-value pair that is applied to one of the elements of the PIM. A marking is a property that has a name-value pair assigned.

MBD *See* Model-based software development.

MDA *See* Model-driven architecture.

MDD *See* Model-driven development.

Metamodel
A model that describes the constructs of another model.

Method
Encapsulates a cohesive behavior responsibility so that it has well-defined scope with respect to software execution.

MLOC
Million Lines of Code

Model

For software, an abstract view of a software solution that provides simplification and tailoring of various views (e.g., static structure versus dynamic).

Model-Based Software Development (MBD

A particular approach to software development that employs the OO paradigm and a translation-based version of MDA. MBD is the primary subject matter of this book.

Model-Driven Architecture (MDA)

An architectural standard for a framework based on models. In particular, MDA uses metamodels to formalize semantics that enables unambiguous transformation between models that are different views of the same software.

Model-Driven Development (MDD)

A generic description of a wide variety of approaches to software development that are based on abstract modeling. MBD is one approach. MDD is defined within the OMG framework as a container for UML, MDA, and other specific modeling standards.

Multiplicity

The number of participants in an association. In MBD this is limited to 1 or * (many). *Contrast:* Cardinality, Conditionality.

Nested State

Any state within a composite state (sometimes called a substate).

Object Oriented Development

A software design paradigm that emphasizes problem space abstraction to ensure that large applications are maintainable in the face of volatile requirements over time. A key notion of OO development is the use of encapsulation and interfaces to decouple (eliminate dependencies among) disparate program modules or units.

OOA (Object Oriented Analysis)

A design technique that results in a problem solution that is described purely in customer terms and is independent of any particular computing environment. Generally OOA resolves only functional requirements. *Contrast:* OOD.

OOD (Object Oriented Design)

A design technique that elaborates on an OOA to address nonfunctional requirements and provide design strategies that are dependent on a particular computing environment.

OOP (Object Oriented Programming)

A design technique for elaborating OOA and OOD to resolve tactical design issues in an OOPL.

OOPL (Object Oriented Programming Language)
A third-generation, text-based computing language that provides specific constructs in support of OOA and OOD.

Operation
The UML term for an object or subsystem behavior responsibility.

OTS
Off The Shelf.

Package
In UML, a general container of a set of model elements that are related. Packages are primarily intended to manage the configuration of the model elements to support things like version control. *Contrast:* Subsystem.

Parent
In a generalization relationship, the generalization of one or more elements, the children.

Pattern
A formal description of an abstract solution that can be tailored to a fairly wide variety of different but related problems.

PIM *See* Platform Independent Model.

Platform
An abstraction of a particular computing environment. It includes things like hardware, 3GL implementation language, operating system, realized libraries, and various computing space technologies used (e.g., J2EE, CORBA, XML, etc.).

Platform Independent Model
An MDA concept: Complete specification of a problem solution in terms of the problem space itself. It is independent of specific computing space technologies like implementation language, operating system, hardware, and so forth. Maps to a traditional OOA model.

Platform Specific Model
A complete specification of a problem solution that is dependent on the specific computing environment. A PSM is an elaboration of a PIM or a more general PSM that provides additional computing space detail. Examples of PSMs are a UML OOD model or a 3GL program.

Property
In an OOA/D/P context, a characteristic of some problem space entity. That property is abstracted in terms of a responsibility to either know something or to do something. In UML a property is synonymous with a knowledge attribute of an object.

PSM *See* Platform Specific Model

Realized Elements
System components that have not been analyzed and are typically handwritten code generated from a specific environment (like a GUI builder or math algorithm environment) or purchased from a third party.

RDM (Relational Data Model)
A specialized branch of relational theory within set theory mathematics. It applies relational theory specifically to persistent data storage where the dominant data collection entity is a table.

Service
An object or subsystem that provides a service in a DbC contract for a collaboration. *Contrast*: Client.

Simple State
A state with no nested states.

Software Architecture
The organization of software, usually at the physical or executable level, which describes how the components interact to achieve the system requirements. We define logical, deployment, and physical views of the architecture.

STD (State Transition Diagram)
A graphical representation of states and transitions in a finite state machine. It is the graphical equivalent of an STT. In UML, an STD is represented as a Statechart.

State Transition Table
A tabular representation of the various valid transitions between states in a finite state machine and the events that trigger them.

Statement Block
A sequence of statements with single entry and exit points.

Stereotype
An extension or modification of a UML modeling element beyond that defined by UML.

STT *See* State Transition Table.

Substate
In a Harel finite state machine, a subdivision of a state triggered by a single event. Actions associated with both the parent state and the substate will execute when the event is consumed. Substates provide a form of generalization for state machines.

In MBD notation, substates are pure notation artifacts used solely to simpify the STD by coalescing multiple transitions to the same state into a single transition, so only a single state's action responds to an event.

Subsystem
A logical unit of application partitioning that captures a single, cohesive subject matter and level of abstraction. Subsystems are related by dependencies in an directed, acyclic graph where the dependencies represent flows of requirements in roughly a client/service relation. Subsystems are encapsulated behind interfaces to decouple their implementations. In UML a subsystem is a stereotype of Component.

Task
An independently running program.

Third Generation Language
A large set of programming languages that were defined from the late 1950s onwards. Those languages were text based, and their common characteristics were abstraction of procedural block structuring, procedural message passing, and stack-based scope.

Thread
An independently running process within a task.

Transformation
The process of executing the Transformation Engine to generate the complete implementation code for all analysis models. In an MBD context, transformation is the act of producing an executable from a PIM.

Transformation Engine
Transforms platform-independent UML models into 3GL or Assembly code.

Transformation rules
Rules used to transform platform-independent models into compilable code or executables.

Transition
A path between states in a statechart diagram.

Type I, Type II
In probability, a Type I error is rejecting a true hypothesis, while a Type II error is accepting a false hypothesis.

UML (Unified Modeling Language)
A modeling language used to specify, visualize, construct, and document the artifacts of an object-oriented software system. The Unified Modeling Language is primarily a

graphical notation. When combined with a platform-independent action language (text-based) and an appropriate UML profile, it becomes a complete fourth generation language.

Unlink
To break the connection between the specified class instances.

XML *See* eXtensible Markup Language.

Index

Information in figures and tables is denoted by *f* and *t*.

A

AAL. *See* Abstract Action Language (AAL)

Abstract Action Language (AAL)
    abstraction and, 475–476
    Action Data Flow Diagram and, 373, 476–478
    ATM example for, 484–488
    garage door opener example for, 480–484
    3GLs *vs.*, 475–476
    methods and, 52
    syntax, 478, 478*t*–480*t*, 480

Abstract data type (ADT), 168, 192, 195–197, 333, 335–336

Abstraction
    abstract action languages and, 475–476
    of aggregates, 335–341
    anthropomorphization and, 206–207, 343–344
    application partitioning and, 116–117, 117*f*
    of associations, 236
    basic, 332
    of behavior, 203–204
    behavior and, 158, 198
    characteristics and, 37–38
    choosing correct, 341–351
    collaboration and, 396
    conditionality and, 252
    definition of, 37, 161–162
    delegation and, 330–331
    domain experts and, 163
    emphasis and, 38
    encapsulation and, 39
    invariants and, 79, 231
    levels of, 35, 36*f*, 116–117, 117*f*, 350–351, 396–397, 397*f*
    Liskov Substitution Principle and, 326

    logical indivisibility and, 396
    of methods, 197–198
    Model-Based Development and, 35
    modification of reality by, 37–38
    in object-oriented paradigm, 35, 36*f*
    of object responsibilities, 399–400
    of people's actions, 343–344
    polymorphism and, 59
    as proactive, 162
    problem space, 31–32, 37–39, 108, 162
    of problem space entities, 163
    representation and, 161–167
    of roles, 163
    to scalar, 193, 228
    sequencing and, 396–397, 397*f*
    in state machine design, 438
    subclasses and, 309
    subject matter and, 308, 345–349
    subsystem implementation and, 110
    of subsystems, 128
    transitions and, 422

Access constraint, associations and, 238, 272

Accessor(s)
    knowledge, 204
    as synchronous service, 371

Action(s)
    definition of, 379, 427–428
    as dynamic, 427
    entity and, 427
    external behavior dependencies and, 428
    in finite state machines, 380
    responsibilities combined in, 440
    self-contained, 429
    timing of execution, 381–382

Action Data Flow Diagram (ADFD), 373, 476–478

Action languages, 373–374

Addresses, memory, 163

ADFD. *See* Action Data Flow Diagram (ADFD)

FREE Online Edition

Your purchase of **Model-Based Development** includes access to a free online edition for 45 days through the Safari Books Online subscription service. Nearly every Addison-Wesley Professional book is available online through Safari Books Online, along with more than 5,000 other technical books and videos from publishers such as Cisco Press, Exam Cram, IBM Press, O'Reilly, Prentice Hall, Que, and Sams.

SAFARI BOOKS ONLINE allows you to search for a specific answer, cut and paste code, download chapters, and stay current with emerging technologies.

Activate your FREE Online Edition at
www.informit.com/safarifree

> **STEP 1:** Enter the coupon code: NZQCIWH.

> **STEP 2:** New Safari users, complete the brief registration form.
>   Safari subscribers, just log in.

If you have difficulty registering on Safari or accessing the online edition, please e-mail customer-service@safaribooksonline.com